LITERARY CRITICISM

AN INTRODUCTORY READER

LITERARY CRITICISM

AN INTRODUCTORY READER

Edited and with an Introduction by
LIONEL TRILLING
Columbia University

HOLT, RINEHART AND WINSTON, INC.

New York • Chicago • San Francisco • Atlanta
Dallas • Montreal • Toronto • London • Sydney

Copyright © 1970 by Lionel Trilling
All rights reserved
Library of Congress Catalog Card Number: 74-97009
SBN: 03-079565-6
Printed in the United States of America
1 2 3 4 5 6 7 8 9

PREFACE FOR THE TEACHER

On the Place of Criticism in Literary Education

For a good many years it has been taken for granted in the United States that the study of literature is an essential part of a liberal education. There are differences of opinion about how much time in the student's college course ought to be given to the study. There are divergent views about the method by which it should be carried on, and about what particular literary works, or kinds of literary works, are best suited to "introducing" the student to literature, by which we mean capturing his interest and reassuring him about the relevance of literature to his own best concerns. But whatever disagreement there may be over details, it is a certitude established in the theory and practice of American college education that some study of literature is indispensable.

The commitment to this idea accounted at least in part for the remarkable efflorescence of literary criticism that occurred in this country some three decades ago. Modern American critcism had its beginnings in England, in the seminal work of I. A. Richards and T. S. Eliot, but the seeds that these men sowed fell on the peculiarly fertile ground of the American academic situation. The majority of critics in this country in recent times have been college and university teachers and what they have written about literature, although eventually directed to a general and anonymous audience, was first worked out face to face with their own students and derived much of its energy and cogency from its awareness of the immediate necessities of the classroom. "How can I correct this particular false or inadequate assumption that stands in the way of a right response to this particular work and to other works of similar kind?"—the simple pedagogic question can be discerned behind most of the American critical writing of our time, especially that which came to be called "New Criticism."

The influence that the critical movement has had upon the educational situation which gave rise to it has been very considerable. In 1948 John Crowe Ransom conceived the idea of a School of Letters to be established at Kenyon College and invited the late F. O. Matthiessen and the present writer to be his coadjutors in planning and directing it. The School of Letters continues in active life in its second home at Indiana University, but its now augmented board of Senior Fellows recognizes that it no longer serves the unique function which Mr. Ransom thought it should have and which, for a time, it did indeed have. When the School was founded, the teachers of literature in our colleges and universities were divided into two antagonistic camps, of which one was the great entrenched force of "scholars," the other a small partisan guerrilla band of "critics." It was Mr. Ransom's purpose to organize the latter into a more or less cohesive body, to give it such force and augmented courage as comes from cohesiveness under an insurgent banner, and to recruit to it those students who were disaffected from the mode of instruction in literature which then prevailed in the colleges and graduate schools. But only a relatively few years were to pass before it became plain that the relation between the two camps had changed. In department after department throughout the country men appeared, or emerged, who were teaching literature in some pretty close approximation to the way in which the School of Letters believed it should be taught. The School's doctrine had never suggested the least abatement of allegiance to the great scholarly virtues of accuracy, attention to detail, comprehensiveness of knowledge. What had made the issue with the dominant mode of teaching literature was the School's insistence that the literary work be understood to have an autonomous existence and be dealt with first in terms proposed by this understanding. This principle of the critical movement has won wide acceptance. No doubt the old issue between scholarship and criticism still exists, but in very much diminished intensity. Differences in temperament make for different emphases in the study and teaching of literature, but it becomes ever harder to maintain the old sense of a great gulf fixed between scholars on the one hand and critics on the other. Nowadays, when a student comes to the School of Letters, it is less likely that he does so because he wants a kind of literary study that he has not been able to get at his own college or university than because he wants more of the kind of study he has already had.

No profession is ever what it should be, but there is reason to believe that the literature-teaching profession is in better condition than it was thirty years ago, that it is in some considerable degree more vivacious and enlightened. If that is so, it is probably fair to say that the improvement is in large part due to the critical movement and to the general credence given to its principles and methods.

And yet the relation which now exists between criticism and the teaching of literature is not wholly simple and may even be thought ambiguous. It is true that the assumptions of the critical movement are at work in the teaching of literature to a far greater extent than three decades ago, sometimes made explicit as principles but usually allowed to remain tacit in practice. And it is true that in many departments of English there are courses devoted to literary criticism as a subject in itself, one which is thought to be valuable for advanced students. But at the same time we may perceive a tendency to denigrate the usefulness of criticism in the educational process and even to judge it to be harmful. This tendency is especially to be observed in what for some students are the beginning years of literary study and for others the only years—that is to say, in the introductory courses, which in most colleges are the "required" courses. In these courses critical writing is often excluded from the reading list not only because poems, plays, and stories or novels make peremptory demands upon the available time, but also because it is thought to have a harmful effect upon the student's experience of literature. This pedagogical judgment is made on grounds that were established—the irony is striking—by criticism itself.

A salient belief of the critical movement which took its rise in our academic institutions is that a work of literature is to be experienced in an unmediated way. The act of reading is properly a "transaction" to which the only parties are the reader and the work. Nothing and no one ought to be permitted to intervene between what the work does and what the reader does by way of apprehending and responding to the work. Of course this does not say what is really meant, which is that no intervention is to be permitted between the activity of the work and the activity of the reader so far as the latter is of the right sort. There is always the chance, that is, that the reader's activity will not be in the ideal condition, that his mind requires to be purified, cleared of the cant and false or inadequate assumptions it has somehow acquired. To effect this purification is the critic's characteristic task, as, presumably, it is the teacher's. But does it not sometimes—often—happen that the critic—but never the teacher!—in going about his job of clearing the reader's mind of what is false, of what impedes a direct response to the work, introduces into the reader's mind what is not the reader's own? By the activity which the critic directs towards making the transaction between the reader and the work an unmediated one, does he not, precisely, mediate? Does he not impose, or insinuate, his own highly developed and formulated response to the work? If the answer is yes, as seems likely, then does it not follow that, in the teaching of literature, critical writing had best be avoided as tending to make the student's experience less immediate and personal, less sincere and authentic?

This objection came to be felt not only in the classroom but also in the wide world of letters. At a certain point in the development of the modern critical movement, the virtues which had once excited enthusiasm began to be charged against it. Its energy was judged to be excessive, its assiduity to be officious. Its authority, once gladly acknowledged, was now accused of preempting that of literature itself. An irritable impatience was expressed even by critics who had made decisive contributions to the movement, eventually by T. S. Eliot himself. In his lecture at the University of Minnesota in 1956, Eliot spoke of the brilliance of the modern critical movement, chiefly American, and went on to ask whether it might not be thought *too* brilliant, whether its bright busyness did not interfere with the independence of the reader.

The reaction is understandable and in some considerable part it was justified. Like much else in modern culture, criticism had become plethoric and hyperactive, taking on something of the aspect of a fashion or an exciting new sport. One reason for the excess is that the most salient mode of American criticism, that which was called "New," seemed to offer a *method*, that of close textual analysis, which could be thought of as available to virtually anyone who wanted to use it. Cleanth Brooks has defended the new critical movement, among whose leaders he is eminent, from the charge of a sterile concern with the particularities of language and technique by pointing out that criticism from Aristotle on has always occupied itself with just such particularities. He is of course right, yet he himself notes that the New Criticism came under fire because "certain of its critical 'methods' " were susceptible of "mechanization" and he instances the "heavy-handed and witless analyses of literary works, often pushed to absurd limits and sometimes becoming an extravagant 'symbol-mongering.' "* In regard to the ready availability of methods, a historian of criticism, George Watson, finds it possible to say that "the average schoolboy of today is probably capable of analysing more closely and more accurately than Dryden or any of Dryden's contemporaries, and the ordinary reviewer often enjoys a similar unearned advantage over the greatest of English critics before the twentieth century."† The average schoolboy Mr. Watson has in mind is English rather than American and even so the estimate of his analytical powers is extravagant, doubtless was meant to be, yet the respect in which, however ironically, the average schoolboy is said to be superior to Dryden vividly suggests the store that for a time was set by the methodical concern with the particularities of language and technique. Such superiority as the average schoolboy has over Dryden, such advantage as the ordinary reviewer has over the greatest English critics before the twentieth century, are bound to be thought of little account, and the temptation naturally presents itself to dismiss as specious the method that is said to have given them their facile abilities.

We may of course be sure that the method of analysis, of close attention to the particularities of language and technique, has not in fact been invalidated by the excess of some of its practitioners. All criticism properly begins with the kind of consciousness that the method of analysis seeks to give. Yet there can be no doubt that the ascendancy of the method had the effect for a time of narrowing the range of critical discourse. It is true, as Mr. Brooks says, that Aristotle concerns himself with the particularities of language and technique, but other and more general or expansive considerations engage him as well, and it is these, I think, that stay best in memory and seem most to lead us to think about literature. What Aristotle says about literature is largely conditioned by his differences with Plato, and even what he says about the particularities of language and technique is therefore involved with questions about the nature of the mind upon which the particularities have their effect, about what effects are desirable or the contrary, the criterion being the health and comfort of the mind and the good of the polity. Such considerations are certainly not absent from the purview of the American critical movement in which the analytical method is salient.‡ But they are present chiefly by implication and do not readily lend themselves to discourse. Granting (again) that discourse about literature best begins with the particular work in all the particular elements of its existence, its range extends well beyond this. It is a true saying about literature that "there are things that are important beyond all this fiddle,"§ yet we are drawn to speculate why all this fiddle manages nevertheless to convince or delude us as to its unique importance, how it leads us to believe that it is the index and even the safeguard of the health of the polity, and we remark

---

* "Literary Criticism: Poet, Poem, and Reader," p. 393 of the present volume.
† *The Literary Critics* (London: Chatto & Windus, 1962; revised edition, 1964), p. 18.
‡ Their presence helps account for the disenchantment with the New Criticism, for its psychological, ethical, and political assumptions came to seem inadequate to the cultural circumstances which prevailed after some point in the mid-Fifties.
§ Marianne Moore, "Poetry."

the extent to which it subverts or supplements the polity's crude explicit moral law by means of its insidious perceptions or by means of its mere tones. It is as engaging in its mystery as in its potency: its potency, indeed, derives in large part from its mystery, which is one of the few beneficent darknesses left to engage our wonder—Keats seems never to have speculated about God, but he lived in a perpetual contemplation of the mystery of Shakespeare.

As it has been traditionally conceived, criticism is (among other things) a speculative discourse about the nature and function of literature. Its etymology reminds us that its practical end in view is the making of judgments, but from the first it understood that it could not proceed to that end without specifying the grounds on which judgment is to be made, and this requires it to say what the thing is that it judges. The discourse that ensues has always been thought highly pleasurable. The pleasure is a natural one—criticism, as Eliot has said, "is as inevitable as breathing."

If this is indeed so, the question must be asked whether literary criticism ought not have a greater place in the teaching of literature than recent pedagogic theory, or sentiment, has been willing to allow it. Criticism is not literature, and the pleasure of criticism is not the pleasure of literature. It is the latter that we seek to lead our beginning students to. But experience suggests that the two pleasures go together, that the pleasure of criticism makes literature and its pleasure the more readily accessible. This view may be supported by a single argument *ad hominem*: Is there anyone engaged in the teaching of literature who will not testify that his own responsiveness to literature has been made the readier by his involvement with criticism, that the categories, the modes and forms of thought, by which he apprehends literature have been made more numerous, that his sense of his subject has become more vivid, his engagement to it more steadfast?

The experience of the teacher proposes the possible experience of the student. For the student, discourse about literature in its generality as well as in its particularity, about literature conceived as a great continuous human enterprise, its greatness attested to by the serious and subtle thought that has been given to its nature and function, has the effect of making his response to literature the more immediate and the more intense. Not the less but the more: American thought about education, especially when it undertakes to examine and revise itself according to "progressive" doctrine, has for a long time manifested an antagonism to generalization and speculative abstraction and a tenderness for what is called "affective education" in contradistinction to "cognitive education." The distinction is a tempting one and long hapituation has led many to accept it as valid. Possibly it has a pragmatic usefulness as a guide to elementary instruction; of this I am not qualified to speak. But as it bears upon college instruction, I am sure that it can only mislead, and I am much inclined to believe that it is scarcely less wrong for secondary schools. At no period of life is generalization and speculation more attractive than in adolescence and early maturity, when the great metaphysical "Why?" of childhood is still a natural condition of the mind and the powers of rational discourse have been sufficiently developed to attempt the answers. It is a grave error of educational theory not to take account of the eagerness with which the young engage in speculation. Where there is so quick a propensity, so lively an appetite, the possibility of instruction is surely great. The fear that the affective life will be desiccated and made less sincere and authentic by such cognitive activity is groundless. William Wordsworth is a legendary defender of the truth and beneficence of the emotions and here is Wordsworth's view of the concord, we might say the continuity, between the affective and the cognitive: "Our continued influxes of feeling are modified and directed by our thoughts, which are indeed the representatives of all our past feelings."*

In making the present volume I have been guided by my conviction that the questions traditionally raised by criticism are of value in the literary education not only of the advanced and committed student but also of the student who is being "introduced" to literature.

Perhaps I can best begin an explanation of the principle on which I chose the essays here included by pointing out that I have not chosen Horace's epistle to the brothers Piso, *The Art of Poetry*, as it is generally called. Here is an anthology of criticism of considerable size even though it does not pretend to be compendious and it begins conformably enough with Plato and goes on expectably enough to Aristotle, but it does not take the presumably inevitable next step, it does not include Horace. Of course no one nowadays thinks that Horace as a critic approaches Plato and Aristotle in interest and value. Yet there was a time when he was preeminent in authority and, if only because this is so, he makes a continuing claim on our attention. For students of literature at a certain advanced stage of their education he is indispensable. Anyone who is committed to a systematic knowledge of the Western tradition of the literary art must have a direct and thoughtful experience of the work which contains the classic statement of the doctrine that literature, ideally conceived, has a double function, that of delighting and that of instructing or edifying, the former being subordinate to the latter. Such a student should also encounter in its original locus the famous doctrine of the affinity between poetry and pictures which once seemed to say so much about poetry until Lessing taught us to reject it as false and misleading.

But the student of whom we can say that he ought to have a knowledge of Horace's poem about literature makes after all a fairly special instance. If the advanced and committed student of literature reads *The Art of Poetry* in translation, as most of us do, he will not be aware of the wit that enlightens the poem in its original language and so he will not be prevented from thinking it dull, as most of us do; but he will know, if only dimly or piously, that in the study of literature there are many things that are dull in themselves or at first, although they become interesting when they are made objects of systematic thought—for example, when they are seen historically. We may reasonably expect that he will come to see that the substantive dullness of *The Art of Poetry* is in itself of the highest interest. Much of what the poem says is memorable chiefly because it suits the rather simple conception of literature that most people have, and the greater part of what it says is mere genial chatter about literature—a beautiful woman should not be depicted as having the tail of a fish; a tragedy should have no more than five acts; characters should speak in character; talent is necessary for the poet but so are good sense

---

* "Preface to *Lyrical Ballads*," p. 144 of the present volume.

and hard work; good poets don't have to go about dirty and unshorn and act as if they were crazy in order to show that they are inspired. The advanced and committed student ought to regard with wonder and curiosity the circumstance that a great poet—such I take Horace to be—should write about his art in so inconsequential a way, and in doing so he will have learned something: nothing much about the nature of literature itself but something of importance about the anomalies of culture.

But a student less committed to literary study and less advanced in it will not respond in the same way and should not be expected to. He will be immediately engaged by what Plato says about poets and poetry and by what Aristotle says about tragedy. In my own experience of reading these authors with freshman students I have never seen this to fail. But I expect no such engagement by what Horace says. And because the intellect or imagination of the beginning student cannot be stirred by the poem, it is courting pedagogic defeat to ask him to read it. If he deals with it dutifully and takes what it says as authoritative doctrine—as why should he not, the text having been assigned? —he can only conclude that criticism is a pretty dull and trivial business.

What I have said about the exclusion of Horace will make it plain that this anthology does not undertake to give a historical conspectus of criticism. I imagine that many teachers will be content that it should not, sharing my belief that it is criticism itself and not its history that should be presented to the beginning student. But I am of course aware that agreement with the principle on which I have made my selection cannot guarantee perfect accord with the result. If, as I expect, no one will quarrel with my exclusion of Horace, there may well be those who will wonder over, say, the exclusion of Sidney's *Apology for Poetry,* or Pope's *Essay on Criticism,* or Shelley's *Defense of Poetry.* I can respond only by avowing my personal admiration for these works and by saying that my experience tells me that they do not engage the speculative interests of beginning students.

Pedagogic considerations controlled my choice not only of older but also of modern texts and induced me to muster up the courage to omit certain of the masters of modern criticism for whose work I personally have very high regard. An acquaintance with this work is an essential part of the education of any person committed to the study of literature. But we have to see that it is written on the assumption that its audience is made up of people already adept in the study of literature, and, what is more, in the study of criticism. With this assumption its manner is in accord: the mode of exposition of some of these preeminent writers—I might mention Ransom, Blackmur, Burke, and Empson— responds to the knowledge, or knowingness, of the audience they address; the premises of their work are often to be found in other works with which it is in dialogue rather than being immediately stated, its idiom is allusive and ironic, and in general it takes more for granted than the beginning student can supply. In the face of great and deserved reputations, I have decided to omit what is likely to baffle and discourage the beginning student.

And of course I have omitted much that I wished to include but could not by reason of the limited space at my disposal.

I have not exercised what has been called "the inalienable right of anthologists" to include anything of my own beyond the Introduction, which

I hope will be read with its modest and merely propaedeutic intention in mind.

I should like to express my deep gratitude to my friend and colleague George Stade for his having supplied the footnotes and for his collaboration on the headnotes, which we have tried to make simple and uninterfering. And I give my warmest thanks to Stanley Burnshaw for his unfailingly helpful advice at every stage in the preparation of this book and to Brian Heald for having made the task easier in all the ways that a gifted and devoted editor can.

L.T.

CONTENTS

LITERARY CRITICISM
AN INTRODUCTORY READER

INTRODUCTION
What Is Criticism?

I

The word criticism derives from the Greek word meaning judgment. A critic does more things with literature than judge it, but his judicial function is involved in everything else that he does. That literature should have called into being an attendant art of judgment tells us something about the nature of literature—that it is an enterprise which is inherently competitive.

In the conventional praise that is nowadays likely to be given to the literary art, this characteristic is overlooked or implicitly denied. The pious view of the serious and dedicated author represents him as being superior to such crass considerations as the acknowledged degree of his excellence in relation to his fellows. He is presumed to be motivated by nothing but a disinterested desire to make his own work as good as his native talent and devoted application will permit. The Greeks, of course, thought otherwise. Their poets and dramatists wrote in open institutional contest with each other—we know how many times Pindar took first prize in music and poetry, we wonder how it could have happened that in one or another year Sophocles was awarded only second place in tragedy.* Dante, Shakespeare, and Milton were overt in their desire for preeminence and spoke shamelessly of the peculiar fame that was its due. In our own day a convention of modesty prevails among writers, making it startling when one of them—Ernest Hemingway, for example, or Norman Mailer—publicly estimates his powers and achievements by comparison with what his predecessors or contemporaries can show, but we may be sure that he is exceptional only in his avowal, not in his competitive concern.

---

* Lemprière's *Classical Dictionary,* after telling us that Pindar "conquered Myrtis in a musical contest," goes on to say, "He was not, however, so successful against Corinna, who obtained five times, while he was competitor, a poetical prize, which according to some, was adjudged rather to the charms of her person than to the brilliancy of her genius, or the superiority of her composition. In the public assemblies of Greece, where females were not permitted to contend, Pindar was awarded the prize in every other competition. . . ." And this is how *The Oxford Companion to French Literature* describes a moment in the career of Racine: "His *Andromaque* (1667) rivalled Corneille's *Le Cid* in its success, and in 1669, after the appearance of his comedy *Les Plaideurs* in 1668, he challenged the older dramatist on his own ground with the political play *Britannicus.* The contest was repeated in 1670, and the younger poet was held the victor, when his *Bérénice* and the *Tite et Bérénice* of Corneille appeared almost simultaneously. . . ."

1

There are several kinds of literary competition that the critic is called upon to judge. One is in essence the rivalry that goes on among tradesmen or craftsmen as to who can give, and be known to give, the best value. A memorable scene in Aristophanes' comedy, *The Frogs,* represents Aeschylus and Euripides in Hades contending over which of the two gives better measure in point of sheer weight. A great pair of scales is brought onto the stage, the dramatists take turns delivering what each takes to be his most ponderous lines, and the scales tip this way or that. The division of literary epochs into those that are "golden" and those that are "silver" is an old one, and the same metals are used to classify poets of any one age: the title of Gerald Bullett's anthology, *Silver Poets of the Sixteenth Century,* suggests that the poets included—Wyatt, Surrey, Sidney, Ralegh, and Davies—although precious indeed, are not so valuable as other poets of the period, such as Spencer and Shakespeare.

"There is no competition among poems," Allen Tate has said. "A good poem suggests the possibility of other poems equally good."* There are occasions in our experience when the first sentence is true. And although the second sentence is always true, it affords the ground for denying the permanent truth of the first. For no sooner have we said "equally good" than we conjure up "not quite so good" and "even better." If the "equally good" poems are peaceable among themselves, it is because the competition has already taken place and been judged. Poems are not competitive as poets are, out of natural depravity. Their competitiveness is imposed on them by us, by our restless need to discriminate among degrees of excellence.

In some sense, a work of art is a commodity. The word artist, to which we now give a highly honorific significance, was once exactly synonymous with the word artisan, that is, a skilled workman who offers the products of his skill for sale. The word "poet" derives from the Greek word meaning "maker," and indeed "maker" was the common English word for poet up to the sixteenth century. Like other objects that are made for the use or pleasure of the customer, the literary object is to be judged by the materials out of which it is fashioned and by the skill of the fashioning. The title of Cleanth Brooks's book about poetry, *The Well-Wrought Urn,* suggests that a poem, whatever else it may be, is an object of *virtu,* prized for its shapeliness and for the ingenious craft that went into the shaping.† We may surmise that Professor Brooks wanted to revive in his readers the sense that was stronger in an older time than it is now, that a poem is a *made* thing, seeking to qualify our modern tendency to think that what we call a work of art is not so much made as *created:* the important place in the moral and spiritual life that we assign to it seems to suggest that it is not really a *thing* at all. In this regard it is useful to reflect that things which in our culture are thought of as the products of "mere" craftsmanship are in other cultures respected in an ultimate degree and considered to have the same transcendent value which we attribute to a work of "high" art. To a Japanese, swords of the thirteenth or fourteenth century, the period of the

---

* See p. 428 of the present volume.

† The Italian word *virtù* when used in English in this context means the aesthetic quality of a work that makes it of interest to a buyer, especially to one who *collects* such works.

great swordsmiths of his country, will yield an experience no less profound, transcendent, and valuable than that which might be afforded by a great poem or painting, and he holds the great smiths in as much reverence as great poets or painters.

In one of his functions, then, the critic is the kind of judge that we call a connoisseur, preferably one who has a pretty thorough knowledge—although not necessarily a practical command—of the technical means the artist or craftsman uses, and the ability to perceive and point out the particular merits of the work, how one or another difficulty was overcome or how this or that detail was scamped or crudely handled. His judgment of any one object involves comparison, whether explicit or implied, with other objects of the same genre. In regard to certain objects, such as Greek or Chinese urns, or Japanese swords, or paintings, or furniture, or gems, the results of these comparative judgments are expressed, in auction rooms and dealers' shops, in monetary terms: the presumed or agreed upon artistic value of the object determines the price it will bring from those who desire to possess objects of this kind.* The expression of artistic value in monetary terms cannot be made in the case of literary objects, but the process of connoisseurship, of making judgments of comparative values, is not essentially different from that which is applied to other artistic works.†

Another kind of literary competition which the critic adjudicates is more grandiose. In it the writer figures not as a craftsman of however exalted a character, pursuing a craftsman's purpose of satisfying the expectations of the customer or patron, but rather as some great feudal lord who asserts his claim to dominion over territories and populations in rivalry with other feudal lords having the same end in view. The critic who exercises his function of judging

---

* Jakob Rosenberg, the eminent historian of art, begins his book, *On Quality in Art: Criteria of Excellence, Past and Present* (Princeton, N.J.: Princeton University Press, Bollingen, 1967), with the following statement: "In recent years we have witnessed an astonishing rise in the prices paid for works of art, both of old and of modern masters. It has been a rise sensational to a degree hardly ever equalled in the past. Naturally one wonders about the causes and the justification for such a development, and this leads to a feeling of uncertainty about the real value of these works of art. We are not concerned [in this book] with the prices of art objects, with their material value, but with their aesthetic value, their quality. Yet if the market acts on a sound basis, the material value should reflect the true artistic value or quality. Thus the problem with which we are concerned in this volume, namely, how to make a proper quality judgment, is as important for the art historian and the art critic as it is for the collector, the museum man, and the serious art dealer."

† Of course a literary work is sold and bought, but the price that the customer pays for it is determined not by its artistic merit but by the cost of printing, binding, and distributing the book in which it appears, and of giving the author some return on his labor and the publisher a profit; we pay no more for a copy of the *Iliad* (perhaps less: Homer does not receive royalties) than for a copy of a detective story. The case is different, to be sure, when what is in question is the original manuscript, the work as it came from the author's hand, or a rare first edition. The artistic value imputed to the work then determines the price it will bring in the open market. The recently discovered manuscript of the first version of T. S. Eliot's *The Waste Land,* a work that can be bought in print for not much more than a dollar, is, as we say, priceless.

in this situation is less the connoisseur than a justice of some high court. He judges the work not primarily in regard to its merit or excellence or degree of preciousness, as a thing to be possessed and cherished, but in regard to its power and "greatness," as claiming possession of us.

There are, it will be seen, two issues to be adjudicated in the contention. One is the legitimacy of any single author's claim to assert dominion over his readers. The other is the conflict of claims among rivals for power.

The latter issue, the jealous rivalry among literary earls and dukes, or, as Hemingway put it, candidates for the presidency, engages the modern critic rather less than might be supposed, and much less than it engaged critics of a former time. D. H. Lawrence and James Joyce are thought by many to be the two preeminent prose writers in English of the first third of the twentieth century. Each disliked the work of the other (thinking it objectionable for, among other reasons, its obscenity); each thought that praise given to the work of the other diminished his own standing, and that the mind of any reader who admired the rival was insofar corrupted as to be unable to respond properly to him. There are indeed critics who undertake to continue the antagonism— for example, the admiration that F. R. Leavis gives Lawrence is sustained by his condemnation of Joyce's methods and sensibility. Most critics, however, do not feel it necessary to make the choice a matter of absolute decision. Perhaps drawn by temperament more to one than to another, they find it possible (even gratifying) to recognize the power of both. To be sure, if one has for a time submitted to the power of Lawrence, it is not easy to submit soon to the power of Joyce, and *vice versa*. Nor, perhaps, should it be. But when one is free from both dominations, it may well seem, as one considers them in recollection, that there is no choice to be made.

This is not to say that the modern critic is wholly indifferent to the hierarchy of literary status. Where the judgment of "great" is made, it is inevitable that judgments of greater and greatest will follow. But the modern critic is less inclined to press toward hierarchical strictness than critics formerly were. Matthew Arnold, in his essay "The Study of Poetry," undertook to designate the canon of the truly great poets of the world and of England. It is not an enterprise that is likely to be repeated in our day.

More than exercising judgment upon the conflicting claims of authors as to how much dominion is their due, the critic, so far as he is a judge, concerns himself with the other issue raised by the *power* of literature— with, that is, the rights of the author as over against those of the reader. What is the legitimacy of the power over us that Shakespeare exercises through *King Lear*? He overcomes our minds, requiring us to behold things from which we want to turn away in horror and disgust. He leads us to the very point of despair, and, as Keats said in the sonnet in which he expressed his fears "on sitting down to read *King Lear* once again," even carries us beyond that point. By what right does he do this? By what right does any author invade our privacy, establish his rule over our emotions, demand of us that we give heed to what he has to say, which may be wholly at odds with what we want to hear said if we are to be comfortable? Joyce said that the ideal reader of his difficult *Finnegans Wake* was someone with an ideal insomnia. By what right does he make this exorbitant demand?

That there is in the abstract such a right is the assumption of any critic.

Not infrequently his judicial task is to affirm the right in some particular instance of its having been unjustly denied, the responsibility for the miscarriage of justice lying, of course, at the door not only of the public but also of impercipient critics. Blake's poems, now so much admired and happily submitted to, were scarcely read for decades after their publication, not until a few critics undertook to declare that this was an impermissible state of affairs. *Moby-Dick* fell virtually into oblivion upon its first appearance in 1851 and was not allowed to exercise its power until critics in the 1920s aroused themselves to say that it should and must. It can happen that time and fashion rescind a right that was once in force, as in the case of John Donne, greatly admired in his own day, then scolded and condescended to in the eighteenth century, then for two centuries largely ignored, and restored to admiration by critical opinion at the beginning of this century.* And of course there are instances of criticism undertaking to reverse favorable judgments made by earlier courts. Matthew Arnold said that Dryden and Pope were not properly to be called poets at all. In our time Milton and Shelley have suffered from influential adverse opinions, of which the best known are those delivered by T. S. Eliot; in the case of Milton, Eliot subsequently reversed himself. When, after an extended advocacy, the high status of Henry James was accepted as legitimate, Maxwell Geismar undertook to question the correctness of the decision and even the disinterestedness of the judges who had made it, but he seems not to have succeeded in sending the case back for review.

II

If we survey the exercise of criticism's judicial function through its long history, we discern certain striking changes in the criteria which have controlled judgment. One such change has already been touched on, the diminishing (but by no means defunct) tendency in modern times to think of the writer as a craftsman and of his work as a made thing. At this point it will be useful to be aware of the successive assumptions about literature on which criticism has operated. These have been systematically and lucidly described by M. H. Abrams in his well-known book, *The Mirror and the Lamp,* and what follows is chiefly a paraphrase of Professor Abrams' admirable first chapter.†

* It is a view commonly held that criticism is insensitive and resistant to new work of high quality and habitually delays its acceptance by the public. On the whole, this is not so. The large majority of notable works in all ages have quite quickly captured the interest and esteem of a significant body of readers. I have noted some exceptions and of course their number could be extended, but they do not support the view that as a rule genius is not readily recognized. It is no doubt true that new work sometimes meets with hostility from influential quarters. But the contemned artist usually (not always) has his own supporting group and the history of modern culture suggests that dissident opinions prevail over conventional ones and in relatively short time. The fullest statement of the opposite view is that made by Henri Peyre in his *The Failures of Criticism* (Ithaca, N.Y.: Cornell University Press, 1944).

† (New York: Oxford University Press, 1953.) I should emphasize *chiefly,* for I have at several points touched upon considerations that were not to Professor Abrams' purpose. And even where I have followed Professor Abrams, the responsibility for the ideas set forth, it goes without saying, is mine.

Professor Abrams begins by observing that in all comprehensive theories of art there are four elements of the artistic situation which are dealt with in one or another degree of emphasis. The first of these is the work of art itself. The second is the maker of the work, the artist. The third is the subject of the work, what the work "is about," and this Professor Abrams denotes by a term that he chooses because it is "neutral and comprehensive": the universe. And finally there is the audience, those who hear or see or read the work. The difference among various theories of art and among the kinds of judgment that follow from these theories lies largely in the varying emphasis that is placed on one or more of the four elements.

The ancient Greeks thought of art primarily in terms of the relation between the work and the universe. Plato takes for granted the common idea that the essence of any work of art is that it represents or imitates some part of the universe. The imitative nature of art makes the ground for the low esteem in which Plato held it, at least for his philosophical purposes. (It is plain that, in what we may speak of as his personal opinion, he held art in high regard; he had a considerable reputation as a poet and some of his philosophical dialogues are intensely admired for being in themselves works of art.) Plato distinguishes three degrees of reality. Of these the universe of things as we know them through the senses is in a median position: the things which we know and use in daily practical life are but imitations of eternal Ideas of things—any object, a bed, a table, a jar, is but the imperfect representation or imitation of the abstract and perfect Idea of the bed, table, or jar, just as the circle we draw on the blackboard in a geometry lesson is but the imperfect representation or imitation of the Idea of the circle. For Plato the Idea is the reality, the real reality. And if the objects of sense that we habitually and unreflectively think of as real are in truth not real at all but copies or shadows of reality, then how much further removed from reality are art's imitations of these objects. They are the copies of copies, the shadows of shadows.

No less than Plato, Aristotle conceived of art as imitative. He speaks of all the arts as being "modes of imitation." But he does not intend this to be in the least a pejorative characterization. For one thing, because he rejects Plato's doctrine of Ideas, he does not conceive of art as imitating reality at two removes; if it is indeed a copy, it is not a copy of a copy. What is more, it is apparent that by imitation Aristotle means something more than mere copying; the two English words by which the Greek word *mimesis* may be translated, imitation and representation, are close in meaning but they are not exactly the same, and it is representation rather than imitation that Aristotle has chiefly in mind. Although it is true that art refers to existing things, it is by no means wholly controlled by what is habitually observed of these things. Each art follows the laws of its own being in its mode of imitation. Aristotle says of tragedy and comedy that they show men as, respectively, "better than they really are" and "worse than they really are" and that each of them uses a selection of language appropriate to its intention. This gives a very considerable latitude to representation. Nowhere does Aristotle speak of a literary genre that represents men just as they really are.

Yet, for all the license that Aristotle grants to representation, his *Poetics* served to establish the mimetic doctrine, the critical mode that concentrates on the relation of the work of art to the universe and on the truth of the imitation that the work achieves. Mimetic theories maintained their force in criticism down to the end of the eighteenth century, had a lesser but still consequential existence in the nineteenth century, and are not without vitality today. In the nineteenth century they appear in the often highly polemical doctrines of realism and naturalism, which have chiefly to do with prose fiction and drama. At present they are most notably to be observed in the doctrine of "socialist realism," which constitutes the official aesthetic of the Soviet Union. And it is probably true that the mimetic assumption is at least one ground—perhaps the first ground—of artistic judgment of the majority of people who participate in Western culture. "Lifelike" and "true to life" are perhaps still the readiest and most common terms of praise of a work of art. It ought to be remarked that the diminished theoretical status of mimetic theories of art does not deny the genuineness of the pleasure that is to be derived from recognition, from perceiving the success of a work of mimetic art in representing what it intended to represent.

In the Renaissance another conception of art generated theories in a line which ran parallel with the mimetic. Professor Abrams calls them pragmatic theories because they look at the work of art "chiefly as a means to an end, an instrument for getting something done." The elements of the artistic situation that pragmatic theories concentrate on are the work of art and the audience: the end to which the work of art directs itself, the thing to be done of which it is the instrument, is to give pleasure to the audience. This, however, is not a final end but a means to yet another end, which is to instruct or edify the audience. The source of this conception of the right purpose of literature is the *Art of Poetry* of the Roman poet, Horace. "Poets," he said, "aim at giving either profit or delight, or at combining the giving of pleasure with some useful precepts of life."* The beneficent moral effect of poetry was a chief preoccupation of criticism during the Renaissance; in England its most notable expression is Sir Philip Sidney's *An Apology for Poetry*. As a basis of critical judgment it survived with at least a degree of vitality into the eighteenth century—Dr. Johnson's essay on Shakespeare, the preface to his edition of the plays, attests to the interest it might still have for a powerful mind. By the nineteenth century its intellectual authority was at an end, although its social authority was still very commanding: that a work had a "high moral purpose" was a ready reason for praising it, and the reviewer or reader who could not discover such a purpose was likely to be disconcerted. Judgments of this kind were not commonly made by the highly developed literary minds of the age; Wordsworth, Shelley, and Matthew Arnold were firm in their belief that literature had a decisive effect for good upon the moral life, but they did not say that this influence was exercised purposefully and by means of precept. At the present time the idea that literature is to be judged by its moral effect has virtually no place in critical theory. In actual critical practice, however, it has a quite considerable vitality. Insofar as literature represents the relations between people, it deals with questions of morality, and a work is judged by the degree to which its treatment of

---

* T. S. Dorsch's translation, *Classical Literary Criticism* (New York: Penguin Books). For a characterization of Horace as a critic, see the Preface to the present volume, pp. x–xi.

moral situations bears in an enlightening way on moral actualities. This, to be sure, is not the same thing as judging a work by the criterion of its ability to inculcate correct moral principles.*

Pragmatic theory in its later stages tended to lighten the emphasis it placed on the moral effect of the work and paid increasing attention to the degree and kind of pleasure the work afforded and to the particular means by which pleasure is given. Horace's *Art of Poetry* had been written as a letter to two young friends of the poet who aspired to be poets themselves and it undertook to advise the aspirants as to what they ought and ought not do if they were to succeed in their ambition. The critics in the line of descent from Horace continue and develop his pedagogic intention: they are pragmatic not only in their assumption that a work of literature has a particular end in view—the giving of pleasure to the further end of giving moral instruction or edification—but also in their purpose of proposing to teach how this end is to be achieved.

The two elements of the artistic situation with which pragmatic criticism is concerned are, it will have been seen, the work of art and the audience. Of the two, the audience is the controlling one; the pragmatic investigation of the particular devices that were most advantageous to the poet took as its criterion the response of the audience: such effects as led the audience to respond in the desired way—which is to say, in the way that the audience itself was presumed to desire—were considered successful and the devices by which these effects were secured were to be recommended. In short, the measure of artistic success

---

* The English critic D. J. Enright, who has taught English literature in Thailand, reports on the high status that direct moral instruction has in the literary thought of that country: "The Thais display a strong and persistent tendency to moralize, or rather to expect other people to moralize, and they often feel unhappy if they cannot indulge this taste. Everything must teach a lesson, preferably a moral one; the lesson does not need to be a complex one, in fact complex moral lessons are suspect (doubtfully moral, that is). That the lesson is one you have learnt before does not detract from its value: in fact this serves to set the seal of approval on the moral—there are not many morals, either, in the world—and also on the medium of the moral (that is, a poem with a good moral is a good poem). If everything is to teach us a lesson, then clearly lessons themselves, at school or at the university, must teach us a lesson. . . .

"Teachers in Thai schools were worried and embarrassed when Daphne du Maurier's *Rebecca* was set as an English reader. Finally one of them went to the Ministry of Education to make representations. The conversation unfolded along these lines:

Teacher: 'The pupils ask us what *Rebecca* teaches us, and we cannot give them an answer. What *is* the answer, please?'

Official: 'The book is intended to teach them English.'

Teacher: 'But that is not enough. It is a book and a book must convey a lesson of some sort. It must *teach*. If it doesn't teach a lesson, then they want to know why they have to read it.'

Official (sophisticated above the average): 'There are some books which we read just for pleasure.'

Teacher: 'Pleasure?'

Official: 'Yes, pleasure. We derive pleasure from reading it.'

Teacher: 'But we can't tell our pupils that! They wouldn't respect us any more!' "

—" 'Reading Poetry Makes You Nice and Neat,' " *Transition* (Kampala, Uganda), Vol. 7, No. 37, October 1968, page 25.

was the approval of the audience, with this proviso only, that the audience must be an enlightened one, its taste properly trained and refined by habituation to the best in art.

The judicial hegemony of the audience was not to last. The focus of criticism gradually shifted from the work of art to its maker, who came to be seen as something other than a maker. Since one of its intentions had been to show how poetry should be written, pragmatic theory necessarily had the poet somewhat in mind, chiefly in his willingness to submit his natural energies to the rational control of precept and tradition. As the eighteenth century advanced, however, criticism became increasingly interested in the natural energies themselves, in the genius with which the poet had been endowed, which came to be identified with the spontaneity of his feelings and the force of his imagination. In the preceding age Ben Jonson, writing in the spirit of Horace, had supplied English pragmatic criticism with the maxim that summarizes its pedagogic mission: "A good poet's made as well as born." Now it became the critical tendency to invert the famous line, to lay the greater stress on the innate abilities of the poet. And in the degree that the interest in the poet grew, the attention paid to the audience and its demands diminished. The more authority criticism assigned to the poet, the less it granted to the audience.

During the late years of the eighteenth century this tendency accelerated dramatically. ". . . All good poetry is the spontaneous overflow of powerful feelings"—Professor Abrams quotes the famous statement of Wordsworth in the 1800 Preface to *Lyrical Ballads* as signalizing in English criticism the displacement of the mimetic and pragmatic theories of art by what he calls expressive theories.* In these the elements of the artistic situation that are considered are the work of art and the artist. As Professor Abrams puts it, "The first test any poem must pass is no longer, 'Is it true to nature?' or 'Is it appropriate to the requirements either of the best judges or the generality of mankind?' but a criterion looking in a different direction; namely, 'Is it sincere? Is it genuine? Does it match the intention, the feeling, and the actual state of mind of the poet while composing?' The work ceases then to be regarded as primarily a reflection of nature . . . ; the mirror held up to nature becomes transparent and yields the reader insight into the mind and heart of the poet himself."

Here it should perhaps be said that the insights that the work yields are into the mind and heart of the poet himself *as poet*. When we ask of a poem whether it matches the actual state of mind of the poet while composing, we limit the range of our question to that part of the poet's state of mind which he has chosen to express. The *whole* state of his mind while composing will include, alas, much else—the discomfort of the rash on his neck, his dislike of the smell of the cabbage that is cooking, his anxiety over his child's persistent sore throat, not to mention all the unconscious but afflicting anxieties and conflicts that psychoanalytical theory says are always at work in us. The "actual state of mind" that we are aware of has been selected and even summoned; in some fairly simple sense of the word and in no pejorative sense, it is histrionic. The

---

* It should always be kept in mind that Wordsworth's statement continues: "but though this be true, poems to which any value can be attached, were never produced on any variety of subjects but by a man who being possessed of more than usual organic sensibility had also thought long and deeply."

sincerity we discern and respond to is not only a function of the poet's intention but also—and perhaps chiefly—an effect of his art. His poem is sincere not only because he means it to be but also because he has a genius for sincere utterance, for using language that has, as we say, the accent of sincerity.

And of course the criterion of sincerity comes into significant use only when the work to which it is applied is judged to be in some way interesting and important. It is after all possible to recognize the sincerity of a work that does not engage our interest, and in such a case the sincerity is thought of not as a quality of art but as a quasi-moral quality; when we remark its presence in a work which we do not admire, we are in effect saying of the poor man who wrote it that at least he did not undertake to deceive us. Perhaps, indeed, the word sincerity is not the most fortunate one to denote the quality that expressive theory makes salient. In any work that does engage our interest it is taken for granted, and perhaps the least likely explicit positive judgment on a successful work that a critic will make is that it is sincere.

To perceive some awkwardness in the word sincerity as denoting the congruity between the poem and the poet's state of mind in the act of composing is not to question the importance that the congruity has in expressive theories. But perhaps an even more important characteristic of these theories is the authority with which they invested the poet. So far from requiring him to submit to the judgment of the audience, they conceived the reverse to be the appropriate state of affairs: the poet made the criterion by which the audience was to be judged. Even the critic approached him with awe; so far from presuming to suggest to the poet how he should go about his business, the critic conceived it as his function to serve the purposes of the poet, to learn to read him, divesting himself of the prejudices and predispositions that stand in the way of comprehension. The poet becomes a law unto himself which he hands down to the audience and critic, if they but have the humility and grace of spirit to receive it.

The latest-developed theories of art, those which Professor Abrams calls the objective theories, transfer to the work of art itself the authority and autonomy that the expressive theories had given to the artist. The objective view of art began to emerge in the late eighteenth and early nineteenth centuries and has had a very considerable influence on the literary thought of our own time. Unlike earlier theories—but Professor Abrams makes exception of "the central portion of Aristotle's *Poetics*"—it does not go about its work with reference to any other of the four elements of the artistic situation than the work itself: neither the audience, the artist, nor the universe is taken into account, only the work of art, which is to be dealt with only in terms of the formal relationships that are to be perceived among its parts. We may conjecture that the objective view of art came into being in response to, or at least concomitantly with, a new attitude among many advanced artists—their desire to liberate themselves from what they thought of as the bondage of personality, their distaste for the idea that they were expressing a state of feeling, which, after all, suggests communication to someone and submission to the conventions that make communication possible. The object that the artist created is understood to have no limiting relation to his own state of feeling, let alone to the audience or the universe; it exists in and for itself. In Joyce's novel, *A Portrait of the Artist as a Young Man*, Stephen Dedalus's remarks on what he calls "didactic" and "pornographic" art

—art that seeks to inculcate a moral attitude and art that stimulates desire of any kind—and his celebrated description of the God-like imperturbability of the artist* will serve to suggest the personal aesthetic of the attitude. It may be questioned whether, in final effect, any artist is capable of carrying out the program to the letter, and Professor Abrams notes the tendency of critics to depart from the strict objective concern with the literary object which they profess. Yet both the artistic program and the critical theory are salutary in reminding us that the work of art in and for itself has a first claim on us.

III

The intention of judgment is a salient motive of all critical theories. They undertake to say what literary excellence consists in and how discriminations between various degrees of excellence are to be made. But if criticism were confined to its judicial function, it would be a far less engaging activity than in fact it is. Actually, however, as has been seen, criticism is anterior to any particular act of judgment in that it defines the nature of the object to be judged and lays out the grounds on which judgment is to proceed. And criticism continues after judgment has been passed, if by judgment we mean simply the attribution to a work, or a canon of work, of a certain degree of excellence. For example, the peculiar excellence of Shakespeare's plays was very fully recognized in their own time and the first superlative judgment has really never been questioned in a decisive way. Yet the body of Shakespeare criticism that has come into being in the intervening years is of such magnitude that it is scarcely to be encompassed by any reader in a lifetime, and there is no likelihood of a falling off in its rate of increase.† What is all this activity about?

It is certainly true that much of it is devoted to judgment—to reaffirming in new and particular ways the general judgment made four centuries back. But judgment thus reiterated in ever-renewed ingenuity is not judgment in any ordinary sense. It is judgment as celebration. Or it is judgment as love. Spinoza spoke of the "intellectual love of God," by which he meant the unremitting activity of mind which ought to be directed to the comprehension of the totality of the universe which, in Spinoza's conception, is one with God. The criticism of Shakespeare may be thought of as just such an activity: its assumption is that the effort to understand its great object is to be perpetual, that it cannot come to an end, that there is always more for it to perceive. What is observed and concluded by one mind does not wholly satisfy another; the discernment that seems sufficient at one time seems inadequate or mistaken a few decades later. About the permanent interest of the object there can be no doubt.

Criticism does not always discharge its function of what might be called simple and primary judgment quite so expeditiously as in the case of Shakespeare, although on the whole it works with reasonable dispatch. Once it has

* See pp. 317–326 of this volume.

† "Over the sixty-year period following the two-volume Variorum Edition of 1877, and covered by the *Hamlet Bibliography* of A. A. Raven it is computed that twelve days have not passed without witnessing the publication of some additional item of Hamletiana"—Harry Levin, *The Question of* HAMLET (New York: Oxford University Press, 1959), pp. 3–4.

done so, the larger part of its activity of understanding begins. This activity manifests itself in a variety of particular forms and purposes, each of which is an expression of what criticism is, the intellectual love of literature.

The scientific implications of Spinoza's original phrase have some relevance to our paraphrase. Criticism in its relation to literary phenomena bears comparison with science in its relation to natural phenomena. The comparison is permissible only if it is not carried beyond a certain point. Aristotle said that "it is the mark of an educated mind to seek only so much exactness in each type of inquiry as may be allowed to the nature of the subject-matter," and certainly the degree of exactness to be sought in criticism is not equal to that sought in a natural science. It should also be said that comparison between the processes of the two disciplines will be valid only if the science referred to is at a relatively early stage of development. These provisos accepted, the connection between the two activities seems a useful one for our purpose.

A first undertaking of criticism in dealing with a work of literature is to describe the object of its interest. This may be expeditiously begun by saying— after an examination which usually, if it is made by a practised eye, need not be more than cursory—what genre of work it belongs to: it is an epic, a certain kind of long poem; or it is a lyric, a certain kind of short poem; or it is a novel, a prose narrative of a certain length setting forth fictive events; and so on.* The naming of the genre to which the work seems to belong is in itself not very enlightening (and sometimes it darkens understanding by raising false issues), but it serves to initiate the next step in description, the observation of the particularities of the work. Milton's *Paradise Lost* is like the *Iliad* and the *Aeneid* in being a long poem about events of high import in which divine beings play a decisive part, and it is like its predecessors in certain linguistic respects. The effect of the work does not, it is true, wholly depend upon the reader's acquaintance with the earlier epics. But Milton obviously intended that it should be thought of in connection with them—to some extent he counted on the connection being apparent, and part of the descriptive work of criticism is to further the reader's consciousness of the tradition in which the author composed. And the noticing of similarities inevitably involves the remarking of differences: the reader and the critic will be at one in their curiosity about what in the work is new.

Here it should be said that the status of the quality of newness in art is an ambiguous one. Probably in all times certain people and groups of people have been made anxious and irritable by artistic novelty. In some cultural epochs the society as a whole is resistant to it. At other times it is one of the chief *desiderata* of art. This seems to be the case in our own time, when new styles and modes

---

* "Just as every animal belongs to a species," José Ortega y Gasset says, "every literary work belongs to a genre (the theory of Benedetto Croce who denies the existence of literary forms in this sense has left no trace in aesthetics)."—"Notes on the Novel," in *The Dehumanization of Art* (Princeton, N.J.: Princeton University Press, 1968), p. 54.

A recently established scholarly journal describes itself as follows: "*Genre* is a quarterly publication devoted to generic criticism. It publishes articles which fall into the following categories: (1) theoretical discussions of the genre concept, (2) historical studies of particular genres and genre debates, (3) attempts to establish and define genres, (4) interpretations of works of literature from the genre point of view."

are likely to be readily accepted and quickly exhausted. As one writer has put it, "for modern art in general, and for avant-garde in particular, the only irremediable and absolute artistic error is a traditional artistic creation, an art that imitates and repeats itself."* But even in cultural epochs much more conservative than ours, art, however traditional in intention, does not remain fixed and static but tends to change, even though sometimes almost imperceptibly. The awareness of its shifts in style, whether these be gradual and slow or radical and sudden, is part of the developed consciousness of any art, and it is one of the purposes of criticism to intensify this consciousness. To be aware of what a particular style evolved from or of what has evolved out of it is to become more sensitive to what in itself it is.

Early in his enterprise of description the critic will take account of the form or structure of the work he is dealing with. He perceives this, and seeks to make us perceive it, both as a shape, interesting and perhaps beautiful in itself, and also as the means by which the reader's emotions and thoughts are organized toward the effect the work intends.

Sometimes the description of form can proceed without difficulty and with the fairly confident expectation that it will be objective. Dante planned *The Divine Comedy* to have a form that would be readily apprehended. The poem is in three parts, each devoted to one of the three states of the after-life, Hell, Purgatory, and Paradise. The verse is *terza rima*, triple rime, i.e. stanzas of three verses, riming in the pattern aba, bcb, cdc, etc. Each book consists of thirty-three cantos, except the first, which has thirty-four; the total is thus 100. The structure of the poem, it is plain to see, intends a symmetry of a precise kind, one that, we know, was controlled by Dante's belief in the aesthetic and symbolic properties of certain numbers, of which 3 and 10 and certain of their multiples are preeminent, although he also attached special value to 7. There is no doubt a peculiar pleasure to be had from a structure so exact and symmetrical as this. And in general it can be said that readers are likely to respond in a positive way to a work whose component elements are arranged in a form that is rigorous and economical. The perception of unity in diversity is one of the gratifications of the experience of art; a unity made readily manifest, as, for example, in *Oedipus Rex*, may be supposed to give the pleasure of reassurance, as if it implied a thoroughly well-ordered and rational universe even though the substance of the play seems to suggest that the universe is incomprehensible.

But not all unity is readily manifest, often it must be discerned by effort, sometimes by controverting the received ideas of what constitutes unity. To Voltaire, who constructed his own plays according to the quite precise rules which governed French drama for a considerable time, *Hamlet* appeared to be virtually inchoate, and his opinion was long shared by the great majority of French readers, who were accustomed to a different conception of form than

* Renato Poggioli, *The Theory of the Avant-Garde* (Cambridge, Mass.: Harvard University Press, 1968), p. 82. The term *avant-garde* refers to that art and its creators which depart radically from the accepted artistic conventions of the time. Literally, it means vanguard, the part of an army that moves in advance of the main body in an attack, but the literal meaning belies the actual character of *avant-garde*, which does not conceive of itself as cooperating with the main body but, on the contrary, seeks to discredit and destroy it.

that which organizes *Hamlet*. Until relatively recent years, *A Winter's Tale* made many of even the most ardent admirers of Shakespeare uncomfortable; it seemed to lack unity because its action falls into two parts, the second separated from the first by an interval of sixteen years. This dichotomy is nowadays generally thought to be of no account in view of the invincible integrity of the play's thematic development and style. For a considerable time *Ulysses* was said by its detractors to be formless—one notable critic called it "an explosion in a cesspool"; now the precision with which it is structured is generally recognized and there are even those who hold that the precision is too great, to the point of its being mechanical! The shifting opinions on questions of form will suggest the extent to which judgment in this matter is likely to be subjective and conditioned by prevailing taste and fashion. The coherence of a Gothic cathedral is now a thing taken for granted, but for a quite considerable period it was a perception beyond the competence of most educated people.

Up to a point, the description of a literary work can proceed with a considerable degree of objectivity. Certain of the elements of description can even be quantitative. Quantified data about literature are in rather bad repute as being contrary to the spirit of literature, but they have their uses. How one poet's management of a given kind of verse differs from another's can be expressed numerically, for traditional English verse is based on the ratio of accented to unaccented syllables, and the act of *counting* once seemed so important to it that the word "numbers" was a common synonym for verse (*Noble Numbers* is the title of one of Herrick's collections of poems; Pope, speaking of his poetic precocity, said, "I lisped in numbers, for the numbers came.") Iambic pentameter normally has five stresses to a line; if it is observed of a poet who uses this form that he inclines to write lines which, if read "for sense" rather than being "scanned," have only four fully stressed syllables, we have learned something about why his verse sounds as it does. It is observed of Yeats that birds figure frequently in his poems. This seems pertinent to our effort to understand his symbolism and, in general, the processes of his imagination. Doubtless there is something absurd in determining that x number of birds appear in the poems and that among them there are this many curlews, that many herons, swans, or hawks. Still, the quantification makes the observation rather the more significant, and it might lead the critic to remark that birds figured more in Yeats's imagination at one period than at another, from which conclusions of some interest might be drawn. Marcel Proust, writing about Stendhal's novel, *The Red and the Black,* says that the "loftiness of soul" of its hero, Julien Sorel, is "linked to actual height"; he has in mind the circumstance that the incidents in which Julien is shown on, or climbing to, a high place run to a quite considerable number—eight by my count. Once we have been put in mind of this repetition, each of these incidents comes into a sharper focus and is seen as a sort of epitome of the whole story of Julien's commitment to a life which will rise above the mediocre and the commonplace. Caroline Spurgeon remarks on the group of grandiose images in *Antony and Cleopatra* which, she says, is peculiar to this play.* They are "images of the world, the firmament, the ocean and vastness generally." And she goes on: "This vastness

---

* *Shakespeare's Imagery and What It Tells Us* (New York: Cambridge University Press, 1958), p. 352.

of scale is kept constantly before us by the word 'world,' which occurs forty-two times, nearly double, or more than double, as often as in most other [of Shakespeare's] plays, and it is continually employed in a way which increases the sense of grandeur, power and space. . . ."

The usefulness of quantitative description can be of only limited extent and the objectivity of description is not to be measured by the degree to which it relies upon quantification. As for objectivity itself, although it is indeed a quality which we look for in criticism and prize when we find it, Aristotle's *caveat* against demanding more exactness than the subject-matter permits is here most relevant. We expect of the critic that he will make every possible effort, in Matthew Arnold's famous words, "to see the object as in itself it really is" and to describe it accordingly. But we know that what is seen by one critic with the best possible will to see accurately is likely to be different from what is seen by another critic with an equally good will. There comes a point at which description becomes interpretation. There is no help for this failure of perfect objectivity, if that is indeed what we ought to call it. It is in the nature of the case that the object as in itself it really is will not appear wholly the same to any two minds. Perhaps this is properly a cause for rejoicing. Mozart as interpreted by Toscanini is not the same as Mozart interpreted by Munch, but both interpretations give us pleasure and win our admiration. And if, apart from either interpretation, there is a Mozart as in himself he really is, we shall never know him: there can only be other interpretations.

Which does not in the least mean that one interpretation of a musical work through performance or one critical interpretation of a literary work is as good as another. Lawrence Olivier's screen production of *Hamlet* was introduced by a descriptive statement which won for itself an unhappy fame. A portentous voice was heard to say, "This is the tragedy of a man who could not make up his mind." On its face, this description of the play is absurd, conjuring up as it does the sad fate of a man who, on being asked, "Vanilla, chocolate, or strawberry?", found it impossible to fix on one flavor in preference to the others and was in consequence destroyed. Yet a certain dim cogency is lent to the description by the influential line of criticism it can be seen to have descended from. In the nineteenth century, critical comment on the play concentrated on Hamlet's not having carried out his quick-conceived intention of killing the King, his uncle and stepfather, in vengeance for the King's having murdered Hamlet's father, the former King. Why did he fail of his purpose? In Goethe's novel, *Wilhelm Meister's Apprenticeship*, the play is a presiding presence, often referred to and discussed. At one point the protagonist Wilhelm undertakes to explain why Hamlet did not do what he had resolved to do. After a long description of the young prince's traits which stresses his gentleness and magnanimity, Wilhelm says:

> Figure to yourselves this youth, . . . this son of princes; conceive him vividly, bring his state before your eyes, and then observe him when he learns that his father's spirit walks; stand by him in the terrors of the night, when the venerable ghost itself appears before him. A horrid shudder passes over him; he follows it, and hears. The fearful accusation of his uncle rings in his ears; the summons to revenge and the piercing oft-repeated prayer, Remember me!

imagery. Yet for many readers these opinions have become part of the existence of the works to which they were directed. They are kept in mind because they are, in all that we now think their wrongness, an aid to understanding: these judgments are made on premises so forthrightly stated that they have the effect both of stimulating and of organizing our controversion of them, of shaping the view that we think right.

A couplet of Blake's lays down the principle on which wrongness in criticism is to be dealt with:

> The errors of the wise man make your rule
> Rather than the perfections of a fool.

This, of course, is advice to the reader of criticism, not to the critic himself, who can scarcely proceed with his task on the assumption that he is one of the wise men whose errors will be of the enlightening kind. He must believe, however aware he may be of the extent to which his perception is conditioned and limited, that it is possible for him to see the object as in itself it really is.

IV

If we pursue the limited analogy that may be made between criticism and science, we observe that criticism, like science, occupies itself with questions of causation. In the modern period, criticism has in large measure committed itself to the belief that the comprehension of a literary work can be advanced by knowledge of the conditions under which it came into being, which may be supposed to explain why it is what it is.

The belief does not go unchallenged. There are critics of notable authority who take the position that a work of literature is an autonomous and self-determining entity and that its nature is violated if it is dealt with in any other terms than those which in itself it proposes. They maintain further that to adduce considerations extrinsic to the work itself inevitably diverts from it some part of the attention it should receive. These objections are not without cogency and to them others might be added. Yet the resistance is but a rearguard action; the belief that causation is a valuable and interesting category of criticism is now pretty firmly established.

The idea that literature, or any art, is a conditioned thing would seem to have taken its rise in the eighteenth century with the striking development of historical thought that occurred at that time. Historical investigation proliferated at an ever-increasing rate and concerned itself not only with the great manifest events of nations, with wars and the succession of rulers and dynasties, but also with social and economic arrangements, with religion and the moral code, with manners and customs, with philosophy and art. The historians' growing sensitivity to these elements of a national life could not but lead to the perception that they were vitally interconnected, that they formed an organic whole which was a controlling condition of the nature of any one of its components. This way of looking at a people's history was but one expression of an idea that was beginning to command the mind of Europe—the idea of *society*. It might seem absurd to speak of this as a new idea, since men have always lived in society and from time immemorial have reflected on this definitive circumstance of their existence. But never before had society been conceived of as having a distinct and substantial being which was susceptible to investigation and predication. Before long it became possible to propose a study, conceived on the model of the physical sciences and to be called sociology, which envisaged the comprehension of the laws by which society lived and moved and had its being; comprehension was eventually to lead to rational control, for part of the conception of society was that it had an autonomous life whose purposes were not in all respects beneficent. The extent to which the idea took dominion over men's minds may be judged from the great novels of the nineteenth century, of which there is perhaps not one in which society is not a presiding presence, commonly thought of as adversary to human happiness and virtue.

In the late nineteenth century certain implications of the concept of society were given sharper focus by the use of the word *culture*. A precise definition of culture in the sense that is now most usually intended must perhaps be despaired of—in 1952 two eminent anthropologists, A. L. Kroeber and Clyde Kluckhohn, thought it worth their while to bring together the diverse and often contradictory definitions that had been advanced up to that date; the compilation, together with its commentative apparatus, makes a sizeable volume.* In its most inclusive meaning, the word denotes all of society's activities, from the most necessary to the most gratuitous, as these are conceived in their observed, or assumed, integrality. Sometimes, however, the meaning is narrowed by the exclusion from its purview of economic and political activity; what then is left is the society's technology, its religious beliefs and organization, its moral code, its manners and customs, its intellectual and artistic pursuits, its systems of valuation, whether expressed or implicit. A considerable part of the attraction of the concept of culture is the credence it gives to the *implicit,* to those conventions and assumptions that the members of a cultural entity share without being conscious of them.

The concept of culture is of decisive importance in contemporary thought. As Kroeber and Kluckhohn put it in the introduction to their book, "In explanatory importance and in generality of application it is comparable to such categories as gravity in physics, disease in medicine, evolution in biology." It permits us—even invites, perhaps requires, us—to think of any one element of a given culture as being conditioned by the other elements and as being appropriate to them all. The perception of the appropriateness to each other of all the elements finds expression in a quasi-aesthetic judgment, that among the elements there is a continuity of *style*. The same spirit seems to have set its mark on each of them.

If anything is definitive of the concept of culture, it is this idea of a unitary spirit at work. Taine, the nineteenth-century French historian, who did much to propagate the idea of cultural causation, speaks in the opening sentence of his *History of English Literature* (1863) of the transformation of history that has taken place "within a hundred years in Germany, within sixty years in France." He attributes this great change to the study of literature, not as it had been traditionally carried on but in a new way. "It was perceived," he says, "that a

* *Culture: A Critical Review of Concepts and Definitions,* Vol. XLVII—No. 1 of the Papers of the Peabody Museum of American Archaeology and Ethnology, Harvard University; also New York: Random House, 1963 (Vintage Books).

literary work is not a mere individual play of imagination, the isolated caprice of an excited brain, but a transcript of contemporary manners, a manifestation of a certain kind of mind," by which he means the habits of thought which differentiate the people of one culture from those of another. "It was concluded that we might recover from the monuments of literature a knowledge of the manner in which men thought and felt centuries ago."

The conclusion was momentous not only for history but also for literature. On first inspection, the new way of thinking about literary works might seem to degrade their status to that of mere documents in evidence. It is scarcely a recognition of the true nature of, for example, the *Iliad* to say of it that it is not a mere individual play of imagination, the isolated caprice of an excited brain, but a transcript of contemporary manners, a manifestation of the mind of the people among whom Homer lived and for whom he composed his poems. But such maltreatment as literature might seem to have suffered is very quickly redressed and the achieved purposes of history are seen to have served literature. For to perceive a work not only in its isolation, as an object of aesthetic contemplation, but also as implicated in the life of a people at a certain time, as expressing that life, and as being in part shaped by it, does not, in most people's experience, diminish the power or charm of the work but, on the contrary, enhances it.

It needs no special knowledge or intention to see a work in this way. Any reasonably practiced reader, in his experience of the literature of another time, is likely to bring the category of cultural causation into play as a matter of course. In reading, say, Molière's *Misanthrope*, he will be divided between a feeling of familiarity and a feeling of strangeness. He has, for example, no difficulty in responding to the question the play asks: Although sincerity is indeed an admirable trait and to be urged on everyone, is it not possible to set excessive store by it? The question is an engaging one, worth trying to answer. As it figures in the play, it implies an ideal of human behavior and a conception of man's life in society which deserves serious consideration. Still, the reader feels that as a question presumed to be of large public import it would not be posed in our present time; it could not be the subject of a contemporary play, certainly not in the terms that Molière devised, for his protagonist's overvaluation of sincerity expresses itself in a contempt for good manners and in rude behavior, and an audience of our time could scarcely be expected to take a grave view of this. But as the subject of a play in France in 1666 it seems wholly appropriate. In order to make that judgment the reader does not have to be learned in the details of French culture at that time. The play itself provides him with a considerable amount of information. The characters, with the exception of servants, are all aristocrats, and presumably the play was written for a predominantly aristocratic audience. Not all aristocracies set store by elegant manners, but this one is represented as doing so. The author would seem to have counted, or gambled, on his audience being intelligent enough to know that his hero, Alceste, is right in thinking that elaborate good manners make a pleasant façade behind which triviality, stupidity, malice, and injustice have their ugly way, and in judging that life in society is ignoble. This is manifestly Molière's own opinion. Yet his play at its conclusion seems to say that despite all the ignobility that may be discovered in it, society must be accepted as a necessary and essentially beneficent circumstance of human existence; its peace and order, though dependent on lies, must not be disturbed. Alceste is doubtless noble in his rage against social falsehood, yet it is suggested that his commitment to sincerity and his scorn of those who lack it spring from something less admirable than the simple love of virtue, that pride and self-love have their part in the disgust that leads him to alienate himself from society. There is every likelihood that the reader, perhaps to his surprise, will not take this conclusion to be a recommendation to acquiescence and "conformity," that he will understand the play to be saying something grave and difficult and that what it says is part of the effort of the men of its time to realize the idea of society in the terms that were available to them.

The awareness of cultural causation which I have ascribed to the reasonably practiced reader in his experience of *The Misanthrope* comes simply from his having the abstract idea of culture as part of his intellectual equipment. With no more fully substantiated awareness than this he generally does very well in most of his reading.

But perhaps he does even better when the abstract concept of culture is given a degree of substantiation. If, for example, the reader learns the simple historical fact that *The Misanthrope* was not very successful when it first appeared, something is pretty sure to happen to his perception of the play. He must at once complicate his idea of what it means for a literary work to be called the product of its culture, the expression of the mind of the people at the time. *The Misanthrope* is now often said to be Molière's greatest play, yet when it was first produced, opinion went against it. This is not to say, however, that it was given no admiration at all; many thoughtful people, some of great intellectual authority, held it in the highest regard. Such a division of opinion might seem to bring into question the idea of the unitary nature of culture. Actually, of course, the cogency and usefulness of that idea depend exactly upon its being discovered in a manifest diversity, and, indeed, in the disputes that, in any highly elaborated culture, go on between diverse preferences and opinions. A culture has its being in activity, in its complex response to possibilities, as these are offered by external circumstances or as they are conceived by the culture itself, and perhaps the most characteristic form of its activity is the opposition which one group in the culture offers to another. *The Misanthrope* represents such an opposition—between, on the one hand, a body of opinion, perhaps amorphous but later to be more articulated, which holds Alceste's view that society is an affront to rationality and virtue, and, on the other hand, a body of opinion which resists this radical conclusion and which, without making any claims for the rationality and goodness of society, affirms its necessity and the wrongness of judging it by absolute moral standards. *The Misanthrope,* in representing this conflict of opinion, participates in it, although not, as at first we have been led to think, by giving credence only to the moderate view. The mockery of Alceste for his intransigence and the hint that it springs from motives not wholly worthy do not finally negate the force of his condemnation of society; the play's resolution in a counsel of moderation and acceptance is no doubt sincere and not merely formal, yet it does not prevent the supposition that, to have imagined Alceste's revulsion from society, Molière must himself have felt it and that he was inviting his audience to share it or at least to acknowledge its validity. The reader who has learned that the play was coolly received will scarcely fail to conjecture that the reason for its having been resisted was its intention of affecting the culture by bringing it under a scrutiny which was in some degree adverse. The single extrinsic fact has suggested to him something more than he might at first have imagined of the extent to which the play is implicated in its culture, and in doing so has made the more likely his recognition of the living *will* of the play, its energy of intention. The intention is an ambiguous one, which is one reason why *The Misanthrope* is the saddest of comedies.

It is a tribute to the cogency of the idea of cultural causation that it won the assent of the eighteenth-century philosopher, David Hume, much of whose fame rests on the doubts he raised about causation in the physical sciences. He found it reasonable to suppose that the culture stood in a causal relation to individual works of genius, the reason being that geniuses—"choice spirits"— arise from and are related to the mass of people of their time. "The question, therefore," he said, "is not altogether concerning the taste, genius, and spirit of a few, but concerning a whole people; and may, therefore, be accounted for, in some measure, by general causes and principles." But before he gave this license for the use of the category of cultural causation in dealing with the arts, he warned of its dangers. "There is no subject," he said, "in which we must proceed with more caution than in tracing the history of the arts and sciences; lest we assign causes which never existed and reduce what is merely contingent to stable and universal principles." And he goes on: "Chance, therefore, or secret or unknown causes must have great influence on the rise and progress of all refined arts."*

By and large, cultural criticism as it has developed over the intervening years shares Hume's view that a culture is an entity so complex that the category of causation used in relation to it can be of but limited potency. Part of the common conception of culture is that, although predications about it can indeed be made, it is in many respects a mystery, perhaps a sacred one, and to be treated with a degree of intellectual diffidence. One line of cultural thought, however, is characterized by its intransigent confidence in the category of causation. It holds that contingency can indeed be reduced to stable and universal principles, that nothing in culture need be attributed to chance, that such causes as are secret and unknown will not remain in the darkness forever. This is the line of thought that derives from Karl Marx and goes by his name.

Like other theorists of the subject, Marx conceived culture as an integral whole, as the necessary interrelationships of all the elements that comprise it. What differentiates his view from others is that he grants culture virtually no autonomy at all; its nature, so far from being self-determining, is strictly conditioned. For Marx the determining condition of a culture is the particular mode of economic production with which it is associated. Marx's statement of the case is succinct and uncompromising: "In the social production which men carry on they enter into definite relations that are indispensable and independent of their will. . . . The sum total of these relations of production constitutes the economic structure of a society—the real foundation on which rises a legal and

* *Essays Moral, Political and Literary* (New York: Oxford University Press, 1966), pp. 114–115.

political superstructure to which correspond definite forms of social consciousness. The mode of production in material life determines the social, political, and intellectual life-processes in general. It is not the consciousness of men that determines their being, but, on the contrary, their social being that determines their consciousness."* Of equal importance with the idea of economic determinism in Marx's theory of culture is the idea of the antagonism between social classes which is intensified in periods when changes occur in the economic structure. The conflict of classes finds expression in "legal, political, religious, aesthetic, or philosophic—in short, ideological—forms" and serves to explain the succession of cultures.

Marx's theory of culture has had a considerable influence on contemporary criticism. Most critics are not willing to make the political commitment it seems to demand, not so much in itself as in its connection with the revolutionary intention of the whole of Marx's thought. Yet any critic who thinks about literature in relation to society and culture cannot fail to be aware of it as a formidable presence. What I have called its intransigent confidence in the category of causation exerts an unremitting pressure on those who use the category more diffidently. It is hard not to feel that there is a large potential for criticism in the Marxist theory. By the same token, it is hard not to be surprised at how little this has been realized. *The Hidden God,* by the French scholar and critic, Lucien Goldmann, an elaborate study of the tragic vision of Pascal and Racine in relation to the religious thought of their time which in turn is seen in relation to the developing ideology of certain social classes, suggests how much can be done with the Marxist assumptions when they are used by a sufficiently complex mind. But of comparable works there have been none in America and England and few in Europe. For the most part Marxist criticism seems to be ignorant of the intellectual possibilities of the doctrine to which it gives lip-service and contents itself with a simplistic moralizing about literature: having taken for granted the badness of capitalist society, it conceives its chief enterprise to be the demonstration of how the social turpitude manifests itself in the corruption of the artistic consciousness.

V

In highly developed cultures an admired work of literature has always been associated with the man who wrote it and its qualities accounted for by his temperament.† Buffon's famous statement, "Style is the man himself," made in 1753, was perhaps, in its being made at all, a portent of the emphasis that Romanticism was to place on the personality of the author, but it expresses what readers have always felt without saying so. For the earlier readers, however, the equation of man and style was a satisfying tautology; for later readers it settled nothing—on the contrary, it opened the way to questions. If the style is the man

* Preface to *A Contribution to the Critique of Political Economy.* Translated by N. I. Stone (New York: International Library, 1904), p. 11. The work first appeared in 1859.
† I specify highly developed cultures because there are simpler cultures in which the author of an admired work is not known and his identity is of no moment, as, for example, the culture in which the ballads of Scotland and northern England were composed.

himself, how did the man become himself, the person who is signalized by this style and no other? And since style is at the service of, and controlled by, the man's emotion seeking expression, would not the emotion be the better understood if its occasion in the author's actual experience were known?

The belief that biography provides a basis for the fuller understanding of a work of literature meets with substantially the same objections as are offered to the belief that such a basis is to be found in culture. A concern with the author's life is said to usurp the attention that should be given to the work itself. And it is held that knowledge of the biographical circumstances of the work's genesis not only is irrelevant to the work as an autonomous aesthetic object but serves to prevent its being seen in this way.

Such validity as these objections have is limited by the consideration that much of our experience of literature is not of single isolated works but, rather, of some sizeable number of the items that make up an author's whole production. If in an anthology we read a story by, say, Henry James, we incline to be aware of it only in itself and to have but little concern with the author's personal existence. But if the story engages and pleases us, we will probably wonder whether the person who made this particular aesthetic object did not make others that would similarly please and engage us. We discover that this is indeed the case, that Henry James wrote a great many stories, in addition to his many novels, enough to fill twelve sizeable volumes, and that most of them are very good. We will not have gone far in our reading of them before we recognize that, although each story does indeed have its own peculiar existence as an aesthetic object, it also has an existence in its relation to the other stories. They all have something in common, a characteristic tone or style and characteristic social and moral assumptions. We come to think of them as not merely stories but as Henry James stories. And it is because of, and in reference to, what they have in common that we remark the differences among them. In accordance with modern editorial practice, the stories are arranged in the order in which they were written, and if we read them in this order, we are conscious of the continuity between those that James wrote at twenty-one and those he wrote in his late sixties, but we are no less conscious of the respects in which they are unlike. As the stories proceed from the early to the late, they show not only an increasing sureness of execution but also an increasing boldness, complexity, and weightiness. We observe, that is to say, a development. Try as we will at the behest of those critics who warn us of the irrelevance and distraction of biography, we do not see this as the development of autonomous aesthetic objects—the stories are Henry James stories, the development we are conscious of is that of the creative powers of Henry James. We cannot suppress the knowledge that a person, a young man, addressed himself to mastering an art which has as one of its criteria of success the ability to evoke interest and deep feeling by telling the truth about life, and that to this end he gave the energies of nearly fifty working years. Try as we may, we cannot down our consciousness of Henry James the man, the man-writing—he becomes part of our experience of his work, which we see not as a collocation of particular aesthetic objects but as an intention, the enterprise of a lifetime, which has its own coherence and form and is thus in itself an aesthetic object of a kind.

As I have suggested, the involvement of our consciousness of the writer in our experience of his work is a relatively new way of experiencing literature. No biography of Shakespeare was undertaken until nearly a century after his death. We of our time would feel at a loss if we did not believe that we could determine at least in a general way the successive stages of Shakespeare's artistic and intellectual development, but the editors of the First Folio, the earliest collection of his plays, published seven years after his death, had no such interest to satisfy and printed the plays without regard to the chronology of their composition. For us the artist is an element of his art, an element so important, indeed, that we call his art by his name—we say that we read *King Lear* but we also say that we read Shakespeare, and *Madame Bovary* but also Flaubert—and we want to see him as intensely as we can, to know "what he is like," what his temperament was, and his moral character, and the circumstances of his career.

Thus described, the interest in the biography of writers may be thought of as essentially aesthetic. There is a pleasure, cognate with the pleasure we take in the work itself, in discerning a consonance between the work and the personality and life of its author. But perhaps inevitably we go beyond the discernment of consonance to look for causal connections. A work of literature is not an exception to the conditioned nature of all things: it is what it is by reason of the circumstances of its genesis, which are the circumstances, both external and internal, of the man who made it; and he in turn, no less than the thing he creates, is a conditioned being susceptible to explanation in terms of the circumstances that determined his nature. His parentage, his social class, the mode of his rearing and education, the surroundings and events of his early years, all contribute to making him the person he is, with the mind and imagination he has. Sometimes he will say so himself, for writers have licensed our personal interest in them and our impulse to explain them by themselves doing that very thing in their autobiographies. Wordsworth, for example, undertook to explain himself in considerable detail in his long autobiographical poem *The Prelude* (which has for its subtitle *The Growth of a Poet's Mind*) by adducing exactly those circumstances that have just been mentioned—he was the man and poet he was because his mother was the woman she was, because the society of his native Cumberland was simple and democratic, because he was allowed great freedom to range the beautiful and somewhat dangerous countryside, because he attended Hawkshead School, because he went to live in France at the age of twenty-one, having two years before witnessed with sympathy the early days of the French Revolution. The explanation is very full and nearly successful—Wordsworth, who believed, correctly, that he was a genius, undertakes to explain how he came to be a genius and almost convinces us that he has done so. Actually, of course, he has not. He gives us a full account of his emotional development, of the steps by which he came to have the view of the world that infuses his great poems, and of his dedication to poetry, but he tells us nothing of how he came to possess the power to write the poems that so deeply affect us. He explains a mind and a temperament that are appropriate to his genius, but the genius itself he does not explain.

And because genius would seem to be beyond the reach of explanation, the attempts to account for Wordsworth's strange loss of genius carry no conviction. Although Wordsworth lived to be eighty and was productive through this long life, virtually all the work for which he is remembered was written within a period of ten years, the "marvelous decade" of 1797–1807. Thereafter, although there are infrequent brief moments when the old magic revives, the work, although not without interest, is not of the same order as that which makes him one of the great poets of the world. This sudden evanescence of genius is a phenomenon that arouses a natural and legitimate curiosity. One proposed explanation is that the beginning of Wordsworth's great period coincided with the beginning of his close friendship with Coleridge and that the end came when the two men quarrelled. Another refers to his relations with Annette Vallon, the French girl by whom he had an illegitimate daughter and whom he would have married had not the outbreak of war prevented his return to France from what was to have been a short visit to England; it is said that Wordsworth's guilt over this affair destroyed his genius. Yet another explanation is that Wordsworth's genius was the effect of his sensory acuity which is said to have deteriorated materially and abruptly at the age of thirty-seven. And still another is based on Wordsworth's disenchantment with and opposition to the French Revolution, to which he had at first given his enthusiastic assent.

All the explanations offered have a superficial plausibility (except the last, which is contradicted by chronology and Wordsworth's own testimony, a consideration that has not kept it from being the most enduring and popular). None of them, however, bears substantiation and all of them make a false assumption: that Wordsworth wrote great poetry by means of a certain faculty whose existence depended on and therefore in some sense was defined by the presence or absence of one particular emotional circumstance. Nothing that we know of the nature of poetic genius lends credibility to this simplistic assumption.

The tendency to speculate about the determinants of genius was given strong impetus by the development of psychoanalysis. Sigmund Freud had not proceeded very far in the shaping of his theory of the mind before he expressed the belief that the technique used in his therapeutic work might disclose something of the nature of the mysterious processes of art. The basic assumption of psychoanalysis is that certain forms of mental illness are the result of painful threatening emotions which the patient entertains without being conscious of them. When these emotions are brought—usually with great difficulty—into the light of consciousness their force is mitigated. A further assumption is that these threatening emotions were established in the unconscious part of the mind in the patient's early childhood. With the help of the psychoanalyst, the patient conducts a research into his past and present life by talking about his conscious feelings as truthfully as he can and, so far as possible, without regard either to coherence or to propriety: he is to say whatever comes into his head, and the hope that unexpected and untoward things will make their entrance there is usually realized. The products of this "free association," together with the patient's remembered dreams, supply the clues to the workings of his unconscious mind, which are interpreted for him by the psychoanalyst.

Freud, of course, was not the first to propose the idea that something other than, or in addition to, the conscious mind was the agent of artistic creation. Plato had called poets "mad," meaning to say that they were "inspired," that their minds were under some other control than that of the conscious intellect, and this conception of the creative process was variously formulated in succeeding times, although it remained for psychoanalysis to develop it in a positive way and to claim that its method could accomplish two things—explain the personality of the artist and discover and explicate in the work of art meanings which were not consciously intended and which, though not manifest, are integral to the nature of the work.

The success of the first enterprise has been of a limited kind. The use of psychoanalytical concepts does indeed lead us to scrutinize more closely and with an enhanced sense of their significance the details of an artist's life and to be more aware of the complex and subtle ways in which personality is determined. But when the psychoanalytical method is used with the degree of elaborateness and systematization to which it can be brought—and to which psychoanalysts often bring it in their studies of literary figures—it all too often obscures what it attempts to explain, and, what is worse, reduces a personality to the sum of its neurotic manifestations. And whatever else the psychoanalytical method may account for in the personality of the artist, it cannot, any more than traditional biography, explain his genius. It is beyond the power of psychoanalysis to say why one artist is great while another is not. The late Ernest Kris, who was one of the most respected theorists and practitioners of psychoanalysis and distinguished for his knowledge of the arts, was explicit on this point.* "We do not at present," he said, "have tools which would permit us to investigate the roots of gift or talent, not to speak of genius." And he goes on to remark another limitation of the psychoanalytical method—it is not able to explain the artist's style, the peculiar way in which he uses the material that his cultural tradition gives him. As Dr. Kris put it, ". . . The psychology of artistic style is unwritten." That it may yet be written is not beyond the range of possibility.

In its other enterprise, that of interpreting the meaning of the work itself, psychoanalysis has been more successful and its concepts have exerted no small influence on literary criticism. Even those critics who do not accept the whole of psychoanalytical doctrine can find something essentially congenial to literature in the complexity, secrecy, and *duplicity* that Freud ascribes to the human mind. They have been quick to respond to the psychoanalytical assumption that in any human expression more goes on than meets the eye, that something more is being said than first appears, that the "manifest content" of a literary work, like that of a patient's dream or free association, is qualified, sometimes contradicted, always enriched, by the "latent content" that can be discovered lying beneath it.

VI

What I have said about the intentions and processes of criticism does not undertake to be a complete account of them, only a first view. As such, it

* *Psychoanalytic Explorations in Art* (New York: International Universities, 1952), pp. 20–21.

requires that one further word be added to it. This relates to what might be called the natural amity between literature and the criticism of literature. I put the matter in this way because it is impossible not to be aware of the opinion—it never prevails but neither does it ever wholly die—that criticism is of its nature essentially alien to the art which is its concern and, in fact, harmful to it. Literature, the opinion goes, directs itself to the feelings while criticism is an activity of the intellect, and therefore, in undertaking to serve literature, can only betray it, interfering with the exercise of its function, diminishing the immediacy with which, if left to itself, it can affect the reader. It would be wrong to say that, as a matter of occasional experience, this is never true. The ineptness or officiousness of a particular piece of criticism may make it true. The mood of a moment may make it true for the moment—there are times when criticism seems beside the point of literature and it is literature beyond the reach of criticism that we want, just as there are times when literature itself seems beside the point of life and it is life itself beyond the reach of literature that we want. But it is not true in principle. And to its not being true in principle the creators of literature itself offer testimony by being themselves practitioners, often especially distinguished ones, of the art of criticism. When, in 1922, the novelist and critic André Gide wrote in homage to the poet and critic Paul Valéry, he prefixed to his essay as an epigraph a passage from the poet and critic Baudelaire which puts the situation succinctly: "Through a natural development, all great poets eventually become critics. I pity those poets guided by instinct alone; for they seem incomplete to me. In the spiritual life of the former, infallibly there comes about a crisis that makes them want to reason out their art, to discover the obscure laws by virtue of which they have created. . . ."*

* Translated by Blanche A. Price in *Pretexts* by André Gide, edited by Justin O'Brien (London: Secker & Warburg, 1960).

Plato

ION

Socrates (c. 469–399 B.C.), the protagonist of truth in most of Plato's
dialogues, did not write anything, but spent much of his time informally
educating himself and a group of devoted followers by the method of
question-and-response, or "dialectics." In part because he refused to participate in the judicial murder of a man named Leon of Salamis, and
largely because he was an all-around "gadfly," as he called himself—a
man who went around trying to get people to examine themselves and
the assumptions upon which they acted—Socrates was brought to trial
on the charges of introducing new gods and corrupting the young. He
was found guilty and executed by being given a cup of hemlock poison
to drink.

Plato (c. 427–347 B.C.), one of the Socratics, or "followers of Socrates," founded in 386 B.C. a school of philosophy, called the Academy,
because it was set in a grove sacred to the hero Academos. The Academy
survived as a functioning institution until A.D. 529. Here Plato taught
Socrates' methods and findings and built upon them something approaching a philosophic system.

The *Ion* was probably written relatively early in Plato's career, not
very long after the death of Socrates.

Socrates. Welcome, Ion. Are you from your native city of Ephesus?

Ion. No, Socrates; but from Epidaurus, where I attended the festival of
Aesculapius.[1]

Soc. Indeed! Do the Epidaurians have a contest of rhapsodes[2] in his
honour?

Ion. O yes; and of other kinds of music.

Soc. And were you one of the competitors—and did you succeed?

Ion. I—we—obtained the first prize of all, Socrates.

Soc. Well done; now we must win another victory, at the Panathenaea.[3]

Ion. It shall be so, please heaven.

Soc. I have often envied the profession of a rhapsode, Ion; for it is a part

From *The Dialogues of Plato,* translated by Benjamin Jowett (fourth edition, revised).
The Clarendon Press, Oxford, 1953. Reprinted by permission of the Clarendon Press,
Oxford.

[1] God of medicine.

[2] A rhapsode or "song-stitcher" was a professional reciter of poems, especially
epic poems, especially by Homer, especially at public festivals.

[3] The most ancient and most important of the Athenian festivals.

of your art to wear fine clothes and to look as beautiful as you can, while at the same time you are obliged to be continually in the company of many good poets, and especially of Homer, who is the best and most divine of them, and to understand his mind, and not merely learn his words by rote; all this is a thing greatly to be envied. I am sure that no man can become a good rhapsode who does not understand the meaning of the poet. For the rhapsode ought to interpret the mind of the poet to his hearers, but how can he interpret him well unless he knows what he means? All this is much to be envied, I repeat.

Ion. Very true, Socrates; interpretation has certainly been the most laborious part of my art; and I believe myself able to speak about Homer better than any man; and that neither Metrodorus of Lampsacus, nor Stesimbrotus of Thasos, nor Glaucon, nor anyone else who ever was, had as good ideas about Homer as I have, or as many.

Soc. I am glad to hear you say so, Ion; I see that you will not refuse to acquaint me with them.

Ion. Certainly, Socrates; and you really ought to hear how exquisitely I display the beauties of Homer. I think that the Homeridae[4] should give me a golden crown.

Soc. I shall take an opportunity of hearing your embellishments of him at some other time. But just now I should like to ask you a question: Does your art extend to Hesiod and Archilochus,[5] or to Homer only?

Ion. To Homer only; he is in himself quite enough.

Soc. Are there any things about which Homer and Hesiod agree?

Ion. Yes; in my opinion there are a good many.

Soc. And can you interpret what Homer says about these matters better than what Hesiod says?

Ion. I can interpret them equally well, Socrates, where they agree.

Soc. But what about matters in which they do not agree? for example, about divination of which both Homer and Hesiod have something to say,—

Ion. Very true.

Soc. Would you or a good prophet be a better interpreter of what these two poets say about divination, not only when they agree, but when they disagree?

Ion. A prophet.

Soc. And if you were a prophet, and could interpret them where they agree, would you not know how to interpret them also where they disagree?

Ion. Clearly.

Soc. But how did you come to have this skill about Homer only, and not about Hesiod or the other poets? Does not Homer speak of the same themes which all other poets handle? Is not war his great argument? and does he not speak of human society and of intercourse of men, good and bad, skilled and unskilled, and of the gods conversing with one another and with mankind, and about what happens in heaven and in the world below, and the generations of gods and heroes? Are not these the themes of which Homer sings?

Ion. Very true, Socrates.

[4] A guild of rhapsodes from Chios, reputed descendants of Homer.
[5] Lyric poet, especially eminent as a writer of lampoons; Hesiod was an epic poet who wrote perhaps a century after Homer.

Soc. And do not the other poets sing of the same?

Ion. Yes, Socrates; but not in the same way as Homer.

Soc. What, in a worse way?

Ion. Yes, in a far worse.

Soc. And Homer in a better way?

Ion. He is incomparably better.

Soc. And yet surely, my dear friend Ion, where many people are discussing numbers, and one speaks better than the rest, there is somebody who can judge which of them is the good speaker?

Ion. Yes.

Soc. And he who judges of the good will be the same as he who judges of the bad speakers?

Ion. The same.

Soc. One who knows the science of arithmetic?

Ion. Yes.

Soc. Or again, if many persons are discussing the wholesomeness of food, and one speaks better than the rest, will he who recognizes the better speaker be a different person from him who recognizes the worse, or the same?

Ion. Clearly the same.

Soc. And who is he, and what is his name?

Ion. The physician.

Soc. And speaking generally, in all discussions in which the subject is the same and many men are speaking, will not he who knows the good know the bad speaker also? For obviously if he does not know the bad, neither will he know the good, when the same topic is being discussed.

Ion. True.

Soc. We find, in fact, that the same person is skilful in both?

Ion. Yes.

Soc. And you say that Homer and the other poets, such as Hesiod and Archilochus, speak of the same things, although not in the same way; but the one speaks well and the other not so well?

Ion. Yes; and I am right in saying so.

Soc. And if you know the good speaker, you ought also to know the inferior speakers to be inferior?

Ion. It would seem so.

Soc. Then, my dear friend, can I be mistaken in saying that Ion is equally skilled in Homer and in other poets, since he himself acknowledges that the same person will be a good judge of all those who speak of the same things; and that almost all poets do speak of the same things?

Ion. Why then, Socrates, do I lose attention and have absolutely no ideas of the least value and practically fall asleep when anyone speaks of any other poet; but when Homer is mentioned, I wake up at once and am all attention and have plenty to say?

Soc. The reason, my friend, is not hard to guess. No one can fail to see that you speak of Homer without any art or knowledge. If you were able to speak of him by rules of art, you would have been able to speak of all other poets; for poetry is a whole.

Ion. Yes.

Soc. And when anyone acquires any other art as a whole, the same may be said of them. Would you like me to explain my meaning, Ion?

Ion. Yes, indeed, Socrates; I very much wish that you would: for I love to hear you wise men talk.

Soc. O that we were wise, Ion, and that you could truly call us so; but you rhapsodes and actors, and the poets whose verses you sing, are wise; whereas I am a common man, who only speak the truth. For consider what a very commonplace and trivial thing is this which I have said—a thing which any man might say: that when a man has acquired a knowledge of a whole art, the inquiry into good and bad is one and the same. Let us consider this matter; is not the art of painting a whole?

Ion. Yes.

Soc. And there are and have been many painters good and bad?

Ion. Yes.

Soc. And did you ever know anyone who was skilful in pointing out the excellences and defects of Polygnotus[6] the son of Aglaophon, but incapable of criticizing other painters; and when the work of any other painter was produced, went to sleep and was at a loss, and had no ideas; but when he had to give his opinion about Polygnotus, or whoever the painter might be, and about him only, woke up and was attentive and had plenty to say?

Ion. No indeed, I have never known such a person.

Soc. Or take sculpture—did you ever know of anyone who was skilful in expounding the merits of Daedalus the son of Metion, or of Epeius the son of Panopeus, or of Theodorus the Samian, or of any individual sculptor; but when the works of sculptors in general were produced, was at a loss and went to sleep and had nothing to say?

Ion. No indeed; no more than the other.

Soc. And if I am not mistaken, you never met with anyone among flute-players or harp-players or singers to the harp or rhapsodes who was able to discourse of Olympus or Thamyras or Orpheus,[7] or Phemius the rhapsode of Ithaca, but was at a loss when he came to speak of Ion of Ephesus, and had no notion of his merits or defects?

Ion. I cannot deny what you say, Socrates. Nevertheless I am conscious in my own self, and the world agrees with me, that I do speak better and have more to say about Homer than any other man; but I do not speak equally well about others. After all, there must be some reason for this; what is it?

Soc. I see the reason, Ion; and I will proceed to explain to you what I imagine it to be. The gift which you possess of speaking excellently about Homer is not an art, but, as I was just saying, an inspiration; there is a divinity moving you, like that contained in the stone which Euripides calls a magnet, but which is commonly known as the stone of Heraclea. This stone not only attracts iron rings, but also imparts to them a similar power of attracting other rings; and sometimes you may see a number of pieces of iron and rings suspended from one another so as to form quite a long chain: and all of them derive their power of suspension from the original stone. In like manner the Muse first of

[6] A Greek painter of the fifth century B.C. He is said to have been the first to give life and character to painting.

[7] Mythical poets and musicians.

all inspires men herself; and from these inspired persons a chain of other persons is suspended, who take the inspiration. For all good poets, epic as well as lyric, compose their beautiful poems not by art, but because they are inspired and possessed. And as the Corybantian[8] revellers when they dance are not in their right mind, so the lyric poets are not in their right mind when they are composing their beautiful strains: but when falling under the power of music and metre they are inspired and possessed; like Bacchic maidens[9] who draw milk and honey from the rivers when they are under the influence of Dionysus but not when they are in their right mind. And the soul of the lyric poet does the same, as they themselves say; for they tell us that they bring songs from honeyed fountains, culling them out of the gardens and dells of the Muses; they, like the bees, winging their way from flower to flower. And this is true. For the poet is a light and winged and holy thing, and there is no invention in him until he has been inspired and is out of his senses, and reason is no longer in him: no man, while he retains that faculty, has the oracular gift of poetry.

Many are the noble words in which poets speak concerning the actions of men; but like yourself when speaking about Homer, they do not speak of them by any rules of art: they are simply inspired to utter that to which the Muse impels them, and that only; and when inspired, one of them will make dithyrambs,[10] another hymns of praise, another choral strains, another epic or iambic verses, but not one of them is of any account in the other kinds. For not by art does the poet sing, but by power divine; had he learned by rules of art, he would have known how to speak not of one theme only, but of all; and therefore God takes away reason from poets, and uses them as his ministers, as he also uses the pronouncers of oracles and holy prophets, in order that we who hear them may know them to be speaking not of themselves, who utter these priceless words while bereft of reason, but that God himself is the speaker, and that through them he is addressing us. And Tynnichus the Chalcidian affords a striking instance of what I am saying: he wrote no poem that anyone would care to remember but the famous paean which is in everyone's mouth, one of the finest lyric poems ever written, simply an invention of the Muses, as he himself says. For in this way God would seem to demonstrate to us and not to allow us to doubt that these beautiful poems are not human, nor the work of man, but divine and the work of God; and that the poets are only the interpreters of the gods by whom they are severally possessed. Was not this the lesson which God intended to teach when by the mouth of the worst of poets he sang the best of songs? Am I not right, Ion?

Ion. Yes, indeed, Socrates, I feel that you are; for your words touch my soul, and I am persuaded that in these works the good poets, under divine inspiration, interpret to us the voice of the Gods.

Soc. And you rhapsodists are the interpreters of the poets?

[8] The Corybantes were legendary attendants on the Phrygian goddess Rhea Cybele; they were supposed to accompany the goddess with wild music and dancing while she wandered by torchlight through mountain forests.

[9] The Maenads: female devotees of Dionysus, who danced perhaps to even madder music than the Corybantes.

[10] The dithyramb was a choral song, originally sung in honor of Dionysus.

Ion. There again you are right.

Soc. Then you are the interpreters of interpreters?

Ion. Precisely.

Soc. I wish you would frankly tell me, Ion, what I am going to ask of you: When you produce the greatest effect upon the audience in the recitation of some striking passage, such as the apparition of Odysseus leaping forth on the floor, recognized by the suitors and shaking out his arrows at his feet, or the description of Achilles springing upon Hector, or the sorrows of Andromache, Hecuba, or Priam,—are you in your right mind? Are you not carried out of yourself, and does not your soul in an ecstasy seem to be among the persons or places of which you are speaking, whether they are in Ithaca or in Troy or whatever may be the scene of the poem?

Ion. That proof strikes home to me, Socrates. For I must frankly confess that at the tale of pity my eyes are filled with tears, and when I speak of horrors, my hair stands on end and my heart throbs.

Soc. Well, Ion, and what are we to say of a man who at a sacrifice or festival, when he is dressed in an embroidered robe, and has golden crowns upon his head, of which nobody has robbed him, appears weeping or panic-stricken in the presence of more than twenty thousand friendly faces, when there is no one despoiling or wronging him;—is he in his right mind or is he not?

Ion. No indeed, Socrates, I must say that, strictly speaking, he is not in his right mind.

Soc. And are you aware that you produce similar effects on most of the spectators?

Ion. Only too well; for I look down upon them from the stage, and behold the various emotions of pity, wonder, sternness, stamped upon their countenances when I am speaking: and I am obliged to give my very best attention to them; for if I make them cry I myself shall laugh, and if I make them laugh I myself shall cry, when the time of payment arrives.

Soc. Do you know that the spectator is the last of the rings which, as I am saying, receive the power of the original magnet from one another? The rhapsode like yourself and the actor are intermediate links, and the poet himself is the first of them. Through all these God sways the souls of men in any direction which He pleases, causing each link to communicate the power to the next. Thus there is a vast chain of dancers and masters and under-masters of choruses, who are suspended, as if from the stone, at the side of the rings which hang down from the Muse. And every poet has some Muse from whom he is suspended, and by whom he is said to be possessed, which is nearly the same thing; for he is taken hold of. And from these first rings, which are the poets, depend others, some deriving their inspiration from Orpheus, others from Musaeus[11]; but the greater number are possessed and held by Homer. Of whom, Ion, you are one, and are possessed by Homer; and when anyone repeats the words of another poet you go to sleep, and know not what to say; but when anyone recites a strain of Homer you wake up in a moment, and your soul leaps within you, and you have plenty to say; for not by art or knowledge about Homer do you say what you say, but by divine inspiration and by possession;

---

[11] Mythical singer and seer.

just as the Corybantian revellers too have a quick perception of that strain only which is appropriated to the god by whom they are possessed, and have plenty of dances and words for that, but take no heed of any other. And you, Ion, when the name of Homer is mentioned have plenty to say, and have nothing to say of others. You ask, "Why is this?" The answer is that your skill in the praise of Homer comes not from art but from divine inspiration.

Ion. That is good, Socrates; and yet I doubt whether you will ever have eloquence enough to persuade me that I praise Homer only when I am mad and possessed; and if you could hear me speak of him I am sure you would never think this to be the case.

Soc. I should like very much to hear you, but not until you have answered a question which I have to ask. On what part of Homer do you speak well?— not surely about every part?

Ion. There is no part, Socrates, about which I do not speak well: of that I can assure you.

Soc. Surely not about things in Homer of which you have no knowledge?

Ion. And what is there in Homer of which I have no knowledge?

Soc. Why, does not Homer speak in many passages about arts? For example, about driving; if I can only remember the lines I will repeat them.

Ion. I remember, and will repeat them.

Soc. Tell me then, what Nestor says to Antilochus, his son, where he bids him to be careful of the turn at the horse-race in honour of Patroclus.

Ion.

"Bend gently," he says, "in the polished chariot to the left of them, and urge the horse on the right hand with whip and voice; and slacken the rein. And when you are at the goal, let the left horse draw near, so that the nave of the well-wrought wheel may appear to graze the extremity; but have a care not to touch the stone." [*Iliad.* xxiii. 335.]

Soc. Enough. Now, Ion, will the charioteer or the physician be the better judge of the propriety of these lines?

Ion. The charioteer, clearly.

Soc. And will the reason be that this is his art, or will there be any other reason?

Ion. No, that will be the reason.

Soc. And every art is appointed by God to have knowledge of a certain work; for that which we know by the art of the pilot we shall not succeed in knowing also by the art of medicine?

Ion. Certainly not.

Soc. Nor shall we know by the art of the carpenter that which we know by the art of medicine?

Ion. Certainly not.

Soc. And this is true of all the arts;—that which we know with one art we shall not know with the other? But let me ask a prior question: You admit that there are differences of arts?

Ion. Yes.

Soc. You would argue, as I should, that if there are two kinds of knowledge, dealing with different things, these can be called different arts?

Ion. Yes.

Soc. Yes, surely; for if the object of knowledge were the same, there would be no meaning in saying that the arts were different,—since they both gave the same knowledge. For example, I know that here are five fingers, and you know the same. And if I were to ask whether I and you became acquainted with this fact by the help of the same art of arithmetic, you would acknowledge that we did?

Ion. Yes.

Soc. Tell me, then, what I was intending to ask you,—whether in your opinion this holds universally? If two arts are the same, must not they necessarily have the same objects? And if one differs from another, must it not be because the object is different?

Ion. That is my opinion, Socrates.

Soc. Then he who has no knowledge of a particular art will have no right judgement of the precepts and practice of that art?

Ion. Very true.

Soc. Then which will be the better judge of the lines which you were reciting from Homer, you or the charioteer?

Ion. The charioteer.

Soc. Why, yes, because you are a rhapsode and not a charioteer.

Ion. Yes.

Soc. And the art of the rhapsode is different from that of the charioteer?

Ion. Yes.

Soc. And if a different knowledge, then a knowledge of different matters?

Ion. True.

Soc. You know the passage in which Hecamede, the concubine of Nestor, is described as giving to the wounded Machaon a posset, as he says,

> Made with Pramnian wine; and she grated cheese of goat's milk with a grater of bronze, and at his side placed an onion which gives a relish to drink. [*Iliad.* xi. 628, 630.]

Now would you say that the art of the rhapsode or the art of medicine was better able to judge of the propriety of these lines?

Ion. The art of medicine.

Soc. And when Homer says,

> And she descended into the deep like a leaden plummet, which, set in the horn of ox that ranges the fields, rushes along carrying death among the ravenous fishes, [*Iliad.* xxiv. 80.]

will the art of the fisherman or of the rhapsode be better able to judge what these lines mean, and whether they are accurate or not?

Ion. Clearly, Socrates, the art of the fisherman.

Soc. Come now, suppose that you were to say to me: "Since you, Socrates, are able to assign different passages in Homer to their corresponding arts, I wish that you would tell me what are the passages of which the excellence ought to be judged by the prophet and prophetic art"; and you will see how readily and truly I shall answer you. For there are many such passages, particularly in the Odyssey; as, for example, the passage in which Theoclymenus the prophet of the house of Melampus says to the suitors:—

> Wretched men! what is happening to you? Your heads and your faces and your limbs underneath are shrouded in night; and the voice of lamentation bursts forth, and your cheeks are wet with tears. And the vestibule is full, and the court is full, of ghosts descending into the darkness of Erebus, and the sun has perished out of heaven, and an evil mist is spread abroad. [*Odyssey.* xx. 351.]

And there are many such passages in the Iliad also; as for example in the description of the battle near the rampart, where he says:—

> As they were eager to pass the ditch, there came to them an omen: a soaring eagle, skirting the people on his left, bore a huge blood-red dragon in his talons, still living and panting; nor had he yet resigned the strife, for he bent back and smote the bird which carried him on the breast by the neck, and he in pain let him fall from him to the ground into the midst of the multitude. And the eagle, with a cry, was borne afar on the wings of the wind. [*Iliad.* xii. 200.]

These are the sort of things which I should say that the prophet ought to consider and determine.

Ion. And you are quite right, Socrates, in saying so.

Soc. Yes, Ion, and you are right also. And as I have selected from the *Iliad* and *Odyssey* for you passages which describe the office of the prophet and the physician and the fisherman, do you, who know Homer so much better than I do, Ion, select for me passages which relate to the rhapsode and the rhapsode's art, and which the rhapsode ought to examine and judge of better than other men.

Ion. All passages, I should say, Socrates.

Soc. Not all, Ion, surely. Have you already forgotten what you were saying? A rhapsode ought to have a better memory.

Ion. Why, what am I forgetting?

Soc. Do you not remember that you declared the art of the rhapsode to be different from the art of the charioteer?

Ion. Yes, I remember.

Soc. And you admitted that being different they would know different objects?

Ion. Yes.

Soc. Then upon your own showing the rhapsode, and the art of the rhapsode, will not know everything?

Ion. I should exclude such things as you mention, Socrates.

Soc. You mean to say that you would exclude pretty much the subjects of the other arts. As he does not know all of them, which of them will he know?

Ion. He will know what a man and what a woman ought to say, and what a freeman and what a slave ought to say, and what a ruler and what a subject.

Soc. Do you mean that a rhapsode will know better than the pilot what the ruler of a sea-tossed vessel ought to say?

Ion. No; the pilot will know best.

Soc. Or will the rhapsode know better than the physician what the ruler of a sick man ought to say?

Ion. Again, no.

Soc. But he will know what a slave ought to say?

Ion. Yes.

Soc. Suppose the slave to be a cowherd; the rhapsode will know better than the cowherd what he ought to say in order to soothe infuriated cows?

Ion. No, he will not.

Soc. But he will know what a spinning-woman ought to say about the working of wool?

Ion. No.

Soc. At any rate he will know what a general ought to say when exhorting his soldiers?

Ion. Yes, that is the sort of thing which the rhapsode will be sure to know.

Soc. What! Is the art of the rhapsode the art of the general?

Ion. I am sure that I should know what a general ought to say.

Soc. Why, yes, Ion, because you may possibly have the knowledge of a general as well as that of a rhapsode; and you might also have a knowledge of horsemanship as well as of the lyre, and then you would know when horses were well or ill managed. But suppose I were to ask you: By the help of which art, Ion, do you know whether horses are well managed, by your skill as a horseman or as a performer on the lyre—what would you answer?

Ion. I should reply, by my skill as a horseman.

Soc. And if you judged of performers on the lyre, you would admit that you judged of them as a performer on the lyre, and not as a horseman?

Ion. Yes.

Soc. And in judging of the general's art, do you judge as a general, or as a good rhapsode?

Ion. To me there appears to be no difference between them.

Soc. What do you mean? Do you mean to say that the art of the rhapsode and of the general is the same?

Ion. Yes, one and the same.

Soc. Then he who is a good rhapsode is also a good general?

Ion. Certainly, Socrates.

Soc. And he who is a good general is also a good rhapsode?

Ion. No; I do not agree to that.

Soc. But you do agree that he who is a good rhapsode is also a good general.

Ion. Certainly.

Soc. And you are the best of Hellenic rhapsodes?

Ion. Far the best, Socrates.

Soc. And are you also the best general, Ion?

Ion. To be sure, Socrates; and Homer was my master.

Soc. But then, Ion, why in the name of goodness do you, who are the best of generals as well as the best of rhapsodes in all Hellas, go about reciting rhapsodies when you might be a general? Do you think that the Hellenes are in grave need of a rhapsode with his golden crown, and have no need at all of a general?

Ion. Why, Socrates, the reason is that my countrymen, the Ephesians, are the servants and soldiers of Athens, and do not need a general; and that you and Sparta are not likely to appoint me, for you think that you have enough generals of your own.

Soc. My good Ion, did you never hear of Apollodorus of Cyzicus?

Ion. Who may he be?

Soc. One who, though a foreigner, has often been chosen their general by the Athenians: and there is Phanosthenes of Andros, and Heraclides of Clazomenae, whom they have also appointed to the command of their armies and to other offices, although aliens, after they had shown their merit. And will they not choose Ion the Ephesian to be their general, and honour him, if they deem him qualified? Were not the Ephesians originally Athenians, and Ephesus is no mean city? But, indeed, Ion, if you are correct in saying that by art and knowledge you are able to praise Homer, you do not deal fairly with me, and after all your professions of knowing many glorious things about Homer, and promises that you would exhibit them, you only deceive me, and so far from exhibiting the art of which you are a master, will not, even after my repeated entreaties, explain to me the nature of it. You literally assume as many forms as Proteus, twisting and turning up and down, until at last you slip away from me in the disguise of a general, in order that you may escape exhibiting your Homeric lore. And if you have art, then, as I was saying, in falsifying your promise that you would exhibit Homer, you are not dealing fairly with me. But if, as I believe, you have no art, but speak all these beautiful words about Homer unconsciously under his inspiring influence, then I acquit you of dishonesty, and shall only say that you are inspired. Which do you prefer to be thought, dishonest or inspired?

Ion. There is a great difference, Socrates, between the two alternatives; and inspiration is by far the nobler.

Soc. Then, Ion, I shall assume the nobler alternative; and attribute to you in your praises of Homer inspiration, and not art.

Plato

THE REPUBLIC
Book X

The *Republic*, written some time after the *Ion*, is usually considered
Plato's greatest work. In it Socrates recounts how he and a group of companions moved from an attempt to define "justice" to a description of
what would be an ideal *polis*, or city having the independent status of a
modern nation. The passage that follows is the first two thirds of Book
X, in which Socrates explains to Glaucon, a half-brother to Plato, what
position poetry and art in general ought to have under their ideal regime.

Of the many excellences which I perceive in the order of our State, there
is none which upon reflection pleases me better than the rule about poetry.

To what do you refer?

To our refusal to admit the imitative kind of poetry, for it certainly ought
not to be received; as I see far more clearly now that the parts of the soul have
been distinguished.

What do you mean?

Speaking in confidence, for you will not denounce me to the tragedians
and the rest of the imitative tribe, all poetical imitations are ruinous to the
understanding of the hearers, unless as an antidote they possess the knowledge
of the true nature of the originals.

Explain the purport of your remark.

Well, I tell you, although I have always from my earliest youth had an
awe and love of Homer which even now makes the words falter on my lips,
for he seems to be the great captain and teacher of the whole of that noble
tragic company; but a man is not to be reverenced more than the truth, and
therefore I will speak out.

Very good, he said.

Listen to me then, or rather, answer me.

Put your question.

Can you give me a general definition of imitation? for I really do not
myself understand what it professes to be.

A likely thing, then, that I should know.

From *The Dialogues of Plato*, translated by Benjamin Jowett (fourth edition, revised).
The Clarendon Press, Oxford, 1953. Reprinted by permission of the Clarendon Press,
Oxford.

There would be nothing strange in that, for the duller eye may often see a thing sooner than the keener.

Very true, he said; but in your presence, even if I had any faint notion, I could not muster courage to utter it. Will you inquire yourself?

Well then, shall we begin the inquiry at this point, following our usual method: Whenever a number of individuals have a common name, we assume that there is one corresponding idea or form:—do you understand me?

I do.

Let us take, for our present purpose, any instance of such a group; there are beds and tables in the world—many of each, are there not?

Yes.

But there are only two ideas or forms of such furniture—one the idea of a bed, the other of a table.

True.

And the maker of either of them makes a bed or he makes a table for our use, in accordance with the idea—that is our way of speaking in this and similar instances—but no artificer makes the idea itself: how could he?

Impossible.

And there is another artificer,—I should like to know what you would say of him.

Who is he?

One who is the maker of all the works of all other workmen.

What an extraordinary man!

Wait a little, and there will be more reason for your saying so. For this is the craftsman who is able to make not only furniture of every kind, but all that grows out of the earth, and all living creatures, himself included; and besides these he can make earth and sky and the gods, and all the things which are in heaven or in the realm of Hades under the earth.

He must be a wizard and no mistake.

Oh! you are incredulous, are you? Do you mean that there is no such maker or creator, or that in one sense there might be a maker of all these things but in another not? Do you see that there is a way in which you could make them all yourself?

And what way is this? he asked.

An easy way enough; or rather, there are many ways in which the feat might be quickly and easily accomplished, none quicker than that of turning a mirror round and round—you would soon enough make the sun and the heavens, and the earth and yourself, and other animals and plants, and furniture and all the other things of which we were just now speaking, in the mirror.

Yes, he said; but they would be appearances only.

Very good, I said, you are coming to the point now. And the painter too is, as I conceive, just such another—a creator of appearances, is he not?

Of course.

But then I suppose you will say that what he creates is untrue. And yet there is a sense in which the painter also creates a bed? Is there not?

Yes, he said, but here again, an appearance only.

And what of the maker of the bed? were you not saying that he too makes, not the idea which according to our view is the real object denoted by the word bed, but only a particular bed?

Yes, I did.

Then if he does not make a real object he cannot make what *is*, but only some semblance of existence; and if any one were to say that the work of the maker of the bed, or of any other workman, has real existence, he could hardly be supposed to be speaking the truth.

Not, at least, he replied, in the view of those who make a business of these discussions.

No wonder, then, that his work too is an indistinct expression of truth.

No wonder.

Suppose now that by the light of the examples just offered we inquire who this imitator is?

If you please.

Well then, here we find three beds: one existing in nature, which is made by God, as I think that we may say—for no one else can be the maker?

No one, I think.

There is another which is the work of the carpenter?

Yes.

And the work of the painter is a third?

Yes.

Beds, then, are of three kinds, and there are three artists who superintend them: God, the maker of the bed, and the painter?

Yes, there are three of them.

God, whether from choice or from necessity, made one bed in nature and one only; two or more such beds neither ever have been nor ever will be made by God.

Why is that?

Because even if He had made but two, a third would still appear behind them of which they again both possessed the form, and that would be the real bed and not the two others.

Very true, he said.

God knew this, I suppose, and He desired to be the real maker of a real bed, not a kind of maker of a kind of bed, and therefore He created a bed which is essentially and by nature one only.

So it seems.

Shall we, then, speak of Him as the natural author or maker of the bed?

Yes, he replied; inasmuch as by the natural process of creation He is the author of this and of all other things.

And what shall we say of the carpenter—is not he also the maker of a bed?

Yes.

But would you call the painter an artificer and maker?

Certainly not.

Yet if he is not the maker, what is he in relation to the bed?

I think, he said, that we may fairly designate him as the imitator of that which the others make.

Good, I said; then you call him whose product is third in the descent from nature, an imitator?

Certainly, he said.

And so if the tragic poet is an imitator, he too is thrice removed from the king and from the truth; and so are all other imitators.

That appears to be so.

Then about the imitator we are agreed. And what about the painter?—Do you think he tries to imitate in each case that which originally exists in nature, or only the creations of artificers?

The latter.

As they are or as they appear? you have still to determine this.

What do you mean?

I mean to ask whether a bed really becomes different when it is seen from different points of view, obliquely or directly or from any other point of view? Or does it simply appear different, without being really so? And the same of all things.

Yes, he said, the difference is only apparent.

Now let me ask you another question: Which is the art of painting designed to be—an imitation of things as they are, or as they appear—of appearance or of reality?

Of appearance, he said.

Then the imitator is a long way off the truth, and can reproduce all things because he lightly touches on a small part of them, and that part an image. For example: A painter will paint a cobbler, carpenter, or any other artisan, though he knows nothing of their arts; and, if he is a good painter, he may deceive children or simple persons when he shows them his picture of a carpenter from a distance, and they will fancy that they are looking at a real carpenter.

Certainly.

And surely, my friend, this is how we should regard all such claims: whenever any one informs us that he has found a man who knows all the arts, and all things else that anybody knows, and every single thing with a higher degree of accuracy than any other man—whoever tells us this, I think that we can only retort that he is a simple creature who seems to have been deceived by some wizard or imitator whom he met, and whom he thought all-knowing, because he himself was unable to analyse the nature of knowledge and ignorance and imitation.

Most true.

And next, I said, we have to consider tragedy and its leader, Homer; for we hear some persons saying that these poets know all the arts; and all things human; where virtue and vice are concerned, and indeed all divine things too; because the good poet cannot compose well unless he knows his subject, and he who has not this knowledge can never be a poet. We ought to consider whether here also there may not be a similar illusion. Perhaps they may have come across imitators and been deceived by them; they may not have remembered when they saw their works that these were thrice removed from the truth, and could easily be made without any knowledge of the truth, because they are appearances only and not realities? Or, after all, they may be in the right and good poets do really know the things about which they seem to the many to speak so well?

The question, he said, should by all means be considered.

Now do you suppose that if a person were able to make the original as well as the image, he would seriously devote himself to the image-making branch? Would he allow imitation to be the ruling principle of his life, as if he had nothing higher in him?

I should say not.

But the real artist, who had real knowledge of those things which he chose also to imitate, would be interested in realities and not in imitations; and would desire to leave as memorials of himself works many and fair; and, instead of being the author of encomiums, he would prefer to be the theme of them.

Yes, he said, that would be to him a source of much greater honour and profit.

Now let us refrain, I said, from calling Homer or any other poet to account regarding those arts to which his poems incidentally refer: we will not ask them, in case any poet has been a doctor and not a mere imitator of medical parlance, to show what patients have been restored to health by a poet, ancient or modern, as they were by Asclepius[1]; or what disciples in medicine a poet has left behind him, like the Asclepiads. Nor shall we press the same question upon them about the other arts. But we have a right to know respecting warfare, strategy, the administration of States and the education of man, which are the chiefest and noblest subjects of his poems, and we may fairly ask him about them. "Friend Homer," then we say to him, "if you are only in the second remove from truth in what you say of virtue, and not in the third—not an image maker, that is, by our definition, an imitator—and if you are able to discern what pursuits make men better or worse in private or public life, tell us what State was ever better governed by your help? The good order of Lacedaemon is due to Lycurgus, and many other cities great and small have been similarly benefited by others; but who says that you have been a good legislator to them and have done them any good? Italy and Sicily boast of Charondas, and there is Solon who is renowned among us; but what city has anything to say about you?" Is there any city which he might name?

I think not, said Glaucon; not even the Homeridæ[2] themselves pretend that he was a legislator.

Well, but is there any war on record which was carried on successfully owing to his leadership or counsel?

There is not.

Or is there anything comparable to those clever improvements in the arts, or in other operations, which are said to have been due to men of practical genius such as Thales the Milesian or Anacharsis the Scythian?[3]

There is absolutely nothing of the kind.

But, if Homer never did any public service, was he privately a guide or teacher of any? Had he in his lifetime friends who loved to associate with him,

[1] The god of medicine.

[2] The Homeridæ: a clan or guild in Chios, claiming descent from Homer, who occupied themselves by reciting his poems.

[3] Thales and Anacharsis are among the classic Seven Wise Men. Thales was credited with predicting eclipses, with having discovered the solstices, with inventions in geometry, and with having given good political advice; Anacharsis was said to have invented the anchor and the potter's wheel.

and who handed down to posterity an Homeric way of life, such as was established by Pythagoras[4] who was especially beloved for this reason and whose followers are to this day conspicuous among others by what they term the Pythagorean way of life?

Nothing of the kind is recorded of him. For surely, Socrates, Creophylus, the companion of Homer, that child of flesh,[5] whose name always makes us laugh, might be more justly ridiculed for his want of breeding, if what is said is true, that Homer was greatly neglected by him in his own day when he was alive?

Yes, I replied, that is the tradition. But can you imagine, Glaucon, that if Homer had really been able to educate and improve mankind—if he had been capable of knowledge and not been a mere imitator—can you imagine, I say, that he would not have attracted many followers, and been honoured and loved by them? Protagoras of Abdera, and Prodicus of Ceos,[6] and a host of others, have only to whisper to their contemporaries: "You will never be able to manage either your own house or your own State until you appoint us to be your ministers of education"—and this ingenious device of theirs has such an effect in making men love them that their companions all but carry them about on their shoulders. And is it conceivable that the contemporaries of Homer, or again of Hesiod, would have allowed either of them to go about as rhapsodists, if they had really been able to help mankind forward in virtue? Would they not have been as unwilling to part with them as with gold, and have compelled them to stay at home with them? Or, if the master would not stay, then the disciples would have followed him about everywhere, until they had got education enough?

Yes, Socrates, that, I think, is quite true.

Then must we not infer that all these poetical individuals, beginning with Homer, are only imitators, who copy images of virtue and the other themes of their poetry, but have no contact with the truth? The poet is like a painter who, as we have already observed, will make a likeness of a cobbler though he understands nothing of cobbling; and his picture is good enough for those who know no more than he does, and judge only by colours and figures.

Quite so.

In like manner the poet with his words and phrases may be said to lay on the colours of the several arts, himself understanding their nature only enough to imitate them; and other people, who are as ignorant as he is, and judge only from his words, imagine that if he speaks of cobbling, or of military tactics, or of anything else, in metre and harmony and rhythm, he speaks very well—such is the sweet influence which melody and rhythm by nature have. For I am sure that you know what a poor appearance the works of poets make when stripped of the colours which art puts upon them, and recited in simple prose. You have seen some examples?

---

[4] Said to have been the first man to call himself a philosopher, or lover of truth; founded a secret religious society, which made contributions to astronomy, medicine, geometry, music; credited with the theorem in geometry that bears his name.

[5] A rough translation of "Creophylus," more literally, "of the meat clan." All we know of this man is that an ancient translator calls him an epic poet.

[6] Sophists: contemporaries of Plato; men who made their living by teaching.

Yes, he said.

They are like faces which were never really beautiful, but only blooming, seen when the bloom of youth has passed away from them?

Exactly.

Come now, and observe this point: The imitator or maker of the image knows nothing, we have said, of true existence; he knows appearances only. Am I not right?

Yes.

Then let us have a clear understanding, and not be satisfied with half an explanation.

Proceed.

Of the painter we say that he will paint reins, and he will paint a bit?

Yes.

And the worker in leather and brass will make them?

Certainly.

But does the painter know the right form of the bit and reins? Nay, hardly even the workers in brass and leather who make them; only the horseman who knows how to use them—he knows their right form.

Most true.

And may we not say the same of all things?

What?

That there are three arts which are concerned with all things: one which uses, another which makes, a third which imitates them?

Yes.

And the excellence and beauty and rightness of every structure, animate or inanimate, and of every action of man, is relative solely to the use for which nature or the artist has intended them.

True.

Then beyond doubt it is the user who has the greatest experience of them, and he must report to the maker the good or bad qualities which develop themselves in use; for example, the flute-player will tell the flute-maker which of his flutes is satisfactory to the performer; he will tell him how he ought to make them, and the other will attend to his instructions?

Of course.

So the one pronounces with knowledge about the goodness and badness of flutes, while the other, confiding in him, will make them accordingly?

True.

The instrument is the same, but about the excellence or badness of it the maker will possess a correct belief, since he associates with one who knows, and is compelled to hear what he has to say; whereas the user will have knowledge?

True.

But will the imitator have either? Will he know from use whether or no that which he paints is correct or beautiful? or will he have right opinion from being compelled to associate with another who knows and gives him instructions about what he should paint?

Neither.

Then an imitator will no more have true opinion than he will have knowledge about the goodness or badness of his models?

I suppose not.

The imitative poet will be in a brilliant state of intelligence about the theme of his poetry?

Nay, very much the reverse.

And still he will go on imitating without knowing what makes a thing good or bad, and may be expected therefore to imitate only that which appears to be good to the ignorant multitude?

Just so.

Thus far then we are pretty well agreed that the imitator has no knowledge worth mentioning of what he imitates. Imitation is only a kind of play or sport, and the tragic poets, whether they write in iambic or in heroic verse, are imitators in the highest degree?

Very true.

And now tell me, I conjure you,—this imitation is concerned with an object which is thrice removed from the truth?

Certainly.

And what kind of faculty in man is that to which imitation makes its special appeal?

What do you mean?

I will explain: The same body does not appear equal to our sight when seen near and when seen at a distance?

True.

And the same objects appear straight when looked at out of the water, and crooked when in the water; and the concave becomes convex, owing to the illusion about colours to which the sight is liable. Thus every sort of confusion is revealed within us; and this is that weakness of the human mind on which the art of painting in light and shadow, the art of conjuring, and many other ingenious devices impose, having an effect upon us like magic.

True.

And the arts of measuring and numbering and weighing come to the rescue of the human understanding—there is the beauty of them—with the result that the apparent greater or less, or more or heavier, no longer have the mastery over us, but give way before the power of calculation and measuring and weighing?

Most true.

And this, surely, must be the work of the calculating and rational principle in the soul?

To be sure.

And often when this principle measures and certifies that some things are equal, or that some are greater or less than others, it is, at the same time, contradicted by the appearance which the objects present?

True.

But did we not say that such a contradiction is impossible—the same faculty cannot have contrary opinions at the same time about the same thing?

We did; and rightly.

Then that part of the soul which has an opinion contrary to measure can hardly be the same with that which has an opinion in accordance with measure?

True.

And the part of the soul which trusts to measure and calculation is likely to be the better one?

Certainly.

And therefore that which is opposed to this is probably an inferior principle in our nature?

No doubt.

This was the conclusion at which I was seeking to arrive when I said that painting or drawing, and imitation in general, are engaged upon productions which are far removed from truth, and are also the companions and friends and associates of a principle within us which is equally removed from reason, and that they have no true or healthy aim.

Exactly.

The imitative art is an inferior who from intercourse with an inferior has inferior offspring.

Very true.

And is this confined to the sight only, or does it extend to the hearing also, relating in fact to what we term poetry?

Probably the same would be true of poetry.

Do not rely, I said, on a probability derived from the analogy of painting; but let us once more go directly to that faculty of the mind with which imitative poetry has converse, and see whether it is good or bad.

By all means.

We may state the question thus:—Imitation imitates the actions of men, whether voluntary or involuntary, on which, as they imagine, a good or bad result has ensued, and they rejoice or sorrow accordingly. Is there anything more?

No, there is nothing else.

But in all this variety of circumstances is the man at unity with himself— or rather, as in the instance of sight there was confusion and opposition in his opinions about the same things, so here also is there not strife and inconsistency in his life? Though I need hardly raise the question again, for I remember that all this has been already admitted; and the soul has been acknowledged by us to be full of these and ten thousand similar oppositions occurring at the same moment?

And we were right, he said.

Yes, I said, thus far we were right; but there was an omission which must now be supplied.

What was the omission?

Were we not saying that a good man, who has the misfortune to lose his son or anything else which is most dear to him, will bear the loss with more equanimity than another?

Yes, indeed.

But will he have no sorrow, or shall we say that although he cannot help sorrowing, he will moderate his sorrow?

The latter, he said, is the truer statement.

Tell me: will he be more likely to struggle and hold out against his sorrow when he is seen by his equals, or when he is alone in a deserted place?

The fact of being seen will make a great difference, he said.

When he is by himself he will not mind saying many things which he would be ashamed of any one hearing, and also doing many things which he would not care to be seen doing?

True.

And doubtless it is the law and reason in him which bids him resist; while it is the affliction itself which is urging him to indulge his sorrow?

True.

But when a man is drawn in two opposite directions, to and from the same object, this, as we affirm, necessarily implies two distinct principles in him?

Certainly.

One of them is ready to follow the guidance of the law?

How do you mean?

The law would say that to be patient under calamity is best, and that we should not give way to impatience, as the good and evil in such things are not clear, and nothing is gained by impatience; also, because no human thing is of serious importance, and grief stands in the way of that which at the moment is most required.

What is most required? he asked.

That we should take counsel about what has happened, and when the dice have been thrown, according to their fall, order our affairs in the way which reason deems best; not, like children who have had a fall, keeping hold of the part struck and wasting time in setting up a howl, but always accustoming the soul forthwith to apply a remedy, raising up that which is sickly and fallen, banishing the cry of sorrow by the healing art.

Yes, he said, that is the true way of meeting the attacks of fortune.

Well then, I said, the higher principle is ready to follow this suggestion of reason?

Clearly.

But the other principle, which inclines us to recollection of our troubles and to lamentation, and can never have enough of them, we may call irrational, useless, and cowardly?

Indeed, we may.

Now does not the principle which is thus inclined to complaint, furnish a great variety of materials for imitation? Whereas the wise and calm temperament, being always nearly equable, is not easy to imitate or to appreciate when imitated, especially at a public festival when a promiscuous crowd is assembled in a theatre. For the feeling represented is one to which they are strangers.

Certainly.

Then the imitative poet who aims at being popular is not by nature made, nor is his art intended, to please or to affect the rational principle in the soul; but he will appeal rather to the lachrymose and fitful temper, which is easily imitated?

Clearly.

And now we may fairly take him and place him by the side of the painter, for he is like him in two ways: first, inasmuch as his creations have an inferior degree of truth—in this, I say, he is like him; and he is also like him in being the associate of an inferior part of the soul; and this is enough to show that we shall be right in refusing to admit him into a State which is to be well ordered, because he awakens and nourishes this part of the soul, and by strengthening it impairs the reason. As in a city when the evil are permitted to wield power and the finer men are put out of the way, so in the soul of each man, as we shall maintain, the imitative poet implants an evil constitution, for he indulges the irrational nature which has no discernment of greater and less, but thinks the same thing at one time great and at another small—he is an imitator of images and is very far removed from the truth.

Exactly.

But we have not yet brought forward the heaviest count in our accusation: —the power which poetry has of harming even the good (and there are very few who are not harmed), is surely an awful thing?

Yes, certainly, if the effect is what you say.

Hear and judge: The best of us, as I conceive, when we listen to a passage of Homer or one of the tragedians, in which he represents some hero who is drawling out his sorrows in a long oration, or singing, and smiting his breast— the best of us, you know, delight in giving way to sympathy, and are in raptures at the excellence of the poet who stirs our feelings most.

Yes, of course I know.

But when any sorrow of our own happens to us, then you may observe that we pride ourselves on the opposite quality—we would fain be quiet and patient; this is considered the manly part, and the other which delighted us in the recitation is now deemed to be the part of a woman.

Very true, he said.

Now can we be right in praising and admiring another who is doing that which any one of us would abominate and be ashamed of in his own person?

No, he said, that is certainly not reasonable.

Nay, I said, quite reasonable from one point of view.

What point of view?

If you consider, I said, that when in misfortune we feel a natural hunger and desire to relieve our sorrow by weeping and lamentation, and that this very feeling which is starved and suppressed in our own calamities is satisfied and delighted by the poets;—the better nature in each of us, not having been sufficiently trained by reason or habit, allows the sympathetic element to break loose because the sorrow is another's; and the spectator fancies that there can be no disgrace to himself in praising and pitying any one who while professing to be a brave man, gives way to untimely lamentation; he thinks that the pleasure is a gain, and is far from wishing to lose it by rejection of the whole poem. Few persons ever reflect, as I should imagine, that the contagion must pass from others to themselves. For the pity which has been nourished and strengthened in the misfortunes of others is with difficulty repressed in our own.

How very true!

And does not the same hold also of the ridiculous? There are jests which you would be ashamed to make yourself, and yet on the comic stage, or indeed in private, when you hear them, you are greatly amused by them, and are not at all disgusted at their unseemliness;—the case of pity is repeated;—there is a principle in human nature which is disposed to raise a laugh, and this, which you once restrained by reason because you were afraid of being thought a buffoon, is now let out again; and having stimulated the risible faculty at the theatre, you are betrayed unconsciously to yourself into playing the comic poet at home.

Quite true, he said.

And the same may be said of lust and anger and all the other affections, of desire and pain and pleasure, which are held to be inseparable from every action —in all of them poetry has a like effect; it feeds and waters the passions instead of drying them up; she lets them rule, although they ought to be controlled if mankind are ever to increase in happiness and virtue.

I cannot deny it.

Therefore, Glaucon, I said, whenever you meet with any of the eulogists of Homer declaring that he has been the educator of Hellas, and that he is profitable for education and for the ordering of human things, and that you should take him up again and again and get to know him and regulate your whole life according to him, we may love and honour those who say these things—they are excellent people, as far as their lights extend; and we are ready to acknowledge that Homer is the greatest of poets and first of tragedy writers; but we must remain firm in our conviction that hymns to the gods and praises of famous men are the only poetry which ought to be admitted into our State. For if you go beyond this and allow the honeyed Muse to enter, either in epic or lyric verse, not law and the reason of mankind, which by common consent have ever been deemed best, but pleasure and pain will be the rulers in our State.

That is most true, he said.

And now since we have reverted to the subject of poetry, let this our defence serve to show the reasonableness of our former judgement in sending away out of our State an art having the tendencies which we have described; for reason constrained us. But that she may not impute to us any harshness or want of politeness, let us tell her that there is an ancient quarrel between philosophy and poetry; of which there are many proofs, such as the saying of "the yelping hound howling at her lord," or of one "mighty in the vain talk of fools," and "the mob of sages circumventing Zeus," and the "subtle thinkers who are beggars after all,"[7] and there are innumerable other signs of ancient enmity between them. Notwithstanding this, let us assure the poetry which aims at pleasure, and the art of imitation, that if she will only prove her title to exist in a well-ordered State we shall be delighted to receive her—we are very conscious of her charms; but it would not be right on that account to betray the truth. I dare say, Glaucon, that you are as much charmed by her as I am, especially when she appears in Homer?

Yes, indeed, I am greatly charmed.

Shall I propose, then, that she be allowed to return from exile, but upon this condition only—that she make a defence of herself in some lyrical or other metre?

Certainly.

And we may further grant to those of her defenders who are lovers of poetry and yet not poets the permission to speak in prose on her behalf: let them show not only that she is pleasant but also useful to States and to human life,

---

[7] These tags are presumably from poets' attacks on philosophers, but they have not been traced.

and we will listen in a kindly spirit; for we shall surely be the gainers if this can be proved, that there is a use in poetry as well as a delight?

Certainly, he said, we shall be the gainers.

If her defence fails, then, my dear friend, like other persons who are enamoured of something, but put a restraint upon themselves when they think their desires are opposed to their interests, so too must we after the manner of lovers give her up, though not without a struggle. We too are inspired by that love of such poetry which the education of noble States has implanted in us, and therefore we shall be glad if she appears at her best and truest; but so long as she is unable to make good her defence, this argument of ours shall be a charm to us, which we will repeat to ourselves while we listen to her strains; that we may not fall away into the childish love of her which captivates the many. At all events we are well aware that poetry, such as we have described, is not to be regarded seriously as attaining to the truth; and he who listens to her, fearing for the safety of the city which is within him, should be on his guard against her seductions and make our words his law.

Yes, he said, I quite agree with you.

Yes, I said, my dear Glaucon, for great is the issue at stake, greater than appears, whether a man is to be good or bad. And what will any one be profited if under the influence of honour or money or power, aye, or under the excitement of poetry, he neglect justice and virtue?

Aristotle

THE POETICS

Aristotle is said to have been born in Stagira, in Macedonia, in 384 B.C.
At the age of eighteen he came to Athens and studied with Plato until
the latter died in 347 B.C. After traveling for a few years, he was asked
by Philip of Macedonia, an old family friend, to become tutor of Philip's
thirteen-year-old son, later Alexander the Great. When Alexander succeeded to the throne, Aristotle returned to Athens and founded a philosophical academy, called the Lyceum because the site was sacred to Apollo
Lyceus. When, after the death of Alexander, agitation against everything
connected with Macedonia swept through Athens, Aristotle fled to Chal-
cis, and, thinking of Socrates' fate, remarked that he would not give the
Athenians an opportunity "to sin twice against philosophy." He died in
322 B.C.

The *Poetics* was probably written around 330 B.C. After the fall of
Rome it was pretty much lost to the West, until the Arabs introduced
much of Aristotle's work to Islam in the ninth century A.D., whence it
was reintroduced to Europe by Arabian and Jewish scholars. Its influence
on criticism has been steady from the time it was translated into Latin
by the Italian humanist Valla in 1498.

I propose to treat of Poetry in itself and of its various kinds, noting the
essential quality of each; to inquire into the structure of the plot as requisite to
a good poem; into the number and nature of the parts of which a poem is composed; and similarly into whatever else falls within the same inquiry. Following,
then, the order of nature, let us begin with the principles which come first.

Epic poetry and Tragedy, Comedy also and Dithyrambic[1] poetry, and the
music of the flute and of the lyre in most of their forms, are all in their general
conception modes of imitation. They differ, however, from one another in three
respects,—the medium, the objects, the manner or mode of imitation, being in
each case distinct.

For as there are persons who, by conscious art or mere habit, imitate and
represent various objects through the medium of colour and form, or again by
the voice; so in the arts above mentioned, taken as a whole, the imitation is
produced by rhythm, language, or "harmony," either singly or combined.

Thus in the music of the flute and of the lyre, "harmony" and rhythm alone

---

[1] The dithyramb was a choral song, originally sung in honor of Dionysus.

From *Aristotle's Theory of Poetry and Fine Art, with a Critical Text and Translation of
the Poetics,* translated by S. H. Butcher (fourth edition, 1907). London, Macmillan and
Co., Ltd.

are employed; also in other arts, such as that of the shepherd's pipe, which are essentially similar to these. In dancing, rhythm alone is used without "harmony"; for even dancing imitates character, emotion, and action, by rhythmical movement.

There is another art which imitates by means of language alone, and that either in prose or verse—which verse, again, may either combine different metres or consist of but one kind—but this has hitherto been without a name. For there is no common term we could apply to the mimes[2] of Sophron and Xenarchus and the Socratic dialogues on the one hand; and, on the other, to poetic imitations in iambic, elegiac, or any similar metre. People do, indeed, add the word "maker" or "poet" to the name of the metre, and speak of elegiac poets, or epic (that is, hexameter) poets, as if it were not the imitation that makes the poet, but the verse that entitles them all indiscriminately to the name. Even when a treatise on medicine or natural science is brought out in verse, the name of poet is by custom given to the author; and yet Homer and Empedocles[3] have nothing in common but the metre, so that it would be right to call the one poet, the other physicist rather than poet. On the same principle, even if a writer in his poetic imitation were to combine all metres, as Chaeremon[4] did in his *Centaur*, which is a medley composed of metres of all kinds, we should bring him too under the general term poet. So much then for these distinctions.

There are, again, some arts which employ all the means above mentioned,— namely, rhythm, tune, and metre. Such are Dithyrambic and Nomic[5] poetry, and also Tragedy and Comedy; but between them the difference is, that in the first two cases these means are all employed in combination, in the latter, now one means is employed, now another.

Such, then, are the differences of the arts with respect to the medium of imitation.

Since the objects of imitation are men in action, and these men must be either of a higher or a lower type (for moral character mainly answers to these divisions, goodness and badness being the distinguishing marks of moral differences), it follows that we must represent men either as better than in real life, or as worse, or as they are. It is the same in painting. Polygnotus depicted men as nobler than they are, Pauson as less noble, Dionysius drew them true to life.

Now it is evident that each of the modes of imitation above mentioned will exhibit these differences, and become a distinct kind in imitating objects that are thus distinct. Such diversities may be found even in dancing, flute-playing, and lyre-playing. So again in language, whether prose or verse unaccompanied by music. Homer, for example, makes men better than they are; Cleophon as they are; Hegemon the Thasian, the inventor of parodies, and Nicochares, the author of the *Deiliad*,[6] worse than they are. The same thing holds good of Dithyrambs and Nomes; here too one may portray different types, as Timotheus

---

2 The *mimos,* as written by Sophron and his son Xenarchus, was a short burlesque sketch, written in rhythmic, but colloquial, prose.

3 Empedocles (fl. 460 B.C.) of Agrigentium wrote philosophical poems in hexameters.

4 Fourth-century B.C. tragedian.

5 The *nomos* as associated with Terpander of Lesbos (seventh century B.C.) was a lyric sung to the accompaniment of a flute or cithera.

6 *Deilos* means "coward"; a *Deiliad* is the narrative of a man whose cowardice is the subject of an epic.

and Philoxenus differed in representing their Cyclopes. The same distinction marks off Tragedy from Comedy; for Comedy aims at representing men as worse, Tragedy as better than in actual life.

There is still a third difference—the manner in which each of these objects may be imitated. For the medium being the same, and the objects the same, the poet may imitate by narration—in which case he can either take another personality as Homer does, or speak in his own person, unchanged—or he may present all his characters as living and moving before us.

These, then, as we said at the beginning, are the three differences which distinguish artistic imitation,—the medium, the objects, and the manner. So that from one point of view, Sophocles is an imitator of the same kind as Homer—for both imitate higher types of character; from another point of view, of the same kind as Aristophanes—for both imitate persons acting and doing. Hence, some say, the name of "drama" is given to such poems, as representing action. For the same reason the Dorians claim the invention both of Tragedy and Comedy. The claim to Comedy is put forward by the Megarians,—not only by those of Greece proper, who allege that it originated under their democracy, but also by the Megarians of Sicily, for the poet Epicharmus, who is much earlier than Chionides and Magnes,[7] belonged to that country. Tragedy too is claimed by certain Dorians of the Peloponnese. In each case they appeal to the evidence of language. The outlying villages, they say, are by them called κῶμαι [komai], by the Athenians δῆμοι [demoi]: and they assume that Comedians were so named not from κωμάζειν [komazein], "to revel," but because they wandered from village to village (κατὰ κώμας) [kata komas], being excluded contemptuously from the city. They add also that the Dorian word for "doing" is δρᾶν [dran], and the Athenian, πράττειν [prattein].

This may suffice as to the number and nature of the various modes of imitation.

Poetry in general seems to have sprung from two causes, each of them lying deep in our nature. First, the instinct of imitation is implanted in man from childhood, one difference between him and other animals being that he is the most imitative of living creatures, and through imitation learns his earliest lessons; and no less universal is the pleasure felt in things imitated. We have evidence of this in the facts of experience. Objects which in themselves we view with pain, we delight to contemplate when reproduced with minute fidelity: such as the forms of the most ignoble animals and of dead bodies. The cause of this again is, that to learn gives the liveliest pleasure, not only to philosophers but to men in general; whose capacity, however, of learning is more limited. Thus the reason why men enjoy seeing a likeness is, that in contemplating it they find themselves learning or inferring, and saying perhaps, "Ah, that is he." For if you happen not to have seen the original, the pleasure will be due not to the imitation as such, but to the execution, the colouring, or some such other cause.

Imitation, then, is one instinct of our nature. Next, there is the instinct for "harmony" and rhythm, metres being manifestly sections of rhythm. Persons, therefore, starting with this natural gift developed by degrees their special aptitudes, till their rude improvisations gave birth to Poetry.

---

[7] Attic writers of comedy of the fifth century B.C.

Poetry now diverged in two directions, according to the individual character of the writers. The graver spirits imitated noble actions, and the actions of good men. The more trivial sort imitated the actions of meaner persons, at first composing satires, as the former did hymns to the gods and the praises of famous men. A poem of the satirical kind cannot indeed be put down to any author earlier than Homer; though many such writers probably there were. But from Homer onward, instances can be cited,—his own *Margites*,[8] for example, and other similar compositions. The appropriate metre was also here introduced; hence the measure is still called the iambic or lampooning measure, being that in which people lampooned one another. Thus the older poets were distinguished as writers of heroic or of lampooning verse.

As, in the serious style, Homer is pre-eminent among poets, for he alone combined dramatic form with excellence of imitation, so he too first laid down the main lines of Comedy, by dramatising the ludicrous instead of writing personal satire. His *Margites* bears the same relation to Comedy that the *Iliad* and *Odyssey* do to Tragedy. But when Tragedy and Comedy came to light, the two classes of poets still followed their natural bent: the lampooners became writers of Comedy, and the Epic poets were succeeded by Tragedians, since the drama was a larger and higher form of art.

Whether Tragedy has as yet perfected its proper types or not; and whether it is to be judged in itself, or in relation also to the audience,—this raises another question. Be that as it may, Tragedy—as also Comedy—was at first mere improvisation. The one originated with the authors of the Dithyramb, the other with those of the phallic songs, which are still in use in many of our cities. Tragedy advanced by slow degrees; each new element that showed itself was in turn developed. Having passed through many changes, it found its natural form, and there it stopped.

Aeschylus first introduced a second actor; he diminished the importance of the Chorus, and assigned the leading part to the dialogue. Sophocles raised the number of actors to three, and added scene-painting. Moreover, it was not till late that the short plot was discarded for one of greater compass, and the grotesque diction of the earlier satyric form for the stately manner of Tragedy. The iambic measure then replaced the trochaic tetrameter, which was orginally employed when the poetry was of the satyric order, and had greater affinities with dancing.[9] Once dialogue had come in, Nature herself discovered the appropriate measure. For the iambic is, of all measures, the most colloquial: we see it in the fact that conversational speech runs into iambic lines more frequently than into any other kind of verse; rarely into hexameters, and only when we drop the colloquial intonation. The additions to the number of "episodes" or acts, and the other accessories of which tradition tells, must be taken as already described; for to discuss them in detail would, doubtless, be a large undertaking.

Comedy is, as we have said, an imitation of characters of a lower type,— not, however, in the full sense of the word bad, the Ludicrous being merely a

---

[8] Comic poem attributed to Homer in Aristotle's time and for a long time after.

[9] Aristotle seems to be saying that tragedy grew out of the satyr-play, which in Aristotle's time was the fourth and comic play that followed the presentation of three tragedies.

subdivision of the ugly. It consists in some defect or ugliness which is not painful or destructive. To take an obvious example, the comic mask is ugly and distorted, but does not imply pain.

The successive changes through which Tragedy passed, and the authors of these changes, are well known, whereas Comedy has had no history, because it was not at first treated seriously. It was late before the Archon granted a comic chorus to a poet;[10] the performers were till then voluntary. Comedy had already taken definite shape when comic poets, distinctively so called, are heard of. Who furnished it with masks, or prologues, or increased the number of actors,—these and other similar details remain unknown. As for the plot, it came originally from Sicily; but of Athenian writers Crates was the first who, abandoning the "iambic" or lampooning form, generalised his themes and plots.

Epic poetry agrees with Tragedy in so far as it is an imitation in verse of characters of a higher type. They differ, in that Epic poetry admits but one kind of metre, and is narrative in form. They differ, again, in their length: for Tragedy endeavours, as far as possible, to confine itself to a single revolution of the sun, or but slightly to exceed this limit; whereas the Epic action has no limits of time. This, then, is a second point of difference; though at first the same freedom was admitted in Tragedy as in Epic poetry.

Of their constituent parts some are common to both, some peculiar to Tragedy: whoever, therefore, knows what is good or bad Tragedy, knows also about Epic poetry. All the elements of an Epic poem are found in Tragedy, but the elements of a Tragedy are not all found in the Epic poem.

Of the poetry which imitates in hexameter verse, and of Comedy, we will speak hereafter. Let us now discuss Tragedy, resuming its formal definition, as resulting from what has been already said.

Tragedy, then, is an imitation of an action that is serious, complete, and of a certain magnitude; in language embellished with each kind of artistic ornament, the several kinds being found in separate parts of the play; in the form of action, not of narrative; through pity and fear effecting the proper purgation of these emotions. By "language embellished," I mean language into which rhythm, "harmony," and song enter. By "the several kinds in separate parts," I mean, that some parts are rendered through the medium of verse alone, others again with the aid of song.

Now as tragic imitation implies persons acting, it necessarily follows, in the first place, that Spectacular equipment will be a part of Tragedy. Next, Song and Diction, for these are the medium of imitation. By "Diction" I mean the mere metrical arrangement of the words: as for "Song," it is a term whose sense every one understands.

Again, Tragedy is the imitation of an action; and an action implies personal agents, who necessarily possess certain distinctive qualities both of character and thought; for it is by these that we qualify actions themselves, and these—thought and character—are the two natural causes from which actions spring, and on actions again all success or failure depends. Hence, the Plot is

[10] The Greek dramatist submitted his play to the archon, or magistrate, in charge of the festival at which he hoped to have it performed. If the play was chosen, the archon "granted it a chorus"; that is, he provided a choregus, a public-minded man of means who paid the expenses of the production.

the imitation of the action:—for by plot I here mean the arrangement of the incidents. By Character I mean that in virtue of which we ascribe certain qualities to the agents. Thought is required wherever a statement is proved, or, it may be, a general truth enunciated. Every Tragedy, therefore, must have six parts, which parts determine its quality—namely, Plot, Character, Diction, Thought, Spectacle, Song. Two of the parts constitute the medium of imitation, one the manner, and three the objects of imitation. And these complete the list. These elements have been employed, we may say, by the poets to a man; in fact, every play contains Spectacular elements as well as Character, Plot, Diction, Song, and Thought.

But most important of all is the structure of the incidents. For Tragedy is an imitation, not of men, but of an action and of life, and life consists in action, and its end is a mode of action, not a quality. Now character determines men's qualities, but it is by their actions that they are happy or the reverse. Dramatic action, therefore, is not with a view to the representation of character: character comes in as subsidiary to the actions. Hence the incidents and the plot are the end of a tragedy; and the end is the chief thing of all. Again, without action there cannot be a tragedy; there may be without character. The tragedies of most of our modern poets fail in the rendering of character; and of poets in general this is often true. It is the same in painting; and here lies the difference between Zeuxis and Polygnotus. Polygnotus delineates character well: the style of Zeuxis is devoid of ethical quality. Again, if you string together a set of speeches expressive of character, and well finished in point of diction and thought, you will not produce the essential tragic effect nearly so well as with a play which, however deficient in these respects, yet has a plot and artistically constructed incidents. Besides which, the most powerful elements of emotional interest in Tragedy—Peripeteia or Reversal of the Situation, and Recognition scenes—are parts of the plot. A further proof is, that novices in the art attain to finish of diction and precision of portraiture before they can construct the plot. It is the same with almost all the early poets.

The Plot, then, is the first principle, and, as it were, the soul of a tragedy: Character holds the second place. A similar fact is seen in painting. The most beautiful colours, laid on confusedly, will not give as much pleasure as the chalk outline of a portrait. Thus Tragedy is the imitation of an action, and of the agents mainly with a view to the action.

Third in order is Thought,—that is, the faculty of saying what is possible and pertinent in given circumstances. In the case of oratory, this is the function of the political art and of the art of rhetoric: and so indeed the older poets make their characters speak the language of civic life; the poets of our time, the language of the rhetoricians. Character is that which reveals moral purpose, showing what kind of things a man chooses or avoids. Speeches, therefore, which do not make this manifest, or in which the speaker does not choose or avoid anything whatever, are not expressive of character. Thought, on the other hand, is found where something is proved to be or not to be, or a general maxim is enunciated.

Fourth among the elements enumerated comes Diction; by which I mean, as has been already said, the expression of the meaning in words; and its essence is the same both in verse and prose.

Of the remaining elements Song holds the chief place among the embellishments.

The Spectacle has, indeed, an emotional attraction of its own, but, of all the parts, it is the least artistic, and connected least with the art of poetry. For the power of Tragedy, we may be sure, is felt even apart from representation and actors. Besides, the production of spectacular effects depends more on the art of the stage machinist than on that of the poet.

These principles being established, let us now discuss the proper structure of the Plot, since this is the first and most important thing in Tragedy.

Now, according to our definition, Tragedy is an imitation of an action that is complete, and whole, and of a certain magnitude; for there may be a whole that is wanting in magnitude. A whole is that which has a beginning, a middle, and an end. A beginning is that which does not itself follow anything by causal necessity, but after which something naturally is or comes to be. An end, on the contrary, is that which itself naturally follows some other thing, either by necessity, or as a rule, but has nothing following it. A middle is that which follows something as some other thing follows it. A well constructed plot, therefore, must neither begin nor end at haphazard, but conform to these principles.

Again, a beautiful object, whether it be a living organism or any whole composed of parts, must not only have an orderly arrangement of parts, but must also be of a certain magnitude; for beauty depends on magnitude and order. Hence a very small animal organism cannot be beautiful; for the view of it is confused, the object being seen in an almost imperceptible moment of time. Nor, again, can one of vast size be beautiful; for as the eye cannot take it all in at once, the unity and sense of the whole is lost for the spectator; as for instance if there were one a thousand miles long. As, therefore, in the case of animate bodies and organisms a certain magnitude is necessary, and a magnitude which may be easily embraced in one view; so in the plot, a certain length is necessary, and a length which can be easily embraced by the memory. The limit of length in relation to dramatic competition and sensuous presentment, is no part of artistic theory. For had it been the rule for a hundred tragedies to compete together, the performance would have been regulated by the water-clock,—as indeed we are told was formerly done. But the limit as fixed by the nature of the drama itself is this:—the greater the length, the more beautiful will the piece be by reason of its size, provided that the whole be perspicuous. And to define the matter roughly, we may say that the proper magnitude is comprised within such limits, that the sequence of events, according to the law of probability or necessity, will admit of a change from bad fortune to good, or from good fortune to bad.

Unity of plot does not, as some persons think, consist in the unity of the hero. For infinitely various are the incidents in one man's life which cannot be reduced to unity; and so, too, there are many actions of one man out of which we cannot make one action. Hence the error, as it appears, of all poets who have composed a *Heracleid*, a *Theseid*, or other poems of the kind. They imagine that as Heracles was one man, the story of Heracles must also be a unity. But Homer, as in all else he is of surpassing merit, here too—whether from art or natural genius—seems to have happily discerned the truth. In composing the

Odyssey he did not include all the adventures of Odysseus—such as his wound
on Parnassus, or his feigned madness at the mustering of the host—incidents
between which there was no necessary or probable connexion: but he made the
Odyssey, and likewise the *Iliad*, to centre round an action that in our sense of
the word is one. As therefore, in the other imitative arts, the imitation is one
when the object imitated is one, so the plot, being an imitation of an action,
must imitate one action and that a whole, the structural union of the parts being
such that, if any one of them is displaced or removed, the whole will be dis-
jointed and disturbed. For a thing whose presence or absence makes no visible
difference, is not an organic part of the whole.

It is, moreover, evident from what has been said, that it is not the function
of the poet to relate what has happened, but what may happen,—what is possible according to the law of probability or necessity. The poet and the historian
differ not by writing in verse or in prose. The work of Herodotus might be put
into verse, and it would still be a species of history, with metre no less than
without it. The true difference is that one relates what has happened, the other
what may happen. Poetry, therefore, is a more philosophical and a higher thing
than history: for poetry tends to express the universal, history the particular.
By the universal I mean how a person of a certain type will on occasion speak
or act, according to the law of probability or necessity; and it is this universality
at which poetry aims in the names she attaches to the personages. The particular
is—for example—what Alcibiades[11] did or suffered. In Comedy this is already
apparent: for here the poet first constructs the plot on the lines of probability,
and then inserts characteristic names;—unlike the lampooners who write about
particular individuals. But tragedians still keep to real names, the reason being
that what is possible is credible: what has not happened we do not at once
feel sure to be possible: but what has happened is manifestly possible: otherwise it would not have happened. Still there are even some tragedies in which
there are only one or two well known names, the rest being fictitious. In others,
none are well known,—as in Agathon's *Antheus*, where incidents and names
alike are fictitious, and yet they give none the less pleasure. We must not,
therefore, at all costs keep to the received legends, which are the usual subjects
of Tragedy. Indeed, it would be absurd to attempt it; for even subjects that are
known are known only to a few, and yet give pleasure to all. It clearly follows
that the poet or "maker" should be the maker of plots rather than of verses;
since he is a poet because he imitates, and what he imitates are actions. And
even if he chances to take an historical subject, he is none the less a poet; for
there is no reason why some events that have actually happened should not
conform to the law of the probable and possible, and in virtue of that quality
in them he is their poet or maker.

Of all plots and actions the epeisodic are the worst. I call a plot "epeisodic"

---

[11] Alcibiades (c. 450–404 B.C.), one of the most dazzling, dangerous, puzzling, yet
somehow characteristic, of ancient Athenians. He was, in his youth, dissolute; then
he became a leader of the popular party; a brilliant general; a deserter to Sparta
during the Peloponnesian Wars; a deserter back to the Athenians, for whom he once
again won brilliant victories; finally, an exile and victim of assassins. The best accounts of his activities are in Plutarch's *Parallel Lives* and in Thucydides' *History
of the Peloponnesian Wars*. He is an important character in Plato's *Symposium*.

in which the episodes or acts succeed one another without probable or necessary sequence. Bad poets compose such pieces by their own fault, good poets, to please the players; for, as they write show pieces for competition, they stretch the plot beyond its capacity, and are often forced to break the natural continuity.

But again, Tragedy is an imitation not only of a complete action, but of events inspiring fear or pity. Such an effect is best produced when the events come on us by surprise; and the effect is heightened when, at the same time, they follow as cause and effect. The tragic wonder will then be greater than if they happened of themselves or by accident; for even coincidences are most striking when they have an air of design. We may instance the statue of Mitys at Argos, which fell upon his murderer while he was a spectator at a festival, and killed him. Such events seem not to be due to mere chance. Plots, therefore, constructed on these principles are necessarily the best.

Plots are either Simple or Complex, for the actions in real life, of which the plots are an imitation, obviously show a similar distinction. An action which is one and continuous in the sense above defined, I call Simple, when the change of fortune takes place without Reversal of the Situation and without Recognition.

A Complex action is one in which the change is accompanied by such Reversal, or by Recognition, or by both. These last should arise from the internal structure of the plot, so that what follows should be the necessary or probable result of the preceding action. It makes all the difference whether any given event is a case of *propter hoc* or *post hoc*.[12]

Reversal of the Situation is a change by which the action veers round to its opposite, subject always to our rule of probability or necessity. Thus in the *Oedipus,* the messenger comes to cheer Oedipus and free him from his alarms about his mother, but by revealing who he is, he produces the opposite effect. Again in the *Lynceus,* Lynceus is being led away to his death, and Danaus goes with him, meaning to slay him; but the outcome of the preceding incidents is that Danaus is killed and Lynceus saved.

Recognition, as the name indicates, is a change from ignorance to knowledge, producing love or hate between the persons destined by the poet for good or bad fortune. The best form of recognition is coincident with a Reversal of the Situation, as in the *Oedipus*. There are indeed other forms. Even inanimate things of the most trivial kind may in a sense be objects of recognition. Again, we may recognize or discover whether a person has done a thing or not. But the recognition which is most intimately connected with the plot and action is, as we have said, the recognition of persons. This recognition, combined with Reversal, will produce either pity or fear; and actions producing these effects are those which, by our definition, Tragedy represents. Moreover, it is upon such situations that the issues of good or bad fortune will depend. Recognition, then, being between persons, it may happen that one person only is recognised by the other—when the latter is already known—or it may be necessary that the recognition should be on both sides. Thus Iphigenia [in Euripides' *Iphigenia*

---

[12] The distinction is between an event that occurs *because of* a preceding action and one that occurs merely *after* it.

in Taurus] is revealed to Orestes by the sending of the letter; but another act of recognition is required to make Orestes known to Iphigenia.

Two parts, then, of the Plot—Reversal of the Situation and Recognition—turn upon surprises. A third part is the Scene of Suffering. The Scene of Suffering is a destructive or painful action, such as death on the stage, bodily agony, wounds and the like.

The parts of Tragedy which must be treated as elements of the whole have been already mentioned. We now come to the quantitative parts—the separate parts into which Tragedy is divided—namely, Prologue, Episode, Exode, Choric song; this last being divided into Parode and Stasimon. These are common to all plays: peculiar to some are the songs of actors from the stage and the Commoi.

The Prologue is that entire part of a tragedy which precedes the Parode[13] of the Chorus. The Episode is that entire part of a tragedy which is between complete choric songs. The Exode is that entire part of a tragedy which has no choric song after it. Of the Choric part the Parode is the first undivided utterance of the Chorus: the Stasimon is a Choric ode without anapaests or trochaic tetrameters:[14] the Commos is a joint lamentation of Chorus and actors. The parts of Tragedy which must be treated as elements of the whole have been already mentioned. The quantitative parts—the separate parts into which it is divided—are here enumerated.

As the sequel to what has already been said, we must proceed to consider what the poet should aim at, and what he should avoid, in constructing his plots; and by what means the specific effect of Tragedy will be produced.

A perfect tragedy should, as we have seen, be arranged not on the simple but on the complex plan. It should, moreover, imitate actions which excite pity and fear, this being the distinctive mark of tragic imitation. It follows plainly, in the first place, that the change of fortune presented must not be the spectacle of a virtuous man brought from prosperity to adversity: for this moves neither pity nor fear; it merely shocks us. Nor, again, that of a bad man passing from adversity to prosperity: for nothing can be more alien to the spirit of Tragedy; it possesses no single tragic quality; it neither satisfies the moral sense nor calls forth pity or fear. Nor, again, should the downfall of the utter villain be exhibited. A plot of this kind would, doubtless, satisfy the moral sense, but it would inspire neither pity nor fear; for pity is aroused by unmerited misfortune, fear by the misfortune of a man like ourselves. Such an event, therefore, will be neither pitiful nor terrible. There remains, then, the character between these two extremes,—that of a man who is not eminently good and just, yet whose misfortune is brought about not by vice or depravity, but by some error or frailty. He must be one who is highly renowned and prosperous,—a personage like Oedipus, Thyestes, or other illustrious men of such families.

A well-constructed plot should, therefore, be single in its issue, rather than double as some maintain. The change of fortune should be not from bad to good, but, reversely, from good to bad. It should come about as the result not of

---

[13] Chanted by the chorus as they entered.

[14] Not entirely true of surviving tragedies. The stasimon is often defined as a "stationary song," delivered by the chorus from its stationary position in the orchestra.

vice, but of some great error or frailty, in a character either such as we have described, or better rather than worse. The practice of the stage bears out our view. At first the poets recounted any legend that came in their way. Now, the best tragedies are founded on the story of a few houses,—on the fortunes of Alcmaeon, Oedipus, Orestes, Meleager, Thyestes, Telephus, and those others who have done or suffered something terrible. A tragedy, then, to be perfect according to the rules of art should be of this construction. Hence they are in error who censure Euripides just because he follows this principle in his plays, many of which end unhappily. It is, as we have said, the right ending. The best proof is that on the stage and in dramatic competition, such plays, if well worked out, are the most tragic in effect; and Euripides, faulty though he may be in the general management of his subject, yet is felt to be the most tragic of the poets.

In the second rank comes the kind of tragedy which some place first. Like the *Odyssey*, it has a double thread of plot, and also an opposite catastrophe for the good and for the bad. It is accounted the best because of the weakness of the spectators; for the poet is guided in what he writes by the wishes of his audience. The pleasure, however, thence derived is not the true tragic pleasure. It is proper rather to Comedy, where those who, in the piece, are the deadliest enemies—like Orestes and Aegisthus—quit the stage as friends at the close, and no one slays or is slain.

Fear and pity may be aroused by spectacular means; but they may also result from the inner structure of the piece, which is the better way, and indicates a superior poet. For the plot ought to be so constructed that, even without the aid of the eye, he who hears the tale told will thrill with horror and melt to pity at what takes place. This is the impression we should receive from hearing the story of the *Oedipus*. But to produce this effect by the mere spectacle is a less artistic method, and dependent on extraneous aids. Those who employ spectacular means to create a sense not of the terrible but only of the monstrous, are strangers to the purpose of Tragedy; for we must not demand of Tragedy any and every kind of pleasure, but only that which is proper to it. And since the pleasure which the poet should afford is that which comes from pity and fear through imitation, it is evident that this quality must be impressed upon the incidents.

Let us then determine what are the circumstances which strike us as terrible or pitiful.

Actions capable of this effect must happen between persons who are either friends or enemies or indifferent to one another. If an enemy kills an enemy, there is nothing to excite pity either in the act or the intention,—except so far as the suffering in itself is pitiful. So again with indifferent persons. But when the tragic incident occurs between those who are near or dear to one another—if, for example, a brother kills, or intends to kill, a brother, a son his father, a mother her son, a son his mother, or any other deed of the kind is done—these are the situations to be looked for by the poet. He may not indeed destroy the framework of the received legends—the fact, for instance, that Clytemnestra was slain by Orestes and Eriphyle by Alcmaeon—but he ought to show invention of his own, and skilfully handle the traditional material. Let us explain more clearly what is meant by skilful handling.

The action may be done consciously and with knowledge of the persons, in the manner of the older poets. It is thus too that Euripides makes Medea slay her children. Or, again, the deed of horror may be done, but done in ignorance, and the tie of kinship or friendship be discovered afterwards. The *Oedipus* of Sophocles is an example. Here, indeed, the incident is outside the drama proper; but cases occur where it falls within the action of the play: one may cite the *Alcmaeon* of Astydamas, or Telegonus in the *Wounded Odysseus*.[15] Again, there is a third case,—to be about to act with knowledge of the persons and then not to act. The fourth case is when some one is about to do an irreparable deed through ignorance, and makes the discovery before it is done. These are the only possible ways. For the deed must either be done or not done,—and that wittingly or unwittingly. But of all these ways, to be about to act knowing the persons, and then not to act, is the worst. It is shocking without being tragic, for no disaster follows. It is, therefore, never, or very rarely, found in poetry. One instance, however, is in the *Antigone* [by Sophocles], where Haemon threatens to kill Creon. The next and better way is that the deed should be perpetrated. Still better, that it should be perpetrated in ignorance, and the discovery made afterwards. There is then nothing to shock us, while the discovery produces a startling effect. The last case is the best, as when in the *Cresphontes* [by Euripides] Merope is about to slay her son, but, recognising who he is, spares his life. So in the *Iphigenia*, the sister recognises the brother just in time. Again in the *Helle*, the son recognises the mother when on the point of giving her up. This, then, is why a few families only, as has been already observed, furnish the subjects of tragedy. It was not art, but happy chance, that led the poets in search of subjects to impress the tragic quality upon their plots. They are compelled, therefore, to have recourse to those houses whose history contains moving incidents like these.

Enough has now been said concerning the structure of the incidents, and the right kind of plot.

In respect of Character there are four things to be aimed at. First, and most important, it must be good. Now any speech or action that manifests moral purpose of any kind will be expressive of character: the character will be good if the purpose is good. This rule is relative to each class. Even a woman may be good, and also a slave; though the woman may be said to be an inferior being, and the slave quite worthless. The second thing to aim at is propriety. There is a type of manly valour; but valour in a woman, or unscrupulous cleverness, is inappropriate. Thirdly, character must be true to life: for this is a distinct thing from goodness and propriety, as here described. The fourth point is consistency: for though the subject of the imitation, who suggested the type, be inconsistent, still he must be consistently inconsistent. As an example of motiveless degradation of character, we have Menelaus in the *Orestes* [by Euripides]: of character indecorous and inappropriate, the lament of Odysseus in the *Scylla*,[16] and the speech of Melanippe:[17] of inconsistency,

15 In a story not in Homer, but used in a number of tragedies, including one by Sophocles, Telegonus, son of Odysseus and Circe, sets out to find his father, but, not recognizing him, wounds him fatally.

16 In that, probably, the lament is unheroic. Nothing is known of the *Scylla*.

17 In that, probably, she is too clever for a woman. The reference is to *Melanippe the Wise*, a lost play by Euripides.

the *Iphigenia at Aulis* [by Euripides],—for Iphigenia the suppliant in no way resembles her later self.

As in the structure of the plot, so too in the portraiture of character, the poet should always aim either at the necessary or the probable. Thus a person of a given character should speak or act in a given way, by the rule either of necessity or of probability; just as this event should follow that by necessary or probable sequence. It is therefore evident that the unravelling of the plot, no less than the complication, must arise out of the plot itself, it must not be brought about by the *Deus ex Machina*[18]—as in the *Medea* [by Euripides], or in the Return of the Greeks in the *Iliad*. The *Deus ex Machina* should be employed only for events external to the drama,—for antecedent or subsequent events, which lie beyond the range of human knowledge, and which require to be reported or foretold; for to the gods we ascribe the power of seeing all things. Within the action there must be nothing irrational. If the irrational cannot be excluded, it should be outside the scope of the tragedy. Such is the irrational element in the *Oedipus* of Sophocles.

Again, since Tragedy is an imitation of persons who are above the common level, the example of good portrait-painters should be followed. They, while reproducing the distinctive form of the original, make a likeness which is true to life and yet more beautiful. So too the poet, in representing men who are irascible or indolent, or have other defects of character, should preserve the type and yet ennoble it. In this way Achilles is portrayed by Agathon[19] and Homer.

These then are rules the poet should observe. Nor should he neglect those appeals to the senses, which, though not among the essentials, are the concomitants of poetry; for here too there is much room for error. But of this enough has been said in our published treatises.

What Recognition is has been already explained. We will now enumerate its kinds.

First, the least artistic form, which, from poverty of wit, is most commonly employed—recognition by signs. Of these some are congenital,—such as "the spear which the earth-born race bear on their bodies," or the stars introduced by Carcinus in his *Thyestes*.[20] Others are acquired after birth; and of these some are bodily marks, as scars; some external tokens, as necklaces, or the little ark in the *Tyro* by which the discovery is effected. Even these admit of more or less skilful treatment. Thus in the recognition of Odysseus by his scar, the discovery is made in one way by the nurse, in another by the swineherds. The use of tokens for the express purpose of proof—and, indeed, any formal proof with or without tokens—is a less artistic mode of recognition.

[18] "God from the machine." A contrivance by means of which the gods were brought on stage, usually on the roof of the scene building. Aristotle is arguing that the action of a drama should not be resolved abruptly, arbitrarily, and, as it were, mechanically, by the introduction of a supernatural agent.

[19] In a tragedy of which nothing is known.

[20] Of the illustrations in the immediately following discussion, only the *Odyssey*, the *Choephori* by Aeschylus, the *Oedipus* by Sophocles, and the *Iphigenia in Taurus* by Euripides are known. In the *Odyssey*, the old nurse Eurycleia sees Odysseus' scar by accident while he is bathing, whereas on the later occasion Odysseus deliberately reveals his scar to herdsmen for the express purpose of establishing his identity.

A better kind is that which comes about by a turn of incident, as in the Bath Scene in the *Odyssey*.

Next come the recognitions invented at will by the poet, and on that account wanting in art. For example, Orestes in the *Iphigenia* [*in Taurus*] reveals the fact that he is Orestes. She, indeed, makes herself known by the letter; but he, by speaking himself, and saying what the poet, not what the plot requires. This, therefore, is nearly allied to the fault above mentioned:— for Orestes might as well have brought tokens with him. Another similar instance is the "voice of the shuttle" in the *Tereus*[21] of Sophocles.

The third kind depends on memory when the sight of some object awakens a feeling: as in the *Cyprians* of Dicaeogenes, where the hero breaks into tears on seeing the picture; or again in the "Lay of Alcinous," where Odysseus, hearing the minstrel play the lyre, recalls the past and weeps; and hence the recognition.

The fourth kind is by process of reasoning. Thus in the *Choephori*:— "Some one resembling me has come: no one resembles me but Orestes: there-fore Orestes has come." Such too is the discovery made by Iphigenia in the play of Polyidus the Sophist. It was a natural reflexion for Orestes to make, "So I too must die at the altar like my sister." So, again, in the *Tydeus* of Theodectes, the father says, "I came to find my son, and I lose my own life." So too in the *Phineidae*: the women, on seeing the place, inferred their fate:— "Here we are doomed to die, for here we were cast forth." Again, there is a composite kind of recognition involving false inference on the part of one of the characters, as in the *Odysseus Disguised as a Messenger*. A said that no one else was able to bend the bow; hence B (the disguised Odysseus) im-agined that A would recognise the bow which, in fact, he had not seen; and to bring about a recognition by this means—the expectation that A would recognize the bow—is false inference.

But, of all recognitions, the best is that which arises from the incidents themselves, where the startling discovery is made by natural means. Such is that in the *Oedipus* of Sophocles, and in the *Iphigenia* [*in Taurus*]; for it was natural that Iphigenia should wish to dispatch a letter. These recognitions alone dispense with the artificial aid of tokens or amulets. Next come the recognitions by process of reasoning.

In constructing the plot and working it out with the proper diction, the poet should place the scene, as far as possible, before his eyes. In this way, seeing everything with the utmost vividness, as if he were a spectator of the action, he will discover what is in keeping with it, and be most unlikely to overlook inconsistencies. The need of such a rule is shown by the fault found in Carcinus. Amphiaraus was on his way from the temple. This fact escaped the observation of one who did not see the situation. On the stage, however, the piece failed, the audience being offended at the oversight.

Again, the poet should work out his play, to the best of his power, with appropriate gestures; for those who feel emotion are most convincing through natural sympathy with the characters they represent; and one who is agitated

---

[21] In most versions of the story, Tereus rapes Philomela and cuts out her tongue, but she weaves the story of her violation into a tapestry. Thus the shuttle speaks.

storms, one who is angry rages, with the most life-like reality. Hence poetry implies either a happy gift of nature or a strain of madness. In the one case a man can take the mould of any character; in the other, he is lifted out of his proper self.

As for the story, whether the poet takes it ready made or constructs it for himself, he should first sketch its general outline, and then fill in the episodes and amplify in detail. The general plan may be illustrated by the *Iphigenia* [*in Taurus*]. A young girl is sacrificed; she disappears mysteriously from the eyes of those who sacrificed her; she is transported to another country, where the custom is to offer up all strangers to the goddess. To this ministry she is appointed. Some time later her own brother chances to arrive. The fact that the oracle for some reason ordered him to go there, is outside the general plan of the play. The purpose, again, of his coming is outside the action proper. However, he comes, he is seized, and, when on the point of being sacrificed, reveals who he is. The mode of recognition may be either that of Euripides or of Polyidus, in whose play he exclaims very naturally:—"So it was not my sister only, but I too, who was doomed to be sacrificed"; and by that remark he is saved.

After this, the names being once given, it remains to fill in the episodes. We must see that they are relevant to the action. In the case of Orestes,[22] for example, there is the madness which led to his capture, and his deliverance by means of the purificatory rite. In the drama, the episodes are short, but it is these that give extension to Epic poetry. Thus the story of the *Odyssey* can be stated briefly. A certain man is absent from home for many years; he is jealously watched by Poseidon, and left desolate. Meanwhile his home is in a wretched plight—suitors are wasting his substance and plotting against his son. At length, tempest-tost, he himself arrives; he makes certain persons acquainted with him; he attacks the suitors with his own hand, and is himself preserved while he destroys them. This is the essence of the plot; the rest is episode.

Every tragedy falls into two parts,—Complication and Unravelling or *Dénouement*. Incidents extraneous to the action are frequently combined with a portion of the action proper, to form the Complication; the rest is the Unravelling. By the Complication I mean all that extends from the beginning of the action to the part which marks the turning-point to good or bad fortune. The Unravelling is that which extends from the beginning of the change to the end. Thus, in the *Lynceus* of Theodectes, the Complication consists of the incidents presupposed in the drama, the seizure of the child, and then again [of the parents]. The Unravelling extends from the accusation of murder to the end.

There are four kinds of Tragedy, the Complex, depending entirely on Reversal of the Situation and Recognition; the Pathetic (where the motive is passion),—such as the tragedies on Ajax and Ixion,[23] the Ethical (where the motives are ethical),—such as the *Phthiotides* and the *Peleus*.[24] The fourth

[22] In the same play.
[23] By Sophocles and Euripides respectively.
[24] Lost plays by Sophocles.

kind is the Simple. We here exclude the purely spectacular element, ex-emplified by the *Phorcides*, the *Prometheus*,[25] and scenes laid in Hades. The poet should endeavour, if possible, to combine all poetic elements; or failing that, the greatest number and those the most important; the more so, in face of the cavilling criticism of the day. For whereas there have hitherto been good poets, each in his own branch, the critics now expect one man to surpass all others in their several lines of excellence.

In speaking of a tragedy as the same or different, the best test to take is the plot. Identity exists where the Complication and Unravelling are the same. Many poets tie the knot well, but unravel it ill. Both arts, however, should always be mastered.

Again, the poet should remember what has been often said, and not make an Epic structure into a Tragedy—by an Epic structure I mean one with a multiplicity of plots—as if, for instance, you were to make a tragedy out of the entire story of the *Iliad*. In the Epic poem, owing to its length, each part assumes its proper magnitude. In the drama the result is far from answering to the poet's expectation. The proof is that the poets who have dramatised the whole story of the Fall of Troy, instead of selecting portions, like Euripides; or who have taken the whole tale of Niobe, and not a part of her story, like Aeschylus, either fail utterly or meet with poor success on the stage. Even Agathon has been known to fail from this one defect. In his Reversals of the Situation, however, he shows a marvellous skill in the effort to hit the popular taste,—to produce a tragic effect that satisfies the moral sense. This effect is produced when the clever rogue, like Sisyphus, is outwitted, or the brave villain defeated. Such an event is probable in Agathon's sense of the word: "it is probable," he says, "that many things should happen contrary to probability."

The Chorus too should be regarded as one of the actors; it should be an integral part of the whole, and share in the action, in the manner not of Euripides but of Sophocles. As for the later poets, their choral songs pertain as little to the subject of the piece as to that of any other tragedy. They are, therefore, sung as mere interludes,—a practice first begun by Agathon. Yet what difference is there between introducing such choral interludes, and transferring a speech, or even a whole act, from one play to another?

It remains to speak of Diction and Thought, the other parts of Tragedy having been already discussed. Concerning Thought, we may assume what is said in the *Rhetoric*, to which inquiry the subject more strictly belongs. Under Thought is included every effect which has to be produced by speech, the subdivisions being,—proof and refutation; the excitation of the feelings, such as pity, fear, anger, and the like; the suggestion of importance or its opposite. Now, it is evident that the dramatic incidents must be treated from the same points of view as the dramatic speeches, when the object is to evoke the sense of pity, fear, importance, or probability. The only difference is, that the in-cidents should speak for themselves without verbal exposition; while the effects aimed at in speech should be produced by the speaker, and as a result of the

[25] Both by Aeschylus; only the second survives.

speech. For what were the business of a speaker, if the Thought were revealed quite apart from what he says?

Next, as regards Diction. One branch of the inquiry treats of the Modes of Utterance. But this province of knowledge belongs to the art of Delivery and to the masters of that science. It includes, for instance,—what is a command, a prayer, a statement, a threat, a question, an answer, and so forth. To know or not to know these things involves no serious censure upon the poet's art. For who can admit the fault imputed to Homer by Protagoras,—that in the words, "Sing, goddess, of the wrath," he gives a command under the idea that he utters a prayer? For to tell some one to do a thing or not to do it is, he says, a command. We may, therefore, pass this over as an inquiry that belongs to another art, not to poetry.[26]

*   *   *

Every word is either current, or strange, or metaphorical, or ornamental, or newly-coined, or lengthened, or contracted, or altered.

By a current or proper word I mean one which is in general use among a people; by a strange word, one which is in use in another country. Plainly, therefore, the same word may be at once strange and current, but not in relation to the same people. The word σίγυνον, "lance," is to the Cyprians a current term but to us a strange one.

Metaphor is the application of an alien name by transference either from genus to species, or from species to genus, or from species to species, or by analogy, that is, proportion. Thus from genus to species, as: "There lies my ship"; for lying at anchor is a species of lying. From species to genus, as: "Verily ten thousand noble deeds hath Odysseus wrought"; for ten thousand is a species of large number, and is here used for a large number generally. From species to species, as: "With blade of bronze drew away the life," and "Cleft the water with the vessel of unyielding bronze." Here ἀρύσαι, "to draw away," is used for ταμεῖν, "to cleave," and ταμεῖν again for ἀρύσαι,—each being a species of taking away.[27] Analogy or proportion is when the second term is to the first as the fourth to the third. We may then use the fourth for the second, or the second for the fourth.[28] Sometimes too we qualify the metaphor by adding the term to which the proper word is relative. Thus the cup is to Dionysus as the shield to Ares. The cup may, therefore, be called "the shield of Dionysus," and the shield "the cup of Ares." Or, again, as old age is to life, so is evening to day. Evening may therefore be called "the old age of the day," and old age, "the evening of life," or, in the phrase of Empedocles, "life's setting sun." For some of the terms of the proportion there is at times no word in existence; still the metaphor may be used. For instance, to scatter seed is called sowing: but the action of the sun in scattering his rays is nameless. Still this process bears to the sun the same relation as sowing to the seed. Hence the expression

---

[26] A short technical passage, largely on the alphabet and on parts of speech, is omitted.

[27] As, presumably, in ritual sacrifice, when the body is cleft with a knife and blood is drawn off in a bronze bowl.

[28] If $a : b = c : d$, then b may be applied to c and d may be applied to a.

of the poet "sowing the god-created light." There is another way in which this kind of metaphor may be employed. We may apply an alien term, and then deny of that term one of its proper attributes; as if we were to call the shield, not "the cup of Ares," but "the wineless cup."[29]

*   *   *

The perfection of style is to be clear without being mean. The clearest style is that which uses only current or proper words; at the same time it is mean:—witness the poetry of Cleophon and of Sthenelus. That diction, on the other hand, is lofty and raised above the commonplace which employs unusual words. By unusual, I mean strange (or rare) words, metaphorical, lengthened,—anything, in short, that differs from the normal idiom. Yet a style wholly composed of such words is either a riddle or a jargon; a riddle, if it consists of metaphors; a jargon, if it consists of strange (or rare) words. For the essence of a riddle is to express true facts under impossible combinations. Now this cannot be done by any arrangement of ordinary words, but by the use of metaphor it can. Such is the riddle:—"A man I saw who on another man had glued the bronze by aid of fire,"[30] and others of the same kind. A diction that is made up of strange (or rare) terms is a jargon. A certain infusion, therefore, of these elements is necessary to style; for the strange (or rare) word, the metaphorical, the ornamental, and the other kinds above mentioned, will raise it above the commonplace and mean, while the use of proper words will make it perspicuous. But nothing contributes more to produce a clearness of diction that is remote from commonness than the lengthening, contraction, and alteration of words. For by deviating in exceptional cases from the normal idiom, the language will gain distinction; while, at the same time, the partial conformity with usage will give perspicuity. The critics, therefore, are in error who censure these licenses of speech, and hold the author up to ridicule. Thus Eucleides, the elder, declared that it would be an easy matter to be a poet if you might lengthen syllables at will. He caricatured the practice in the very form of his diction, as in the verse:

Ἐπιχάρην εἶδον Μαραθῶνάδε βαδίζοντα,[31]

or,

οὐκ ἄν γ' ἐράμενος τὸν ἐκείνου ἐλλέβορον.[32]

To employ such license at all obtrusively is, no doubt, grotesque; but in any mode of poetic diction there must be moderation. Even metaphors, strange (or rare) words, or any similar forms of speech, would produce the like effect if used without propriety and with the express purpose of being ludicrous. How great a difference is made by the appropriate use of lengthening, may be seen in Epic poetry by the insertion of ordinary forms in the verse. So, again, if we take a strange (or rare) word, a metaphor, or any similar mode of expression, and replace it by the current or proper term, the truth of our observation will be manifest. For example Aeschylus and Euripides each composed the same iambic line. But the alteration of a single word by Euripides,

[29] Another short passage is omitted.
[30] Refers to the medical practice of "cupping."
[31] "I saw Epichares a-walking Marathon-ward," with distortions to make the line scan.
[32] Obscure: the line has something to do with a lover and hellebore.

who employed the rarer term instead of the ordinary one, makes one verse appear beautiful and the other trivial. Aeschylus in his *Philoctetes* says:

φαγέδαινα δ' ἣ μου σάρκας ἐσθίει ποδός.[33]

Euripides substitutes θοινᾶται "feasts on" for ἐσθίει "feeds on." Again, in the line,

νῦν δέ μ' ἐὼν ὀλίγος τε καὶ οὐτιδανὸς καὶ ἀεικής,[34]

the difference will be felt if we substitute the common words,

νῦν δέ μ' ἐὼν μικρός τε καὶ ἀσθενικὸς καὶ ἀειδής.[35]

Or, if for the line,

δίφρον ἀεικέλιον καταθεὶς ὀλίγην τε τράπεζαν,[36]

we read,

δίφρον μοχθηρὸν καταθεὶς μικράν τε τράπεζαν.[37]

Or, for ἠιόνες βοόωσιν, ἠιόνες κράζουσιν.[38]

Again, Ariphrades ridiculed the tragedians for using phrases which no one would employ in ordinary speech: for example, δωμάτων ἄπο instead of ἀπὸ δωμάτων, σέθεν, ἐγὼ δέ νιν, Ἀχιλλέως, πέρι instead of περὶ Ἀχιλλέως, and the like.[39] It is precisely because such phrases are not part of the current idiom that they give distinction to the style. This, however, he failed to see.

It is a great matter to observe propriety in these several modes of expression, as also in compound words, strange (or rare) words, and so forth. But the greatest thing by far is to have a command of metaphor. This alone cannot be imparted by another; it is the mark of genius, for to make good metaphors implies an eye for resemblances.

Of the various kinds of words, the compound are best adapted to dithyrambs, rare words to heroic poetry, metaphors to iambic. In heroic poetry, indeed, all these varieties are serviceable. But in iambic verse, which reproduces, as far as may be, familiar speech, the most appropriate words are those which are found even in prose. These are,—the current or proper, the metaphorical, the ornamental.

Concerning Tragedy and imitation by means of action this may suffice.

As to that poetic imitation which is narrative in form and employs a single metre, the plot manifestly ought, as in a tragedy, to be constructed on dramatic principles. It should have for its subject a single action, whole and complete, with a beginning, a middle, and an end. It will thus resemble a living organism in all its unity, and produce the pleasure proper to it. It will differ in structure from historical compositions, which of necessity present not a single action, but a single period, and all that happened within that period to one person or to many, little connected together as the events may be. For as the sea-fight at Salamis and the battle with the Carthaginians in Sicily took place at the same time, but did not tend to any one result, so in the sequence of events, one thing sometimes follows another, and yet no single result is

[33] "This cancer is eating up my foot." This play and the next-mentioned, by Euripides, are lost.
[34] "And now, a man feeble, ungoodly, and ephemeral."
[35] "And now, a man small, weak, ugly."
[36] "He put at his disposal a chaise unseemly and a table scant."
[37] "He brought him a sorry stool and a small table."
[38] "The beach makes a noise" for "The sea resounds."
[39] The point of these examples is that the preposition is made to follow, rather than precede, the noun: "from the house away" and "Achilles about."

thereby produced. Such is the practice, we may say, of most poets. Here again, then, as has been already observed, the transcendent excellence of Homer is manifest. He never attempts to make the whole war of Troy the subject of his poem, though that war had a beginning and an end. It would have been too vast a theme, and not easily embraced in a single view. If, again, he had kept it within moderate limits, it must have been over-complicated by the variety of the incidents. As it is, he detaches a single portion, and admits as episodes many events from the general story of the war—such as the Catalogue of the ships and others—thus diversifying the poem. All other poets take a single hero, a single period, or an action single indeed, but with a multiplicity of parts. Thus did the author of the *Cypria* and of the *Little Iliad*.[40] For this reason the *Iliad* and the *Odyssey* each furnish the subject of one tragedy, or, at most, of two; while the *Cypria* supplies materials for many, and the *Little Iliad* for eight—the *Award of the Arms*, the *Philoctetes*, the *Neoptolemus*, the *Eurypylus*, the *Mendicant Odysseus*, the *Laconian Women*, the *Fall of Ilium*, the *Departure of the Fleet*.[41]

Again, Epic poetry must have as many kinds as Tragedy: it must be simple, or complex, or "ethical," or "pathetic." The parts also, with the exception of song and spectacle, are the same; for it requires Reversals of the Situation, Recognitions, and Scenes of Suffering. Moreover, the thoughts and the diction must be artistic. In all these respects Homer is our earliest and sufficient model. Indeed each of his poems has a twofold character. The *Iliad* is at once simple and "pathetic," and the *Odyssey* complex (for Recognition scenes run through it), and at the same time "ethical." Moreover, in diction and thought they are supreme.

Epic poetry differs from Tragedy in the scale on which it is constructed, and in its metre. As regards scale or length, we have already laid down an adequate limit:—the beginning and the end must be capable of being brought within a single view. This condition will be satisfied by poems on a smaller scale than the old epics, and answering in length to the group of tragedies presented at a single sitting.

Epic poetry has, however, a great—a special—capacity for enlarging its dimensions, and we can see the reason. In Tragedy we cannot imitate several lines of actions carried on at one and the same time; we must confine ourselves to the action on the stage and the part taken by the players. But in Epic poetry, owing to the narrative form, many events simultaneously transacted can be presented; and these, if relevant to the subject, add mass and dignity to the poem. The Epic has here an advantage, and one that conduces to grandeur of effect, to diverting the mind of the hearer, and relieving the story with varying episodes. For sameness of incident soon produces satiety, and makes tragedies fail on the stage.

As for the metre, the heroic measure has proved its fitness by the test of experience. If a narrative poem in any other metre or in many metres were now composed, it would be found incongruous. For of all measures the heroic is the stateliest and the most massive; and hence it most readily admits rare

[40] Non-Homeric early epics, of which only small fragments survive.
[41] Only the *Philoctetes* of Sophocles survives.

words and metaphors, which is another point in which the narrative form of imitation stands alone. On the other hand, the iambic and the trochaic tetrameter are stirring measures, the latter being akin to dancing, the former expressive of action. Still more absurd would it be to mix together different metres, as was done by Chaeremon. Hence no one has ever composed a poem on a great scale in any other than heroic verse. Nature herself, as we have said, teaches the choice of the proper measure.

Homer, admirable in all respects, has the special merit of being the only poet who rightly appreciates the part he should take himself. The poet should speak as little as possible in his own person, for it is not this that makes him an imitator. Other poets appear themselves upon the scene throughout, and imitate but little and rarely. Homer, after a few prefatory words, at once brings in a man, or woman, or other personage; none of them wanting in characteristic qualities, but each with a character of his own.

The element of the wonderful is required in Tragedy. The irrational, on which the wonderful depends for its chief effects, has wider scope in Epic poetry, because there the person acting is not seen. Thus, the pursuit of Hector would be ludicrous if placed upon the stage—the Greeks standing still and not joining in the pursuit, and Achilles waving them back. But in the Epic poem the absurdity passes unnoticed. Now the wonderful is pleasing: as may be inferred from the fact that every one tells a story with some addition of his own, knowing that his hearers like it. It is Homer who has chiefly taught other poets the art of telling lies skilfully. The secret of it lies in a fallacy. For, assuming that if one thing is or becomes, a second is or becomes, men imagine that, if the second is, the first likewise is or becomes. But this is a false inference. Hence, where the first thing is untrue, it is quite unnecessary, provided the second be true, to add that the first is or has become. For the mind, knowing the second to be true, falsely infers the truth of the first. There is an example of this in the Bath Scene of the *Odyssey*.[42]

Accordingly, the poet should prefer probable impossibilities to improbable possibilities. The tragic plot must not be composed of irrational parts. Everything irrational should, if possible, be excluded; or, at all events, it should lie outside the action of the play (as, in the *Oedipus*, the hero's ignorance as to the manner of Laius' death); not within the drama,—as in the *Electra* [by Sophocles], the messenger's account of the Pythian games; or, as in the *Mysians*,[43] the man who has come from Tegea to Mysia and is still speechless. The plea that otherwise the plot would have been ruined, is ridiculous; such a plot should not in the first instance be constructed. But once the irrational has been introduced and an air of likelihood imparted to it, we must accept it in spite of the absurdity. Take even the irrational incidents in the *Odyssey*, where Odysseus is left upon the shore of Ithaca.[44] How intolerable even these might have been would be apparent if an inferior poet were to treat the subject. As it is, the absurdity is veiled by the poetic charm with which the poet invests it.

[42] Odysseus, in disguise, tells Penelope a tale; he also accurately describes Odysseus' dress; she believes the antecedent falsehood because of the subsequent truth.
[43] Lost play by Aeschylus.
[44] Odysseus is brought home in a magical ship; further, he does not awake from sleep when this ship runs aground and he is carried ashore.

The diction should be elaborated in the pauses of the action, where there is no expression of character or thought. For, conversely, character and thought are merely obscured by a diction that is over brilliant.

With respect to critical difficulties and their solutions, the number and nature of the sources from which they may be drawn may be thus exhibited.

The poet being an imitator, like a painter or any other artist, must of necessity imitate one of three objects,—things as they were or are, things as they are said or thought to be, or things as they ought to be. The vehicle of expression is language,—either current terms or, it may be, rare words or metaphors. There are also many modifications of language, which we concede to the poets. Add to this, that the standard of correctness is not the same in poetry and politics, any more than in poetry and any other art. Within the art of poetry itself there are two kinds of faults,—those which touch its essence, and those which are accidental. If a poet has chosen to imitate something, but has imitated it incorrectly through want of capacity, the error is inherent in the poetry. But if the failure is due to a wrong choice—if he has represented a horse as throwing out both his off legs at once, or introduced technical inaccuracies in medicine, for example, or in any other art—the error is not essential to the poetry. These are the points of view from which we should consider and answer the objections raised by the critics.

First as to matters which concern the poet's own art. If he describes the impossible, he is guilty of an error; but the error may be justified, if the end of the art be thereby attained (the end being that already mentioned),—if, that is, the effect of this or any other part of the poem is thus rendered more striking. A case in point is the pursuit of Hector. If, however, the end might have been as well, or better, attained without violating the special rules of the poetic art, the error is not justified: for every kind of error should, if possible, be avoided.

Again, does the error touch the essentials of the poetic art, or some accident of it? For example,—not to know that a hind has no horns is a less serious matter than to paint it inartistically.

Further, if it be objected that the description is not true to fact, the poet may perhaps reply,—"But the objects are as they ought to be": just as Sophocles said that he drew men as they ought to be; Euripides, as they are. In this way the objection may be met. If, however, the representation be of neither kind, the poet may answer,—"This is how men say the thing is." This applies to tales about the gods. It may well be that these stories are not higher than fact nor yet true to fact: they are, very possibly, what Xenophanes says of them.[45] But anyhow, "this is what is said." Again, a description may be no better than the fact: "still, it was the fact"; as in the passage about the arms: "Upright upon their butt-ends stood the spears." This was the custom then, as it now is among the Illyrians.

Again, in examining whether what has been said or done by some one is poetically right or not, we must not look merely to the particular act or saying, and ask whether it is poetically good or bad. We must consider by whom it is

[45] Xenophanes of Colophon, poet-philosopher, said that Homer told wickedly untrue tales of the gods.

said or done, to whom, when, by what means, or for what end; whether, for instance, it be to secure a greater good, or avert a greater evil.

Other difficulties may be resolved by due regard to the usage of language. We may note a rare word, as in οὐρῆας μὲν πρῶτον,[46] where the poet perhaps employs οὐρῆας not in the sense of mules, but of sentinels. So, again, of Dolon: "ill-favoured indeed he was to look upon." It is not meant that his body was ill-shaped, but that his face was ugly; for the Cretans use the word εὐειδές, "well-favoured," to denote a fair face. Again, ζωρότερον δὲ κέραιε, "mix the drink livelier," does not mean "mix it stronger" as for hard drinkers, but "mix it quicker."

Sometimes an expression is metaphorical, as "Now all gods and men were sleeping through the night,"—while at the same time the poet says: "Often indeed as he turned his gaze to the Trojan plain, he marvelled at the sound of flutes and pipes." "All" is here used metaphorically for "many," all being a species of many. So in the verse,—"alone she hath no part . . ," οἴη, "alone," is metaphorical; for the best known may be called the only one.

Again, the solution may depend upon accent or breathing. Thus Hippias of Thasos solved the difficulties in the lines,—δίδομεν (δίδόμεν) δέ οἱ,[47] and τὸ μὲν οὗ (οὐ) καταπύθεται ὄμβρῳ.[48]

Or again, the question may be solved by punctuation, as in Empedocles,— "Of a sudden things became mortal that before had learnt to be immortal, and things unmixed before mixed."

Or again, by ambiguity of meaning,—as παρῴχηκεν δὲ πλέω νύξ,[49] where the word πλέω is ambiguous.

Or by the usage of language. Thus any mixed drink is called οἶνος, "wine." Hence Ganymede is said "to pour the wine to Zeus," though the gods do not drink wine. So too workers in iron are called χαλκέας, or workers in bronze. This, however, may also be taken as a metaphor.

Again, when a word seems to involve some inconsistency of meaning, we should consider how many senses it may bear in the particular passage. For example: "there was stayed the spear of bronze"—we should ask in how many ways we may take "being checked there."[50] The true mode of interpretation is the precise opposite of what Glaucon mentions. Critics, he says, jump at certain groundless conclusions; they pass adverse judgment and then proceed to reason on it; and, assuming that the poet has said whatever they happen to think, find fault if a thing is inconsistent with their own fancy. The question about Icarius has been treated in this fashion. The critics imagine he was a

---

[46] "Upon the mules," or, says Aristotle, "upon the sentinels."

[47] Hippias' emendation would transfer from Zeus to the Dream-God the onus of the responsibility of a deceiving dream sent to Agamemnon.

[48] Hippias emends "the wood of which [stump] is rotten with rain" to "the wood is not rotten."

[49] "The night has advanced more than two-thirds [but the third part is still to come]. This is illogical; Aristotle suggests that the word translated as "more than" be taken as meaning "fully."

[50] Achilles' shield is made up of layers of metal, with gold on the outside. Homer says the spear pierced two layers, but was stopped by the gold. Aristotle presumably means that the gold may have stopped the spear even if it did penetrate a layer or so further.

Lacedaemonian. They think it strange, therefore, that Telemachus should not have met him when he went to Lacedaemon. But the Cephallenian story may perhaps be the true one. They allege that Odysseus took a wife from among themselves, and that her father was Icadius not Icarius. It is merely a mistake, then, that gives plausibility to the objection.

In general, the impossible must be justified by reference to artistic requirements, or to the higher reality, or to received opinion. With respect to the requirements of art, a probable impossibility is to be preferred to a thing improbable and yet possible. Again, it may be impossible that there should be men such as Zeuxis painted. "Yes," we say, "but the impossible is the higher thing; for the ideal type must surpass the reality." To justify the irrational, we appeal to what is commonly said to be. In addition to which, we urge that the irrational sometimes does not violate reason; just as "it is probable that a thing may happen contrary to probability."

Things that sound contradictory should be examined by the same rules as in dialectical refutation—whether the same thing is meant, in the same relation, and in the same sense. We should therefore solve the question by reference to what the poet says himself, or to what is tacitly assumed by a person of intelligence.

The element of the irrational, and, similarly, depravity of character, are justly censured when there is no inner necessity for introducing them. Such is the irrational element in the introduction of Aegeus by Euripides and the badness of Menelaus in the *Orestes*.[51]

Thus, there are five sources from which critical objections are drawn. Things are censured either as impossible, or irrational, or morally hurtful, or contradictory, or contrary to artistic correctness. The answers should be sought under the twelve heads above mentioned.

The question may be raised whether the Epic or Tragic mode of imitation is the higher. If the more refined art is the higher, and the more refined in every case is that which appeals to the better sort of audience, the art which imitates anything and everything is manifestly most unrefined. The audience is supposed to be too dull to comprehend unless something of their own is thrown in by the performers, who therefore indulge in restless movements. Bad flute-players twist and twirl, if they have to represent "the quoit-throw," or hustle the coryphaeus[52] when they perform the *Scylla*. Tragedy, it is said, has this same defect. We may compare the opinion that the older actors entertained of their successors. Mynniscus used to call Callippides "ape" on account of the extravagance of his action, and the same view was held of Pindarus. Tragic art, then, as a whole, stands to Epic in the same relation as the younger to the elder actors. So we are told that Epic poetry is addressed to a cultivated audience, who do not need gesture; Tragedy, to an inferior public. Being then unrefined, it is evidently the lower of the two.

Now, in the first place, this censure attaches not to the poetic but to the histrionic art; for gesticulation may be equally overdone in epic recitation, as by Sosistratus, or in lyrical competition, as by Mnasitheus the Opuntian. Next,

---

[51] The appearance of Aegeus in the *Medea* is improbable and the wickedness of Menelaus is gratuitous.
[52] Chorus leader.

all action is not to be condemned—any more than all dancing—but only that of bad performers. Such was the fault found in Callippides, as also in others of our own day, who are censured for representing degraded women.[53] Again, Tragedy like Epic poetry produces its effect even without action; it reveals its power by mere reading. If, then, in all other respects it is superior, this fault, we say, is not inherent in it.

And superior it is, because it has all the epic elements—it may even use the epic metre—with the music and spectacular effects as important accessories; and these produce the most vivid of pleasures. Further, it has vividness of impression in reading as well as in representation. Moreover, the art attains its end within narrower limits; for the concentrated effect is more pleasurable than one which is spread over a long time and so diluted. What, for example, would be the effect of the *Oedipus* of Sophocles, if it were cast into a form as long as the *Iliad?* Once more, the Epic imitation has less unity; as is shown by this, that any Epic poem will furnish subjects for several tragedies. Thus if the story adopted by the poet has a strict unity, it must either be concisely told and appear truncated; or, if it conform to the Epic canon of length, it must seem weak and watery. Such length implies some loss of unity, if, I mean, the poem is constructed out of several actions, like the *Iliad* and the *Odyssey,* which have many such parts, each with a certain magnitude of its own. Yet these poems are as perfect as possible in structure; each is, in the highest degree attainable, an imitation of a single action.

If, then, Tragedy is superior to Epic poetry in all these respects, and, moreover, fulfills its specific function better as an art—for each art ought to produce, not any chance pleasure, but the pleasure proper to it, as already stated—it plainly follows that Tragedy is the higher art, as attaining its end more perfectly.

Thus much may suffice concerning Tragic and Epic poetry in general; their several kinds and parts, with the number of each and their differences; the causes that make a poem good or bad; the objections of the critics and the answers to these objections.

---

[53] Female roles were played by male actors.

Dante Alighieri

LETTER TO CAN GRANDE DELLA SCALA

Dante Alighieri (1265–1321) was born into a family of Florentine nobles with an illustrious past. By the time he was eighteen, he had associated with the most notable poets, painters, and musicians of his city, had become known as a lyric poet of distinction, and had fallen in love with Beatrice Portinari, whom he celebrated in verse and prose. After the death of Beatrice in 1290 and his marriage in 1295, he entered Florentine politics in what seems to have been a responsibly patriotic, rather than factional, spirit. But his attempts to take the larger view won him no gratitude from the opposed factions—Guelphs and Ghibellines, Pope's men and Emperor's men—contending for control of Florence: he was convicted on trumped-up charges in 1302, and thereafter roamed through Europe, under sentence of death. For a while he found refuge in Verona, which was under the rule of the della Scala family. At the head of this family was Can Grande, in gratitude to whom Dante in the letter printed below dedicates the third part of the *Divine Comedy*, the *Paradiso*.

The *Comedy* may not have been finished until the year of Dante's death. The letter to Can Grande seems to have been written in 1319.

To the magnificent and victorious lord, Lord Can Grande della Scala, vicar-general of the most sacred imperial princedom in the city of Verona and in the state of Vicenza, his most devoted servant Dante Alighieri, a Florentine by birth, not by character, wishes long protracted life and felicity, and the perpetual growth of the glory of his name.

The illustrious praise of your munificence, which wakeful fame scatters abroad as she flies, draws divers in such divers directions as to exalt these in the hope of prosperous success and hurl down those into terror of destruction. Now this report, exceeding all deeds of moderns, I was once wont to think extravagant, as stretching beyond the warrant of truth; but, lest continued doubt should keep me too much in suspense, even as the queen of the south sought Jerusalem or as Pallas sought Helicon,[1] so did I seek Verona, to scrutinise by the faithful

[1] Pallas visited Helicon in order to test the truth of stories about Hippocrene, the fountain which was said to inspire poets.

From *A Translation of the Latin Works of Dante Alighieri*, by Philip H. Wicksteed. London, J. M. Dent & Sons, Ltd., 1904 (A Temple Classic).

testimony of my own eyes the things which I had heard. And there I beheld your splendour, I beheld and at the same time handled your bounty; and even as I had formerly suspected excess on the side of the reports, so did I afterwards recognise that it was the facts themselves that exceeded. Wherefore it came to pass that whereas the mere report had already secured my good will, with a certain submission of mind, at the sight of the source and origin itself I became your most devoted servant and friend.

Nor do I think I am laying myself open to a charge of presumption (as some perhaps might urge) by arrogating to myself the name of friend, since unequals no less than equals are united in the sacrament of friendship. For should one care to examine those friendships from which delight and advantage have sprung, right often will he discover on inspection that such have united pre-eminent persons to their inferiors. And if attention be turned to the true friendship which exists for its own sake, will it not abundantly appear that the friends of illustrious and supreme princes have for the most part been men obscure in fortune but shining in integrity? Why not? Since even the friendship of God and man is in no sort hindered by disparity. But if any one thinks my assertions too bold, let him hearken to the Holy Spirit declaring that certain men share his own friendship, for in *Wisdom*[2] we read, concerning Wisdom, "For she is an infinite treasure to men, and they that use it are made partakers of the friendship of God." But the artlessness of the vulgar herd judges without discrimination, and even as it supposes the sun to be a foot across, so is it deceived by vain credulity as to chacacter. But it is not fitting for us, to whom it has been granted to know the best that is in us, to follow the footprints of the herd; nay, rather are we bounden to oppose its wanderings; for we who have vigour of intellect and reason, being endowed with a certain divine liberty, are held to no precedents. And no wonder, for such are not directed by the laws but rather the laws by them. It is clear, then, that what I said above, namely, that I am your most devoted servant and your friend, is in no sort presumptuous.

Cherishing your friendship, then, as my dearest treasure, I desire to preserve it with loving forethought and considered care; and therefore, since in the teaching of ethics we are instructed that friendship is equalised and preserved by what is proportionate, it is in my vows to keep the path of proportion in my return for bounty received. Wherefore I have often and eagerly scrutinised such small gifts as I have, and have set them side by side, and then conned them over again, considering which would be the more worthy and the more acceptable to you. And I have found nothing more suited to your pre-eminence than the sublime cantica of the *Comedy* which is adorned with the title of *Paradise;* which cantica, under cover of the present epistle, as though dedicated under its own special heading, I inscribe, I offer, and conclusively commend to you.

Neither will my glowing affection permit me to pass over in absolute silence the thought that in this dedication there may seem to be greater measure of honour and fame conferred on the patron than on the gift. And what wonder? since in its very inscription I appeared to those who looked closely, to have already uttered a presage of the destined increase of the glory to your name, and

---

[2] That is, the apocryphal book of the Bible, *The Wisdom of Solomon.*

this of set purpose. But now, zeal for your glory, for which I thirst, making little of my own, urges me forward to the goal set before me from the beginning.

And so, having brought to a close what I have written in the shape of a letter, I will at once assume the office of lecturer, and sketch in outline something by way of introduction to the work I offer you.

As the Philosopher[3] said in the second book of the *Metaphysics,* "as a thing is related to existence, so is it related to truth," the reason of which is that the truth about a thing (which is established in the truth as in its subject) is a perfect likeness of the thing as it is. Now of things which exist some so exist as to have absolute being in themselves; others so exist as to have a being dependent on something else, by some kind of relation, for example "being at the same time" or "being related to something else," like the correlatives "father and son," "master and servant," "double and half," "whole and part," and the like, as such; and because the being of such depends on something else, it follows that the truth of them also depends on something else; for if we have no knowledge of half we can never understand double, and so of the rest.

Therefore if we desire to furnish some introduction to a part of any work, it behoves us to furnish some knowledge of the whole of which it is a part. Wherefore I too, desiring to furnish something by way of introduction to the above-named portion of the *Comedy,* have thought that something concerning the whole work should be premised, that the approach to the part should be the easier and more complete. There are six things then which must be inquired into at the beginning of any work of instruction; to wit, the *subject, agent, form,* and *end,* the *title of the work,* and the *branch of philosophy* it concerns. And there are three of these wherein this part which I purposed to design for you differs from the whole; to wit, *subject, form,* and *title;* whereas in the others it differs not, as is plain on inspection. And so, an inquiry concerning these three must be instituted specially with reference to the work as a whole; and when this has been done the way will be sufficiently clear to the introduction of the part. After that we shall examine the other three, not only with reference to the whole but also with reference to that special part which I am offering to you.

To elucidate, then, what we have to say, be it known that the sense of this work is not simple, but on the contrary it may be called polysemous, that is to say, "of more senses than one"; for it is one sense which we get through the letter, and another which we get through the thing the letter signifies; and the first is called literal, but the second allegorical or mystic. And this mode of treatment, for its better manifestation, may be considered in this verse: "When Israel came out of Egypt, and the house of Jacob from a people of strange speech, Judæa became his sanctification, Israel his power." For if we inspect the letter alone the departure of the children of Israel from Egypt in the time of Moses is presented to us; if the allegory, our redemption wrought by Christ; if the moral sense, the conversion of the soul from the grief and misery of sin to the state of grace is presented to us; if the anagogical, the departure of the holy soul from the slavery of this corruption to the liberty of eternal glory is presented to us. And although these mystic senses have each their special denominations, they may all in general be called allegorical, since they differ

[3] Aristotle.

from the literal and historical; for *allegory* is derived from *alleon,* in Greek, which means the same as the Latin *alienum* or *diversum.*[4]

When we understand this we see clearly that the *subject* round which the alternative senses play must be twofold. And we must therefore consider the subject of this work as literally understood, and then its subject as allegorically intended. The subject of the whole work, then, taken in the literal sense only, is "the state of souls after death" without qualification, for the whole progress of the work hinges on it and about it. Whereas if the work be taken allegorically the subject is "man, as by good or ill deserts, in the exercise of the freedom of his choice, he becomes liable to rewarding or punishing justice."

Now the *form* is twofold, the form of the treatise and the form of the treatment. The form of the treatise is threefold, according to its threefold division.[5] The first division is that by which the whole work is divided into three *cantiche;* the second that whereby each *cantica* is divided into cantos; the third, that whereby each canto is divided into lines. The form or method of treatment is poetic, fictive, descriptive, digressive, transumptive;[6] and likewise proceeding by definition, division, proof, refutation, and setting forth of examples.

The *title of the work* is, "Here beginneth the *Comedy* of Dante Alighieri, a Florentine by birth, not by character." To understand which, be it known that *comedy* is derived from *comus,* "a village," and *oda,* which is, "song"; whence comedy is, as it were, "rustic song." So comedy is a certain kind of poetic narration differing from all others. It differs, then, from tragedy in its content, in that tragedy begins admirably and tranquilly, whereas its end or exit is foul and terrible; and it derives its name from *tragus* which is a "goat" and *oda,* as though to say "goat-song," that is fetid like a goat, as appears from Seneca in his tragedies; whereas comedy introduces some harsh complication, but brings its matter to a prosperous end, as appears from Terence, in his comedies. And hence certain writers, on introducing themselves, have made it their practice to give the salutation: "I wish you a tragic beginning and a comic end." They likewise differ in their mode of speech, tragedy being exalted and sublime, comedy lax and humble, as Horace has it in his *Poetica,* where he gives comedians leave sometimes to speak like tragedians and conversely:—

> *Interdum tamen et vocem comædia tollit,*
> *Iratusque Chremes tumido delitigat ore;*
> *Et tragicus plerumque dolet sermone pedestri.*[7]

And hence it is evident that the title of the present work is *"the Comedy."* For if we have respect to its content, at the beginning it is horrible and fetid, for it is hell; and in the end it is prosperous, desirable, and gracious, for it is *Paradise.* If we have respect to the method of speech the method is lax and

[4] *Allegory* is now said to be derived from the Greek *Allegoria,* from *allegorein,* "to speak figuratively," from *alla* (neuter plural of *allos,* "other") + *agorein,* "to speak publicly."

[5] The *Inferno,* the *Purgatorio,* the *Paradiso.* Each of these is a *cantica,* the plural of which word is *cantiche.*

[6] The word means "figurative" or "metaphorical."

[7] "Sometimes Comedy herself raises her voice, and wrathful Chremes denounces with tempestuous lips. And the tragedian often lowers his wail to pedestrian tone." "Chremes" is a type-name for an old man.

humble, for it is the vernacular speech in which very women communicate. There are also other kinds of poetic narration, as the bucolic song, elegy, satire, and the utterance of prayer, as may also be seen from Horace in his *Poetica*. But concerning them nought need at present be said.

There can be no difficulty in assigning the *subject* of the part I am offering you; for if the subject of the whole, taken literally, is "the state of souls after death," not limited but taken without qualification, it is clear that in this part that same state is the subject, but with a limitation, to wit, "the state of blessed souls after death"; and if the subject of the whole work taken allegorically is "man as by good or ill deserts, in the exercise of the freedom of his choice, he becomes liable to rewarding or punishing justice," it is manifest that the subject in this part is contracted to "man as by good deserts, he becomes liable to rewarding justice."

And in like manner the *form* of the part is clear from the form assigned to the whole; for if the form of the treatise as a whole is threefold, in this part it is twofold only, namely, division of the cantiche and of the cantos. The first division cannot be a part of its special form, since it is itself a part under that first division.

The *title of the work* is also clear, for if the title of the whole work is "Here beginneth the Comedy," and so forth as set out above, the title of this part will be "Here beginneth the third cantica of Dante's Comedy, which is entitled Paradise."

Having investigated the three things in which the part differs from the whole, we must examine the other three, in which there is no variation from the whole. The *agent,* then, of the whole and of the part is the man already named,[8] who is seen throughout to be such.

The *end* of the whole and of the part may be manifold, to wit, the proximate and the ultimate, but dropping all subtle investigation, we may say briefly that the end of the whole and of the part is to remove those living in this life from the state of misery and lead them to the state of felicity.

But the *branch of philosophy* which regulates the work in its whole and in its parts, is morals or ethics, because the whole was undertaken not for speculation but for practical results. For albeit in some parts or passages it is handled in the way of speculation, this is not for the sake of speculation, but for the sake of practical results; because, as the Philosopher says in the second book of the *Metaphysics,* "practical men sometimes speculate on things in their relative and temporal bearings."

These, then, premised, we must approach the exposition of the letter, after the fashion of a kind of prelibation; but we must announce in advance that the exposition of the letter is nought else than the development of the form of the work. This part, then, namely the third cantica, which is called *Paradise,* falls by its main division into two parts, to wit, the *prologue* and the *executive portion.* The second begins here, "riseth unto mortals through divers straits."

Concerning the first part you are to know that although it might, in the common way, be called an *exordium,* yet in strict propriety it should have no

---

[8] Dante himself, who is not only the author of the *Comedy,* but its principal character.

other name than *prologue,* which is what the Philosopher seems to be at in the third book of the *Rhetoric,* where he says that "the proem is the beginning of a rhetorical discourse, as a prologue is of a poetic one, and a prelude in flute-playing." It is further to be noted that the prefatory enunciation, commonly called an exordium, is differently conducted by poets and by orators; for orators are wont to make a prelibation of what they are about to utter, calculated to prepare the mind of the hearer; whereas poets not only do this, but also utter some certain invocation after this. And this is to their purpose, for they have need of ample invocation, since they have to implore something above the common scope of man from the higher beings, as in some sort a divine gift. Therefore the present prologue is divided into two parts; in the first of which is premised what is to be said; in the second Apollo is invoked. And the second part begins here, "O, good Apollo, for the crowning task," and the rest.

With reference to the first part be it noted, that for a good exordium three things are needed, as saith Tully in the *Nova Rhetorica,* to wit, that one should render his hearer benevolent and attentive and tractable;[9] and this, especially in a marvellous kind of matter, as Tully himself says. And since the matter with which the present treatise is concerned is marvellous, the intention is, at the beginning of the exordium or prologue, to excite those said dispositions, in connection with the marvellous. For he says that he will tell such part as he could retain of what he saw in the first heaven; in which utterance all those three things are comprehended. For the profit of the things to be said secures benevolence, their wondrous nature attention, their being possible docility. He gives their profitableness to be understood, when he declares that he is going to relate those things which chiefly attract the longing of mankind, to wit, the joys of Paradise; he touches on their wondrous nature when he promises to tell of such lofty and sublime things, to wit, the conditions of the celestial kingdom; he shows that they are possible when he says that he will tell those things which he had power to retain in his mind; and if he had such power, then shall others have it too. All these things are indicated in those words, wherein he says that he was in the first heaven, and that he is purposed to tell concerning the celestial kingdom whatsoever he had power to retain in his mind, as a treasure. Having therefore taken note of the excellence and perfection of the first part of the prologue, let us proceed to the letter.

He says, then, that the "glory of the first mover," who is God, "reglows in all parts of the universe," yet so as to be in "some part more" and in "another less." Now that it reglows everywhere reason and authority declare. Reason thus: Everything that is has its being either from itself or from another. But it is obvious that to have being from itself is competent only to one, to wit the first or initial being, which is God. And since to have being does not imply self-necessity of being, and self-necessity of being is competent to one only, to wit the first or initial Being, which is the Cause of all; therefore all things that are, save that one itself, have their being from another. If, then, we take any one of the individual phenomena of the universe it must evidently have its existence from something; and that from which it has it has [its existence]

---

[9] The passage occurs in a work called the *Rhetorica ad Herennium,* in Dante's time known as the *Nova Rhetorica* and incorrectly attributed to Cicero ("Tully").

either from itself or from something else; if from itself then it is the prime existence; if from something else, then that again must have its existence from itself or from something else. And so we should go on to infinity along a line of effective causes, as is proved in the second book of the *Metaphysics,* and since this is impossible we must at last come to the prime existence, which is God, and thus mediately or immediately everything which is has its being from him; for it is by what the second cause received from the first cause that it has influence upon that which it causes, after the fashion of a body that receives and reflects a ray. Wherefore the first cause is cause in a higher degree; and this is what the book *De Causis*[10] says, to wit, that "every primary cause is more influential on that which it causes, than a universal secondary cause." So much as to being.

But as to essence I prove it thus: Every essence, except the primary, is caused; otherwise there would be more than one existence of self-necessity, which is impossible. What is caused is either of nature or of intelligence; and what is of nature is consequentially caused by intellect, since nature is the work of intelligence. Everything, therefore, which is caused, is caused by some intellect, mediately or immediately. Since, then, virtue follows the essence whose virtue it is, if the essence be intellectual the whole virtue is of one [intelligence] which causes it; and thus, like as before we had to come to a first cause of being itself, so now of essence and of virtue. Wherefore it is clear that every essence and virtue proceeds from the primal one, and the lower intelligences receive it as from a radiating source, and throw the rays of their superior upon their inferior, after the fashion of mirrors. Which Dionysius, speaking of the celestial hierarchy,[11] seems to handle clearly enough, and therefore it is said in the book *De Causis,* that "every intelligence is full of forms." It is clear, then, how reason declares the divine light, that is, the divine excellence, wisdom, and virtue, to reglow everywhere.

And authority does the same as science; for the Holy Spirit says by Jeremiah, "Do I not fill heaven and earth?" and in the psalm, "Whither shall I go from thy spirit, and whither shall I flee from thy presence? If I ascend into heaven thou art there; if I descend into hell thou art present. If I take my wings," and the rest. And *Wisdom* says that "the spirit of the Lord filled the whole world," and *Ecclesiasticus,*[12] in the forty-second, "His work is full of the glory of the Lord." Whereto the scripture of the pagans bears co-witness, for Lucan in the ninth [book of the *Pharsalia*]:

Juppiter est quodcumque vides quocumque moveris.[13]

It is therefore well said when it says that the divine ray, or divine glory *pierces and reglows* through the universe. It pierces as to essence; it reglows as to being. And what he adds as to *more and less* is manifest truth; since we see that one thing has its being in a more exalted grade, and another in a lower,

---

[10] The *Liber De Causis,* although attributed to Aristotle in Dante's time, was an adaptation of a work by Proclus, a fifth-century neo-Platonic philosopher.
[11] The actual author of the *Celestial Hierarchy* is unknown and is usually referred to as the Pseudo-Dionysius.
[12] An apocryphal book of proverbs.
[13] "Whatsoever thou seest, wheresoever thou goest, is Jupiter."

as is evident with respect to the heaven and the elements, whereof that is incorruptible and these corruptible.

And having premised this truth, he goes on from it with a circumlocution for Paradise, and says that he "was in that heaven which receives most abundantly of the glory or the light of God"; wherefore you are to know that that heaven is the supreme heaven, containing all the bodies of the universe and contained by love, within which all bodies move (itself abiding in eternal rest), receiving its virtue from no corporeal substance. And it is called the *Empyrean,* which is the same as the heaven flaming with fire or heat, not because there is any material fire or heat in it, but spiritual, to wit holy love or charity.

Now that it receives more of the divine light can be proved by two things. First, by its containing all things and being contained by none; secondly, by its eternal rest or peace. As to the first the proof is this: That which contains is related by natural position to that which is contained, as the formative to the formable, as is stated in the fourth book of the *Physics* [of Aristotle]. But in the natural position of the whole universe the first heaven contains all things; therefore it is related to all things as the formative to the formable, which is the same as being related by way of cause. And since every causative power is a certain ray emanating from the first cause, which is God, it is manifest that that heaven which is most of the nature of cause receives most of the divine light.

As to the second point it is proved thus: Everything that moves, moves for the sake of something which it has not, and which is the goal of its motion; as the heaven of the moon moves because of some part of itself which has not the position towards which it is moving; and inasmuch as every part of it, not having attained every position (which is impossible), moves to some other, it follows that it always moves and never rests, in accordance with its appetite. And what I say of the heaven of the moon must be understood of all the rest except the first. Everything that moves, then, has some defect, and does not grasp its whole being at once. That heaven, therefore, which is not moved by anything has in itself and in its every part, in perfect fashion, everything which it is capable of having; so that it needs no motion for its perfecting. And since all perfection is a ray of the primal perfection, which realises the highest degree of perfection, it is manifest that the first heaven receives most of the light of the primal being, which is God. It is true that this argument appears to proceed from the negation of the antecedent, which is not in itself conclusive, as a form of argument; but, if we consider its content, it is conclusive, because it refers to an eternal being, the defect in which would be susceptible of being eternalised. Wherefore if God gave it no movement it is clear that he did not give it material that was defective in anything; and on this supposition the argument holds, by reason of its content. It is the same way of arguing as if I were to say: "If he is a man he is able to laugh"; for in all convertibles the like reasoning holds, in virtue of the content. So it is evident that when he says, "in that heaven which receives most of the light of God," he means to describe Paradise, or the empyrean heaven, by circumlocution.

And concordantly with all this the Philosopher declares in the first book of *On the Heavens* that heaven has matter more honourable than the things below it in proportion as it is more remote from the things here; and we might further adduce what the apostle [St. Paul] says in *Ephesians* concerning Christ, "who ascended above all the heavens, that he might fill all things." This is that heaven of the "delights of the Lord," concerning which delights it is said against Lucifer through Ezekiel, "Thou, the seal of similitude, full of wisdom and perfect in beauty, wast in the delights of the Paradise of God."

And when he[14] has said that he was in that place of Paradise, described by circumlocution, he goes on to say "that he saw certain things which he who thence descends cannot relate"; and he tells the reason, saying that "the intellect is so engulfed" in the very thing for which it longs, which is God, "that memory cannot follow." To understand which things be it known that the human intellect, when it is exalted in this life, because of its being co-natural and having affinity with a sejunct intellectual substance, it is so far exalted that after its return memory fails it, because it has transcended the measure of humanity. And this we are given to understand by the apostle, speaking to the Corinthians, where he says, "I know such a man (whether in the body or out of the body I know not, God knoweth), who was rapt into Paradise and heard hidden words, which it is not lawful for a man to utter." Behold, when the intellect had transcended human measure in its ascent, it remembered not the things that took place beyond its own range. And this we are also given to understand in Matthew, where the three disciples fell upon their faces, and record nothing thereafter, as though they had forgotten. And in Ezekiel it is written, "I saw and fell upon my face." And if all this suffices not the carpers, let them read Richard of St. Victor[15] in his book *De Contemplatione*, let them read Bernard's[16] *De Consideratione*, let them read Augustine's[17] *De Quantitate Animae*, and they will cease to carp. But if they yelp against the assignment of so great exaltation, because of the sin of the speaker, let them read Daniel, where they will find that Nabuchodonosor, too, was divinely enabled to see certain things against sinners, and then dropped them into oblivion; for he "who makes his sun to rise upon the good and the evil, and sends his rain upon the just and the unjust," sometimes in compassion, for their conversion, sometimes in wrath, for their punishment, reveals his glory, in greater or less measure, as he wills, to those who live never so evilly.

He saw, then, as he says, certain things "which he who returns has not knowledge, nor power to relate"; and it must be noted carefully that he says, has "not knowledge, nor power." He has not knowledge, because he has forgotten; and he has not power, because if he remembered and retained the matter, nevertheless language fails: for we see many things by the intellect for which there are no vocal signs, of which Plato gives sufficient hint in his books by having recourse to metaphors; for he saw many things by intellectual light which he could not express in direct speech.

Then he says that "he will tell those things which he was able to retain

---

[14] "He," that is, Dante as a character in the *Divine Comedy*.

[15] Scottish monk and mystic who died in 1173.

[16] St. Bernard of Clairvaux (c. 1090–1153), mystic, churchman, one of the most influential men in the Western Europe of his time.

[17] St. Augustine (354–430), Doctor of the Church, one of the four Latin fathers, bishop of Hippo, the greatest Christian theologian before St. Thomas Aquinas. Dante cites Victor, St. Bernard, and St. Augustine as men who have had mystical experiences of the sort he claims for himself in the earlier part of this paragraph.

concerning the celestial kingdom"; and this, he says, is "the matter of his work"; and of what nature and extent these things are will be revealed in the executive part.

Then when he says, "O good Apollo," and the rest, he makes his invocation. And that part is divided into two parts: in the first he makes petition in his invocation; in the second he suasively urges upon Apollo the petition he has made, announcing a kind of remuneration. And the second part begins here, "O divine power." The first part is divided into two parts, in the first of which he seeks the divine aid, and in the second touches upon the necessity of his petition, which is its justification. And it begins here: "up to this point one peak of Parnassus," and the rest.

This is the general purport of the second part of the Prologue; but I will not at present expound it in detail, for I am pressed by my narrow domestic circumstances, so that I must needs relinquish this and other matters profitable to the common good. But I hope from your munificence that I may have opportunity, at some other time, to proceed to a profitable exposition.

Now concerning the executive part, which was co-ordinate in the division of the whole with the Prologue, nought shall be said at present either concerning its divisions or its purport, save this, that there will be a process of ascending from heaven to heaven; and the narrative will tell of blessed souls discovered in each orb, and how true blessedness consists in the sense of the prime source of truth, as is evident by John[18] in the passage: "This is true blessedness, to know thee, the true God," and the rest; and by Boethius in the third book of *De Consolatione,* in the passage: "To behold thee is the end." Whence it comes about that to make manifest the glory of blessedness in those souls, many things will be asked of them (as of those who look upon all truth) which have much profit and delight. And inasmuch as, when the source or origin has been found, to wit, God, there is nought to seek beyond, since he is A and O,[19] that is, the beginning and the end, as the vision of John calls him, the treatise ends in God himself, who is blessed in *sæcula sæculorum.*[20]

---

[18] St. John, the disciple of Christ, supposed author of the Gospel of John and the three epistles of the New Testament bearing his name.
[19] Alpha and Omega, the first and last letters of the Greek alphabet.
[20] For ages of ages.

John Dryden

PREFACE TO
TROILUS AND CRESSIDA:
THE GROUNDS OF
CRITICISM IN
TRAGEDY

John Dryden (1631–1700) was born in Northamptonshire and reared there in a Puritan family environment. He was educated at Westminster School and Trinity College, Cambridge, from which he graduated B.A. in 1654. After settling in London and marrying, he turned playwright in order to support himself. His first play was produced in 1663; from then until 1678 he wrote on the average one play a year. He achieved great fame, considerable wealth, and a number of official recognitions, including, in 1670, the Poet Laureateship. In 1687, after the accession of the Catholic James II, he converted to Catholicism, but lost the patronage and favor of the court, along with his laureateship, on the accession of the Protestant William III in 1689. He lived out his life in industrious retirement, making numerous translations of Greek and Latin works.

Dryden's *Troilus and Cressida,* an adaptation of Shakespeare's play of the same name, was first acted in 1679. When it was published later in the same year, a short preface introduced not only the play, but a separate critical essay, "The Grounds of Criticism in Tragedy."

The poet Aeschylus was held in the same veneration by the Athenians of after ages as Shakespeare is by us; and Longinus has judged, in favour of him, that he had a noble boldness of expression, and that his imaginations were lofty and heroic; but, on the other side, Quintilian[1] affirms that he was daring to extravagance. 'Tis certain that he affected pompous words, and that his sense too often was obscured by figures; notwithstanding these imperfections, the value of his writings after his decease was such that his countrymen ordained an equal reward to those poets who could alter his plays to be acted on the

[1] Dryden refers to a passage in Quintilian's *Institutio oratoria,* a survey of rhetoric. From the book *Of Dramatic Poesy and Other Critical Essays,* by John Dryden. London: J. M. Dent & Sons, Ltd.; New York: E. P. Dutton & Co., Inc. Everyman's Library Edition. Used by permission of J. M. Dent & Sons, Ltd., and E. P. Dutton & Co., Inc.

theatre, with those whose productions were wholly new, and of their own. The case is not the same in England; though the difficulties of altering are greater, and our reverence for Shakespeare much more just than that of the Grecians for Aeschylus. In the age of that poet, the Greek tongue was arrived to its full perfection; they had then amongst them an exact standard of writing and of speaking. The English language is not capable of such a certainty; and we are at present so far from it that we are wanting in the very foundation of it, a perfect grammar. Yet it must be allowed to the present age that the tongue in general is so much refined since Shakespeare's time that many of his words, and more of his phrases, are scarce intelligible. And of those which we understand, some are ungrammatical, others coarse; and his whole style is so pestered with figurative expressions, that it is as affected as it is obscure. 'Tis true, that in his later plays he had worn off somewhat of the rest; but the tragedy which I have undertaken to correct was, in all probability, one of his first endeavours on the stage.[2]

The original story was written by one Lollius,[3] a Lombard, in Latin verse and translated by Chaucer into English; intended, I suppose, a satire on the inconstancy of women: I find nothing of it among the Ancients; not so much as the name Cressida once mentioned.[4] Shakespeare (as I hinted), in the apprenticeship of his writing, modelled it into that play which is now called by the name of *Troilus and Cressida*; but so lamely is it left to us, that it is not divided into acts; which fault I ascribe to the actors who printed it after Shakespeare's death; and that too so carelessly, that a more uncorrect copy I never saw.[5] For the play itself, the author seems to have begun it with some fire; the characters of Pandarus and Thersites are promising enough; but as if he grew weary of his task, after an entrance or two, he lets 'em fall: and the later part of the tragedy is nothing but a confusion of drums and trumpets, excursions and alarms. The chief persons, who give name to the tragedy, are left alive; Cressida is false, and is not punished. Yet, after all, because the play was Shakespeare's, and that there appeared in some places of it the admirable genius of the author, I undertook to remove that heap of rubbish under which many excellent thoughts lay wholly buried. Accordingly, I new modelled the plot; threw out many unnecessary persons, improved those characters which were begun and left unfinished, as Hector, Troilus, Pandarus, and Thersites; and added that of Andromache. After this I made, with no small trouble, an order and connection of all the scenes; removing them from the places where they were inartificially set; and though it was impossible to keep 'em all unbroken, because the scene must be sometimes in the city and sometimes in the camp, yet I have so ordered them that there is a coherence of 'em with one

[2] Dryden's *Troilus and Cressida* was "undertaken to correct" Shakespeare's *Troilus and Cressida,* a play that Shakespeare probably wrote in mid-career, around 1602.
[3] Chaucer claims that he received much of his material from "myn autour called Lollius," about whom nothing other than what Chaucer tells us is known. Lollius is probably a hoax. Boccaccio's *Filostrato* is the main source for Chaucer's poem.
[4] Cressida's story is post-classical. But her name derives from the accusative of "Chryseis," the name of a character in the *Iliad.*
[5] Many of the plays in the First Folio (1623) of Shakespeare's plays lack complete scene-divisions. John Heminge and Henry Condell, former colleagues of Shakespeare's, edited the First Folio.

another, and a dependence on the main design: no leaping from Troy to the
Grecian tents, and thence back again in the same act; but a due proportion of
time allowed for every motion. I need not say that I have refined his language,
which before was obsolete; but I am willing to acknowledge that as I have often
drawn his English nearer to our times, so I have sometimes conformed my own
to his; and consequently, the language is not altogether so pure as it is significant. The scenes of Pandarus and Cressida, of Troilus and Pandarus, of Andromache with Hector and the Trojans, in the second act, are wholly new; together
with that of Nestor and Ulysses with Thersites, and that of Thersites with Ajax
and Achilles. I will not weary my reader with the scenes which are added of
Pandarus and the lovers, in the third; and those of Thersites, which are wholly
altered; but I cannot omit the last scene in it, which is almost half the act,
betwixt Troilus and Hector. The occasion of raising it was hinted to me by
Mr Betterton:[6] the contrivance and working of it was my own. They who
think to do me an injury by saying that it is an imitation of the scene betwixt
Brutus and Cassius,[7] do me an honour by supposing I could imitate the incomparable Shakespeare; but let me add that if Shakespeare's scene, or the
faulty copy of it in *Amintor and Melantius*,[8] had never been, yet Euripides had
furnished me with an excellent example in his *Iphigenia* [*in Aulis*], between
Agamemnon and Menelaus; and from thence, indeed, the last turn of it is
borrowed. The occasion which Shakespeare, Euripides, and Fletcher have all
taken is the same; grounded upon friendship: and the quarrel of two virtuous
men, raised by natural degrees to the extremity of passion, is conducted in all
three to the declination of the same passion, and concludes with a warm re-
newing of their friendship. But the particular groundwork which Shakespeare
has taken is incomparably the best; because he has not only chosen two of
the greatest heroes of their age, but has likewise interested the liberty of Rome,
and their own honours who were the redeemers of it, in this debate. And if he
has made Brutus, who was naturally a patient man, to fly into excess at first,
let it be remembered in his defence that, just before, he has received the news
of Portia's death; whom the poet, on purpose neglecting a little chronology,
supposes to have died before Brutus, only to give him an occasion of being
more easily exasperated. Add to this that the injury he had received from
Cassius had long been brooding in his mind; and that a melancholy man, upon
consideration of an affront, especially from a friend, would be more eager in
his passion than he who had given it, though naturally more choleric.

Euripides, whom I have followed, has raised the quarrel betwixt two
brothers who were friends. The foundation of the scene was this: the Grecians
were windbound at the port of Aulis, and the oracle had said that they could
not sail, unless Agamemnon delivered up his daughter to be sacrificed: he
refuses; his brother Menelaus urges the public safety; the father defends himself by arguments of natural affection, and hereupon they quarrel. Agamemnon
is at last convinced, and promises to deliver up Iphigenia, but so passionately
laments his loss that Menelaus is grieved to have been the occasion of it and,

---

[6] Thomas Betterton (1635?–1710), perhaps the greatest actor of his time.
[7] In *Julius Caesar* (1599).
[8] In *The Maid's Tragedy* (1619) by Francis Beaumont (c. 1584–1616) and John
Fletcher (1584–1625) there is a quarrel between the friends Amintor and Melantius.

by a return of kindness, offers to intercede for him with the Grecians, that his daughter might not be sacrificed. But my friend Mr. Rymer[9] has so largely, and with so much judgment, described this scene, in comparing it with that of Melantius and Amintor, that it is superfluous to say more of it; I only named the heads of it, that any reasonable man might judge it was from thence I modelled my scene betwixt Troilus and Hector. I will conclude my reflexions on it with a passage of Longinus, concerning Plato's imitation of Homer: "We ought not to regard a good imitation as a theft, but as a beautiful idea of him who undertakes to imitate, by forming himself on the invention and the work of another man; for he enters into the lists like a new wrestler, to dispute the prize with the former champion. This sort of emulation, says Hesiod, is honourable, ἀγαθὴ δ' ἔρις ἐστὶ βροτοῖσιν,[10] when we combat for victory with a hero, and are not without glory even in our overthrow. Those great men whom we propose to ourselves as patterns of our imitation serve us as a torch, which is lifted up before us to enlighten our passage; and often elevate our thoughts as high as the conception we have of our author's genius."

I have been so tedious in three acts that I shall contract myself in the two last. The beginning scenes of the fourth act are either added or changed wholly by me; the middle of it is Shakespeare altered, and mingled with my own; three or four of the last scenes are altogether new. And the whole fifth act, both the plot and the writing, are my own additions.

But having written so much for imitation of what is excellent, in that part of the preface which related only to myself, methinks it would neither be unprofitable nor unpleasant to inquire how far we ought to imitate our own poets, Shakespeare and Fletcher, in their tragedies: and this will occasion another inquiry how those two writers differ between themselves. But since neither of these questions can be solved unless some measures be first taken by which we may be enabled to judge truly of their writings, I shall endeavour, as briefly as I can, to discover the grounds and reason of all criticism, applying them in this place only to tragedy. Aristotle with his interpreters, and Horace, and Longinus, are the authors to whom I owe my lights; and what part soever of my own plays, or of this, which no mending could make regular, shall fall under the condemnation of such judges, it would be impudence in me to defend. I think it no shame to retract my errors, and am well pleased to suffer in the cause, if the art may be improved at my expense: I therefore proceed to

THE GROUNDS OF CRITICISM IN TRAGEDY

Tragedy is thus defined by Aristotle (omitting what I thought unnecessary in his definition). 'Tis an imitation of one entire, great, and probable action; not told, but represented; which, by moving in us fear and pity; is conducive to the purging of those two passions in our minds. More largely thus, tragedy describes or paints an action, which action must have all the properties above

---

[9] Thomas Rymer (1643?–1713), was a critic and historiographer, who in 1678, the year before Dryden wrote this preface, had rather savagely attacked the contemporary and preceding English dramatists in his *The Tragedies of the Last Age*.
[10] "This strife is wholesome to men"; from the *Works and Days* of Hesiod.

named. First, it must be one or single, that is, it must not be a history of one man's life; suppose of Alexander the Great, or Julius Caesar, but one single action of theirs. This condemns all Shakespeare's historical plays, which are rather chronicles represented than tragedies, and all double action of plays. As to avoid a satire upon others, I will make bold with my own *Marriage a-la-Mode* [1671], where there are manifestly two actions, not depending on one another: but in *Oedipus* [1679] there cannot properly be said to be two actions, because the love of Adrastus and Eurydice has a necessary dependence on the principal design, into which it is woven. The natural reason of this rule is plain; for two different independent actions distract the attention and concernment of the audience, and consequently destroy the intention of the poet: if his business be to move terror and pity, and one of his actions be comical, the other tragical, the former will divert the people, and utterly make void his greater purpose. Therefore, as in perspective, so in tragedy, there must be a point of sight in which all the lines terminate; otherwise the eye wanders, and the work is false. This was the practice of the Grecian stage. But Terence made an innovation in the Roman: all his plays have double actions; for it was his custom to translate two Greek comedies, and to weave them into one of his, yet so that both the actions were comical, and one was principal, the other but secondary or subservient. And this has obtained on the English stage, to give us the pleasure of variety.

As the action ought to be one, it ought, as such, to have order in it, that is, to have a natural beginning, a middle, and an end. A natural beginning, says Aristotle, is that which could not necessarily have been placed after another thing, and so of the rest. This consideration will arraign all plays after the new model of Spanish plots,[11] where accident is heaped upon accident, and that which is first might as reasonably be last: an inconvenience not to be remedied but by making one accident naturally produce another, otherwise 'tis a farce and not a play. Of this nature is the *Slighted Maid*,[12] where there is no scene in the first act which might not by as good reason be in the fifth. And if the action to be one, the tragedy ought likewise to conclude with the action of it. Thus in *Mustapha*,[13] the play should naturally have ended with the death of Zanger, and not have given us the grace cup after dinner of Solyman's divorce from Roxolana.

The following properties of the action are so easy that they need not my explaining. It ought to be great, and to consist of great persons, to distinguish it from comedy, where the action is trivial, and the persons of inferior rank. The last quality of the action is that it ought to be probable, as well as admirable and great. 'Tis not necessary that there should be historical truth in it; but always necessary that there should be a likeness of truth, something that is more than barely possible, *probable* being that which succeeds or happens oftener than it misses. To invent therefore a probability, and to make it wonderful, is the most difficult undertaking in the art of poetry; for that which is not

---

[11] A name for adaptations into English of plays by Pedro Calderón de la Barca (1600–1681).

[12] A romantic comedy, published in 1663, by Sir Robert Stapylton (d. 1669).

[13] *Mustapha* (1665) is a heroic tragedy by Roger Boyle, Earl of Orrery (1621–1679).

wonderful is not great; and that which is not probable will not delight a reasonable audience. This action, thus described, must be represented and not told, to distinguish dramatic poetry from epic: but I hasten to the end or scope of tragedy, which is, to rectify or purge our passions, fear and pity.

To instruct delightfully is the general end of all poetry. Philosophy instructs, but it performs its work by precept: which is not delightful, or not so delightful as example. To purge the passions by example is therefore the particular instruction which belongs to tragedy. Rapin, a judicious critic, has observed from Aristotle that pride and want of commiseration are the most predominant vices in mankind,[14] therefore, to cure us of these two, the inventors of tragedy have chosen to work upon two other passions, which are fear and pity. We are wrought to fear by their setting before our eyes some terrible example of misfortune, which happened to persons of the highest quality; for such an action demonstrates to us that no condition is privileged from the turns of fortune; this must of necessity cause terror in us, and consequently abate our pride. But when we see that the most virtuous, as well as the greatest, are not exempt from such misfortunes, that consideration moves pity in us, and insensibly works us to be helpful to, and tender over, the distressed, which is the noblest and most god-like of moral virtues. Here 'tis observable that it is absolutely necessary to make a man virtuous, if we desire he should be pitied: we lament not, but detest, a wicked man, we are glad when we behold his crimes are punished, and that poetical justice[15] is done upon him. Euripides was censured by the critics of his time for making his chief characters too wicked: for example, Phaedra,[16] though she loved her son-in-law with reluctancy, and that it was a curse upon her family for offending Venus, yet was thought too ill a pattern for the stage. Shall we therefore banish all characters of villainy? I confess I am not of that opinion; but it is necessary that the hero of the play be not a villain; that is, the characters which should move our pity ought to have virtuous inclinations, and degrees of moral goodness in them. As for a perfect character of virtue, it never was in nature, and therefore there can be no imitation of it; but there are allays of frailty to be allowed for the chief persons, yet so that the good which is in them shall outweigh the bad, and consequently leave room for punishment on the one side, and pity on the other.

After all, if any one will ask me whether a tragedy cannot be made upon any other grounds than those of exciting pity and terror in us, Bossu,[17] the best of modern critics, answers thus in general: that all excellent arts, and particularly that of poetry, have been invented and brought to perfection by men of a transcendent genius; and that therefore they who practise afterwards the same arts are obliged to tread in their footsteps, and to search in their writings the foundation of them; for it is not just that new rules should

[14] Thomas Rymer had translated René Rapin's *Reflections on Aristotle's Treatise of Poesie* in 1674.

[15] The expression appears to have been coined by Rymer in *The Tragedies of the Last Age*.

[16] In *Hippolytus* (428 B.C.).

[17] Dryden is referring to the critical study *Traité du poème épique* (1675) of René Le Bossu (1631–1680), a work that was translated by "W. J." as *Treatise of the Epick Poem* in 1695.

destroy the authority of the old. But Rapin writes more particularly thus: that no passions in a story are so proper to move our concernment as fear and pity; and that it is from our concernment we receive our pleasure, is undoubted; when the soul becomes agitated with fear for one character, or hope for another, then it is that we are pleased in tragedy by the interest which we take in their adventures.

Here, therefore, the general answer may be given to the first question, how far we ought to imitate Shakespeare and Fletcher in their plots; namely, that we ought to follow them so far only as they have copied the excellencies of those who invented and brought to perfection dramatic poetry: those things only excepted which religion, customs of countries, idioms of languages, etc., have altered in the superstructures, but not in the foundation of the design.

How defective Shakespeare and Fletcher have been in all their plots, Mr. Rymer has discovered in his criticisms: neither can we who follow them be excused from the same or greater errors; which are the more unpardonable in us, because we want their beauties to countervail our faults. The best of their designs, the most approaching to antiquity, and the most conducing to move pity, is the *King and No King*;[18] which, if the farce of Bessus were thrown away, is of that inferior sort of tragedies which end with a prosperous event. 'Tis probably derived from the story of Oedipus, with the character of Alexander the Great, in his extravagancies, given to Arbaces. The taking of this play, amongst many others, I cannot wholly ascribe to the excellency of the action; for I find it moving when it is read: 'tis true, the faults of the plot are so evidently proved that they can no longer be denied. The beauties of it must therefore lie either in the lively touches of the passion: or we must conclude, as I think we may, that even in imperfect plots there are less degrees of nature, by which some faint emotions of pity and terror are raised in us: as a less engine will raise a less proportion of weight, though not so much as one of Archimedes' making; for nothing can move our nature, but by some natural reason, which works upon passions. And since we acknowledge the effect, there must be something in the cause.

The difference between Shakespeare and Fletcher in their plotting seems to be this: that Shakespeare generally moves more terror, and Fletcher more compassion. For the first had a more masculine, a bolder and more fiery genius; the second, a more soft and womanish. In the mechanic beauties of the plot, which are the observation of the three unities, time, place, and action, they are both deficient; but Shakespeare most. Ben Jonson reformed those errors in his comedies, yet one of Shakespeare's was regular before him; which is, *The Merry Wives of Windsor* [1599]. For what remains concerning the design, you are to be referred to our English critic.[19] That method which he has prescribed to raise it from mistake, or ignorance of the crime, is certainly the best, though 'tis not the only: for amongst all the tragedies of Sophocles, there is but one, *Oedipus,* which is wholly built after that model.

After the plot, which is the foundation of the play, the next thing to which we ought to apply our judgment is the manners, for now the poet

18 This play was written by Beaumont *and* Fletcher, the larger part of it probably by Beaumont.
19 That is, Rymer.

comes to work above ground: the ground-work indeed is that which is most necessary, as that upon which depends the firmness of the whole fabric; yet it strikes not the eye so much as the beauties or imperfections of the manners, the thoughts, and the expressions.

The first rule which Bossu prescribes to the writer of an heroic poem, and which holds too by the same reason in all dramatic poetry, is to make the moral of the work, that is, to lay down to yourself what that precept of morality shall be, which you would insinuate into the people; as namely Homer's (which I have copied in my *Conquest of Granada*),[20] was that union preserves a commonwealth, and discord destroys it; Sophocles, in his *Oedipus*, that no man is to be accounted happy before his death. 'Tis the moral that directs the whole action of the play to one centre; and that action or fable is the example built upon the moral, which confirms the truth of it to our experience: when the fable is designed, then, and not before, the persons are to be introduced with their manners, characters, and passions.

The manners in a poem are understood to be those inclinations, whether natural or acquired, which move and carry us to actions, good, bad, or in-different, in a play; or which incline the persons to such or such actions. I have anticipated part of this discourse already, in declaring that a poet ought not to make the manners perfectly good in his best persons; but neither are they to be more wicked in any of his characters than necessity requires. To produce a villain, without other reason than a natural inclination to villainy is, in poetry, to produce an effect without a cause; and to make him more a villain than he has just reason to be, is to make an effect which is stronger than the cause.

The manners arise from many causes; and are either distinguished by complexion, as choleric and phlegmatic,[21] or by the differences of age or sex, of climates, or quality of the persons, or their present condition: they are likewise to be gathered from the several virtues, vices, or passions, and many other commonplaces which a poet must be supposed to have learned from natural philosophy, ethics, and history; of all which whosoever is ignorant, does not deserve the name of poet.

But as the manners are useful in this art, they may be all comprised under these general heads: first, they must be apparent; that is, in every character of the play, some inclinations of the person must appear; and these are shown in the actions and discourse. Secondly, the manners must be suitable, or agreeing to the persons; that is, to the age, sex, dignity, and the other general heads of manners: thus, when a poet has given the dignity of a king to one of his persons, in all his actions and speeches, that person must dis-cover majesty, magnanimity, and jealousy of power, because these are suitable to the general manners of a king. The third property of manners is re-semblance; and this is founded upon the particular characters of men, as we have them delivered to us by relation or history; that is, when a poet has the

---

[20] A play in two parts (1670, 1671).

[21] According to an ancient theory, a man's temperament or psychological complexion was sanguine, phlegmatic, choleric, or melancholic depending upon which of four fluids or humours (blood, phlegm, black bile, or yellow bile) predominated in his body.

known character of this or that man before him, he is bound to represent him such, at least not contrary to that which fame has reported him to have been. Thus, it is not a poet's choice to make Ulysses choleric, or Achilles patient, because Homer has described 'em quite otherwise. Yet this is a rock on which ignorant writers daily split; and the absurdity is as monstrous as if a painter should draw a coward running from a battle, and tell us it was the picture of Alexander the Great.

The last property of manners is that they be constant and equal, that is, maintained the same through the whole design: thus, when Virgil had once given the name of *pious* to Aeneas, he was bound to show him such, in all his words and actions through the whole poem. All these properties Horace has hinted to a judicious observer: 1. *notandi sunt tibi mores;* 2. *aut famam sequere;* 3. *aut sibi convenientia finge;* 4. *servetur ad imum, qualis ab incepto processerit, et sibi constet.*[22]

From the manners, the characters of persons are derived; for indeed the characters are no other than the inclinations, as they appear in the several persons of the poem; a character being thus defined, that which distinguishes one man from another. Not to repeat the same things over again which have been said of the manners, I will only add what is necessary here. A character, or that which distinguishes one man from all others, cannot be supposed to consist of one particular virtue, or vice, or passion only; but 'tis a composition of qualities which are not contrary to one another in the same person; thus the same man may be liberal and valiant, but not liberal and covetous; so in a comical character or humour (which is an inclination to this or that particular folly), Falstaff[23] is a liar, and a coward, a glutton, and a buffoon, because all these qualities may agree in the same man; yet it is still to be observed that one virtue, vice, and passion ought to be shown in every man as predominant over all the rest; as covetousness in Crassus,[24] love of his country in Brutus;[25] and the same in characters which are feigned.

The chief character or hero in a tragedy, as I have already shown, ought in prudence to be such a man who has so much more in him of virtue than of vice, that he may be left amiable to the audience, which otherwise cannot have any concernment for his sufferings; and 'tis on this one character that the pity and terror must be principally, if not wholly, founded. A rule which is extremely necessary, and which none of the critics that I know have fully enough discovered to us. For terror and compassion work but weakly when they are divided into many persons. If Creon had been the chief character in *Oedipus,* there had neither been terror nor compassion moved; but only detestation of

---

22 "1. Observe the manners of each age; 2. either follow established usage; 3. or create conventions for yourself; 4. let each character proceed as he began, and let him remain self-consistent." From the *Art of Poetry.*

23 In Shakespeare's *Henry IV,* Part I; *Henry IV,* Part II; and *The Merry Wives of Windsor,* all written between 1597 and 1599.

24 Marcus Licinius Crassus (d. 533 B.C.), a member of the First Triumvirate with Caesar and Pompey, was known as a man of unbounded avarice and ambition in his own day, and so represented on the English stage.

25 In Dryden's century, Marcus Junius Brutus (c. 85–42 B.C.) was often treated sympathetically as a man who reluctantly assassinated Julius Caesar in order to save the Roman republic from becoming an empire. See Shakespeare's *Julius Caesar.*

the man and joy for his punishment; if Adrastus and Eurydice had been made more appearing characters, then the pity had been divided, and lessened on the part of Oedipus: but making Oedipus the best and bravest person, and even Jocasta but an underpart to him, his virtues and the punishment of his fatal crime drew both the pity and the terror to himself.

By what had been said of the manners, it will be easy for a reasonable man to judge whether the characters be truly or falsely drawn in a tragedy; for if there be no manners appearing in the characters, no concernment for the persons can be raised; no pity or horror can be moved, but by vice or virtue; therefore, without them, no person can have any business in the play. If the inclinations be obscure, 'tis a sign the poet is in the dark, and knows not what manner of man he presents to you; and consequently you can have no idea, or very imperfect, of that man; nor can judge what resolutions he ought to take; or what words or actions are proper for him. Most comedies made up of accidents or adventures are liable to fall into this error; and tragedies with many turns are subject to it; for the manners never can be evident where the surprises of fortune take up all the business of the stage; and where the poet is more in pain to tell you what happened to such a man than what he was. 'Tis one of the excellencies of Shakespeare that the manners of his persons are generally apparent, and you see their bent and inclinations. Fletcher comes far short of him in this, as indeed he does almost in every thing: there are but glimmerings of manners in most of his comedies, which run upon adventures; and in his tragedies, *Rollo, Otto*, the *King and No King, Melantius*,[26] and many others of his best, are but pictures shown you in the twilight; you know not whether they resemble vice or virtue, and they are either good, bad, or indifferent, as the present scene requires it. But of all poets, this commendation is to be given to Ben Jonson, that the manners even of the most inconsiderable persons in his plays are everywhere apparent.

By considering the second quality of manners, which is that they be suitable to the age, quality, country, dignity, etc., of the character, we may likewise judge whether a poet has followed nature. In this kind, Sophocles and Euripides have more excelled among the Greeks than Aeschylus; and Terence more than Plautus[27] among the Romans. Thus Sophocles gives to Oedipus the true qualities of a king, in both those plays which bear his name; but in the latter, which is the *Oedipus Colonœus*, he lets fall on purpose his tragic style; his hero speaks not in the arbitrary tone; but remembers, in the softness of his complaints, that he is an unfortunate blind old man; that he is banished from his country, and persecuted by his next relations. The present French poets are generally accused that wheresoever they lay the scene, or in whatsoever age, the manners of their heroes are wholly French. Racine's Bajazet[28] is bred at Constantinople; but his civilities are conveyed to him, by some secret passage, from Versailles into the Seraglio. But our Shakespeare, having ascribed to Henry the Fourth the character of a king and of a father, gives him the perfect manners of each relation, when either he transacts with his son or with his subjects. Fletcher, on the other side, gives neither to Arbaces, nor to

[26] I.e., *The Maid's Tragedy* (1619).
[27] Writer of comedies (c. 254–184 B.C.).
[28] A character in the play (1672) in which he is the titular hero.

his King in the *Maid's Tragedy*, the qualities which are suitable to a monarch; though he may be excused a little in the latter, for the King there is not uppermost in the character; 'tis the lover of Evadne, who is King only in a second consideration; and though he be unjust, and has other faults which shall be nameless, yet he is not the hero of the play. 'Tis true, we find him a lawful prince (though I never heard of any King that was in Rhodes), and therefore Mr. Rymer's criticism stands good; that he should not be shown in so vicious a character. Sophocles has been more judicious in his *Antigona*; for though he represents in Creon a bloody prince, yet he makes him not a lawful king, but an usurper, and Antigona herself is the heroine of the tragedy. But when Philaster wounds Arethusa and the boy; and Perigot his mistress, in the *Faithful Shepherdess*,[29] both these are contrary to the character of manhood. Nor is Valentinian managed much better, for though Fletcher has taken his picture truly, and shown him as he was, an effeminate, voluptuous man, yet he has forgotten that he was an Emperor, and has given him none of those royal marks which ought to appear in a lawful successor of the throne. If it be inquired what Fletcher should have done on this occasion; ought he not to have represented Valentinian as he was? Bossu shall answer this question for me, by an instance of the like nature: Mauritius, the Greek Emperor, was a prince far surpassing Valentinian, for he was endued with many kingly virtues; he was religious, merciful, and valiant, but withal he was noted of extreme covetousness, a vice which is contrary to the character of a hero, or a prince: therefore, says the critic, that emperor was no fit person to be represented in a tragedy, unless his good qualities were only to be shown, and his covetousness (which sullied them all) were slurred over by the artifice of the poet. To return once more to Shakespeare: no man ever drew so many characters, or generally distinguished 'em better from one another, excepting only Jonson. I will instance but in one, to show the copiousness of his invention: 'tis that of Caliban, or the Monster in the *Tempest*. He seems there to have created a person which was not in nature, a boldness which at first sight would appear intolerable; for he makes him a species of himself, begotten by an incubus on a witch; but this, as I have elsewhere proved, is not wholly beyond the bounds of credibility, at least the vulgar still believe it. We have the separated notions of a spirit, and of a witch; (and spirits, according to Plato, are vested with a subtle body; according to some of his followers, have different sexes); therefore, as from the distinct apprehensions of a horse, and of a man, imagination has formed a centaur; so from those of an incubus and a sorceress, Shakespeare has produced his monster. Whether or no his generation can be defended, I leave to philosophy; but of this I am certain, that the poet has most judiciously furnished him with a person, a language, and a character, which will suit him, both by father's and mother's side: he has all the discontents and malice of a witch, and of a devil, besides a convenient proportion of the deadly sins; gluttony, sloth, and lust are manifest; the dejectedness of a slave is likewise given him, and the ignorance of one bred up in a desert island. His person is monstrous, as he is the product of unnatural lust; and his language is as hobgoblin as his person; in all things he is distinguished from other mortals. The characters of

[29] A play by John Fletcher, first produced in 1608.

Fletcher are poor and narrow, in comparison of Shakespeare's; I remember not one which is not borrowed from him; unless you will accept that strange mixture of a man in the *King and No King*; so that in this part Shakespeare is generally worth our imitation; and to imitate Fletcher is but to copy after him who was a copier.

Under this general head of manners, the passions are naturally included as belonging to the characters. I speak not of pity and of terror, which are to be moved in the audience by the plot; but of anger, hatred, love, ambition, jealousy, revenge, etc., as they are shown in this or that person of the play. To describe these naturally, and to move them artfully, is one of the greatest commendations which can be given to a poet: to write pathetically, says Longinus, cannot proceed but for a lofty genius. A poet must be born with this quality; yet, unless he help himself by an acquired knowledge of the passions, what they are in their own nature, and by what springs they are to be moved, he will be subject either to raise them where they ought not to be raised, or not to raise them by the just degrees of nature, or to amplify them beyond the natural bounds, or not to observe the crisis and turns of them, in their cooling and decay: all which errors proceed from want of judgment in the poet, and from being unskilled in the principles of moral philosophy. Nothing is more frequent in a fanciful writer than to foil himself by not managing his strength; therefore, as in a wrestler, there is first required some measure of force, a well-knit body, and active limbs, without which all instruction would be vain; yet, these being granted, if he want the skill which is necessary to a wrestler, he shall make but small advantage of his natural robustuousness: so, in a poet, his inborn vehemence and force of spirit will only run him out of breath the sooner, if it be not supported by the help of art. The roar of passion, indeed, may please an audience, three parts of which are ignorant enough to think all is moving which is noise, and it may stretch the lungs of an ambitious actor, who will die upon the spot for a thundering clap; but it will move no other passion than indignation and contempt from judicious men. Longinus, whom I have hitherto followed, continues thus: *If the passions be artfully employed, the discourse becomes vehement and lofty: if otherwise, there is nothing more ridiculous than a great passion out of season:* and to this purpose he animadverts severely upon Aeschylus, who writ nothing in cold blood, but was always in a rapture, and in fury with his audience: the inspiration was still upon him, he was ever tearing it upon the tripos;[30] or (to run off as madly as he does, from one similitude to another) he was always at high flood of passion, even in the dead ebb and lowest water-mark of the scene. He who would raise the passion of a judicious audience, says a learned critic, must be sure to take his hearers along with him; if they be in a calm, 'tis in vain for him to be in a huff: he must move them by degrees, and kindle with 'em; otherwise he will be in danger of setting his own heap of stubble on fire, and of burning out by himself without warming the company that stand about him. They who would justify the madness of poetry from the authority of Aristotle have mistaken the text, and consequently the interpretation: I imagine it to be false read, where he says of poetry that it is

[30] That is, tripod, a bowl or cauldron on three legs; the priestess of Apollo's shrine at Delphi used one in the passionate delivery of her oracles.

εὐφυοῦς ἢ μανικοῦ, that it had always somewhat in it either of a genius, or of a madman. 'Tis more probable that the original ran thus, that poetry was εὐφυοῦς οὐ μανικοῦ, that it belongs to a witty man, but not to a madman. Thus then the passions, as they are considered simply and in themselves, suffer violence when they are perpetually maintained at the same height; for what melody can be made on that instrument, all whose strings are screwed up at first to their utmost stretch, and to the same sound? But this is not the worst: for the characters likewise bear a part in the general calamity, if you consider the passions as embodied in them; for it follows of necessity that no man can be distinguished from another by his discourse, when every man is ranting, swaggering, and exclaiming with the same excess: as if it were the only business of all the characters to contend with each other for the prize at Billingsgate;[31] or that the scene of the tragedy lay in Bet'lem.[32] Suppose the poet should intend this man to be choleric, and that man to be patient; yet when they are confounded in the writing, you cannot distinguish them from one another: for the man who was called patient and tame is only so before he speaks; but let his clack be set a-going, and he shall tongue it as impetuously, and as loudly, as the errantest hero in the play. By this means, the characters are only distinct in name; but, in reality, all the men and women in the play are the same person. No man should pretend to write who cannot temper his fancy with his judgment: nothing is more dangerous to a raw horseman than a hot-mouthed jade without a curb.

'Tis necessary therefore for a poet who would concern an audience by describing of a passion, first to prepare it, and not to rush upon it all at once. Ovid has judiciously shown the difference of these two ways, in the speeches of Ajax and Ulysses: Ajax, from the very beginning, breaks out into his exclamations, and is swearing by his Maker, *agimus, proh Jupiter, inquit.*[33] Ulysses, on the contrary, prepares his audience with all the submissiveness he can practise, and all the calmness of a reasonable man; he found his judges in a tranquillity of spirit, and therefore set out leisurely and softly with 'em, till he had warmed 'em by degrees; and then he began to mend his pace, and to draw them along with his own impetuousness: yet so managing his breath, that it might not fail him at his need, and reserving his utmost proofs of ability even to the last. The success, you see, was answerable; for the crowd only applauded the speech of Ajax:

> vulgique secutum
> ultima murmur erat:[34]

But the judges awarded the prize for which they contended to Ulysses:

> mota manus procerum est; et quid facundia posset
> tum patuit, fortisque viri tulit arma disertus.[35]

31 A gate in the old wall of London, near which there was a fish market, long noted for its atmosphere of obscene and abusive language.
32 Bedlam, the hospital of St. Mary of Bethlehem in Lambeth, an asylum for the insane.
33 *Metamorphoses*, xiii. 5. "We are pleading [our case], O Jupiter, he said."
34 *Ibid.*, 123. "The murmur of the crowd that followed the end [of his speech]."
35 *Ibid.*, 382-3 (*re patuit . . .*): "The assembly was much moved, and it was revealed what eloquence could do: and the expert orator carried off the hero's arms."

The next necessary rule is to put nothing into the discourse which may hinder your moving of the passions. Too many accidents, as I have said, encumber the poet, as much as the arms of Saul did David; for the variety of passions which they produce are ever crossing and jostling each other out of the way. He who treats of joy and grief together is in a fair way of causing neither of those effects. There is yet another obstacle to be removed, which is pointed wit, and sentences affected out of season; these are nothing of kin to the violence of passion: no man is at leisure to make sentences and similes when his soul is in an agony. I the rather name this fault that it may serve to mind me of my former errors; neither will I spare myself, but give an example of this kind from my *Indian Emperor*. Montezuma, pursued by his enemies, and seeking sanctuary, stands parleying without the fort, and describing his danger to Cydaria, in a simile of six lines:

> As on the sands the frighted traveller
> Sees the high seas come rolling from afar, etc.

My Indian potentate was well skilled in the sea for an inland prince, and well improved since the first act, when he sent his son to discover it. The image had not been amiss from another man, at another time: *sed nunc non erat hisce locus:*[36] he destroyed the concernment which the audience might otherwise have had for him; for they could not think the danger near when he had the leisure to invent a simile.

If Shakespeare be allowed, as I think he must, to have made his characters distinct, it will easily be inferred that he understood the nature of the passions: because it has been proved already that confused passions make undistinguishable characters: yet I cannot deny that he has his failings; but they are not so much in the passions themselves as in his manner of expression: he often obscures his meaning by his words, and sometimes makes it unintelligible. I will not say of so great a poet that he distinguished not the blown puffy style from true sublimity; but I may venture to maintain that the fury of his fancy often transported him beyond the bounds of judgment, either in coining of new words and phrases, or racking words which were in use into the violence of a catachresis.[37] 'Tis not that I would explode the use of metaphors from passions, for Longinus thinks 'em necessary to raise it: but to use 'em at every word, to say nothing without a metaphor, a simile, an image, or description, is I doubt to smell a little too strongly of the buskin.[38] I must be forced to give an example of expressing passion figuratively; but that I may do it with respect to Shakespeare, it shall not be taken from anything of his: 'tis an exclamation against Fortune, quoted in his *Hamlet* but written by some other poet:[39]

> Out, out, thou strumpet Fortune! all you gods,
> In general synod, take away her power;
> Break all the spokes and felleys from her wheel,

[36] From Horace: "But this was not the place." *The Art of Poetry* I. 19.
[37] Misuse of a word, as by a misapplication of terminology or in a strained metaphor.
[38] The high boot worn by Greek tragic actors; hence, the tragic in general; hence, a display of extreme and theatrical emotion.
[39] There is now little doubt that Shakespeare wrote the passage.

> And bowl the round nave down the hill of Heav'n,
> As low as to the fiends.

And immediately after, speaking of Hecuba, when Priam was killed before her eyes:

> The mobbled queen ran up and down,
> Threatening the flame with bisson rheum; a clout about that head
> Where late the diadem stood; and for a robe,
> About her lank and all o'er-teemed loins,
> A blanket in th'alarm of fear caught up.
> Who this had seen, with tongue in venom steep'd
> 'Gainst Fortune's state would treason have pronounced;
> But if the gods themselves did see her then,
> When she saw Pyrrhus make malicious sport
> In mincing with his sword her husband's limbs,
> The instant burst of clamour that she made
> (Unless things mortal move them not at all)
> Would have made milch the burning eyes of Heaven,
> And passion in the gods.

What a pudder is here kept in raising the expression of trifling thoughts! Would not a man have thought that the poet had been bound prentice to a wheelwright, for his first rant? and had followed a ragman for the clout and blanket, in the second? Fortune is painted on a wheel, and therefore the writer, in a rage, will have poetical justice done upon every member of that engine: after this execution, he bowls the nave down hill, from Heaven to the fiends (an unreasonable long mark, a man would think); 'tis well there are no solid orbs to stop it in the way, or no element of fire to consume it:[40] but when it came to the earth, it must be monstrous heavy, to break ground as low as to the centre. His making milch the burning eyes of Heaven was a pretty tolerable flight too: and I think no man ever drew milk out of eyes before him: yet, to make the wonder greater, these eyes were burning. Such a sight indeed were enough to have raised passion in the gods; but to excuse the effects of it, he tells you, perhaps they did not see it. Wise men would be glad to find a little sense couched under all these pompous words; for bombast is commonly the delight of that audience which loves poetry, but understands it not: and as commonly has been the practice of those writers who, not being able to infuse a natural passion into the mind, have made it their business to ply the ears and to stun their judges by the noise. But Shakespeare does not often thus; for the passions in his scene between Brutus and Cassius are extremely natural, the thoughts are such as arise from the matter, the expression of 'em not viciously figurative. I cannot leave this subject, before I do justice to that divine poet by giving you one of his passionate descriptions: 'tis of Richard the Second when he was deposed, and led in triumph through the streets of London by Henry of Bullingbrook:[41] the painting of it is so lively, and the words so moving, that I have scarce read any thing comparable to it in any

---

[40] Dryden is alluding to the demise of the Ptolemaic conception of the universe.
[41] Henry Bolingbroke, Duke of Hereford, in Shakespeare's *Richard II* (c. 1595). He became Henry IV.

other language. Suppose you have seen already the fortunate usurper passing
through the crowd, and followed by the shouts and acclamations of the people;
and now behold King Richard entering upon the scene: consider the wretchedness of his condition, and his carriage in it; and refrain from pity if you can:

> As in a theatre, the eyes of men,
> After a well-graced actor leaves the stage,
> Are idly bent on him that enters next,
> Thinking his prattle to be tedious:
> Even so, or with much more contempt, men's eyes
> Did scowl on Richard: no man cried, God save him:
> No joyful tongue gave him his welcome home,
> But dust was thrown upon his sacred head,
> Which with such gentle sorrow he shook off,
> His face still combating with tears and smiles
> (The badges of his grief and patience),
> That had not God (for some strong purpose) steel'd
> The hearts of men, they must perforce have melted,
> And barbarism itself have pitied him.

To speak justly of this whole matter: 'tis neither height of thought that
is discommended, nor pathetic vehemence, nor any nobleness of expression in
its proper place; but 'tis a false measure of all these, something which is like
'em, and is not them; 'tis the Bristol-stone,[42] which appears like a diamond; 'tis
an extravagant thought, instead of a sublime one; 'tis roaring madness, instead
of vehemence; and a sound of words, instead of sense. If Shakespeare were
stripped of all the bombast in his passions, and dressed in the most vulgar words,
we should find the beauties of his thoughts remaining; if his embroideries were
burnt down, there would still be silver at the bottom of the melting-pot: but I
fear (at least let me fear it for myself) that we who ape his sounding words
have nothing of his thought, but are all outside; there is not so much as a
dwarf within our giant's clothes. Therefore, let not Shakespeare suffer for our
sakes; 'tis our fault, who succeed him in an age which is more refined, if we
imitate him so ill that we copy his failings only, and make a virtue of that in
our writings which in his was an imperfection.

For what remains, the excellency of that poet was, as I have said, in the
more manly passions; Fletcher's in the softer: Shakespeare writ better betwixt
man and man; Fletcher, betwixt man and woman: consequently, the one
described friendship better; the other love: yet Shakespeare taught Fletcher
to write love: and Juliet, and Desdemona,[43] are originals. 'Tis true, the scholar
had the softer soul; but the master had the kinder. Friendship is both a virtue
and a passion essentially; love is a passion only in its nature, and is not a
virtue but by accident: good nature makes friendship; but effeminacy love.
Shakespeare had an universal mind, which comprehended all characters and
passions; Fletcher a more confined and limited: for though he treated love in
perfection, yet honour, ambition, revenge, and generally all the stronger passions,

---

[42] I.e., rock-crystal, also called "Bristol-diamond."
[43] In *Romeo and Juliet* (1595) and *Othello* (1604) respectively.

he either touched not, or not masterly. To conclude all, he was a limb of Shakespeare.

I had intended to have proceeded to the last property of manners, which is that they must be constant, and the characters maintained the same from the beginning to the end; and from thence to have proceeded to the thoughts and expressions suitable to a tragedy: but I will first see how this will relish with the age. 'Tis, I confess, but cursorily written; yet the judgment which is given here is generally founded upon experience: but because many men are shocked at the name of rules, as if they were a kind of magisterial prescription upon poets, I will conclude with the words of Rapin, in his reflections on Aristotle's work of poetry: "If the rules be well considered, we shall find them to be made only to reduce nature into method, to trace her step by step, and not to suffer the least mark of her to escape us: 'tis only by these that probability in fiction is maintained, which is the soul of poetry. They are founded upon good sense, and sound reason, rather than on authority; for though Aristotle and Horace are produced, yet no man must argue that what they write is true because they writ it; but 'tis evident, by the ridiculous mistakes and gross absurdities which have been made by those poets who have taken their fancy only for their guide, that if this fancy be not regulated, 'tis a mere caprice, and utterly incapable to produce a reasonable and judicious poem."

Samuel Johnson

MILTON'S POETICAL WORKS

Samuel Johnson (1709–1784) was born in Lichfield, the only child of a
learned bookseller whose financial condition was in decline. Partly
because of his intellectual precocity, partly because he was afflicted
with scrofula, a disfiguring disease of the tissues, the young Johnson
lived much to himself among the books of his father's shop, accumulating
the erudition which astonished his teachers and fellow-students when
he entered Pembroke College. He had gone to Oxford on the promise
of help from a wealthy neighbor which was but minimally redeemed
and Johnson endured the humiliation of visible poverty for two years
and left the university without taking his degree. (Many years later,
when he had become famous, Oxford awarded him the honorary
doctorate which became part of his name: he is still commonly referred
to as "Dr. Johnson.") He returned to Lichfield, where for six years he
sold books, worked as a schoolmaster, and tried his hand at journalism
and translation. In 1735 he married Mrs. Elizabeth Porter, a widow twice
his age, and opened a private school, which soon failed. In 1737 he set
off for London to seek his fortune as a man of letters. Over nearly a
quarter of a century Johnson's life was an unremitting struggle against
extreme poverty. For some years he kept himself alive by the meanest
sort of anonymous hackwork. He did, however, begin to achieve a
degree of reputation with the publication of his poem *London* (1738)
and this was augmented by the critical success of his brilliant *Life of
Savage* (1743); by 1747 his abilities were so far recognized that, when
a syndicate of publishers planned a dictionary of the English language,
it was to him that they turned for the carrying out of the project. The
famous *Dictionary*, when it was published in 1755, established Johnson's
fame but was far from making his fortune or even from compensating
him for the eight years of labor he had bestowed on the undertaking,
nor did his semi-weekly essay-periodical *The Rambler* (1750–1752) and
his classical philosophical romance *Rasselas* (1759) give him a financial
return commensurate with their success. But in 1762 he was offered a
pension of £300 a year by King George III. In his *Dictionary* Johnson
had defined a pension as pay given to a state hireling for treason to his
country and a pensioner as a slave of state hired to obey his master;
it is perhaps the measure of the special admiration and affection in

From the book *Lives of the English Poets,* Volume II, by Samuel Johnson ("The Life of
Milton"). London: J. M. Dent & Sons, Ltd.; New York: E. P. Dutton & Co., Inc. Every-
man's Library Edition. Used by permission of J. M. Dent & Sons, Ltd., and E. P. Dutton
& Co., Inc.

which Johnson is held that no one thinks seriously to accuse him of moral inconsistency in his having accepted what was offered.

His financial needs secured, Johnson wrote less but cultivated his passion for conversation; his talk became the chief attraction of "The Club," formed in 1764 by some of the most famous and gifted Londoners of the time. One of its members was James Boswell, whom Johnson had met in 1763, whose *Life* of his beloved friend is generally thought to be the greatest biography in English, perhaps in any language. It was this work that made Johnson into the legendary figure he now is—the huge, awkward, ugly man, plagued by ill-health, the prey of melancholia and morbid fear, his social deportment impossible, his opinions absolute and brooking no contradiction, loved and cherished by his friends for the kindness of his heart and the loyalty of his affections, for his wit, common sense, and detestation of cant.

In 1765 Johnson published his edition of Shakespeare's plays, a work no doubt deficient in the requisite scholarship—Macaulay makes much of Johnson's ignorance of the writers contemporary with Shakespeare—but rich in critical perception. But Johnson's greatest achievement in criticism was still to come, in *The Lives of the English Poets* (1779, 1781), a series of fifty-two biographical and critical studies that appeared as the prefaces to a compendious collection of poets issued by a group of booksellers. The two essays given here are parts of the *Lives* of Milton and Cowley, respectively. Johnson's criticism engages by being at once so strikingly individual and so encompassingly characteristic— the writer is his own man speaking his own mind in his own voice, but in what he says we hear also the general informed opinion of his age finding its clearest and most emphatic utterance. For that reason a comparison of Johnson's remarks on the "metaphysical" poets with T. S. Eliot's clear and emphatic announcement (pp. 368 ff.) of how a later age was to regard these poets is peculiarly instructive.

. . . In the examination of Milton's poetical works I shall pay so much regard to time as to begin with his juvenile productions. For his early pieces he seems to have had a degree of fondness not very laudable; what he has once written he resolves to preserve, and gives to the public an unfinished poem, which he broke off because he was *nothing satisfied with what he had done,* supposing his readers less nice than himself. These preludes to his future labours are in Italian, Latin, and English. Of the Italian I cannot pretend to speak as a critic; but I have heard them commended by a man well qualified to decide their merit. The Latin pieces are lusciously elegant; but the delight which they afford is rather by the exquisite imitation of the ancient writers, by the purity of the diction, and the harmony of the numbers, than by any power of invention, or vigour of sentiment. They are not all of equal value; the elegies excel the odes; and some of the exercises on *Gunpowder Treason*[1] might have been spared.

[1] Milton wrote five poems in Latin, essentially school exercises, on the so-called Gunpowder Plot, the unsuccessful attempt by Guy Fawkes and eight others to blow up the British Houses of Parliament, along with James I, when the session opened on November 5, 1605.

The English poems, though they make no promises of *Paradise Lost,* have this evidence of genius, that they have a cast original and unborrowed. But their peculiarity is not excellence: if they differ from verses of others, they differ for the worse; for they are too often distinguished by repulsive harshness; the combinations of words are new, but they are not pleasing; the rhymes and epithets seem to be laboriously sought, and violently applied.

That in the early parts of his life he wrote with much care appears from his manuscripts, happily preserved at Cambridge, in which many of his smaller works are found as they were first written, with the subsequent corrections. Such relics show how excellence is acquired; what we hope ever to do with ease we must learn first to do with diligence.

Those who admire the beauties of this great poet sometimes force their own judgment into false approbation of his little pieces, and prevail upon themselves to think that admirable which is only singular. All that short compositions can commonly attain is neatness and elegance. Milton never learned the art of doing little things with grace; he overlooked the milder excellence of suavity and softness; he was a *lion* that had no skill *in dandling the kid.*[2]

One of the poems on which much praise has been bestowed is *Lycidas,* of which the diction is harsh, the rhymes uncertain, and the numbers unpleasing. What beauty there is we must therefore seek in the sentiments and images. It is not to be considered as the effusion of real passion; for passion runs not after remote allusions and obscure opinions. Passion plucks no berries from the myrtle and ivy, nor calls upon Arethuse and Mincius,[3] nor tells of rough *satyrs* and *fauns with cloven heel.* Where there is leisure for fiction there is little grief.

In this poem there is no nature, for there is nothing new. Its form is that of a pastoral, easy, vulgar, and therefore disgusting; whatever images it can supply are long ago exhausted, and its inherent improbability always forces dissatisfaction on the mind. When Cowley tells of Hervey, that they studied together, it is easy to suppose how much he must miss the companion of his labours, and the partner of his discoveries;[4] but what image of tenderness can be excited by these lines?—

> We drove a field, and both together heard
> What time the grey fly winds her sultry horn,
> Battening our flocks with the fresh dews of night.

We know that they never drove a field, and that they had no flocks to batten; and though it be allowed that the representation may be allegorical, the true meaning is so uncertain and remote that it is never sought because it cannot be known when it is found.

Among the flocks, and copses, and flowers, appear the heathen deities— Jove and Phoebus, Neptune and Aeolus, with a long train of mythological

---

[2] In *Paradise Lost* Milton had written "Sporting the lion ramp'd, and in his paw / Dandl'd the kid." IV. 343.

[3] Mythical bodies of water mentioned in *Lycidas.*

[4] Abraham Cowley (1618–1678) wrote an elegy on his Cambridge friend, William Hervey, in 1642.

imagery, such as a college easily supplies. Nothing can less display knowledge, or less exercise invention, than to tell how a shepherd has lost his companion, and must now feed his flocks alone, without any judge of his skill in piping; and how one god asks another god what is become of Lycidas, and how neither god can tell. He who thus grieves will excite no sympathy; he who thus praises will confer no honour.

This poem has yet a grosser fault. With these trifling fictions are mingled the most awful and sacred truths, such as ought never to be polluted with such irreverend combinations. The shepherd likewise is now a feeder of sheep, and afterwards an ecclesiastical pastor, a superintendent of a Christian flock. Such equivocations are always unskilful; but here they are indecent, and at least approach to impiety, of which, however, I believe the writer not to have been conscious.

Such is the power of reputation justly acquired, that its blaze drives away the eye from nice examination. Surely no man could have fancied that he read *Lycidas* with pleasure had he not known its author.

Of the two pieces, *L'Allegro* and *Il Penseroso,* I believe opinion is uniform; every man that reads them reads them with pleasure. The author's design is not, what Theobald[5] has remarked, merely to show how objects derive their colours from the mind, by representing the operation of the same things upon the gay and the melancholy temper, or upon the same man as he is differently disposed; but rather how, among the successive variety of appearances, every disposition of mind takes hold on those by which it may be gratified.

The *cheerful* man hears the lark in the morning; the *pensive* man hears the nightingale in the evening. The *cheerful* man sees the cock strut, and hears the horn and hounds echo in the wood; then walks, *not unseen,* to observe the glory of the rising sun, or listen to the singing milkmaid, and view the labours of the ploughman and the mower; then casts his eyes about him over scenes of smiling plenty, and looks up to the distant tower, the residence of some fair inhabitant; thus he pursues rural gaiety through a day of labour or of play, and delights himself at night with the fanciful narratives of superstitious ignorance.

The *pensive* man, at one time, walks *unseen* to muse at mid-night; and at another hears the sullen curfew. If the weather drives him home, he sits in a room lighted only by *glowing embers,* or by a lonely lamp outwatches the north star, to discover the habitation of separate souls, and varies the shades of meditation by contemplating the magnificent or pathetic scenes of tragic and epic poetry. When the morning comes, a morning gloomy with rain and wind, he walks into the dark trackless woods, falls asleep by some murmuring water, and with melancholy enthusiasm expects some dream of prognostication, or some music played by aerial performers.

Both Mirth and Melancholy are solitary, silent inhabitants of the breast, that neither receive nor transmit communication; no mention is therefore made of a philosophical friend, or a pleasant companion. The seriousness does not arise from any participation of calamity, nor the gaiety from the pleasures of the bottle.

---

[5] Lewis Theobald (1688–1744) critic and editor of Shakespeare's works.

The man of *cheerfulness*, having exhausted the country, tries what *towered cities* will afford, and mingles with scenes of splendour gay assemblies and nuptial festivities; but he mingles a mere spectator, as, when the learned comedies of Jonson or the wild dramas of Shakespeare are exhibited, he attends the theatre.

The *pensive* man never loses himself in crowds, but walks the cloister, or frequents the cathedral. Milton probably had not yet forsaken the Church.

Both his characters delight in music; but he seems to think that cheerful notes would have obtained from Pluto a complete dismission of Eurydice,[6] of whom solemn sounds only procured a conditional release.

For the old age of Cheerfulness he makes no provision; but Melancholy he conducts with great dignity to the close of life. His cheerfulness is without levity, and his pensiveness without asperity.

Through these two poems the images are properly selected, and nicely distinguished; but the colours of the diction seem not sufficiently discriminated. I know not whether the characters are kept sufficiently apart. No mirth can indeed be found in his melancholy; but I am afraid that I always meet some melancholy in his mirth. They are two noble efforts of imagination.

The greatest of his juvenile performances is the *Masque of Comus,* in which may very plainly be discovered the dawn or twilight of *Paradise Lost.* Milton appears to have formed very early that system of diction, and mode of verse, which his maturer judgment approved, and from which he never endeavoured nor desired to deviate.

Nor does *Comus* afford only a specimen of his language; it exhibits likewise his power of description and his vigour of sentiment employed in the praise and defence of virtue. A work more truly poetical is rarely found; allusions, images, and descriptive epithets, embellish almost every period with lavish decoration. As a series of lines, therefore, it may be considered as worthy of all the admiration with which the votaries have received it.

As a drama it is deficient. The action is not probable. A masque, in those parts where supernatural intervention is admitted, must indeed be given up to all the freaks of imagination; but, so far as the action is merely human, it ought to be reasonable, which can hardly be said of the conduct of the two brothers, who, when their sister sinks with fatigue in a pathless wilderness, wander both away together in search of berries too far to find their way back, and leave a helpless Lady to all the sadness and danger of solitude. This, however, is a defect overbalanced by its convenience.

What deserves more reprehension is, that the prologue spoken in the wild wood by the attendant Spirit is addressed to the audience; a mode of communication so contrary to the nature of dramatic representation, that no precedents can support it.

The discourse of the Spirit is too long—an objection that may be made to almost all the following speeches; they have not the sprightliness of a dialogue animated by reciprocal contention, but seem rather declamations deliberately composed, and formally repeated, on a moral question. The auditor therefore listens as to a lecture, without passion, without anxiety.

[6] In the Greek myth Eurydice was held captive by Hades (or "Pluto," his name among the Romans) in the Underworld.

The song of Comus has airiness and jollity; but, what may recommend Milton's morals as well as his poetry, the invitations to pleasure are so general, that they excite no distinct images of corrupt enjoyment, and take no dangerous hold on the fancy.

The following soliloquies of Comus and the Lady are elegant, but tedious. The song must owe much to the voice, if it ever can delight. At last the Brothers enter, with too much tranquillity; and when they have feared lest their sister should be in danger, and hoped that she is not in danger, the Elder makes a speech in praise of chastity, and the Younger finds how fine it is to be a philosopher.

Then descends the Spirit in form of a shepherd, and the Brother, instead of being in haste to ask his help, praises his singing, and inquires his business in that place. It is remarkable, that at this interview the Brother is taken with a short fit of rhyming. The Spirit relates that the Lady is in the power of Comus; the Brother moralises again; and the Spirit makes a long narration, of no use because it is false, and therefore unsuitable to a good being.

In all these parts the language is poetical, and the sentiments are generous; but there is something wanting to allure attention.

The dispute between the Lady and Comus is the most animated and affecting scene of the drama, and wants nothing but a brisker reciprocation of objections and replies to invite attention and detain it.

The songs are vigorous, and full of imagery; but they are harsh in their diction, and not very musical in their numbers.

Throughout the whole the figures are too bold, and the language too luxuriant for dialogue. It is a drama in the epic style, inelegantly splendid, and tediously instructive.

The *Sonnets* were written in different parts of Milton's life, upon different occasions. They deserve not any particular criticism; for of the best it can only be said, that they are not bad; and perhaps only the eighth and twenty-first are truly entitled to this slender commendation. The fabric of a sonnet, however adapted to the Italian language, has never succeeded in ours, which, having greater variety of termination, requires the rhymes to be often changed.

Those little pieces may be despatched without much anxiety; a greater work calls for greater care. I am now to examine *Paradise Lost*; a poem which, considered with respect to design, may claim the first place, and with respect to performance, the second, among the productions of the human mind.

By the general consent of critics the first praise of genius is due to the writer of an epic poem, as it requires an assemblage of all the powers which are singly sufficient for other compositions. Poetry is the art of uniting pleasure with truth, by calling imagination to the help of reason. Epic poetry undertakes to teach the most important truths by the most pleasing precepts, and therefore relates some great event in the most affecting manner. History must supply the writer with the rudiments of narration, which he must improve and exalt by a nobler art, must animate by dramatic energy, and diversify by retrospection and anticipation; morality must teach him the exact bounds, and different shades, of vice and virtue; from policy, and the practice of life, he has to learn the discriminations of character, and the tendency of the passions, either single or combined; and physiology must supply him with illustrations and images. To put these materials to poetical use, is required an imagination capable of painting nature and realising fiction. Nor is he yet a poet till he has attained the whole extension of his language, distinguished all the delicacies of phrase, and all the colours of words, and learned to adjust their different sounds to all the varieties of metrical modulation.

Bossu is of opinion that the poet's first work is to find a *moral,* which his fable is afterwards to illustrate and establish.[7] This seems to have been the process only of Milton; the moral of other poems is incidental and consequent; in Milton's only it is essential and intrinsic. His purpose was the most useful and the most arduous; *to vindicate the ways of God to man;* to show the reasonableness of religion, and the necessity of obedience to the Divine Law.

To convey this moral, there must be a *fable,* a narration artfully constructed, so as to excite curiosity, and surprise expectation. In this part of his work Milton must be confessed to have equalled every other poet. He has involved in his account of the Fall of Man the events which preceded, and those that were to follow it: he has interwoven the whole system of theology with such propriety that every part appears to be necessary; and scarcely any recital is wished shorter for the sake of quickening the progress of the main action.

The subject of an epic poem is naturally an event of great importance. That of Milton is not the destruction of a city, the conduct of a colony, or the foundation of an empire. His subject is the fate of worlds, the revolutions of heaven and of earth; rebellion against the Supreme King, raised by the highest order of created beings; the overthrow of their host, and the punishment of their crime; the creation of a new race of reasonable creatures; their original happiness and innocence, their forfeiture of immortality, and their restoration to hope and peace.

Great events can be hastened or retarded only by persons of elevated dignity. Before the greatness displayed in Milton's poem, all other greatness shrinks away. The weakest of his agents are the highest and noblest of human beings, the original parents of mankind; with whose actions the elements consented; on whose rectitude, or deviation of will, depended the state of terrestrial nature, and the condition of all the future inhabitants of the globe.

Of the other agents in the poem, the chief are such as it is irreverence to name on slight occasions. The rest were lower powers;

> — of which the least could wield
> Those elements, and arm him with the force
> Of all their regions;

powers which only the control of Omnipotence restrains from laying creation waste, and filling the vast expanse of space with ruin and confusion. To display the motives and actions of beings thus superior, so far as human reason can examine them, or human imagination represent them, is the task which this mighty poet has undertaken and performed.

In the examination of epic poems much speculation is commonly employed upon the *characters.* The characters in the *Paradise Lost,* which admit

[7] Johnson is referring to *Traité du poème épique* (1675) by René Le Bossu (1631–1680).

of examination, are those of angels and of man; of angels good and evil; of man in his innocent and sinful state.

Among the angels, the virtue of Raphael is mild and placid, of easy condescension and free communication; that of Michael is regal and lofty, and, as may seem, attentive to the dignity of his own nature. Abdiel and Gabriel appear occasionally, and act as every incident requires; the solitary fidelity of Abdiel is very amiably painted.

Of the evil angels the characters are more diversified. To Satan, as Addison[8] observes, such sentiments are given as suit *the most exalted and most depraved being.* Milton has been censured by Clarke[9] for the impiety which sometimes breaks from Satan's mouth. For there are thoughts, as he justly remarks, which no observation of character can justify, because no good man would willingly permit them to pass, however transiently, through his own mind. To make Satan speak as a rebel, without any such expressions as might taint the reader's imagination, was indeed one of the greatest difficulties in Milton's undertaking, and I cannot but think that he has extricated himself with great happiness. There is in Satan's speeches little that can give pain to a pious ear. The language of rebellion cannot be the same with that of obedience. The malignity of Satan foams in haughtiness and obstinacy; but his expressions are commonly general, and no otherwise offensive than as they are wicked.

The other chiefs of the celestial rebellion are very judiciously discriminated in the first and second books; and the ferocious character of Moloch appears, both in the battle and the council, with exact consistency.

To Adam and to Eve are given, during their innocence, such sentiments as innocence can generate and utter. Their love is pure benevolence and mutual veneration; their repasts are without luxury, and their diligence without toil. Their addresses to their Maker have little more than the voice of admiration and gratitude. Fruition left them nothing to ask; and Innocence left them nothing to fear.

But with guilt enter distrust and discord, mutual accusation and stubborn self-defence; they regard each other with alienated minds, and dread their Creator as the avenger of their transgression. At last they seek shelter in his mercy, soften to repentance, and melt in supplication. Both before and after the Fall the superiority of Adam is diligently sustained.

Of the *probable* and the *marvellous,* two parts of a vulgar epic poem which immerge the critic in deep consideration, the *Paradise Lost* requires little to be said. It contains the history of a miracle, of Creation and Redemption; it displays the power and the mercy of the Supreme Being; the probable therefore is marvellous, and the marvellous is probable. The substance of the narrative is truth; and as truth allows no choice, it is, like necessity, superior to rule. To the accidental or adventitious parts, as to everything human, some slight exceptions may be made. But the main fabric is immoveably supported.

It is justly remarked by Addison, that this poem has, by the nature of its subject, the advantage above all others, that it is universally and perpetually

---

[8] Joseph Addison (1672–1719), chiefly known as an essayist, wrote a number of papers on Milton for a famous journal of the time, the *Spectator.*
[9] John Clarke, a schoolmaster, author of the *Essay on Study* (1713).

interesting. All mankind will, through all ages, bear the same relation to Adam
and to Eve, and must partake of that good and evil which extend to themselves.

Of the *machinery,* so called from θεὸς ἀπὸ μηχανῆς,[10] by which is meant the
occasional interposition of supernatural power, another fertile topic of critical
remarks, here is no room to speak, because everything is done under the
immediate and visible direction of Heaven; but the rule is so far observed,
that no part of the action could have been accomplished by any other means.

Of *episodes,* I think there are only two, contained in Raphael's relation
of the war in heaven, and Michael's prophetic account of the changes to
happen in this world. Both are closely connected with the great action; one was
necessary to Adam as a warning, the other as a consolation.

To the completeness or *integrity* of the design nothing can be objected;
it has distinctly and clearly what Aristotle requires, a beginning, a middle, and
an end. There is perhaps no poem, of the same length, from which so little
can be taken without apparent mutilation. Here are no funeral games, nor is
there any long description of a shield.[11] The short digressions at the beginning
of the third, seventh, and ninth books might doubtless be spared; but super-
fluities so beautiful, who would take away? or who does not wish that the
author of the *Iliad* had gratified succeeding ages with a little knowledge of
himself? Perhaps no passages are more frequently or more attentively read
than those extrinsic paragraphs; and, since the end of poetry is pleasure, that
cannot be unpoetical with which all are pleased.

The questions, whether the action of the poem be strictly *one,* whether
the poem can be properly termed *heroic,* and who is the hero, are raised by
such readers as draw their principles of judgment rather from books than from
reason. Milton, though he entitled *Paradise Lost* only a *poem,* yet calls it
himself *heroic song.* Dryden, petulantly and indecently, denies the heroism of
Adam, because he was overcome; but there is no reason why the hero should
not be unfortunate, except established practice, since success and virtue do not
go necessarily together. Cato is the hero of Lucan; but Lucan's authority will
not be suffered by Quintilian to decide.[12] However, if success be necessary,
Adam's deceiver was at last crushed; Adam was restored to his Maker's favour,
and therefore may securely resume his human rank.

After the scheme and fabric of the poem, must be considered as component parts, the sentiments and the diction.

The *sentiments,* as expressive of manners, or appropriated to characters,
are for the greater part unexceptionally just.

Splendid passages, containing lessons of morality, or precepts of prudence,
occur seldom. Such is the original formation of this poem, that as it admits no
human manners till the Fall, it can give little assistance to human conduct. Its
end is to raise the thoughts above sublunary cares or pleasures. Yet the praise
of that fortitude with which Abdiel maintained his singularity of virtue against

---

[10] "God from the machine." A contrivance by means of which the gods were brought
on stage, usually on the roof of the scene building.

[11] As there are, for example, in Homer's *Iliad* and Virgil's *Aeneid.*

[12] Cato the Younger (95–46 B.C.) was treated sympathetically by Lucan (A.D. 39–
65) in his poem on the civil war between Caesar and Pompey, but Quintilian (A.D.
35–95), a rhetorician and a political enemy of Lucan's, did not agree about Cato.

the scorn of multitudes, may be accommodated to all times; and Raphael's reproof of Adam's curiosity after the planetary motions, with the answer returned by Adam, may be confidently opposed to any rule of life which any poet has delivered.

The thoughts which are occasionally called forth in the progress are such as could only be produced by an imagination in the highest degree fervid and active, to which materials were supplied by incessant study and unlimited curiosity. The heat of Milton's mind might be said to suplimate his learning, to throw off into his work the spirit of science, unmingled with its grosser parts.

He had considered creation in its whole extent, and his descriptions are therefore learned. He had accustomed his imagination to unrestrained indulgence, and his conceptions therefore were extensive. The characteristic quality of his poem is sublimity. He sometimes descends to the elegant, but his element is the great. He can occasionally invest himself with grace; but his natural port is gigantic loftiness. He can please when pleasure is required; but it is his peculiar power to astonish.

He seems to have been well acquainted with his own genius, and to know what it was that nature had bestowed upon him more bountifully than upon others; the power of displaying the vast, illuminating the splendid, enforcing the awful, darkening the gloomy, and aggravating the dreadful; he therefore chose a subject on which too much could not be said, on which he might tire his fancy without the censure of extravagance.

The appearances of nature, and the occurrences of life, did not satiate his appetite of greatness. To paint things as they are requires a minute attention, and employs the memory rather than the fancy. Milton's delight was to sport in the wide regions of possibility; reality was a scene too narrow for his mind. He sent his faculties out upon discovery, into worlds where only imagination can travel, and delighted to form new modes of existence, and furnish sentiment and action to superior beings, to trace the counsels of hell, or accompany the choirs of heaven.

But he could not be always in other worlds; he must sometimes revisit earth, and tell of things visible and known. When he cannot raise wonder by the sublimity of his mind, he gives delight by its fertility.

Whatever be his subject, he never fails to fill the imagination. But his images and descriptions of the scenes or operations of nature do not seem to be always copied from original form, nor to have the freshness, raciness, and energy of immediate observation. He saw nature, as Dryden expresses it, *through the spectacles of books;* and on most occasions calls learning to his assistance. The garden of Eden brings to his mind the vale of Enna, where Proserpine was gathering flowers. Satan makes his way through fighting elements, like Argo between the Cyanean rocks, or Ulysses between the two Sicilian whirlpools, when he shunned Charybdis on the *larboard.* The mythological allusions have been justly censured, as not being always used with notice of their vanity; but they contribute variety to the narration, and produce an alternate exercise of the memory and the fancy.

His similes are are less numerous and more various than those of his predecessors. But he does not confine himself within the limits of rigorous comparison: his great excellence is ampltitude, and he expands the adventitious image beyond the dimensions which the occasion required. Thus, comparing the shield of Satan to the orb of the moon, he crowds the imagination with the discovery of the telescope, and all the wonders which the telescope discovers.

Of his moral sentiments it is hardly praise to affirm that they excel those of all other poets; for this superiority he was indebted to his acquaintance with the sacred writings. The ancient epic poets, wanting the light of revelation, were very unskilful teachers of virtue: their principal characters may be great, but they are not amiable. The reader may rise from their works with a greater degree of active or passive fortitude, and sometimes of prudence; but he will be able to carry away few precepts of justice, and none of mercy.

From the Italian writers it appears that the advantages of even Christian knowledge may be possessed in vain. Ariosto's[13] pravity is generally known; and though the *Deliverance of Jerusalem*[14] may be considered as a sacred subject, the poet has been very sparing of moral instruction.

In Milton every line breathes sanctity of thought and purity of manners, except when the train of the narration requires the introduction of the rebellious spirits; and even they are compelled to acknowledge their subjection to God, in such a manner as excites reverence and confirms piety.

Of human beings there are but two; but those two are the parents of mankind, venerable before their fall for dignity and innocence, and amiable after it for repentance and submission. In their first state their affection is tender without weakness, and their piety sublime without presumption. When they have sinned, they show how discord begins in mutual frailty, and how it ought to cease in mutual forbearance, how confidence of the Divine favour is forfeited by sin, and how hope of pardon may be obtained by penitence and prayer. A state of innocence we can only conceive, if indeed in our present misery it be possible to conceive it; but the sentiments and worship proper to a fallen and offending being we have all to learn, as we have all to practise.

The poet, whatever be done, is always great. Our progenitors in their first state conversed with angels; even when folly and sin had degraded them, they had not in their humiliation *the port of mean suitors;* and they rise again to reverential regard when we find that their prayers were heard.

As human passions did not enter the world before the Fall, there is in the *Paradise Lost* little opportunity for the pathetic; but what little there is has not been lost. That passion which is peculiar to rational nature, the anguish arising from the consciousness of transgression, and the horrors attending the sense of the Divine displeasure, are very justly described and forcibly impressed. But the passions are moved only on one occasion; sublimity is the general and prevailing quality of this poem; sublimity variously modified, sometimes descriptive, sometimes argumentative.

The defects and faults of *Paradise Lost*—for faults and defects every work of man must have—it is the business of impartial criticism to discover. As, in displaying the excellence of Milton, I have not made long quotations, because

[13] Ludovico Ariosto (1474–1533), Italian poet, is chiefly known for his *Orlando Furioso,* an epic treatment of the Roland story.
[14] *Gerusalemme liberata* was written by Torquato Tasso (1544–1595), an Italian poet. It is an epic poem of the exploits of Godfrey of Boulogne in the First Crusade.

of selecting beauties there had been no end, I shall in the same general manner mention that which seems to deserve censure; for what Englishman can take delight in transcribing passages which, if they lessen the reputation of Milton, diminish in some degree the honour of our country?

The generality of my scheme does not admit the frequent notice of verbal inaccuracies; which Bentley,[15] perhaps better skilled in grammar than poetry, has often found, though he sometimes made them, and which he imputed to the obtrusions of a reviser, whom the author's blindness obliged him to employ; a supposition rash and groundless if he thought it true, and vile and pernicious if, as is said, he in private allowed it to be false.

The plan of *Paradise Lost* has this inconvenience, that it comprises neither human actions nor human manners. The man and woman who act and suffer are in a state which no other man or woman can ever know. The reader finds no transaction in which he can by any effort of imagination place himself; he has therefore little natural curiosity or sympathy.

We all, indeed, feel the effects of Adam's disobedience; we all sin like Adam, and like him must all bewail our offenses: we have restless and insidious enemies in the fallen angels, and in the blessed spirits we have guardians and friends; in the redemption of mankind we hope to be included; in the description of heaven and hell we are surely interested, as we are all to reside hereafter either in the regions of horror or bliss.

But these truths are too important to be new; they have been taught to our infancy; they have mingled with our solitary thoughts and familiar conversation, and are habitually interwoven with the whole texture of life. Being therefore not new, they raise no unaccustomed emotion in the mind; what we knew before, we cannot learn; what is not unexpected, cannot surprise.

Of the idea suggested by these awful scenes, from some we recede with reverence, except when stated hours require their association; and from others we shrink with horror, or admit them only as salutary inflictions, as counterpoises to our interests and passions. Such images rather obstruct the career of fancy than incite it.

Pleasure and terror are indeed the genuine sources of poetry; but poetical pleasure must be such as human imagination can at least conceive, and poetical terrors such as human strength and fortitude may combat. The good and evil of eternity are too ponderous for the wings of wit; the mind sinks under them in passive helplessness, content with calm belief and humble adoration.

Known truths, however, may take a different appearance, and be conveyed to the mind by a new train of intermediate images. This Milton has undertaken, and performed with pregnancy and vigour of mind peculiar to himself. Whoever considers the few radical positions which the Scriptures afforded him, will wonder by what energetic operation he expanded them to such extent, and ramified them to so much variety, restrained as he was by religious reverence from licentiousness of fiction.

Here is a full display of the united force of study and genius; of a great accumulation of materials, with judgment to digest, and fancy to combine them:

[15] Richard Bentley (1662–1742), critic, scholar, and disputant in the early eighteenth-century quarrel over the relative merits of ancient and modern writers, made many fussy emendations in his edition of *Paradise Lost* of 1732.

Milton was able to select from nature, or from story, from an ancient fable, or from modern science, whatever could illustrate or adorn his thoughts. An accumulation of knowledge impregnated his mind, fermented by study, and exalted by imagination.

It has been therefore said, without an indecent hyperbole, by one of his encomiasts, that in reading *Paradise Lost* we read a book of universal knowledge.

But original deficience cannot be supplied. The want of human interest is always felt. *Paradise Lost* is one of the books which the reader admires and lays down, and forgets to take up again. None ever wished it longer than it is. Its perusal is a duty rather than a pleasure. We read Milton for instruction, retire harassed and overburdened, and look elsewhere for recreation; we desert our master and seek for companions.

Another inconvenience of Milton's design is, that it requires the description of what cannot be described, the agency of spirits. He saw that immateriality supplied no images, and that he could not show angels acting but by instruments of action; he therefore invested them with form and matter. This, being necessary, was therefore defensible; and he should have secured the consistency of his system, by keeping immateriality out of sight, and enticing his reader to drop it from his thoughts. But he has unhappily perplexed his poetry with his philosophy. His infernal and celestial powers are sometimes pure spirit, and sometimes animated body. When Satan walks with his lance upon the *burning marle,* he has a body; when, in his passage between hell and the new world, he is in danger of sinking in the vacuity, and is supported by a gust of rising vapours, he has a body; when he animates the toad, he seems to be mere spirit, that can penetrate matter at pleasure; when he *starts up in his own shape,* he has at least a determined form; and when he is brought before Gabriel he has *a spear and a shield,* which he had the power of hiding in the toad, though the arms of the contending angels are evidently material.

The vulgar inhabitants of Pandæmonium, being *incorporeal spirits,* are *at large, though without number,* in a limited space: yet in the battle, when they were overwhelmed by mountains, their armour hurt them, *crushed in upon their substance, now grown gross by sinning.* This likewise happened to the uncorrupted angels, who were overthrown the *sooner for their arms, for unarmed they might easily as spirit have evaded by contraction or remove.* Even as spirits they are hardly spiritual; for *contraction* and *remove* are images of matter; but if they could have escaped without their armour, they might have escaped from it, and left only the empty cover to be battered. Uriel, when he rides on a sunbeam, is material; Satan is material when he is afraid of the prowess of Adam.

The confusion of spirit and matter which pervades the whole narration of the war of heaven fills it with incongruity; and the book in which it is related is, I believe, the favourite of children, and gradually neglected as knowledge is increased.

After the operation of immaterial agents, which cannot be explained, may be considered that of allegorical persons, which have no real existence. To exalt causes into agents, to invest abstract ideas with form, and animate them with activity, has always been the right of poetry. But such airy beings are, for the most part, suffered only to do their natural office, and retire. Thus Fame tells a tale, and Victory hovers over a general, or perches on a standard; but Fame and Victory can do more. To give them any real employment, or ascribe to them any material agency, is to make them allegorical no longer, but to shock the mind by ascribing effects to non-entity. In the *Prometheus* of Aeschylus we see Violence and Strength, and in the *Alcestis* of Euripides we see Death brought upon the stage, all as active persons of the drama; but no precedents can justify absurdity.

Milton's allegory of Sin and Death is undoubtedly faulty. Sin is indeed the mother of Death, and may be allowed to be the portress of hell; but when they stop the journey of Satan, a journey described as real, and when Death offers him battle, the allegory is broken. That Sin and Death should have shown the way to hell, might have been allowed; but they cannot facilitate the passage by building a bridge, because the difficulty of Satan's passage is described as real and sensible, and the bridge ought to be only figurative. The hell assigned to the rebellious spirits is described as not less local than the residence of man. It is placed in some distant part of space, separated from the regions of harmony and order by a chaotic waste and an unoccupied vacuity; but Sin and Death worked up a *mole* of *aggravated soil,* cemented with *asphaltus;* a work too bulky for ideal architects.

This unskilful allegory appears to me one of the greatest faults of the poem; and to this there was no temptation but the author's opinion of its beauty.

To the conduct of the narrative some objection may be made. Satan is with great expectation brought before Gabriel in Paradise, and is suffered to go away unmolested. The creation of man is represented as the consequence of the vacuity left in heaven by the expulsion of the rebels; yet Satan mentions it as a report *rife in heaven* before his departure.

To find sentiments for the state of innocence was very difficult; and something of anticipation perhaps is now and then discovered. Adam's discourse of dreams seems not to be the speculation of a new-created being. I know not whether his answer to the angel's reproof for curiosity does not want something of propriety; it is the speech of a man acquainted with many other men. Some philosophical notions, especially when the philosophy is false, might have been better omitted. The angel, in a comparison, speaks of *timorous* deer before deer were yet timorous, and before Adam could understand the comparison.

Dryden remarks, that Milton has some flats among his elevations. This is only to say that all the parts are not equal. In every work one part must be for the sake of others; a palace must have passages; a poem must have transitions. It is no more to be required that wit should always be blazing than that the sun should always stand at noon. In a great work there is a vicissitude of luminous and opaque parts, as there is in the world a succession of day and night. Milton, when he has expatiated in the sky, may be allowed sometimes to revisit earth; for what other author ever soared so high, or sustained his flight so long?

Milton, being well versed in the Italian poets, appears to have borrowed often from them; and as every man catches something from his companions, his desire of imitating Ariosto's levity has disgraced his work with the "Paradise of Fools"—a fiction not in itself ill-imagined, but too ludicrous for its place.

His play on words, in which he delights too often; his equivocations, which

Bentley endeavours to defend by the example of the ancients; his unnecessary and ungraceful use of terms of art, it is not necessary to mention, because they are easily remarked, and generally censured, and at last bear so little proportion to the whole that they scarcely deserve the attention of a critic.

Such are the faults of that wonderful performance *Paradise Lost,* which he who can put in balance with its beauties must be considered not as nice but as dull, as less to be censured for want of candour, than pitied for want of sensibility.

Of *Paradise Regained,* the general judgment seems now to be right, that it is in many parts elegant, and everywhere instructive. It was not to be supposed that the writer of *Paradise Lost* could ever write without great effusions of fancy, and exalted precepts of wisdom. The basis of *Paradise Regained* is narrow: a dialogue without action can never please like an union of the narrative and dramatic powers. Had this poem been written not by Milton, but by some imitator, it would have claimed and received universal praise.

If *Paradise Regained* has been too much depreciated, *Samson Agonistes* has in requital been too much admired. It could only be by long prejudice, and the bigotry of learning, that Milton could prefer the ancient tragedies, with their encumbrance of a chorus, to the exhibitions of the French and English stages; and it is only by a blind confidence in the reputation of Milton that a drama can be praised in which the intermediate parts have neither cause nor consequence, neither hasten nor retard the catastrophe.

In this tragedy are however many particular beauties, many just sentiments and striking lines; but it wants that power of attracting the attention which a well-connected plan produces.

Milton would not have excelled in dramatic writing; he knew human nature only in the gross, and had never studied the shades of character, nor the combinations of concurring, or the perplexity of contending, passions. He had read much, and knew what books could teach, but had mingled little in the world, and was deficient in the knowledge which experience must confer.

Through all his greater works there prevails an uniform peculiarity of *diction,* a mode and cast of expression which bears little resemblance to that of any former writer, and which is so far removed from common use that an unlearned reader, when he first opens his book, finds himself surprised by a new language.

This novelty has been, by those who can find nothing wrong in Milton, imputed to his laborious endeavours after words suitable to the grandeur of his ideas. *Our language,* says Addison, *sunk under him.* But the truth is that, both in prose and verse, he had formed his style by a perverse and pedantic principle. He was desirous to use English words with a foreign idiom. This in all his prose is discovered and condemned; for there judgment operates freely, neither softened by the beauty nor awed by the dignity of his thoughts; but such is the power of his poetry, that his call is obeyed without resistance, the reader feels himself in captivity to a higher and nobler mind, and criticism sinks in admiration.

Milton's style was not modified by his subject; what is shown with greater extent in *Paradise Lost* may be found in *Comus.* One source of his peculiarity was his familiarity with the Tuscan poets; the disposition of his words is, I think, frequently Italian, perhaps sometimes combined with other tongues. Of him, at last may be said what Jonson[16] says of Spenser,[17] that *he wrote no language,* but has formed what Butler calls a *Babylonish dialect,*[18] in itself harsh and barbarous, but made, by exalted genius and extensive learning, the vehicle of so much instruction and so much pleasure that, like other lovers, we find grace in its deformity.

Whatever be the faults of his diction, he cannot want the praise of copiousness and variety: he was master of his language in its full extent; and has selected the melodious words with such diligence, that from his book alone the Art of English Poetry might be learned.

After his diction, something must be said of his *versification.* The *measure,* he says, *is the English heroic verse without rhyme.* Of this mode he had many examples among the Italians, and some in his own country. The Earl of Surrey is said to have translated one of Virgil's books without rhyme,[19] and, besides our tragedies, a few short poems had appeared in blank verse, particularly one tending to reconcile the nation to Raleigh's wild attempt upon Guiana,[20] and probably written by Raleigh himself. These petty performances cannot be supposed to have much influenced Milton, who more probably took his hint from Trissino's *Italia Liberata,*[21] and, finding blank verse easier than rhyme, was desirous of persuading himself that it is better.

Rhyme, he says, and says truly, *is no necessary adjunct of true poetry.* But, perhaps, of poetry as a mental operation, metre or music is no necessary adjunct: it is, however, by the music of metre that poetry has been discriminated in all languages; and, in languages melodiously constructed with a due proportion of long and short syllables, metre is sufficient. But one language cannot communicate its rules to another: where metre is scanty and imperfect, some help is necessary. The music of the English heroic line strikes the ear so faintly, that it is easily lost, unless all the syllables of every line co-operate together; this co-operation can be only obtained by the preservation of every verse unmingled with another as a distinct system of sounds; and this distinctness is obtained and preserved by the artifice of rhyme. The variety of pauses, so much boasted by the lovers of blank verse, changes the measures of an English poet to the periods of a declaimer; and there are only a few happy readers of Milton who enable their audience to perceive where the lines end or begin. *Blank verse,* said an ingenious critic, *seems to be verse only to the eye.*

Poetry may subsist without rhyme, but English poetry will not often please; nor can rhyme ever be safely spared but where the subject is able to

[16] Ben Jonson (1572–1637), English playwright and lyric poet.

[17] Edmund Spenser (1552?–1599), English poet, best known as author of *The Faerie Queene.* Ben Jonson was referring to the many archaic expressions used in that poem.

[18] The phrase is used by Samuel Butler (1612–1680) in *Hudibras,* a mock-heroic attack on the Puritans.

[19] A translation of a portion of Virgil's *Aeneid* by Henry Howard, Earl of Surrey (c. 1517–1547), may have been the first appearance of blank verse in English.

[20] The poem in question, *De Guiana Carmen,* was almost certainly not written by Sir Walter Raleigh (c. 1552–1618), courtier, poet, adventurer.

[21] Gian Giorgio Trissino (1478–1550) completed his unrhymed epic poem *Italia liberata dai Goti* in 1547.

support itself. Blank verse makes some approach to that which is called the *lapidary style;* has neither the easiness of prose, nor the melody of numbers, and therefore tires by long continuance. Of the Italian writers without rhyme, whom Milton alleges as precedents, not one is popular; what reason could urge in its defense has been confuted by the ear.

But whatever be the advantage of rhyme, I cannot prevail on myself to wish that Milton had been a rhymer; for I cannot wish his work to be other than it is; yet, like other heroes, he is to be admired rather than imitated. He that thinks himself capable of astonishing may write blank verse; but those that hope only to please must condescend to rhyme.

The highest praise of genius is original invention. Milton cannot be said to have contrived the structure of an epic poem, and therefore owes reverence to that vigour and amplitude of mind to which all generations must be indebted for the art of poetical narration, for the texture of the fable, the variation of incidents, the interposition of dialogue, and all the stratagems that surprise and enchain attention. But, of all the borrowers from Homer, Milton is perhaps the least indebted. He was naturally a thinker for himself, confident of his own abilities, and disdainful of help or hindrance: he did not refuse admission to the thoughts or images of his predecessors, but he did not seek them. From his contemporaries he neither courted nor received support; there is in his writings nothing by which the pride of other authors might be gratified, or favour gained; no exchange of praise, nor solicitation of support. His great works were performed under discountenance, and in blindness, but difficulties vanished at his touch; he was born for whatever is arduous; and his work is not the greatest of heroic poems, only because it is not the first.

Samuel Johnson

THE METAPHYSICAL POETS

. . . Cowley, like other poets who have written with narrow views, and, instead of tracing intellectual pleasures in the mind of man, paid their court to temporary prejudices, has been at one time too much praised, and too much neglected at another.

Wit, like all other things subject by their nature to the choice of man, has its changes and fashions, and at different times takes different forms. About the beginning of the seventeenth century appeared a race of writers that may be termed the *metaphysical poets*,[1] of whom, in a criticism on the works of Cowley, it is not improper to give some account.

The metaphysical poets were men of learning, and to show their learning was their whole endeavour; but unluckily resolving to show it in rhyme, instead of writing poetry they only wrote verses, and very often such verses as stood the trial of the finger better than of the ear; for the modulation was so imperfect, that they were only found to be verses by counting the syllables.

If the father of criticism[2] has rightly denominated poetry τέχνη μιμητική, *an imitative art*, these writers will, without great wrong, lose their right to the name of poets, for they cannot be said to have imitated anything; they neither copied nature nor life, neither painted the forms of matter, nor represented the operations of intellect.

Those, however, who deny them to be poets, allow them to be wits. Dryden[3] confesses of himself and his contemporaries, that they fall below Donne in wit, but maintains that they surpass him in poetry.

If wit be well described by Pope,[4] as being "that which has been often

From the book *Lives of the English Poets*, Volume I, by Samuel Johnson ("The Life of Cowley"). London: J. M. Dent & Sons, Ltd.; New York: E. P. Dutton & Co., Inc. Everyman's Library Edition. Used by permission of J. M. Dent & Sons, Ltd., and E. P. Dutton & Co., Inc.

[1] Since Johnson's time different critics have included different poets among the "metaphysicals"; most lists include John Donne (1572–1631); George Herbert (1593–1633); Richard Crashaw (1612–1649); and Andrew Marvell (1621–1678). These poets and others, some of whom are discussed by Johnson below, did not comprise a "school" in their own eyes; they are grouped together by critics who believe that the poems of these writers have distinctive traits in common.

[2] That is, Aristotle.

[3] For John Dryden, see p. 88 of this volume.

[4] Alexander Pope (1688–1744). Johnson paraphrases the following from Pope's *An Essay on Criticism:*

thought, but was never before so well expressed," they certainly never attained, nor ever sought it; for they endeavoured to be singular in their thoughts, and were careless of their diction. But Pope's account of wit is undoubtedly erroneous: he depresses it below its natural dignity, and reduces it from strength of thought to happiness of language.

If by a more noble and more adequate conception that be considered as wit which is at once natural and new, that which, though not obvious, is, upon its first production, acknowledged to be just; if it be that which he that never found it wonders how he missed, to wit of this kind the metaphysical poets have seldom risen. Their thoughts are often new, but seldom natural; they are not obvious, but neither are they just; and the reader, far from wondering that he missed them, wonders more frequently by what perverseness of industry they were ever found.

But wit, abstracted from its effects upon the hearer, may be more rigorously and philosophically considered as a kind of *discordia concors*,[5] a combination of dissimilar images, or discovery of occult resemblances in things apparently unlike. Of wit, thus defined, they have more than enough. The most heterogeneous ideas are yoked by violence together; nature and art are ransacked for illustrations, comparisons, and allusions; their learning instructs, and their subtlety surprises; but the reader commonly thinks his improvement dearly bought, and, though he sometimes admires, is seldom pleased.

From this account of their compositions it will be readily inferred that they were not successful in representing or moving the affections. As they were wholly employed on something unexpected and surprising, they had no regard to that uniformity of sentiment which enables us to conceive and to excite the pains and the pleasure of other minds: they never inquired what, on any occasion, they should have said or done, but wrote rather as beholders than partakers of human nature; as beings looking upon good and evil, impassive and at leisure; as Epicurean deities,[6] making remarks on the actions of men, and the vicissitudes of life, without interest and without emotion. Their courtship was void of fondness, and their lamentation of sorrow. Their wish was only to say what they hoped had been never said before.

Nor was the sublime more within their reach than the pathetic; for they never attempted that comprehension and expanse of thought which at once fills the whole mind, and of which the first effect is sudden astonishment, and the second rational admiration. Sublimity is produced by aggregation, and littleness by dispersion. Great thoughts are always general, and consist in positions not limited by exceptions, and in descriptions not descending to minuteness. It is with great propriety that subtlety, which in its original import means exility[7] of particles, is taken in its metaphorical meaning for nicety of distinction. Those writers who lay on the watch for novelty could have little hope of greatness; for great things cannot have escaped former observation. Their attempts were al-

---

True Wit is Nature to advantage dress'd,
What oft was thought, but ne'er so well express'd.

[5] A "concordant discord."

[6] In the philosophy of Epicurus (341–270 B.C.), the gods are said to be as Johnson here describes them.

[7] That is, smallness, fineness, tenuity.

ways analytic; they broke every image into fragments; and could no more repre-sent, by their slender conceits and laboured particularities, the prospects of nature, or the scenes of life, than he who dissects a sunbeam with a prism can exhibit the wide effulgence of a summer noon.

What they wanted however of the sublime, they endeavoured to supply by hyperbole; their amplification had no limits; they left not only reason but fancy behind them; and produced combinations of confused magnificence, that not only could not be credited, but could not be imagined.

Yet great labour, directed by great abilities, is never wholly lost: if they fre-quently threw away their wit upon false conceits, they likewise sometimes struck out unexpected truth; if their conceits were far-fetched, they were often worth the carriage. To write on their plan, it was at least necessary to read and think. No man could be born a metaphysical poet, nor assume the dignity of a writer, by descriptions copied from descriptions, by imitations borrowed from imitations, by traditional imagery, and hereditary similes, by readiness of rhyme, and volubility of syllables.

In perusing the works of this race of authors, the mind is exercised either by recollection or inquiry; either something already learned is to be retrieved, or something new is to be examined. If their greatness seldom elevates, their acute-ness often surprises; if the imagination is not always gratified, at least the powers of reflection and comparison are employed; and in the mass of materials which ingenious absurdity has thrown together, genuine wit and useful knowl-edge may be sometimes found buried perhaps in grossness of expression, but useful to those who know their value; and such as, when they are expanded to perspicuity, and polished to elegance, may give lustre to works which have more propriety though less copiousness of sentiment.

This kind of writing, which was, I believe, borrowed from Marino[8] and his followers, had been recommended by the example of Donne, a man of a very extensive and various knowledge; and by Jonson,[9] whose manner resembled that of Donne more in the ruggedness of his lines than in the cast of his senti-ments.

When their reputation was high, they had undoubtedly more imitators than time has left behind. Their immediate successors, of whom any remembrance can be said to remain, were Suckling, Waller, Denham, Cowley, Cleveland,[10] and Milton. Denham and Waller sought another way to fame, by improving the harmony of our numbers. Milton tried the metaphysic style only in his lines upon Hobson the Carrier.[11] Cowley adopted it, and excelled his predecessors, having as much sentiment and more music. Suckling neither improved versifica-tion, nor abounded in conceits. The fashionable style remained chiefly with Cowley; Suckling could not reach it, and Milton disdained it.

[8] Giovanni Battista Marini, or Marino (1569–1625), Italian poet, of whom Byron said, "No one has ever denied genius to Marino, who corrupted not merely the taste of Italy, but that of all Europe, for nearly a century."

[9] Ben Jonson (1572–1637).

[10] Sir John Suckling (1609–1642); Edmund Waller (1606–1687); Sir John Denham (1615–1669); John Cleveland (1613–1658).

[11] Milton wrote two poems on Thomas Hobson, who drove a weekly coach between London and Cambridge until shortly before his death in 1631, one year before Milton received an M.A. degree at Cambridge.

Critical remarks are not easily understood without examples; and I have therefore collected instances of the modes of writing by which this species of poets, for poets they were called by themselves and their admirers, was eminently distinguished.[12]

As the authors of this race were perhaps more desirous of being admired than understood, they sometimes drew their conceits from recesses of learning not very much frequented by common readers of poetry. Thus Cowley on *Knowledge:*

> The sacred tree midst the fair orchard grew;
>> The phoenix Truth did on it rest,
>> And built his perfum'd nest,
> That right Porphyrian tree which did true logic show.
>> Each leaf did learned notions give,
>> And th' apples were demonstrative:
> So clear their colour and divine,
> The very shade they cast did other lights outshine

On Anacreon[13] continuing a lover in his old age:

> Love was with thy life entwin'd,
> Close as heat with fire is join'd,
> A powerful brand prescrib'd the date
> Of thine, like Meleager's fate,
> Th' antiperistasis of age
> More inflam'd thy amorous rage.
>> *Elegy upon Anacreon.*

In the following verses we have an allusion to a Rabbinical opinion concerning Manna:

> Variety I ask not: give me one
> To live perpetually upon.
> The person Love does to us fit,
> Like manna, has the taste of all in it.

Thus Donne shows his medicinal knowledge in some encomiastic verses:

> In every thing there naturally grows
> A balsamum to keep it fresh and new,
>> If 't were not injur'd by extrinsique blows;
> Your birth and beauty are this balm in you.
>> But you, of learning and religion,
> And virtue, and such ingredients, have made
>> A mithridate, whose operation
> Keeps off, or cures what can be done or said.
>> DONNE, *To the Countess of Bedford.*

---

[12] Johnson's principle of exemplification is, of course, unexceptional, but in this essay his practice of it runs rather to excess and some of the many examples he collected have been omitted. These omissions are indicated by asterisks.
[13] Greek lyric poet of the sixth cent. B.C.

Though the following lines of Donne, on the last night of the year, have something in them too scholastic, they are not inelegant:

> This twilight of two years, not past nor next,
>   Some emblem is of me, or I of this,
> Who, meteor-like, of stuff and form perplext,
>   Whose what and where in disputation is,
>   If I should call me anything, should miss.
> I sum the years and me, and find me not
>   Debtor to th' old, nor creditor to th' new;
> That cannot say, my thanks I have forgot,
>   Nor trust I this with hopes; and yet scarce true
>   This bravery is, since these times show'd me you.
>   DONNE, *To the Countess of Bedford.*

Yet more abstruse and profound is Donne's reflection upon man as a microcosm:

> If men be worlds, there is in every one
> Something to answer in some proportion
> All the world's riches: and in good men, this
> Virtue, our form's form, and our soul's soul is.

Of thoughts so far fetched, as to be not only unexpected but unnatural, all their books are full.

> *To a Lady, who made posies for rings*
>
> They, who above do various circles find,
> Say, like a ring th' aequator heaven does bind.
> When heaven shall be adorn'd by thee,
> (Which then more heaven than 'tis, will be,)
> 'Tis thou must write the poesy there,
> For it wanteth one as yet,
> Though the sun pass through 't twice a year,
> The sun, who is esteem'd the god of wit.
>   COWLEY.

The difficulties which have been raised about identity in philosophy, are by Cowley with still more perplexity applied to love:

> Five years ago (says story) I lov'd you,
> For which you call me most inconstant now:
> Pardon me, madam, you mistake the man;
> For I am not the same that I was then;
> No flesh is now the same 'twas then in me,
> And that my mind is chang'd yourself may see.
> The same thoughts to retain still, and intents,
> Were more inconstant far: for accidents
> Must of all things most strangely inconstant prove,
> If from one subject they t' another move:
> My members then, the father members were

From whence these take their birth, which now are here.
If then this body love what th' other did,
'Twere incest, which by nature is forbid.

Inconstancy.

*   *   *

The tears of lovers are always of great poetical account; but Donne has extended them into worlds. If the lines are not easily understood, they may be read again:

On a round ball
A workman, that hath copies by, can lay
An Europe, Afric, and an Asia,
And quickly make that, which was nothing, All.
So doth each tear,
Which thee doth wear,
A globe, yea would, by that impression grow,
Till thy tears mixt with mine do overflow
This world, by waters sent from thee my heaven dissolved so.

A Valediction of Weeping.

On reading the following lines, the reader may perhaps cry out—*Confusion worse confounded:*

Here lies a she sun, and a he moon there,
She gives the best light to his sphere,
Or each is both, and all, and so
They unto one another nothing owe.

DONNE, *Epithalamion on the Count Palatine, etc.*

Who but Donne would have thought that a good man is a telescope?

Though God be our true glass through which we see
All, since the being of all things is he,
Yet are the trunks, which do to us derive
Things in proportion fit, by perspective
Deeds of good men; for by their living here,
Virtues, indeed remote, seem to be near.

Who would imagine it possible that in a very few lines so many remote ideas could be brought together?

Since 'tis my doom, Love's undershrieve,
Why this reprieve?
Why doth my she advowson fly
Incumbency?
To sell thyself dost thou intend
By candle's end,
And hold the contract thus in doubt,
Life's taper out?
Think but how soon the market fails,
Your sex lives faster than the males;

And if to measure age's span,
The sober Julian were th' account of man,
Whilst you live by the fleet Gregorian.
      CLEVELAND, *To Julia to expedite her Promise.*

Of enormous and disgusting hyperboles, these may be examples:

By every wind that comes this way,
      Send me at least a sigh or two,
Such and so many I'll repay
      As shall themselves make winds to get to you.
                                          COWLEY.

In tears I'll waste these eyes,
      By Love so vainly fed;
So lust of old the Deluge punished.
                                          COWLEY.

All arm'd in brass, the richest dress of war,
(A dismal glorious sight,) he shone afar.
The sun himself started with sudden fright,
To see his beams return so dismal bright.
                                          COWLEY.

          *   *   *

As they sought only for novelty, they did not much inquire whether their allusions were to things high or low, elegant or gross; whether they compared the little to the great, or the great to the little.

Physic and Chirurgery for a Lover

Gently, ah gently, madam, touch
      The wound which you yourself have made;
That pain must needs be very much,
      Which makes me of your hand afraid.
Cordials of pity give me now,
      For I too weak for purgings grow.
                                    COWLEY, *Counsel.*

The World and a Clock

Mahol, th' inferior world's fantastic face
Thro' all the turns of matter's maze did trace,
Great Nature's well-set clock in pieces took;
On all the springs and smallest wheels did look
Of life and motion, and with equal art
Made up again the whole of every part.
                              COWLEY, *Davideis,* book i.

A coal-pit has not often found its poet; but that it may not want its due honour, Cleveland has parallelled it with the sun:

The moderate value of our guiltless ore
Makes no man atheist, nor no woman whore;
Yet why should hallow'd vestal's sacred shrine
Deserve more honour than a flaming mine?
These pregnant wombs of heat would fitter be,
Than a few embers, for a deity.
Had he our pits, the Persian would admire
No sun, but warm 's devotion at our fire:
He'd leave the trotting whipster, and prefer
Our profound Vulcan 'bove that waggoner.
For wants he heat, or light? or would have store,
Of both? 'tis here: and what can suns give more?
Nay, what's the sun but, in a different name,
A coal-pit rampant, or a mine on flame?
Then let this truth reciprocally run,
The sun's heaven's coalery, and coals our sun.

CLEVELAND, *News from Newcastle.*

Death, a Voyage

No family
E'er rigg'd a soul for heaven's discovery,
With whom more venturers might boldly dare
Venture their stakes, with him in joy to share.

DONNE

Their thoughts and expressions were sometimes grossly absurd, and such as no figures or licence can reconcile to the understanding.

*   *   *

A Lover's Heart, a hand grenado

Wo to her stubborn heart, if once mine come
  Into the self-same room,
    'Twill tear and blow up all within,
Like a grenado shot into a magazine.
Then shall Love keep the ashes, and torn parts,
  Of both our broken hearts:
    Shall out of both one new one make;
From her's th' allay; from mine, the metal take..

COWLEY, *The Given Heart.*

*   *   *

They were sometimes indelicate and disgusting. Cowley thus apostrophises beauty:

—— Thou tyrant, which leav'st no man free!
Thou subtle thief, from whom nought safe can be!
Thou murtherer, which hast kill'd, and devil, which woulds't damn me!

COWLEY, *Beauty.*

Thus he addresses his mistress:

> Thou who, in many a propriety
> So truly art the sun to me,
> Add one more likeness, which I'm sure you can,
> And let me and my sun beget a man.
>
> COWLEY, The Parting.

Thus he represents the meditations of a lover:

> Though in thy thoughts scarce any tracts have been
> So much as of original sin,
> Such charms thy beauty wears as might
> Desires in dying confest saints excite.
>   Thou with strange adultery
> Dost in each breast a brothel keep;
>   Awake, all men do lust for thee,
> And some enjoy thee when they sleep.
>
> COWLEY.

*   *   *

They were not always strictly curious, whether the opinions from which they drew their illustrations were true; it was enough that they were popular. Bacon remarks, that some falsehoods are continued by tradition, because they supply commodious allusions.

> It gave a piteous groan, and so it broke:
> In vain it something would have spoke:
> The love within too strong for 't was,
> Like poison put into a Venice-glass.
>
> COWLEY, The Heartbreaking.

In forming descriptions, they looked out, not for images, but for conceits. Night has been a common subject which poets have contended to adorn. Dryden's *Night* is well known; Donne's is as follows:

> Thou seest me here at midnight, now all rest:
> Time's dead low-water; when all minds divest
> To-morrow's business, when the labourers have
> Such rest in bed, that their last church-yard grave,
> Subject to change, will scarce be a type of this,
> Now when the client, whose last hearing is
> To-morrow, sleeps; when the condemned man,
> Who, when he opes his eyes, must shut them then
> Again by death, although sad watch he keep,
> Doth practise dying by a little sleep,
> Thou at this midnight seest me.

It must be however confessed of these writers, that if they are upon common subjects often unnecessarily and unpoetically subtle, yet where scholastic speculation can be properly admitted, their copiousness and acuteness may justly be admired. What Cowley has written upon Hope shows an unequalled fertility of invention:

> Hope, whose weak being ruin'd is,
>   Alike if it succeed, and if it miss;
> Whom good or ill does equally confound,
>   And both the horns of Fate's dilemma wound;
>   Vain shadow! which dost vanquish quite,
>   Both at full noon and perfect night!
>   The stars have not a possibility
>   Of blessing thee;
> If things then from their end we happy call,
> 'Tis Hope is the most hopeless thing of all.
>   Hope, thou bold taster of delight,
>   Who, whilst thou should'st but taste, devour'st it quite!
>   Thou bring'st us an estate, yet leav'st us poor,
>   By clogging it with legacies before!
>   The joys which we entire should wed,
>   Come deflower'd virgins to our bed;
> Good fortunes without gain imported be,
>   Such mighty custom's paid to thee:
> For joy, like wine kept close, does better taste,
> If it take air before its spirits waste.
>
> COWLEY, *Against Hope.*

To the following comparison of a man that travels, and his wife that stays at home, with a pair of compasses, it may be doubted whether absurdity or ingenuity has the better claim:

> Our two souls therefore, which are one,
>   Though I must go, endure not yet
> A breach, but an expansion,
>   Like gold to airy thinness beat.
> If they be two, they are two so
>   As stiff twin-compasses are two;
> Thy soul the fixt foot, makes no show
>   To move, but doth, if th' other do.
> And though it in the centre sit,
>   Yet, when the other far doth roam,
> It leans, and hearkens after it,
>   And grows erect, as that comes home.
> Such wilt thou be to me, who must
>   Like th' other foot obliquely run.
> Thy firmness makes my circle just,
>   And makes me end, where I begun.
>
> DONNE, *A Valediction forbidding Mourning.*

In all these examples it is apparent, that whatever is improper or vicious is produced by a voluntary deviation from nature in pursuit of something new and strange; and that the writers fail to give delight, by their desire of exciting admiration.

*   *   *

Friedrich Schiller

OF THE CAUSE OF THE PLEASURE WE DERIVE FROM TRAGIC OBJECTS

The place of Friedrich Schiller (1759–1805) in German literature is second only to that of Goethe, the close friend of his last decade and his collaborator in many cultural ventures. His first fame came to him through his achievement as a dramatist and lyric poet; he was highly regarded as a historian; at the present time, it is perhaps chiefly his criticism that engages attention. Born in Marbach, in the German State of Württemberg, the son of an army officer, the young Schiller would have prepared for a career in the church had not the Duke of Württemberg obliged him to attend the military academy he had established at his castle and to engage—at the age of thirteen!—in the study of law. Two years later he was required to change his course of study to that of medicine. In 1780, at the age of twenty-one, he was posted to a regiment at Stuttgart as its surgeon. The next year, to the intense displeasure of the Duke, he published his first play, *The Robbers,* which, the year following, was produced at Mannheim with great success. Escaping from the tyranny of the Duke, Schiller devoted the next years to writing for the theater, becoming one of the leaders of the German literary movement known as *Sturm und Drang* (Storm and Stress) which had as its informing ideal the daemonic energies of the individual as they put themselves into opposition to the conventional, static, and repressive order of society. This first period of Schiller's dramatic production came to an end in 1787. The work of his second dramatic period, beginning in 1798 and going on to the close of his life, was in a different mode, stricter both in its form and in its moral and social speculation. In the decade between the two periods, Schiller devoted himself to lyric poetry and, most especially, to aesthetic theory. His masterpiece in the latter genre is the *Letters on the Aesthetic Education of Man* (1795) in which he derives the principle, and the hope, of political freedom from the human instinct for play, which expresses itself in the creation of, and the response to, art. A defining characteristic of the Romantic attitude to art was the belief that art was essential to man's moral development, and Schiller's influence in promulgating this belief—in England it is especially apparent in Coleridge's thought—was decisive.

From *Schiller's Works: Essays Aesthetical and Philosophical.* Bohn's Libraries, 1875.

Whatever pains some modern aesthetics give themselves to establish, contrary to general belief, that the arts of imagination and of feeling have not pleasure for their object, and to defend them against this degrading accusation, this belief will not cease: it reposes upon a solid foundation, and the fine arts would renounce with a bad grace the beneficent mission which has in all times been assigned to them, to accept the new employment to which it is generously proposed to raise them. Without troubling themselves whether they lower themselves in proposing our pleasure as object, they become rather proud of the advantages of reaching immediately an aim never attained except mediately in other routes followed by the activity of the human mind. That the aim of nature, with relation to man, is the happiness of man,—although he ought of himself, in his moral conduct, to take no notice of this aim,—is what, I think, cannot be doubted in general by any one who admits that nature has an aim. Thus the fine arts have the same aim as nature, or rather as the Author of nature, namely, to spread pleasure and render people happy. It procures for us in play what at other more austere sources of good to man we extract only with difficulty. It lavishes as a pure gift that which elsewhere is the price of many hard efforts. With what labour, what application, do we not pay for the pleasures of the understanding; with what painful sacrifices the approbation of reason; with what hard privations the joys of sense! And if we abuse these pleasures, with what a succession of evils do we expiate excess! Art alone supplies an enjoyment which requires no appreciable effort, which costs no sacrifice, and which we need not repay with repentance. But who could class the merit of charming in this manner with the poor merit of amusing? who would venture to deny the former of these two aims of the fine arts solely because they have a tendency higher than the latter.

The praiseworthy object of pursuing everywhere moral good as the supreme aim, which has already brought forth in art so much mediocrity, has caused also in theory a similar prejudice. To assign to the fine arts a really elevated position, to conciliate for them the favour of the State, the veneration of all men, they are pushed beyond their true domain, and a vocation is imposed upon them contrary to their nature. It is supposed that a great service is awarded them by substituting for a frivolous aim,—that of charming—a moral aim; and their influence upon morality, which is so apparent, necessarily militates in favour of this pretension. It is found illogical that the art, which contributes in so great a measure to the development of all that is most elevated in man, should produce but accessorily this effect, and make its chief object an aim so vulgar as we imagine pleasure to be. But this apparent contradiction it would be very easy to conciliate if we had a good theory of pleasure, and a complete system of aesthetic philosophy.

It would result from this theory that a free pleasure, as that which the fine arts procure for us, rests wholly upon moral conditions, and all the moral faculties of man are exercised in it. It would further result that this pleasure is an aim which can never be attained but by moral means, and consequently that art, to tend and perfectly attain to pleasure, as to a real aim, must follow the road of healthy morals. Thus it is perfectly indifferent for the dignity of art whether its aim should be a moral aim, or whether it should reach only through moral means; for in both cases it has always to do with the morality, and must be rigorously in unison with the sentiment of duty; but for the perfection of art, it is by no means indifferent which of the two should be the aim and which the means. If it is the aim that is moral, art loses all that by which it is powerful,—I mean its freedom, and that which gives it so much influence over us—the charm of pleasure. The play which recreates is changed into serious occupation, and yet it is precisely in recreating us that art can the better complete the great affair—the moral work. It cannot have a salutary influence upon the morals but in exercising its highest aesthetic action, and it can only produce the aesthetic effect in its highest degree in fully exercising its liberty.

It is certain, besides, that all pleasure, the moment it flows from a moral source, renders man morally better, and then the effect in its turn becomes cause. The pleasure we find in what is beautiful, or touching, or sublime, strengthens our moral sentiments, as the pleasure we find in kindness, in love, &c., strengthens these inclinations. And just as contentment of mind is the sure lot of the morally excellent man, so moral excellence willingly accompanies satisfaction of heart. Thus the moral efficacity of art is, not only because it employs moral means in order to charm us, but also because even the pleasure which it procures us is a means of morality.

There are as many means by which art can attain its aim as there are in general sources from which a free pleasure for the mind can flow. I call a free pleasure that which brings into play the spiritual forces—reason and imagination —and which awakens in us a sentiment by the representation of an idea, in contradistinction to physical or sensuous pleasure, which places our soul under the dependence of the blind forces of nature, and where sensation is immediately awakened in us by a physical cause. Sensual pleasure is the only one excluded from the domain of the fine arts; and the talent of exciting this kind of pleasure could never raise itself to the dignity of an art, except in the case where the sensual impressions are ordered, reinforced or moderated, after a plan which is the production of art, and which is recognized by representation. But, in this case even, that alone here can merit the name of art which is the object of a free pleasure, I mean good taste in the regulation, which pleases our understanding, and not physical charms themselves, which alone flatter our sensibility.

The general source of all pleasure, even of sensual pleasure, is propriety, the conformity with the aim. Pleasure is sensual when this propriety is manifested by means of some necessary law of nature which has for physical result the sensation of pleasure. Thus the movement of the blood, and of the animal life, when in conformity with the aim of nature, produces in certain organs, or in the entire organism, corporeal pleasure with all its varieties and all its modes. We feel this conformity by the means of agreeable sensation, but we arrive at no representation of it, either clear or confused.

Pleasure is free when we represent to ourselves the conformability, and when the sensation that accompanies this representation is agreeable. Thus all the representations by which we have notice that there is propriety and harmony between the end and the means, are for us the sources of free pleasure, and consequently can be employed to this end by the fine arts. Thus, all the representations can be placed under one of these heads: the good, the true, the perfect, the beautiful, the touching, the sublime. The good especially occupies our reason; the true and perfect, our intelligence; the beautiful interests both the intelligence and the imagination; the touching and the sublime, the reason and the imagination. It is true that we also take pleasure in the charm [*Reiz*] or the power called out by action from play, but art uses charm only to accompany the higher enjoyments which the idea of propriety gives to us. Considered in itself the charm or attraction is lost amid the sensations of life, and art disdains it together with all merely sensual pleasures.

We could not establish a classification of the fine arts only upon the difference of the sources from which each of them draws the pleasure which it affords us; for in the same class of the fine arts many sorts of pleasures may enter, and often all together. But in as far as a certain sort of pleasure is pursued as a principal aim, we can make of it, if not a specific character of a class properly so called, at least the principle and the tendency of a class in the works of art. Thus, for example, we could take the arts which, above all, satisfy the intelligence and imagination—consequently, those which have as chief object the true, the perfect, and the beautiful—and unite them under the name of fine arts (arts of taste, arts of intelligence); those on the other hand, which especially occupy the imagination and the reason, and which, in consequence, have for principal object the good, the sublime, and the touching, could be limited in a particular class under the denomination of touching arts (arts of sentiment, arts of the heart). Without doubt it is impossible to separate absolutely the touching from the beautiful, but the beautiful can perfectly subsist without the touching. Thus, although we are not authorised to base upon this difference of principle a rigorous classification of the liberal arts, it can at least serve to determine with more of precision the criterion, and prevent the confusion in which we are inevitably involved, when drawing up laws of aesthetic things, we confound two absolutely different domains, as that of the touching and that of the beautiful.

The touching and the sublime resemble in this point, that both one and the other produce a pleasure by a feeling at first of displeasure, and that consequently (pleasure proceeding from suitability, and displeasure from the contrary) they give us a feeling of suitability which presupposes an unsuitability.

The feeling of the sublime is composed in part of the feeling of our feebleness, of our impotence to embrace an object; and, on the other side, of the feeling of our moral power—of this superior faculty which fears no obstacle, no limit, and which subdues spiritually that even to which our physical forces give way. The object of the sublime thwarts, then, our physical power; and this contrariety (impropriety) must necessarily excite a displeasure in us. But it is, at the same time, an occasion to recall to our conscience another faculty which is in us—a faculty which is even superior to the objects before which our imagination yields. In consequence, a sublime object, precisely because it thwarts the senses, is suitable with relation to reason, and it gives to us a joy by means of a higher faculty, at the same time that it wounds us in an inferior one.

The touching, in its proper sense, designates this mixed sensation, into which enters at the same time suffering and the pleasure that we find in suffering. Thus we can only feel this kind of emotion in the case of a personal misfortune, only when the grief that we feel is sufficiently tempered to leave some place for that impression of pleasure that would be felt by a compassionate spectator. The loss of a great good prostrates for the time, and the remembrance itself of the grief will make us experience emotion after a year. The feeble man is always the prey of his grief; the hero and the sage, whatever the misfortune that strikes them, never experience more than emotion.

Emotion, like the sentiment of the sublime, is composed of two affections—grief and pleasure. There is, then, at the bottom a propriety, here as well as there, and under this propriety a contradiction. Thus it seems that it is a contradiction in nature that man, who is not born to suffer, is nevertheless a prey to suffering, and this contradiction hurts us. But the evil which this contradiction does us is a propriety with regard to our reasonable nature in general, insomuch as this evil solicits us to act: it is a propriety also with regard to human society; consequently, even displeasure, which excites in us this contradiction, ought necessarily to make us experience a sentiment of pleasure, because this displeasure is a propriety. To determine in an emotion if it is pleasure or displeasure which triumphs, we must ask ourselves if it is the idea of impropriety or that of propriety which affects us the more deeply. That can depend either on the number of the aims reached or abortive, or on their connection with the final aim of all.

The suffering of the virtuous man moves us more painfully than that of the perverse man, because in the first case there is contradiction not only to the general destiny of man, which is happiness, but also to this other particular principle, which is, that virtue renders happy; whilst in the second case there is contradiction only with regard to the end of man in general. Reciprocally, the happiness of the wicked also offends us much more than the misfortune of the good man, because we find in it a double contradiction: in the first place vice itself, and, in the second place, the recompense of vice.

There is also this other consideration, that virtue is much more able to recompense itself than vice, when it triumphs, is to punish itself; and it is precisely for this that the virtuous man in misfortune would much more remain faithful to the cultus of virtue than the perverse man would dream of converting himself in prosperity.

But what is above all important in determining in the emotions the relation of pleasure and displeasure, is to compare the two ends—that which has been fulfilled and that which has been ignored—and to see which is the most considerable. There is no propriety which touches us so nearly as moral propriety, and no superior pleasure to that which we feel from it. Physical propriety could well be a problem, and a problem for ever unsolvable. Moral propriety is already demonstrated. It alone is founded upon our reasonable nature and upon internal necessity. It is our nearest interest, the most considerable, and, at the same time, the most easily recognised, because it is not determined by any external element but by an internal principle of our reason: it is the palladium of our liberty.

This moral propriety is never more vividly recognised than when it is found in conflict with another propriety, and still keeps the upper hand; then only the moral law awakens in full power, when we find it struggling against all the other forces of nature, and when all those forces lose in its presence their empire over a human soul. By these words, "the other forces of nature," we must understand all that is not moral force, all that is not subject to the supreme legislation of reason: that is to say, feelings, affections, instincts, passions, as well as physical necessity and destiny. The more redoubtable the adversary, the more glorious the victory; resistance alone brings out the strength of the force and renders it visible. It follows that the highest degree of moral consciousness can only exist in strife, and the highest moral pleasure is always accompanied by pain.

Consequently, the kind of poetry which secures us a high degree of moral pleasure, must employ mixed feelings, and please us through pain or distress,— this is what tragedy does specially; and her realm embraces all that sacrifices a physical propriety to a moral one; or one moral propriety to a higher one. It might be possible, perhaps, to form a measure of moral pleasure, from the lowest to the highest degree, and to determine by this principle of propriety the degree of pain or pleasure experienced. Different orders of tragedy might be classified on the same principle, so as to form a complete exhaustive tabulation of them. Thus a tragedy being given, its place could be fixed, and its genus determined. Of this subject more will be said separately, in its proper place.

A few examples will show how far moral propriety commands physical propriety in our souls.

Hüon and Amanda[1] are both tied to the stake as martyrs, and free to choose life or death by the terrible ordeal of fire—they select the latter. What is it which gives such pleasure to us in this scene? Their position so conflicting with the smiling destiny they reject, the reward of misery given to virtue— all here awakens in us the feeling of impropriety: it ought to fill us with great distress. What is nature, and what are her ends and laws, if all this impropriety shows us moral propriety in its full light. We here see the triumph of the moral law, so sublime an experience for us that we might even hail the calamity which elicits it. For harmony in the world of moral freedom gives us infinitely more pleasure than all the discords in nature give us pain.

When Coriolanus,[2] obedient to duty as husband, son, and citizen, raises the siege of Rome, then almost conquered, withdrawing his army, and silencing his vengeance, he commits a very contradictory act evidently. He loses all the fruit of previous victories, he runs spontaneously to his ruin: yet what moral excellence and grandeur he offers! How noble to prefer any impropriety rather than wound moral sense; to violate natural interests and prudence in order to be in harmony with the higher moral law! Every sacrifice of a life is a contradiction, for life is the condition of all good; but in the light of morality the sacrifice of life is in a high degree proper, because life is not great in itself, but only as a means of accomplishing the moral law. If then the sacrifice of life be the way to do this, life must go. "It is not necessary for me to live, but it is necessary for Rome to be saved from famine," said Pompey,[3] when the

---

[1] Hüon and Amanda are characters in *Oberon* (1766), an epic by Christoph Martin Wieland (1733–1813), Canto XII, Stanzas 56 ff.

[2] The story of Coriolanus is told in Plutarch's *The Parallel Lives*. But see also Shakespeare's play *Coriolanus* (c. 1609).

[3] Cneius Pompeius, often called Pompey the Great (106–48 b.c.), Roman general and triumvir, whose biography was also written by Plutarch.

Romans embarked for Africa, and his friends begged him to defer his departure till the gale was over.

But the sufferings of a criminal are as charming to us tragically as those of a virtuous man; yet here is the idea of moral impropriety. The antagonism of his conduct to moral law, and the moral imperfection which such conduct presupposes, ought to fill us with pain. Here there is no satisfaction in the morality of his person, nothing to compensate for his misconduct. Yet both supply a valuable object for art; this phænomenon can easily be made to agree with what has been said.

We find pleasure not only in obedience to morality, but in the punishment given to its infraction. The pain resulting from moral imperfection agrees with its opposite, the satisfaction at conformity with the law. Repentance, even despair, have nobleness morally, and can only exist if an incorruptible sense of justice exists at the bottom of the criminal heart, and if conscience maintains its ground against self-love. Repentance comes by comparing our acts with the moral law, hence in the moment of repenting the moral law speaks loudly in man. Its power must be greater than the gain resulting from the crime as the infraction poisons the enjoyment. Now a state of mind where duty is sovereign is morally proper, and therefore a source of moral pleasure. What, then, sublimer than the heroic despair that tramples even life underfoot, because it cannot bear the judgment within? A good man sacrificing his life to conform to the moral law, or a criminal taking his own life because of the morality he has violated: in both cases our respect for the moral law is raised to the highest power. If there be any advantage it is in the case of the latter; for the good man may have been encouraged in his sacrifice by an approving conscience, thus detracting from his merit. Repentance and regret at past crimes show us some of the sublimest pictures of morality in active condition. A man who violates morality comes back to the moral law by repentance.

But moral pleasure is sometimes obtained only at the cost of moral pain. Thus one duty may clash with another. Let us suppose Coriolanus encamped with a Roman army before Antium or Corioli, and his mother a Volscian;[4] if her prayers move him to desist, we now no longer admire him. His obedience to his mother would be at strife with a higher duty, that of a citizen. The governor to whom the alternative is proposed, either of giving up the town or of seeing his son stabbed, decides at once on the latter, his duty as father being beneath that of citizen. At first our heart revolts at this conduct in a father, but we soon pass to admiration that moral instinct, even combined with inclination, could not lead reason astray in the empire where it commands. When Timoleon of Corinth[5] puts to death his beloved but ambitious brother Timophanes, he does it because his idea of duty to his country bids him to do so. The act here inspires horror and repulsion as against nature and the moral sense, but this feeling is soon succeeded by the highest admiration for his heroic virtue, pronouncing, in a tumultuous conflict of emotions, freely

[4] In fact, Coriolanus, although a Roman, was encamped with the Volscian army, of which he had become co-commander, outside Rome. His mother's pleas led him to withdraw his troops to Corioli, which, like Antium, was a Volscian city.

[5] Greek statesman and general of the fourth century B.C.

and calmly, with perfect rectitude. If we differ with Timoleon about his duty as a republican, this does not change our view. Nay, in those cases, where our understanding judges differently, we see all the more clearly how high we put moral propriety above all other.

But the judgments of men on this moral phænomenon are exceedingly various, and the reason of it is clear. Moral sense is common to all men, but differs in strength. To most men it suffices that an act be partially conformable with the moral law to make them obey it; and to make them condemn an action it must glaringly violate the law. But to determine the relation of moral duties with the highest principle of morals, requires an enlightened intelligence and an emancipated reason. Thus an action which to a few will be a supreme propriety, will seem to the crowd a revolting impropriety, though both judge morally; and hence the emotion felt at such actions is by no means uniform. To the mass the sublimest and highest is only exaggeration, because sublimity is perceived by reason, and all men have not the same share of it. A vulgar soul is oppressed or over-stretched by those sublime ideas, and the crowd sees dreadful disorder where a thinking mind sees the highest order.

This is enough about moral propriety as a principle of tragic emotion, and the pleasure it elicits. It must be added that there are cases where natural propriety also seems to charm our mind even at the cost of morality. Thus we are always pleased by the sequence of machinations of a perverse man, though his means and end are immoral. Such a man deeply interests us, and we tremble lest his plan fail, though we ought to wish it to do so. But this fact does not contradict what has been advanced about moral propriety, and the pleasure resulting from it.

Propriety, the reference of means to an end, is to us, in all cases, a source of pleasure, even disconnected with morality. We experience this pleasure unmixed, so long as we do not think of any moral end which disallows action before us. Animal instincts give us pleasure—as the industry of bees—without reference to morals; and in like manner human actions are a pleasure to us when we consider in them only the relation of means to ends. But if a moral principle be added to these, and impropriety be discovered, if the idea of moral agent comes in, a deep indignation succeeds our pleasure, which no intellectual propriety can remedy. We must not call to mind too vividly that Richard III, Iago, and Lovelace are *men*;[6] otherwise our sympathy for them infallibly turns into an opposite feeling. But, as daily experience teaches, we have the power to direct our attention to different sides of things; and pleasure, only possible through this abstraction, invites us to exercise it, and to prolong its exercise.

Yet it is not rare for intelligent perversity to secure our favour by being the means of procuring us the pleasure of moral propriety. The triumph of moral propriety will be great in proportion as the snares set by Lovelace for the virtue of Clarissa are formidable, and as the trials of an innocent victim by a cruel tyrant are severe. It is a pleasure to see the craft of a seducer foiled by

---

[6] Schiller is referring to the villainous King Richard III in Shakespeare's play (c. 1593); to Iago, the villain of Shakespeare's *Othello* (1604); to the Colonel Lovelace who pursues the heroine through the seven volumes of the novel by Samuel Richardson (1689–1761) which bears her name, *Clarissa Harlowe* (1748).

the omnipotence of the moral sense. On the other hand, we reckon as a sort of merit the victory of a malefactor over his moral sense, because it is the proof of a certain strength of mind, and intellectual propriety.

Yet this propriety in vice can never be the source of a perfect pleasure, except when it is humiliated by morality. In that case it is an essential part of our pleasure, because it brings moral sense into stronger relief. The last impression left on us by the author of Clarissa is a proof of this. The intellectual propriety in the plan of Lovelace is greatly surpassed by the rational propriety of Clarissa. This allows us to feel in full the satisfaction caused by both.

When the tragic poet has for object to awaken in us the feeling of moral propriety, and chooses his means skilfully for that end, he is sure to charm doubly the connoisseur, by moral and by natural propriety. The first satisfies the heart, the second the mind. The crowd is impressed through the heart without knowing the cause of the magic impression. But, on the other hand, there is a class of connoisseurs on whom that which affects the heart is entirely lost, and who can only be gained by the appropriateness of the means; a strange contradiction resulting from over-refined taste, especially when moral culture remains behind intellectual. This class of connoisseurs seek only the intellectual side in touching and sublime themes. They appreciate this in the justest manner, but you must beware how you appeal to their heart! The over-culture of the age leads to this shoal, and nothing becomes the cultivated man so much as to escape by a happy victory this twofold and pernicious influence. Of all other European nations, our neighbours the French lean most to this extreme, and we, as in all things, strain every nerve to imitate this model.

William Wordsworth

PREFACE TO
LYRICAL BALLADS (1802)

The reputation of William Wordsworth (1770–1850) as a poet has always been touched by ambiguity. There are those who admire him passionately and give his work a unique devotion; there are those who can make but little connection with him. Yet whenever the question is raised what English poet deserves to stand as a third beside Shakespeare and Milton, it is Wordsworth who is most often thought to assert the strongest claim. His statement of his poetic creed in the Preface to the 1802 edition of *Lyrical Ballads* is one of the most memorable and influential documents in the history of literature. The first edition had appeared in 1798, the joint work of Wordsworth and his close friend Coleridge. By far the greater number of the poems the volume contained were by Wordsworth: Coleridge's chief contribution, a very considerable one indeed, was the first version of *The Ancient Mariner*. The poems were prefaced by an "Advertisement" written by Wordsworth which said (1) that the materials of poetry "are to be found in every subject which can interest the human heart" and (2) that most of the poems in the volume were "to be considered as experiments . . . to ascertain how far the language of conversation in the middle and lower classes of society is adapted to the purposes of poetic pleasure." In 1800 a second edition of *Lyrical Ballads* was brought out, this time in two volumes. The poems of the first volume are nearly identical with those of the first edition; the poems of the second volume are all Wordsworth's. To this edition Wordsworth prefixed a preface which states again the substance of the "Advertisement" and develops it with eloquent passion. For the edition of 1802 Wordsworth, no doubt in order to meet objections that Coleridge had expressed to him, revised certain of the formulations in the interests of precision, and added the passage which undertakes to answer the question "What is a Poet?" The Preface has lost nothing of its interest and importance with the passage of time. Doubtless many modern readers will incline to withhold assent from its grandiose view of the function of poetry, but they cannot fail to be engaged by its discussion of language and subject. Coleridge's disagreement with Wordsworth's views on these questions appears on pages 161–181.

From *Wordsworth's Literary Criticism*, edited by Nowell C. Smith. Oxford, Oxford University Press, 1905.

The first volume of these Poems has already been submitted to general perusal. It was published, as an experiment, which, I hoped, might be of some use to ascertain, how far, by fitting to metrical arrangement a selection of the real language of men in a state of vivid sensation, that sort of pleasure and that quantity of pleasure may be imparted, which a Poet may rationally endeavour to impart.

I had formed no very inaccurate estimate of the probable effect of those Poems: I flattered myself that they who should be pleased with them would read them with more than common pleasure: and, on the other hand, I was well aware, that by those who should dislike them, they would be read with more than common dislike. The result has differed from my expectation in this only, that a greater number have been pleased than I ventured to hope I should please.

For the sake of variety and from a consciousness of my own weakness I was induced to request the assistance of a Friend, who furnished me with the Poems of the ANCIENT MARINER, the FOSTER-MOTHER'S TALE, the NIGHTINGALE, the DUNGEON, and the Poem entitled LOVE.[1] I should not, however, have requested this assistance, had I not believed that the Poems of my Friend would in a great measure have the same tendency as my own, and that, though there would be found a difference, there would be found no discordance in the colours of our style; as our opinions on the subject of poetry do almost entirely coincide.

Several of my Friends are anxious for the success of these Poems, from a belief, that if the views with which they were composed were indeed realized, a class of Poetry would be produced, well adapted to interest mankind permanently, and not unimportant in the quality, and in the multiplicity of its moral relations: and on this account they have advised me to prefix a systematic defence of the theory upon which the Poems were written. But I was unwilling to undertake the task, knowing that on this occasion the Reader would look coldly upon my arguments, since I might be suspected of having been principally influenced by the selfish and foolish hope of *reasoning* him into an approbation of these particular Poems: and I was still more unwilling to undertake the task, because, adequately to display the opinions, and fully to enforce the arguments, would require a space wholly disproportionate to a preface. For, to treat the subject with the clearness and coherence of which it is susceptible, it would be necessary to give a full account of the present state of the public taste in this country, and to determine how far this taste is healthy or depraved; which, again, could not be determined, without pointing out in what manner language and the human mind act and re-act on each other, and without retracing the revolutions, not of literature alone, but likewise of society itself. I have therefore altogether declined to enter regularly upon this defence; yet I am sensible, that there would be something like impropriety in abruptly obtruding upon the Public, without a few words of introduction, Poems so materially different from those upon which general approbation is at present bestowed.

It is supposed, that by the act of writing in verse an Author makes a

---

[1] The Friend, of course, is Coleridge.

formal engagement that he will gratify certain known habits of association; that he not only thus apprises the Reader that certain classes of ideas and expressions will be found in his book, but that others will be carefully excluded. This exponent or symbol held forth by metrical language must in different eras of literature have excited very different expectations: for example, in the age of Catullus, Terence, and Lucretius,[2] and that of Statius or Claudian;[3] and in our own country, in the age of Shakespeare and Beaumont and Fletcher, and that of Donne and Cowley, or Dryden, or Pope.[4] I will not take upon me to determine the exact import of the promise which, by the act of writing in verse, an Author in the present day makes to his reader: but it will undoubtedly appear to many persons that I have not fulfilled the terms of an engagement thus voluntarily contracted. They who have been accustomed to the gaudiness and inane phraseology of many modern writers, if they persist in reading this book to its conclusion, will, no doubt, frequently have to struggle with feelings of strangeness and awkwardness: they will look round for poetry, and will be induced to inquire by what species of courtesy these attempts can be permitted to assume that title. I hope therefore the reader will not censure me for attempting to state what I have proposed to myself to perform; and also (as far as the limits of a preface will permit) to explain some of the chief reasons which have determined me in the choice of my purpose: that at least he may be spared any unpleasant feeling of disappointment, and that I myself may be protected from one of the most dishonourable accusations which can be brought against an Author; namely, that of an indolence which prevents him from endeavouring to ascertain what is his duty, or, when his duty is ascertained, prevents him from performing it.

The principal object, then, proposed in these Poems was to choose incidents and situations from common life, and to relate or describe them, throughout, as far as was possible in a selection of language really used by men, and, at the same time, to throw over them a certain colouring of imagination, whereby ordinary things should be presented to the mind in an unusual aspect; and, further, and above all, to make these incidents and situations interesting by tracing in them, truly though not ostentatiously, the primary laws of our nature: chiefly, as far as regards the manner in which we associate ideas in a state of excitement. Humble and rustic life was generally chosen, because, in that condition, the essential passions of the heart find a better soil in which they can attain their maturity, are less under restraint, and speak a plainer and more emphatic language; because in that condition of life our elementary feelings coexist in a state of greater simplicity, and, consequently, may be more accurately contemplated, and more forcibly communicated; because the manners of rural life germinate from those elementary feelings, and, from the necessary character of rural occupations, are more easily comprehended, and are more durable; and, lastly, because in that condition the passions of men are incorporated with the beautiful and permanent forms of nature.

[2] Latin poets of the last two centuries B.C.
[3] Latin poets of, respectively, the first and fourth centuries A.D.
[4] William Shakespeare (1564–1616); Francis Beaumont (c. 1584–1616); John Fletcher (1579–1625); John Donne (1572–1631); Abraham Cowley (1618–1667); John Dryden (1631–1700); Alexander Pope (1688–1744).

The language, too, of these men has been adopted (purified indeed from what appear to be its real defects, from all lasting and rational causes of dislike or disgust) because such men hourly communicate with the best objects from which the best part of language is originally derived; and because, from their rank in society and the sameness and narrow circle of their intercourse, being less under the influence of social vanity, they convey their feelings and notions in simple and unelaborated expressions. Accordingly, such a language, arising out of repeated experience and regular feelings, is a more permanent, and a far more philosophical language, than that which is frequently substituted for it by Poets, who think that they are conferring honour upon themselves and their art, in proportion as they separate themselves from the sympathies of men, and indulge in arbitrary and capricious habits of expression, in order to furnish food for fickle tastes, and fickle appetites, of their own creation.*

I cannot, however, be insensible to the present outcry against the triviality and meanness, both of thought and language, which some of my contemporaries have occasionally introduced into their metrical compositions; and I acknowledge that this defect, where it exists, is more dishonourable to the Writer's own character than false refinement or arbitrary innovation, though I should contend at the same time, that it is far less pernicious in the sum of its consequences. From such verses the Poems in these volumes will be found distinguished at least by one mark of difference, that each of them has a worthy *purpose*. Not that I always began to write with a distinct purpose formally conceived; but habits of meditation have, I trust, so prompted and regulated my feelings, that my descriptions of such objects as strongly excite those feelings, will be found to carry along with them a *purpose*. If this opinion be erroneous, I can have little right to the name of a Poet. For all good poetry is the spontaneous overflow of powerful feelings: and though this be true, Poems to which any value can be attached were never produced on any variety of subjects but by a man who, being possessed of more than usual organic sensibility, had also thought long and deeply. For our continued influxes of feeling are modified and directed by our thoughts, which are indeed the representatives of all our past feelings; and, as by contemplating the relation of these general representatives to each other, we discover what is really important to men, so, by the repetition and continuance of this act, our feelings will be connected with important subjects, till at length, if we be originally possessed of much sensibility, such habits of mind will be produced, that, by obeying blindly and mechanically the impulses of those habits, we shall describe objects, and utter sentiments, of such a nature, and in such connexion with each other, that the understanding of the Reader must necessarily be in some degree enlightened, and his affections strengthened and purified.

It has been said that each of these poems has a purpose. Another circumstance must be mentioned which distinguishes these Poems from the popular Poetry of the day; it is this, that the feeling therein developed gives importance to the action and situation, and not the action and situation to the feeling.

A sense of false modesty shall not prevent me from asserting, that the

---

* It is worth while here to observe, that the affecting parts of Chaucer are almost always expressed in language pure and universally intelligible even to this day. [Wordsworth's note.]

Reader's attention is pointed to this mark of distinction, far less for the sake of these particular Poems than from the general importance of the subject. The subject is indeed important! For the human mind is capable of being excited without the application of gross and violent stimulants; and he must have a very faint perception of its beauty and dignity who does not know this, and who does not further know, that one being is elevated above another, in proportion as he possesses this capability. It has therefore appeared to me, that to endeavour to produce or enlarge this capability is one of the best services in which, at any period, a Writer can be engaged; but this service, excellent at all times, is especially so at the present day. For a multitude of causes, unknown to former times, are now acting with a combined force to blunt the discriminating powers of the mind, and, unfitting it for all voluntary exertion, to reduce it to a state of almost savage torpor. The most effective of these causes are the great national events which are daily taking place, and the increasing accumulation of men in cities, where the uniformity of their occupations produces a craving for extraordinary incident, which the rapid communication of intelligence hourly gratifies. To this tendency of life and manners the literature and theatrical exhibitions of the country have conformed themselves. The invaluable works of our elder writers, I had almost said the works of Shakespeare and Milton, are driven into neglect by frantic novels, sickly and stupid German Tragedies, and deluges of idle and extravagant stories in verse.—When I think upon this degrading thirst after outrageous stimulation, I am almost ashamed to have spoken of the feeble endeavour made in these volumes to counteract it; and, reflecting upon the magnitude of the general evil, I should be oppressed with no dishonourable melancholy, had I not a deep impression of certain inherent and indestructible qualities of the human mind, and likewise of certain powers in the great and permanent objects that act upon it, which are equally inherent and indestructible; and were there not added to this impression a belief, that the time is approaching when the evil will be systematically opposed, by men of greater powers, and with far more distinguished success.

Having dwelt thus long on the subjects and aim of these Poems, I shall request the Reader's permission to apprise him of a few circumstances relating to their *style,* in order, among other reasons, that he may not censure me for not having performed what I never attempted. The Reader will find that personifications of abstract ideas rarely occur in these volumes; and are utterly rejected, as an ordinary device to elevate the style, and raise it above prose. My purpose was to imitate, and, as far as possible, to adopt the very language of men; and assuredly such personifications do not make any natural or regular part of that language. They are, indeed, a figure of speech occasionally prompted by passion, and I have made use of them as such; but have endeavoured utterly to reject them as a mechanical device of style, or as a family language which Writers in metre seem to lay claim to by prescription. I have wished to keep the Reader in the company of flesh and blood, persuaded that by so doing I shall interest him. Others who pursue a different track will interest him likewise; I do not interefere with their claim, but wish to prefer a claim of my own. There will also be found in these volumes little of what is usually called poetic diction; as much pains has been taken to avoid it as is ordinarily taken to produce it; this has been done for the reason already alleged, to bring my language near to the language of men; and further, because the pleasure which I have proposed to myself to impart, is of a kind very different from that which is supposed by many persons to be the proper object of poetry. Without being culpably particular, I do not know how to give my Reader a more exact notion of the style in which it was my wish and intention to write, than by informing him that I have at all times endeavoured to look steadily at my subject; consequently, there is I hope in these Poems little falsehood of description, and my ideas are expressed in language fitted to their respective importance. Something must have been gained by this practice, as it is friendly to one property of all good poetry, namely, good sense: but it has necessarily cut me off from a large portion of phrases and figures of speech which from father to son have long been regarded as the common inheritance of Poets. I have also thought it expedient to restrict myself still further, having abstained from the use of many expressions, in themselves proper and beautiful, but which have been foolishly repeated by bad Poets, till such feelings of disgust are connected with them as it is scarcely possible by any art of association to overpower.

If in a poem there should be found a series of lines, or even a single line, in which the language, though naturally arranged, and according to the strict laws of metre, does not differ from that of prose, there is a numerous class of critics, who, when they stumble upon these prosaisms, as they call them, imagine that they have made a notable discovery, and exult over the Poet as over a man ignorant of his own profession. Now these men would establish a canon of criticism which the Reader will conclude he must utterly reject, if he wishes to be pleased with these volumes. And it would be a most easy task to prove to him, that not only the language of a large portion of every good poem, even of the most elevated character, must necessarily, except with reference to the metre, in no respect differ from that of good prose, but likewise that some of the most interesting parts of the best poems will be found to be strictly the language of prose when prose is well written. The truth of this assertion might be demonstrated by innumerable passages from almost all the poetical writings, even of Milton himself. To illustrate the subject in a general manner, I will here adduce a short composition of Gray,[5] who was at the head of those who, by their reasonings, have attempted to widen the space of separation betwixt Prose and Metrical composition, and was more than any other man curiously elaborate in the structure of his own poetic diction.

> In vain to me the smiling mornings shine,
> And reddening Phoebus lifts his golden fire:
> The birds in vain their amorous descant join,
> Or cheerful fields resume their green attire.
> These ears, alas! for other notes repine;
> *A different object do these eyes require:*
> *My lonely anguish melts no heart but mine:*
> *And in my breast the imperfect joys expire:*
> Yet morning smiles the busy race to cheer,

---

[5] Thomas Gray (1716–1771), whose "Sonnet on the Death of Richard West" Wordsworth quotes.

> And new-born pleasure brings to happier men;
> The fields to all their wonted tribute bear;
> To warm their little loves the birds complain.
> *I fruitless mourn to him that cannot hear,*
> *And weep the more because I weep in vain.*

It will easily be perceived, that the only part of this Sonnet which is of any value is the lines printed in Italics; it is equally obvious, that, except in the rhyme, and in the use of the single word "fruitless" for fruitlessly, which is so far a defect, the language of these lines does in no respect differ from that of prose.

By the foregoing quotation it has been shown that the language of Prose may yet be well adapted to Poetry; and it was previously asserted, that a large portion of the language of every good poem can in no respect differ from that of good Prose. We will go further. It may be safely affirmed, that there neither is, nor can be, any *essential* difference between the language of prose and metrical composition. We are fond of tracing the resemblance between Poetry and Painting, and, accordingly, we call them Sisters: but where shall we find bonds of connexion sufficiently strict to typify the affinity betwixt metrical and prose composition? They both speak by and to the same organs; the bodies in which both of them are clothed may be said to be of the same substance, their affections are kindred and almost identical, not necessarily differing even in degree; Poetry* sheds no tears "such as Angels weep,"[6] but natural and human tears; she can boast of no celestial ichor[7] that distinguishes her vital juices from those of prose; the same human blood circulates through the veins of them both.

If it be affirmed that rhyme and metrical arrangement of themselves constitute a distinction which overturns what has just been said on the strict affinity of metrical language with that of prose, and paves the way for other artificial distinctions which the mind voluntarily admits, I answer that the language of such Poetry as is here recommended is, as far as is possible, a selection of the language really spoken by men; that this selection, wherever it is made with true taste and feeling, will of itself form a distinction far greater than would at first be imagined, and will entirely separate the composition from the vulgarity and meanness of ordinary life; and, if metre be superadded thereto, I believe that a dissimilitude will be produced altogether sufficient for the gratification of a rational mind. What other distinction would we have? Whence is it to come? And where is it to exist? Not, surely, where the Poet speaks through the mouths of his characters: it cannot be necessary here, either for elevation of style, or any of its supposed ornaments: for, if the

---

* I here use the word "Poetry" (though against by own judgement) as opposed to the word Prose, and synonymous with metrical composition. But much confusion has been introduced into criticism by this contradistinction of Poetry and Prose, instead of the more philosophical one of Poetry and Matter of Fact, or Science. The only strict antithesis to Prose is Metre; nor is this, in truth, a *strict* antithesis, because lines and passages of metre so naturally occur in writing prose, that it would be scarcely possible to avoid them, even were it desirable. [Wordsworth's note.]

[6] Quoted from *Paradise Lost*, I, 620.

[7] An ethereal fluid which, instead of blood, ran through the veins of the Greek gods.

Poet's subject be judiciously chosen, it will naturally, and upon fit occasion, lead him to passions the language of which, if selected truly and judiciously, must necessarily be dignified and variegated, and alive with metaphors and figures. I forbear to speak of an incongruity which would shock the intelligent Reader, should the Poet interweave any foreign splendour of his own with that which the passion naturally suggests: it is sufficient to say that such addition is unnecessary. And, surely, it is more probable that those passages, which with propriety abound with metaphors and figures, will have their due effect, if, upon other occasions where the passions are of a milder character, the style also be subdued and temperate.

But, as the pleasure which I hope to give by the Poems now presented to the Reader must depend entirely on just notions upon this subject, and, as it is in itself of high importance to our taste and moral feelings, I cannot content myself with these detached remarks. And if, in what I am about to say, it shall appear to some that my labour is unnecessary, and that I am like a man fighting a battle without enemies, such persons may be reminded, that, whatever be the language outwardly holden by men, a practical faith in the opinions which I am wishing to establish is almost unknown. If my conclusions are admitted, and carried as far as they must be carried if admitted at all, our judgements concerning the works of the greatest Poets both ancient and modern will be far different from what they are at present, both when we praise, and when we censure; and our moral feelings influencing and influenced by these judgements will, I believe, be corrected and purified.

Taking up the subject, then, upon general grounds, let me ask, what is meant by the word Poet? What is a Poet? To whom does he address himself? And what language is to be expected from him?—He is a man speaking to men: a man, it is true, endowed with more lively sensibility, more enthusiasm and tenderness, who has a greater knowledge of human nature, and a more comprehensive soul, than are supposed to be common among mankind; a man pleased with his own passions and volitions, and who rejoices more than other men in the spirit of life that is in him; delighting to contemplate similar volitions and passions as manifested in the goings-on of the Universe, and habitually impelled to create them where he does not find them. To these qualities he has added a disposition to be affected more than other men by absent things as if they were present; an ability of conjuring up in himself passions, which are indeed far from being the same as those produced by real events, yet (especially in those parts of the general sympathy which are pleasing and delightful) do more nearly resemble the passions produced by real events, than anything which, from the motions of their own minds merely, other men are accustomed to feel in themselves:—whence, and from practice, he has acquired a greater readiness and power in expressing what he thinks and feels, and especially those thoughts and feelings which, by his own choice, or from the structure of his own mind, arise in him without immediate external excitement.

But whatever portion of this faculty we may suppose even the greatest Poet to possess, there cannot be a doubt that the language which it will suggest to him, must often, in liveliness and truth, fall short of that which is uttered by men in real life, under the actual pressure of those passions, certain shadows of which the Poet thus produces, or feels to be produced, in himself.

However exalted a notion we would wish to cherish of the character of a Poet, it is obvious, that while he describes and imitates passions, his employment is in some degree mechanical, compared with the freedom and power of real and substantial action and suffering. So that it will be the wish of the Poet to bring his feelings near to those of the persons whose feelings he describes, nay, for short spaces of time, perhaps, to let himself slip into an entire delusion, and even confound and identify his own feelings with theirs; modifying only the language which is thus suggested to him by a consideration that he describes for a particular purpose, that of giving pleasure. Here, then, he will apply the principle of selection which has been already insisted upon. He will depend upon this for removing what would otherwise be painful or disgusting in the passion; he will feel that there is no necessity to trick out or to elevate nature: and, the more industriously he applies this principle, the deeper will be his faith that no words, which *his* fancy or imagination can suggest, will be to be compared with those which are the emanations of reality and truth.

But it may be said by those who do not object to the general spirit of these remarks, that, as it is impossible for the Poet to produce upon all occasions language as exquisitely fitted for the passion as that which the real passion itself suggests, it is proper that he should consider himself as in the situation of a translator, who does not scruple to substitute excellencies of another kind for those which are unattainable by him; and endeavours occasionally to surpass his original, in order to make some amends for the general inferiority to which he feels that he must submit. But this would be to encourage idleness and unmanly despair. Further, it is the language of men who speak of what they do not understand; who talk of Poetry as of a matter of amusement and idle pleasure; who will converse with us as gravely about a *taste* for Poetry, as they express it, as if it were a thing as indifferent as a taste for rope-dancing, or Frontiniac or Sherry. Aristotle, I have been told, has said, that Poetry is the most philosophic of all writing: it is so: its object is truth, not individual and local, but general, and operative; not standing upon external testimony, but carried alive into the heart by passion; truth which is its own testimony, which gives competence and confidence to the tribunal to which it appeals, and receives them from the same tribunal. Poetry is the image of man and nature. The obstacles which stand in the way of the fidelity of the Biographer and Historian, and of their consequent utility, are incalculably greater than those which are to be encountered by the Poet who comprehends the dignity of his art. The Poet writes under one restriction only, namely, the necessity of giving immediate pleasure to a human Being possessed of that information which may be expected from him, not as a lawyer, a physician, a mariner, an astronomer, or a natural philosopher, but as a Man. Except this one restriction, there is no object standing between the Poet and the image of things; between this, and the Biographer and Historian, there are a thousand.

Nor let this necessity of producing immediate pleasure be considered as a degradation of the Poet's art. It is far otherwise. It is an acknowledgement of the beauty of the universe, an acknowledgement the more sincere, because not formal, but indirect; it is a task light and easy to him who looks at the world in the spirit of love: further, it is a homage paid to the native and naked dignity of man, to the grand elementary principle of pleasure, by which he knows, and feels, and lives, and moves.[8] We have no sympathy but what is propagated by pleasure: I would not be misunderstood; but wherever we sympathize with pain, it will be found that the sympathy is produced and carried on by subtle combinations with pleasure. We have no knowledge, that is, no general principles drawn from the contemplation of particular facts, but what has been built up by pleasure, and exists in us by pleasure alone. The Man of science, the Chemist and Mathematician, whatever difficulties and disgusts they may have had to struggle with, know and feel this. However painful may be the objects with which the Anatomist's knowledge is connected, he feels that his knowledge is pleasure; and where he has no pleasure he has no knowledge. What then does the Poet? He considers man and the objects that surround him as acting and re-acting upon each other, so as to produce an infinite complexity of pain and pleasure; he considers man in his own nature and in his ordinary life as contemplating this with a certain quantity of immediate knowledge, with certain convictions, intuitions, and deductions, which from habit acquire the quality of intuitions; he considers him as looking upon this complex scene of ideas and sensations, and finding everywhere objects that immediately excite in him sympathies which, from the necessities of his nature, are accompanied by an overbalance of enjoyment.

To this knowledge which all men carry about with them, and to these sympathies in which, without any other discipline than that of our daily life, we are fitted to take delight, the Poet principally directs his attention. He considers man and nature as essentially adapted to each other, and the mind of man as naturally the mirror of the fairest and most interesting properties of nature. And thus the Poet, prompted by this feeling of pleasure, which accompanies him through the whole course of his studies, converses with general nature, with affections akin to those, which, through labour and length of time, the Man of science has raised up in himself, by conversing with those particular parts of nature which are the objects of his studies. The knowledge both of the Poet and the Man of science is pleasure; but the knowledge of the one cleaves to us as a necessary part of our existence, our natural and unalienable inheritance; the other is a personal and individual acquisition, slow to come to us, and by no habitual and direct sympathy connecting us with our fellow-beings. The Man of science seeks truth as a remote and unknown benefactor; he cherishes and loves it in his solitude: the Poet, singing a song in which all human beings join with him, rejoices in the presence of truth as our visible and hourly companion. Poetry is the breath and finer spirit of all knowledge; it is the impassioned expression which is in the countenance of all Science. Emphatically may it be said of the Poet, as Shakespeare hath said of man, "that he looks before and after."[9] He is the rock of defence for human nature; an upholder and preserver, carrying everywhere with him relationship and love. In spite of difference of soil and climate, of language and manners, of laws and customs: in spite of things silently gone out of mind, and things violently destroyed; the Poet binds together by passion and knowledge the vast

[8] In Acts 17:28, St. Paul is quoted as saying that "we live, and move, and have our being" in God.
[9] *Hamlet*, IV. iv. 37.

empire of human society, as it is spread over the whole earth, and over all time. The objects of the Poet's thoughts are everywhere; though the eyes and senses of man are, it is true, his favourite guides, yet he will follow wheresoever he can find an atmosphere of sensation in which to move his wings. Poetry is the first and last of all knowledge—it is as immortal as the heart of man. If the labours of Men of science should ever create any material revolution, direct or indirect, in our condition, and in the impressions which we habitually receive, the Poet will sleep then no more than at present; he will be ready to follow the steps of the Man of science, not only in those general indirect effects, but he will be at his side, carrying sensation into the midst of the objects of the science itself. The remotest discoveries of the Chemist, the Botanist, or Mineralogist, will be as proper objects of the Poet's art as any upon which it can be employed, if the time should ever come when these things shall be familiar to us, and the relations under which they are contemplated by the followers of these respective sciences shall be manifestly and palpably material to us as enjoying and suffering beings. If the time should ever come when what is now called science, thus familiarized to men, shall be ready to put on, as it were, a form of flesh and blood, the Poet will lend his divine spirit to aid the transfiguration, and will welcome the Being thus produced, as a dear and genuine inmate of the household of man.—It is not, then, to be supposed that any one, who holds that sublime notion of Poetry which I have attempted to convey, will break in upon the sanctity and truth of his pictures by transitory and accidental ornaments, and endeavour to excite admiration of himself by arts, the necessity of which must manifestly depend upon the assumed meanness of his subject.

What has been thus far said applies to Poetry in general; but especially to those parts of composition where the Poet speaks through the mouths of his characters; and upon this point it appears to authorize the conclusion that there are few persons of good sense, who would not allow that the dramatic parts of composition are defective, in proportion as they deviate from the real language of nature, and are coloured by a diction of the Poet's own, either peculiar to him as an individual Poet or belonging simply to Poets in general; to a body of men who, from the circumstance of their compositions being in metre, it is expected will employ a particular language.

It is not, then, in the dramatic parts of composition that we look for this distinction of language; but still it may be proper and necessary where the Poet speaks to us in his own person and character. To this I answer by referring the Reader to the description before given of a Poet. Among the qualities there enumerated as principally conducing to form a Poet, is implied nothing differing in kind from other men, but only in degree. The sum of what was said is, that the Poet is chiefly distinguished from other men by a greater promptness to think and feel without immediate external excitement, and a greater power in expressing such thoughts and feelings as are produced in him in that manner. But these passions and thoughts and feelings are the general passions and thoughts and feelings of men. And with what are they connected? Undoubtedly with our moral sentiments and animal sensations, and with the causes which excite these; with the operations of the elements, and the appearances of the visible universe; with storm and sunshine, with the revolutions of the seasons, with cold and heat, with loss of friends and kindred, with injuries and resentments, gratitude and hope, with fear and sorrow. These, and the like, are the sensations and objects which the Poet describes, as they are the sensations of other men, and the objects which interest them. The Poet thinks and feels in the spirit of human passions. How, then, can his language differ in any material degree from that of all other men who feel vividly and see clearly? It might be *proved* that it is impossible. But supposing that this were not the case, the Poet might then be allowed to use a peculiar language when expressing his feelings for his own gratification, or that of men like himself. But Poets do not write for Poets alone, but for men. Unless therefore we are advocates for that admiration which subsists upon ignorance, and that pleasure which arises from hearing what we do not understand, the Poet must descend from this supposed height; and, in order to excite rational sympathy, he must express himself as other men express themselves. To this it may be added, that while he is only selecting from the real language of men, or, which amounts to the same thing, composing accurately in the spirit of such selection, he is treading upon safe ground, and we know what we are to expect from him. Our feelings are the same with respect to metre; for, as it may be proper to remind the Reader, the distinction of metre is regular and uniform, and not, like that which is produced by what is usually called POETIC DICTION, arbitrary, and subject to infinite caprices upon which no calculation whatever can be made. In the one case, the Reader is utterly at the mercy of the Poet, respecting what imagery or diction he may choose to connect with the passion; whereas, in the other, the metre obeys certain laws, to which the Poet and Reader both willingly submit because they are certain, and because no interference is made by them with the passion, but such as the concurring testimony of ages has shown to heighten and improve the pleasure which co-exists with it.

It will now be proper to answer an obvious question, namely, Why, professing these opinions, have I written in verse? To this, in addition to such answer as is included in what has been already said, I reply, in the first place, Because, however I may have restricted myself, there is still left open to me what confessedly constitutes the most valuable object of all writing, whether in prose or verse; the great and universal passions of men, the most general and interesting of their occupations, and the entire world of nature before me —to supply endless combinations of forms and imagery. Now, supposing for a moment that whatever is interesting in these objects may be as vividly described in prose, why should I be condemned for attempting to superadd to such description the charm which, by the consent of all nations, is acknowledged to exist in metrical language? To this, by such as are yet unconvinced, it may be answered that a very small part of the pleasure given by Poetry depends upon the metre, and that it is injudicious to write in metre, unless it be accompanied with the other artificial distinctions of style with which metre is usually accompanied, and that, by such deviation, more will be lost from the shock which will thereby be given to the Reader's associations than will be counterbalanced by any pleasure which he can derive from the general power of numbers. In answer to those who still contend for the necessity of accompanying metre with certain appropriate colours of style in order to the accomplishment of its appropriate end, and who also, in my opinion, greatly underrate the power of metre in itself, it might, perhaps, as far as relates to these Volumes, have been almost sufficient to observe, that poems are extant, written upon more humble subjects, and in a still more naked and simple style, which have continued to give pleasure from generation to generation. Now, if nakedness and simplicity be a defect, the fact here mentioned affords a strong presumption that poems somewhat less naked and simple are capable of affording pleasure at the present day; and, what I wished *chiefly* to attempt, at present, was to justify myself for having written under the impression of this belief.

But various causes might be pointed out why, when the style is manly, and the subject of some importance, words metrically arranged will long continue to impart such a pleasure to mankind as he who proves the extent of that pleasure will be desirous to impart. The end of Poetry is to produce excitement in co-existence with an overbalance of pleasure; but, by the supposition, excitement is an unusual and irregular state of the mind; ideas and feelings do not, in that state, succeed each other in accustomed order. If the words, however, by which this excitement is produced be in themselves powerful, or the images and feelings have an undue proportion of pain connected with them, there is some danger that the excitement may be carried beyond its proper bounds. Now the co-presence of something regular, something to which the mind has been accustomed in various moods and in a less excited state, cannot but have great efficacy in tempering and restraining the passion by an intertexture of ordinary feeling, and of feeling not strictly and necessarily connected with the passion. This is unquestionably true; and hence, though the opinion will at first appear paradoxical, from the tendency of metre to divest language, in a certain degree, of its reality, and thus to throw a sort of half-consciousness of unsubstantial existence over the whole composition, there can be little doubt but that more pathetic situations and sentiments, that is, those which have a greater proportion of pain connected with them, may be endured in metrical composition, especially in rhyme, than in prose. The metre of the old ballads is very artless; yet they contain many passages which would illustrate this opinion; and, I hope, if the following Poems be attentively perused, similar instances will be found in them. This opinion may be further illustrated by appealing to the Reader's own experience of the reluctance with which he comes to the re-perusal of the distressful parts of *Clarissa Harlowe*,[10] or *The Gamester*;[11] while Shakespeare's writings, in the most pathetic scenes, never act upon us, as pathetic, beyond the bounds of pleasure—an effect which, in a much greater degree than might at first be imagined, is to be ascribed to small, but continual and regular impulses of pleasurable surprise from the metrical arrangement.—On the other hand (what it must be allowed will much more frequently happen) if the Poet's words should be incommensurate with the passion, and inadequate to raise the Reader to a height of desirable excitement, then (unless the Poet's choice of his metre has been grossly injudicious), in the feelings of pleasure which the Reader has been accustomed to connect with metre in general, and in the feeling, whether cheerful or melancholy, which he has been accustomed to connect

[10] A novel by Samuel Richardson (1689–1761).
[11] A domestic tragedy of 1753 by Edward Moore (1712–1757).

with that particular movement of metre, there will be found something which will greatly contribute to impart passion to the words, and to effect the complex end which the Poet proposes to himself.

If I had undertaken a SYSTEMATIC defence of the theory here maintained, it would have been my duty to develop the various causes upon which the pleasure received from metrical language depends. Among the chief of these causes is to be reckoned a principle which must be well known to those who have made any of the Arts the object of accurate reflection; namely, the pleasure which the mind derives from the perception of similitude in dissimilitude. This principle is the great spring of the activity of our minds, and their chief feeder. From this principle the direction of the sexual appetite, and all the passions connected with it, take their origin: it is the life of our ordinary conversation; and upon the accuracy with which similitude in dissimilitude, and dissimilitude in similitude are perceived, depend our taste and our moral feelings. It would not be a useless employment to apply this principle to the consideration of metre, and to show that metre is hence enabled to afford much pleasure, and to point out in what manner that pleasure is produced. But my limits will not permit me to enter upon this subject, and I must content myself with a general summary.

I have said that poetry is the spontaneous overflow of powerful feelings: it takes its origin from emotion recollected in tranquillity: the emotion is contemplated till, by a species of reaction, the tranquillity gradually disappears, and an emotion, kindred to that which was before the subject of contemplation, is gradually produced, and does itself actually exist in the mind. In this mood successful composition generally begins, and in a mood similar to this it is carried on; but the emotion, of whatever kind, and in whatever degree, from various causes, is qualified by various pleasures, so that in describing any passions whatsoever, which are voluntarily described, the mind will, upon the whole, be in a state of enjoyment. If Nature be thus cautious to preserve in a state of enjoyment a being so employed, the Poet ought to profit by the lesson held forth to him, and ought especially to take care, that, whatever passions he communicates to his Reader, those passions, if his Reader's mind be sound and vigorous, should always be accompanied with an overbalance of pleasure. Now the music of harmonious metrical language, the sense of difficulty overcome, and the blind association of pleasure which has been previously received from works of rhyme or metre of the same or similar construction, an indistinct perception perpetually renewed of language closely resembling that of real life, and yet, in the circumstance of metre, differing from it so widely—all these imperceptibly make up a complex feeling of delight, which is of the most important use in tempering the painful feeling always found intermingled with powerful descriptions of the deeper passions. This effect is always produced in pathetic and impassioned poetry; while, in lighter compositions, the ease and gracefulness with which the Poet manages his numbers are themselves confessedly a principal source of the gratification of the Reader. All that it is *necessary* to say, however, upon this subject, may be effected by affirming, what few persons will deny, that, of two descriptions, either of passions, manners, or characters, each of them equally well executed, the one in prose and the other in verse, the verse will be read a hundred times where the prose is read once.

Having thus explained a few of my reasons for writing in verse, and why I have chosen subjects from common life, and endeavoured to bring my language near to the real language of men, if I have been too minute in pleading my own cause, I have at the same time been treating a subject of general interest; and for this reason a few words shall be added with reference solely to these particular poems, and to some defects which will probably be found in them. I am sensible that my associations must have sometimes been particular instead of general, and that, consequently, giving to things a false importance, I may have sometimes written upon unworthy subjects; but I am less apprehensive on this account, than that my language may frequently have suffered from those arbitrary connexions of feelings and ideas with particular words and phrases, from which no man can altogether protect himself. Hence I have no doubt, that, in some instances, feelings, even of the ludicrous, may be given to my Readers by expressions which appeared to me tender and pathetic. Such faulty expressions, were I convinced they were faulty at present, and that they must necessarily continue to be so, I would willingly take all reasonable pains to correct. But it is dangerous to make these alterations on the simple authority of a few individuals, or even of certain classes of men; for where the understanding of an Author is not convinced, or his feelings altered, this cannot be done without great injury to himself: for his own feelings are his stay and support; and, if he set them aside in one instance, he may be induced to repeat this act till his mind shall lose all confidence in itself, and become utterly debilitated. To this it may be added, that the critic ought never to forget that he is himself exposed to the same errors as the Poet, and, perhaps, in a much greater degree: for there can be no presumption in saying of most readers, that it is not probable they will be so well acquainted with the various stages of meaning through which words have passed, or with the fickleness or stability of the relations of particular ideas to each other; and, above all, since they are so much less interested in the subject, they may decide lightly and carelessly.

Long as the Reader has been detained, I hope he will permit me to caution him against a mode of false criticism which has been applied to Poetry, in which the language closely resembles that of life and nature. Such verses have been triumphed over in parodies, of which Dr. Johnson's stanza is a fair specimen:—

> I put my hat upon my head
> And walked into the Strand,
> And there I met another man
> Whose hat was in his hand.[12]

Immediately under these lines let us place one of the most justly admired stanzas of the "Babes in the Wood."

> These pretty Babes with hand in hand
> Went wandering up and down;
> But never more they saw the Man
> Approaching from the Town.[13]

[12]Wordsworth apparently saw the stanza in *The London Magazine* for April, 1785.
[13] Wordsworth probably first saw this anonymous poem in Thomas Percy's *Reliques of Ancient English Poetry* (1765), but he seems to be quoting from a version published in a pamphlet of around 1800.

In both these stanzas the words, and the order of the words, in no respect differ from the most unimpassioned conversation. There are words in both, for example, "the Strand," and "the Town," connected with none but the most familiar ideas; yet the one stanza we admit as admirable, and the other as a fair example of the superlatively contemptible. Whence arises this difference? Not from the metre, not from the language, not from the order of the words; but the *matter* expressed in Dr. Johnson's stanza is contemptible. The proper method of treating trivial and simple verses, to which Dr. Johnson's stanza would be a fair parallelism, is not to say, this is a bad kind of poetry, or, this is not poetry; but, this wants sense; it is neither interesting in itself, nor can *lead* to anything interesting; the images neither originate in that sane state of feeling which arises out of thought, nor can excite thought or feeling in the Reader. This is the only sensible manner of dealing with such verses. Why trouble yourself about the species till you have previously decided upon the genus? Why take pains to prove that an ape is not a Newton, when it is self-evident that he is not a man?

One request I must make of my reader, which is, that in judging these Poems he would decide by his own feelings genuinely, and not by reflection upon what will probably be the judgement of others. How common is it to hear a person say, I myself do not object to this style of composition, or this or that expression, but, to such and such classes of people it will appear mean or ludicrous! This mode of criticism, so destructive of all sound unadulterated judgement, is almost universal: let the Reader then abide, independently, by his own feelings, and, if he finds himself affected, let him not suffer such conjectures to interfere with his pleasure.

If an Author, by any single composition, has impressed us with respect for his talents, it is useful to consider this as affording a presumption, that on other occasions where we have been displeased, he, nevertheless, may not have written ill or absurdly; and further, to give him so much credit for this one composition as may induce us to review what has displeased us, with more care than we should otherwise have bestowed upon it. This is not only an act of justice, but, in our decisions upon poetry especially, may conduce, in a high degree, to the improvement of our own taste; for an *accurate* taste in poetry, and in all the other arts, as Sir Joshua Reynolds[14] has observed, is an *acquired* talent, which can only be produced by thought and a long continued intercourse with the best models of composition. This is mentioned, not with so ridiculous a purpose as to prevent the most inexperienced Reader from judging for himself (I have already said that I wish him to judge for himself), but merely to temper the rashness of decision, and to suggest, that, if Poetry be a subject on which much time has not been bestowed, the judgement may be erroneous; and that, in many cases, it necessarily will be so.

Nothing would, I know, have so effectually contributed to further the end which I have in view, as to have shown of what kind the pleasure is, and how that pleasure is produced, which is confessedly produced by metrical composition essentially different from that which I have here endeavoured to recom-

---

[14] Sir Joshua Reynolds (1723–1792) was a portrait painter and first president of the Royal Academy. His yearly discourses before that body were widely attended and discussed.

mend: for the Reader will say that he has been pleased by such composition; and what more can be done for him? The power of any art is limited; and he will suspect, that, if it be proposed to furnish him with new friends, that can be only upon condition of his abandoning his old friends. Besides, as I have said, the Reader is himself conscious of the pleasure which he has received from such composition, composition to which he has peculiarly attached the endearing name of Poetry; and all men feel an habitual gratitude, and something of an honourable bigotry, for the objects which have long continued to please them: we not only wish to be pleased, but to be pleased in that particular way in which we have been accustomed to be pleased. There is in these feelings enough to resist a host of arguments; and I should be the less able to combat them successfully, as I am willing to allow, that, in order entirely to enjoy the Poetry which I am recommending, it would be necessary to give up much of what is ordinarily enjoyed. But, would my limits have permitted me to point out how this pleasure is produced, many obstacles might have been removed, and the Reader assisted in perceiving that the powers of language are not so limited as he may suppose; and that it is possible for poetry to give other enjoyments, of a purer, more lasting, and more exquisite nature. This part of the subject has not been altogether neglected, but it has not been so much my present aim to prove, that the interest excited by some other kinds of poetry is less vivid, and less worthy of the nobler powers of the mind, as to offer reasons for presuming, that if my purpose were fulfilled, a species of poetry would be produced, which is genuine poetry; in its nature well adapted to interest mankind permanently, and likewise important in the multiplicity and quality of its moral relations.

From what has been said, and from a perusal of the Poems, the Reader will be able clearly to perceive the object which I had in view: he will determine how far it has been attained; and, what is a much more important question, whether it be worth attaining: and upon the decision of these two questions will rest my claim to the approbation of the Public.

Appendix

Perhaps, as I have no right to expect that attentive perusal, without which, confined, as I have been, to the narrow limits of a preface, my meaning cannot be thoroughly understood, I am anxious to give an exact notion of the sense in which the phrase poetic diction has been used; and for this purpose, a few words shall here be added, concerning the origin and characteristics of the phraseology, which I have condemned under that name.

The earliest poets of all nations generally wrote from passion excited by real events; they wrote naturally, and as men: feeling powerfully as they did, their language was daring, and figurative. In succeeding times, Poets, and Men ambitious of the fame of Poets, perceiving the influence of such language, and desirous of producing the same effect without being animated by the same passion, set themselves to a mechanical adoption of these figures of speech, and made use of them, sometimes with propriety, but much more frequently applied them to feelings and thoughts with which they had no natural connexion whatsoever. A language was thus insensibly produced, differing materially from the real language of men in *any situation*. The Reader or Hearer of this distorted language found himself in a perturbed and unusual state of mind: when affected by the genuine language of passion he had been in a perturbed and unusual state of mind also: in both cases he was willing that his common judgement and understanding should be laid asleep, and he had no instinctive and infallible perception of the true to make him reject the false; the one served as a passport for the other. The motion was in both cases delightful, and no wonder if he confounded the one with the other, and believed them both to be produced by the same, or similar causes. Besides, the Poet spake to him in the character of a man to be looked up to, a man of genius and authority. Thus, and from a variety of other causes, this distorted language was received with admiration; and Poets, it is probable, who had before contented themselves for the most part with misapplying only expressions which at first had been dictated by real passion, carried the abuse still further, and introduced phrases composed apparently in the spirit of the original figurative language of passion, yet altogether of their own invention, and characterized by various degrees of wanton deviation from good sense and nature.

It is indeed true, that the language of the earliest Poets was felt to differ materially from ordinary language, because it was the language of extraordinary occasions; but it was really spoken by men, language which the Poet himself had uttered when he had been affected by the events which he described, or which he had heard uttered by those around him. To this language it is probable that metre of some sort or other was early superadded. This separated the genuine language of Poetry still further from common life, so that whoever read or heard the poems of these earliest Poets felt himself moved in a way in which he had not been accustomed to be moved in real life, and by causes manifestly different from those which acted upon him in real life. This was the great temptation to all the corruptions which have followed: under the protection of this feeling succeeding Poets constructed a phraseology which had one thing, it is true, in common with the genuine language of poetry, namely, that it was not heard in ordinary conversation; that it was unusual. But the first Poets, as I have said, spake a language which, though unusual, was still the language of men. This circumstance, however, was disregarded by their successors; they found that they could please by easier means: they became proud of modes of expression which they themselves had invented, and which were uttered only by themselves. In process of time metre became a symbol or promise of this unusual language, and whoever took upon him to write in metre, according as he possessed more or less of true poetic genius, introduced less or more of this adulterated phraseology into his compositions, and the true and the false were inseparably interwoven until, the taste of men becoming gradually perverted, this language was received as a natural language: and at length, by the influence of books upon men, did to a certain degree really become so. Abuses of this kind were imported from one nation to another, and with the progress of refinement this diction became daily more and more corrupt, thrusting out of sight the plain humanities of nature by a motley masquerade of tricks, quaintnesses, hieroglyphics, and enigmas.

It would not be uninteresting to point out the causes of the pleasure given by this extravagant and absurd diction. It depends upon a great variety of causes, but upon none, perhaps, more than its influence in impressing a notion of the peculiarity and exaltation of the Poet's character, and in flattering the Reader's self-love by bringing him nearer to a sympathy with that character; an effect which is accomplished by unsettling ordinary habits of thinking, and thus assisting the Reader to approach to that perturbed and dizzy state of mind in which if he does not find himself, he imagines that he is *balked* of a peculiar enjoyment which poetry can and ought to bestow.

The sonnet quoted from Gray, in the Preface, except the lines printed in Italics, consists of little else but this diction, though not of the worst kind; and indeed, if one may be permitted to say so, it is far too common in the best writers both ancient and modern. Perhaps in no way, by positive example, could more easily be given a notion of what I mean by the phrase *poetic diction* than by referring to a comparison between the metrical paraphrase which we have of passages in the Old and New Testament, and those passages as they exist in our common Translation. See Pope's *Messiah* throughout; Prior's "Did sweeter sounds adorn my flowing tongue,"[15] &c. &c. "Though I speak with the tongues of men and of angels," &c. &c., 1st Corinthians, ch. xiii. By way of immediate example take the following of Dr. Johnson:—

> Turn on the prudent Ant thy heedless eyes,
> Observe her labours, Sluggard, and be wise;
> No stern command, no monitory voice,
> Prescribes her duties, or directs her choice;
> Yet, timely provident, she hastes away
> To snatch the blessings of a plenteous day;
> When fruitful Summer loads the teeming plain,
> She crops the harvest, and she stores the grain.
> How long shall sloth usurp thy useless hours,
> Unnerve thy vigour, and enchain thy powers?
> While artful shades thy downy couch enclose,
> And soft solicitation courts repose,
> Amidst the drowsy charms of dull delight,
> Year chases year with unremitted flight,
> Till Want now following, fraudulent and slow,
> Shall spring to seize thee, like an ambush'd foe.[16]

From this hubbub of words pass to the original. "Go to the Ant, thou Sluggard, consider her ways, and be wise: which having no guide, overseer, or ruler, provideth her meat in the summer, and gathereth her food in the harvest. How long wilt thou sleep, O Sluggard? when wilt thou arise out of thy sleep? Yet a little sleep, a little slumber, a little folding of the hands to sleep. So shall thy poverty come as one that travelleth, and thy want as an armed man," Proverbs, ch. vi.

---

[15] Wordsworth is referring to the "Charity. A Paraphrase on the Thirteenth Chapter of the First Epistle to the Corinthians," by Matthew Prior (1664–1721). Pope's *Messiah* was first published in 1712.
[16] From Samuel Johnson's "The Ant."

One more quotation, and I have done. It is from Cowper's Verses supposed to be written by Alexander Selkirk:—[17]

> Religion! what treasure untold
> Resides in that heavenly word!
> More precious than silver and gold,
> Or all that this earth can afford.
> But the sound of the church-going bell
> These valleys and rocks never heard,
> Ne'er sighed at the sound of a knell,
> Or smiled when a sabbath appeared.
>
> Ye winds, that have made me your sport
> Convey to this desolate shore
> Some cordial endearing report
> Of a land I must visit no more.
> My Friends, do they now and then send
> A wish or a thought after me?
> O tell me I yet have a friend,
> Though a friend I am never to see.

This passage is quoted as an instance of three different styles of composition. The first four lines are poorly expressed; some Critics would call the language prosaic; the fact is, it would be bad prose, so bad, that it is scarcely worse in metre. The epithet "church-going" applied to a bell, and that by so chaste a writer as Cowper, is an instance of the strange abuses which poets have introduced into their language, till they and their Readers take them as matters of course, if they do not single them out expressly as objects of admiration. The two lines "Ne'er sighed at the sound," &c., are, in my opinion, an instance of the language of passion wrested from its proper use, and, from the mere circumstance of the composition being in metre, applied upon an occasion that does not justify such violent expressions; and I should condemn the passage, though perhaps few Readers will agree with me, as vicious poetic diction. The last stanza is throughout admirably expressed: it would be equally good whether in prose or verse, except that the Reader has an exquisite pleasure in seeing such natural language so naturally connected with metre. The beauty of this stanza tempts me to conclude with a principle which ought never to be lost sight of, and which has been my chief guide in all I have said,—namely, that in works of *imagination and sentiment,* for of these only have I been treating, in proportion as ideas and feelings are valuable, whether the composition be in prose or in verse, they require and exact one and the same language. Metre is but adventitious to composition, and the phraseology for which that passport is necessary, even where it may be graceful at all, will be little valued by the judicious.

[17] See Cowper's *Poems,* ed. H. S. Milford, fourth edition (New York: Oxford University Press, 1934), p. 312.

Samuel Taylor Coleridge

BIOGRAPHIA LITERARIA

Among English writers Samuel Taylor Coleridge is unique in having possessed a genius both for poetry and for speculative thought. As an abstract thinker he is perhaps not of the very first order of originality, but he put his mark on every intellectual discipline he practiced, making seminal contributions to political theory, psychology, metaphysics, logic, and theology. Upon literary criticism his influence has been decisive—it is to the point that I. A. Richards, often credited with having inaugurated the modern critical movement, brought his own critical theory to its climax with a book entitled *Coleridge on Imagination* (1935).

Coleridge was born in 1772, the ninth son and the thirteenth child of the vicar of Ottery St. Mary's, in Devonshire. On the death of his father when Samuel was nine, a place was found for the boy at Christ's Hospital, the famous charity school in London. He spent eight years there, some of them in company with Charles Lamb, who was to be his lifelong friend, and distinguished himself by his brilliance and erudition. In 1791 he entered Jesus College, Cambridge, where he responded to the temper of the time and the influence of some of his college mates by adopting radical opinions in both religion and politics. In 1793 he expressed his dissatisfaction with the university by leaving it and going to London. Finding himself penniless, he enlisted in a regiment of dragoons (under the ever-memorable name of Silas Tomkyn Comberbacke); his discharge was secured by his family and he returned to Cambridge, only to leave again in 1794, without taking a degree. With Robert Southey, who had also been stirred by the ideals of the French Revolution, he involved himself in planning a utopian community—a "pantisocracy," a government by all—to be established in America, on the banks of the Susquehanna. If only because it proved impossible to finance the project, it was abandoned in 1795. In that year Coleridge made the marriage which was to be unhappy almost from the first and that ended in separation some twelve years later. In that year too he met William Wordsworth for the first time.

The famous friendship between the two poets was of decisive importance in the lives of both and its monument is the volume of poems, *Lyrical Ballads,* which they published jointly in 1798. Coleridge's chief contribution to it was "The Rime of the Ancient Mariner." That they were not wholly at one in their theories of poetry, at least not after 1800, when Wordsworth published his Preface to a new edition of the work, is made plain by Coleridge in *Biographia Literaria,* but

From *Biographia Literaria,* Edited with His Aesthetical Essays by John Shawcross. Oxford: The Clarendon Press, 1907.

161

this did not prevent their stimulation and nourishment of each others' minds during the period of their intimacy. It was in company with Wordsworth and his sister Dorothy that Coleridge set out for Germany in 1798. Here he came under influence of the German thinkers—Kant primarily and also Lessing, Herder, the Schlegels, and Schilling—which was to give direction to his own mature thought, of which a salient element is an extreme subjectivism, a belief that the objects of perception are not so much "given" as "taken," that they are what they are through the creative power of the human imagination. At this time he lost his enthusiasm for revolutionary ideas and began to move toward his characteristic conservative-liberal theory of society and the state which later won the admiration of the radical-liberal John Stuart Mill and had no small part in the shaping of modern England.

In his youth, perhaps in his university time, Coleridge had fallen prey to the opium habit as the result of having taken the drug to relieve severe chronic pain. The addiction increased with the years and Coleridge's letters and poems bear testimony to the misery it brought him in the form of depression and night-terrors. Although at no time did Coleridge wholly lose his power of work, the habit did impede his application to his many ambitious projects, and in 1816 he put himself into the charge of a young surgeon, James Gillman. At Gillman's house in Highgate, then a town outside London, he spent his days until his death in 1834, reading, writing, and talking; he had always been known for the brilliance of his conversation and in the Highgate years he was sought out by admiring visitors who delighted to hear him on all manner of subjects.

The *Biographia Literaria,* or "Life in Literature," from which the following chapters have been selected, was first published in 1817.

Chapter XIV

During the first year that Mr. Wordsworth and I were neighbours,[1] our conversations turned frequently on the two cardinal points of poetry, the power of exciting the sympathy of the reader by a faithful adherence to the truth of nature, and the power of giving the interest of novelty by the modifying colors of imagination. The sudden charm, which accidents of light and shade, which moon-light or sun-set diffused over a known and familiar landscape, appeared to represent the practicability of combining both. These are the poetry of nature. The thought suggested itself (to which of us I do not recollect) that a series of poems might be composed of two sorts. In the one, the incidents and agents were to be, in part at least, supernatural; and the excellence aimed at was to consist in the interesting of the affections by the dramatic truth of such emotions, as would naturally accompany such situations, supposing them real. And real in *this* sense they have been to every human being who, from whatever source of delusion, has at any time believed himself under supernatural agency. For the second class, subjects were to be chosen from ordinary life; the char-

---

[1] In 1797, at Nether Stowey and Alfoxden, Somerset. The reader might compare Coleridge's account of the origin of the *Lyrical Ballads* with Wordsworth's on pp. 142 ff. of this volume.

acters and incidents were to be such, as will be found in every village and its vicinity, where there is a meditative and feeling mind to seek after them, or to notice them, when they present themselves.

In this idea originated the plan of the "Lyrical Ballads"; in which it was agreed, that my endeavours should be directed to persons and characters supernatural, or at least romantic; yet so as to transfer from our inward nature a human interest and a semblance of truth sufficient to procure for these shadows of imagination that willing suspension of disbelief for the moment, which constitutes poetic faith. Mr. Wordsworth, on the other hand, was to propose to himself as his object, to give the charm of novelty to things of every day, and to excite a feeling analogous to the supernatural, by awakening the mind's attention from the lethargy of custom, and directing it to the loveliness and the wonders of the world before us; an inexhaustible treasure, but for which, in consequence of the film of familiarity and selfish solicitude we have eyes, yet see not, ears that hear not, and hearts that neither feel nor understand.

With this view I wrote "The Ancient Mariner," and was preparing among other poems, "The Dark Ladie," and the "Christabel," in which I should have more nearly realized my ideal, than I had done in my first attempt. But Mr. Wordsworth's industry had proved so much more successful, and the number of his poems so much greater, that my compositions, instead of forming a balance, appeared rather an interpolation of heterogeneous matter. Mr. Wordsworth added two or three poems written in his own character, in the impassioned, lofty, and sustained diction, which is characteristic of his genius. In this form the "Lyrical Ballads" were published; and were presented by him, as an *experiment,* whether subjects, which from their nature rejected the usual ornaments and extra-colloquial style of poems in general, might not be so managed in the language of ordinary life as to produce the pleasureable interest, which it is the peculiar business of poetry to impart. To the second edition he added a preface of considerable length; in which, notwithstanding some passages of apparently a contrary import, he was understood to contend for the extension of this style to poetry of all kinds, and to reject as vicious and indefensible all phrases and forms of style that were not included in what he (unfortunately, I think, adopting an equivocal expression) called the language of *real* life. From this preface, prefixed to poems in which it was impossible to deny the presence of original genius, however mistaken its direction might be deemed, arose the whole long-continued controversy.[2] For from the conjunction of perceived power with supposed heresy I explain the inveteracy and in some instances, I grieve to say, the acrimonious passions, with which the controversy has been conducted by the assailants.

Had Mr. Wordsworth's poems been the silly, the childish things, which they were for a long time described as being; had they been really distinguished from the compositions of other poets merely by meanness of language and inanity of thought; had they indeed contained nothing more than what is found in the parodies and pretended imitations of them; they must have sunk at once, a dead weight, into the slough of oblivion, and have dragged the preface along

---

[2] That is, the controversy over Wordsworth's theory and his poetical practice in the literary journals of the time.

with them. But year after year increased the number of Mr. Wordsworth's admirers. They were found too not in the lower classes of the reading public, but
chiefly among young men of strong sensibility and meditative minds; and their
admiration (inflamed perhaps in some degree by opposition) was distinguished
by its intensity, I might almost say, by its *religious* fervor. These facts, and the
intellectual energy of the author, which was more or less consciously felt, where
it was outwardly and even boisterously denied, meeting with sentiments of
aversion to his opinions, and of alarm at their consequences, produced an eddy
of criticism, which would of itself have borne up the poems by the violence,
with which it whirled them round and round. With many parts of this preface,
in the sense attributed to them, and which the words undoubtedly seem to
authorize, I never concurred; but on the contrary objected to them as erroneous
in principle, and as contradictory (in appearance at least) both to other parts of
the same preface, and to the author's own practice in the greater number of the
poems themselves. Mr. Wordsworth in his recent collection[3] has, I find, degraded this prefatory disquisition to the end of his second volume, to be read
or not at the reader's choice. But he has not, as far as I can discover, announced
any change in his poetic creed. At all events, considering it as the source of a
controversy, in which I have been honored more than I deserve by the frequent
conjunction of my name with his, I think it expedient to declare once for all,
in what points I coincide with his opinions, and in what points I altogether
differ. But in order to render myself intelligible I must previously, in as few
words as possible, explain my ideas, first, of a POEM; and secondly, of POETRY
itself, in *kind,* and in *essence.*

 The office of philosophical *disquisition* consists in just *distinction;* while it
is the privilege of the philosopher to preserve himself constantly aware, that
distinction is not division. In order to obtain adequate notions of any truth, we
must intellectually separate its distinguishable parts; and this is the technical
process of philosophy. But having so done, we must then restore them in our
conceptions to the unity, in which they actually co-exist; and this is the *result*
of philosophy. A poem contains the same elements as a prose composition; the
difference therefore must consist in a different combination of them, in consequence of a different object being proposed. According to the difference of
the object will be the difference of the combination. It is possible, that the object
may be merely to facilitate the recollection of any given facts or observations by
artificial arrangement; and the composition will be a poem, merely because it is
distinguished from prose by metre, or by rhyme, or by both conjointly. In this,
the lowest sense, a man might attribute the name of a poem to the well-known
enumeration of the days in the several months;

> Thirty days hath September,
> April, June, and November, &c.

and others of the same class and purpose. And as a particular pleasure is found
in anticipating the recurrence of sounds and quantities, all compositions that
have this charm super-added, whatever be their contents, *may* be entitled poems.

 So much for the superficial *form.* A difference of object and contents sup-

---

[3] In the two-volume collection of his poems published in 1815.

plies an additional ground of distinction. The immediate purpose may be the communication of truths; either of truth absolute and demonstrable, as in works of science; or of facts experienced and recorded, as in history. Pleasure, and that of the highest and most permanent kind, may *result* from the *attainment* of the end; but it is not itself the immediate end. In other works the communication of pleasure may be the immediate purpose; and though truth, either moral or intellectual, ought to be the *ultimate* end, yet this will distinguish the character of the author, not the class to which the work belongs. Blest indeed is that state of society, in which the immediate purpose would be baffled by the perversion of the proper ultimate end; in which no charm of diction or imagery could exempt the Bathyllus even of an Anacreon, or the Alexis of Virgil,[4] from disgust and aversion!

But the communication of pleasure may be the immediate object of a work not metrically composed; and that object may have been in a high degree attained, as in novels and romances. Would then the mere superaddition of metre, with or without rhyme, entitle *these* to the name of poems? The answer is, that nothing can permanently please, which does not contain in itself the reason why it is so, and not otherwise. If metre be superadded, all other parts must be made consonant with it. They must be such, as to justify the perpetual and distinct attention to each part, which an exact correspondent recurrence of accent and sound are calculated to excite. The final definition then, so deduced, may be thus worded. A poem is that species of composition, which is opposed to works of science, by proposing for its *immediate* object pleasure, not truth; and from all other species (having *this* object in common with it) it is discriminated by proposing to itself such delight from the *whole,* as is compatible with a distinct gratification from each component *part.*

Controversy is not seldom excited in consequence of the disputants attaching each a different meaning to the same word; and in few instances has this been more striking, than in disputes concerning the present subject. If a man chooses to call every composition a poem, which is rhyme, or measure, or both, I must leave his opinion uncontroverted. The distinction is at least competent to characterize the writer's intention. If it were subjoined, that the whole is likewise entertaining or affecting, as a tale, or as a series of interesting reflections, I of course admit this as another fit ingredient of a poem, and an additional merit. But if the definition sought for be that of a *legitimate* poem, I answer, it must be one, the parts of which mutually support and explain each other; all in their proportion harmonizing with, and supporting the purpose and known influences of metrical arrangement. The philosophic critics of all ages coincide with the ultimate judgement of all countries, in equally denying the praises of a just poem, on the one hand, to a series of striking lines or distiches,[5] each of which, absorbing the whole attention of the reader to itself, disjoins it from its context, and makes it a separate whole, instead of an harmonizing part; and on the other hand, to an unsustained composition, from which the reader collects rapidly the general result, unattracted by the component parts. The reader should be carried forward, not merely or chiefly by the mechanical impulse of

---

[4] Anacreon (c. 560–c. 475 B.C.), a Greek lyric poet, lovingly praised "Bathyllus," a handsome boy; "Alexis" is a young man loved by a shepherd in Virgil's *Eclogue II.*
[5] Pairs of lines.

curiosity, or by a restless desire to arrive at the final solution; but by the pleasureable activity of mind excited by the attractions of the journey itself. Like the motion of a serpent, which the Egyptians made the emblem of intellectual power; or like the path of sound through the air; at every step he pauses and half recedes, and from the retrogressive movement collects the force which again carries him onward. "Praecipitandus est *liber* spiritus,"[6] says Petronius Arbiter most happily. The epithet, *liber*, here balances the preceding verb; and it is not easy to conceive more meaning condensed in fewer words.

But if this should be admitted as a satisfactory character of a poem, we have still to seek for a definition of poetry. The writings of PLATO, and Bishop TAYLOR,[7] and the "Theoria Sacra" of BURNET,[8] furnish undeniable proofs that poetry of the highest kind may exist without metre, and even without the contra-distinguishing objects of a poem. The first chapter of Isaiah (indeed a very large portion of the whole book) is poetry in the most emphatic sense; yet it would be not less irrational than strange to assert, that pleasure, and not truth, was the immediate object of the prophet. In short, whatever *specific* import we attach to the word, poetry, there will be found involved in it, as a necessary consequence, that a poem of any length neither can be, or ought to be, all poetry. Yet if an harmonious whole is to be produced, the remaining parts must be preserved *in keeping* with the poetry; and this can be no otherwise effected than by such a studied selection and artificial arrangement, as will partake of *one,* though not a *peculiar* property of poetry. And this again can be no other than the property of exciting a more continuous and equal attention than the language of prose aims at, whether colloquial or written.

My own conclusions on the nature of poetry, in the strictest use of the word, have been in part anticipated in the preceding disquisition on the fancy and imagination. What is poetry? is so nearly the same question with, what is a poet? that the answer to the one is involved in the solution of the other. For it is a distinction resulting from the poetic genius itself, which sustains and modifies the images, thoughts, and emotions of the poet's own mind.

The poet, described in *ideal* perfection, brings the whole soul of man into activity, with the subordination of its faculties to each other, according to their relative worth and dignity. He diffuses a tone and spirit of unity, that blends, and (as it were) *fuses,* each into each, by that synthetic and magical power, to which we have exclusively appropriated the name of imagination. This power, first put in action by the will and understanding, and retained under their irremissive, though gentle and unnoticed, controul (*laxis effertur habenis*)[9] reveals itself in the balance or reconciliation of opposite or discordant qualities: of sameness, with difference; of the general, with the concrete; the idea, with the image; the individual, with the representative; the sense of novelty and freshness, with old and familiar objects; a more than usual state of emotion, with

---

[6] "The free spirit [of the epic poet] must be propelled onward." From the *Satyricon.* Petronius was responsible for directing the emperor Nero's entertainments, but fell out of favor and committed suicide in 66 B.C.
[7] Jeremy Taylor (1613–1667), author of *Holy Living* and *Holy Dying.*
[8] Thomas Burnet (1635–1715), author of *Telluris Theoria Sacra,* "The Sacred Theory of the Earth."
[9] "Is driven with loose reins."

more than usual order; judgement ever awake and steady self-possession, with enthusiasm and feeling profound or vehement; and while it blends and harmonizes the natural and the artificial, still subordinates art to nature; the manner to the matter; and our admiration of the poet to our sympathy with the poetry. "Doubtless," as Sir John Davies[10] observes of the soul (and his words may with slight alteration be applied, and even more appropriately, to the poetic IMAGINATION)

> Doubtless this could not be, but that she turns
> Bodies to spirit by sublimation strange,
> As fire converts to fire the things it burns,
> As we our food into our nature change.
>
> From their gross matter she abstracts their forms,
> And draws a kind of quintessence from things;
> Which to her proper nature she transforms,
> To bear them light on her celestial wings.
>
> Thus does she, when from individual states
> She doth abstract the universal kinds;
> Which then re-clothed in divers names and fates
> Steal access through our senses to our minds.

Finally, GOOD SENSE is the BODY of poetic genius, FANCY its DRAPERY, MOTION its LIFE, and IMAGINATION the SOUL that is everywhere, and in each; and forms all into one graceful and intelligent whole.

Chapter XV

In the application of these principles to purposes of practical criticism as employed in the appraisal of works more or less imperfect, I have endeavoured to discover what the qualities in a poem are, which may be deemed promises and specific symptoms of poetic power, as distinguished from general talent determined to poetic composition by accidental motives, by an act of the will, rather than by the inspiration of a genial and productive nature. In this investigation, I could not, I thought, do better, than keep before me the earliest work of the greatest genius, that perhaps human nature has yet produced, our *myriad-minded** Shakespeare. I mean the "Venus and Adonis," and the "Lucrece";[11] works which give at once strong promises of the strength, and yet obvious proofs of the immaturity, of his genius. From these I abstracted the following marks, as characteristics of original poetic genius in general.

1. In the "Venus and Adonis," the first and most obvious excellence is the

---

[10] English lawyer and poet (1569–1626), noted for his ingenuity. Coleridge quotes, with minor changes, from Davies' "On the Soul of Man."

* Ἀνὴρ μυριόνους, a phrase which I have borrowed from a Greek monk [Naucritius], who applies it to a Patriarch of Constantinople [Theodorus Chersites]. I might have said, that I have *reclaimed,* rather than borrowed it: for it seems to belong to Shakespeare, "de jure singulari, et ex privilegio naturæ." [Coleridge's note.]

[11] Long narrative poems written by Shakespeare early in his career.

perfect sweetness of the versification; its adaptation to the subject; and the power displayed in varying the march of the words without passing into a loftier and more majestic rhythm than was demanded by the thoughts, or permitted by the propriety of preserving a sense of melody predominant. The delight in richness and sweetness of sound, even to a faulty excess, if it be evidently original, and not the result of an easily imitable mechanism, I regard as a highly favourable promise in the compositions of a young man. "The man that hath not music in his soul"[12] can indeed never be a genuine poet. Imagery (even taken from nature, much more when transplanted from books, as travels, voyages, and works of natural history); affecting incidents; just thoughts; interesting personal or domestic feelings; and with these the art of their combination or intertexture in the form of a poem; may all by incessant effort be acquired as a trade, by a man of talents and much reading, who, as I once before observed, has mistaken an intense desire of poetic reputation for a natural poetic genius; the love of the arbitrary end for a possession of the peculiar means. But the sense of musical delight, with the power of producing it, is a gift of imagination; and this together with the power of reducing multitude into unity of effect, and modifying a series of thoughts by some one predominant thought or feeling, may be cultivated and improved, but can never be learned. It is in these that "poeta nascitur non fit."[13]

2. A second promise of genius is the choice of subjects very remote from the private interests and circumstances of the writer himself. At least I have found, that where the subject is taken immediately from the author's personal sensations and experiences, the excellence of a particular poem is but an equivocal mark, and often a fallacious pledge, of genuine poetic power. We may perhaps remember the tale of the statuary, who had acquired considerable reputation for the legs of his goddesses, though the rest of the statue accorded but indifferently with ideal beauty; till his wife, elated by her husband's praises, modestly acknowledged that she herself had been his constant model. In the "Venus and Adonis" this proof of poetic power exists even to excess. It is throughout as if a superior spirit more intuitive, more intimately conscious, even than the characters themselves, not only of every outward look and act, but of the flux and reflux of the mind in all its subtlest thoughts and feelings, were placing the whole before our view; himself meanwhile unparticipating in the passions, and actuated only by that pleasureable excitement, which had resulted from the energetic fervor of his own spirit in so vividly exhibiting, what it had so accurately and profoundly contemplated. I think, I should have conjectured from these poems, that even then the great instinct, which impelled the poet to the drama, was secretly working in him, prompting him by a series and never broken chain of imagery, always vivid and, because unbroken, often minute; by the highest effort of the picturesque in words, of which words are capable, higher perhaps than was ever realized by any other poet, even Dante not excepted; to provide a substitute for that visual language, that constant intervention and running comment by tone, look and gesture, which in his dramatic works he was entitled to expect from the players. His "Venus and Adonis" seem

---

[12] Quoted almost correctly from Shakespeare's *Merchant of Venice*, V. i. 83.
[13] "A poet is born, not made."

at once the characters themselves, and the whole representation of those characters by the most consummate actors. You seem to be told nothing, but to see and hear everything. Hence it is, that from the perpetual activity of attention required on the part of the reader; from the rapid flow, the quick change, and the playful nature of the thoughts and images; and above all from the alienation, and, if I may hazard such an expression, the utter *aloofness* of the poet's own feelings, from those of which he is at once the painter and the analyst; that though the very subject cannot but detract from the pleasure of a delicate mind, yet never was poem less dangerous on a moral account. Instead of doing as Ariosto[14] and as, still more offensively, Wieland[15] has done, instead of degrading and deforming passion into appetite, the trials of love into the struggles of concupiscence; Shakespeare has here represented the animal impulse itself, so as to preclude all sympathy with it, by dissipating the reader's notice among the thousand outward images, and now beautiful, now fanciful circumstances, which form its dresses and its scenery; or by diverting our attention from the main subject by those frequent witty or profound reflections, which the poet's ever active mind has deduced from, or connected with, the imagery and the incidents. The reader is forced into too much action to sympathize with the merely passive of our nature. As little can a mind thus roused and awakened be brooded on by mean and indistinct emotion, as the low, lazy mist can creep upon the surface of a lake, while a strong gale is driving it onward in waves and billows.

3. It has been before observed that images, however beautiful, though faithfully copied from nature, and as accurately represented in words, do not of themselves characterize the poet. They become proofs of original genius only as far as they are modified by a predominant passion; or by associated thoughts or images awakened by that passion; or when they have the effect of reducing multitude to unity, or succession to an instant; or lastly, when a human and intellectual life is transferred to them from the poet's own spirit,

> Which shoots its being through earth, sea and air.[16]

In the two following lines for instance, there is nothing objectionable, nothing which would preclude them from forming, in their proper place, part of a descriptive poem:

> Behold yon row of pines, that shorn and bow'd
> Bend from the sea-blast, seen at twilight eve.

But with a small alteration of rhythm, the same words would be equally in their place in a book of topography, or in a descriptive tour. The same image will rise into semblance of poetry if thus conveyed:

> Yon row of bleak and visionary pines,
> By twilight glimpse discerned, mark! how they flee
> From the fierce sea-blast, all their tresses wild
> Streaming before them.

[14] Ludovico Ariosto (1474–1533), Italian poet.
[15] Christoph Martin Wieland (1733–1813), German poet and belle-lettrist, sometimes called the German Voltaire.
[16] An altered line from Coleridge's own poem, "France: an Ode."

I have given this as an illustration, by no means as an instance, of that particular excellence which I had in view, and in which Shakespeare even in his
earliest, as in his latest, works surpasses all other poets. It is by this, that he still
gives a dignity and a passion to the objects which he presents. Unaided by any
previous excitement, they burst upon us at once in life and in power.

> Full many a glorious morning have I seen
> *Flatter* the mountain tops with sovereign eye.
>   Shakespeare, Sonnet 33rd.

> Not mine own fears, nor the prophetic soul
> Of the wide world dreaming on things to come—
>
>   *   *   *
>
> The mortal moon hath her eclipse endur'd,
> And the sad augurs mock their own presage;
> Incertainties now crown themselves assur'd,
> And Peace proclaims olives of endless age.
> Now with the drops of this most balmy time
> My Love looks fresh, and DEATH to me subscribes!
> Since spite of him, I'll live in this poor rhyme,
> While he insults o'er dull and speechless tribes.
> And thou in this shalt find thy monument,
> When tyrants' crests, and tombs of brass are spent.
>   Sonnet 107.

As of higher worth, so doubtless still more characteristic of poetic genius
does the imagery become, when it moulds and colors itself to the circumstances,
passion, or character, present and foremost in the mind. For unrivalled instances
of this excellence, the reader's own memory will refer him to the LEAR,
OTHELLO, in short to which not of the *"great, ever living, dead man's"* dramatic
works? "Inopem me copia fecit."[17] How true it is to nature, he has himself
finely expressed in the instance of love in Sonnet 98.

> From you have I been absent in the spring,
> When proud pied April drest in all its trim
> Hath put a spirit of youth in every thing,
> That heavy Saturn laugh'd and leap'd with him.
> Yet nor the lays of birds, nor the sweet smell
> Of different flowers in odour and in hue,
> Could make me any summer's story tell,
> Or from their proud lap pluck them, where they grew:
> Nor did I wonder at the lilies white,
> Nor praise the deep vermilion in the rose;
> They were, tho' sweet, but figures of delight,
> Drawn after you, you pattern of all those.
> Yet seem'd it winter still, and, you away,
> *As with your shadow I with these did play!*

[17] "Plenty has made me poor." From the *Metamorphoses* of Ovid (43 B.C–A.D. 18),
Latin poet.

Scarcely less sure, or if a less valuable, not less indispensable mark

Γονίμου μὲν ποιητοῦ——
——ὅστις ῥῆμα γενναῖον λάκοι,[18]

will the imagery supply, when, with more than the power of the painter, the poet gives us the liveliest image of succession with the feeling of simultaneousness!

> With this, he breaketh from the sweet embrace
> Of those fair arms, that held him to her heart,
> And homeward through the dark lawns runs apace:
> *Look! how a bright star shooteth from the sky,*
> *So glides he in the night from Venus' eye.*[19]

4. The last character I shall mention, which would prove indeed but little, except as taken conjointly with the former; yet without which the former could scarce exist in a high degree, and (even if this were possible) would give promises only of transitory flashes and a meteoric power; is DEPTH, and ENERGY of THOUGHT. No man was ever yet a great poet, without being at the same time a profound philosopher. For poetry is the blossom and the fragrancy of all human knowledge, human thoughts, human passions, emotions, language. In Shakespeare's *poems* the creative power and the intellectual energy wrestle as in a war embrace. Each in its excess of strength seems to threaten the extinction of the other. At length in the DRAMA they were reconciled, and fought each with its shield before the breast of the other. Or like two rapid streams, that, at their first meeting within narrow and rocky banks, mutually strive to repel each other and intermix reluctantly and in tumult; but soon finding a wider channel and more yielding shores blend, and dilate, and flow on in one current and with one voice. The "Venus and Adonis" did not perhaps allow the display of the deeper passions. But the story of Lucretia seems to favor and even demand their intensest workings. And yet we find in *Shakespeare's* management of the tale neither pathos, nor any other *dramatic* quality. There is the same minute and faithful imagery as in the former poem, in the same vivid colors, inspirited by the same impetuous vigor of thought, and diverging and contracting with the same activity of the assimilative and of the modifying faculties; and with a yet larger display, a yet wider range of knowledge and reflection; and lastly, with the same perfect dominion, often *domination,* over the whole world of language. What then shall we say? even this; that Shakespeare, no mere child of nature; no automaton of genius; no passive vehicle of inspiration possessed by the spirit, not possessing it; first studied patiently, meditated deeply, understood minutely, till knowledge, become habitual and intuitive, wedded itself to his habitual feelings, and at length gave birth to that stupendous power, by which he stands alone, with no equal or second in his own class; to that power which seated him on one of the two glory-smitten summits of the poetic mountain, with Milton as his compeer, not rival. While the former darts himself forth, and passes into all the forms of human character and passion, the one Proteus of the

---

[18] You will never find a true poet to utter notable things." From the *Frogs* of Aristophanes (c. 448–385 B.C.), Greek writer of comedies.
[19] *Venus and Adonis,* ll. 811–813 and 815–816.

fire and the flood; the other attracts all forms and things to himself, into the
unity of his own IDEAL. All things and modes of action shape themselves anew
in the being of MILTON; while SHAKESPEARE becomes all things, yet for ever
remaining himself. O what great men hast thou not produced, England! my
country! truly indeed—

> Must *we* be free or die, who speak the tongue,
> Which SHAKESPEARE spake; the faith and morals hold,
> Which MILTON held. In every thing we are sprung
> Of earth's first blood, have titles manifold![20]
>   WORDSWORTH.

*   *   *

Chapter XVII

As far then as Mr. Wordsworth in his preface contended, and most ably
contended, for a reformation in our poetic diction, as far as he has evinced the
truth of passion, and the *dramatic* propriety of those figures and metaphors in
the original poets, which, stripped of their justifying reasons, and converted into
mere artifices of connection or ornament, constitute the characteristic falsity in
the poetic style of the moderns; and as far as he has, with equal acuteness and
clearness, pointed out the process by which this change was effected, and the
resemblances between that state into which the reader's mind is thrown by the
pleasureable confusion of thought from an unaccustomed train of words and
images; and that state which is induced by the natural language of empassioned
feeling; he undertook a useful task, and deserves all praise, both for the attempt
and for the execution. The provocations to this remonstrance in behalf of truth
and nature were still of perpetual recurrence before and after the publication of
this preface. I cannot likewise but add, that the comparison of such poems of
merit, as have been given to the public within the last ten or twelve years, with
the majority of those produced previously to the appearance of that preface, leave
no doubt on my mind, that Mr. Wordsworth is fully justified in believing his
efforts to have been by no means ineffectual. Not only in the verses of those
who have professed their admiration of his genius, but even of those who have
distinguished themselves by hostility to his theory, and depreciation of his
writings, are the impressions of his principles plainly visible. It is possible, that
with these principles others may have been blended, which are not equally
evident; and some which are unsteady and subvertible from the narrowness or
imperfection of their basis. But it is more than possible, that these errors of
defect or exaggeration, by kindling and feeding the controversy, may have con-
duced not only to the wider propagation of the accompanying truths, but that,
by their frequent presentation to the mind in an excited state, they may have
won for them a more permanent and practical result. A man will borrow a part
from his opponent the more easily, if he feels himself justified in continuing to
reject a part. While there remain important points in which he can still feel

[20] Slightly adapted from Wordsworth's sonnet beginning "It is not to be thought of
that the Flood."

himself in the right, in which he still finds firm footing for continued resistance, he will gradually adopt those opinions, which were the least remote from his own convictions, as not less congruous with his own theory than with that which he reprobates. In like manner with a kind of instinctive prudence, he will abandon by little and little his weakest posts, till at length he seems to forget that they had ever belonged to him, or affects to consider them at most as accidental and "petty annexments," the removal of which leaves the citadel unhurt and unendangered.

My own differences from certain supposed parts of Mr. Wordsworth's theory ground themselves on the assumption, that his words had been rightly interpreted, as purporting that the proper diction for poetry in general consists altogether in a language taken, with due exceptions, from the mouths of men in real life, a language which actually constitutes the natural conversation of men under the influence of natural feelings.[21] My objection is, first, that in *any* sense this rule is applicable only to *certain* classes of poetry; secondly, that even to these classes it is not applicable, except in such a sense, as hath never by any one (as far as I know or have read) been denied or doubted; and lastly, that as far as, and in that degree in which it is *practicable*, yet as a *rule* it is useless, if not injurious, and therefore either need not, or ought not to be practised. The poet informs his reader, that he had generally chosen *low and rustic* life; but not *as* low and rustic, or in order to repeat that pleasure of doubtful moral effect, which persons of elevated rank and of superior refinement oftentimes derive from a happy *imitation* of the rude unpolished manners and discourse of their inferiors. For the pleasure so derived may be traced to three exciting causes. The first is the naturalness, in *fact*, of the things represented. The second is the apparent naturalness of the *representation*, as raised and qualified by an imperceptible infusion of the author's own knowledge and talent, which infusion does, indeed, constitute it an *imitation* as distinguished from a mere *copy*. The third cause may be found in the reader's conscious feeling of his superiority awakened by the contrast presented to him; even as for the same purpose the kings and great barons of yore retained sometimes *actual* clowns and fools, but more frequently shrewd and witty fellows in that *character*. These, however, were not Mr. Wordsworth's objects. *He* chose low and rustic life, "because in that condition the essential passions of the heart find a better soil, in which they can attain their maturity, are less under restraint, and speak a plainer and more emphatic language; because in that condition of life our elementary feelings coexist in a state of greater simplicity, and consequently may be more accurately contemplated, and more forcibly communicated; because the manners of rural life germinate from those elementary feelings; and from the necessary character of rural occupations are more easily comprehended, and are more durable; and lastly, because in that condition the passions of men are incorporated with the beautiful and permanent forms of nature."

Now it is clear to me, that in the most interesting of the poems, in which the author is more or less dramatic, as "the Brothers," "Michael," "Ruth," "the Mad Mother," &c., the persons introduced are by no means taken *from low or*

---

[21] Wordsworth in his *Preface* commends "the real language of men in a state of vivid sensation, . . ." the language of men of "humble and rustic life."

rustic life in the common acceptation of those words; and it is not less clear, that the sentiments and language, as far as they can be conceived to have been really transferred from the minds and conversation of such persons, are attributable to causes and circumstances not necessarily connected with "their occupations and abode." The thoughts, feelings, language, and manners of the shepherd-farmers in the vales of Cumberland and Westmoreland, as far as they are actually adopted in those poems, may be accounted for from causes, which will and do produce the same results in *every* state of life, whether in town or country. As the two principal I rank that INDEPENDENCE, which raises a man above servitude, or daily toil for the profit of others, yet not above the necessity of industry and a frugal simplicity of domestic life; and the accompanying unambitious, but solid and religious, EDUCATION, which has rendered few books familiar, but the Bible, and the liturgy or hymn book. To this latter cause, indeed, which is so far *accidental,* that it is the blessing of particular countries and a particular age, not the product of particular places or employments, the poet owes the show of probability, that his personages might really feel, think, and talk with any tolerable resemblance to his representation. It is an excellent remark of Dr. Henry More's, (*Enthusiasmus triumphatus,* Sec. XXXV.), that "a man of confined education, but of good parts, by constant reading of the Bible will naturally form a more winning and commanding rhetoric than those that are learned; the intermixture of tongues and of artificial phrases debasing *their* style."

It is, moreover, to be considered that to the formation of healthy feelings, and a reflecting mind, *negations* involve impediments not less formidable than sophistication and vicious intermixture. I am convinced, that for the human soul to prosper in rustic life a certain vantage-ground is pre-requisite. It is not every man that is likely to be improved by a country life or by country labors. Education, or original sensibility, or both, must pre-exist, if the changes, forms, and incidents of nature are to prove a sufficient stimulant. And where these are not sufficient, the mind contracts and hardens by want of stimulants: and the man becomes selfish, sensual, gross, and hard-hearted. Let the management of the POOR LAWS in Liverpool, Manchester, or Bristol be compared with the ordinary dispensation of the poor rates in agricultural villages, where the *farmers* are the overseers and guardians of the poor. If my own experience have not been particularly unfortunate, as well as that of the many respectable country clergymen with whom I have conversed on the subject, the result would engender more than scepticism concerning the desireable influences of low and rustic life in and for itself. Whatever may be concluded on the other side, from the stronger local attachments and enterprising spirit of the Swiss, and other mountaineers, applies to a particular mode of pastoral life, under forms of property that permit and beget manners truly republican, not to rustic life in general, or to the absence of artificial cultivation. On the contrary the mountaineers, whose manners have been so often eulogized, are in general better educated and greater readers than men of equal rank elsewhere. But where this is not the case, as among the peasantry of North Wales, the ancient mountains, with all their terrors and all their glories, are pictures to the blind, and music to the deaf.

I should not have entered so much into detail upon this passage, but here seems to be the point, to which all the lines of difference converge as to their source and centre. (I mean, as far as, and in whatever respect, my poetic creed *does* differ from the doctrines promulged in this preface.) I adopt with full faith the principle of Aristotle, that poetry as poetry is essentially* *ideal*, that it avoids and excludes all *accident;* that its apparent individualities of rank, character, or occupation must be *representative* of a class; and that the *persons* of poetry must be clothed with *generic* attributes, with the *common* attributes of the class: not with such as one gifted individual might *possibly* possess, but such as from his situation it is most probable before-hand that he *would* possess. If my premises are right and my deductions legitimate, it follows that there can be no *poetic* medium between the swains of Theocritus[22] and those of an imaginary golden age.

The characters of the vicar and the shepherd-mariner in the poem of "THE BROTHERS," that of the shepherd of Greenhead Ghyll in the "MICHAEL," have all the verisimilitude and representative quality, that the purposes of poetry can require. They are persons of a known and abiding class, and their manners and sentiments the natural product of circumstances common to the class. Take "MICHAEL"[23] for instance:

> An old man stout of heart, and strong of limb:
> His bodily frame had been from youth to age
> Of an unusual strength: his mind was keen,
> Intense, and frugal, apt for all affairs,
> And in his shepherd's calling he was prompt

* Say not that I am recommending abstractions; for these class-characteristics which constitute the instructiveness of a character, are so modified and particularized in each person of the Shakespearean Drama, that life itself does not excite more distinctly that sense of individuality which belongs to real existence. Paradoxical as it may sound, one of the essential properties of Geometry is not less essential to dramatic excellence; and Aristotle has accordingly required of the poet an involution of the universal in the individual. The chief differences are, that in Geometry it is the universal truth, which is uppermost in the consciousness; in poetry the individual form, in which the truth is clothed. With the ancients, and not less with the elder dramatists of England and France, both comedy and tragedy were considered as kinds of poetry. They neither sought in comedy to make us laugh merely; much less to make us laugh by wry faces, accidents of jargon, *slang* phrases for the day, or the clothing of common-place morals drawn from the shops or mechanic occupations of their characters. Nor did they condescend in tragedy to wheedle away the applause of the spectators, by representing before them facsimiles of their own mean selves in all their existing meanness, or to work on the sluggish sympathies by a pathos not a whit more respectable than the maudlin tears of drunkenness. Their tragic scenes were meant to *affect* us indeed; but yet within the bounds of pleasure, and in union with the activity both of our understanding and imagination. They wished to transport the mind to a sense of its possible greatness, and to implant the germs of that greatness, during the temporary oblivion of the worthless "thing we are," and of the peculiar state in which each man *happens* to be, suspending our individual recollections and lulling them to sleep amid the music of nobler thoughts.

The Friend, Pages 251, 252

[Coleridge's note. This extract is taken from the second of *Satyrane's Letters,* originally published in *The Friend,* in 1809.]

[22] Hellenistic Greek poet of the third century A.D., known chiefly as a writer of pastoral verse.

[23] Coleridge quotes from "Michael, a Pastoral Poem," as it appeared in the 1802 edition of the *Lyrical Ballads.*

And watchful more than ordinary men.
Hence he had learnt the meaning of all winds,
Of blasts of every tone; and oftentimes
When others heeded not, he heard the South
Make subterraneous music, like the noise
Of bagpipers on distant Highland hills.
The shepherd, at such warning, of his flock
Bethought him, and he to himself would say,
The winds are now devising work for me!
And truly at all times the storm, that drives
The traveller to a shelter, summon'd him
Up to the mountains. He had been alone
Amid the heart of many thousand mists,
That came to him and left him on the heights.
So liv'd he, till his eightieth year was pass'd.
And grossly that man errs, who should suppose
That the green vallies, and the streams and rocks,
Were things indifferent to the shepherd's thoughts.
Fields, where with chearful spirits he had breath'd
The common air; the hills, which he so oft
Had climb'd with vigorous steps; which had impress'd
So many incidents upon his mind
Of hardship, skill or courage, joy or fear;
Which, like a book, preserved the memory
Of the dumb animals, whom he had sav'd,
Had fed or shelter'd, linking to such acts,
So grateful in themselves, the certainty
Of honorable gain; these fields, these hills
Which were his living being, even more
Than his own blood—what could they less? had laid
Strong hold on his affections, were to him
A pleasureable feeling of blind love,
The pleasure which there is in life itself.

On the other hand, in the poems which are pitched at a lower note, as the "HARRY GILL," "IDIOT BOY," the *feelings* are those of human nature in general; though the poet has judiciously laid the *scene* in the country, in order to place *himself* in the vicinity of interesting images, without the necessity of ascribing a sentimental perception of their beauty to the persons of his drama. In the "Idiot Boy," indeed, the mother's character is not so much a real and native product of a "situation where the essential passions of the heart find a better soil, in which they can attain their maturity and speak a plainer and more emphatic language," as it is an impersonation of an instinct abandoned by judgement. Hence the two following charges seem to me not wholly groundless: at least, they are the only plausible objections, which I have heard to that fine poem. The one is, that the author has not, in the poem itself, taken sufficient care to preclude from the reader's fancy the disgusting images of *ordinary morbid idiocy*, which yet it was by no means his intention to represent. He has even by the "burr, burr, burr," uncounteracted by any preceding description of the boy's beauty, assisted in recalling them. The other is, that the idiocy of the *boy* is so evenly balanced by the folly of the *mother*, as to present to the general reader rather a laughable burlesque on the blindness of anile dotage, than an analytic display of maternal affection in its ordinary workings.

In the "Thorn" the poet himself acknowledges in a note the necessity of an introductory poem, in which he should have pourtrayed the character of the person from whom the words of the poem are supposed to proceed: a superstitious man moderately imaginative, of slow faculties and deep feelings, "a captain of a small trading vessel, for example, who, being past the middle age of life, had retired upon an annuity, or small independent income, to some village or country town of which he was not a native, or in which he had not been accustomed to live. Such men having nothing to do become credulous and talkative from indolence." But in a poem, still more in a lyric poem (and the NURSE in Shakespeare's Romeo and Juliet alone prevents me from extending the remark even to dramatic *poetry*, if indeed the Nurse itself can be deemed altogether a case in point) it is not possible to imitate truly a dull and garrulous discourser, without repeating the effects of dullness and garrulity. However this may be, I dare assert, that the parts (and these form the far larger portion of the whole) which might as well or still better have proceeded from the poet's own imagination, and have been spoken in his own character, are those which have given, and which will continue to give, universal delight; and that the passages exclusively appropriate to the supposed narrator, such as the last couplet of the third stanza;* the seven last lines of the tenth;† and the five

* I've measured it from side to side;
'Tis three feet long, and two feet wide.
[Coleridge's note.].
† Nay, rack your brain—'tis all in vain,
I'll tell you every thing I know;
But to the Thorn, and to the Pond
Which is a little step beyond,
I wish that you would go:
Perhaps when you are at the place,
You something of her tale may trace.

I'll give you the best help I can:
Before you up the mountain go,
Up to the dreary mountain-top,
I'll tell you all I know.
'Tis now some two-and-twenty years
Since she (her name is Martha Ray)
Gave, with a maiden's true good will,
Her company to Stephen Hill;
And she was blithe and gay,
And she was happy, happy still
Whene'er she thought of Stephen Hill.

And they had fix'd the wedding-day,
The morning that must wed them both;
But Stephen to another maid
Had sworn another oath;
And, with this other maid, to church

following stanzas, with the exception of the four admirable lines at the commencement of the fourteenth, are felt by many unprejudiced and unsophisticated hearts, as sudden and unpleasant sinkings from the height to which the poet had previously lifted them, and to which he again re-elevates both himself and his reader.

If then I am compelled to doubt the theory, by which the choice of *characters* was to be directed, not only *a priori,* from grounds of reason, but both from the few instances in which the poet himself *need* be supposed to have been governed by it, and from the comparative inferiority of those instances; still more must I hesitate in my assent to the sentence which immediately follows the former citation; and which I can neither admit as particular fact, or as general rule. "The language too of these men is adopted (purified indeed from what appear to be its real defects, from all lasting and rational causes of dislike or disgust) because such men hourly communicate with the best objects

---

Unthinking Stephen went—
Poor Martha! on that woeful day
A pang of pitiless dismay
Into her soul was sent;
A fire was kindled in her breast,
Which might not burn itself to rest.

They say, full six months after this,
While yet the summer leaves were green,
She to the mountain-top would go,
And there was often seen.
'Tis said a child was in her womb,
As now to any eye was plain;
She was with child, and she was mad;
Yet often she was sober sad
From her exceeding pain.
Oh me! ten thousand times I'd rather
That he had died, that cruel father!

　　　　　　*　　　　*　　　　*

Last Christmas when we talked of this,
Old farmer Simpson did maintain,
That in her womb the infant wrought
About its mother's heart, and brought
Her senses back again:
And, when at last her time drew near,
Her looks were calm, her senses clear.

No more I know, I wish I did,
And I would tell it all to you:
For what became of this poor child
There's none that ever knew:
And if a child was born or no,
There's no one that could ever tell;
And if 'twas born alive or dead,
There's no one knows, as I have said:
But some remember well,
That Martha Ray about this time
Would up the mountain often climb.
[Coleridge's note.]

from which the best part of language is originally derived; and because, from their rank in society and the sameness and narrow circle of their intercourse, being less under the action of social vanity, they convey their feelings and notions in simple and unelaborated expressions." To this I reply; that a rustic's language, purified from all provincialism and grossness, and so far reconstructed as to be made consistent with the rules of grammar (which are in essence no other than the laws of universal logic, applied to psychological materials) will not differ from the language of any other man of common-sense, however learned or refined he may be, except as far as the notions, which the rustic has to convey, are fewer and more indiscriminate. This will become still clearer, if we add the consideration (equally important though less obvious) that the rustic, from the more imperfect developement of his faculties, and from the lower state of their cultivation, aims almost solely to convey *insulated facts,* either those of his scanty experience or his traditional belief; while the educated man chiefly seeks to discover and express those *connections* of things, or those relative *bearings* of fact to fact, from which some more or less general law is deducible. For *facts* are valuable to a wise man, chiefly as they lead to the discovery of the indwelling *law,* which is the true *being* of things, the sole solution of their modes of existence, and in the knowledge of which consists our dignity and our power.

As little can I agree with the assertion, that from the objects with which the rustic hourly communicates the best part of language is formed. For first, if to communicate with an object implies such an acquaintance with it, as renders it capable of being discriminately reflected on; the distinct knowledge of an uneducated rustic would furnish a very scanty vocabulary. The few things, and modes of action, requisite for his bodily conveniences, would alone be individualized; while all the rest of nature would be expressed by a small number of confused general terms. Secondly, I deny that the words and combinations of words derived from the objects, with which the rustic is familiar, whether with distinct or confused knowledge, can be justly said to form the *best* part of language. It is more than probable, that many classes of the brute creation possess discriminating sounds, by which they can convey to each other notices of such objects as concern their food, shelter, or safety. Yet we hesitate to call the aggregate of such sounds a language, otherwise than metaphorically. The best part of human language, properly so called, is derived from reflection on the acts of the mind itself. It is formed by a voluntary appropriation of fixed symbols to internal acts, to processes and results of imagination, the greater part of which have no place in the consciousness of uneducated man; though in civilized society, by imitation and passive remembrance of what they hear from their religious instructors and other superiors, the most uneducated share in the harvest which they neither sowed or reaped. If the history of the phrases in hourly currency among our peasants were traced, a person not previously aware of the fact would be surprised at finding so large a number, which three or four centuries ago were the exclusive property of the universities and the schools; and, at the commencement of the Reformation, had been transferred from the school to the pulpit, and thus gradually passed into common life. The extreme difficulty, and often the impossibility, of finding words for the simplest moral and intellectual processes of the languages of uncivilized tribes has proved perhaps the weightiest obstacle to the progress of our most zealous and adroit missionaries. Yet these tribes are surrounded by the same nature as our peasants are; but in still more impressive forms; and they are, moreover, obliged to *particularize* many more of them. When, therefore, Mr. Wordsworth adds, "accordingly, such a language" (meaning, as before, the language of rustic life purified from provincialism) "arising out of repeated experience and regular feelings, is a more permanent, and a far more philosophical language, than that which is frequently substituted for it by poets, who think they are conferring honor upon themselves and their art in proportion as they indulge in arbitrary and capricious habits of expression:" it may be answered, that the language, which he has in view, can be attributed to rustics with no greater right, than the style of Hooker or Bacon to Tom Brown or Sir Roger L'Estrange.[24] Doubtless, if what is peculiar to each were omitted in each, the result must needs be the same. Further, that the poet, who uses an illogical diction, or a style fitted to excite only the low and changeable pleasure of wonder by means of groundless novelty, substitutes a language of *folly* and *vanity*, not for that of the *rustic*, but for that of *good sense* and *natural feeling*.

Here let me be permitted to remind the reader, that the positions, which I controvert, are contained in the sentences—"*a selection of the* REAL *language of men;*"—"*the language of these men*" (i.e. men in low and rustic life) "*I propose to myself to imitate, and, as far as is possible, to adopt the very language of men.*" "*Between the language of prose and that of metrical composition, there neither is, nor can be any essential difference.*" It is against these exclusively that my opposition is directed.

I object, in the very first instance, to an equivocation in the use of the word "real." Every man's language varies, according to the extent of his knowledge, the activity of his faculties, and the depth or quickness of his feelings. Every man's language has, first, its *individualities;* secondly, the common properties of the *class* to which he belongs; and thirdly, words and phrases of *universal* use. The language of Hooker, Bacon, Bishop Taylor,[25] and Burke[26] differs from the common language of the learned class only by the superior number and novelty of the thoughts and relations which they had to convey. The language of Algernon Sidney[27] differs not at all from that, which every well-educated gentleman would wish to write, and (with due allowances for the undeliberateness, and less connected train, of thinking natural and proper to conversation) such as he would wish to talk. Neither one nor the other differ half so much from the general language of cultivated society, as the language of Mr. Wordsworth's homeliest composition differs from that of a common peasant. For "real" therefore, we must substitute *ordinary,* or *lingua communis.* And this, we have proved, is no more to be found in the phraseology of low and rustic life than

[24] Richard Hooker (1554–1600), author of *Ecclesiastical Polity,* and Francis Bacon (1561–1626) were great prose writers. Thomas Brown (1663–1704) was dull and Sir Roger L'Estrange (1616–1704) was scurrilous.

[25] Jeremy Taylor (1613–1667), whose devotional writings were noted for the beauty of their style.

[26] Edmund Burke (1729–1797), political writer and statesman.

[27] Algernon Sidney (1622–1683), republican soldier and statesman, whose *Discourses Concerning Government* appeared posthumously.

in that of any other class. Omit the peculiarities of each, and the result of course must be common to all. And assuredly the omissions and changes to be made in the language of rustics, before it could be transferred to any species of poem, except the drama or other professed imitation, are at least as numerous and weighty, as would be required in adapting to the same purpose the ordinary language of tradesmen and manufacturers. Not to mention, that the language so highly extolled by Mr. Wordsworth varies in every county, nay in every village, according to the accidental character of the clergyman, the existence or non-existence of schools; or even, perhaps, as the exciseman, publican, or barber, happen to be, or not to be, zealous politicians, and readers of the weekly newspaper *pro bono publico.*[28] Anterior to cultivation, the lingua communis of every country, as Dante has well observed, exists every where in parts, and no where as a whole.[29]

Neither is the case rendered at all more tenable by the addition of the words, *in a state of excitement:* For the nature of a man's words, where he is strongly affected by joy, grief, or anger, must necessarily depend on the number and quality of the general truths, conceptions and images, and of the words expressing them, with which his mind had been previously stored. For the property of passion is not to *create;* but to set in increased activity. At least, whatever new connections of thoughts or images, or (which is equally, if not more than equally, the appropriate effect of strong excitement) whatever generalizations of truth or experience, the heat of passion may produce; yet the terms of their conveyance must have pre-existed in his former conversations, and are only collected and crowded together by the unusual stimulation. It is indeed very possible to adopt in a poem the unmeaning repetitions, habitual phrases, and other blank counters, which an unfurnished or confused understanding interposes at short intervals, in order to keep hold of his subject, which is still slipping from him, and to give him time for recollection; or in mere aid of vacancy, as in the scanty companies of a country stage the same player pops backwards and forwards, in order to prevent the appearance of empty spaces, in the procession of *Macbeth,* or *Henry VIIIth.* But what assistance to the poet, or ornament to the poem, these can supply, I am at a loss to conjecture. Nothing assuredly can differ either in origin or in mode more widely from the *apparent* tautologies of intense and turbulent feeling, in which the passion is greater and of longer endurance than to be exhausted or satisfied by a single representation of the image or incident exciting it. Such repetitions I admit to be a beauty of the highest kind; as illustrated by Mr. Wordsworth himself from the song of Deborah. *"At her feet he bowed, he fell, he lay down; at her feet he bowed, he fell; where he bowed, there he fell down dead."*[30]

[28] "For the public welfare."

[29] In *De vulgari eloquentia* ("On the Vulgar Tongue") Dante argues that the Italian vernacular is fit for poetry and common to all of Italy.

[30] Judges 5:27, quoted by Wordsworth to show that "repetition and apparent tautology are frequently beauties of the highest kind."

Charles Lamb

SANITY OF TRUE GENIUS

The critical gifts of Charles Lamb (1775–1834) were of a high order but he did not often bring them into play and the relatively few forays that he did make into criticism have been thrust into relative obscurity by his more characteristic work, of which the best is to be found in *The Essays of Elia* (1823) and *The Last Essays of Elia* (1833). Lamb was born in London—which he loved with a passion that is often compared with Wordsworth's love of the Lake Country—the son of a domestic servant, later a lawyer's clerk. He was educated at Christ's Hospital, an admirable school for poor children, known also as the Blue coat School from the costume, including yellow stockings, still worn by the pupils. Here he first met Coleridge, with whom he formed a lifelong friendship. The outward course of his life was determined when his sister Mary, in a fit of the insanity which was hereditary in the family, stabbed their mother to death. Rather than commit Mary to an institution, Lamb undertook to make a home for her and a quiet existence which was occasionally interrupted by recurrences of her disorder; she shared her brother's tastes and pursuits, and collaborated with him in the once popular children's book, *Tales from Shakespeare*.

Lamb derived his chief support from his position as a clerk in East India House. In his early days he attempted poems and plays; of the former a few have merit, but as much cannot be said for the latter. It was not until middle age that he found his true genre, the personal essay, in which free rein is given to speculation and to the exploitation of idiosyncrasy, touched with pathos and irony and written in a style derived from the prose of certain authors of the seventeenth century whom he admired and helped win admiration for. Of his critical essays, "Sanity of True Genius" is one of the most notable for its good sense bluntly stated and its precise discriminations. Its pertinence is maintained by the continuing life of the fallacy to which it directs itself. It was first published in the *New Monthy Magazine*, May 1826.

So far from the position holding true, that great wit (or genius, in our modern way of speaking) has a necessary alliance with insanity, the greatest

From *The Essays of Elia* by Charles Lamb, with notes by Alfred Ainger. London, Macmillan and Co., Limited, 1898.

wits, on the contrary, will ever be found to be the sanest writers. It is impossible
for the mind to conceive of a mad Shakespeare. The greatness of wit, by which
the poetic talent is here chiefly to be understood, manifests itself in the admirable balance of all the faculties. Madness is the disproportionate straining
or excess of any one of them. "So strong a wit," says Cowley, speaking of a
poetical friend,

> ——did Nature to him frame,
> As all things but his judgment overcame;
> His judgment like the heavenly moon did show,
> Tempering that mighty sea below.[1]

The ground of the mistake is, that men, finding in the raptures of the
higher poetry a condition of exaltation, to which they have no parallel in their
own experience, besides the spurious resemblance of it in dreams and fevers,
impute a state of dreaminess and fever to the poet. But the true poet dreams
being awake. He is not possessed by his subject, but has dominion over it. In
the groves of Eden he walks familiar as in his native paths. He ascends the
empyrean heaven, and is not intoxicated. He treads the burning marl without
dismay; he wins his flight without self-loss through realms of chaos "and old
night."[2] Or if, abandoning himself to that severer chaos of a "human mind
untuned," he is content awhile to be mad with Lear, or to hate mankind (a sort
of madness) with Timon,[3] neither is that madness, nor this misanthropy, so
unchecked, but that,—never letting the reins of reason wholly go, while most he
seems to do so,—he has his better genius still whispering at his ear, with the
good servant Kent suggesting saner counsels, or with the honest steward
Flavius[4] recommending kindlier resolutions. Where he seems most to recede
from humanity, he will be found the truest to it. From beyond the scope of
Nature if he summon possible existences, he subjugates them to the law of
her consistency. He is beautifully loyal to that sovereign directress, even when
he appears most to betray and desert her. His ideal tribes submit to policy; his
very monsters are tamed to his hand, even as that wild sea-brood, shepherded
by Proteus.[5] He tames, and he clothes them with attributes of flesh and blood,
till they wonder at themselves, like Indian Islanders forced to submit to European vesture. Caliban,[6] the Witches,[7] are as true to the laws of their own
nature (ours with a difference), as Othello, Hamlet, and Macbeth. Herein the
great and the little wits are differenced; that if the latter wander ever so little
from nature or actual existence, they lose themselves and their readers. Their
phantoms are lawless; their visions nightmares. They do not create, which implies shaping and consistency. Their imaginations are not active—for to be
active is to call something into act and form—but passive, as men in sick dreams.

---

[1] From "Ode on the Death of Mr. William Hervey."
[2] "And old night" and "burning marl" are phrases from Milton's *Paradise Lost.*
[3] Semi-legendary Greek misanthrope. See Shakespeare's *Timon of Athens.*
[4] Characters in *King Lear* and *Timon of Athens* respectively.
[5] An ocean deity, son of Poseidon, and the tender of the monsters of the deep.
[6] A character in Shakespeare's *The Tempest,* "a freckled whelp . . . not honor'd
with a human shape."
[7] In Macbeth.

For the super-natural, or something super-added to what we know of nature, they give you the plainly non-natural. And if this were all, and that these mental hallucinations were discoverable only in the treatment of subjects out of nature, or transcending it, the judgment might with some plea be pardoned if it ran riot, and a little wantonized: but even in the describing of real and every-day life, that which is before their eyes, one of these lesser wits shall more deviate from nature—show more of that inconsequence, which has a natural alliance with frenzy,—than a great genius in his "maddest fits," as Wither somewhere calls them.[8] We appeal to any one that is acquainted with the common run of Lane's novels,[9]—as they existed some twenty of thirty years back,—those scanty intellectual viands of the whole female reading public, till a happier genius arose,[10] and expelled for ever the innutritious phantoms,—whether he has not found his brain more "betossed," his memory more puzzled, his sense of when and where more confounded, among the improbable events, the incoherent incidents, the inconsistent characters, or no characters, of some third-rate love-intrigue—where the persons shall be a Lord Glendamour and a Miss Rivers, and the scene only alternate between Bath and Bond Street—a more bewildering dreaminess induced upon him than he has felt wandering over all the fairy-grounds of Spenser.[11] In the productions we refer to, nothing but names and places is familiar; the persons are neither of this world nor of any other conceivable one; an endless stream of activities without purpose, of purposes destitute of motive:—we meet phantoms in our known walks; *fantasques* only christened. In the poet we have names which announce fiction; and we have absolutely no place at all, for the things and persons of the Fairy Queen prate not of their "whereabout." But in their inner nature, and the law of their speech and actions, we are at home, and upon acquainted ground. The one turns life into a dream; the other to the wildest dreams gives the sobrieties of everyday occurrences. By what subtle art of tracing the mental processes it is effected, we are not philosophers enough to explain, but in that wonderful episode of the cave of Mammon, in which the Money God appears first in the lowest form of a miser, is then a worker of metals, and becomes the god of all the treasures of the world; and has a daughter, Ambition, before whom all the world kneels for favours—with the Hesperian fruit,[12] the waters of Tantalus,[13] with Pilate washing his hands vainly, but not impertinently, in the same stream—that we should be at one moment in the cave of an old hoarder of treasures, at the next at the forge of the Cyclops, in a palace and yet in hell, all at once, with the shifting mutations of the most rambling dream, and our

---

[8] George Wither (1588–1667) used the phrase in his *The Shepherd's Hunting,* a group of pastorals written by Wither while he was in prison.

[9] Between 1790 and 1820, William Lane's Minerva Press turned out a good deal of extravagant fiction, much of it gothic romances.

[10] Probably Sir Walter Scott (1771–1832).

[11] Edmund Spenser (1552–1599), author of *The Faerie Queene.* "That wonderful episode," mentioned below, is in Book II, Canto 7.

[12] The Golden Apples of Greek myth.

[13] Tantalus, in Greek myth, was doomed to the torment of perpetual hunger and thirst. He was immersed in water up to his chin; luscious fruits dangled before his eyes. When he opened his mouth to eat or drink, the fruits vanished and the water dried up.

judgment yet all the time awake, and neither able nor willing to detect the fallacy,—is a proof of that hidden sanity which still guides the poet in the wildest seeming-aberrations.

It is not enough to say that the whole episode is a copy of the mind's conceptions in sleep; it is, in some sort—but what a copy! Let the most romantic of us, that has been entertained all night with the spectacle of some wild and magnificent vision, recombine it in the morning, and try it by his waking judgment. That which appeared so shifting, and yet so coherent, while that faculty was passive, when it comes under cool examination shall appear so reasonless and so unlinked, that we are ashamed to have been so deluded; and to have taken though but in sleep, a monster for a god. But the transitions in this episode are every whit as violent as in the most extravagant dream, and yet the waking judgment ratifies them.

William Hazlitt

CORIOLANUS

William Hazlitt (1778–1830), the son of a Unitarian clergyman, was destined by his father for a career in the ministry. At the age of fifteen he was sent to the Unitarian seminary at Hackney, then a suburb of London. His interest in divinity was but slight and he followed his own intellectual bent, reading widely in many subjects, with a special predilection for philosophy and political theory. A decisive event in his life was his meeting, when he was twenty, with Coleridge, who at the time was making a living by lecturing to Unitarian congregations, among them that of Hazlitt's father. Coleridge, as Hazlitt tells us in his famous essay of 1823, "My First Acquaintance with Poets," introduced him not only to Wordsworth and Southey but to the life of the imagination and literature. It was, however, some years before Hazlitt actually turned to literature as a practitioner, for his first love in the arts was painting, which he studied assiduously for some years until he became convinced that he lacked sufficient talent for success. (One of his surviving works is an attractive portrait of Charles Lamb in the dress of a Renaissance gentleman.)

Although Hazlitt published philosophical and political works earlier, it was not until the age of thirty that he began the characteristic work upon which his fame rests. The larger part of it is perhaps to be called journalism, since it was contributed, on order and under the pressure of deadlines, to the periodicals of the day, but it is journalism of a superlative—indeed, of a transcendant—order. His essays range widely over politics, literature, painting, the drama, sports, moral and psychological speculation, public personalities, personal reminiscences. Whatever his subject, he brought to its development a first-rate critical intelligence. His powerful, quick-glancing mind and his vivid style, in which a colloquial abruptness consorts happily with a precision of rhetorical structure, make him one of the great figures of the English Romantic period.

In the early days of their friendship, Coleridge, Wordsworth, and Southey shared with Hazlitt an enthusiasm for the French Revolution. But their feeling waned while Hazlitt's did not, and the difference of opinion made the occasion of Hazlitt's permanent quarrel with them; he was a man of quick and violent temper. His commitment to the radical democratic position in politics was maintained all his life, which makes the more remarkable the view advanced in his lecture on *Coriolanus*—

From the book *The Round Table. Characters of Shakespeare's Plays*, by William Hazlitt. London: J. M. Dent & Sons, Ltd.; New York: E. P. Dutton & Co., Inc. Everyman's Library Edition. Used by permission of J. M. Dent & Sons, Ltd., and E. P. Dutton & Co., Inc.

included in his *Characters of Shakespeare's Plays* (1817)—that poetry is essentially anti-democratic in the principle of its being and even in its substance.

Shakespeare has in this play shewn himself well versed in history and state-affairs. CORIOLANUS is a store-house of political common-places. Any one who studies it may save himself the trouble of reading Burke's Reflections,[1] or Paine's Rights of Man,[2] or the Debates in both Houses of Parliament since the French Revolution or our own. The arguments for and against aristocracy or democracy, on the privileges of the few and the claims of the many, on liberty and slavery, power and the abuse of it, peace and war, are here very ably handled, with the spirit of a poet and the acuteness of a philosopher. Shakespeare himself seems to have had a leaning to the arbitrary side of the question, perhaps from some feeling of contempt for his own origin; and to have spared no occasion of baiting the rabble. What he says of them is very true: what he says of their betters is also very true, though he dwells less upon it.—The cause of the people is indeed but little calculated as a subject for poetry: it admits of rhetoric, which goes into argument and explanation, but it presents no immediate or distinct images to the mind, "no jutting frieze, buttress, or coigne of vantage" for poetry "to make its pendant bed and procreant cradle in." The language of poetry naturally falls in with the language of power. The imagination is an exaggerating and exclusive faculty: it takes from one thing to add to another: it accumulates circumstances together to give the greatest possible effect to a favourite object. The understanding is a dividing and measuring faculty: it judges of things not according to their immediate impression on the mind, but according to their relations to one another. The one is a monopolising faculty, which seeks the greatest quantity of present excitement by inequality and disproportion; the other is a distributive faculty, which seeks the greatest quantity of ultimate good, by justice and porportion. The one is an aristocratical, the other a republican faculty. The principle of poetry is a very anti-levelling principle. It aims at effect, it exists by contrast. It admits of no medium. It is every thing by excess. It rises above the ordinary standard of sufferings and crimes. It presents a dazzling appearance. It shows its head turretted, crowned, and crested. Its front is gilt and blood-stained. Before it "it carries noise, and behind it leaves tears." It has its altars and its victims, sacrifices, human sacrifices. Kings, priests, nobles, are its train-bearers, tyrants and slaves its executioners.—"Carnage is its daughter."—Poetry is right-royal. It puts the individual for the species, the one above the infinite many, might before right. A lion hunting a flock of sheep or a herd of wild asses is a more poetical object than they; and we even take part with the lordly beast, because our vanity or some other feeling makes us disposed to place ourselves in the situation of the strongest party. So we feel some concern for the poor citizens of Rome when they meet together to compare their wants and grievances, till Coriolanus comes

[1] Edmund Burke (1729–1797), English political writer and statesman, author of *Reflections on the Revolution in France* (1790).
[2] Thomas Paine (1737–1809), American political writer, author of *The Rights of Man* (1792), a book largely directed against Burke's *Reflections*.

in and with blows and big words drives this set of "poor rats," this rascal scum, to their homes and beggary before him. There is nothing heroical in a multitude of miserable rogues not wishing to be starved, or complaining that they are like to be so: but when a single man comes forward to brave their cries and to make them submit to the last indignities, from mere pride and self-will, our admiration of his prowess is immediately converted into contempt for their pusillanimity. The insolence of power is stronger than the plea of necessity. The tame submission to usurped authority or even the natural resistance to it has nothing to excite or flatter the imagination: it is the assumption of a right to insult or oppress others that carries an imposing air of superiority with it. We had rather be the oppressor than the oppressed. The love of power in ourselves and the admiration of it in others are both natural to man: the one makes him a tyrant, the other a slave. Wrong dressed out in pride, pomp, and circumstance, has more attraction than abstract right.—Coriolanus complains of the fickleness of the people: yet, the instant he cannot gratify his pride and obstinacy at their expense, he turns his arms against his country. If his country was not worth defending, why did he build his pride on its defence? He is a conquerer and a hero; he conquers other countries, and makes this a plea for enslaving his own; and when he is prevented from doing so, he leagues with its enemies to destroy his country. He rates the people "as if he were a God to punish, and not a man of their infirmity." He scoffs at one of their tribunes for maintaining their rights and franchises: "Mark you his absolute *shall?*" not marking his own absolute *will* to take every thing from them, his impatience of the slightest opposition to his own pretensions being in proportion to their arrogance and absurdity. If the great and powerful had the beneficence and wisdom of Gods, then all this would have been well: if with a greater knowledge of what is good for the people, they had as great a care for their interest as they have themselves, if they were seated above the world, sympathising with the welfare, but not feeling the passions of men, receiving neither good nor hurt from them, but bestowing their benefits as free gifts on them, they might then rule over them like another Providence. But this is not the case. Coriolanus is unwilling that the senate should shew their "cares" for the people, lest their "cares" should be construed into "fears," to the subversion of all due authority; and he is no sooner disappointed in his schemes to deprive the people not only of the cares of the state, but of all power to redress themselves, than Volumnia is made madly to exclaim,

> Now the red pestilence strike all trades in Rome,
> And occupations perish.

This is but natural: it is but natural for a mother to have more regard for her son than for a whole city; but then the city should be left to take some care of itself. The care of the state cannot, we here see, be safely entrusted to maternal affection, or to the domestic charities of high life. The great have private feelings of their own, to which the interests of humanity and justice must courtesy. Their interests are so far from being the same as those of the community, that they are in direct and necessary opposition to them; their power is at the expense of *our* weakness; their riches of *our* poverty; their pride of *our* degradation; their splendour of *our* wretchedness; their tyranny of *our* servitude. If they had the superior knowledge ascribed to them (which they have not) it would only render them so much more formidable; and from Gods would convert them into Devils. The whole dramatic moral of CORIOLANUS is that those who have little shall have less, and that those who have much shall take all that others have left. The people are poor; therefore they ought to be starved. They are slaves; therefore they ought to be beaten. They work hard; therefore they ought to be treated like beasts of burden. They are ignorant; therefore they ought not to be allowed to feel that they want food, or clothing, or rest, that they are enslaved, oppressed, and miserable. This is the logic of the imagination and the passions; which seek to aggrandize what excites admiration and to heap contempt on misery, to raise power into tyranny, and to make tyranny absolute; to thrust down that which is low still lower, and to make wretches desperate: to exalt magistrates into kings, kings into gods; to degrade subjects to the rank of slaves, and slaves to the condition of brutes. The history of mankind is a romance, a mask, a tragedy, constructed upon the principles of *poetical justice;* it is a noble or royal hunt, in which what is sport to the few is death to the many, and in which the spectators halloo and encourage the strong to set upon the weak, and cry havoc in the chase though they do not share in the spoil. We may depend upon it that what men delight to read in books, they will put in practice in reality.

*   *   *

Thomas De Quincey

THE LITERATURE OF KNOWLEDGE AND THE LITERATURE OF POWER

Thomas De Quincey (1785–1859) was born in Manchester, the son of a merchant of that city. As a schoolboy he distinguished himself by his extraordinary proficiency in Greek. In the winter of 1802–1803 he ran off to Wales, then to London, where he lived by his wits and in great privation; when at last he was found by his family, he was sent to Worcester College, Oxford, where he stayed five years, leaving without taking a degree. In 1809 he took up residence at Grasmere, in the Lake Country, to be near Wordsworth and Coleridge, whom he greatly admired; his friendship with Wordsworth came to an end after a marriage touched by scandal and the development of his addiction to opium. He had first taken the drug at Oxford to relieve the pains of neuralgia; at Grasmere the addiction was for a time quite severe. It was never wholly broken but eventually was brought under control. His first-published and most famous book was *The Confessions of an English Opium-Eater* (1821; revised and expanded 1856), an autobiographical memoir centering in, though not exclusively devoted to, his use of the drug. De Quincey's characteristic genre was the long discursive essay, speculative, meditative, erudite, often fanciful. Although his explicitly critical essays are few, two of them, the passage (originally a portion of "The Poetry of Pope," *North British Review,* August 1848) here included and "On the Knocking at the Gate in *Macbeth*" are among the best known in the whole range of English criticism.

Books, therefore, do not suggest an idea coextensive and interchangeable with the idea of Literature; since much literature, scenic, forensic, or didactic (as from lecturers and public orators), may never come into books, and much that *does* come into books may connect itself with no literary interest.*

From *Thomas De Quincy,* edited by Bonomy Dobree. New York: Schocken Books; London: B. T. Batsford, Ltd., 1965.

* What are called *The Blue Books,*—by which title are understood the folio Reports issued every session of Parliament by committees of the two Houses, and stitched

But a far more important correction, applicable to the common vague idea of literature, is to be sought not so much in a better definition of literature as in a sharper distinction of the two functions which it fulfils. In that great social organ which, collectively, we call literature, there may be distinguished two separate offices that may blend and often *do* so, but capable, severally, of a severe insulation, and naturally fitted for reciprocal repulsion. There is, first, the literature of *knowledge;* and, secondly, the literature of *power.* The function of the first is—to *teach;* the function of the second is—to *move:* the first is a rudder; the second, an oar or a sail. The first speaks to the *mere* discursive understanding; the second speaks ultimately, it may happen, to the higher understanding or reason, but always *through* affections of pleasure and sympathy. Remotely, it may travel towards an object seated in what Lord Bacon calls *dry* light;[1] but, proximately, it does and must operate,—else it ceases to be a literature of *power,*—on and through that *humid* light which clothes itself in the mists and glittering *iris* of human passions, desires, and genial emotions. Men have so little reflected on the higher functions of literature as to find it a paradox if one should describe it as a mean or subordinate purpose of books to give information. But this is a paradox only in the sense which makes it honourable to be paradixocal. Whenever we talk in ordinary language of seeking information or gaining knowledge, we understand the words as connected with something of absolute novelty. But it is the grandeur of all truth which *can* occupy a very high place in human interests that it is never absolutely novel to the meanest of minds; it exists eternally by way of germ or latent principle in the lowest as in the highest, needing to be developed, but never to be planted. To be capable of transplantation is the immediate criterion of a truth that ranges on a lower scale. Besides which, there is a rarer thing than truth,—namely, *power,* or deep sympathy with truth. What is the effect, for instance, upon society, of children? By the pity, by the tenderness, and by the peculiar modes of admiration, which connect themselves with the helplessness, with the innocence, and with the simplicity of children, not only are the primal affections strengthened and continually renewed, but the qualities which are dearest in the sight of heaven,—the frailty, for instance, which appeals to forbearance, the innocence which symbolises the heavenly, and the simplicity which is most alien from the worldly,—are kept up in perpetual remembrance, and their ideals are continually refreshed. A purpose of the same nature is answered by the higher literature, viz., the literature of power. What do you learn from *Paradise Lost?* Nothing at all. What do you learn from a cookery-book? Something new, something that you did not know before, in every paragraph. But would you therefore put the wretched cookery-book on a higher level of estimation than the divine poem? What you owe to Milton is not any knowledge, of which a million separate items are still but a million of advancing steps on the same earthly level;

---

into blue covers,—though often sneered at by the ignorant as so much waste paper, will be acknowledged gratefully by those who have used them diligently as the main wellheads of all accurate information as to the Great Britain of this day. As an immense depository of faithful (*and not super-annuated*) statistics, they are indispensable to the honest student. But no man would therefore class the *Blue Books* as literature. [De Quincey's note.]

[1] Francis Bacon (1561–1626), in his essay "Of Friendship."

what you owe is *power*,—that is, exercise and expansion to your own latent capacity of sympathy with the infinite, where every pulse and each separate influx is a step upwards, a step ascending as upon a Jacob's ladder from earth to mysterious altitudes above the earth. *All* the steps of knowledge, from first to last, carry you further on the same plane, but could never raise you one foot above your ancient level of earth: whereas the very *first* step in power is a flight—is an ascending movement into another element where earth is forgotten.

Were it not that human sensibilities are ventilated and continually called out into exercise by the great phenomena of infancy, or of real life as it moves through chance and change, or of literature as it recombines these elements in the mimicries of poetry, romance, &c., it is certain that, like any animal power or muscular energy falling into disuse, all such sensibilities would gradually droop and dwindle. It is in relation to these great *moral* capacities of man that the literature of power, as contradistinguished from that of knowledge, lives and has its field of action. It is concerned with what is highest in man; for the Scriptures themselves never condescended to deal by suggestion or co-operation with the mere discursive understanding: when speaking of man in his intellectual capacity, the Scriptures speak not of the understanding, but of *"the understanding heart,"*—making the heart, *i.e.* the great *intuitive* (or non-discursive) organ, to be the interchangeable formula for man in his highest state of capacity for the infinite. Tragedy, romance, fairy tale, or epopee,[2] all alike restore to man's mind the ideals of justice, of hope, of truth, of mercy, of retribution, which else (left to the support of daily life in its realities) would languish for want of sufficient illustration. What is meant, for instance, by *poetic justice?* —It does not mean a justice that differs by its object from the ordinary justice of human jurisprudence; for then it must be confessedly a very bad kind of justice; but it means a justice that differs from common forensic justice by the degree in which it *attains* its object, a justice that is more omnipotent over its own ends, as dealing—not with the refractory elements of earthly life, but with the elements of its own creation, and with materials flexible to its own purest preconceptions. It is certain that, were it not for the Literature of Power, these ideals would often remain amongst us as mere arid notional forms; whereas, by the creative forces of man put forth in literature, they gain a vernal life of restoration, and germinate into vital activities. The commonest novel, by moving in alliance with human fears and hopes, with human instincts of wrong and right, sustains and quickens those affections. Calling them into action, it rescues them from torpor. And hence the pre-eminency over all authors that merely *teach* of the meanest that *moves,* or that teaches, if at all, indirectly *by* moving. The very highest work that has ever existed in the Literature of Knowledge is but a *provisional* work: a book upon trial and sufferance, and *quamdiu bene se gesserit.*[3] Let its teaching be even partially revised, let it be but expanded,— nay, even let its teaching be but placed in a better order,—and instantly it is superseded. Whereas the feeblest works in the Literature of Power, surviving at all, survive as finished and unalterable amongst men. For instance, the *Principia* of Sir Isaac Newton was a book *militant* on earth from the first. In all stages of its progress it would have to fight for its existence: 1st, as regards absolute truth;

[2] The genre of epic.
[3] "As long as it shall have conducted itself well"—i.e., on probation.

2dly, when that combat was over, as regards its form or mode of presenting the truth. And as soon as a La Place,[4] or anybody else, builds higher upon the foundations laid by this book, effectually he throws it out of the sunshine into decay and darkness; by weapons won from this book he superannuates and destroys this book, so that soon the name of Newton remains as a mere *nominis umbra,* but his book, as a living power, has transmigrated into other forms. Now, on the contrary, the Iliad, the Prometheus of Aeschylus, the Othello or King Lear, the Hamlet or Macbeth, and the Paradise Lost, are not militant, but triumphant for ever as long as the languages exist in which they speak or can be taught to speak. They never *can* transmigrate into new incarnations. To reproduce *these* in new forms, or variation, even if in some things they should be improved, would be to plagiarise. A good steam-engine is properly superseded by a better. But one lovely pastoral valley is not superseded by another, nor a statue of Praxiteles[5] by a statue of Michael Angelo. These things are separated not by imparity, but by disparity. They are not thought of as unequal under the same standard, but as different in *kind,* and, if otherwise equal, as equal under a different standard. Human works of immortal beauty and works of nature in one respect stand on the same footing: they never absolutely repeat each other, never approach so near as not to differ; and they differ not as better and worse, or simply by more and less: they differ by undecipherable and incommunicable differences, that cannot be caught by mimicries, that cannot be reflected in the mirror of copies, that cannot become ponderable in the scales of vulgar comparison.

Applying these principles to Pope as a representative of fine literature in general, we would wish to remark the claim which he has, or which any equal writer has, to the attention and jealous winnowing of those critics in particular who watch over public morals. Clergymen, and all organs of public criticism put in motion by clergymen, are more especially concerned in the just appreciation of such writers, if the two canons are remembered which we have endeavoured to illustrate, viz. that all works in this class, as opposed to those in the literature of knowledge, 1st, work by far deeper agencies, and, 2dly, are more permanent; in the strictest sense they are κτήματα ἐς ἀεί:[6] and what evil they do, or what good they do, is commensurate with the national language, sometimes long after the nation has departed. At this hour, five hundred years since their creation, the tales of Chaucer never equalled on this earth for their tenderness, and for life of picturesqueness, are read familiarly by many in the charming language of their natal day, and by others in the modernisations of Dryden, of Pope, and Wordsworth. At this hour, one thousand eight hundred years since their creation, the Pagan tales of Ovid, never equalled on this earth for the gaiety of their movement and the capricious graces of their narrative, are read by all Christendom. This man's people and their monuments are dust; but *he* is alive: he has survived them, as he told us that he had it in his commission to do, by a thousand years; "and *shall* a thousand more."

[4] Pierre Simon, Marquis de Laplace (1749–1827), French astronomer and mathematician.

[5] Most celebrated of the classical sculptors. He lived in the middle of the fourth century B.C.

[6] "Possessions for ever."

All the literature of knowledge builds only ground-nests, that are swept away by floods, or confounded by the plough; but the literature of power builds nests in aerial altitudes of temples sacred from violation, or of forests inaccessible to fraud. *This* is a great prerogative of the *power* literature; and it is a greater which lies in the mode of its influence. The *knowledge* literature, like the fashion of this world, passeth away. An Encyclopædia is its abstract; and, in this respect, it may be taken for its speaking symbol—that before one generation has passed an Encyclopædia is superannuated; for it speaks through the dead memory and unimpassioned understanding, which have not the repose of higher faculties, but are continually enlarging and varying their phylacteries. But all literature properly so called—literature κατ' ἐξοχὴν,[7]—for the very same reason that it is so much more durable than the literature of knowledge, is (and by the very same proportion it is) more intense and electrically searching in its impressions. The directions in which the tragedy of this planet has trained our human feelings to play, and the combinations into which the poetry of this planet has thrown our human passions of love and hatred, of admiration and contempt, exercise a power for bad or good over human life that cannot be contemplated, when stretching through many generations, without a sentiment allied to awe.* And of this let every one be assured—that he owes to the impassioned books which he has read many a thousand more of emotions than he can consciously trace back to them. Dim by their origination, these emotions yet arise in him, and mould him through life, like forgotten incidents of his childhood.

---

[7] *"Par excellence."*

* The reason why the broad distinctions between the two literatures of power and knowledge so little fix the attention lies in the fact that a vast proportion of books,—history, biography, travels, miscellaneous essays, &c.,—lying in a middle zone, confound these distinctions by interblending them. All that we call "amusement" or "entertainment" is a diluted form of the power belonging to passion, and also a mixed form; and, where threads of direct *instruction* intermingle in the texture with these threads of *power,* this absorption of the duality into one representative nuance neutralises the separate perception of either. Fused into a *tertium quid,* or neutral state, they disappear to the popular eye as the repelling forces which, in fact, they are. [De Quincey's note.]

Walt Whitman

PREFACE TO
LEAVES OF GRASS

In 1837, Ralph Waldo Emerson was the speaker at the Phi Beta Kappa exercises at Harvard. The address that he gave was "The American Scholar," one of the famous documents of American cultural history— "our intellectual Declaration of Independence," as Oliver Wendell Holmes called it. In it Emerson reviewed the state of the intellectual contemporary life, noting that all the energies of the young nation had gone into practical work but predicting that "our day of dependence, our long apprenticeship" to the learning and literature of Europe was drawing to a close, that there would soon be great American poets and thinkers to deal with American themes in an American way. Eighteen years were to pass before Emerson's prophecy as to poetry was fulfilled; in 1855 a New York journalist (and printer, carpenter, and contractor) published a volume of twelve untitled poems called *Leaves of Grass,* the first truly great American poems. Emerson, to whom Walt Whitman (1819–1892) sent the volume, was one of the few readers who did not find it barbaric or eccentric or vulgar; his letter to Whitman greeted the poet "at the beginning of a great career." He might well have been gratified, for his oration had been not only the prophecy of *Leaves of Grass* but its inspiration.

An enlarged edition of the volume appeared in 1856 and Whitman continued to add to it and to rearrange its contents until his death. Only the first edition contained the preface. If its insistence on the particular American mode seems now excessively polemical, it should be remembered that Matthew Arnold could tell Americans in the 1880s that there was no such thing as American literature, only English literature written by Americans.

The three dots (. . .) are Whitman's own punctuation and do not indicate omissions.

America does not repel the past or what it has produced under its forms or amid other politics or the idea of castes or the old religions . . . . accepts the lesson with calmness . . . is not so impatient as has been supposed that the slough still sticks to opinions and manners and literature while the life which served its requirements has passed into the new life of the new forms . . . perceives that the corpse is slowly borne from the eating and sleeping rooms of the

From *Leaves of Grass and Selected Prose* by Walt Whitman, edited by John Kouwenhoven. New York: Random House, 1950 (Modern Library).

house . . . perceives that it waits a little while in the door . . . that it was fittest for its days . . . that its action has descended to the stalwart and wellshaped heir who approaches . . . and that he shall be fittest for his days.

The Americans of all nations at any time upon the earth have probably the fullest poetical nature. The United States themselves are essentially the greatest poem. In the history of the earth hitherto the largest and most stirring appear tame and orderly to their ampler largeness and stir. Here at last is something in the doings of man that corresponds with the broadcast doings of the day and night. Here is not merely a nation but a teeming nation of nations. Here is action untied from strings necessarily blind to particulars and details magnificently moving in vast masses. Here is the hospitality which forever indicates heroes . . . . Here are the roughs and beards and space and ruggedness and nonchalance that the soul loves. Here the performance disdaining the trivial unapproached in the tremendous audacity of its crowds and groupings and the push of its perspective spreads with crampless and flowing breadth and showers its prolific and splendid extravagance. One sees it must indeed own the riches of the summer and winter, and need never be bankrupt while corn grows from the ground or the orchards drop apples or the bays contain fish or men beget children upon women.

Other states indicate themselves in their deputies . . . . but the genius of the United States is not best or most in its executives or legislatures, nor in its ambassadors or authors or colleges or churches or parlors, nor even in its newspapers or inventors . . . but always most in the common people. Their manners speech dress friendships—the freshness and candor of their physiognomy—the picturesque looseness of their carriage . . . their deathless attachment to freedom —their aversion to anything indecorous or soft or mean—the practical acknowledgment of the citizens of one state by the citizens of all other states—the fierceness of their roused resentment—their curiosity and welcome of novelty—their self-esteem and wonderful sympathy—their susceptibility to a slight—the air they have of persons who never knew how it felt to stand in the presence of superiors—the fluency of their speech—their delight in music, the sure symptom of manly tenderness and native elegance of soul . . . their good temper and openhandedness—the terrible significance of their elections—the President's taking off his hat to them not they to him—these too are unrhymed poetry. It awaits the gigantic and generous treatment worthy of it.

The largeness of nature or the nation were monstrous without a corresponding largeness and generosity of the spirit of the citizen. Not nature nor swarming states nor streets and steamships nor prosperous business nor farms nor capital nor learning may suffice for the ideal of man . . . nor suffice the poet. No reminiscences may suffice either. A live nation can always cut a deep mark and can have the best authority the cheapest . . . namely from its own soul. This is the sum of the profitable uses of individuals or states and of present action and grandeur and of the subjects of poets.—As if it were necessary to trot back generation after generation to the eastern records! As if the beauty and sacredness of the demonstrable must fall behind that of the mythical! As if men do not make their mark out of any times! As if the opening of the western continent by discovery and what has transpired since in North and South America were less than the small theatre of the antique or the aimless sleepwalking of the middle ages! The pride of the United States leaves the wealth and finesse of the cities and all returns of commerce and agriculture and all the magnitude of geography or shows of exterior victory to enjoy the breed of fullsized men or one fullsized man unconquerable and simple.

The American poets are to enclose old and new [,] for America is the race of races. Of them a bard is to be commensurate with a people. To him the other continents arrive as contributions . . . he gives them reception for their sake and his own sake. His spirit responds to his country's spirit . . . . he incarnates its geography and natural life and rivers and lakes. Mississippi with annual freshets and changing chutes, Missouri and Columbia and Ohio and Saint Lawrence with the falls and beautiful masculine Hudson, do not embouchure where they spend themselves more than they embouchure into him. The blue breadth over the inland sea of Virginia and Maryland and the sea off Massachusetts and Maine and over Manhattan bay and over Champlain and Erie and over Ontario and Huron and Michigan and Superior, and over the Texan and Mexican and Floridian and Cuban seas and over the seas off California and Oregon, is not tallied by the blue breadth of the waters below more than the breadth of above and below is tallied by him. When the long Atlantic coast stretches longer and the Pacific coast stretches longer he easily stretches with them north or south. He spans between them also from east to west and reflects what is between them. On him rise solid growths that offset the growths of pine and cedar and hemlock and liveoak and locust and chestnut and cypress and hickory and limetree and cottonwood and tuliptree and cactus and wildvine and tamarind and persimmon . . . . and tangles as tangled as any canebrake or swamp . . . . and forests coated with transparent ice and icicles hanging from the boughs and crackling in the wind . . . . and sides and peaks of mountains . . . . and pasturage sweet and free as savannah or upland or prairie . . . . with flights and songs and screams that answer those of the wild-pigeon and highhold and orchard-oriole and coot and surf-duck and redshouldered-hawk and fish-hawk and white-ibis and indian-hen and cat-owl and water-pheasant and qua-bird and pied-sheldrake and blackbird and mockingbird and buzzard and condor and night-heron and eagle. To him the hereditary countenance descends both mother's and father's. To him enter the essences of the real things and past and present events—of the enormous diversity of temperature and agriculture and mines—the tribes of red aborigines—the weatherbeaten vessels entering new ports or making landings on rocky coasts—the first settlements north or south—the rapid stature and muscle—the haughty defiance of '76, and the war and peace and formation of the constitution . . . . the union always surrounded by blatherers and always calm and impregnable—the perpetual coming of immigrants—the wharfhem'd cities and superior marine—the unsurveyed interior—the loghouses and clearings and wild animals and hunters and trappers . . . . the free commerce—the fisheries and whaling and gold-digging—the endless gestation of new states— the convening of Congress every December, the members duly coming up from all climates and the uttermost parts . . . . the noble character of the young mechanics and of all free American workmen and workwomen . . . . the general ardor and friendliness and enterprise—the perfect equality of the female with the male . . . . the large amativeness—the fluid movement of the population—the factories and mercantile life and laborsaving machinery—the

Yankee swap—the New-York firemen and the target excursion—the southern plantation life—the character of the northeast and of the northwest and southwest—slavery and the tremulous spreading of hands to protect it, and the stern opposition to it which shall never cease till it ceases or the speaking of tongues and the moving of lips cease. For such the expression of the American poet is to be transcendant and new. It is to be indirect and not direct or descriptive or epic. Its quality goes through these to much more. Let the age and wars of other nations be chanted and their eras and characters be illustrated and that finish the verse. Not so the great psalm of the republic. Here the theme is creative and has vista. Here comes one among the wellbeloved stonecutters and plans with decision and science and sees the solid and beautiful forms of the future where there are now no solid forms.

Of all nations the United States with veins full of poetical stuff most need poets and will doubtless have the greatest and use them the greatest. Their Presidents shall not be their common referee so much as their poets shall. Of all mankind the great poet is the equable man. Not in him but off from him things are grotesque or eccentric or fail of their sanity. Nothing out of its place is good and nothing in its place is bad. He bestows on every object or quality its fit proportions neither more nor less. He is the arbiter of the diverse and he is the key. He is the equalizer of his age and land . . . . he supplies what wants supplying and checks what wants checking. If peace is the routine out of him speaks the spirit of peace, large, rich, thrifty, building vast and populous cities, encouraging agriculture and the arts and commerce—lighting the study of man, the soul, immortality—federal, state or municipal government, marriage, health, free-trade, intertravel by land and sea . . . . nothing too close, nothing too far off . . . the stars not too far off. In war he is the most deadly force of the war. Who recruits him recruits horse and foot . . . he fetches parks of artillery the best that engineer ever knew. If the time becomes slothful and heavy he knows how to arouse it . . . he can make every word he speaks draw blood. Whatever stagnates in the flat of custom or obedience or legislation he never stagnates. Obedience does not master him, he masters it. High up out of reach he stands turning a concentrated light . . . he turns the pivot with his finger . . . he baffles the swiftest runners as he stands and easily overtakes and envelops them. The time straying toward infidelity and confections and persiflage he withholds by his steady faith . . . he spreads out his dishes . . . he offers the sweet firmfibred meat that grows men and women. His brain is the ultimate brain. He is no arguer . . . he is judgment. He judges not as the judge judges but as the sun falling around a helpless thing. As he sees the farthest he has the most faith. His thoughts are the hymns of the praise of things. In the talk on the soul and eternity and God off of his equal plane he is silent. He sees eternity less like a play with a prologue and denouement . . . . he sees eternity in men and women . . . he does not see men and women as dreams or dots. Faith is the antiseptic of the soul . . . it pervades the common people and preserves them . . . they never give up believing and expecting and trusting. There is that indescribable freshness and unconsciousness about an illiterate person that humbles and mocks the power of the noblest expressive genius. The poet sees for a certainty how one not a great artist may be just as sacred and perfect as the greatest artist. . . . . . The power to destroy or remould is freely used by him but never the power of attack. What is past is past. If he does not expose superior models and prove himself by every step he takes he is not what is wanted. The presence of the greatest poet conquers . . . not parleying or struggling or any prepared attempts. Now he has passed that way see after him! there is not left any vestige of despair or misanthropy or cunning or exclusiveness or the ignominy of a nativity or color or delusion of hell or the necessity of hell . . . . . and no man thenceforward shall be degraded for ignorance or weakness or sin.

The greatest poet hardly knows pettiness or triviality. If he breathes into any thing that was before thought small it dilates with the grandeur and life of the universe. He is a seer . . . . he is individual . . . he is complete in himself . . . . the others are as good as he, only he sees it and they do not. He is not one of the chorus . . . . he does not stop for any regulation . . . he is the president of regulation. What the eyesight does to the rest he does to the rest. Who knows the curious mystery of the eyesight? The other senses corroborate themselves, but this is removed from any proof but its own and foreruns the identities of the spiritual world. A single glance of it mocks all the investigations of man and all the instruments and books of the earth and all reasoning. What is marvellous? what is unlikely? what is impossible or baseless or vague? after you have once just opened the space of a peachpit and given audience to far and near and to the sunset and had all things enter with electric swiftness softly and duly without confusion or jostling or jam.

The land and sea, the animals fishes and birds, the sky of heaven and the orbs, the forests mountains and rivers, are not small themes . . . but folks expect of the poet to indicate more than the beauty and dignity which always attach to dumb real objects . . . . they expect him to indicate the path between reality and their souls. Men and women perceive the beauty well enough . . probably as well as he. The passionate tenacity of hunters, woodmen, early risers, cultivators of gardens and orchards and fields, the love of healthy women for the manly form, seafaring persons, drivers of horses, the passion for light and the open air, all is an old varied sign of the unfailing perception of beauty and of a residence of the poetic in outdoor people. They can never be assisted by poets to perceive . . . some may but they never can. The poetic quality is not marshalled in rhyme or uniformity or abstract addresses to things nor in melancholy complaints or good precepts, but is the life of these and much else and is in the soul. The profit of rhyme is that it drops seeds of a sweeter and more luxuriant rhyme, and of uniformity that it conveys itself into its own roots in the ground out of sight. The rhyme and uniformity of perfect poems show the free growth of metrical laws and bud from them as unerringly and loosely as lilacs or roses on a bush, and take shapes as compact as the shapes of chestnuts and oranges and melons and pears, and shed the perfume impalpable to form. The fluency and ornaments of the finest poems or music or orations or recitations are not independent but dependent. All beauty comes from beautiful blood and a beautiful brain. If the greatnesses are in conjunction in a man or woman it is enough . . . . the fact will prevail through the universe . . . . but the gaggery and gilt of a million years will not prevail. Who troubles himself about his ornaments or fluency is lost. This is what you shall do: Love the earth and sun and the animals, despise riches, give alms to every one that asks, stand up for the stupid and crazy, devote your income and labor to others, hate tyrants, argue not concerning God, have patience and indulgence toward the people, take off your hat to nothing known or unkown or to any man or number of men, go freely with powerful uneducated persons and with the young and with the mothers of families, read these leaves[1] in the open air every season of every year of your life, reexamine all you have been told at school or church or in any book, dismiss whatever insults your own soul, and your very flesh shall be a great poem and have the richest fluency not only in its words but in the silent lines of its lips and face and between the lashes of your eyes and in every motion and joint of your body . . . . The poet shall not spend his time in unneeded work. He shall know that the ground is always ready ploughed and manured . . . . others may not know it but he shall. He shall go directly to the creation. His trust shall master the trust of everything he touches . . . . and shall master all attachment.

The known universe has one complete lover and that is the greatest poet. He consumes an eternal passion and is indifferent which chance happens and which possible contingency of fortune or misfortune and persuades daily and hourly his delicious pay. What balks or breaks others is fuel for his burning progress to contact and amorous joy. Other proportions of the reception of pleasure dwindle to nothing to his proportions. All expected from heaven or from the highest he is rapport with in the sight of the daybreak or a scene of the winter woods or the presence of children playing or with his arm round the neck of a man or woman. His love above all love has leisure and expanse . . . . he leaves room ahead of himself. He is no irresolute or suspicious lover . . . he is sure . . . he scorns intervals. His experience and the showers and thrills are not for nothing. Nothing can jar him . . . . suffering and darkness cannot— death and fear cannot. To him complaint and jealousy and envy are corpses buried and rotten in the earth . . . . he saw them buried. The sea is not surer of the shore or the shore of the sea than he is of the fruition of his love and of all perfection and beauty.

The fruition of beauty is no chance of hit or miss . . . it is inevitable as life . . . . it is exact and plumb as gravitation. From the eyesight proceeds another eyesight and from the hearing proceeds another hearing and from the voice proceeds another voice eternally curious of the harmony of things with man. To these respond perfections not only in the committees that were supposed to stand for the rest but in the rest themselves just the same. These understand the law of perfection in masses and floods . . . that its finish is to each for itself and onward from itself . . . that it is profuse and impartial . . . that there is not a minute of the light or dark nor an acre of the earth or sea without it— nor any direction of the sky nor any trade or employment nor, any turn of events. This is the reason that about the proper expression of beauty there is precision and balance . . . one part does not need to be thrust above another. The best singer is not the one who has the most lithe and powerful organ . . . the pleasure of poems is not in them that take the handsomest measure and similes and sound.

Without effort and without exposing in the least how it is done the greatest

---

[1] That is, the pages and poems in *Leaves of Grass*.

poet brings the spirit of any or all events and passions and scenes and persons some more and some less to bear on your individual character as you hear or read. To do this well is to compete with the laws that pursue and follow time. What is the purpose must surely be there and the clue of it must be there . . . . and the faintest indication is the indication of the best and then becomes the clearest indication. Past and present and future are not disjoined but joined. The greatest poet forms the consistence of what is to be from what has been and is. He drags the dead out of their coffins and stands them again on their feet . . . . he says to the past, Rise and walk before me that I may realize you. He learns the lesson . . . . he places himself where the future becomes present. The greatest poet does not only dazzle his rays over character and scenes and passions . . . he finally ascends and finishes all . . . he exhibits the pinnacles that no man can tell what they are for or what is beyond . . . . he glows a moment on the extremest verge. He is most wonderful in his last half-hidden smile or frown . . . by that flash of the moment of parting the one that sees it shall be encouraged or terrified afterward for many years. The greatest poet does not moralize or make applications of morals . . . he knows the soul. The soul has that measureless pride which consists in never acknowledging any lessons but its own. But it has sympathy as measureless as its pride and the one balances the other and neither can stretch too far while it stretches in company with the other. The inmost secrets of art sleep with the twain. The greatest poet has lain close betwixt both and they are vital in his style and thoughts.

The art of art, the glory of expression and the sunshine of the light of letters is simplicity. Nothing is better than simplicity . . . . nothing can make up for excess or for the lack of definiteness. To carry on the heave of impulse and pierce intellectual depths and give all subjects their articulations are powers neither common nor very uncommon. But to speak in literature with the perfect rectitude and insouciance of the movements of animals and the unimpeach-ableness of the sentiment of trees in the woods and grass by the roadside is the flawless triumph of art. If you have looked on him who has achieved it you have looked on one of the masters of the artists of all nations and times. You shall not contemplate the flight of the graygull over the bay or the mettlesome action of the blood horse or the tall leaning of sunflowers on their stalk or the appearance of the sun journeying through heaven or the appearance of the moon afterward with any more satisfaction than you shall contemplate him. The greatest poet has less a marked style and is more the channel of thoughts and things without increase or diminution, and is the free channel of himself. He swears to his art, I will not be meddlesome, I will not have in my writing any elegance or effect or originality to hang in the way between me and the rest like curtains. I will have nothing hang in the way, not the richest curtains. What I tell I tell for precisely what it is. Let who may exalt or startle or fascinate or sooth I will have purposes as health or heat or snow has and be as regardless of observation. What I experience or portray shall go from my composition without a shred of my composition. You shall stand by my side and look in the mirror with me.

The old red blood and stainless gentility of great poets will be proved by their unconstraint. A heroic person walks at his ease through and out of that custom or precedent or authority that suits him not. Of the traits of the brotherhood of writers savants musicians inventors and artists nothing is finer than silent defiance advancing from new free forms. In the need of poems philosophy politics mechanism science behaviour, the craft of art, an appropriate native grand-opera, shipcraft, or any craft, he is greatest forever and forever who contributes the greatest original practical example. The cleanest expression is that which finds no sphere worthy of itself and makes one.

The messages of great poets[2] to each man and woman are, Come to us on equal terms, Only then can you understand us, We are no better than you, What we enclose you enclose, What we enjoy you may enjoy. Did you suppose there could be only one Supreme? We affirm there can be unnumbered Supremes, and that one does not countervail another any more than one eyesight countervails another . . and that men can be good or grand only of the consciousness of their supremacy within them. What do you think is the grandeur of storms and dismemberments and the deadliest battles and wrecks and the wildest fury of the elements and the power of the sea and the motion of nature and of the throes of human desires and dignity and hate and love? It is that something in the soul which says, Rage on, Whirl on, I tread master here and everywhere, Master of the spasms of the sky and of the shatter of the sea, Master of nature and passion and death, And of all terror and all pain.

The American bards shall be marked for generosity and affection and for encouraging competitors . . They shall be kosmos . . without monopoly or secrecy . . glad to pass any thing to any one . . hungry for equals night and day. They shall not be careful of riches and privilege . . . . they shall be riches and privilege . . . . they shall perceive who the most affluent man is. The most affluent man is he that confronts all the shows he sees by equivalents out of the stronger wealth of himself. The American bard shall delineate no class of persons nor one or two out of the strata of interests nor love most nor truth most nor the soul most nor the body most . . . . and not be for the eastern states more than the western or the northern states more than the southern.

Exact science and its practical movements are no checks on the greatest poet but always his encouragement and support. The outset and remembrance are there . . there the arms that lifted him first and brace him best . . . . there he returns after all his goings and comings. The sailor and traveler . . the anatomist chemist astonomer geologist phrenologist spiritualist mathematician historian and lexicographer are not poets, but they are the lawgivers of poets and their construction underlies the structure of every perfect poem. No matter what rises or is uttered they sent the seed of the conception of it . . . of them and by them stand the visible proofs of souls . . . . . always of their fatherstuff must be begotten the sinewy races of bards. If there shall be love and content between the father and the son and if the greatness of the son is the exuding of the greatness of the father there shall be love between the poet and the man of demonstrable science. In the beauty of poems are the tuft and final applause of science.

Great is the faith of the flush of knowledge and of the investigation of the depths of qualities and things. Cleaving and circling here swells the soul of the poet yet is president of itself always. The depths are fathomless and

---

[2] Whitman changed this word to "poems" in later editions.

therefore calm. The innocence and nakedness are resumed . . . they are neither modest nor immodest. The whole theory of the special and supernatural and all that was twined with it or educed out of it departs as a dream. What has ever happened . . . . what happens and whatever may or shall happen, the vital laws enclose all . . . . they are sufficent for any case and for all cases . . . none to be hurried or retarded . . . . any miracle of affairs or persons inadmissible in the vast clear scheme where every motion and every spear of grass and the frames and spirits of men and women and all that concerns them are unspeakably perfect miracles all referring to all and each distinct and in its place. It is also not consistent with the reality of the soul to admit that there is anything in the known universe more divine than men and women.

Men and women and the earth and all upon it are simply to be taken as they are, and the investigation of their past and present and future shall be unintermitted and shall be done with perfect candor. Upon this basis philosophy speculates ever looking toward the poet, ever regarding the eternal tendencies of all toward happiness never inconsistent with what is clear to the senses and to the soul. For the eternal tendencies of all toward happiness make the only point of sane philosophy. Whatever comprehends less than that . . . whatever is less than the laws of light and of astronomical motion . . . or less than the laws that follow the thief the liar the glutton and the drunkard through his life and doubtless afterward . . . . . or less than vast stretches of time or the slow formation of density or the patient upheaving of strata—is of no account. Whatever would put God in a poem or system of philosophy as contending against some being or influence is also of no account. Sanity and ensemble characterise the great master . . . spoilt in one principle all is spoilt. The great master has nothing to do with miracles. He sees health for himself in being one of the mass . . . . he sees the hiatus in singular eminence. To the perfect shape comes common ground. To be under the general law is great for that is to correspond with it. The master knows that he is unspeakably great and that all are unspeakably great . . . . that nothing for instance is greater than to conceive children and bring them up well . . . that to be is just as great as to perceive or tell.

In the make of the great masters the idea of political liberty is indispensable. Liberty takes the adherence of heroes wherever men and women exist . . . . but never takes any adherence or welcome from the rest more than from poets. They are the voice and exposition of liberty. They out of ages are worthy the grand idea . . . . to them it is confided and they must sustain it. Nothing has precedence of it and nothing can warp or degrade it. The attitude of great poets is to cheer up slaves and horrify despots. The turn of their necks, the sound of their feet, the motions of their wrists, are full of hazard to the one and hope to the other. Come nigh them awhile and though they neither speak or advise you shall learn the faithful American lesson. Liberty is poorly served by men whose good intent is quelled from one failure or two failures or any number of failures, or from the casual indifference or ingratitude of the people, or from the sharp show of the tushes[3] of power, or the bringing to bear soldiers and cannon or any penal statutes. Liberty relies upon itself, invites no one, promises nothing, sits in calmness and light, is positive and composed, and knows no dis-

---

[3] Tusks.

couragement. The battle rages with many a loud alarm and frequent advance and retreat . . . . the enemy triumphs . . . . the prison, the handcuffs, the iron necklace and anklet, the scaffold, garrote and leadballs do their work . . . . the cause is asleep . . . . the strong throats are choked with their own blood . . . . the young men drop their eyelashes toward the ground when they pass each other . . . . and is liberty gone out of that place? No never. When liberty goes it is not the first to go nor the second or third to go . . it waits for all the rest to go . . it is the last . . . When the memories of the old martyrs are faded utterly away . . . . when the large names of patriots are laughed at in the public halls from the lips of the orators . . . . when the boys are no more christened after the same but christened after tyrants and traitors instead . . . . when the laws of the free are grudgingly permitted and laws for informers and bloodmoney are sweet to the taste of the people . . . . when I and you walk abroad upon the earth stung with compassion at the sight of numberless brothers answering our equal friendship and calling no man master—and when we are elated with noble joy at the sight of slaves . . . . when the soul retires in the cool communion of the night and surveys its experience and has much extasy over the word and deed that put back a helpless innocent person into the gripe of the gripers or into any cruel inferiority . . . . when those in all parts of these states who could easier realize the true American character but do not yet—when the swarms of cringers, suckers, doughfaces, lice of politics, planners of sly involutions for their own preferment to city officers or state legislatures or the judiciary or congress or the presidency, obtain a response of love and natural deference from the people whether they get the offices or no . . . . when it is better to be a bound booby and rogue in office at a high salary than the poorest free mechanic or farmer with his hat unmoved from his head and firm eyes and a candid and generous heart . . . . and when servility by town or state or the federal government or any oppression on a large scale or small scale can be tried on without its own punishment following duly after in exact proportion against the smallest chance of escape . . . . or rather when all life and all the souls of men and women are discharged from any part of the earth—then only shall the instinct of liberty be discharged from that part of the earth.

As the attributes of the poets of the kosmos concentre in the real body and soul and in the pleasure of things they possess the superiority of genuineness over all fiction and romance. As they emit themselves facts are showered over with light . . . . the daylight is lit with more volatile light . . . . also the deep between the setting and rising sun goes deeper many fold. Each precise object or condition or combination or process exhibits a beauty . . . . the multiplication table its—old age its—the carpenter's trade its—the grand-opera its . . . . the huge-hulled cleanshaped New-York clipper at sea under steam or full sail gleams with unmatched beauty . . . . the American circles and large harmonies of government gleam with theirs . . . . and the commonest definite intentions and actions with theirs. The poets of the kosmos advance through all interpositions and coverings and turmoils and stratagems to first principles. They are of use . . . . they dissolve poverty from its need and riches from its conceit. You large proprietor they say shall not realize or perceive more than any one else. The owner of the library is not he who holds a legal title to it having bought and paid for it. Any one and every one is owner of the library who can read the same through all the varieties of tongues and subjects and styles, and in whom they enter with ease and take residence and force toward paternity and maternity, and make supple and powerful and rich and large. . . . . These American states strong and healthy and accomplished shall receive no pleasure from violations of natural models and must not permit them. In paintings or mouldings or carvings in mineral or wood, or in the illustrations of books or newspapers, or in any comic or tragic prints, or in the patterns of woven stuffs or any thing to beautify rooms or furniture or costumes, or to put upon cornices or monuments or on the prows or sterns of ships, or to put anywhere before the human eye indoors or out, that which distorts honest shapes or which creates unearthly beings or places or contingencies is a nuisance and revolt. Of the human form especially it is so great it must never be made ridiculous. Of ornaments to a work nothing outré[4] can be allowed . . but those ornaments can be allowed that conform to the perfect facts of the open air and that flow out of the nature of the work and come irrepressibly from it and are necessary to the completion of the work. Most works are most beautiful without ornament. . . Exaggerations will be revenged in human physiology. Clean and vigorous children are jetted and conceived only in those communities where the models of natural forms are public every day. . . . . Great genius and the people of these states must never be demeaned to romances. As soon as histories are properly told there is no more need of romances.

The great poets are also to be known by the absence in them of tricks and by the justification of perfect personal candor. Then folks echo a new cheap joy and a divine voice leaping from their brains: How beautiful is candor! All faults may be forgiven of him who has perfect candor. Henceforth let no man of us lie, for we have seen that openness wins the inner and outer world and that there is no single exception, and that never since our earth gathered itself in a mass have deceit or subterfuge or prevarication attracted its smallest particle or the faintest tinge of a shade—and that through the enveloping wealth and rank of a state or the whole republic of states a sneak or sly person shall be discovered and despised . . . . and that the soul has never been once fooled and never can be fooled . . . . and thrift without the loving nod of the soul is only a fœtid puff . . . . and there never grew up in any of the continents of the globe nor upon any planet or satellite or star, nor upon the asteroids, nor in any part of ethereal space, nor in the midst of density, nor under the fluid wet of the sea, nor in that condition which precedes the birth of babes, nor at any time during the changes of life, nor in that condition that follows what we term death, nor in any stretch of abeyance or action afterward of vitality, nor in any process of formation or reformation anywhere, a being whose instinct hated the truth.

Extreme caution or prudence, the soundest organic health, large hope and comparison and fondness for women and children, large alimentiveness and destructiveness and causality, with a perfect sense of the oneness of nature and the propriety of the same spirit applied to human affairs . . these are called up of the float of the brain of the world to be parts of the greatest poet from his birth out of his mother's womb and from her birth out of her mother's. Caution seldom goes far enough. It has been thought that the prudent citizen

---

[4] Exaggerated or eccentric or bizarre (Fr.).

was the citizen who applied himself to solid gains and did well for himself and his family and completed a lawful life without debt or crime. The greatest poet sees and admits these economies as he sees the economies of food and sleep, but has higher notions of prudence than to think he gives much when he gives a few slight attentions at the latch of the gate. The premises of the prudence of life are not the hospitality of it or the ripeness and harvest of it. Beyond the independence of a little sum laid aside for burial-money, and of a few clapboards around and shingles overhead on a lot of American soil owned, and the easy dollars that supply the year's plain clothing and meals, the melancholy prudence of the abandonment of such a great being as a man is to the toss and pallor of years of moneymaking with all their scorching days and icy nights and all their stifling deceits and underhanded dodgings, or infinitesimals of parlors, or shameless stuffing while others starve . . and all the loss of the bloom and odor of the earth and of the flowers and atmosphere and of the sea and of the true taste of the women and men you pass or have to do with in youth or middle age, and the issuing sickness and desperate revolt at the close of a life without elevation or naivete, and the ghastly chatter of a death without serenity or majesty, is the great fraud upon modern civilization and forethought, blotching the surface and system which civilization undeniably drafts, and moistening with tears the immense features it spreads and spreads with such velocity before the reached kisses of the soul. . . Still the right explanation remains to be made about prudence. The prudence of the mere wealth and respectability of the most esteemed life appears too faint for the eye to observe at all when little and large alike drop quietly aside at the thought of the prudence suitable for immortality. What is wisdom that fills the thinness of a year or seventy or eighty years to wisdom spaced out by ages and coming back at a certain time with strong reinforcements and rich presents and the clear faces of wedding-guests as far as you can look in every direction running gaily toward you? Only the soul is of itself . . . . all else has reference to what ensues. All that a person does or thinks is of consequence. Not a move can a man or woman make that affects him or her in a day or a month or any part of the direct lifetime or the hour of death but the same affects him or her onward afterward through the indirect lifetime. The indirect is always as great and real as the direct. The spirit receives from the body just as much as it gives to the body. Not one name of word or deed . . not of venereal sores or discolorations . . not the privacy of the onanist . . not of the putrid veins of gluttons or rumdrinkers . . . not peculation or cunning or betrayal or murder . . no serpentine poison of those that seduce women . . not the foolish yielding of women . . not prostitution . . not of any depravity of young men . . not of the attainment of gain by discreditable means . . not any nastiness of appetite . . not any harshness of officers to men or judges to prisoners or fathers to sons or sons to fathers or of husbands to wives or bosses to their boys . . not of greedy looks or malignant wishes . . . nor any of the wiles practised by people upon themselves . . . ever is or ever can be stamped on the programme but it is duly realized and returned, and that returned in further performances . . . and they returned again. Nor can the push of charity or personal force ever be any thing else than the profoundest reason, whether it bring arguments to hand or no. No specification is necessary . . to add or subtract or divide is in vain. Little or big, learned or unlearned, white or black, legal or illegal, sick or well, from the first inspiration down the windpipe to the last expiration out of it, all that a male or female does that is vigorous and benevolent and clean is so much sure profit to him or her in the unshakable order of the universe and through the whole scope of it forever. If the savage or felon is wise it is well . . . . if the greatest poet or savant is wise it is simply the same . . if the President or chief justice is wise it is the same . . . if the young mechanic or farmer is wise it is no more or less . . if the prostitute is wise it is no more nor less. The interest will come round . . all will come round. All the best actions of war and peace . . . all help given to relatives and strangers and the poor and old and sorrowful and young children and widows and the sick, and to all shunned persons . . all furtherance of fugitives and of the escape of slaves . . all the self-denial that stood steady and aloof on wrecks and saw others take the seats of the boats . . . all offering of substance or life for the good old cause, or for a friend's sake or opinion's sake . . . all pains of enthusiasts scoffed at by their neighbors . . all the vast sweet love and precious suffering of mothers . . . all honest men baffled in strifes recorded or unrecorded . . . . all the grandeur and good of the few ancient nations whose fragments of annals we inherit . . and all the good of the hundreds of far mightier and more ancient nations unknown to us by name or date or location . . . . all that was ever manfully begun, whether it succeeded or no . . . . all that has at any time been well suggested out of the divine heart of man or by the divinity of his mouth or by the shaping of his great hands . . and all that is well thought or done this day on any part of the surface of the globe . . or on any of the wandering stars or fixed stars by those there as we are here . . or that is henceforth to be well thought or done by you whoever you are, or by any one—these singly and wholly inured at their time and inure now and will inure always to the identities from which they sprung or shall spring . . . Did you guess any of them lived only its moment? The world does not so exist . . no parts palpaple or impalpable so exist . . . no result exists now without being from its long antecedent result, and that from its antecedent, and so backward without the farthest mentionable spot coming a bit nearer the beginning than any other spot. . . . . Whatever satisfies the soul is truth. The prudence of the greatest poet answers at last the craving and glut of the soul, is not contemptuous of less ways of prudence if they conform to its ways, puts off nothing, permits no let-up for its own case or any case, has no particular sabbath or judgment-day, divides not the living from the dead or the righteous from the unrighteous, is satisfied with the present, matches every thought or act by its correlative, knows no possible forgiveness or deputed atonement . . knows that the young man who composedly periled his life and lost it has done exceeding well for himself, while the man who has not periled his life and retains it to old age in riches and ease has perhaps achieved nothing for himself worth mentioning . . and that only that person has no great prudence to learn who has learnt to prefer real longlived things, and favors body and soul the same, and perceives the indirect assuredly following the direct, and what evil or good he does leaping onward and waiting to meet him again—and who in his spirit in any emergency whatever neither hurries or avoids death.

The direct trial of him who would be the greatest poet is today. If he does not flood himself with the immediate age as with vast oceanic tides . . . . . and if he does not attract his own land body and soul to himself and hang on its neck with incomparable love and plunge his semitic[5] muscle into its merits and demerits . . . and if he be not himself the age transfigured . . . . and if to him is not opened the eternity which gives similitude to all periods and locations and processes and animate and inanimate forms, and which is the bond of time, and rises up from its inconceivable vagueness and infiniteness in the swimming shape of today, and is held by the ductile anchors of life, and makes the present spot the passage from what was to what shall be, and commits itself to the representation of this wave of an hour and this one of the sixty beautiful children of the wave—let him merge in the general run and wait his development . . . . Still the final test of poems or any character or work remains. The prescient poet projects himself centuries ahead and judges performer or performance after the changes of time. Does it live through them? Does it still hold on untired? Will the same style and the direction of genius to similar points be satisfactory now? Has no new discovery in science or arrival at superior planes of thought and judgment and behavior fixed him or his so that either can be looked down upon? Have the marches of tens and hundreds and thousands of years made willing detours to the right hand and the left hand for his sake? Is he beloved long and long after he is buried? Does the young man think often of him? and the young woman think often of him? and do the middleaged and the old think of him?

A great poem is for ages and ages in common and for all degrees and complexions and all departments and sects and for a woman as much as a man and a man as much as a woman. A great poem is no finish to a man or woman but rather a beginning. Has any one fancied he could sit at last under some due authority and rest satisfied with explanations and realize and be content and full? To no such terminus does the greatest poet bring . . . he brings neither cessation or sheltered fatness and ease. The touch of him tells in action. Whom he takes he takes with firm sure grasp into live regions previously unattained . . . . thenceforward is no rest . . . . they see the space and ineffable sheen that turn the old spots and lights into dead vacuums. The companion of him beholds the birth and progress of stars and learns one of the meanings. Now there shall be a man cohered out of tumult and chaos . . . . the elder encourages the younger and shows him how . . . they two shall launch off fearlessly together till the new world fits an orbit for itself and looks unabashed on the lesser orbits of the stars and sweeps through the ceaseless rings and shall never be quiet again.

There will soon be no more priests. Their work is done. They may wait a while . . perhaps a generation or two . . dropping off by degrees. A superior breed shall take their place . . . . the gangs of kosmos and prophets en masse shall take their place. A new order shall arise and they shall be the priests of man, and every man shall be his own priest. The churches built under their umbrage shall be the churches of men and women. Through the divinity of themselves shall the kosmos and the new breed of poets be interpreters of men and women and of all events and things. They shall find their inspiration in real

[5] Whitman probably meant to write "seminal," as in Canto 6, line 8, of his poem "By Blue Ontario's Shore." Then again, he may have meant "semitic."

objects today, symptoms of the past and future . . . . They shall not deign to defend immortality or God or the perfection of things or liberty or the exquisite beauty and reality of the soul. They shall arise in America and be responded to from the remainder of the earth.

The English language befriends the grand American expression . . . . it is brawny enough and limber and full enough. On the tough stock of a race who through all change of circumstance was never without the idea of political liberty, which is the animus of all liberty, it has attracted the terms of daintier and gayer and subtler and more elegant tongues. It is the powerful language of resistance . . . it is the dialect of common sense. It is the speech of the proud and melancholy races and of all who aspire. It is the chosen tongue to express growth faith self-esteem freedom justice equality friendliness amplitude prudence decision and courage. It is the medium that shall well nigh express the inexpressible.

No great literature nor any like style of behaviour or oratory or social intercourse or household arrangements or public institutions or the treatment by bosses of employed people, nor executive detail or detail of the army or navy, nor spirit of legislation or courts or police or tuition or architecture or songs or amusements or the costumes of young men, can long elude the jealous and passionate instinct of American standards. Whether or no the sign appears from the mouths of the people, it throbs a live interrogation in every freeman's and freewoman's heart after that which passes by or this built to remain. Is it uniform with my country? Are its disposals without ignominious distinctions? Is it for the evergrowing communes of brothers and lovers, large, well-united, proud beyond the old models, generous beyond all models? Is it something grown fresh out of the fields or drawn from the sea for use to me today here? I know that what answers for me an American must answer for any individual or nation that serves for a part of my materials. Does this answer? or is it without reference to universal needs? or sprung of the needs of the less developed society of special ranks? or old needs of pleasure overlaid by modern science and forms? Does this acknowledge liberty with audible and absolute acknowledgement, and set slavery at nought for life and death? Will it help breed one good-shaped and wellhung man, and a woman to be his perfect and independent mate? Does it improve manners? Is it for the nursing of the young of the republic? Does it solve readily with the sweet milk of the nipples of the breasts of the mother of many children? Has it too the old ever-fresh forbearance and impartiality? Does it look with the same love on the last born and on those hardening toward stature, and on the errant, and on those who disdain all strength of assault outside of their own?

The poems distilled from other poems will probably pass away. The coward will surely pass away. The expectation of the vital and great can only be satisfied by the demeanor of the vital and great. The swarms of the polished deprecating and reflectors and the polite float off and leave no remembrance. America prepares with composure and good will for the visitors that have sent word. It is not intellect that is to be their warrant and welcome. The talented, the artist, the ingenious, the editor, the statesman, the erudite . . they are not unappreciated . . they fall in their place and do their work. The soul of the nation also does its work. No disguise can pass on it . . no disguise can conceal from it. It rejects none, it permits all. Only toward as good as itself and toward the like of itself will it advance half-way. An individual is as superb as a nation when he has the qualities which make a superb nation. The soul of the largest and wealthiest and proudest nation may well go half-way to meet that of its poets. The signs are effectual. There is no fear of mistake. If the one is true the other is true. The proof of a poet is that his country absorbs him as affectionately as he has absorbed it.

Hippolyte Taine

INTRODUCTION TO
HISTORY OF ENGLISH LITERATURE

The influence of Hippolyte Taine (1828–1893) on thoughtful minds in the latter part of the nineteenth century was very great, especially in his native France but in other countries as well. Some account of the part he played in establishing the interest and validity of the category of causation in thinking about cultural events has been given in the Introduction to the present volume (pp. 19 ff.) and the reader will find a fuller treatment of Taine's achievement and influence in Harry Levin's essay, "Literature as an Institution" (pp. 406 ff.). Taine was trained at the École Normale Supérieure, France's famous and exigent school for future university teachers. He was a brilliant student but he failed to pass his examination (1851) because the views he expressed seemed to his examiners to be too daring. He taught for a time in provincial schools, then supported himself by private tutoring and literary journalism, adding to his already great learning. By the time he was thirty, he had established a considerable reputation with his scholarly but always vivivacious historical studies of literature and philosophy. In 1864 he was appointed Professor of Aesthetics and of the History of Art at the École des Beaux Arts. His *History of English Literature* (3 volumes), the Introduction to which has gained a special fame among his writings, was published in 1863.

The historian might place himself for a given period, say a series of ages, or in the human soul, or with some particular people; he might study, describe, relate, all the events, all the transformations, all the revolutions which had been accomplished in the internal man; and when he had finished his work, he would have a history of civilisation amongst the people and in the period he had selected.—Guizot, *Civilisation in Europe*, p. 25.

History has been transformed, within a hundred years in Germany, within sixty years in France, and that by the study of their literatures.

From *History of English Literature*, by Hippolyte A. Taine, translated by H. Van Laun. New York: Leypoldt and Holt, Inc., 1883; Frederick Unger Publishing Co., 1965.

It was perceived that a literary work is not a mere individual play of imagination, the isolated caprice of an excited brain, but a transcript of contemporary manners, a manifestation of a certain kind of mind. It was concluded that we might recover, from the monuments of literature, a knowledge of the manner in which men thought and felt centuries ago. The attempt was made, and it succeeded.

Pondering on these modes of feeling and thought, men decided that they were facts of the highest kind. They saw that these facts bore reference to the most important occurrences, that they explained and were explained by them, that it was necessary thenceforth to give them a rank, and a most important rank, in history. This rank they have received, and from that moment history has undergone a complete change: in its subject-matter, its system, its machinery, the appreciation of laws and of causes. It is this change, such as it is and must be, that we shall here endeavour to exhibit.

I

What is your first remark on turning over the great, stiff leaves of a folio, the yellow sheets of a manuscript,—a poem, a code of laws, a confession of faith? This, you say, did not come into existence all alone. It is but a mould, like a fossil shell, an imprint, like one of those shapes embossed in stone by an animal which lived and perished. Under the shell there was an animal, and behind the document there was a man. Why do you study the shell, except to bring before you the animal? So you study the document only to know the man. The shell and the document are lifeless wrecks, valuable only as a clue to the entire and living existence. We must get hold of this existence, endeavour to re-create it. It is a mistake to study the document, as if it were isolated. This were to treat things like a simple scholar, to fall into the error of the bibliomaniac. Neither mythology nor languages exist in themselves; but only men, who arrange words and imagery according to the necessities of their organs and the original bent of their intellects. A dogma is nothing in itself; look at the people who have made it,—a portrait, for instance, of the sixteenth century, say the stern powerful face of an English archbishop or martyr. Nothing exists except through some individual man; it is this individual with whom we must become acquainted. When we have established the parentage of dogmas, or the classification of poems, or the progress of constitutions, or the transformation of idioms, we have only cleared the soil: genuine history is brought into existence only when the historian begins to unravel, across the lapse of time, the living man, toiling, impassioned, entrenched in his customs, with his voice and features, his gestures and his dress, distinct and complete as he from whom we have just parted in the street. Let us endeavour, then, to annihilate as far as possible this great interval of time, which prevents us from seeing man with our eyes, with the eyes of our head. What have we under the fair glazed pages of a modern poem? A modern poet, who has studied and travelled, a man like Alfred de Musset, Victor Hugo, Lamartine, or Heine,[1] in a black coat and gloves,

---

[1] Alfred de Musset (1810–1857), French poet, dramatist, and fiction writer; Victor Hugo (1802–1888), French poet, dramatist, and novelist; Alphonse de Lamartine

welcomed by the ladies, and making every evening his fifty bows and his score of bon-mots in society, reading the papers in the morning, lodging as a rule on a second floor; not over gay, because he has nerves, and especially because, in this dense democracy where we choke one another, the discredit of the dignities of office has exaggerated his pretensions while increasing his importance, and because the keenness of his feelings in general disposes him somewhat to believe himself a deity. This is what we take note of under modern Meditations or Sonnets. Even so, under a tragedy of the seventeenth century we have a poet, like Racine for instance, elegant, staid, a courtier, a fine talker, with a majestic wig and ribboned shoes, at heart a royalist and a Christian, who says, "God has been so gracious to me, that in whatever company I find myself I never have occasion to blush for the gospel or the king;" clever at entertaining the prince, and rendering for him into good French the "old French of Amyot;"[2] very respectful to the great, always "knowing his place;" as assiduous and reserved at Marly[3] as at Versailles,[4] amidst the regular pleasures of polished and ornate nature, amidst the salutations, graces, airs, and fopperies of the braided lords, who rose early in the morning to obtain the promise of being appointed to some office in case of the death of the present holder, and amongst charming ladies who count their genealogies on their fingers in order to obtain the right of sitting down in the presence of the King or Queen. On that head consult St. Simon[5] and the engravings of Pérelle, as for the present age you have consulted Balzac and the water colours of Eugène Lami. Similarly, when we read a Greek tragedy, our first care should be to realise to ourselves the Greeks, that is, the men who live half naked, in the gymnasia, or in the public squares, under a glowing sky, face to face with the most beautiful and the most noble landscapes, bent on making their bodies lithe and strong, on conversing, discussing, voting, carrying on patriotic piracies, nevertheless lazy and temperate, with three urns for their furniture, two anchovies in a jar of oil for their food, waited on by slaves, so as to give them leisure to cultivate their understanding and exercise their limbs, with no desire beyond that of having the most beautiful town, the most beautiful processions, the most beautiful ideas, the most beautiful men. On this subject, a statue such as the Meleager or the Theseus of the Parthenon, or still more, the sight of the Mediterranean, blue and lustrous as a silken tunic, and the islands that stud it with their massive marble outlines: add to these twenty select phrases from Plato and Aristophanes, and they will teach you much more than a multitude of dissertations and commentaries. And so again, in order to understand an Indian Purána,[6] begin by imagining to yourself the father of a family, who, "having seen a son on his son's knees," retires, according to the law, into solitude, with an axe and a pitcher under a banyan tree, by the brook-side,

---

(1790–1869), French poet, novelist, and statesman; Heinrich Heine (1797–1856), German lyric poet.

[2] Jacques Amyot (1513–1593), humanist and translator.

[3] Town on the Seine, where Louis XIV had a chateau.

[4] Where Louis XIV built a palace in extensive grounds and established his royal residence.

[5] Louis de Rouvroy, Duc de Saint-Simon (1675–1755), whose memoirs in seven large volumes detail the goings-on in the court of Louis XIV.

[6] One of the four classes of Shastras, or sacred books.

talks no more, adds fast to fast, dwells naked between four fires, and under that terrible sun, which devours and renews without end all things living; who, for weeks at a time, fixes his imagination first upon the feet of Brahma, next upon his knee, next upon his thigh, next upon his navel, and so on, until, beneath the strain of this intense meditation, hallucinations begin to appear, until all the forms of existence, mingled and transformed the one with the other, quaver before a sight dazzled and giddy, until the motionless man, catching in his breath, with fixed gaze, beholds the universe vanishing like a smoke in the universal void of Being into which he hopes to be absorbed. To this end a voyage to India would be the best instructor; or for want of better, the accounts of travellers, books of geography, botany, ethnology, will serve their turn. In each case the search must be the same. Language, legislation, creeds, are only abstract things: the complete thing is the man who acts, the man corporeal and visible, who eats, walks, fights, labours. Leave aside the theory and the mechanism of constitutions, religions and their systems, and try to see men in their workshops, in their offices, in their fields, with their sky and soil, their houses, their dress, cultivations, meals, as you do when, landing in England or Italy, you look at faces and motions, roads and inns, a citizen taking his walk, a workman drinking. Our great care should be to supply as much as possible the want of present, personal, direct, and sensible observation which we can no longer practise; for it is the only means of knowing men. Let us make the past present: in order to judge of a thing, it must be before us; there is no experience in respect of what is absent. Doubtless this reconstruction is always incomplete; it can produce only incomplete judgments; but that we cannot help. It is better to have an imperfect knowledge than none at all; and there is no other means of acquainting ourselves approximately with the events of other days, than to *see* approximately the men of other days.

This is the first step in history; it was made in Europe at the revival of imagination, toward the close of the last century, by Lessing[7] and Walter Scott; a little later in France, by Chateaubriand, Augustin Thierry, Michelet,[8] and others. And now for the second step.

II

When you consider with your eyes the visible man, what do you look for? The man invisible. The words which enter your ears, the gestures, the motions of his head, the clothes he wears, visible acts and deeds of every kind, are expressions merely; somewhat is revealed beneath them, and that is a soul. An inner man is concealed beneath the outer man; the second does but reveal the first. You look at his house, furniture, dress; and that in order to discover in them the marks of his habits and tastes, the degree of his refinement or rusticity, his extravagance or his economy, his stupidity or his acuteness. You

[7] Gotthold Ephrain Lessing (1729–1781), German philosopher, dramatist, and critic.
[8] François René, vicomte de Chateaubriand (1768–1848), writer and statesman; Augustin Thierry (1795–1856), historian; Jules Michelet (1798–1874), historian. All three had much to do with making romanticism conscious of itself in French, with formulating and advancing new ideas about history.

listen to his conversation, and you note the inflexions of his voice, the changes in his attitudes; and that in order to judge of his vivacity, his self-forgetfulness or his gaiety, his energy or his constraint. You consider his writings, his artistic productions, his business transactions or political ventures; and that in order to measure the scope and limits of his intelligence, his inventiveness, his coolness, to find out the order, the character, the general force of his ideas, the mode in which he thinks and resolves. All these externals are but avenues converging towards a centre; you enter them simply in order to reach that centre; and that centre is the genuine man, I mean that mass of faculties and feelings which are the inner man. We have reached a new world, which is infinite, because every action which we see involves an infinite association of reasonings, emotions, sensations new and old, which have served to bring it to light, and which, like great rocks deep-seated in the ground, find in it their end and their level. This underworld is a new subject-matter, proper to the historian. If his critical education is sufficient, he can lay bare, under every detail of architecture, every stroke in a picture, every phrase in a writing, the special sensation whence detail, stroke, or phrase had issue; he is present at the drama which was enacted in the soul of artist or writer; the choice of a word, the brevity or length of a sentence, the nature of a metaphor, the accent of a verse, the development of an argument—everything is a symbol to him; while his eyes read the text, his soul and mind pursue the continuous development and the everchanging succession of the emotions and conceptions out of which the text has sprung: in short, he works out its psychology. If you would observe this operation, consider the originator and model of all grand contemporary culture, Goethe, who, before writing *Iphigenia*, employed day after day in making drawings of the most finished statues, and who at last, his eyes filled with the noble forms of ancient scenery, his mind penetrated by the harmonious loveliness of antique life, succeeded in reproducing so exactly in himself the habits and peculiarities of the Greek imagination, that he gives us almost the twin sister of the Antigone of Sophocles, and the goddesses of Phidias.[9] This precise and proved interpretation of past sensations has given to history, in our days, a second birth; hardly anything of the sort was known to the preceding century. They thought men of every race and century were all but identical; the Greek, the barbarian, the Hindoo, the man of the Renaissance, and the man of the eighteenth century, as if they had been turned out of a common mould; and all in conformity to a certain abstract conception, which served for the whole human race. They knew man, but not men; they had not penetrated to the soul; they had not seen the infinite diversity and marvellous complexity of souls; they did not know that the moral constitution of a people or an age is as particular and distinct as the physical structure of a family of plants or an order of animals. Now-a-days, history, like zoology, has found its anatomy; and whatever the branch of history to which you devote yourself, philology, linguistic lore, mythology, it is by these means you must strive to produce new fruit. Amid so many writers who, since the time of Herder,[18]

---

[9] Greek sculptor of the Fifth century B.C.
[10] Johann Gottfried von Herder (1744–1803), German philosopher, poet, and critic.

Otfried Müller,[11] and Goethe, have continued and still improve this great method, let the reader consider only two historians and two works, Carlyle's *Cromwell*, and Sainte-Beuve's *Port-Royal*: he will see with what fairness, exactness, depth of insight, a man may discover a soul beneath its actions and its works; how behind the old general, in place of a vulgar hypocritical schemer, we recover a man troubled with the obscure reveries of a melancholic imagination, but with practical instincts and faculties, English to the core, strange and incomprehensible to one who has not studied the climate and the race; how, with about a hundred meagre letters and a score of mutilated speeches, we may follow him from his farm and team, to the general's tent and to the Protector's throne, in his transmutation and development, in his pricks of conscience and his political sagacity, until the machinery of his mind and actions becomes visible, and the inner tragedy, ever changing and renewed, which exercised this great, darkling soul, passes, like one of Shakespeare's, through the soul of the looker-on. He will see (in the other case) how, behind the squabbles of the monastery, or the contumacies of nuns, he may find a great province of human psychology; how about fifty characters, that had been buried under the uniformity of a circumspect narrative, reappear in the light of day, each with its own specialty and its countless diversities; how, beneath theological disquisitions and monotonous sermons, we can unearth the beatings of living hearts, the convulsions and apathies of monastic life, the unforeseen reassertions and wavy turmoil of nature, the inroads of surrounding worldliness, the intermittent victories of grace, with such a variety of lights and shades, that the most exhaustive description and the most elastic style can hardly gather the inexhaustible harvest, which the critic has caused to spring up on this abandoned field. And so it is throughout. Germany, with its genius so pliant, so comprehensive, so apt for transformation, so well calculated to reproduce the most remote and anomalous conditions of human thought; England, with its intellect so precise, so well calculated to grapple closely with moral questions, to render them exact by figures, weights and measures, geography, statistics, by quotation and by common sense; France, with her Parisian culture, with her drawing-room manners, with her untiring analysis of characters and actions, her irony so ready to hit upon a weakness, her finesse so practised in the discrimination of shades of thought;—all have worked the same soil, and we begin to understand that there is no region of history where it is not imperative to till this deep level, if we would see a serviceable harvest rise between the furrows.

This is the second step; we are in a fair way to its completion. It is the fit work of the contemporary critic. No one has done it so justly and grandly as Sainte-Beuve: in this respect we are all his pupils, his method has revolutionised, in our days, in books, and even in newspapers, every kind of literary, of philosophical and religious criticism. From it we must set out in order to begin the further development. I have more than once endeavoured to indicate this development; there is here, in my mind, a new path open to history, and I will try to describe it more in detail.

[11] Karl Otfried Müller (1797–1840), German classical scholar and archeologist.

III

When you have observed and noted in man one, two, three, then a multitude of sensations, does this suffice, or does your knowledge appear complete? Is Psychology only a series of observations? No; here as elsewhere we must search out the causes after we have collected the facts. No matter if the facts be physical or moral, they all have their causes; there is a cause for ambition, for courage, for truth, as there is for digestion, for muscular movement, for animal heat. Vice and virtue are products, like vitriol and sugar; and every complex phenomenon arises from other more simple phenomena on which it hangs. Let us then seek the simple phenomena for moral qualities, as we seek them for physical qualities; and let us take the first fact that presents itself: for example, religious music, that of a Protestant Church. There is an inner cause which has turned the spirit of the faithful toward these grave and monotonous melodies, a cause broader than its effect; I mean the general idea of the true, external worship which man owes to God. It is this which has modelled the architecture of Protestant places of worship, thrown down the statues, removed the pictures, destroyed the ornaments, curtailed the ceremonies, shut up the worshippers in high pews which prevent them from seeing anything, and regulated the thousand details of decoration, posture, and general externals. This again comes from another more general cause, the idea of human conduct in all its comprehensiveness, internal and external, prayers, actions, duties of every kind which man owes to God; it is this which has enthroned the doctrine of grace, lowered the status of the clergy, transformed the sacraments, suppressed various practices, and changed religion from a discipline to a morality. This second idea in its turn depends upon a third still more general, that of moral perfection, such as is met with in the perfect God, the unerring judge, the stern watcher of souls, before whom every soul is sinful, worthy of punishment, incapable of virtue or salvation, except by the power of conscience which He calls forth, and the renewal of heart which He produces. That is the master idea, which consists in erecting duty into an absolute king of human life, and in prostrating all ideal models before a moral model. Here we track the root of man; for to explain this conception it is necessary to consider the race itself, the German and Northman, the structure of his character and mind, his general processes of thought and feeling, the sluggishness and coldness of sensation which prevent his falling easily and headlong under the sway of pleasure, the bluntness of his taste, the irregularity and revolutions of his conception, which arrest in him the birth of fair dispositions and harmonious forms, the disdain of appearances, the desire for truth, the attachment to bare and abstract ideas, which develop in him conscience, at the expense of all else. There the search is at an end; we have arrived at a primitive disposition; at a feature peculiar to all the sensations, and to all the conceptions of a century or a race, at a particularity inseparable from all the motions of his intellect and his heart. Here lie the grand causes, for they are the universal and permanent causes, present at every moment and in every case, everywhere and always acting, indestructible, and finally infallibly supreme, since the accidents which

thwart them, being limited and partial, end by yielding to the dull and incessant repetition of their efforts; in such a manner that the general structure of
things, and the grand features of events, are their work; and religions, philosophies, poetries, industries, the framework of society and of families, are in
fact only the imprints stamped by their seal.

IV

There is, then, a system in human sentiments and ideas: and this system
has for its motive power certain general traits, certain characteristics of the intellect and the heart common to men of one race, age, or country. As in
mineralogy the crystals, however diverse, spring from certain simple physical
forms, so in history, civilisations, however diverse, are derived from certain
simple spiritual forms. The one are explained by a primitive geometrical element, as the others are by a primitive psychological element. In order to master
the classification of mineralogical systems, we must first consider a regular and
general solid, its sides and angles, and observe in this the numberless transformations of which it is capable. So, if you would realise the system of historical
varieties, consider first a human soul generally, with its two or three fundamental faculties, and in this compendium you will perceive the principal forms
which it can present. After all, this kind of ideal picture, geometrical as well as
psychological, is not very complex, and we speedily see the limits of the outline in which civilisations, like crystals, are constrained to exist.

What is really the mental structure of man? Images or representations of
things, which float within him, exist for a time, are effaced, and return again,
after he has been looking upon a tree, an animal, any visible object. This is the
subject-matter, the development whereof is double, either speculative or practical, according as the representations resolve themselves into a *general conception*
or an *active resolution*. Here we have the whole of man in an abridgment; and
in this limited circle human diversities meet, sometimes in the womb of the
primordial matter, sometimes in the twofold primordial development. However
minute in their elements, they are enormous in the aggregate, and the least
alteration in the factors produces vast alteration in the results. According as the
representation is clear and as it were punched out or confused and faintly defined, according as it embraces a great or small number of the characteristics of
the object, according as it is violent and accompanied by impulses, or quiet and
surrounded by calm, all the operations and processes of the human machine
are transformed. So, again, according as the ulterior development of the representation varies, the whole human development varies. If the general conception in which it results is a mere dry notation (in Chinese fashion), language
becomes a sort of algebra, religion and poetry dwindle, philosophy is reduced to
a kind of moral and practical common sense, science to a collection of utilitarian
formulas, classifications, mnemonics, and the whole intellect takes a positive
bent. If, on the contrary, the general representation in which the conception
results is a poetical and figurative creation, a living symbol, as among the
Aryan races, language becomes a sort of delicately-shaded and coloured epic
poem, in which every word is a person, poetry and religion assume a mag-

nificent and inexhaustible grandeur, metaphysics are widely and subtly developed, without regard to positive applications; the whole intellect, in spite of the inevitable deviations and shortcomings of its effort, is smitten with the beautiful and the sublime, and conceives an ideal capable by its nobleness and its harmony of rallying round it the tenderness and enthusiasm of the human race. If, again, the general conception in which the representation results is poetical but not graduated; if man arrives at it not by an uninterrupted gradation, but by a quick intuition; if the original operation is not a regular development, but a violent explosion,—then, as with the Semitic races, metaphysics are absent, religion conceives God only as a king solitary and devouring, science cannot grow, the intellect is too rigid and unbending to reproduce the delicate operations of nature, poetry can give birth only to vehement and grandiose exclamations, language cannot unfold the web of argument and of eloquence, man is reduced to a lyric enthusiasm, an unchecked passion, a fanatical and limited action. In this interval between the particular representation and the universal conception are found the germs of the greatest human differences. Some races, as the classical, pass from the first to the second by a graduated scale of ideas, regularly arranged, and general by degrees; others, as the Germanic, traverse the same ground by leaps, without uniformity, after vague and prolonged groping. Some, like the Romans and English, halt at the first steps; others, like the Hindoos and Germans, mount to the last. If, again, after considering the passage from the representation to the idea, we consider that from the representation to the resolution, we find elementary differences of the like importance and the like order, according as the impression is sharp, as in southern climates, or dull, as in northern; according as it results in instant action, as among barbarians, or slowly, as in civilised nations; as it is capable or not of growth, inequality, persistence, and relations. The whole network of human passions, the chances of peace and public security, the sources of labour and action, spring from hence. Such is the case with all primordial differences: their issues embrace an entire civilisation; and we may compare them to those algebraical formulas which, in a narrow limit, contain in advance the whole curve of which they form the law. Not that this law is always developed to its issue; there are perturbing forces; but when it is so, it is not that the law was false, but that it was not single. New elements become mingled with the old; great forces from without counteract the primitive. The race emigrates, like the Aryan, and the change of climate has altered in its case the whole economy, intelligence, and organisation of society. The people has been conquered, like the Saxon nation, and a new political structure has imposed on it customs, capacities, and inclinations which it had not. The nation has installed itself in the midst of a conquered people, downtrodden and threatening, like the ancient Spartans; and the necessity of living like troops in the field has violently distorted in an unique direction the whole moral and social constitution. In each case, the mechanism of human history is the same. We continually find, as the original mainspring, some very general disposition of mind and soul, innate and appended by nature to the race, or acquired and produced by some circumstance acting upon the race. These mainsprings, once admitted, produce their effect gradually: I mean that after some centuries they bring the nation into a new condition, religious, literary, social, economic; a new condition

which, combined with their renewed effort, produces another condition, sometimes good, sometimes bad, sometimes slowly, sometimes quickly, and so forth;
so that we may regard the whole progress of each distinct civilisation as the
effect of a permanent force which, at every stage, varies its operation by modifying the circumstances of its action.

V

Three different sources contribute to produce this elementary moral state—
RACE, SURROUNDINGS, and EPOCH. What we call the race are the innate and
hereditary dispositions which man brings with him into the world, and which,
as a rule, are united with the marked differences in the temperament and structure of the body. They vary with various peoples. There is a natural variety of
men, as of oxen and horses, some brave and intelligent, some timid and dependent, some capable of superior conceptions and creations, some reduced to
rudimentary ideas and inventions, some more specially fitted to special works,
and gifted more richly with particular instincts, as we meet with species of dogs
better favoured than others,—these for coursing, those for fighting, those for
hunting, these again for house dogs or shepherds' dogs. We have here a distinct
force,—so distinct, that amidst the vast deviations which the other two motive
forces produce in him, one can recognise it still; and a race, like the old
Aryans, scattered from the Ganges as far as the Hebrides, settled in every clime,
and every stage of civilisation, transformed by thirty centuries of revolutions,
nevertheless manifests in its languages, religions, literatures, philosophies, the
community of blood and of intellect which to this day binds its offshoots together. Different as they are, their parentage is not obliterated; barbarism, culture and grafting, differences of sky and soil, fortunes good and bad, have
laboured in vain: the great marks of the original model have remained, and we
find again the two or three principal lineaments of the primitive stamp underneath the secondary imprints which time has laid upon them. There is nothing
astonishing in this extraordinary tenacity. Although the vastness of the distance
lets us but half perceive—and by a doubtful light—the origin of species,* the
events of history sufficiently illumine the events anterior to history, to explain
the almost immovable steadfastness of the primordial marks. When we meet
with them, fifteen, twenty, thirty centuries before our era, in an Aryan, an
Egyptian, a Chinese, they represent the work of a great many ages, perhaps of
several myriads of centuries. For as soon as an animal begins to exist, it has to
reconcile itself with its surroundings; it breathes and renews itself, is differently
affected according to the variations in air, food, temperature. Different climate
and situation bring it various needs, and consequently a different course of
activity; and this, again, a different set of habits; and still again, a different set
of aptitudes and instincts. Man, forced to accommodate himself to circumstances, contracts a temperament and a character corresponding to them; and
his character, like his temperament, is so much more stable, as the external impression is made upon him by more numerous repetitions, and is transmitted
to his progeny by a more ancient descent. So that at any moment we may con-

* Darwin, *The Origin of Species*. Prosper Lucas, *de l'Hérédité*. [Taine's note.]

sider the character of a people as an abridgment of all its preceding actions and sensations; that is, as a quantity and as a weight, not infinite,* since everything in nature is finite, but disproportioned to the rest, and almost impossible to lift, since every moment of an almost infinite past has contributed to increase it, and because, in order to raise the scale, one must place in the opposite scale a still greater number of actions and sensations. Such is the first and richest source of these master-faculties from which historical events take their rise; and one sees at the outset, that if it be powerful, it is because this is no simple spring, but a kind of lake, a deep reservoir wherein other springs have, for a multitude of centuries, discharged their several streams.

Having thus outlined the interior structure of a race, we must consider the surroundings in which it exists. For a man is not alone in the world; nature surrounds him, and his fellow-men surround him; accidental and secondary tendencies overlay his primitive tendencies, and physical or social circumstances disturb or confirm the character committed to their charge. Sometimes the climate has had its effect. Though we can follow but obscurely the Aryan peoples from their common fatherland to their final settlements, we can yet assert that the profound differences which are manifest between the German races on the one side, and the Greek and Latin on the other, arise for the most part from the difference between the countries in which they are settled: some in cold moist lands, deep in rugged marshy forests or on the shores of a wild ocean, beset by melancholy or violent sensations, prone to drunkenness and gluttony, bent on a fighting, blood-spilling life; others, again, within the loveliest landscapes, on a bright and pleasant sea-coast, enticed to navigation and commerce, exempt from gross cravings of the stomach, inclined from the beginning to social ways, to a settled organisation of the state, to feelings and dispositions such as develop the art of oratory, the talent for enjoyment, the inventions of science, letters, arts. Sometimes the state policy has been at work, as in the two Italian civilisations: the first wholly turned to action, conquest, government, legislation, on account of the original site of its city of refuge, its border-land emporium, its armed aristocracy, who, by importing and drilling strangers and conquered, created two hostile armies, having no escape from its internal discords and its greedy instincts but in systematic warfare; the other, shut out from unity and any great political ambition by the stability of its municipal character, the cosmopolitan position of its pope, and the military intervention of neighbouring nations, directed by the whole bent of its magnificent and harmonious genius towards the worship of pleasure and beauty. Sometimes the social conditions have impressed their mark, as eighteen centuries ago by Christianity, and twenty-five centuries ago by Buddhism, when around the Mediterranean, as well as in Hindostan, the extreme results of Aryan conquest and civilisation induced intolerable oppression, the subjugation of the individual, utter despair, the thought that the world was cursed, with the development of metaphysics and myth, so that man in this dungeon of misery, feeling his heart softened, begot the idea of abnegation, charity, tender love, gentleness, humility, brotherly love—there, in a notion of universal nothingness, here under the Fatherhood of God.

* Spinoza, *Ethics,* Part iv, axiom. [Taine's note.]

Look around you upon the regulating instincts and faculties implanted in a race—in short, the mood of intelligence in which it thinks and acts at the present time: you will discover most often the work of some one of these prolonged situations, these surrounding circumstances, persistent and gigantic pressures, brought to bear upon an aggregate of men who, singly and together, from generation to generation, are continually moulded and modelled by their action; in Spain, a crusade against the Mussulmans which lasted eight centuries, protracted even beyond and until the exhaustion of the nation by the expulsion of the Moors, the spoliation of the Jews, the establishment of the Inquisition, the Catholic wars; in England, a political establishment of eight centuries, which keeps a man erect and respectful, in independence and obedience, and accustoms him to strive unitedly, under the authority of the law; in France, a Latin organisation, which, imposed first upon docile barabarians, then shattered in the universal crash, was reformed from within under a lurking conspiracy of the national instinct, was developed under hereditary kings, ends in a sort of levelling republic, centralised, administrative, under dynasties exposed to revolution. These are the most efficacious of the visible causes which mould the primitive man: they are to nations what education, career, condition, abode, are to individuals; and they seem to comprehend everything, since they comprehend all external powers which mould human matter, and by which the external acts on the internal.

There is yet a third rank of causes; for, with the forces within and without, there is the work which they have already produced together, and this work itself contributes to produce that which follows. Beside the permanent impulse and the given surroundings, there is the acquired momentum. When the national character and surrounding circumstances operate, it is not upon a *tabula rasa*,[12] but on a ground on which marks are already impressed. According as one takes the ground at one moment or another, the imprint is different; and this is the cause that the total effect is different. Consider, for instance, two epochs of a literature or art,—French tragedy under Corneille and under Voltaire, the Greek drama under Æschylus and under Euripides,[13] Italian painting under da Vinci and under Guido.[14] Truly, at either of these two extreme points the general idea has not changed; it is always the same human type which is its subject of representation or painting; the mould of verse, the structure of the drama, the form of body has endured. But among several differences there is this, that the one artist is the precursor, the other the successor; the first has no model, the second has; the first sees objects face to face, the second sees them through the first; that many great branches of art are lost, many details are perfected, that simplicity and grandeur of impression have diminished, pleasing and refined forms have increased,—in short, that the first work has influenced the second. Thus it is with a people as with a plant; the same sap, under the same temperature, and in the same soil, produces, at different steps of its progressive development, different formations, buds, flowers, fruits, seed-

---

[12] A "smoothed tablet," a blank slate.
[13] Aeschylus wrote his tragedies in the first half of the fifth century B.C., Euripides in the second half.
[14] Leonardo da Vinci (1452–1519); Guido Reni (1575–1642).

vessels, in such a manner that the one which follows must always be preceded by the former, and must spring up from its death. And if now you consider no longer a brief epoch, as our own time, but one of those wide intervals which embrace one or more centuries, like the middle ages, or our last classic age, the conclusion will be similar. A certain dominant idea has had sway; men, for two, for five hundred years, have taken to themselves a certain ideal model of man: in the middle ages, the knight and the monk; in our classic age, the courtier, the man who speaks well. This creative and universal idea is displayed over the whole field of action and thought; and after covering the world with its involuntarily systematic works, it has faded, it has died away, and lo, a new idea springs up, destined to a like domination, and as manifold creations. And here remember that the second depends in part upon the first, and that the first, uniting its effect with those of national genius and surrounding circumstances, imposes on each new creation its bent and direction. The great historical currents are formed after this law—the long dominations of one intellectual pattern, or a master idea, such as the period of spontaneous creations called the Renaissance, or the period of oratorical models called the Classical Age, or the series of mystical systems called the Alexandrian and Christian eras, or the series of mythological efflorescences which we meet with in the infancy of the German people, of the Indian and the Greek. Here as elsewhere we have but a mechanical problem; the total effect is a result, depending entirely on the magnitude and direction of the producing causes. The only difference which separates these moral problems from physical ones is, that the magnitude and direction cannot be valued or computed in the first as in the second. If a need or a faculty is a quantity, capable of degrees, like a pressure or a weight, this quantity is not measurable like the pressure or the weight. We cannot define it in an exact or approximative formula; we cannot have more, or give more, in respect of it, than a literary impression; we are limited to marking and quoting the salient points by which it is manifested, and which indicate approximately and roughly the part of the scale which is its position. But though the means of notation are not the same in the moral and physical sciences, yet as in both the matter is the same, equally made up of forces, magnitudes, and directions, we may say that in both the final result is produced after the same method. It is great or small, as the fundamental forces are great or small and act more or less exactly in the same sense, according as the distinct effects of race, circumstance, and epoch combine to add the one to the other, or to annul one another. Thus are explained the long impotences and the brilliant triumphs which make their appearance irregularly and without visible cause in the life of a people; they are caused by internal concords or contrarieties. There was such a concord when in the seventeenth century the sociable character and the conversational aptitude, innate in France, encountered the drawing-room manners and the epoch of oratorical analysis; when in the nineteenth century the profound and pliant genius of Germany encountered the age of philosophical systems and of cosmopolitan criticism. There was such a contrariety when in the seventeenth century the harsh and lonely English genius tried blunderingly to adopt a new-born politeness; when in the sixteenth century the lucid and prosaic French spirit tried vainly to bring forth a living poetry. That hidden concord of creative forces produced the finished urbanity and the noble and regular literature under Louis XIV. and Bossuet,[15] the grand metaphysics and broad critical sympathy of Hegel and Goethe. That hidden contrariety of creative forces produced the imperfect literature, the scandalous comedy, the abortive drama under Dryden and Wycherley,[16] the feeble Greek importations, the groping elaborate efforts, the scant half-graces under Ronsard and the Pleiad.[17] So much we can say with confidence, that the unknown creations towards which the current of the centuries conducts us, will be raised up and regulated altogether by the three primordial forces; that if these forces could be measured and computed, we might deduce from them as from a formula the characteristics of future civilisation; and that if, in spite of the evident crudeness of our notations, and the fundamental inexactness of our measures, we try now to form some idea of our general destiny, it is upon an examination of these forces that we must base our prophecy. For in enumerating them, we traverse the complete circle of the agencies; and when we have considered RACE, SURROUNDINGS, and EPOCH, which are the internal mainsprings, the external pressure, and the acquired momentum, we have exhausted not only the whole of the actual causes, but also the whole of the possible causes of motion.

VI

It remains for us to examine how these causes, when applied to a nation or an age, produce their results. As a spring, rising from a height and flowing downwards spreads its streams, according to the depth of the descent, stage after stage, until it reaches the lowest level of the soil, so the disposition of intellect or soul impressed on a people by race, circumstance, or epoch, spreads in different proportions and by regular descents, down the diverse orders of facts which make up its civilisation.* If we arrange the map of a country, starting from the watershed, we find that below this common point the streams are divided into five or six principal basins, then each of these into several secondary basins, and so on, until the whole country with its thousand details is included in the ramifications of this network. So, if we arrange the psychological map of the events and sensations of a human civilisation, we find first of all five or six well-defined provinces—religion, art, philosophy, the state, the family, the industries; then in each of these provinces natural departments; and in each of these, smaller territories, until we arrive at the numberless details of life such as may be observed within and around us every day. If now we examine and compare these diverse groups of

[15] Jacques Bénigne Bossuet (1627–1704), French prelate and writer, noted for the eloquence of his prose and oratory.

[16] John Dryden and William Wycherley wrote most of their plays during the last thirty-five years of the seventeenth century.

[17] A group of seven poets, among them Ronsard, in 1553 took on the name *Pléiade*, in imitation of seven tragic poets of ancient Alexandria.

* For this scale of co-ordinate effects, consult Renan, *Langues Sémitiques*, ch. i.; Mommsen, *Comparison between the Greek and Roman Civilizations*, ch. ii, vol. i. 3d ed.; Tocqueville, *Conséquences de la Démocratie in Amérique*, vol. iii. [Taine's note.]

facts, we find first of all that they are made up of parts, and that all have parts in common. Let us take first the three chief works of human intelligence—religion, art, philosophy. What is a philosophy but a conception of nature and its primordial causes, under the form of abstractions and formulas? What is there at the bottom of a religion or of an art but a conception of this same nature and of these same causes under form of symbols more or less precise, and personages more or less marked; with this difference, that in the first we believe that they exist, in the second we believe that they do not exist? Let the reader consider a few of the great creations of the intelligence in India, Scandinavia, Persia, Rome, Greece, and he will see that, throughout, art is a kind of philosophy made sensible, religion a poem taken for true, philosophy an art and a religion dried up, and reduced to simple ideas. There is therefore, at the core of each of these three groups, a common element, the conception of the world and its principles; and if they differ among themselves, it is because each combines with the common, a distinct element: now the power of abstraction, again the power to personify and to believe, and finally the power to personify and not believe. Let us now take the two chief works of human association, the family and the state. What forms the state but a sentiment of obedience, by which the many unite under the authority of a chief? And what forms the family but the sentiment of obedience by which wife and children act under the direction of a father and husband? The family is a natural state, primitive and restrained, as the state is an artificial family, ulterior and expanded; and underneath the differences arising from the number, origin, and condition of its members, we discover in the small society as in the great, a like disposition of the fundamental intelligence which assimilates and unites them. Now suppose that this element receives from circumstance, race, or epoch certain special marks, it is clear that all the groups into which it enters will be modified proportionately. If the sentiment of obedience is merely fear,* you will find, as in most Oriental states, a brutal despotism, exaggerated punishment, oppression of the subject, servility of manners, insecurity of property, impoverished production, the slavery of women, and the customs of the harem. If the sentiment of obedience has its root in the instinct of order, sociality, and honour, you will find, as in France, a perfect military organisation, a fine administrative hierarchy, a want of public spirit with occasional jerks of patriotism, ready docility of the subject with a revolutionary impatience, the cringing courtier with the counter-efforts of the high-bred man, the refined pleasure of conversation and society on the one hand, and the worry at the fireside and among the family on the other, the equality of husband and wife, the imperfection of the married state, and consequently the necessary constraint of the law. If, again, the sentiment of obedience has its root in the instinct of subordination and the idea of duty, you will find, as among the Germans, security and happiness in the household, a solid basis of domestic life, a tardy and incomplete development of social and conversational life, an innate respect for established dignities, a superstitious reverence for the past, the keeping up of social inequalities, natural and habitual regard for the law. So in a race, according as the aptitude

* Montesquieu, *Esprit des Lois, Principes des trois gouvernements.* [Taine's note.]

for general ideas varies, religion, art, and philosophy vary. If man is naturally inclined to the widest universal conceptions, and apt to disturb them at the same time by the nervous delicacy of his over-sensitive organisation, you will find, as in India, an astonishing abundance of gigantic religious creations, a glowing outgrowth of vast and transparent epic poems, a strange tangle of subtle and imaginative philosophies, all so well interwoven, and so penetrated with a common essence, as to be instantly recognised, by their breadth, their colouring, and their want of order, as the products of the same climate and the same intelligence. If, on the other hand, a man naturally staid and balanced in mind limits of his own accord the scope of his ideas, in order the better to define their form, you will find, as in Greece, a theology of artists and tale-tellers; distinctive gods, soon considered distinct from things, and transformed, almost at the outset, into recognised personages; the sentiment of universal unity all but effaced, and barely preserved in the vague notion of Destiny; a philosophy rather close and delicate than grand and systematic, with shortcomings in higher metaphysics,* but incomparable for logic, sophistry, and morals; poetry and arts superior for clearness, artlessness, just proportions, truth, and beauty, to all that have ever been known. If, once more, man, reduced to narrow conceptions, and deprived of all speculative refinement, is at the same time altogether absorbed and straitened by practical occupations, you will find, as in Rome, rudimentary deities, mere hollow names, serving to designate the trivial details of agriculture, generation, household concerns, customs about marriage, rural life, producing a mythology, hence a philosophy, a poetry, either worth nothing or borrowed. Here, as everywhere, the law of mutual dependence† comes into play. A civilisation forms a body, and its parts are connected with each other like the parts of an organic body. As in an animal, instincts, teeth, limbs, osseous structure, muscular envelope, are mutually connected, so that a change in one produces a corresponding change in the rest, and a clever naturalist can by a process of reasoning reconstruct out of a few fragments almost the whole body; even so in a civilisation, religion, philosophy, the organisation of the family, literature, the arts, make up a system in which every local change induces a general change, so that an experienced historian, studying some particular part of it, sees in advance and half predicts the character of the rest. There is nothing vague in this interdependence. In the living body the regulator is, first, its tendency to manifest a certain primary type; then its necessity for organs whereby to satisfy its wants and to be in harmony with itself in order that it may live. In a civilisation, the regulator is the presence, in every great human creation, of a productive element, present also in other surrounding creations,—to wit, some faculty, aptitude, disposition, effective and discernible, which, being possessed of its proper character, introduces it into all the operations in which

---

* The Alexandrian philosophy had its birth from the West. The metaphysical notions of Aristotle are isolated; moreover, with him as with Plato, they are but a sketch. By way of contrast consider the systematic vigour of Plotinus, Proclus, Schelling, and Hegel, or the wonderful boldness of Brahminical and Buddhistic speculation. [Taine's note.]

† I have endeavoured on several occasions to give expression to this law, notably in the preface to *Essais de Critique et d'Histoire*. [Taine's note.]

it assists, and, according to its variations, causes all the works in which it co-operates to vary also.

VII

At this point we can obtain a glimpse of the principal features of human transformations, and begin to search for the general laws which regulate, not events only, but classes of events, not such and such religion or literature, but a group of literatures or religions. If, for instance, it were admitted that a religion is a metaphysical poem, accompanied by belief; and remarking at the same time that there are certain epochs, races, and circumstances in which belief, the poetical and metaphysical faculty, show themselves with an unwonted vigour; if we consider that Christianity and Buddhism were produced at periods of high philosophical conceptions, and amid such miseries as raised up the fanatics of the Cévennes,[18] if we recognise, on the other hand, that primitive religions are born at the awakening of human reason, during the richest blossoming of human imagination, at a time of the fairest artlessness and the greatest credulity; if we consider, also, that Mohammedanism appeared with the dawning of poetic prose, and the conception of national unity, amongst a people destitute of science, at a period of sudden development of the intellect, —we might then conclude that a religion is born, declines, is reformed and transformed according as circumstances confirm and combine with more or less exactitude and force its three generative instincts; and we should understand why it is endemic in India, amidst imaginative, philosophic, eminently fanatic brains; why it blossomed forth so strangely and grandly in the middle ages, amidst an oppressive organisation, new tongues and literatures; why it was aroused in the sixteenth century with a new character and heroic enthusiasm, amid universal regeneration, and during the awakening of the German races; why it breaks out into eccentric sects amid the coarse American democracy, and under the bureaucratic Russian despotism; why, in short, it is spread, at the present day, over Europe in such different dimensions and such various characteristics, according to the differences of race and civilisation. And so for every kind of human production—for literature, music, the fine arts, philosophy, science, the state, industries, and the rest. Each of these has for its direct cause a moral disposition, or a combination of moral dispositions: the cause given, they appear; the cause withdrawn, they vanish: the weakness or intensity of the cause measures their weakness or intensity. They are bound up with their causes, as a physical phenomenon with its condition, as the dew with the fall of the variable temperature, as dilatation with heat. There are similarly connected data in the moral as in the physical world, as rigorously bound together, and as universally extended in the one as in the other. Whatever in the one case produces, alters, or suppresses the first term, produces, alters, or suppresses the second as a necessary consequence. Whatever lowers the surrounding temperature, deposits the dew. Whatever develops credulity

---

[18] In 1702 Protestant peasants of the Cévennes region of France rebelled against the persecutions that followed the revocation (1685) of the Edict of Nantes (which had guaranteed Protestants many rights).

side by side with a poetical conception of the world, engenders religion. Thus phenomena have been produced; thus they will be produced. As soon as we know the sufficient and necessary condition of one of these vast occurences, our understanding grasps the future as well as the past. We can say with confidence in what circumstances it will reappear, foretell without presumption many portions of its future history, and sketch cautiously some features of its ulterior development.

VIII

History now attempts, or rather is very near attempting this method of research. The question propounded now-a-days is of this kind. Given a litera-ture, philosophy, society, art, group of arts, what is the moral condition which produced it? what the conditions of race, epoch, circumstance, the most fitted to produce this moral condition? There is a distinct moral condition for each of these formations, and for each of their branches; one for art in general, one for each kind of art—for architecture, painting, sculpture, music, poetry; each has its special germ in the wide field of human psychology; each has its law, and it is by virtue of this law that wesee it raised, by chance, as it seems, wholly alone, amid the miscarriage of its neighbours, like painting in Flanders and Holland in the seventeenth century, poetry in England in the sixteenth, music in Germany in the eighteenth. At this moment, and in these countries, the conditions have been fulfilled for one art, not for others, and a single branch has budded in the general barrenness. History must search now-a-days for these rules of human growth; with the special psychology of each special formation it must occupy itself; the finished picture of these characteristic con-ditions it must now labour to compose. No task is more delicate or more difficult; Montesquieu[19] tried it, but in his time history was too new to admit of his success; they had not yet even a suspicion of the road necessary to be travelled, and hardly now do we begin to catch sight of it. Just as in its elements astron-omy is a mechanical and physiology a chemical problem, so history in its elements is a psychological problem. There is a particular system of inner impressions and operations which makes an artist, a believer, a musician, a painter, a man in a nomadic or social state; and of each the birth and growth, the energy, the connection of ideas and emotions, are different: each has his moral history and his special structure, with some governing disposition and some dominant feature. To explain each, it would be necessary to write a chapter of psychological analysis, and barely yet has such a method been rudely sketched. One man alone, Stendhal, with a peculiar bent of mind and a strange education, has undertaken it, and to this day the majority of readers find his books paradoxical and obscure: his talent and his ideas were premature; his admirable divinations were not understood, any more than his profound sayings thrown out cursorily, or the astonishing precision of his system and of his logic. It was not perceived that, under the exterior of a conversationalist and a man of the world, he explained the most complicated of esoteric mechan-

[19] Charles Louis de Secondat, Baron de la Brède et la Montesquieu (1689–1755), French jurist, historian, politican, philosopher.

isms; that he laid his finger on the mainsprings; that he introduced into the history of the heart scientific processes, the art of notation, decomposition, deduction; that he first marked the fundamental causes of nationality, climate, temperament; in short, that he treated sentiments as they should be treated,— in the manner of the naturalist, and of the natural philosopher, who classifies and weighs forces. For this very reason he was considered dry and eccentric: he remained solitary, writing novels, voyages, notes, for which he sought and obtained a score of readers. And yet we find in his books at the present day essays the most suitable to open the path which I have endeavoured to describe. No one has better taught us how to open our eyes and see, to see first the men that surround us and the life that is present, then the ancient and authentic documents, to read between the black and white lines of the pages, to recognise beneath the old impression, under the scribbling of a text, the precise sentiment, the movement of ideas, the state of mind in which they were written. In his writings, in Sainte-Beuve, in the German critics, the reader will see all the wealth that may be drawn from a literary work: when the work is rich, and people know how to interpret it, we find there the psychology of a soul, frequently of an age, now and then of a race. In this light, a great poem, a fine novel, the confessions of a superior man, are more instructive than a heap of historians with their histories. I would give fifty volumes of charters and a hundred volumes of state papers for the memoirs of Cellini,[20] the epistles of St. Paul, the Table-talk of Luther, or the comedies of Aristophanes. In this consists the importance of literary works: they are instructive because they are beautiful: their utility grows with their perfection; and if they furnish documents it is because they are monuments. The more a book brings sentiments into light, the more it is a work of literature; for the proper office of literature is to make sentiments visible. The more a book represents important sentiments, the higher is its place in literature; for it is by representing the mode of being of a whole nation and a whole age, that a writer rallies round him the sympathies of an entire age and an entire nation. This is why, amid the writings which set before our eyes the sentiments of preceding generations, a literature, and notably a grand literature, is incomparably the best. It resembles those admirable apparatus of extraordinary sensibility, by which physicians disentangle and measure the most recondite and delicate changes of a body. Constitutions, religions, do not approach it in importance; the articles of a code of laws and of a creed only show us the spirit roughly and without delicacy. If there are any writings in which politics and dogma are full of life, it is in the eloquent discourses of the pulpit and the tribune, memoirs, unrestrained confessions; and all this belongs to literature: so that, in addition to itself, it has all the advantage of other works. It is then chiefly by the study of literatures that one may construct a moral history, and advance toward the knowledge of psychological laws, from which events spring.

I intend to write the history of a literature, and to seek in it for the psychology of a people: if I have chosen this nation in particular, it is not without a reason. I had to find a people with a grand and complete literature, and this is rare: there are few nations who have, during their whole existence,

[20] Benvenuto Cellini (1500–1571), Italian sculptor, metal-smith, and autobiographer.

really thought and written. Among the ancients, the Latin literature is worth nothing at the outset, then it borrowed and became imitative. Among the moderns, German literature does not exist for nearly two centuries.* Italian literature and Spanish literature end at the middle of the seventeenth century. Only ancient Greece, modern France and England, offer a complete series of great significant monuments. I have chosen England, because being still living, and subject to direct examination, it may be better studied than a destroyed civilisation, of which we retain but the relics, and because, being different from France, it has in the eyes of a Frenchman a more distinct character. Besides, there is a peculiarity in this civilisation, that apart from its spontaneous development, it presents a forced deviation, it has suffered the last and most effectual of all conquests, and the three grounds whence it has sprung, race, climate, the Norman invasion, may be observed in its remains with perfect exactness; so that we may examine in this history the two most powerful moving springs of human transformation, natural bent and constraining force, and we may examine them without uncertainty or gap, in a series of authentic and unmutilated memorials.

I have endeavoured to define these primary springs, to exhibit their gradual effects, to explain how they have ended by bringing to light great political, religious, and literary works, and by developing the recondite mechanism whereby the Saxon barbarian has been transformed into the Englishman of to-day.

---

* From 1550 to 1750. [Taine's note.]

Matthew Arnold

THE STUDY OF POETRY

Matthew Arnold (1822–1888) is generally accounted the most influential English literary critic of the nineteenth century. He was the son of Dr. Thomas Arnold, who is chiefly famous for his reform of English upper- and middle-class education but who is also notable for his liberal influence on English social and political thought. Arnold went from Rugby School, of which his father was Headmaster, to Balliol College, Oxford. He first came to public notice as a poet. The body of his poetical work is small by comparison with that of Tennyson and Browning and it was less celebrated in its time than theirs, but Arnold now stands with them as one of the three most memorable poets of the Victorian age. And of the three it is Arnold who speaks most intimately to readers today—perhaps no one of his time expressed so immediately the discomfort and confusion of the individual's relation to the modern world.

For the greater part of his mature life Arnold served as an inspector of elementary schools. It was a fatiguing profession and he disliked it, the more because it made the writing of poetry nearly impossible. But it did not stand in the way of criticism and perhaps it provided that acute sense of the actualities of English society that gives Arnold's criticism its peculiar force. One of the most frequently quoted of his utterances is his description of poetry, and of literature in general, as "a criticism of life"—his conception of literature was based on the assumption that the sensibility and thought of a nation, and eventually the quality of its life, could to some considerable extent be influenced by its literature. This assumption informs all that he wrote about literature and is made most fully explicit in *Culture and Anarchy* (1869), the book—it is one of the classics of English political thought—in which he inquired into the right relation of the national State to the newly enfranchised democratic masses.

In the latter part of his life Arnold turned his mind for a time to certain of the questions that had been raised by the crisis of religious faith that England experienced in the nineteenth century. The position he took is perhaps to be called radical-conservative. He held that religion was a precious possession of mankind but not by reason of truth of its dogmatic statements about the universe and its moral governance, rather because it expresses and encourages the human aspiration to goodness. The Bible was to be read as providing the ground not of dogmatic sys-

From *Essays in Criticism,* Second Series, by Matthew Arnold. London: Macmillan and Co., Limited, 1905.

tems but of insight into the nature of the moral life; its statements were not to be taken literally as in any sense "scientific"—they were poetic and conveyed such truth as poetry can convey, the truth of feeling, or, as we sometimes call it, wisdom. For Arnold, the Bible was the greatest of all works of literature and, by that token, all truly great works of literature were to be thought of as entitled to share the authority and the love that had long been given to the Bible, as being of their nature essentially religious. It is plain that the criteria that govern Arnold's selection of the "touchstones" by which we may test the greatness of poetry are the qualities generally associated with the experience of worship—all have the "high seriousness" Arnold valued, most are touched with solemnity, or awe, or the sense of the inscrutability of life.

"The Study of Poetry" was written to serve as the general introduction to a four-volume anthology of English poetry edited by T. H. Ward and published in 1880. The passage with which Arnold begins the essay is quoted (in somewhat abbreviated form) from the introduction he had contributed to a now forgotten volume called *The Hundred Greatest Men* (1879).

"The future of poetry is immense, because in poetry, where it is worthy of its high destinies, our race, as time goes on, will find an ever surer and surer stay. There is not a creed which is not shaken, not an accredited dogma which is not shown to be questionable, not a received tradition which does not threaten to dissolve. Our religion has materialised itself in the fact, in the supposed fact; it has attached its emotion to the fact, and now the fact is failing it. But for poetry the idea is everything; the rest is a world of illusion, of divine illusion. Poetry attaches its emotion to the idea; the idea *is* the fact. The strongest part of our religion to-day is its unconscious poetry."

Let me be permitted to quote these words of my own, as uttering the thought which should, in my opinion, go with us and govern us in all our study of poetry. In the present work[1] it is the course of one great contributory stream to the world-river of poetry that we are invited to follow. We are here invited to trace the stream of English poetry. But whether we set ourselves, as here, to follow only one of the several streams that make the mighty river of poetry, or whether we seek to know them all, our governing thoughts should be the same. We should conceive of poetry worthily, and more highly than it has been the custom to conceive of it. We should conceive of it as capable of higher uses, and called to higher destinies, than those which in general men have assigned to it hitherto. More and more mankind will discover that we have to turn to poetry to interpret life for us, to console us, to sustain us. Without poetry, our science will appear incomplete; and most of what now passes with us for religion and philosophy will be replaced by poetry. Science, I say, will appear incomplete without it. For finely and truly does Wordsworth call poetry "the impassioned expression which is in the countenance of all science";[2] and what is a countenance without its expression? Again, Wordsworth finely

---

[1] That is, the anthology to which the essay served as introduction—see the headnote.
[2] See Wordsworth's *Preface*, p. 150 of the present volume.

and truly calls poetry "the breath and finer spirit of all knowledge": our religion, parading evidences such as those on which the popular mind relies now; our philosophy, pluming itself on its reasonings about causation and finite and infinite being; what are they but the shadows and dreams and false shows of knowledge? The day will come when we shall wonder at ourselves for having trusted to them, for having taken them seriously; and the more we perceive their hollowness, the more we shall prize "the breath and finer spirit of knowledge" offered to us by poetry.

But if we conceive thus highly of the destinies of poetry, we must also set our standard for poetry high, since poetry, to be capable of fulfilling such high destinies, must be poetry of a high order of excellence. We must accustom ourselves to a high standard and to a strict judgment. Sainte-Beuve[3] relates that Napoleon one day said, when somebody was spoken of in his presence as a charlatan: "Charlatan as much as you please; but where is there *not* charlatanism?"—"Yes," answers Sainte-Beuve, "in politics, in the art of governing mankind, that is perhaps true. But in the order of thought, in art, the glory, the eternal honour is that charlatanism shall find no entrance; herein lies the inviolableness of that noble portion of man's being." It is admirably said, and let us hold fast to it. In poetry, which is thought and art in one, it is the glory, the eternal honour, that charlatanism shall find no entrance; that this noble sphere be kept inviolate and inviolable. Charlatanism is for confusing or obliterating the distinctions between excellent and inferior, sound and unsound or only half-sound, true and untrue or only half-true. It is charlatanism, conscious or unconscious, whenever we confuse or obliterate these. And in poetry, more than anywhere else, it is unpermissible to confuse or obliterate them. For in poetry the distinction between excellent and inferior, sound and unsound or only half-sound, true and untrue or only half-true, is of paramount importance. It is of paramount importance because of the high destinies of poetry. In poetry, as a criticism of life under the conditions fixed for such a criticism by the laws of poetic truth and poetic beauty, the spirit of our race will find, we have said, as time goes on and as other helps fail, its consolation and stay. But the consolation and stay will be of power in proportion to the power of the criticism of life. And the criticism of life will be of power in proportion as the poetry conveying it is excellent rather than inferior, sound rather than unsound or half-sound, true rather than untrue or half-true.

The best poetry is what we want; the best poetry will be found to have a power of forming, sustaining, and delighting us, as nothing else can. A clearer, deeper sense of the best in poetry, and of the strength and joy to be drawn from it, is the most precious benefit which we can gather from a poetical collection such as the present. And yet in the very nature and conduct of such a collection there is inevitably something which tends to obscure in us the consciousness of what our benefit should be, and to distract us from the pursuit of it. We should therefore steadily set it before our minds at the outset, and should compel ourselves to revert constantly to the thought of it as we proceed.

Yes; constantly in reading poetry, a sense for the best, the really excellent, and of the strength and joy to be drawn from it, should be present in our

---

[3] Charles Sainte-Beuve (1804–1869), French critic much admired by Arnold.

minds and should govern our estimate of what we read. But this real estimate, the only true one, is liable to be superseded, if we are not watchful, by two other kinds of estimate, the historic estimate and the personal estimate, both of which are fallacious. A poet or a poem may count to us historically, they may count to us on grounds personal to ourselves, and they may count to us really. They may count to us historically. The course of development of a nation's language, thought, and poetry, is profoundly interesting; and by regarding a poet's work as a stage in this course of development we may easily bring ourselves to make it of more importance as poetry than in itself it really is, we may come to use a language of quite exaggerated praise in criticising it; in short, to over-rate it. So arises in our poetic judgments the fallacy caused by the estimate which we may call historic. Then, again, a poet or a poem may count to us on grounds personal to ourselves. Our personal affinities, likings, and circumstances, have great power to sway our estimate of this or that poet's work, and to make us attach more importance to it as poetry than in itself it really possesses, because to us it is, or has been, of high importance. Here also we over-rate the object of our interest, and apply to it a language of praise which is quite exaggerated. And thus we get the source of a second fallacy in our poetic judgments—the fallacy caused by an estimate which we may call personal.

Both fallacies are natural. It is evident how naturally the study of the history and development of a poetry may incline a man to pause over reputations and works once conspicuous but now obscure, and to quarrel with a careless public for skipping, in obedience to mere tradition and habit, from one famous name or work in its national poetry to another, ignorant of what it misses, and of the reason for keeping what it keeps, and of the whole process of growth in its poetry. The French have become diligent students of their own early poetry, which they long neglected; the study makes many of them dissatisfied with their so-called classical poetry, the court-tragedy of the seventeenth century, a poetry which Pellisson[4] long ago reproached with its want of the true poetic stamp, with its *politesse stérile et rampante*,[5] but which nevertheless has reigned in France as absolutely as if it had been the perfection of classical poetry indeed. The dissatisfaction is natural; yet a lively and accomplished critic, M. Charles d'Héricault, the editor of Clément Marot,[6] goes too far when he says that "the cloud of glory playing round a classic is a mist as dangerous to the future of a literature as it is intolerable for the purposes of history." "It hinders," he goes on, "it hinders us from seeing more than one single point, the culminating and exceptional point; the summary, fictitious and arbitrary, of a thought and of a work. It substitutes a halo for a physiognomy, it puts a statue where there was once a man, and hiding from us all trace of the labour, the attempts, the weaknesses, the failures, it claims not study but veneration; it does not show us how the thing is done, it imposes upon us a model. Above all, for the historian this creation of classic personages is inadmissable; for it withdraws the poet from his time, from his proper life, it breaks historical relationships, it blinds criticism by conventional admiration, and renders the investigation of literary origins unacceptable. It gives us a human personage no longer, but

[4] Paul Pellisson (1624–1693), French critic.
[5] "Sterile and ostentatious conventionality."
[6] D'Héricault's edition of Clément Marot (c. 1495–1544) was published in 1868.

a God seated immovable amidst His perfect work, like Jupiter on Olympus; and hardly will it be possible for the young student, to whom such work is exhibited at such a distance from him, to believe that it did not issue ready made from that divine head."

All this is brilliantly and tellingly said, but we must plead for a distinction. Everything depends on the reality of a poet's classic character. If he is a dubious classic, let us sift him; if he is a false classic, let us explode him. But if he is a real classic, if his work belongs to the class of the very best (for this is the true and right meaning of the word *classic, classical*), then the great thing for us is to feel and enjoy his work as deeply as ever we can, and to appreciate the wide difference between it and all work which has not the same high character. This is what is salutary, this is what is formative; this is the great benefit to be got from the study of poetry. Everything which interferes with it, which hinders it, is injurious. True, we must read our classic with open eyes, and not with eyes blinded with superstition; we must perceive when his work comes short, when it drops out of the class of the very best, and we must rate it, in such cases, at its proper value. But the use of this negative criticism is not in itself, it is entirely in its enabling us to have a clearer sense and a deeper enjoyment of what is truly excellent. To trace the labour, the attempts, the weaknesses, the failures of a genuine classic, to acquaint oneself with his time and his life and his historical relationships, is mere literary dilettantism unless it has that clear sense and deeper enjoyment for its end. It may be said that the more we know about a classic the better we shall enjoy him; and, if we lived as long as Methuselah and had all of us heads of perfect clearness and wills of perfect steadfastness, this might be true in fact as it is plausible in theory. But the case here is much the same as the case with the Greek and Latin studies of our schoolboys. The elaborate philological ground-work which we require them to lay is in theory an admirable preparation for appreciating the Greek and Latin authors worthily. The more thoroughly we lay the groundwork, the better we shall be able, it may be said, to enjoy the authors. True, if time were not so short, and schoolboys' wits not so soon tired and their power of attention exhausted; only, as it is, the elaborate philological preparation goes on, but the authors are little known and less enjoyed. So with the investigator of "historic origins" in poetry. He ought to enjoy the true classic all the better for his investigations; he often is distracted from the enjoyment of the best, and with the less good he overbusies himself, and is prone to over-rate it in proportion to the trouble which it has cost him.

The idea of tracing historic origins and historical relationships cannot be absent from a compilation like the present. And naturally the poets to be exhibited in it will be assigned to those persons for exhibition who are known to prize them highly, rather than to those who have no special inclination towards them. Moreover the very occupation with an author, and the business of exhibiting him, disposes us to affirm and amplify his importance. In the present work, therefore, we are sure of frequent temptation to adopt the historic estimate, or the personal estimate, and to forget the real estimate; which latter, nevertheless, we must employ if we are to make poetry yield us its full benefit. So high is that benefit, the benefit of clearly feeling and of deeply enjoying the really excellent, the truly classic in poetry, that we do well, I say, to set it fixedly before our minds as our object in studying poets and poetry, and to make the desire of attaining it the one principle to which, as the *Imitation* says, whatever we may read or come to know, we always return. *Cum multa legeris et cognoveris, ad unum semper oportet redire principium.*[7]

The historic estimate is likely in especial to affect our judgment and our language when we are dealing with ancient poets; the personal estimate when we are dealing with poets our contemporaries, or at any rate modern. The exaggerations due to the historic estimate are not in themselves, perhaps, of very much gravity. Their report hardly enters the general ear; probably they do not always impose even on the literary men who adopt them. But they lead to a dangerous abuse of language. So we hear Cædmon,[8] amongst our own poets, compared to Milton. I have already noticed the enthusiasm of one accomplished French critic for "historic origins." Another eminent French critic, M. Vitet, comments upon that famous document of the early poetry of his nation, the *Chanson de Roland.*[9] It is indeed a most interesting document. The *joculator or jongleur*[10] Taillefer, who was with William the Conqueror's army at Hastings, marched before the Norman troops, so said the tradition, singing "of Charlemagne and of Roland and of Oliver, and of the vassals who died at Roncevaux"; and it is suggested that in the *Chanson de Roland* by one Turoldus or Théroulde, a poem preserved in a manuscript of the twelfth century in the Bodleian Library at Oxford, we have certainly the matter, perhaps even some of the words, of the chant which Taillefer sang. The poem has vigour and freshness; it is not without pathos. But M. Vitet is not satisfied with seeing in it a document of some poetic value, and of very high historic and linguistic value; he sees in it a grand and beautiful work, a monument of epic genius. In its general design he finds the grandiose conception, in its details he finds the constant union of simplicity with greatness, which are the marks, he truly says, of the genuine epic, and distinguish it from the artificial epic of literary ages. One thinks of Homer; this is the sort of praise which is given to Homer, and justly given. Higher praise there cannot well be, and it is the praise due to epic poetry of the highest order only, and to no other. Let us try, then, the *Chanson de Roland* at its best. Roland, mortally wounded, lays himself down under a pine-tree, with his face turned towards Spain and the enemy—

> De plusurs choses à remembrer li prist,
> De tantes teres cume li bers cunquist,
> De dulce France, des humes de sun lign,
> De Carlemagne sun seignor ki l'nurrit.*

[7] "When you have read and learned much, you should still return to the one principle." From *The Imitation of Christ,* a devotional work by Thomas à Kempis (1380?–1471), German churchman.
[8] Seventh-century Old English poet, reputed to be the first to write religious verse in the vernacular.
[9] Eleventh-century epic poem in Old French, describing an heroic rearguard defense by Roland and Oliver when Charlemagne's troops were ambushed at Roncevaux by Moors.
[10] Minstrel.
* "Then began he to call many things to remembrance,—all the lands which his valour conquered, and pleasant France, and the men of his lineage, and Charlemagne his liege lord who nourished him."—*Chanson de Roland,* iii, 939–942. [Arnold's note.]

That is primitive work, I repeat, with an undeniable poetic quality of its own. It deserves such praise, and such praise is sufficient for it. But now turn to Homer—

$$\text{῝Ως φάτο· τοὺς δ᾽ ἤδη κατέχεν φυσίζοος αἶα}$$
$$\text{ἐν Λακεδαίμονι αὖθι, φίλῃ ἐν πατρίδι γαίῃ.*}$$

We are here in another world, another order of poetry altogether; here is rightly due such supreme praise as that which M. Vitet gives to the *Chanson de Roland*. If our words are to have any meaning, if our judgments are to have any solidity, we must not heap that supreme praise upon poetry of an order immeasurably inferior.

Indeed there can be no more useful help for discovering what poetry belongs to the class of the truly excellent, and can therefore do us most good, than to have always in one's mind lines and expressions of the great masters, and to apply them as a touchstone to other poetry. Of course we are not to require this other poetry to resemble them; it may be very dissimilar. But if we have any tact we shall find them, when we have lodged them well in our minds, an infallible touchstone for detecting the presence or absence of high poetic quality, and also the degree of this quality, in all other poetry which we may place beside them. Short passages, even single lines, will serve our turn quite sufficiently. Take the two lines which I have just quoted from Homer, the poet's comment on Helen's mention of her brothers;—or take his

$$\text{᾽Α δειλώ, τί σφῶϊ δόμεν Πηλῆϊ ἄνακτι}$$
$$\text{θνητᾷ; ὑμεῖς δ᾽ ἐστὸν ἀγήρω τ᾽ ἀθανάτω τε.}$$
$$\text{ἦ ἵνα δυστήνοισι μετ᾽ ἀνδράσιν ἄλγε᾽ ἔχητον;†}$$

the address of Zeus to the horses of Peleus;—or take finally his

$$\text{Καὶ σέ, γέρον, τὸ πρὶν μὲν ἀκούομεν ὄλβιον εἶναι.‡}$$

the words of Achilles to Priam, a suppliant before him. Take that incomparable line and a half of Dante, Ugolino's tremendous words—

> Io no piangeva; sì dentro impietrai.
> Piangevan elli . . .§

take the lovely words of Beatrice to Virgil—

> Io son fatta da Dio, sua mercè, tale,
> Che la vostra miseria non mi tange,
> Nè fiamma d'esto incendio non m'assale . . .||

---

* "So said she; they long since in Earth's soft arms were reposing,
   There, in their own dear land, their fatherland, Lacedæmon."
                 Iliad, iii, 243, 244 (translated by Dr. Hawtrey.) [Arnold's note.]
† "Ah, unhappy pair, why gave we you to King Peleus, to a mortal? but ye are without old age, and immortal. Was it that with men born to misery ye might have sorrow?"—*Iliad*, xvii. 443–445. [Arnold's note.]
‡ "Nay, and thou too, old man, in former days wast, as we hear, happy,"—*Iliad*, xxiv. 543. [Arnold's note.]
§ "I wailed not, so of stone grew I within;—*they* wailed."—*Inferno*, xxxiii. 39, 40. [Arnold's note.]
|| Of such sort hath God, thanked be His mercy, made me, that your misery toucheth me not, neither doth the flame of this fire strike me."—*Inferno*, ii, 91–93. [Arnold's note.]

take the simple, but perfect, single line—

In la sua volontade è nostra pace.*

Take of Shakespeare a line or two of Henry the Fourth's expostulation with sleep—

> Wilt thou upon the high and giddy mast
> Seal up the ship-boy's eyes, and rock his brains
> In cradle of the rude imperious surge . . .
> [*Henry IV*, III, i, 18–20.]

and take, as well, Hamlet's dying request to Horatio—

> If thou didst ever hold me in thy heart,
> Absent thee from felicity awhile,
> And in this harsh world draw thy breath in pain
> To tell my story . . . [*Hamlet, V*, ii, 357–360.]

Take of Milton that Miltonic passage—

> Darken'd so, yet shone
> Above them all the archangel; but his face
> Deep scars of thunder had intrench'd, and care
> Sat on his faded cheek . . . [*Paradise Lost*, I, 599–602.]

add two such lines as—

> And courage never to submit or yield
> And what is else not to be overcome . . . [*Paradise Lost*, I, 108–109.]

and finish with the exquisite close to the loss of Proserpine, the loss

> . . . which cost Ceres all that pain
> To seek her through the world. [*Paradise Lost, IV*, 271–272.]

These few lines, if we have tact and can use them, are enough even of themselves to keep clear and sound our judgments about poetry, to save us from fallacious estimates of it, to conduct us to a real estimate.

The specimens I have quoted differ widely from one another, but they have in common this: the possession of the very highest poetical quality. If we are thoroughly penetrated by their power, we shall find that we have acquired a sense enabling us, whatever poetry may be laid before us, to feel the degree in which a high poetical quality is present or wanting there. Critics give themselves great labour to draw out what in the abstract constitutes the characters of a high quality of poetry. It is much better simply to have recourse to concrete examples;—to take specimens of poetry of the high, the very highest quality, and to say: The characters of a high quality of poetry are what is expressed *there*. They are far better recognised by being felt in the verse of the master, than by being perused in the prose of the critic. Nevertheless if we are urgently pressed to give some critical account of them, we may safely, perhaps, venture on laying down, not indeed how and why the characters

---

* "In His will is our peace."—*Paradiso*, iii, 85. [Arnold's note.]

arise, but where and in what they arise. They are in the matter and substance of the poetry, and they are in its manner and style. Both of these, the substance and matter on the one hand, the style and manner on the other, have a mark, an accent, of high beauty, worth, and power. But if we are asked to define this mark and accent in the abstract, our answer must be: No, for we should thereby be darkening the question, not clearing it. The mark and accent are as given by the substance and matter of that poetry, by the style and manner of that poetry, and of all other poetry which is akin to it in quality.

Only one thing we may add as to the substance and matter of poetry, guiding ourselves by Aristotle's profound observation that the superiority of poetry over history consists in its possessing a higher truth and a higher seriousness (φιλοσοφώτερον καὶ σπουδαιότερον). Let us add, therefore, to what we have said, this: that the substance and matter of the best poetry acquire their special character from possessing, in an eminent degree, truth and seriousness. We may add yet further, what is in itself evident, that to the style and manner of the best poetry their special character, their accent, is given by their diction, and, even yet more, by their movement. And though we distinguish between the two characters, the two accents, of superiority, yet they are nevertheless vitally connected one with the other. The superior character of truth and seriousness, in the matter and substance of the best poetry, is inseparable from the superiority of diction and movement marking its style and manner. The two superiorities are closely related, and are in steadfast proportion one to the other. So far as high poetic truth and seriousness are wanting to a poet's matter and substance, so far also, we may be sure, will a high poetic stamp of diction and movement be wanting to his style and manner. In proportion as this high stamp of diction and movement, again, is absent from a poet's style and manner, we shall find, also, that high poetic truth and seriousness are absent from his substance and matter.

So stated, these are but dry generalities; their whole force lies in their application. And I could wish every student of poetry to make the application of them for himself. Made by himself, the application would impress itself upon his mind far more deeply than made by me. Neither will my limits allow me to make any full application of the generalities above propounded; but in the hope of bringing out, at any rate, some significance in them, and of establishing an important principle more firmly by their means, I will, in the space which remains to me, follow rapidly from the commencement the course of our English poetry with them in my view.

Once more I return to the early poetry of France, with which our own poetry, in its origins, is indissolubly connected. In the twelfth and thirteenth centuries, that seed-time of all modern language and literature, the poetry of France had a clear predominance in Europe. Of the two divisions of that poetry, its productions in the *langue d'oil* and its productions in the *langue d'oc*,[11] the poetry of the *langue d'oc*, of southern France, of the troubadours, is of importance because of its effect on Italian literature;—the first literature of modern Europe to strike the true and grand note, and to bring forth, as

[11] Medieval dialects of France. The two phrases mean something like, "the dialect in which 'yes' (*oui*) is pronounced *oil*" and "the dialect in which 'yes' is pronounced *oc*"; that is, the northern and southern dialects, respectively.

in Dante and Petrarch[12] it brought forth, classics. But the predominance of French poetry in Europe, during the twelfth and thirteenth centuries, is due to its poetry of the *langue d'oil*, the poetry of northern France and of the tongue which is now the French language. In the twelfth century the bloom of this romance-poetry was earlier and stronger in England, at the court of our Anglo-Norman kings, than in France itself. But it was a bloom of French poetry; and as our native poetry formed itself, it formed itself out of this. The romance-poems which took possession of the heart and imagination of Europe in the twelfth and thirteenth centuries are French; "they are," as Southey justly says, "the pride of French literature, nor have we anything which can be placed in competition with them." Themes were supplied from all quarters; but the romance setting which was common to them all, and which gained the ear of Europe, was French. This constituted for the French poetry, literature, and language, at the height of the Middle Age, an unchallenged predominance. The Italian Brunetto Latini, the master of Dante, wrote his *Treasure* in French because, he says, "la parleure en est plus délitable et plus commune à toutes gens."[13] In the same century, the thirteenth, the French romance-writer, Christian of Troyes, formulates the claims, in chivalry and letters, of France, his native country, as follows:—

> Or vous ert par ce livre apris,
> Que Gresse ot de chevalerie
> Le premier los et de clergie;
> Puis vint chevalerie à Rome,
> Et de la clergie la some,
> Qui ore est en France venue.
> Diex doinst qu'ele i soit retenue,
> Et que li lius li abelisse
> Tant que de France n'isse
> L'onor qui s'i est arestée!

Now by this book you will learn that first Greece had the renown for chivalry and letters: then chivalry and the primacy in letters passed to Rome, and now it is come to France. God grant it may be kept there; and that the place may please it so well, that the honour which has come to make stay in France may never depart thence!

Yet it is now all gone, this French romance-poetry, of which the weight of substance and the power of style are not unfairly represented by this extract from Christian of Troyes. Only by means of the historic estimate can we persuade ourselves now to think that any of it is of poetical importance.

But in the fourteenth century there comes an Englishman nourished on this poetry, taught his trade by this poetry, getting words, rhyme, metre from this poetry; for even of that stanza which the Italians used, and which Chaucer derived immediately from the Italians, the basis and suggestion was probably given in France. Chaucer (I have already named him) fascinated his

---

[12] Francesco Petrarca (1304–1374), Italian humanist and poet.
[13] Brunetto Latini (c. 1220–1295) wrote his *Trésor*, or encyclopedic survey of knowledge, in French, because "the language is most delightful and most commonly known among all peoples."

contemporaries, but so did Christian of Troyes and Wolfram of Eschenbach.[14] Chaucer's power of fascination, however, is enduring; his poetical importance does not need the assistance of the historic estimate; it is real. He is a genuine source of joy and strength, which is flowing still for us and will flow always. He will be read, as time goes on, far more generally than he is read now. His language is a cause of difficulty for us; but so also, and I think in quite as great a degree, is the language of Burns. In Chaucer's case, as in that of Burns, it is a difficulty to be unhesitatingly accepted and overcome.

If we ask ourselves wherein consists the immense superiority of Chaucer's poetry over the romance-poetry—why it is that in passing from this to Chaucer we suddenly feel ourselves to be in another world, we shall find that his superiority is both in the substance of his poetry and in the style of his poetry. His superiority in substance is given by his large, free, simple, clear yet kindly view of human life,—so unlike the total want, in the romance-poets, of all intelligent command of it. Chaucer has not their helplessness; he has gained the power to survey the world from a central, a truly human point of view. We have only to call to mind the Prologue to *The Canterbury Tales.* The right comment upon it is Dryden's: "It is sufficient to say, according to the proverb, that *here is God's plenty.*" And again: "He is a perpetual fountain of good sense." It is by a large, free, sound representation of things, that poetry, this high criticism of life, has truth of substance; and Chaucer's poetry has truth of substance.

Of his style and manner, if we think first of the romance-poetry and then of Chaucer's divine liquidness of diction, his divine fluidity of movement, it is difficult to speak temperately. They are irresistible, and justify all the rapture with which his successors speak of his "gold dew-drops of speech." Johnson misses the point entirely when he finds fault with Dryden for ascribing to Chaucer the first refinement of our numbers, and says that Gower[15] also can show smooth numbers and easy rhymes. The refinement of our numbers means something far more than this. A nation may have versifiers with smooth numbers and easy rhymes, and yet may have no real poetry at all. Chaucer is the father of our splendid English poetry; he is our "well of English undefiled," because by the lovely charm of his diction, the lovely charm of his movement, he makes an epoch and founds a tradition. In Spenser, Shakespeare, Milton, Keats, we can follow the tradition of the liquid diction, the fluid movement, of Chaucer; at one time it is his liquid diction of which in these poets we feel the virtue, and at another time it is his fluid movement. And the virtue is irresistible.

Bounded as is my space, I must yet find room for an example of Chaucer's virtue, as I have given examples to show the virtue of the great classics. I feel disposed to say that a single line is enough to show the charm of Chaucer's verse; that merely one line like this—

O martyr souded* in virginitee!

---

[14] Twelfth-cent. German poet, author of *Parzival.*
[15] John Gower (c. 1325–1408), a friend of Chaucer, chiefly known as author of the *Confessio Amantis,* a long poem in octosyllabic couplets.
* The French *soudé;* soldered, fixed fast. [Arnold's note.]

has a virtue of manner and movement such as we shall not find in all the verse of romance-poetry;—but this is saying nothing. The virtue is such as we shall not find, perhaps, in all English poetry, outside the poets whom I have named as the special inheritors of Chaucer's tradition. A single line, however, is too little if we have not the strain of Chaucer's verse well in our memory; let us take a stanza. It is from *The Prioress's Tale,* the story of the Christian child murdered in a Jewry—

> My throte is cut unto my nekke-bone
> Saidè this child, and as by way of kinde
> I should have deyd, yea, longè time agone;
> But Jesu Christ, as ye in bookès finde,
> Will that his glory last and be in minde,
> And for the worship of his mother dere
> Yet may I sing O *Alma* loud and clere.

Wordsworth has modernised this Tale, and to feel how delicate and evanescent is the charm of verse, we have only to read Wordsworth's first three lines of this stanza after Chaucer's—

> My throat is cut unto the bone, I trow,
> Said this young child, and by the law of kind
> I should have died, yea, many hours ago.

The charm is departed. It is often said that the power of liquidness and fluidity in Chaucer's verse was dependent upon a free, a licentious dealing with language, such as is now impossible; upon a liberty, such as Burns too enjoyed, of making words like *neck, bird,* into a dissyllable by adding to them, and words like *cause, rhyme,* into a dissyllable by sounding the e mute. It is true that Chaucer's fluidity is conjoined with this liberty, and is admirably served by it; but we ought not to say that it was dependent upon it. It was dependent upon his talent. Other poets with a like liberty do not attain to the fluidity of Chaucer; Burns himself does not attain to it. Poets, again, who have a talent akin to Chaucer's, such as Shakespeare or Keats, have known how to attain to his fluidity without the like liberty.

   And yet Chaucer is not one of the great classics. His poetry transcends and effaces, easily and without effort, all the romance-poetry of Catholic Christendom; it transcends and effaces all the English poetry contemporary with it, it transcends and effaces all the English poetry subsequent to it down to the age of Elizabeth. Of such avail is poetic truth of substance, in its natural and necessary union with poetic truth of style. And yet, I say, Chaucer is not one of the great classics. He has not their accent. What is wanting to him is suggested by the mere mention of the name of the first great classic of Christendom, the immortal poet who died eighty years before Chaucer,— Dante. The accent of such verse as

> In la sua volontade è nostra pace . . .

is altogether beyond Chaucer's reach; we praise him, but we feel that this accent is out of the question for him. It may be said that it was necessarily out of the reach of any poet in the England of that stage of growth. Possibly; but we are to adopt a real, not a historic, estimate of poetry. However we may account for its absence, something is wanting, then, to the poetry of Chaucer, which poetry must have before it can be placed in the glorious class of the best. And there is no doubt what that something is. It is the σπουδαιότης, the high and excellent seriousness, which Aristotle assigns as one of the grand virtues of poetry. The substance of Chaucer's poetry, his view of things and his criticism of life, has largeness, freedom, shrewdness, benignity; but it has not this high seriousness. Homer's criticism of life has it, Dante's has it, Shakespeare's has it. It is this chiefly which gives to our spirits what they can rest upon; and with the increasing demands of our modern ages upon poetry, this virtue of giving us what we can rest upon will be more and more highly esteemed. A voice from the slums of Paris, fifty or sixty years after Chaucer, the voice of poor Villon[16] out of his life of riot and crime, has at its happy moments (as, for instance, in the last stanza of *La Belle Heaulmière**) more of this important poetic virtue of seriousness than all the production of Chaucer. But its apparition in Villon, and in men like Villon, is fitful; the greatness of the great poets, the power of their criticism of life, is that their virtue is sustained.

To our praise, therefore, of Chaucer as a poet there must be this limitation; he lacks the high seriousness of the great classics, and therewith an important part of their virtue. Still, the main fact for us to bear in mind about Chaucer is his sterling value according to that real estimate which we firmly adopt for all poets. He has poetic truth of substance, though he has not high poetic seriousness, and corresponding to his truth of substance he has an exquisite virtue of style and manner. With him is born our real poetry.

For my present purpose I need not dwell on our Elizabethan poetry, or on the continuation and close of this poetry in Milton. We all of us profess to be agreed in the estimate of this poetry; we all of us recognise it as great poetry, our greatest, and Shakespeare and Milton as our poetical classics. The real estimate, here, has universal currency. With the next age of our poetry divergency and difficulty begin. An historic estimate of that poetry has established itself; and the question is, whether it will be found to coincide with the real estimate.

The age of Dryden, together with our whole eighteenth century which

---

[16] Francois Villon (1431–1484), French poet, B.A., M.A., and jailbird.

* The name *Heaulmière* is said to be derived from a headdress (helm) worn as a mark by courtesans. In Villon's ballad, a poor old creature of this class laments her days of youth and beauty. The last stanza of the ballad runs thus—

> Ainsi le bon temps regretons
> Entre nous, pauvres vielles sottes,
> Assises bas, à croppetons,
> Tout en ung tas comme pelottes;
> A petit feu de chenevottes
> Tost allumées, tost estainctes.
> Et jadis fusmes si mignottes!
> Ainsi en prend à maintz et maintes.

"Thus amongst ourselves we regret the good time, poor silly old things, low-seated on our heels, all in a heap like so many balls; by a little fire of hemp-stalks, soon lighted, soon spent. And once we were such darlings! So fares it with many and many a one." [Arnold's note.]

followed it, sincerely believed itself to have produced poetical classics of its own, and even to have made advance, in poetry, beyond all its predecessors. Dryden regards as not seriously disputable the opinion "that the sweetness of English verse was never understood or practised by our fathers." Cowley could see nothing at all in Chaucer's poetry. Dryden heartily admired it, and, as we have seen, praised its matter admirably; but of its exquisite manner and movement all he can find to say is that "there is the rude sweetness of a Scotch tune in it, which is natural and pleasing, though not perfect." Addison, wishing to praise Chaucer's numbers, compares them with Dryden's own. And all through the eighteenth century, and down even into our own times, the stereotyped phrase of approbation for good verse found in our early poetry has been, that it even approached the verse of Dryden, Addison, Pope, and Johnson.

Are Dryden and Pope poetical classics? Is the historic estimate, which represents them as such, and which has been so long established that it cannot easily give way, the real estimate? Wordsworth and Coleridge, as is well known, denied it; but the authority of Wordsworth and Coleridge does not weigh much with the young generation, and there are many signs to show that the eighteenth century and its judgments are coming into favour again. Are the favourite poets of the eighteenth century classics?

It is impossible within my present limits to discuss the question fully. And what man of letters would not shrink from seeming to dispose dictatorially of the claims of two men who are, at any rate, such masters in letters as Dryden and Pope; two men of such admirable talent, both of them, and one of them, Dryden, a man, on all sides, of such energetic and genial power? And yet, if we are to gain the full benefit from poetry, we must have the real estimate of it. I cast about for some mode of arriving, in the present case, at such an estimate without offence. And perhaps the best way is to begin, as it is easy to begin, with cordial praise.

When we find Chapman, the Elizabethan translator of Homer, expressing himself in his preface thus: "Though truth in her very nakedness sits in so deep a pit, that from Gades to Aurora and Ganges few eyes can sound her, I hope yet those few here will so discover and confirm that, the date being out of her darkness in this morning of our poet, he shall now gird his temples with the sun,"—we pronounce that such a prose is intolerable. When we find Milton writing: "And long it was not after, when I was confirmed in this opinion, that he, who would not be frustrate of his hope to write well hereafter in laudable things, ought himself to be a true poem,"—we pronounce that such a prose has its own grandeur, but that it is obsolete and inconvenient. But when we find Dryden telling us: "What Virgil wrote in the vigour of his age, in plenty and at ease, I have undertaken to translate in my declining years; struggling with wants, oppressed with sickness, curbed in my genius, liable to be misconstrued in all I write,"—then we exclaim that here at last we have the true English prose, a prose such as we would all gladly use if we only knew how. Yet Dryden was Milton's contemporary.

But after the Restoration the time had come when our nation felt the imperious need of a fit prose. So, too, the time had likewise come when our nation felt the imperious need of freeing itself from the absorbing preoccupation which religion in the Puritan age had exercised. It was impossible that this freedom should be brought about without some negative excess, without some neglect and impairment of the religious life of the soul; and the spiritual history of the eighteenth century shows us that the freedom was not achieved without them. Still, the freedom was achieved; the preoccupation, an undoubtedly baneful and retarding one if it had continued, was got rid of. And as with religion amongst us at that period, so it was also with letters. A fit prose was a necessity; but it was impossible that a fit prose should establish itself amongst us without some touch of frost to the imaginative life of the soul. The needful qualities for a fit prose are regularity, uniformity, precision, balance. The men of letters, whose destiny it may be to bring their nation to the attainment of a fit prose, must of necessity, whether they work in prose or in verse, give a predominating, an almost exclusive attention to the qualities of regularity, uniformity, precision, balance. But an almost exclusive attention to these qualities involves some repression and silencing of poetry.

We are to regard Dryden as the puissant and glorious founder, Pope as the splendid high priest, of our age of prose and reason, of our excellent and indispensable eighteenth century. For the purposes of their mission and destiny their poetry, like their prose, is admirable. Do you ask me whether Dryden's verse, take it almost where you will, is not good?

> A milk-white Hind, immortal and unchanged,
> Fed on the lawns and in the forest ranged.

I answer: Admirable for the purposes of the inaugurator of an age of prose and reason. Do you ask me whether Pope's verse, take it almost where you will, is not good?

> To Hounslow Heath I point, and Banstead Down;
> Thence comes your mutton, and these chicks my own.

I answer: Admirable for the purposes of the high priest of an age of prose and reason. But do you ask me whether such verse proceeds from men with an adequate poetic criticism of life, from men whose criticism of life has a high seriousness, or even, without that high seriousness, has poetic largeness, freedom, insight, benignity? Do you ask me whether the application of ideas to life in the verse of these men, often a powerful application, no doubt, is a powerful *poetic* application? Do you ask me whether the poetry of these men has either the matter or the inseparable manner of such an adequate poetic criticism; whether it has the accent of

> Absent thee from felicity awhile . . .

or of

> And what is else not to be overcome . . .

or of

> O martyr souded in virginitee!

I answer: It has not and cannot have them; it is the poetry of the builders of an age of prose and reason. Though they may write in verse, though they

may in a certain sense be masters of the art of versification, Dryden and Pope
are not classics of our poetry, they are classics of our prose.

Gray is our poetical classic of that literature and age; the position of Gray
is singular, and demands a word of notice here. He has not the volume or the
power of poets who, coming in times more favourable, have attained to an
independent criticism of life. But he lived with the great poets, he lived, above
all, with the Greeks, through perpetually studying and enjoying them; and he
caught their poetic point of view for regarding life, caught their poetic manner.
The point of view and the manner are not self-sprung in him, he caught them
of others; and he had not the free and abundant use of them. But whereas
Addison and Pope never had the use of them, Gray had the use of them at
times. He is the scantiest and frailest of classics in our poetry, but he is a
classic.

And now, after Gray, we are met, as we draw towards the end of the
eighteenth century, we are met by the great name of Burns. We enter now
on times where the personal estimate of poets begins to be rife, and where the
real estimate of them is not reached without difficulty. But in spite of the disturbing pressures of personal partiality, of national partiality, let us try to reach
a real estimate of the poetry of Burns.

By his English poetry Burns in general belongs to the eighteenth century,
and has little importance for us.

> Mark ruffian Violence, distain'd with crimes,
> Rousing elate in these degenerate times;
> View unsuspecting Innocence a prey,
> As guileful Fraud points out the erring way;
> While subtle Litigation's pliant tongue
> The life-blood equal sucks of Right and Wrong!

Evidently this is not the real Burns, or his name and fame would have disappeared long ago. Nor is Clarinda's love-poet, Sylvander,[17] the real Burns
either. But he tells us himself: "These English songs gravel me to death. I have
not the command of the language that I have of my native tongue. In fact, I
think that my ideas are more barren in English than in Scotch. I have been
at *Duncan Gray* to dress it in English, but all I can do is desperately stupid."
We English turn naturally, in Burns, to the poems in our own language, because we can read them easily; but in those poems we have not the real Burns.

The real Burns is of course in his Scotch poems. Let us boldly say that of
much of this poetry, a poetry dealing perpetually with Scotch drink, Scotch
religion, and Scotch manners, a Scotchman's estimate is apt to be personal. A
Scotchman is used to this world of Scotch drink, Scotch religion, and Scotch
manners; he has a tenderness for it; he meets its poet half way. In this tender
mood he reads pieces like the *Holy Fair* or *Halloween*. But this world of Scotch
drink, Scotch religion, and Scotch manners is against a poet, not for him, when
it is not a partial countryman who reads him; for in itself it is not a beautiful
world, and no one can deny that it is of advantage to a poet to deal with a

---

[17] Burns, styling himself "Sylvander," carried on a flowery correspondence with a
Mrs. Maclehose, whom he addressed as "Clarinda."

beautiful world. Burns's world of Scotch drink, Scotch religion, and Scotch
manners is often a harsh, a sordid, a repulsive world: even the world of his
Cotter's Saturday Night is not a beautiful world. No doubt a poet's criticism of
life may have such truth and power that it triumphs over its world and delights
us. Burns may triumph over his world, often he does triumph over his world,
but let us observe how and where. Burns is the first case we have had where
the bias of the personal estimate tends to mislead; let us look at him closely,
he can bear it.

Many of his admirers will tell us that we have Burns, convivial, genuine,
delightful, here—

> Leeze me on drink! it gies us mair
>   Than either school or college;
> It kindles wit, it waukens lair,
>   It pangs us fou o' knowledge.
> Be 't whisky gill or penny wheep
>   Or ony stronger potion,
> It never fails, on drinking deep,
>   To kittle up our notion
>   By night or day.

There is a great deal of that sort of thing in Burns, and it is unsatisfactory,
not because it is bacchanalian poetry, but because it has not that accent of sincerity which bacchanalian poetry, to do it justice, very often has. There is something in it of bravado, something which makes us feel that we have not the
man speaking to us with his real voice; something, therefore, poetically unsound.

With still more confidence will his admirers tell us that we have the
genuine Burns, the great poet, when his strain asserts the independence, equality, dignity, of men, as in the famous song *For a' that and a' that*—

> A prince can mak' a belted knight,
>   A marquis, duke, and a' that;
> But an honest man's aboon his might,
>   Guid faith he mauna fa' that!
>   For a' that, and a' that,
>   Their dignities, and a' that,
>   The pith o' sense, and pride o' worth,
>   Are higher rank than a' that.

Here they find his grand, genuine touches; and still more, when this puissant
genius, who so often set morality at defiance, falls moralising—

> The sacred lowe o' weel-placed love
>   Luxuriantly indulge it;
> But never tempt th' illicit rove,
>   Tho' naething should divulge it.
> I waive the quantum o' the sin,
>   The hazard o' concealing,
> But och! it hardens a' within,
>   And petrifies the feeling.

Or in a higher strain—

> Who made the heart, 'tis He alone
>   Decidedly can try us;
> He knows each chord, its various tone;
>   Each spring, its various bias.
> Then at the balance let's be mute,
>   We never can adjust it;
> What's *done* we partly may compute,
>   But know not what's resisted.

Or in a better strain yet, a strain, his admirers will say, unsurpassable—

> To make a happy fire-side clime
>   To weans and wife,
> That's the true pathos and sublime
>   Of human life.

There is criticism of life for you, the admirers of Burns will say to us; there is the application of ideas to life! There is, undoubtedly. The doctrine of the last-quoted lines coincides almost exactly with what was the aim and end, Xenophon[18] tells us, of all the teaching of Socrates. And the application is a powerful one; made by a man of vigorous understanding, and (need I say?) a master of language.

But for supreme poetical success more is required than the powerful application of ideas to life; it must be an application under the conditions fixed by the laws of poetic truth and poetic beauty. Those laws fix as an essential condition, in the poet's treatment of such matters as are here in question, high seriousness;—the high seriousness which comes from absolute sincerity. The accent of high seriousness, born of absolute sincerity, is what gives to such verse as

> In la sua volontade è nostra pace . . .

to such criticism of life as Dante's, its power. Is this accent felt in the passages which I have been quoting from Burns? Surely not; surely, if our sense is quick, we must perceive that we have not in those passages a voice from the very inmost soul of the genuine Burns; he is not speaking to us from these depths, he is more or less preaching. And the compensation for admiring such passages less, from missing the perfect poetic accent in them, will be that we shall admire more the poetry where that accent is found.

No; Burns, like Chaucer, comes short of the high seriousness of the great classics, and the virtue of matter and manner which goes with that high seriousness is wanting to his work. At moments he touches it in a profound and passionate melancholy, as in those four immortal lines taken by Byron as a motto for *The Bride of Abydos,* but which have in them a depth of poetic quality such as resides in no verse of Byron's own—

---

[18] Xenophon (c. 430–355 B.C.), Greek historian and disciple of Socrates, known best as author of *Anabasis.*

> Had we never loved sae kindly,
> Had we never loved sae blindly,
> Never met, or never parted,
> We had ne'er been broken-hearted.

But a whole poem of that quality Burns cannot make; the rest, in the *Farewell to Nancy,* is verbiage.

We arrive best at the real estimate of Burns, I think, by conceiving his work as having truth of matter and truth of manner, but not the accent or the poetic virtue of the highest masters. His genuine criticism of life, when the sheer poet in him speaks, is ironic; it is not—

> Thou Power Supreme, whose mighty scheme
>   These woes of mine fulfil,
> Here firm I rest, they must be best
>   Because they are Thy will!

It is far rather: *Whistle owre the lave o't!*[19] Yet we may say of him as of Chaucer, that of life and the world, as they come before him, his view is large, free, shrewd, benignant,—truly poetic, therefore; and his manner of rendering what he sees is to match. But we must note, at the same time, his great difference from Chaucer. The freedom of Chaucer is heightened, in Burns, by a fiery, reckless energy; the benignity of Chaucer deepens, in Burns, into an overwhelming sense of the pathos of things;—of the pathos of human nature, the pathos, also, of non-human nature. Instead of the fluidity of Chaucer's manner, the manner of Burns has spring, bounding swiftness. Burns is by far the greater force, though he has perhaps less charm. The world of Chaucer is fairer, richer, more significant than that of Burns; but when the largeness and freedom of Burns get full sweep, as in *Tam o' Shanter,* or still more in that puissant and splendid production, *The Jolly Beggars,* his world may be what it will, his poetic genius triumphs over it. In the world of *The Jolly Beggars* there is more than hideousness and squalor, there is bestiality; yet the piece is a superb poetic success. It has a breadth, truth, and power which make the famous scene in Auerbach's Cellar, of Goethe's *Faust,* seem artificial and tame beside it, and which are only matched by Shakespeare and Aristophanes.[20]

Here, where his largeness and freedom serve him so admirably, and also in those poems and songs where to shrewdness he adds infinite archness and wit, and to benignity infinite pathos, where his manner is flawless, and a perfect poetic whole is the result,—in things like the address to the mouse whose home he had ruined, in things like *Duncan Gray, Tam Glen, Whistle and I'll come to you my Lad, Auld Lang Syne* (this list might be made much longer),—here we have the genuine Burns, of whom the real estimate must be high indeed. Not a classic, nor with the excellent σπουδαιότης[21] of the great classics, nor with a verse rising to a criticism of life and a virtue like theirs; but a poet with thorough truth of substance and an answering truth of style, giving us a poetry

---

[19] "Whistle over what's left of it," the refrain of one of Burns' poems.
[20] Athenian comic poet, greatest of the ancient writers of comedies (c. 448–385 B.C.)
[21] "High seriousness."

sound to the core. We all of us have a leaning towards the pathetic, and may be inclined perhaps to prize Burns most for his touches of piercing, sometimes almost intolerable, pathos; for verse like—

> We twa hae paidl't i' the burn
> From mornin' sun till dine;
> But seas between us braid hae roar'd
> Sin auld lang syne . . .

where he is as lovely as he is sound. But perhaps it is by the perfection of soundness of his lighter and archer masterpieces that he is poetically most wholesome for us. For the votary misled by a personal estimate of Shelley, as so many of us have been, are, and will be,—of that beautiful spirit building his many-coloured haze of words and images

> Pinnacled dim in the intense inane—

no contact can be wholesomer than the contact with Burns at his archest and soundest. Side by side with the

> On the brink of the night and the morning
> My coursers are wont to respire,
> But the Earth has just whispered a warning
> That their flight must be swifter than fire . . .

of *Prometheus Unbound,* how salutary, how very salutary, to place this from *Tam Glen—*

> My minnie does constantly deave me
> And bids me beware o' young men;
> They flatter, she says, to deceive me;
> But wha can think sae o' Tam Glen?

But we enter on burning ground as we approach the poetry of times so near to us—poetry like that of Byron, Shelley, and Wordsworth—of which the estimates are so often not only personal, but personal with passion. For my purpose, it is enough to have taken the single case of Burns, the first poet we come to of whose work the estimate formed is evidently apt to be personal, and to have suggested how we may proceed, using the poetry of the great classics as a sort of touchstone, to correct this estimate, as we had previously corrected by the same means the historic estimate where we met with it. A collection like the present, with its succession of celebrated names and celebrated poems, offers a good opportunity to us for resolutely endeavouring to make our estimates of poetry real. I have sought to point out a method which will help us in making them so, and to exhibit it in use so far as to put any one who likes in a way of applying it for himself.

At any rate the end to which the method and the estimate are designed to lead, and from leading to which, if they do lead to it, they get their whole value,—the benefit of being able clearly to feel and deeply to enjoy the best, the truly classic, in poetry,—is an end, let me say it once more at parting, of supreme importance. We are often told that an era is opening in which we are to see multitudes of a common sort of readers, and masses of a common sort of literature; that such readers do not want and could not relish anything better than such literature, and that to provide it is becoming a vast and profitable industry. Even if good literature entirely lost currency with the world, it would still be abundantly worth while to continue to enjoy it by oneself. But it never will lose currency with the world, in spite of momentary appearances; it never will lose supremacy. Currency and supremacy are insured to it, not indeed by the world's deliberate and conscious choice, but by something far deeper,—by the instinct of self-preservation in humanity.

Walter Pater

STYLE

Walter Pater (1839–1894) was educated at King's School, Canterbury, and at Queen's College, Oxford. At neither place did he distinguish himself scholastically, but he impressed some of his elders, among them the redoubtable Benjamin Jowett, with his intellectual promise, and in 1864, two years after taking his degree in the second class, he was elected a fellow of Brasenose College. In 1866 he published the first of his critical essays—on Coleridge—and proceeded to the series of studies of Renaissance artistic and intellectual figures which was to make his reputation. When these essays were collected as *Studies in the History of the Renaissance,* Pater appended a "Conclusion" which is one of the most celebrated and significant documents of Victorian culture. In its time it was something of a scandal, and on two counts. For one, it defined "success in life" in wholly hedonistic, aesthetic terms which could not but be offensive to the earnest, utilitarian ethic of Victorian respectability—speaking of an ultimate intensity of perception and enjoyment, Pater said that "to burn always with this hard gemlike flame, to maintain this ecstasy, is success in life." For another, it implied that religion was not to be looked to for any comfort or guidance in life; it ends with these words: "We are all under a sentence of death but with a sort of indefinite reprieve . . . we have an interval, and then our place knows us no more. Some spend this interval in listlessness, some in high passions, the wisest, at least among 'the children of this world,' in art and song. For our one chance lies in expanding that interval, in getting as many pulsations as possible into the given time. Great passions may give us this quickened sense of life, ecstasy and sorrow of love, the various forms of enthusiastic activity, disinterested or otherwise, which come naturally to many of us. Only be sure it is passion—that it does yield you this fruit of a quickened, multiplied consciousness. Of this wisdom, the poetic passion, the desire of beauty, the love of art for art's sake, has most; for art comes to you professing frankly to give nothing but the highest quality to your moments as they pass, and simply for those moments' sake."

As an undergraduate at Oxford, Pater had lost, with great pain, his once-fervent religious faith. The issue of an event of an earlier time supplied this loss, so far as anything could—as a pupil at King's School he had read Ruskin's *Modern Painters,* one of the early gospels of the new valuation of art and of its importance in the spiritual life that established itself in the nineteenth century concomitantly with the

From *Appreciations,* by Walter Pater. London: Macmillan and Co., Limited, 1884 (reprinted 1967).

general decline of religion; another such gospel is Matthew Arnold's "The Study of Poetry" (pp. 231 ff.). The Conclusion to *The Renaissance* was the most extreme statement of the position and it made Pater the reluctant leader of the so-called Aesthetic Movement in England. The aesthetic creed had a natural tendency to edge toward a-morality or at least toward the discrediting of the simple morality of respectability, if only because it insisted that art need not, serve any moral purpose, and Pater, a quiet-souled and essentially pious man, apprehensive that his words might have the effect of corrupting the young men who admired him and sought his company suppressed the Conclusion when a new edition of *The Renaissance* was called for. But he restored it to its place in subsequent editions.

Pater's novel, *Marius the Epicurean* (1885), elaborates and confirms his doctrine of cultivated hedonism and gives fuller expression to his sense of the sadness of human life which it was devised to meet. *Imaginary Portraits* (1887) is a series of philosophic fictions. *Plato and Platonism* (1893) is still highly regarded as a learned and perceptive introduction to its subject. The essay reprinted here was published in *Appreciations, with an Essay on Style* (1889). Partly because of his reluctant association with the Aesthetic Movement, which was characterized by its affectation of disengagement, and partly because his prose is occasionally rather mannered, the opinion has grown up that Pater as a critic is deficient in cogency and force. A reading of the essay printed here on style should controvert this facile and mistaken view.

Since all progress of mind consists for the most part in differentiation, in the resolution of an obscure and complex object into its component aspects, it is surely the stupidest of losses to confuse things which right reason has put asunder, to lose the sense of achieved distinctions, the distinction between poetry and prose, for instance, or, to speak more exactly, between the laws and characteristic excellences of verse and prose composition. On the other hand, those who have dwelt most emphatically on the distinction between prose and verse, prose and poetry, may sometimes have been tempted to limit the proper functions of prose too narrowly; and this again is at least false economy, as being, in effect, the renunciation of a certain means or faculty, in a world where after all we must needs make the most of things. Critical efforts to limit art *a priori*, by anticipations regarding the natural incapacity of the material with which this or that artist works, as the sculptor with solid form, or the prose-writer with the ordinary language of men, are always liable to be discredited by the facts of artistic production; and while prose is actually found to be a coloured thing with Bacon, picturesque with Livy and Carlyle, musical with Cicero and Newman, mystical and intimate with Plato and Michelet and Sir Thomas Browne, exalted or florid, it may be, with Milton and Taylor,[1] it will

[1] Francis Bacon (1561–1626), English philosopher, essayist, statesman; Titus Livius Livy (59 B.C.–A.D. 17), Roman historian; Thomas Carlyle (1795–1881), English historian and writer on public affairs; Marcus Tullius Cicero (106–43 B.C.), Roman orator, philosopher, politician; John Henry Newman (1801–1890), English

be useless to protest that it can be nothing at all, except something very tamely and narrowly confined to mainly practical ends—a kind of "good round-hand"; as useless as the protest that poetry might not touch prosaic subjects as with Wordsworth, or an abstruse matter as with Browning, or treat contemporary life nobly as with Tennyson. In subordination to one essential beauty in all good literary style, in all literature as a fine art, as there are many beauties of poetry so the beauties of prose are many, and it is the business of criticism to estimate them as such; as it is good in the criticism of verse to look for those hard, logical, and quasi-prosaic excellences which that too has, or needs. To find in the poem, amid the flowers, the allusions, the mixed perspectives, of *Lycidas*[2] for instance, the thought, the logical structure:—how wholesome! how delightful! as to identify in prose what we call the poetry, the imaginative power, not treating it as out of place and a kind of vagrant intruder, but by way of an estimate of its rights, that is, of its achieved powers, there.

Dryden, with the characteristic instinct of his age, loved to emphasise the distinction between poetry and prose, the protest against their confusion with each other, coming with somewhat diminished effect from one whose poetry was so prosaic. In truth, his sense of prosaic excellence affected his verse rather than his prose, which is not only fervid, richly figured, poetic, as we say, but vitiated, all unconsciously, by many a scanning line. Setting up correctness, that humble merit of prose, as the central literary excellence, he is really a less correct writer than he may seem, still with an imperfect mastery of the relative pronoun. It might have been foreseen that, in the rotations of mind, the province of poetry in prose would find its assertor; and, a century after Dryden, amid very different intellectual needs, and with the need therefore of great modifications in literary form, the range of the poetic force in literature was effectively enlarged by Wordsworth. The true distinction between prose and poetry he regarded as the almost technical or accidental one of the absence or presence of metrical beauty, or, say! metrical restraint; and for him the opposition came to be between verse and prose of course; but, as the essential dichotomy in this matter, between imaginative and unimaginative writing, parallel to De Quincey's distinction between "the literature of power and the literature of knowledge," in the former of which the composer gives us not fact, but his peculiar sense of fact, whether past or present.

Dismissing then, under sanction of Wordsworth, that harsher opposition of poetry to prose, as savouring in fact of the arbitrary psychology of the last century, and with it the prejudice that there can be but one only beauty of prose style, I propose here to point out certain qualities of all literature as a fine art, which, if they apply to the literature of fact, apply still more to the litera-ture of the imaginative sense of fact, while they apply indifferently to verse and prose, so far as either is really imaginative—certain conditions of true art in both alike, which conditions may also contain in them the secret of the proper discrimination and guardianship of the peculiar excellences of either.

---

churchman and author; Jules Michelet (1798–1874), French historian; Sir Thomas Browne (1605–1682), English author and physician; Jeremy Taylor (1613–1667), English bishop and devotional writer.

[2] A pastoral elegy by John Milton.

The line between fact and something quite different from external fact is, indeed, hard to draw. In Pascal, for instance, in the persuasive writers generally, how difficult to define the point where, from time to time, argument which, if it is to be worth anything at all, must consist of facts or groups of facts, becomes a pleading—a theorem no longer, but essentially an appeal to the reader to catch the writer's spirit, to think with him, if one can or will—an expression no longer of fact but of his sense of it, his peculiar intuition of a world, prospective, or discerned below the faulty conditions of the present, in either case changed somewhat from the actual world. In science, on the other hand, in history so far as it conforms to scientific rule, we have a literary domain where the imagination may be thought to be always an intruder. And as, in all science, the functions of literature reduce themselves eventually to the transcribing of fact, so all the excellences of literary form in regard to science are reducible to various kinds of pains-taking; this good quality being involved in all "skilled work" whatever, in the drafting of an act of parliament, as in sewing. Yet here again, the writer's sense of fact, in history especially, and in all those complex subjects which do but lie on the borders of science, will still take the place of fact, in various degrees. Your historian, for instance, with absolutely truthful intention, amid the multitude of facts presented to him must needs select, and in selecting assert something of his own humour, something that comes not of the world without but of a vision within. So Gibbon[3] moulds his unwieldy material to a preconceived view. Livy, Tacitus, Michelet, moving full of poignant sensibility amid the records of the past, each, after his own sense, modifies—who can tell where and to what degree?—and becomes something else than a transcriber; each, as he thus modifies, passing into the domain of art proper. For just in proportion as the writer's aim, consciously or unconsciously, comes to be the transcribing, not of the world, not of mere fact, but of his sense of it, he becomes an artist, his work *fine* art; and good art (as I hope ultimately to show) in proportion to the truth of his presentment of that sense; as in those humbler or plainer functions of literature also, truth—truth to bare fact, there—is the essence of such artistic quality as they may have. Truth! there can be no merit, no craft at all, without that. And further, all beauty is in the long run only *fineness* of truth, or what we call expression, the finer accommodation of speech to that vision within.

—The transcript of his sense of fact rather than the fact, as being preferable, pleasanter, more beautiful to the writer himself. In literature, as in every other product of human skill, in the moulding of a bell or a platter for instance, wherever this sense asserts itself, wherever the producer so modifies his work as, over and above its primary use or intention, to make it pleasing (to himself, of course, in the first instance) there, "fine" as opposed to merely serviceable art, exists. Literary art, that is, like all art which is in any way imitative or reproductive of fact—form, or colour, or incident—is the representation of such fact as connected with soul, of a specific personality, in its preferences, its volition and power.

Such is the matter of imaginative or artistic literature—this transcript, not of mere fact, but of fact in its infinite variety, as modified by human pre-

---

[3] Edward Gibbon (1737–1794), English historian.

ference in all its infinitely varied forms. It will be good literary art not because
it is brilliant or sober, or rich, or impulsive, or severe, but just in proportion
as its representation of that sense, that soul-fact, is true, verse being only one
department of such literature, and imaginative prose, it may be thought, being
the special art of the modern world. That imaginative prose should be the
special and opportune art of the modern world results from two important
facts about the latter: first, the chaotic variety and complexity of its interests,
making the intellectual issue, the really master currents of the present time
incalculable—a condition of mind little susceptible of the restraint proper to
verse form, so that the most characteristic verse of the nineteenth century
has been lawless verse; and secondly, an all-pervading naturalism, a curiosity
about everything whatever as it really is, involving a certain humility of attitude,
cognate to what must, after all, be the less ambitious form of literature. And
prose thus asserting itself as the special and privileged artistic faculty of the
present day, will be, however critics may try to narrow its scope, as varied
in its excellence as humanity itself reflecting on the facts of its latest experience—
an instrument of many stops, meditative, observant, descriptive, eloquent,
analytic, plaintive, fervid. Its beauties will be not exclusively "pedestrian":
it will exert, in due measure, all the varied charms of poetry, down to the
rhythm which, as in Cicero, or Michelet, or Newman, at their best, gives its
musical value to every syllable.*

The literary artist is of necessity a scholar, and in what he proposes to
do will have in mind, first of all, the scholar and the scholarly conscience—
the male conscience in this matter, as we must think it, under a system of
education which still to so large an extent limits real scholarship to men.
In his self-criticism, he supposes always that sort of reader who will go
(full of eyes) warily, considerately, though without consideration for him,
over the ground which the female conscience traverses so lightly, so amiably.
For the material in which he works is no more a creation of his own than
the sculptor's marble. Product of a myriad various minds and contending
tongues, compact of obscure and minute association, a language has its
own abundant and often recondite laws, in the habitual and summary recognition of which scholarship consists. A writer, full of a matter he is before all
things anxious to express, may think of those laws, the limitations of vocabulary, structure, and the like, as a restriction, but if a real artist will find in them
an opportunity. His punctilious observance of the proprieties of his medium
will diffuse through all he writes a general air of sensibility, of refined usage.
Exclusiones debitæ naturæ—the exclusions, or rejections, which nature demands—we know how large a part these play, according to Bacon, in the science
of nature. In a somewhat changed sense, we might say that the art of the

---

* Mr. Saintsbury, in his *Specimens of English Prose, from Malory to Macaulay*,
has succeeded in tracing, through successive English prose-writers, the tradition of
that severer beauty in them, of which this admirable scholar of our literature is
known to be a lover. *English Prose, from Mandeville to Thackeray*, more recently
"chosen and edited" by a younger scholar, Mr. Arthur Galton, of New College,
Oxford, a lover of our literature at once enthusiastic and discreet, aims at a more
various illustration of the eloquent powers of English prose, and is a delightful
companion. [Pater's note.]

scholar is summed up in the observance of those rejections demanded by the nature of his medium, the material he must use. Alive to the value of an atmosphere in which every term finds its utmost degree of expression, and with all the jealousy of a lover of words, he will resist a constant tendency on the part of the majority of those who use them to efface the distinctions of language, the facility of writers often reinforcing in this respect the work of the vulgar. He will feel the obligation not of the laws only, but of those affinities, avoidances, those mere preferences, of his language, which through the associations of literary history have become a part of its nature, prescribing the rejection of many a neology, many a license, many a gipsy phrase which might present itself as actually expressive. His appeal, again, is to the scholar, who has great experience in literature, and will show no favour to short-cuts, or hackneyed illustration, or an affectation of learning designed for the un-learned. Hence a contention, a sense of self-restraint and renunciation, having for the susceptible reader the effect of a challenge for minute consideration; the attention of the writer, in every minutest detail, being a pledge that it is worth the reader's while to be attentive too, that the writer is dealing scrupu-lously with his instrument, and therefore, indirectly, with the reader himself also, that he has the science of the instrument he plays on, perhaps, after all, with a freedom which in such case will be the freedom of a master.

For meanwhile, braced only by those restraints, he is really vindicating his liberty in the making of a vocabulary, an entire system of composition, for himself, his own true manner; and when we speak of the manner of a true master we mean what is essential in his art. Pedantry being only the scholarship of *le cuistre*[4] (we have no English equivalent) he is no pedant, and does but show his intelligence of the rules of language in his freedoms with it, addition or expansion, which like the spontaneities of manner in a well-bred person will still further illustrate good taste.—The right vocabulary! Translators have not invariably seen how all-important that is in the work of translation, driving for the most part at idiom or construction; whereas, if the original be first-rate, one's first care should be with its elementary particles, Plato, for instance, being often reproducible by an exact following, with no variation in structure, of word after word, as the pencil follows a drawing under tracing-paper, so only each word or syllable be not of false colour, to change my illustration a little.

Well! that is because any writer worth translating at all has winnowed and searched through his vocabulary, is conscious of the words he would select in systematic reading of a dictionary, and still more of the words he would reject were the dictionary other than Johnson's;[5] and doing this with his peculiar sense of the world ever in view, in search of an instrument for the adequate expression of that, he begets a vocabulary faithful to the colouring of his own spirit, and in the strictest sense original. That living authority which language needs lies, in truth, in its scholars, who recognising always that every language possesses a genius, a very fastidious genius, of its own, ex-pand at once and purify its very elements, which must needs change along

[4] The French word originally meant a servingman in a college, now a vulgar, pedantic person.
[5] Samuel Johnson, whose *Dictionary of the English Language* appeared in 1755.

with the changing thoughts of living people. Ninety years ago, for instance, great mental force, certainly, was needed by Wordsworth, to break through the consecrated poetic associations of a century, and speak the language that was his, that was to become in a measure the language of the next generation. But he did it with the tact of a scholar also. English, for a quarter of a century past, has been assimilating the phraseology of pictorial art; for half a century, the phraseology of the great German metaphysical movement of eighty years ago; in part also the language of mystical theology: and none but pedants will regret a great consequent increase of its resources. For many years to come its enterprise may well lie in the naturalisation of the vocabulary of science, so only it be under the eye of a sensitive scholarship—in a liberal naturalisation of the ideas of science too, for after all the chief stimulus of good style is to possess a full, rich, complex matter to grapple with. The literary artist, therefore, will be well aware of physical science; science also attaining, in its turn, its true literary ideal. And then, as the scholar is nothing without the historic sense, he will be apt to restore not really obsolete or really worn-out words, but the finer edge of words still in use: *ascertain, communicate, discover*—words like these it has been part of our "business" to misuse. And still, as language was made for man, he will be no authority for correctnesses which, limiting freedom of utterance, were yet but accidents in their origin; as if one vowed not to say *"its,"* which ought to have been in Shakespeare; *"his"* and *"hers,"* for inanimate objects, being but a barbarous and really inexpressive survival. Yet we have known many things like this. Racy Saxon monosyllables, close to us as touch and sight, he will intermix readily with those long, savoursome, Latin words, rich in "second intention." In this late day certainly, no critical process can be conducted reasonably without eclecticism. Of such eclecticism we have a justifying example in one of the first poets of our time. How illustrative of monosyllabic effect, of sonorous Latin, of the phraseology of science, of metaphysic, of colloquialism even, are the writings of Tennyson; yet with what a fine, fastidious scholarship throughout!

A scholar writing for the scholarly, he will of course leave something to the willing intelligence of his reader. "To go preach to the first passer-by," says Montaigne, "to become tutor to the ignorance of the first I meet, is a thing I abhor;" a thing, in fact, naturally distressing to the scholar, who will therefore ever be shy of offering uncomplimentary assistance to the reader's wit. To really strenuous minds there is a pleasurable stimulus in the challenge for a continuous effort on their part, to be rewarded by securer and more intimate grasp of the author's sense. Self-restraint, a skilful economy of means, *ascêsis,*[6] that too has a beauty of its own; and for the reader supposed there will be an æsthetic satisfaction in that frugal closeness of style which makes the most of a word, in the exaction from every sentence of a precise relief, in the just spacing out of word to thought, in the logically filled space connected always with the delightful sense of difficulty overcome.

Different classes of persons, at different times, make, of course, very various demands upon literature. Still, scholars, I suppose, and not only scholars, but all disinterested lovers of books, will always look to it, as to all other fine

---

[6] Self-denial, asceticism.

art, for a refuge, a sort of cloistral refuge, from a certain vulgarity in the actual world. A perfect poem like *Lycidas,* a perfect fiction like *Esmond,*[7] the perfect handling of a theory like Newman's *Idea of a University,* has for them something of the uses of a religious "retreat." Here, then, with a view to the central need of a select few, those "men of a finer thread" who have formed and maintain the literary ideal, everything, every component element, will have undergone exact trial, and, above all, there will be no uncharacteristic or tarnished or vulgar decoration, permissible ornament being for the most part structural, or necessary. As the painter in his picture, so the artist in his book, aims at the production by honourable artifice of a peculiar atmosphere. "The artist," says Schiller, "may be known rather by what he *omits*"; and in literature, too, the true artist may be best recognised by his tact of omission. For to the grave reader words too are grave; and the ornamental word, the figure, the accessory form or colour or reference, is rarely content to die to thought precisely at the right moment, but will inevitably linger awhile, stirring a long "brain-wave" behind it of perhaps quite alien associations.

Just there, it may be, is the detrimental tendency of the sort of scholarly attentiveness of mind I am recommending. But the true artist allows for it. He will remember that, as the very word ornament indicates what is in itself non-essential, so the "one beauty" of all literary style is of its very essence, and independent, in prose and verse alike, of all removable decoration; that it may exist in its fullest lustre, as in Flaubert's *Madame Bovary,* for instance, or in Stendhal's *Le Rouge et Le Noir,*[8] in a composition utterly unadorned, with hardly a single suggestion of visibly beautiful things. Parallel, allusion, the allusive way generally, the flowers in the garden:—he knows the narcotic force of these upon the negligent intelligence to which any *diversion,* literally, is welcome, any vagrant intruder, because one can go wandering away with it from the immediate subject. Jealous, if he have a really quickening motive within, of all that does not hold directly to that, of the facile, the otiose, he will never depart from the strictly pedestrian process, unless he gains a ponderable something thereby. Even assured of its congruity, he will still question its serviceableness. Is it worth while, can we afford, to attend to just that, to just that figure or literary reference, just then?—Surplusage! he will dread that, as the runner on his muscles. For in truth all art does but consist in the removal of surplusage, from the last finish of the gem-engraver blowing away the last particle of invisible dust, back to the earliest divination of the finished work to be, lying somewhere, according to Michelangelo's fancy, in the rough-hewn block of stone.

And what applies to figure or flower must be understood of all other accidental or removable ornaments of writing whatever; and not of specific ornament only, but of all that latent colour and imagery which language as such carries in it. A lover of words for their own sake, to whom nothing about them is unimportant, a minute and constant observer of their physiognomy, he will be on the alert not only for obviously mixed metaphors of course, but for the metaphor that is mixed in all our speech, though a rapid use may

[7] *Henry Esmond* (1852), by William Makepeace Thackeray (1811–1863).
[8] *The Red and the Black.*

involve no cognition of it. Currently recognising the incident, the colour, the physical elements or particles in words like *absorb, consider, extract,* to take the first that occur, he will avail himself of them, as further adding to the resources of expression. The elementary particles of language will be realised as colour and light and shade through his scholarly living in the full sense of them. Still opposing the constant degradation of language by those who use it carelessly, he will not treat coloured glass as if it were clear; and while half the world is using figure unconsciously, will be fully aware not only of all that latent figurative texture in speech, but of the vague, lazy, half-formed personification—a rhetoric, depressing, and worse than nothing, because it has no really rhetorical motive—which plays so large a part there, and, as in the case of more ostentatious ornament, scrupulously exact of it, from syllable to syllable, its precise value.

So far I have been speaking of certain conditions of the literary art arising out of the medium or material in or upon which it works, the essential qualities of language and its aptitudes for contingent ornamentation, matters which define scholarship as science and good taste respectively. They are both subservient to a more intimate quality of good style: more intimate, as coming nearer to the artist himself. The otiose, the facile, surplusage: why are these abhorrent to the true literary artist, except because, in literary as in all other art, structure is all-important, felt, or painfully missed, everywhere? —that architectural conception of work, which foresees the end in the beginning and never loses sight of it, and in every part is conscious of all the rest, till the last sentence does but, with undiminished vigour, unfold and justify the first—a condition of literary art, which, in contradistinction to another quality of the artist himself, to be spoken of later, I shall call the necessity of *mind* in style.

An acute philosophical writer, the late Dean Mansel[9] (a writer whose works illustrate the literary beauty there may be in closeness, and with obvious repression or economy of a fine rhetorical gift) wrote a book,[10] of fascinating precision in a very obscure subject, to show that all the technical laws of logic are but means of securing, in each and all of its apprehensions, the unity, the strict identity with itself, of the apprehending mind. All the laws of good writing aim at a similar unity or identity of the mind in all the processes by which the word is associated to its import. The term is right, and has its essential beauty, when it becomes, in a manner, what it signifies, as with the names of simple sensations. To give the phrase, the sentence, the structural member, the entire composition, song, or essay, a similar unity with its subject and with itself:—style is in the right way when it tends towards that. All depends upon the original unity, the vital wholeness and identity, of the initiatory apprehension or view. So much is true of all art, which therefore requires always its logic, its comprehensive reason—insight, foresight, retrospect, in simultaneous action—true, most of all, of the literary art, as being of all the arts most closely cognate to the abstract intelligence. Such logical coherency may be evidenced not merely in the lines of composition as a whole, but in the

[9] Henry L. Mansel (1820–1871), professor of Philosophy at Oxford and afterwards Dean of St. Paul's.
[10] *The Limits of Religious Thought* (1858).

choice of a single word, while it by no means interferes with, but may even prescribe, much variety, in the building of the sentence for instance, or in the manner, argumentative, descriptive, discursive, of this or that part or member of the entire design. The blithe, crisp sentence, decisive as a child's expression of its needs, may alternate with the long-contending, victoriously intricate sentence; the sentence, born with the integrity of a single word, relieving the sort of sentence in which, if you look closely, you can see much contrivance, much adjustment, to bring a highly qualified matter into compass at one view. For the literary architecture, if it is to be rich and expressive, involves not only foresight of the end in the beginning, but also development or growth of design, in the process of execution, with many irregularities, surprises, and afterthoughts; the contingent as well as the necessary being subsumed under the unity of the whole. As truly, to the lack of such architectural design, of a single, almost visual, image, vigorously informing an entire, perhaps very intricate, composition, which shall be austere, ornate, argumentative, fanciful, yet true from first to last to that vision within, may be attributed those weaknesses of conscious or unconscious repetition of word, phrase, motive, or member of the whole matter, indicating, as Flaubert was aware, an original structure in thought not organically complete. With such foresight, the actual conclusion will most often get itself written out of hand, before, in the more obvious sense, the work is finished. With some strong and leading sense of the world, the tight hold of which secures true *composition* and not mere loose accretion, the literary artist, I suppose, goes on considerately, setting joint to joint, sustained by yet restraining the productive ardour, retracing the negligences of his first sketch, repeating his steps only that he may give the reader a sense of secure and restful progress, readjusting mere assonances even, that they may soothe the reader, or at least not interrupt him on his way; and then, somewhere before the end comes, is burdened, inspired, with his conclusion, and betimes delivered of it, leaving off, not in weariness and because he finds *himself* at an end, but in all the freshness of volition. His work now structurally complete, with all the accumulating effect of secondary shades of meaning, he finishes the whole up to the just proportion of that ante-penultimate conclusion, and all becomes expressive. The house he has built is rather a body he has informed. And so it happens, to its greater credit, that the better interest even of a narrative to be recounted, a story to be told, will often be in its second reading. And though there are instances of great writers who have been no artists, an unconscious tact sometimes directing work in which we may detect, very pleasurably, many of the effects of conscious art, yet one of the greatest pleasures of really good prose literature is in the critical tracing out of that conscious artistic structure, and the pervading sense of it as we read. Yet of poetic literature too; for, in truth, the kind of constructive intelligence here supposed is one of the forms of the imagination.

That is the special function of mind, in style. Mind and soul:—hard to ascertain philosophically, the distinction is real enough practically, for they often interfere, are sometimes in conflict, with each other. Blake, in the last century, is an instance of preponderating soul, embarrassed, at a loss, in an era of preponderating mind. As a quality of style, at all events, soul is a fact, in certain writers—the way they have of absorbing language, of attracting it into the peculiar spirit they are of, with a subtlety which makes the actual result seem like some inexplicable inspiration. By mind, the literary artist reaches us, through static and objective indications of design in his work, legible to all. By soul, he reaches us, somewhat capriciously perhaps, one and not another, through vagrant sympathy and a kind of immediate contact. Mind we cannot choose but approve where we recognise it; soul may repel us, not because we misunderstand it. The way in which theological interests sometimes avail themselves of language is perhaps the best illustration of the force I mean to indicate generally in literature, by the word *soul*. Ardent religious persuasion may exist, may make its way, without finding any equivalent heat in language: or, again, it may enkindle words to various degrees, and when it really takes hold of them doubles its force. Religious history presents many remarkable instances in which, through no mere phrase-worship, an unconscious literary tact has, for the sensitive, laid open a privileged pathway from one to another. "The altar-fire," people say, "has touched those lips!" The Vulgate, the English Bible, the English Prayer-Book, the writings of Swedenborg,[11] the Tracts for the Times:[12]—there, we have instances of widely different and largely diffused phases of religious feeling in operation as soul in style. But something of the same kind acts with similar power in certain writers of quite other than theological literature, on behalf of some wholly personal and peculiar sense of theirs. Most easily illustrated by theological literature, this quality lends to profane writers a kind of religious influence. At their best, these writers become, as we say sometimes, "prophets"; such character depending on the effect not merely of their matter, but of their matter as allied to, in "electric affinity" with, peculiar form, and working in all cases by an immediate sympathetic contact, on which account it is that it may be called soul, as opposed to mind, in style. And this too is a faculty of choosing and rejecting what is congruous or otherwise, with a drift towards unity—unity of atmosphere here, as there of design—soul securing colour (or perfume, might we say?) as mind secures form, the latter being essentially finite, the former vague or infinite, as the influence of a living person is practically infinite. There are some to whom nothing has any real interest, or real meaning, except as operative in a given person; and it is they who best appreciate the quality of soul in literary art. They seem to know a *person*, in a book, and make way by intuition: yet, although they thus enjoy the completeness of a personal information, it is still a characteristic of soul, in this sense of the word, that it does but suggest what can never be uttered, not as being different from, or more obscure than, what actually gets said, but as containing that plenary substance of which there is only one phase or facet in what is there expressed.

If all high things have their martyrs, Gustave Flaubert might perhaps rank as the martyr of literary style. In his printed correspondence, a curious

---

[11] Emanuel Swedenborg (1688–1772), Swedish scientist, religious teacher, and mystic.
[12] A series of pamphlets written by inspirers of the Oxford Movement, the "Tractarians," as they came to be called. The Movement, which began around 1833, was led by such men as J. H. Newman, John Keble, R. H. Froude, and E. B. Pusey. Put simply and not quite accurately, the aim of the Movement was to bring the Church of England closer to Catholicism, to reform it once again by regrafting it onto its ancient roots.

series of letters, written in his twenty-fifth year, records what seems to have been his one other passion—a series of letters which, with its fine casuistries, its firmly repressed anguish, its tone of harmonious grey, and the sense of disillusion in which the whole matter ends, might have been, a few slight changes supposed, one of his own fictions. Writing to Madame X. certainly he does display, by "taking thought" mainly, by constant and delicate pondering, as in his love for literature, a heart really moved, but still more, and as the pledge of that emotion, a loyalty to his work. Madame X., too, is a literary artist, and the best gifts he can send her are precepts of perfection in art, counsels for the effectual pursuit of that better love. In his love-letters it is the pains and pleasures of art he insists on, its solaces: he communicates secrets, reproves, encourages, with a view to that. Whether the lady was dissatisfied with such divided or indirect service, the reader is not enabled to see; but sees that, on Flaubert's part at least, a living person could be no rival of what was, from first to last, his leading passion, a somewhat solitary and exclusive one.

I must scold you (he writes) for one thing, which shocks, scandalises me, the small concern, namely, you show for art just now. As regards glory be it so: there, I approve. But for art!—the one thing in life that is good and real—can you compare with it an earthly love?—prefer the adoration of a relative beauty to the *cultus* of the true beauty? Well! I tell you the truth. That is the one thing good in me: the one thing I have, to me estimable. For yourself, you blend with the beautiful a heap of alien things, the useful, the agreeable, what not?—

The only way not to be unhappy is to shut yourself up in art, and count everything else as nothing. Pride takes the place of all beside when it is established on a large basis. Work! God wills it. That, it seems to me, is clear.—

I am reading over again the *Æneid,* certain verses of which I repeat to myself to satiety. There are phrases there which stay in one's head, by which I find myself beset, as with those musical airs which are for ever returning, and cause you pain, you love them so much. I observe that I no longer laugh much, and am no longer depressed. I am ripe. You talk of my serenity, and envy me. It may well surprise you. Sick, irritated, the prey a thousand times a day of cruel pain, I continue my labour like a true working-man, who, with sleeves turned up, in the sweat of his brow, beats away at his anvil, never troubling himself whether it rains or blows, for hail or thunder. I was not like that formerly. The change has taken place naturally, though my will has counted for something in the matter.—

Those who write in good style are sometimes accused of a neglect of ideas, and of the moral end, as if the end of the physician were something else than healing, of the painter than painting—as if the end of art were not, before all else, the beautiful.

What, then, did Flaubert understand by beauty, in the art he pursued with so much fervour, with so much self-command? Let us hear a sympathetic commentator:—[13]

[13] Guy de Maupassant, in his introduction to the collection of letters Flaubert wrote to George Sand.

Possessed of an absolute belief that there exists but one way of expressing one thing, one word to call it by, one adjective to qualify, one verb to animate it, he gave himself to superhuman labour for the discovery, in every phrase, of that word, that verb, that epithet. In this way, he believed in some mysterious harmony of expression, and when a true word seemed to him to lack euphony still went on seeking another, with invincible patience, certain that he had not yet got hold of the *unique* word. . . . A thousand preoccupations would beset him at the same moment, always with this desperate certitude fixed in his spirit: Among all the expressions in the world, all forms and turns of expression, there is but *one*—one form, one mode—to express what I want to say.

The one word for the one thing, the one thought, amid the multitude of words, terms, that might just do: the problem of style was there!—the unique word, phrase, sentence, paragraph, essay, or song, absolutely proper to the single mental presentation or vision within. In that perfect justice, over and above the many contingent and removable beauties with which beautiful style may charm us, but which it can exist without, independent of them yet dexterously availing itself of them, omnipresent in good work, in function at every point, from single epithets to the rhythm of a whole book, lay the specific, indispensable, very intellectual, beauty of literature, the possibility of which constitutes it a fine art.

One seems to detect the influence of a philosophic idea there, the idea of a natural economy, of some pre-existent adaptation, between a relative, somewhere in the world of thought, and its correlative, somewhere in the world of language—both alike, rather, somewhere in the mind of the artist, desiderative, expectant, inventive—meeting each other with the readiness of "soul and body reunited," in Blake's rapturous design; and, in fact, Flaubert was fond of giving his theory philosophical expression.—

> There are no beautiful thoughts (he would say) without beautiful forms, and conversely. As it is impossible to extract from a physical body the qualities which really constitute it—colour, extension, and the like—without reducing it to a hollow abstraction, in a word, without destroying it; just so it is impossible to detach the form from the idea, for the idea only exists by virtue of the form.

All the recognised flowers, the removable ornaments of literature (including harmony and ease in reading aloud, very carefully considered by him) counted, certainly; for these too are part of the actual value of what one says. But still, after all, with Flaubert, the search, the unwearied research, was not for the smooth, or winsome, or forcible word, as such, as with false Ciceronians, but quite simply and honestly, for the word's adjustment to its meaning. The first condition of this must be, of course, to know yourself, to have ascertained your own sense exactly. Then, if we suppose an artist, he says to the reader,—I want you to see precisely what I see. Into the mind sensitive to "form," a flood of random sounds, colours, incidents, is ever penetrating from the world without, to become, by sympathetic selection, a part of its very structure, and, in turn, the visible vesture and expression of that other world it sees so steadily within, nay, already with a partial conformity thereto, to be refined, enlarged, corrected, at a hundred points; and it is just there, just at those doubtful points that the function of style, as tact or taste, intervenes. The unique term will come more quickly to one than another, at one time than another, according also to the kind of matter in question. Quickness and slowness, ease and closeness alike, have nothing to do with the artistic character of the true word found at last. As there is a charm of ease, so there is also a special charm in the signs of discovery, of effort and contention towards a due end, as so often with Flaubert himself—in the style which has been pliant, as only obstinate, durable metal can be, to the inherent perplexities and recusancy of a certain difficult thought.

If Flaubert had not told us, perhaps we should never have guessed how tardy and painful his own procedure really was, and after reading his confession may think that his almost endless hesitation had much to do with diseased nerves. Often, perhaps, the felicity supposed will be the product of a happier, a more exuberant nature than Flaubert's. Aggravated, certainly, by a morbid physical condition, that anxiety in "seeking the phrase," which gathered all the other small *ennuis* of a really quiet existence into a kind of battle, was connected with his lifelong contention against facile poetry, facile art—art, facile and flimsy; and what constitutes the true artist is not the slowness or quickness of the process, but the absolute success of the result. As with those labourers in the parable, the prize is independent of the mere length of the actual day's work. "You talk," he writes, odd, trying lover, to Madame X.—

> You talk of the exclusiveness of my literary tastes. That might have enabled you to divine what kind of a person I am in the matter of love. I grow so hard to please as a literary artist, that I am driven to despair. I shall end by not writing another line.

"Happy," he cries, in a moment of discouragement at that patient labour, which for him, certainly, was the condition of a great success—

> Happy those who have no doubts of themselves! who lengthen out, as the pen runs on, all that flows forth from their brains. As for me, I hesitate, I disappoint myself, turn round upon myself in despite: my taste is augmented in proportion as my natural vigour decreases, and I afflict my soul over some dubious word out of all proportion to the pleasure I get from a whole page of good writing. One would have to live two centuries to attain a true idea of any matter whatever. What Buffon[14] said is a big blasphemy: genius is not long-continued patience. Still, there is some truth in the statement, and more than people think, especially as regards our own day. Art! art! art! bitter deception! phantom that glows with light, only to lead one on to destruction.

Again—

> I am growing so peevish about my writing. I am like a man whose ear is true but who plays falsely on the violin: his fingers refuse to repro-

[14] Georges Louis Leclerc, Comte de Buffon (1707–1788), French naturalist and author.

duce precisely those sounds of which he has the inward sense. Then the tears come rolling down from the poor scraper's eyes and the bow falls from his hand.

Coming slowly or quickly, when it comes, as it came with so much labour of mind, but also with so much lustre, to Gustave Flaubert, this discovery of the word will be, like all artistic success and felicity, incapable of strict analysis: effect of an intuitive condition of mind, it must be recognised by like intuition on the part of the reader, and a sort of immediate sense. In every one of those masterly sentences of Flaubert there was, below all mere contrivance, shaping and afterthought, by some happy instantaneous concourse of the various faculties of the mind with each other, the exact apprehension of what was *needed* to carry the meaning. And that it fits with absolute justice will be a judgment of immediate sense in the appreciative reader. We all feel this in what may be called inspired translation. Well! all language involves translation from inward to outward. In literature, as in all forms of art, there are the absolute and the merely relative or accessory beauties; and precisely in that exact proportion of the term to its purpose is the absolute beauty of style, prose or verse. All the good qualities, the beauties, of verse also, are such, only as precise expression.

In the highest as in the lowliest literature, then, the one indispensable beauty is, after all, truth:—truth to bare fact in the latter, as to some personal sense of fact, diverted somewhat from men's ordinary sense of it, in the former; truth there as accuracy, truth here as expression, that finest and most intimate form of truth, the *vraie vérité*. And what an eclectic principle this really is! employing for its one sole purpose—that absolute accordance of expression to idea—all other literary beauties and excellences whatever: how many kinds of style it covers, explains, justifies, and at the same time safeguards! Scott's facility, Flaubert's deeply pondered evocation of "the phrase," are equally good art. Say what you have to say, what you have a will to say, in the simplest, the most direct and exact manner possible, with no surplusage:— there, is the justification of the sentence so fortunately born, "entire, smooth, and round," that it needs no punctuation, and also (that is the point!) of the most elaborate period, if it be right in its elaboration. Here is the office of ornament: here also the purpose of restraint in ornament. As the exponent of truth, that austerity (the beauty, the function, of which in literature Flaubert understood so well) becomes not the correctness or purism of the mere scholar, but a security against the otiose, a jealous exclusion of what does not really tell towards the pursuit of relief, of life and vigour in the portraiture of one's sense. License again, the making free with rule, if it be indeed, as people fancy, a habit of genius, flinging aside or transforming all that opposes the liberty of beautiful production, will be but faith to one's own meaning. The seeming baldness of *Le Rouge et Le Noir* is nothing in itself; the wild ornament of *Les Misérables*[15] is nothing in itself; and the restraint of Flaubert, amid a real natural opulence, only redoubled beauty—the phrase so large and so precise at the same time, hard as bronze, in service to the more perfect adaptation of words to their matter. Afterthoughts, retouchings, finish, will be of profit

---

[15] A novel by Victor Hugo (1802–1885), published in 1862.

only so far as they too really serve to bring out the original, initiative, generative, sense in them.

In this way, according to the well-known saying, "The style is the man,"[16] complex or simple, in his individuality, his plenary sense of what he really has to say, his sense of the world; all cautions regarding style arising out of so many natural scruples as to the medium through which alone he can expose that inward sense of things, the purity of this medium, its laws or tricks of refraction: nothing is to be left there which might give conveyance to any matter save that. Style in all its varieties, reserved or opulent, terse, abundant, musical, stimulant, academic, so long as each is really characteristic or expressive, finds thus its justification, the sumptuous good taste of Cicero being as truly the man himself, and not another, justified, yet insured inalienably to him, thereby, as would have been his portrait by Raffaelle,[17] in full consular splendour, on his ivory chair.

A relegation, you may say perhaps—a relegation of style to the subjectivity, the mere caprice, of the individual, which must soon transform it into mannerism. Not so! since there is, under the conditions supposed, for those elements of the man, for every lineament of the vision within, the one word, the one acceptable word, recognisable by the sensitive, by others "who have intelligence" in the matter, as absolutely as ever anything can be in the evanescent and delicate region of human language. The style, the manner, would be the man, not in his unreasoned and really uncharacteristic caprices, involuntary or affected, but in absolutely sincere apprehension of what is most real to him. But let us hear our French guide again.—[18]

> Styles (says Flaubert's commentator), *Styles,* as so many peculiar moulds, each of which bears the mark of a particular writer, who is to pour into it the whole content of his ideas, were no part of his theory. What he believed in was *Style:* that is to say, a certain absolute and unique manner of expressing a thing, in all its intensity and colour. For him the *form* was the work itself. As in living creatures, the blood, nourishing the body, determines its very contour and external aspect, just so, to his mind, the *matter,* the basis, in a work of art, imposed, necessarily, the unique, the just expression, the measure, the rhythm—the *form* in all its characteristics.

If the style be the man, in all the colour and intensity of a veritable apprehension, it will be in a real sense "impersonal."

I said, thinking of books like Victor Hugo's *Les Misérables,* that prose literature was the characteristic art of the nineteenth century, as others, thinking of its triumphs since the youth of Bach, have assigned that place to music. Music and prose literature are, in one sense, the opposite terms of art; the art of literature presenting to the imagination, through the intelligence, a range of interests, as free and various as those which music presents to it through sense. And certainly the tendency of what has been here said is to bring literature too under those conditions, by conformity to which music takes rank as the typically perfect art. If music be the ideal of all art whatever, precisely because in music

---

[16] The author of this famous phrase is Buffon.
[17] Raphael (1483–1520), Italian painter, one of the greatest of the Renaissance.
[18] Maupassant again.

it is impossible to distinguish the form from the substance or matter, the subject from the expression, then, literature, by finding its specific excellence in the absolute correspondence of the term to its import, will be but fulfilling the condition of all artistic quality in things everywhere, of all good art.

Good art, but not necessarily great art; the distinction between great art and good art depending immediately, as regards literature at all events, not on its form, but on the matter. Thackeray's *Esmond,* surely, is greater art than *Vanity Fair,*[19] by the greater dignity of its interests. It is on the quality of the matter it informs or controls, its compass, its variety, its alliance to great ends, or the depth of the note of revolt, or the largeness of hope in it, that the greatness of literary art depends, as *The Divine Comedy, Paradise Lost, Les Misérables, The English Bible,* are great art. Given the conditions I have tried to explain as constituting good art;—then, if it be devoted further to the increase of men's happiness, to the redemption of the oppressed, or the enlargement of our sympathies with each other, or to such presentment of new or old truth about ourselves and our relation to the world as may ennoble and fortify us in our sojourn here, or immediately, as with Dante, to the glory of God, it will be also great art; if, over and above those qualities I summed up as mind and soul—that colour and mystic perfume, and that reasonable structure, it has something of the soul of humanity in it, and finds its logical, its architectural place, in the great structure of human life.

---

[19] Also by Thackeray, published in 1848.

A. C. Bradley

POETRY FOR
POETRY'S SAKE

A[ndrew] C[ecil] Bradley (1851–1935) is best known for his
Shakespearean Tragedy, unquestionably the most famous critical study
of Shakespeare of the twentieth century. It was published in 1904 and
has been in print ever since. Bradley (who was the elder brother of the
influential philosopher F. H. Bradley) was educated at Cheltenham
College and at Balliol College, Oxford. He was made a fellow of
Balliol in 1874 and taught there until 1881. He then served as professor of literature at the University of Liverpool and, briefly, at the University of Glasgow. In 1901 he was elected to the Professorship of
Poetry at Oxford, a partly honorary post which at one time had been
held by Matthew Arnold. "Poetry for Poetry's Sake," first published as a
pamphlet in 1901 and later included in his *Oxford Lectures on Poetry*
(1909), was his inaugural lecture. Its closely reasoned exposition of the
relation of the subject and substance of a poem to its style is a classic
statement of what we mean, or should mean, when we speak of the
meaning of poetry. To the lecture in its published form Bradley added
an appendix of extensive notes which has been omitted.

One who, after twenty years, is restored to the University where he was
taught and first tried to teach, and who has received at the hands of his
Alma Mater an honour of which he never dreamed,[1] is tempted to speak
both of himself and of her. But I remember that you have come to listen to
my thoughts about a great subject, and not to my feelings about myself; and
of Oxford who that holds this Professorship could dare to speak, when he
recalls the exquisite verse in which one of his predecessors[2] described her
beauty, and the prose in which he gently touched on her illusions and pro-
tested that they were as nothing when set against her age-long warfare with
the Philistine?[3] How, again, remembering him and others, should I venture

[1] Election as Professor of Poetry at Oxford.

[2] Bradley refers to Matthew Arnold, who was Professor of Poetry from 1857 to 1867.

[3] The word used by Arnold in his *Culture and Anarchy* for the middle class as it
showed itself smug and conventional and indifferent to cultural and aesthetic values.

From *Oxford Lectures on Poetry,* by A. C. Bradley. London: Macmillan and Company,
Limited; New York: St. Martin's Press, Incorporated. Reprinted by permission of Macmillan and Company, Ltd., and St. Martin's Press, Inc.

to praise my predecessors? It would be pleasant to do so, and even pleasanter to me and you if, instead of lecturing, I quoted to you some of their best passages. But I could not do this for five years. Sooner or later, my own words would have to come, and the inevitable contrast. Not to sharpen it now, I will be silent concerning them also; and will only assure you that I do not forget them, or the greatness of the honour of succeeding them, or the responsibility which it entails.

The words "Poetry for poetry's sake" recall the famous phrase "Art for Art." It is far from my purpose to examine the possible meanings of that phrase, or all the questions it involves. I propose to state briefly what I understand by "Poetry for poetry's sake," and then, after guarding against one or two misapprehensions of the formula, to consider more fully a single problem connected with it. And I must premise, without attempting to justify them, certain explanations. We are to consider poetry in its essence, and apart from the flaws which in most poems accompany their poetry. We are to include in the idea of poetry the metrical form, and not to regard this as a mere accident or a mere vehicle. And, finally, poetry being poems, we are to think of a poem as it actually exists; and, without aiming here at accuracy, we may say that an actual poem is the succession of experiences—sounds, images, thoughts, emotions—through which we pass when we are reading as poetically as we can. Of course this imaginative experience—if I may use the phrase for brevity —differs with every reader and every time of reading: a poem exists in innumerable degrees. But that insurmountable fact lies in the nature of things and does not concern us now.

What then does the formula "Poetry for poetry's sake" tell us about this experience? It says, as I understand it, these things. First, this experience is an end in itself, is worth having on its own account, has an intrinsic value. Next, its *poetic* value is this intrinsic worth alone. Poetry may have also an ulterior value as a means to culture or religion; because it conveys instruction, or softens the passions, or furthers a good cause; because it brings the poet fame or money or a quiet conscience. So much the better: let it be valued for these reasons too. But its ulterior worth neither is nor can directly determine its poetic worth as a satisfying imaginative experience; and this is to be judged entirely from within. And to these two positions the formula would add, though not of necessity, a third. The consideration of ulterior ends, whether by the poet in the act of composing or by the reader in the act of experiencing, tends to lower poetic value. It does so because it tends to change the nature of poetry by taking it out of its own atmosphere. For its nature is to be not a part, nor yet a copy, of the real world (as we commonly understand that phrase), but to be a world by itself, independent, complete, autonomous; and to possess it fully you must enter that world, conform to its laws, and ignore for the time the beliefs, aims, and particular conditions which belong to you in the other world of reality.

Of the more serious misapprehensions to which these statements may give rise I will glance only at one or two. The offensive consequences often drawn from the formula "Art for Art" will be found to attach not to the doctrine that Art is an end in itself, but to the doctrine that Art is the whole or supreme end of human life. And as this latter doctrine, which seems to me absurd, is in any case quite different from the former, its consequences fall outside my subject. The formula "Poetry is an end in itself" has nothing to say on the various questions of moral judgment which arise from the fact that poetry has its place in a many-sided life. For anything it says, the intrinsic value of poetry might be so small, and its ulterior effects so mischievous, that it had better not exist. The formula only tells us that we must not place in antithesis poetry and human good, for poetry is one kind of human good; and that we must not determine the intrinsic value of this kind of good by direct reference to another. If we do, we shall find ourselves maintaining what we did not expect. If poetic value lies in the stimulation of religious feelings, *Lead, kindly Light* is no better a poem than many a tasteless version of a Psalm: if in the excitement of patriotism, why is *Scots, wha hae* superior to *We don't want to fight?* if in the mitigation of the passions, the Odes of Sappho will win but little praise: if in instruction, Armstrong's *Art of preserving Health*[4] should win much.

Again, our formula may be accused of cutting poetry away from its connection with life. And this accusation raises so huge a problem that I must ask leave to be dogmatic as well as brief. There is plenty of connection between life and poetry, but it is, so to say, a connection underground. The two may be called different forms of the same thing: one of them having (in the usual sense) reality, but seldom fully satisfying imagination; while the other offers something which satisfies imagination but has not full "reality." They are parallel developments which nowhere meet, or, if I may use loosely a word which will be serviceable later, they are analogues. Hence we understand one by help of the other, and even, in a sense, care for one because of the other; but hence also, poetry neither is life, nor, strictly speaking, a copy of it. They differ not only because one has more mass and the other a more perfect shape, but because they have different *kinds* of existence. The one touches us as beings occupying a given position in space and time, and having feelings, desires, and purposes due to that position: it appeals to imagination, but appeals to much besides. What meets us in poetry has not a position in the same series of time and space, or, if it has or had such a position, it is taken apart from much that belonged to it there; and therefore it makes no direct appeal to those feelings, desires, and purposes, but speaks only to contemplative imagination—imagination the reverse of empty or emotionless, imagination saturated with the results of "real" experience, but still contemplative. Thus, no doubt, one main reason why poetry has poetic value for us is that it presents to us in its own way something which we meet in another form in nature or life; and yet the test of its poetic value for us lies simply in the question whether it satisfies our imagination; the rest of us, our knowledge or conscience, for example, judging it only so far as they appear transmuted in our imagination. So also Shakespeare's knowledge or his moral insight, Milton's greatness of soul, Shelley's "hate of hate" and "love of love," and that desire to help men or make them happier which may have influenced a poet in hours of meditation

---

[4] The point is that the first item of each of the three pairs is superior aesthetically, as poem, whereas the second item is just as efficient in performing an extrapoetic function.

—all these have, as such, no poetical worth: they have that worth only when, passing through the unity of the poet's being, they reappear as qualities of imagination, and then are indeed mighty powers in the world of poetry.

I come to a third misapprehension, and so to my main subject. This formula, it is said, empties poetry of its meaning: it is really a doctrine of form for form's sake. "It is of no consequence what a poet says, so long as he says the thing well. The *what* is poetically indifferent: it is the *how* that counts. Matter, subject, content, substance, determines nothing; there is no subject with which poetry may not deal: the form, the treatment, is everything. Nay, more: not only is the matter indifferent, but it is the secret of Art to 'eradicate the matter by means of the form,'"—phrases and statements like these meet us everywhere in current criticism of literature and the other arts. They are the stock-in-trade of writers who understand of them little more than the fact that somehow or other they are not "bourgeois." But we find them also seriously used by writers whom we must respect, whether they are anonymous or not; something like one or another of them might be quoted, for example, from Professor Saintsbury, the late R. A. M. Stevenson,[5] Schiller, Goethe himself; and they are the watchwords of a school in the one country where Aesthetics has flourished. They come, as a rule, from men who either practise one of the arts, or, from study of it, are interested in its methods. The general reader— a being so general that I may say what I will of him—is outraged by them. He feels that he is being robbed of almost all that he cares for in a work of art. "You are asking me," he says, "to look at the Dresden Madonna[6] as if it were a Persian rug. You are telling me that the poetic value of *Hamlet* lies solely in its style and versification, and that my interest in the man and his fate is only an intellectual or moral interest. You allege that, if I want to enjoy the poetry of *Crossing the Bar,* I must not mind what Tennyson says there, but must consider solely his way of saying it. But in that case I can care no more for a poem than I do for a set of nonsense verses; and I do not believe that the authors of *Hamlet* and *Crossing the Bar* regarded their poems thus."

These antitheses of subject, matter, substance on the one side, form, treatment, handling on the other, are the field through which I especially want, in this lecture, to indicate a way. It is a field of battle; and the battle is waged for no trivial cause; but the cries of the combatants are terribly ambiguous. Those phrases of the so-called formalist may each mean five or six different things. Taken in one sense they seem to me chiefly true; taken as the general reader not unnaturally takes them, they seem to me false and mischievous. It would be absurd to pretend that I can end in a few minutes a controversy which concerns the ultimate nature of Art, and leads perhaps to problems not yet soluble; but we can at least draw some plain distinctions which, in this controversy, are too often confused.

In the first place, then, let us take "subject" in one particular sense; let us understand by it that which we have in view when, looking at the title of an un-read poem, we say that the poet has chosen this or that for his

[5] Robert Alan Mowbray Stevenson (1847–1900), art critic.
[6] Also called the "Sistine Madonna," by Raphael (1483–1520), great Renaissance Italian painter.

subject. The subject, in this sense, so far as I can discover, is generally something, real or imaginary, as it exists in the minds of fairly cultivated people. The subject of *Paradise Lost* would be the story of the Fall as that story exists in the general imagination of a Bible-reading people. The subject of Shelley's stanzas *To a Skylark* would be the ideas which arise in the mind of an educated person when, without knowing the poem, he hears the word "skylark." If the title of a poem conveys little or nothing to us, the "subject" appears to be either what we should gather by investigating the title in a dictionary or other book of the kind, or else such a brief suggestion as might be offered by a person who had read the poem, and who said, for example, that the subject of *The Ancient Mariner* was a sailor who killed an albatross and suffered for his deed.

Now the subject, in this sense (and I intend to use the word in no other), is not, as such, inside the poem, but outside it. The contents of the stanzas *To a Skylark* are not the ideas suggested by the word "skylark" to the average man; they belong to Shelley just as much as the language does. The subject, therefore, is not the matter *of* the poem at all; and its opposite is not the *form* of the poem, but the whole poem. The subject is one thing; the poem, matter and form alike, another thing. This being so, it is surely obvious that the poetic value cannot lie in the subject, but lies entirely in its opposite, the poem. How can the subject determine the value when on one and the same subject poems may be written of all degrees of merit and demerit; or when a perfect poem may be composed on a subject so slight as a pet sparrow, and, if Macaulay[7] may be trusted, a nearly worthless poem on a subject so stupendous as the omnipresence of the Deity? The "formalist" is here perfectly right. Nor is he insisting on something unimportant. He is fighting against our tendency to take the work of art as a mere copy or reminder of something already in our heads, or at the best as a suggestion of some idea as little removed as possible from the familiar. The sightseer who promenades a picture-gallery, remarking that this portrait is so like his cousin, or that landscape the very image of his birthplace, or who, after satisfying himself that one picture is about Elijah, passes on rejoicing to discover the subject, and nothing but the subject, of the next—what is he but an extreme example of this tendency? Well, but the very same tendency vitiates much of our criticism, much criticism of Shakespeare, for example, which, with all its cleverness and partial truth, still shows that the critic never passed from his own mind into Shakespeare's; and it may be traced even in so fine a critic as Coleridge, as when he dwarfs the sublime struggle of Hamlet into the image of his own unhappy weakness. Hazlitt by no means escaped its influence. Only the third of that great trio, Lamb, appears almost always to have rendered the conception of the composer.

Again, it is surely true that we cannot determine beforehand what subjects are fit for Art, or name any subject on which a good poem might not possibly be written. To divide subjects into two groups, the beautiful or elevating, and the ugly or vicious, and to judge poems according as their subjects belong to one of these groups or the other, is to fall into the same pit, to confuse

[7] Thomas Babington Macaulay (1800–1859), English historian and essayist.

with our pre-conceptions the meaning of the poet. What the thing is in the poem he is to be judged by, not by the thing as it was before he touched it; and how can we venture to say beforehand that he cannot make a true poem out of something which to us was merely alluring or dull or revolting? The question whether, having done so, he ought to publish his poem; whether the thing in the poet's work will not be still confused by the incompetent Puritan or the incompetent sensualist with the thing in *his* mind, does not touch this point: it is a further question, one of ethics, not of art. No doubt the up-holders of "Art for art's sake" will generally be in favour of the courageous course, of refusing to sacrifice the better or stronger part of the public to the weaker or worse; but their maxim in no way binds them to this view. Rossetti[8] suppressed one of the best of his sonnets, a sonnet chosen for admiration by Tennyson, himself extremely sensitive about the moral effect of poetry; suppressed it, I believe, because it was called fleshly. One may regret Rossetti's judgment and at the same time respect his scrupulousness; but in any case he judged in his capacity of citizen, not in his capacity of artist.

So far then the "formalist" appears to be right. But he goes too far, I think, if he maintains that the subject is indifferent and that all subjects are the same to poetry. And he does not prove his point by observing that a good poem might be written on a pin's head, and a bad one on the Fall of Man. That truth shows that the subject *settles* nothing, but not that it counts for nothing. The Fall of Man is really a more favourable subject than a pin's head. The Fall of Man, that is to say, offers opportunities of poetic effects wider in range and more penetrating in appeal. And the fact is that such a subject, as it exists in the general imagination, has some aesthetic value before the poet touches it. It is, as you may choose to call it, an inchoate poem or the débris of a poem. It is not an abstract idea or a bare isolated fact, but an assemblage of figures, scenes, actions, and events, which already appeal to emotional imagination; and it is already in some degree organized and formed. In spite of this a bad poet would make a bad poem on it; but then we should say he was unworthy of the subject. And we should not say this if he wrote a bad poem on a pin's head. Conversely, a good poem on a pin's head would almost certainly transform its subject far more than a good poem on the Fall of Man. It might revolutionize its subject so completely that we should say, "The subject may be a pin's head, but the substance of the poem has very little to do with it."

This brings us to another and a different antithesis. Those figures, scenes, events, that form part of the subject called the Fall of Man, are not the substance of *Paradise Lost*; but in *Paradise Lost* there are figures, scenes, and events resembling them in some degree. These, with much more of the same kind, may be described as its substance, and may then be con-trasted with the measured language of the poem, which will be called its form. Subject is the opposite not of form but of the whole poem. Substance is within the poem, and its opposite, form, is also within the poem. I am not criticizing this antithesis at present, but evidently it is quite different from the other. It is practically the distinction used in the old-fashioned criticism of

[8] Dante Gabriel Rossetti (1828–1882), English poet and painter.

epic and drama, and it flows down, not unsullied, from Aristotle. Addison, for example, in examining *Paradise Lost* considers in order the fable, the characters, and the sentiments; these will be the substance: then he considers the language, that is, the style and numbers; this will be the form. In like manner, the substance or meaning of a lyric may be distinguished from the form.

Now I believe it will be found that a large part of the controversy we are dealing with arises from a confusion between these two distinctions of substance and form, and of subject and poem. The extreme formalist lays his whole weight on the form because he thinks its opposite is the mere subject. The general reader is angry, but makes the same mistake, and gives to the subject praises that rightly belong to the substance.* I will read an example of what I mean. I can only explain the following words of a good critic by supposing that for the moment he has fallen into this confusion: "The mere matter of all poetry—to wit, the appearances of nature and the thoughts and feelings of men—being unalterable, it follows that the difference between poet and poet will depend upon the manner of each in applying language, metre, rhyme, cadence, and what not, to this invariable material." What has become here of the substance of *Paradise Lost*—the story, scenery, characters, sentiments, as they are in the poem? They have vanished clean away. Nothing is left but the form on one side, and on the other not even the subject, but a supposed invariable material, the appearances of nature and the thoughts and feelings of men. Is it surprising that the whole value should then be found in the form?

So far we have assumed that this antithesis of substance and form is valid, and that it always has one meaning. In reality it has several, but we will leave it in its present shape, and pass to the question of its validity. And this question we are compelled to raise, because we have to deal with the two contentions that the poetic value lies wholly or mainly in the substance, and that it lies wholly or mainly in the form. Now these contentions, whether false or true, may seem at least to be clear; but we shall find, I think, that they are both of them false, or both of them nonsense: false if they concern anything outside the poem, nonsense if they apply to something in it. For what do they evidently imply? They imply that there are in a poem two parts, factors, or components, a substance and a form; and that you can conceive them distinctly and separately, so that when you are speaking of the one you are not speaking of the other. Otherwise how can you ask the question, In which of them does the value lie? But really in a poem, apart from defects, there are no such factors or components; and therefore it is strictly nonsense to ask in which of them the value lies. And on the other hand, if the substance and the form referred to are not in the poem, then both the contentions are false, for its poetic value lies in itself.

---

* What is here called "substance" is what people generally mean when they use the word "subject" and insist on the value of the subject. I am not arguing against this usage, or in favour of the usage which I have adopted for the sake of clearness. It does not matter which we employ, so long as we and others know what we mean. (I use "substance" and "content" indifferently.) [Bradley's note.]

What I mean is neither new nor mysterious; and it will be clear, I believe, to any one who reads poetry poetically and who closely examines his experience. When you are reading a poem, I would ask—not analysing it, and much less criticizing it, but allowing it, as it proceeds, to make its full impression on you through the exertion of your recreating imagination—do you then apprehend and enjoy as one thing a certain meaning or substance, and as another thing certain articulate sounds, and do you somehow compound these two? Surely you do not, any more than you apprehend apart, when you see some one smile, those lines in the face which express a feeling, and the feeling that the lines express. Just as there the lines and their meaning are to you one thing, not two, so in poetry the meaning and the sounds are one: there is, if I may put it so, a resonant meaning, or a meaning resonance. If you read the line, "The sun is warm, the sky is clear," you do not experience separately the image of a warm sun and clear sky, on the one side, and certain unintelligible rhythmical sounds on the other; nor yet do you experience them together, side by side; but you experience the one *in* the other. And in like manner, when you are really reading *Hamlet,* the action and the characters are not something which you conceive apart from the words; you apprehend them from point to point *in* the words, and the words as expressions of them. Afterwards, no doubt, when you are out of the poetic experience but remember it, you may by analysis decompose this unity, and attend to a substance more or less isolated, and a form more or less isolated. But these are things in your analytic head, not in the poem, which is *poetic* experience. And if you want to have the poem again, you cannot find it by adding together these two products of decomposition; you can only find it by passing back into poetic experience. And then what you recover is no aggregate of factors, it is a unity in which you can no more separate a substance and a form than you can separate living blood and the life in the blood. This unity has, if you like, various "aspects" or "sides," but they are not factors or parts; if you try to examine one, you find it is also the other. Call them substance and form if you please, but these are not the reciprocally exclusive substance and form to which the two contentions *must* refer. They do not "agree," for they are not apart; they are one thing from different points of view, and in that sense identical. And this identity of content and form, you will say, is no accident; it is of the essence of poetry in so far as it is poetry, and of all art in so far as it is art. Just as there is in music not sound on one side and a meaning on the other, but expressive sound, and if you ask what is the meaning you can only answer by pointing to the sounds; just as in painting there is not a meaning *plus* paint, but a meaning *in* paint, or significant paint, and no man can really express the meaning in any other way than in paint and in *this* paint; so in a poem the true content and the true form neither exist nor can be imagined apart. When then you are asked whether the value of a poem lies in a substance got by decomposing the poem, and present, as such, only in reflective analysis, or whether the value lies in a form arrived at and existing in the same way, you will answer, "It lies neither in one, nor in the other, nor in any addition of them, but in the poem, where they are not."

We have then, first, an antithesis of subject and poem. This is clear and valid; and the question in which of them does the value lie is intelligible;

and its answer is, In the poem. We have next a distinction of substance and form. If the substance means ideas, images, and the like taken alone, and the form means the measured language taken by itself, this is a possible distinction, but it is a distinction of things not in the poem, and the value lies in neither of them. If substance and form mean anything *in* the poem, then each is involved in the other, and the question in which of them the value lies has no sense. No doubt you may say, speaking loosely, that in this poet or poem the aspect of substance is the more noticeable, and in that the aspect of form; and you may pursue interesting discussions on this basis, though no principle or ultimate question of value is touched by them. And apart from that question, of course, I am not denying the usefulness and necessity of the distinction. We cannot dispense with it. To consider separately the action or the characters of a play, and separately its style or versification, is both legitimate and valuable, so long as we remember what we are doing. But the true critic in speaking of these apart does not really think of them apart; the whole, the poetic experience, of which they are but aspects, is always in his mind; and he is always aiming at a richer, truer, more intense repetition of that experience. On the other hand, when the question of principle, of poetic value, is raised, these aspects *must* fall apart into components, separately conceivable; and then there arise two heresies, equally false, that the value lies in one of two things, both of which are outside the poem, and therefore where its value cannot lie.

On the heresy of the separable substance a few additional words will suffice. This heresy is seldom formulated, but perhaps some unconscious holder of it may object: "Surely the action and the characters of *Hamlet* are in the play; and surely I can retain these, though I have forgotten all the words. I admit that I do not possess the whole poem, but I possess a part, and the most important part." And I would answer: "If we are not concerned with any question of principle, I accept all that you say except the last words, which do raise such a question. Speaking loosely, I agree that the action and characters, as you perhaps conceive them, together with a great deal more, are in the poem. Even then, however, you must not claim to possess all of this kind that is in the poem; for in forgetting the words you must have lost innumerable details of the action and the characters. And, when the question of value is raised, I must insist that the action and characters, as you conceive them, are not in *Hamlet* at all. If they are, point them out. You cannot do it. What you find at any moment of that succession of experiences called *Hamlet* is words. In these words, to speak loosely again, the action and characters (more of them than you can conceive apart) are focussed; but your experience is not a combination of them, as ideas, on the one side, with certain sounds on the other; it is an experience of something in which the two are indissolubly fused. If you deny this, to be sure I can make no answer, or can only answer that I have reason to believe that you cannot read poetically, or else are misinterpreting your experience. But if you do not deny this, then you will admit that the action and characters of the poem, as you separately imagine them, are no part of it, but a product of it in your reflective imagination, a faint analogue of one aspect of it taken in detachment from the whole. Well, I do not dispute, I would even insist, that, in the case of so long a poem as *Hamlet*, it may be necessary from time to time to interrupt the poetic experience, in order to enrich it by forming such a product and dwelling on it. Nor, in a wide sense of 'poetic,' do I question the poetic value of this product, as you think of it apart from the poem. It resembles our recollections of the heroes of history or legend, who move about in our imaginations, 'forms more real than living man,' and are worth much to us though we do not remember anything they said. Our ideas and images of the 'substance' of a poem have this poetic value, and more, if they are at all adequate. But they cannot determine the poetic value of the poem, for (not to speak of the competing claims of the 'form') nothing that is outside the poem can do that, and they, as such, are outside it."*

Let us turn to the so-called form—style and versification. There is no such thing as mere form in poetry. All form is expression. Style may have indeed a certain aesthetic worth in partial abstraction from the particular matter it conveys, as in a well-built sentence you may take pleasure in the build almost apart from the meaning. Even so, style is expressive—presents to sense, for example, the order, ease, and rapidity with which ideas move in the writer's mind—but it is not expressive of the meaning of that particular sentence. And it is possible, interrupting poetic experience, to decompose it and abstract for comparatively separate consideration this nearly formal element of style. But the aesthetic value of style so taken is not considerable,† you could not read with pleasure for an hour a composition which had no other merit. And in poetic experience you never apprehend this value by itself; the style is here expressive also of a particular meaning, or rather is one aspect of that unity whose other aspect is meaning. So that what you apprehend may be called indifferently an expressed meaning or a significant form. Perhaps on this point I may in Oxford appeal to authority, that of Matthew Arnold and Walter Pater, the latter at any rate an authority whom the formalist will not despise. What is the gist of Pater's teaching about style, if it is not that in the end the one virtue of style is truth or adequacy; that the word, phrase, sentence, should express perfectly the writer's perception, feeling, image, or thought; so that, as we read a descriptive phrase of Keats's, we exclaim, "That is the thing itself"; so that, to quote Arnold, the words are "symbols equivalent with the thing symbolized," or in our technical language, a form identical with its content? Hence in true poetry it is, in strictness, impossible to express the meaning in any but its own words, or to change the words without changing the meaning. A translation of such poetry is not really the old meaning in a fresh dress; it is a new product, something like the poem, though, if one chooses to say so, more like it in the aspect of meaning than in the aspect of form.

No one who understands poetry, it seems to me, would dispute this, were it not that, falling away from his experience, or misled by theory, he takes the word "meaning" in a sense almost ludicrously inapplicable to poetry. People

---

* These remarks will hold good, *mutatis mutandis,* if by "substance" is understood the "moral" or the "idea" of a poem, although perhaps in one instance out of five thousand this may be found in so many words in the poem. [Bradley's note.]

† On the other hand, the absence, or worse than absence, of style, in this sense, is a serious matter. [Bradley's note.]

say, for instance, "steed" and "horse" have the same meaning; and in bad poetry they have, but not in poetry that *is* poetry.

> "Bring forth the horse!" The horse was brought:
> In truth he was a noble steed!

says Byron in *Mazeppa*. If the two words mean the same here, transpose them:

> "Bring forth the steed!" The steed was brought:
> In truth he was a noble horse!

and ask again if they mean the same. Or let me take a line certainly very free from "poetic diction":

> To be or not to be, that is the question.

You may say that this means the same as "What is just now occupying my attention is the comparative disadvantages of continuing to live or putting an end to myself." And for practical purposes—the purpose, for example, of a coroner—it does. But as the second version altogether misrepresents the speaker at that moment of his existence, while the first does represent him, how can they for any but a practical or logical purpose be said to have the same sense? Hamlet was well able to "unpack his heart with words," but he will not unpack it with our paraphrases.

These considerations apply equally to versification. If I take the famous line which describes how the souls of the dead stood waiting by the river, imploring a passage from Charon:[9]

> Tendebantque manus ripae ulterioris amore;

and if I translate it, "and were stretching forth their hands in longing for the further bank," the charm of the original has fled. Why has it fled? Partly (but we have dealt with that) because I have substituted for five words, and those the words of Virgil, twelve words, and those my own. In some measure because I have turned into rhythmless prose a line of verse which, as mere sound, has unusual beauty. But much more because in doing so I have also changed the *meaning* of Virgil's line. What that meaning is *I* cannot say: Virgil has said it. But I can see this much, that the translation conveys a far less vivid picture of the outstretched hands and of their remaining outstretched, and a far less poignant sense of the distance of the shore and the longing of the souls. And it does so partly because this picture and this sense are conveyed not only by the obvious meaning of the words, but through the long-drawn sound of "tendebantque," through the time occupied by the five syllables and therefore by the idea of "ulterioris," and through the identity of the long sound "or" in the penultimate syllables of "ulterioris amore"—all this, and much more, apprehended not in this analytical fashion, nor as *added* to the beauty of mere sound and to the obvious meaning, but in unity with them and so as expressive of the poetic meaning of the whole.

---

[9] In the *Aeneid*, Book VI, by Virgil (70–19 B.C.). Charon transported the souls of the dead across the river Styx into the underworld proper.

It is always so in fine poetry. The value of versification, when it is indissolubly fused with meaning, can hardly be exaggerated. The gift for feeling
it, even more perhaps than the gift for feeling the value of style, is the *specific*
gift for poetry, as distinguished from other arts. But versification, taken, as
far as possible, all by itself, has a very different worth. Some aesthetic worth
it has; how much, you may experience by reading poetry in a language of
which you do not understand a syllable. The pleasure is quite appreciable,
but it is not great; nor in actual poetic experience do you meet with it, as such,
at all. For, I repeat, it is not *added* to the pleasure of the meaning when you
read poetry that you do understand: by some mystery the music is then the
music *of* the meaning, and the two are one. However fond of versification you
might be, you would tire very soon of reading verses in Chinese; and before
long of reading Virgil and Dante if you were ignorant of their languages. But
take the music as it is *in* the poem, and there is a marvellous change. Now

> It gives a very echo to the seat
> Where love is throned;

or "carries far into your heart," almost like music itself, the sound

> Of old, unhappy, far-off things
> And battles long ago.

What then is to be said of the following sentence of the critic quoted before:
"But when any one who knows what poetry is reads—

> Our noisy years seem moments in the being
> Of the eternal silence,

he sees that, quite independently of the meaning, . . . there is one note added
to the articulate music of the world—a note that never will leave off resounding
till the eternal silence itself gulfs it"? I must think that the writer is deceiving
himself. For I could quite understand his enthusiasm, if it were an enthusiasm
for the music of the meaning; but as for the music, "quite independently of
the meaning," so far as I can hear it thus (and I doubt if any one who knows
English can quite do so), I find it gives some pleasure, but only a trifling
pleasure. And indeed I venture to doubt whether, considered as mere sound,
the words are at all exceptionally beautiful, as Virgil's line certainly is.

When poetry answers to its idea and is purely or almost purely poetic, we
find the identity of form and content; and the degree of purity attained may
be tested by the degree in which we feel it hopeless to convey the effect of a
poem or passage in any form but its own. Where the notion of doing so is simply
ludicrous, you have quintessential poetry. But a great part even of good poetry,
especially in long works, is of a mixed nature; and so we find in it no more
than a partial agreement of a form and substance which remain to some extent
distinct. This is so in many passages of Shakespeare (the greatest of poets when
he chose, but not always a conscientious poet); passages where something was
wanted for the sake of the plot, but he did not care about it or was hurried. The
conception of the passage is then distinct from the execution, and neither is
inspired. This is so also, I think, wherever we can truly speak of merely decora-

tive effect. We seem to perceive that the poet had a truth or fact—philosophical, agricultural, social—distinctly before him, and then, as we say, clothed it in metrical and coloured language. Most argumentative, didactic, or satiric poems are partly of this kind; and in imaginative poems anything which is really a mere "conceit" is mere decoration. We often deceive ourselves in this matter, for what we call decoration has often a new and genuinely poetic content of its own; but wherever there is mere decoration, we judge the poetry to be not wholly poetic. And so when Wordsworth inveighed against poetic diction, though he hurled his darts rather wildly, what he was rightly aiming at was a phraseology, not the living body of a new content, but the mere worn-out body of an old one.

In pure poetry it is otherwise. Pure poetry is not the decoration of a pre-conceived and clearly defined matter: it springs from the creative impulse of a vague imaginative mass pressing for development and definition. If the poet already knew exactly what he meant to say, why should he write the poem? The poem would in fact already be written. For only its completion can reveal, even to him, exactly what he wanted. When he began and while he was at work, he did not possess his meaning; it possessed him. It was not a fully formed soul asking for a body: it was an inchoate soul in the inchoate body of perhaps two or three vague ideas and a few scattered phrases. The growing of this body into its full stature and perfect shape was the same thing as the gradual self-definition of the meaning. And this is the reason why such poems strike us as creations, not manufactures, and have the magical effect which mere decoration cannot produce. This is also the reason why, if we insist on asking for the meaning of such a poem, we can only be answered "It means itself."

And so at last I may explain why I have troubled myself and you with what may seem an arid controversy about mere words. It is not so. These heresies which would make poetry a compound of two factors—a matter common to it with the merest prose, *plus* a poetic form, as the one heresy says: a poetical substance *plus* a negligible form, as the other says—are not only untrue, they are injurious to the dignity of poetry. In an age already inclined to shrink from those higher realms where poetry touches religion and philosophy, the formalist heresy encourages men to taste poetry as they would a fine wine, which has indeed an aesthetic value, but a small one. And then the natural man, finding an empty form, hurls into it the matter of cheap pathos, rancid sentiment, vulgar humour, bare lust, ravenous vanity—everything which, in Schiller's phrase,* the form should extirpate, but which no mere form can extirpate. And the other heresy—which is indeed rather a practice than a creed—encourages us in the habit so dear to us of putting our own thoughts or fancies into the place of the poet's creation. What he meant by *Hamlet*, or the *Ode to a Nightingale*, or *Abt Vogler*,[10] we say, is this or that which we knew already; and so we lose what he had to tell us. But he meant what he said, and said what he meant.

Poetry in this matter is not, as good critics of painting and music often affirm, different from the others arts; in all of them the content is one thing with

---

* Not that to Schiller "form" meant mere style and versification. [Bradley's note.]
[10] A dramatic monologue by Robert Browning, spoken by "Abt Volger," a German organ virtuoso, composer, founder of musical institutes (1749–1814).

the form. What Beethoven meant by his symphony, or Turner[11] by his picture, was not something which you can name, but the picture and the symphony. Meaning they have, but *what* meaning can be said in no language but their own: and we know this, though some strange delusion makes us think the meaning has less worth because we cannot put it into words. Well, it is just the same with poetry. But because poetry is words, we vainly fancy that some other words than its own will express its meaning. And they will do so no more—or, if you like to speak loosely, only a trifle more—than words will express the meaning of the Dresden Madonna. Something a little like it they may indeed express. And we may find analogues of the meaning of poetry outside it, which may help us to appropriate it. The other arts, the best ideas of philosophy or religion, much that nature and life offer us or force upon us, are akin to it. But they are only akin. Nor is it the expression of them. Poetry does not present to imagination our highest knowledge or belief, and much less our dreams and opinions; but it, content and form in unity, embodies in its own irreplaceable way something which embodies itself also in other irreplaceable ways, such as philosophy or religion. And just as each of these gives a satisfaction which the other cannot possibly give, so we find in poetry, which cannot satisfy the needs they meet, that which by their natures they cannot afford us. But we shall not find it fully if we look for something else.

And now, when all is said, the question will still recur, though now in quite another sense, What does poetry mean? This unique expression, which cannot be replaced by any other, still seems to be trying to express something beyond itself. And this, we feel, is also what the other arts, and religion, and philosophy are trying to express: and that is what impels us to seek in vain to translate the one into the other. About the best poetry, and not only the best, there floats an atmosphere of infinite suggestion. The poet speaks to us of one thing, but in this one thing there seems to lurk the secret of all. He said what he meant, but his meaning seems to beckon away beyond itself, or rather to expand into something boundless which is only focussed in it; something also which, we feel, would satisfy not only the imagination, but the whole of us; that something within us, and without, which everywhere

> makes us seem
> To patch up fragments of a dream,
> Part of which comes true, and part
> Beats and trembles in the heart.

Those who are susceptible to this effect of poetry find it not only, perhaps not most, in the ideals which she has sometimes described, but in a child's song by Christina Rossetti[12] about a mere crown of wind-flowers, and in tragedies like *Lear*, where the sun seems to have set for ever. They hear this spirit murmuring its undertone through the *Aeneid*, and catch its voice in the song of Keats's nightingale, and its light upon the figures on the Urn, and it pierces them no less in Shelley's hopeless lament, *O world, O life, O time,* than in the rapturous

---

[11] J. M. W. Turner (1775–1851), English landscape painter.
[12] Christina Georgina Rossetti (1830–1894), English poet, sister of Dante Gabriel Rossetti.

ecstasy of his *Life of Life*. This all-embracing perfection cannot be expressed in poetic words or words of any kind, nor yet in music or in colour, but the suggestion of it is in much poetry, if not all, and poetry has in this suggestion, this "meaning," a great part of its value. We do it wrong, and we defeat our own purposes, when we try to bend it to them:

> We do it wrong, being so majestical,
> To offer it the show of violence;
> For it is as the air invulnerable,
> And our vain blows malicious mockery.

It is a spirit. It comes we know not whence. It will not speak at our bidding, nor answer in our language. It is not our servant; it is our master.

W. B. Yeats

THE SYMBOLISM OF POETRY

William Butler Yeats (1865–1939) is one of the great poets of the modern age; of his contemporaries writing in English only T. S. Eliot challenges his preeminence. He was born of an Anglo-Irish family in Dublin. His mother was a woman of unworldly, traditional mind, and from her he derived his passion for the lore and literature of the folk and his readiness to give credence to the supernatural. His father, John Butler Yeats (1839–1922), was of an opposite mental disposition. A gifted though not successful painter, he was a man of the liveliest intelligence; his devotion to rationalism did nothing to inhibit his love of poetry, and he had, as his son makes plain in his recollections of him, the gift of talking well about it. In his late years the elder Yeats emigrated to America, where he had a notable influence on the generation of American poets who were beginning to make their reputations around 1912; his published letters, especially those to his famous son, attest to the cogency and vivacity of his ideas about poetry. Both parents have their part in the son's essay printed here. In his stern correction of the common view—he implies it is the vulgar view—that the poet writes out of nothing but instinct and impulse, without a formulated theory of what he is undertaking to do, Yeats in effect commemorates his father, from whom he had first learned to speculate about poetry. And by the intensity of feeling for symbolism that he expresses, Yeats is at one with his mother.

Symbolism as an organized "movement" of French poetry, with a manifesto and a program, took its rise in France in the 1880s, deriving its impetus from the practice of poets of a somewhat earlier date, Baudelaire, Verlaine, Rimbaud, and Mallarmé. As an aesthetic doctrine, Symbolism sought to enhance the evocative power of poetry and to communicate emotions that were not susceptible to more explicit modes of expression. Exactly what a symbol is in literature makes a vexed question for criticism, but the following explanation of the method of symbolism by G. Wilson Knight (see pp. 483 ff.) will provide at least some illumination: "The word 'symbolism' as used in current literary and dramatic disquisition is not covered by the dictionary definition of it as a *conventional* sign. Rather it means some effect, person, object, or descriptive passage which automatically radiates significances flowing from that effect's intrinsic nature. The meanings are not imposed by a convention, as they may be in allegory, but spring inevitably from the symbol used" (Article SYMBOLISM in *A Shakespeare Dictionary*, edited by O. J. Campbell). Professor Knight goes on to speak of the extent to which symbolism implies the supernatural. For Yeats this implication was very strong, and, under the influence of certain hermetic cults, had for him the force of a doctrine.

I

Symbolism, as seen in the writers of our day, would have no value if it were not seen also, under one "disguise or another, in every great imaginative writer," writes Mr. Arthur Symons in *The Symbolist Movement in Literature*, a subtle book which I cannot praise as I would, because it has been dedicated to me; and he goes on to show how many profound writers have in the last few years sought for a philosophy of poetry in the doctrine of symbolism, and how even in countries where it is almost scandalous to seek for any philosophy of poetry, new writers are following them in their search. We do not know what the writers of ancient times talked of among themselves, and one bull is all that remains of Shakespeare's talk, who was on the edge of modern times; and the journalist is convinced, it seems, that they talked of wine and women and politics, but never about their art, or never quite seriously about their art. He is certain that no one who had a philosophy of his art, or a theory of how he should write, has ever made a work of art, that people have no imagination who do not write without forethought and afterthought as he writes his own articles. He says this with enthusiasm, because he has heard it at so many comfortable dinner-tables, where some one had mentioned through carelessness, or foolish zeal, a book whose difficulty had offended indolence, or a man who had not forgotten that beauty is an accusation. Those formulas and generalisations, in which a hidden sergeant has drilled the ideas of journalists and through them the ideas of all but all the modern world, have created in their turn a forgetfulness like that of soldiers in battle, so that journalists and their readers have forgotten, among many like events, that Wagner[1] spent seven years arranging and explaining his ideas before he began his most characteristic music; that opera, and with it modern music, arose from certain talks at the house of one Giovanni Bardi of Florence; and that the Pléiade[2] laid the foundations of modern French literature with a pamphlet. Goethe has said, "a poet needs all philosophy, but he must keep it out of his work," though that is not always necessary; and almost certainly no great art, outside England, where journalists are more powerful and ideas less plentiful than elsewhere, has arisen without a great criticism, for its herald or its interpreter and protector, and it may be for this reason that great art, now that vulgarity has armed itself and multiplied itself, is perhaps dead in England.

[1] Richard Wagner (1813–1883), German composer.
[2] A group of seven French poets who took the name *Pléiade* (in 1553) after seven tragic poets who wrote in ancient Alexandria. The French seven encouraged poets to take certain classical and Italian works as their models.

All writers, all artists of any kind, in so far as they have had any philosophical or critical power, perhaps just in so far as they have been deliberate artists at all, have had some philosophy, some criticism of their art; and it has often been this philosophy, or this criticism, that has evoked their most startling inspiration, calling into outer life some portion of the divine life, or of the buried reality, which could alone extinguish in the emotions what their philosophy or their criticism would extinguish in the intellect. They have sought for no new thing, it may be, but only to understand and to copy the pure inspiration of early times, but because the divine life wars upon our outer life, and must needs change its weapons and its movements as we change ours, inspiration has come to them in beautiful startling shapes. The scientific movement brought with it a literature which was always tending to lose itself in externalities of all kinds, in opinion, in declamation, in picturesque writing, in word-painting, or in what Mr. Symons has called an attempt "to build in brick and mortar inside the covers of a book"; and now writers have begun to dwell upon the element of evocation, of suggestion, upon what we call the symbolism in great writers.

II

In "Symbolism in Painting,"[3] I tried to describe the element of symbolism that is in pictures and sculpture, and described a little the symbolism of poetry, but did not describe at all the continuous indefinable symbolism which is the substance of all style.

There are no lines with more melancholy beauty than these by Burns:—

> The white moon is setting behind the white wave,
> And Time is setting with me, O![4]

and these lines are perfectly symbolical. Take from them the whiteness of the moon and of the wave, whose relation to the setting of Time is too subtle for the intellect, and you take from them their beauty. But, when all are together, moon and wave and whiteness and setting Time and the last melancholy cry, they evoke an emotion which cannot be evoked by any other arrangement of colours and sounds and forms. We may call this metaphorical writing, but it is better to call it symbolical writing, because metaphors are not profound enough to be moving, when they are not symbols, and when they are symbols they are the most perfect of all, because the most subtle, outside of pure sound, and through them one can best find out what symbols are. If one begins the reverie with any beautiful lines that one can remember, one finds they are like those by Burns. Begin with this line by Blake:—

> The gay fishes on the wave when the moon sucks up the dew;[5]

or these lines py Nashe:—

[3] An essay that first appeared as an introduction to *A Book of Images,* drawn by W. T. Horton, published in 1898.
[4] From "Open the Door to Me, O"; Burns' first line reads "The wan moon is setting ayont the white wave."
[5] From Blake's "Europe; a Prophecy," 1794.

> Brightness falls from the air,
> Queens have died young and fair,
> Dust hath closed Helen's eye;[6]

or these lines by Shakespeare: —

> Timon hath made his everlasting mansion
> Upon the beached verge of the salt flood;
> Who once a day with his embossed froth
> The turbulent surge shall cover;[7]

or take some line that is quite simple, that gets its beauty from its place in a story, and see how it flickers with the light of the many symbols that have given the story its beauty, as a sword-blade may flicker with the light of burning towers.

All sounds, all colours, all forms, either because of their preordained energies or because of long association, evoke indefinable and yet precise emotions, or, as I prefer to think, call down among us certain disembodied powers, whose footsteps over our hearts we call emotions; and when sound, and colour, and form are in a musical relation, a beautiful relation to one another, they become, as it were, one sound, one colour, one form, and evoke an emotion that is made out of their distinct evocations and yet is one emotion. The same relation exists between all portions of every work of art, whether it be an epic or a song, and the more perfect it is, and the more various and numerous the elements that have flowed into its perfection, the more powerful will be the emotion, the power, the god it calls among us. Because an emotion does not exist, or does not become perceptible and active among us, till it has found its expression, in colour or in sound or in form, or in all of these, and because no two modulations or arrangements of these evoke the same emotion, poets and painters and musicians, and in a less degree because their effects are momentary, day and night and cloud and shadow, are continually making and unmaking mankind. It is indeed only those things which seem useless or very feeble that have any power, and all those things that seem useful or strong, armies, moving wheels, modes of architecture, modes of government, speculations of the reason, would have been a little different if some mind long ago had not given itself to some emotion, as a woman gives herself to her lover, and shaped sounds or colours or forms, or all of these, into a musical relation, that their emotion might live in other minds. A little lyric evokes an emotion, and this emotion gathers others about it and melts into their being in the making of some great epic; and at last, needing an always less delicate body, or symbol, as it grows more powerful, it flows out, with all it has gathered, among the blind instincts of daily life, where it moves a power within powers, as one sees ring within ring in the stem of an old tree. This is maybe what Arthur O'Shaughnessy[8] meant when he made his poets say they had built Nineveh with their sighing; and I am certainly never sure, when I hear of some war, or of some religious excitement, or of some new manufacture, or of anything else that fills the ear

[6] From "In Time of Pestilence," by Thomas Nashe (1567–1601).
[7] *Timon of Athens*, V. i. 216–219.
[8] Arthur W. E. O'Shaughnessy (1844–1881), Pre-Raphaelite poet.

of the world, that it has not all happened because of something that a boy piped in Thessaly.[9] I remember once telling a seeress to ask one among the gods who, as she believed, were standing about her in their symbolic bodies, what would come of a charming but seeming trivial labour of a friend, and the form answering, "the devastation of peoples and the overwhelming of cities." I doubt indeed if the crude circumstance of the world, which seems to create all our emotions, does more than reflect, as in multiplying mirrors, the emotions that have come to solitary men in moments of poetical contemplation; or that love itself would be more than an animal hunger but for the poet and his shadow the priest, for unless we believe that outer things are the reality, we must believe that the gross is the shadow of the subtle, that things are wise before they become foolish, and secret before they cry out in the market-place. Solitary men in moments of contemplation receive, as I think, the creative impulse from the lowest of the Nine Hierarchies,[10] and so make and unmake mankind, and even the world itself, for does not "the eye altering alter all"?

> Our towns are copied fragments from our breast;
> And all man's Babylons strive but to impart
> The grandeurs of his Babylonian heart.

III

The purpose of rhythm, it has always seemed to me, is to prolong the moment of contemplation, the moment when we are both asleep and awake, which is the one moment of creation, by hushing us with an alluring monotony, while it holds us waking by variety, to keep us in that state of perhaps real trance, in which the mind liberated from the pressure of the will is unfolded in symbols. If certain sensitive persons listen persistently to the ticking of a watch, or gaze persistently on the monotonous flashing of a light, they fall into the hypnotic trance; and rhythm is but the ticking of a watch made softer, that one must needs listen, and various, that one may not be swept beyond memory or grow weary of listening; while the patterns of the artist are but the monotonous flash woven to take the eyes in a subtler enchantment. I have heard in meditation voices that were forgotten the moment they had spoken; and I have been swept, when in more profound meditation, beyond all memory but of those things that came from beyond the threshold of waking life. I was writing once at a very symbolical and abstract poem, when my pen fell on the ground; and as I stooped to pick it up, I remembered some fantastic adventure that yet did not seem fantastic, and then another like adventure, and when I asked myself when these things had happened, I found that I was remembering my dreams for

[9] Largest ancient region of Greece, a common setting of the literature of pastoral romance.

[10] Yeats, who was much interested in theosophy and the occult, was co-founder of the Dublin Hermetic Society in 1885. According to a belief common throughout educated Europe until the sixteenth century and maintained either literally or symbolically by theosophists, the universe consisted of nine concentric spheres, each with a presiding spirit, the lowest sphere being that of the moon, traditional source of poetic inspiration.

many nights. I tried to remember what I had done the day before, and then what I had done that morning; but all my waking life had perished from me, and it was only after a struggle that I came to remember it again, and as I did so that more powerful and startling life perished in its turn. Had my pen not fallen on the ground and so made me turn from the images that I was weaving into verse, I would never have known that meditation had become trance, for I would have been like one who does not know that he is passing through a wood because his eyes are on the pathway. So I think that in the making and in the understanding of a work of art, and the more easily if it is full of patterns and symbols and music, we are lured to the threshold of sleep, and it may be far beyond it, without knowing that we have ever set our feet upon the steps of horn or of ivory.

IV

Besides emotional symbols, symbols that evoke emotions alone,—and in this sense all alluring or hateful things are symbols, although their relations with one another are too subtle to delight us fully, away from rhythm and pattern,— there are intellectual symbols, symbols that evoke ideas alone, or ideas mingled with emotions; and outside the very definite traditions of mysticism and the less definite criticism of certain modern poets, these alone are called symbols. Most things belong to one or another kind, according to the way we speak of them and the companions we give them, for symbols, associated with ideas that are more than fragments of the shadows thrown upon the intellect by the emotions they evoke, are the playthings of the allegorist or the pedant, and soon pass away. If I say "white" or "purple" in an ordinary line of poetry, they evoke emotions so exclusively that I cannot say why they move me; but if I bring them into the same sentence with such obvious intellectual symbols as a cross or a crown of thorns, I think of purity and sovereignty. Furthermore, innumerable meanings, which are held to "white" or to "purple" by bonds of subtle suggestion, and alike in the emotions and in the intellect, move visibly through my mind, and move invisibly beyond the threshold of sleep, casting lights and shadows of an indefinable wisdom on what had seemed before, it may be, but sterility and noisy violence. It is the intellect that decides where the reader shall ponder over the procession of the symbols, and if the symbols are merely emotional, he gazes from amid the accidents and destinies of the world; but if the symbols are intellectual too, he becomes himself a part of pure intellect, and he is himself mingled with the procession. If I watch a rushy pool in the moonlight, my emotion at its beauty is mixed with memories of the man that I have seen ploughing by its margin, or of the lovers I saw there a night ago; but if I look at the moon herself and remember any of her ancient names and meanings, I move among divine people, and things that have shaken off our mortality, the tower of ivory, the queen of waters, the shining stag among enchanted woods, the white hare sitting upon the hilltop, the fool of Faery with his shining cup full of dreams, and it may be "make a friend of one of these images of wonder," and "meet the Lord in the air." So, too, if one is moved by Shakespeare, who is content with emotional symbols that he may come the nearer to our sympathy, one is mixed with the whole spectacle of the world; while if one is moved by Dante, or by the myth of Demeter,[11] one is mixed into the shadow of God or of a goddess. So, too, one is furthest from symbols when one is busy doing this or that, but the soul moves among symbols and unfolds in symbols when trance, or madness, or deep meditation has withdrawn it from every impulse but its own. "I then saw," wrote Gérard de Nerval[12] of his madness, "vaguely drifting into form, plastic images of antiquity, which outlined themselves, became definite, and seemed to represent symbols of which I only seized the idea with difficulty." In an earlier time he would have been of that multitude whose souls austerity withdrew, even more perfectly than madness could withdraw his soul, from hope and memory, from desire and regret, that they might reveal those processions of symbols that men bow to before altars, and woo with incense and offerings. But being of our time, he has been like Maeterlinck,[13] like Villiers de l'Isle-Adam[14] in *Axël*, like all who are preoccupied with intellectual symbols in our time, a foreshadower of the new sacred book, of which all the arts, as somebody has said, are beginning to dream. How can the arts overcome the slow dying of men's hearts that we call the progress of the world, and lay their hands upon men's heartstrings again, without becoming the garment of religion as in old times?

V

If people were to accept the theory that poetry moves us because of its symbolism, what change should one look for in the manner of our poetry? A return to the way of our fathers, a casting out of descriptions of nature for the sake of nature, of the moral law for the sake of the moral law, a casting out of all anecdotes and of that brooding over scientific opinion that so often extinguished the central flame in Tennyson, and of that vehemence that would make us do or not do certain things; or, in other words, we should come to understand that the beryl stone was enchanted by our fathers that it might unfold the pictures in its heart, and not to mirror our own excited faces, or the boughs waving outside the window. With this change of substance, this return to imagination, this understanding that the laws of art, which are the hidden laws of the world, can alone bind the imagination, would come a change of style, and we would cast out of serious poetry those energetic rhythms, as of a man running, which are the invention of the will with its eyes always on something to be done or undone; and we would seek out those wavering, meditative, organic rhythms, which are the embodiment of the

[11] In Greek mythology, the goddess of harvest and fertility. When Hades abducted her daughter Persephone, she made the earth barren in grief and wrath, until Hades agreed to allow Persephone to spend two-thirds of every year above-ground with her mother.

[12] Pseudonym of Gerard Labrunie (1808–1855), one of the writers discussed in Symons' *The Symbolist Movement in Literature*.

[13] Maurice Maeterlinck (1862–1949), Belgian author who wrote in French, winner of Nobel Prize in 1911. Also discussed by Symons.

[14] Philippe Auguste Mathias, Comte de Villiers de l'Isle-Adam (1838–1889), poet and author of the visionary drama *Axël*. Also discussed by Symons.

imagination, that neither desires nor hates, because it has done with time, and only wishes to gaze upon some reality, some beauty; nor would it be any longer possible for anybody to deny the importance of form, in all its kinds, for although you can expound an opinion, or describe a thing, when your words are not quite well chosen, you cannot give a body to something that moves beyond the senses, unless your words are as subtle, as complex, as full of mysterious life, as the body of a flower or of a woman. The form of sincere poetry, unlike the form of the "popular poetry," may indeed be sometimes obscure, or ungrammatical as in some of the best of the *Songs of Innocence and Experience*,[15] but it must have the perfections that escape analysis, the subtleties that have a new meaning every day, and it must have all this whether it be but a little song made out of a moment of dreamy indolence, or some great epic made out of the dreams of one poet and of a hundred generations whose hands were never weary of the sword.

---

[15] *The Songs of Innocence* (1789) and *The Songs of Experience* (1794), by William Blake.

Ezra Pound

THE SERIOUS ARTIST

Ezra Pound was born in 1885 in Hailey, Idaho. After his graduation
from Hamilton College he attended the University of Pennsylvania
where he studied Romance languages, taking the degree of Master of
Arts in 1906. Appointed to an instructorship in French and Spanish at
Wabash College, he was dismissed from the post after one semester in
consequence of the scandal caused by his having given a night's lodging
to a stranded burlesque dancer. Shortly after this episode, he left for
Europe and was soon at the center of a number of *avant-garde* movements. His early poems, critical essays, and translations exerted a decisive influence on the artistic theory and practice of his contemporaries
and his driving organizational energies brought him an ultimate authority in the busy world of what was then called "experimental" literature. He became foreign editor of *Poetry,* London editor of the *Chicago
Little Review,* Paris correspondent for *The Dial,* co-editor of *Blast,* and
founder and editor of *Exile.* Horace Gregory and Marya Zaturenska
remark in their *History of American Poetry* that "Pound's influence can
be traced through the files of at least fifty 'little' magazines published
on both sides of the Atlantic from 1916 to 1939." It is fair to say that
Pound, more than any other single person, is responsible for the direction taken by *avant-garde* poetry in the English-speaking countries, in
Scandinavia, and in South America.

During the Twenties Mr. Pound turned his attention to economic
and political matters. He characterized his views as those of a "Jeffer-
sonian Republican" and, to the dismay of that large part of the literary
world which held Fascism in abhorrence, he announced that he had
found "the heritage of Jefferson" in Mussolini's Italy. He maintained
his residence in Italy during World War II and broadcast from Rome
to American troops what he called "personal propaganda in support of
the U.S. Constitution." After the war he was indicted for treason and
brought to the United States for trial, but was judged mentally incompetent to prepare a defense and committed to St. Elizabeth's Hospital in Washington, D.C. In 1958 the indictment was withdrawn and
he was released. He returned to Italy, where he has since lived in
retirement.

The bulk of Pound's poetry may be found in *Personae: The
Collected Shorter Poems of Ezra Pound* (1952), *The Translations of
Ezra Pound* (1953), *Thrones* (1960), and *The Cantos (1-95)* (1965).
The last two volumes contain all that has been published in book form

of Pound's *Cantos,* a long discontinuous epic poem. *The Letters of Ezra Pound, 1907–1941,* edited by D. D. Paige, were published in 1950. For Pound's criticism, see *The Spirit of Romance* (1910), *ABC of Reading* (1934), *Make it New* (1934), and *Literary Essays of Ezra Pound,* ed. T. S. Eliot (1954), from which "The Serious Artist" (first published in the *Egoist* in 1913) is reprinted.

I

It is curious that one should be asked to rewrite Sidney's *Defence of Poesy* in the year of grace 1913.[1] During the intervening centuries, and before them, other centres of civilization had decided that good art was a blessing and that bad art was criminal, and they had spent some time and thought in trying to find means whereby to distinguish the true art from the sham. But in England now, in the age of Gosse[2] as in the age of Gosson we are asked if the arts are moral. We are asked to define the relation of the arts to economics, we are asked what position the arts are to hold in the ideal republic. And it is obviously the opinion of many people less objectionable than the Sydney Webbs[3] than the arts had better not exist at all.

I take no great pleasure in writing prose about æsthetic. I think one work of art is worth forty prefaces and as many apologiæ. Nevertheless I have been questioned earnestly and by a person certainly of good will. It is as if one said to me: what is the use of open spaces in this city, what is the use of rose-trees and why do you wish to plant trees and lay out parks and gardens? There are some who do not take delight in these things. The rose springs fairest from some buried Cæsar's throat and the dogwood with its flower of four petals (our dogwood, not the tree you call by that name) is grown from the heart of Aucassin,[4] or perhaps this is only fancy. Let us pursue the matter in ethic.

It is obvious that ethics are based on the nature of man, just as it is obvious that civics are based upon the nature of men when living together in groups.

It is obvious that the good of the greatest number cannot be attained until we know in some sort of what that good must consist. In other words we must know what sort of an animal man is, before we can contrive his maximum happiness, or before we can decide what percentage of that happiness he can have without causing too great a percentage of unhappiness to those about him.

The arts, literature, poesy, are a science, just as chemistry is a science. Their subject is man, mankind and the individual. The subject of chemistry is matter considered as to its composition.

The arts give us a great percentage of the lasting and unassailable data re-

[1] Sir Philip Sidney (1554–1586) wrote his *The Defense of Poesy* (1595) in rebuttal to Stephen Gosson's *The School of Abuse.*
[2] Sir Edmund Gosse (1849–1928), English biographer and critic.
[3] Beatrice (1858–1943) and Sidney (1859–1947) Webb, English socialists, economists, and reformers.
[4] The hero of *Aucassin et Nicolette,* a thirteenth-century French *chante-fable* or song-story. In many tales flowers grow from the hearts of dead lovers, but Aucassin and Nicolette live happily ever after.

garding the nature of man, of immaterial man, of man considered as a thinking and sentient creature. They begin where the science of medicine leaves off or rather they overlap that science. The borders of the two arts overcross.

From medicine we learn that man thrives best when duly washed, aired and sunned. From the arts we learn that man is whimsical, that one man differs from another. That men differ among themselves as leaves upon trees differ. That they do not resemble each other as do buttons cut by machine.

From the arts also we learn in what ways man resembles and in what way he differs from certain other animals. We learn that certain men are often more akin to certain animals than they are to other men of different composition. We learn that all men do not desire the same things and that it would therefore be inequitable to give to all men two acres and a cow.

It would be manifestly inequitable to treat the ostrich and the polar bear in the same fashion, granted that it is not unjust to have them pent up where you can treat them at all.

An ethic based on a belief that men are different from what they are is manifestly stupid. It is stupid to apply such an ethic as it is to apply laws and morals designed for a nomadic tribe, or for a tribe in the state of barbarism, to a people crowded into the slums of a modern metropolis. Thus in the tribe it is well to beget children, for the more strong male children you have in the tribe the less likely you are to be bashed on the head by males of the neighbouring tribes, and the more female children the more rapidly the tribe will increase. Conversely it is a crime rather worse than murder to beget children in a slum, to beget children for whom no fitting provision is made, either as touching their physical or economic wellbeing. The increase not only afflicts the child born but the increasing number of the poor keeps down the wage. On this count the bishop of London, as an encourager of this sort of increase, is a criminal of a type rather lower and rather more detestable than the souteneur.[5]

I cite this as one example of inequity persisting because of a continued refusal to consider a code devised for one state of society, in its (the code's) relation to a different state of society. It is as if, in physics or engineering, we refused to consider a force designed to affect one mass, in its relation (i.e. the force's) to another mass wholly differing, or in some notable way differing, from the first mass.

As inequities can exist because of refusals to consider the actualities of a law in relation to a social condition, so can inequities exist through refusal to consider the actualities of the composition of the masses, or of the individuals to which they are applied.

If all men desired above everything else two acres and a cow, obviously the perfect state would be that state which gave to each man two acres and a cow.

If any science save the arts were able more precisely to determine what the individual does not actually desire, then that science would be of more use in providing the data for ethics.

In the like manner, if any sciences save medicine and chemistry were more able to determine what things were compatible with physical wellbeing, then those sciences would be of more value for providing the data of hygiene.

---

[5] That is, pimp.

This brings us to the immorality of bad art. Bad art is inaccurate art. It is art that makes false reports. If a scientist falsifies a report either deliberately or through negligence we consider him as either a criminal or a bad scientist according to the enormity of his offence, and he is punished or despised accordingly.

If he falsifies the reports of a maternity hospital in order to retain his position and get profit and advancement from the city board, he may escape detection. If he declines to make such falsification he may lose financial rewards, and in either case his baseness or his pluck may pass unknown and unnoticed save by a very few people. Nevertheless one does not have to argue his case. The layman knows soon enough on hearing it whether the physician is to be blamed or praised.

If an artist falsifies his report as to the nature of man, as to his own nature, as to the nature of his ideal of the perfect, as to the nature of his ideal of this, that or the other, of god, if god exist, of the life force, of the nature of good and evil, if good and evil exist, of the force with which he believes or disbelieves this, that or the other, of the degree in which he suffers or is made glad; if the artist falsifies his reports on these matters or on any other matter in order that he may conform to the taste of his time, to the proprieties of a sovereign, to the conveniences of a preconceived code of ethics, then that artist lies. If he lies out of deliberate will to lie, if he lies out of carelessness, out of laziness, out of cowardice, out of any sort of negligence whatsoever, he nevertheless lies and he should be punished or despised in proportion to the seriousness of his offence. His offence is of the same nature as the physician's and according to his position and the nature of his lie he is responsible for future oppressions and for future misconceptions. Albeit his lies are known to only a few, or his truth-telling to only a few. Albeit he may pass without censure for one and without praise for the other. Albeit he can only be punished on the plane of his crime and by nothing save the contempt of those who know of his crime. Perhaps it is caddishness rather than crime. However there is perhaps nothing worse for a man than to know that he is a cur and to know that someone else, if only one person, knows it.

We distinguish very clearly between the physician who is doing his best for a patient, who is using drugs in which he believes, or who is in a wilderness, let us say, where the patient can get no other medical aid. We distinguish, I say, very clearly between the failure of such a physician, and the act of that physician, who ignorant of the patient's disease, being in reach of more skilful physicians, deliberately denies an ignorance of which he is quite conscious, refuses to consult other physicians, tries to prevent the patient's having access to more skilful physicians, or deliberately tortures the patient for his own ends.

One does not need to read black print to learn this ethical fact about physicians. Yet it takes a deal of talking to convince a layman that bad art is "immoral." And that good art however "immoral" it is, is wholly a thing of virtue. Purely and simply that good art can NOT be immoral. By good art I meant art that bears true witness, I mean the art that is most precise. You can be wholly precise in representing a vagueness. You can be wholly a liar in pretending that the particular vegueness was precise in its outline. If you cannot understand this with regard to poetry, consider the matter in terms of painting.

If you have forgotten my statement that the arts bear witness and define for us the inner nature and conditions of man, consider the Victory of Samothrace[6] and the Taj of Agra.[7] The man who carved the one and the man who designed the other may either or both of them have looked like an ape, or like two apes respectively. They may have looked like other apelike or swinelike men. We have the Victory and the Taj to witness that there was something within them differing from the contents of apes and of the other swinelike men. Thus we learn that humanity is a species or genus of animals capable of a variation that will produce the desire for a Taj or a Victory, and moreover capable of effecting that Taj or Victory in stone. We know from other testimony of the arts and from ourselves that the desire often overshoots the power of efficient presentation; we therefore conclude that other members of the race may have desired to effect a Taj or a Victory. We even suppose that men have desired to effect more beautiful things although few of us are capable of forming any precise mental image of things, in their particular way, more beautiful than this statue or this building. So difficult is this that no one has yet been able to effect a restoration for the missing head of the Victory. At least no one has done so in stone, so far as I know. Doubtless many people have stood opposite the statue and made such heads in their imagination.

As there are in medicine the art of diagnosis and the art of cure, so in the arts, so in the particular arts of poetry and of literature, there is the art of diagnosis and there is the art of cure. They call one the cult of ugliness and the other the cult of beauty.

The cult of beauty is the hygiene, it is sun, air and the sea and the rain and the lake bathing. The cult of ugliness, Villon, Baudelaire, Corbière, Beardsley are diagnosis.[8] Flaubert is diagnosis.[8] Satire, if we are to ride this metaphor to staggers, satire is surgery, insertions and amputations.

Beauty in art reminds one what is worth while. I am not now speaking of shams. I mean beauty, not slither, not sentimentalizing about beauty, not telling people that beauty is the proper and respectable thing. I mean beauty. You don't argue about an April wind, you feel bucked up when you meet it. You feel bucked up when you come on a swift moving thought in Plato or on a fine line in a statue.

Even this pother about gods reminds one that something is worth while. Satire reminds one that certain things are not worth while. It draws one to consider time wasted.

The cult of beauty and the delineation of ugliness are not in mutual opposition.

[6] Statute of Nike, goddess of victory, now in the Louvre.

[7] The Taj Mahal, located in Agra, in North India, was designed by a Turkish architect for the emperor Shah Jehan.

[8] François Villon (c. 1431–1463), French poet; Charles Baudelaire (1821–1867), French poet, who, like Villon, used the grotesque, the squalid, the disreputable as subjects for his poetry; Édouard Corbière (1845–1875), French poet; Aubrey Beardsley (1872–1898), English illustrator associated with the "Decadent" movement of the 1890s; Gustave Flaubert (1821–1880), often cited by Pound as the novelist's novelist.

II

I have said that the arts give us our best data for determining what sort of creature man is. As our treatment of man must be determined by our knowledge or conception of what man is, the arts provide data for ethics.

These data are sound and the data of generalizing psychologists and social theoricians are usually unsound, for the serious artist is scientific and the theorist is usually empiric in the medieval fashion. That is to say a good biologist will make a reasonable number of observations of any given phenomenon before he draws a conclusion, thus we read such phrases as "over 100 cultures from the secretions of the respiratory tracts of over 500 patients and 30 nurses and attendants." The results of each observation must be precise and no single observation must in itself be taken as determining a general law, although, after experiment, certain observations may be held as typical or normal. The serious artist is scientific in that he presents the image of his desire, of his hate, of his indifference as precisely that, as precisely the image of his own desire, hate or indifference. The more precise his record the more lasting and unassailable his work of art.

The theorist, and we see this constantly illustrated by the English writers on sex, the theorist constantly proceeds as if his own case, his own limits and predilections were the typical case, or even as if it were the universal. He is constantly urging someone else to behave as he, the theorist, would like to behave. Now art never asks anybody to do anything, or to think anything, or to be anything. It exists as the trees exist, you can admire, you can sit in the shade, you can pick bananas, you can cut firewood, you can do as you jolly well please.

Also you are a fool to seek the kind of art you don't like. You are a fool to read classics because you are told to and not because you like them. You are a fool to aspire to good taste if you haven't naturally got it. If there is one place where it is idiotic to sham that place is before a work of art. Also you are a fool not to have an open mind, not to be eager to enjoy something you might enjoy but don't know how to. But it is not the artist's place to ask you to learn, or to defend his particular works of art, or to insist on your reading his books. Any artist who wants your particular admiration is, by just so much, the less artist.

The desire to stand on the stage, the desire of plaudits has nothing to do with serious art. The serious artist may like to stand on the stage, he may, apart from his art, be any kind of imbecile you like, but the two things are not connected, at least they are not concentric. Lots of people who don't even pretend to be artists have the same desire to be slobbered over, by people with less brains than they have.

The serious artist is usually, or is often as far from the ægrum vulgus[9] as is the serious scientist. Nobody has heard of the abstract mathematicians who

[9] Sick herd.

worked out the determinants that Marconi[10] made use of in his computations for the wireless telegraph. The public, the public so dear to the journalistic heart, is far more concerned with the shareholders in the Marconi company.

The permanent property, the property given to the race at large is precisely these data of the serious scientist and of the serious artist; of the scientist as touching the relations of abstract numbers, of molecular energy, of the composition of matter, etc.; of the serious artist, as touching the nature of man, of individuals.

Men have ceased trying to conquer the world* and to acquire universal knowledge. Men still try to promote the ideal state. No perfect state will be founded on the theory, or on the working hypothesis that all men are alike. No science save the arts will give us the requisite data for learning in what ways men differ.

The very fact that many men hate the arts is of value, for we are enabled by finding out what part of the arts they hate, to learn something of their nature. Usually when men say they hate the arts we find that they merely detest quackery and bad artists.

In the case of a man's hating one art and not the others we may learn that he is of defective hearing or of defective intelligence. Thus an intelligent man may hate music or a good musician may detest very excellent authors.

And all these things are very obvious.

Among thinking and sentient people the bad artist is contemned as we would contemn a negligent physician or a sloppy, inaccurate scientist, and the serious artist is left in peace, or even supported and encouraged. In the fog and the outer darkness no measures are taken to distinguish between the serious and the unserious artist. The unserious artist being the commoner brand and greatly outnumbering the serious variety, and it being to the temporary and apparent advantage of the false artist to gain the rewards proper to the serious artist, it is natural that the unserious artist should do all in his power to obfuscate the lines of demarcation.

Whenever one attempts to demonstrate the difference between serious and unserious work, one is told that "it is merely a technical discussion." It has rested at that—in England it has rested at that for more than three hundred years. The people would rather have patent medicines than scientific treatment. They will occasionally be told that art as art is not a violation of God's most holy laws. They will not have a specialist's opinion as to what art is good. They will not consider the "problem of style." They want "The value of art to life" and "Fundamental issues."

As touching fundamental issues: The arts give us our data of psychology, of man as to his interiors, as to the ratio of his thought to his emotions, etc., etc., etc.

The touchstone of an art is its precision. This precision is of various and complicated sorts and only the specialist can determine whether certain works of art possess certain sorts of precision. I don't mean to say that any intelligent

[10] Gugliemo Marconi (1874–1937), Italian physicist who developed wireless telegraphy, patented his system in England (1896), and organized a wireless telegraph company in 1897 to develop its commercial possibilities.
* *Blind Optimism* A.D. 1913 [Pound's note.]

person cannot have more or less sound judgement as to whether a certain work of art is good or not. An intelligent person can usually tell whether or not a person is in good health. It is none the less true that it takes a skilful physician to make certain diagnoses or to discern the lurking disease beneath the appearance of vigour.

It is no more possible to give in a few pages full instructions for knowing a masterpiece than it would be to give full instructions for all medical diagnosis.

III. EMOTION AND POESY

Obviously, it is not easy to be a great poet. If it were, many more people would have done so. At no period in history has the world been free of people who have mildly desired to be great poets and not a few have endeavoured conscientiously to be such.

I am aware that adjectives of magnitude are held to savour of barbarism. Still there is no shame in desiring to give great gifts and an enlightened criticism does not draw ignominious comparisons between Villon and Dante. The so-called major poets have most of them given their *own* gift but the peculiar term "major" is rather a gift to them from Chronos. I mean that they have been born upon the stroke of their hour and that it has been given them to heap together and arrange and harmonize the results of many men's labour. This very faculty for amalgamation is a part of their genius and it is, in a way, a sort of modesty, a sort of unselfishness. They have not wished for property.

The men from whom Dante borrowed are remembered as much for the fact that he did borrow as for their own compositions. At the same time he gave of his own, and no mere compiler and classifier of other men's discoveries is given the name of "major poet" for more than a season.

If Dante had not done a deal more than borrow rhymes from Arnaut Daniel[11] and theology from Aquinas[12] he would not be published by Dent in the year of grace 1913.

We might come to believe that the thing that matters in art is a sort of energy, something more or less like electricity or radioactivity, a force transfusing, welding, and unifying. A force rather like water when it spurts up through very bright sand and sets it in swift motion. You may make what image you like.

I do not know that there is much use in composing an answer to the often asked question: What is the difference between poetry and prose?

I believe that poetry is the more highly energized. But these things are relative. Just as we say that a certain temperature is hot and another cold. In the same way we say that a certain prose passage "is poetry" meaning to praise it, and that a certain passage of verse is "only prose" meaning dispraise. And at the same time "Poetry!!!" is used as a synonym for "Bosh! Rott!! Rubbish!!!" The thing that counts is "Good writing."

[11] Provençal troubadour poet who wrote at the end of the twelfth century. In the *Purgatorio* (xxvi, 117) Dante refers to him as *miglior fabbro,* the better craftsman, a phrase T. S. Eliot was later to apply to Pound.
[12] St. Thomas Aquinas (1225–1274), Doctor of the Church, whose theology provided much of the conceptual structure of Dante's *Divine Comedy*.

And "Good writing" is perfect control. And it is quite easy to control a thing that has in it no energy—provided that it be not too heavy and that you do not wish to make it move.

And, as all the words that one would use in writing about these things are the vague words of daily speech, it is nearly impossible to write with scientific preciseness about "prose and verse" unless one writes a complete treatise on the "art of writing," defining each word as one would define the terms in a treatise on chemistry. And on this account all essays about "poetry" are usually not only dull but inaccurate and wholly useless. And on like account if you ask a good painter to tell you what he is trying to do to a canvas he will very probably wave his hands helplessly and murmur that "He—eh—eh—he can't talk about it." And that if you "see anything at all, he is quite—eh—more or less—eh—satisfied."

Nevertheless it has been held for a shameful thing that a man should not be able to give a reason for his acts and words. And if one does not care about being taken for a mystificateur one may as well try to give approximate answers to questions asked in good faith. It might be better to do the thing thoroughly, in a properly accurate treatise, but one has not always two or three spare years at one's disposal, and one is dealing with very subtle and complicated matter, and even so, the very algebra of logic is itself open to debate.

Roughly then, Good writing is writing that is perfectly controlled, the writer says just what he means. He says it with complete clarity and simplicity. He uses the smallest possible number of words. I do not mean that he skimps paper, or that he screws about like Tacitus[13] to get his thought crowded into the least possible space. But, granting that two sentences are at times easier to understand than one sentence containing the double meaning, the author tries to communicate with the reader with the greatest possible despatch, save where for any one of forty reasons he does not wish to do so.

Also there are various kinds of clarity. There is the clarity of the request: Send me four pounds of ten-penny nails. And there is the syntactical simplicity of the request: Buy me the kind of Rembrandt I like. This last is an utter cryptogram. It presupposes a more complex and intimate understanding of the speaker than most of us ever acquire of anyone. It has as many meanings, almost, as there are persons who might speak it. To a stranger it conveys nothing at all.

It is the almost constant labour of the prose artist to translate this latter kind of clarity into the former; to say "Send me the kind of Rembrandt I like" in the terms of "Send me four pounds of ten-penny nails."

The whole thing is an evolution. In the beginning simple words were enough: Food; water; fire. Both prose and poetry are but an extension of language. Man desires to communicate with his fellows. He desires an ever increasingly complicated communication. Gesture serves up to a point. Symbols may serve. When you desire something not present to the eye or when you desire to communicate ideas, you must have recourse to speech. Gradually you wish to communicate something less bare and ambiguous than ideas. You wish

---

[13] Cornelius Tacitus (*ca.* A.D. 55–117), Roman historian, whose prose is sometimes described as "crabbed."

to communicate an idea and its modifications, an idea and a crowd of its effects, atmospheres, contradictions. You wish to question whether a certain formula works in every case, or in what per cent of cases, etc., etc., etc., you get the Henry James[14] novel.

You wish to communicate an idea and its concomitant emotions, or an emotion and its concomitant ideas, or a sensation and its derivative emotions, or an impression that is emotive, etc., etc., etc. You begin with the yeowl and the bark, and you develop into the dance and into music, and into music with words, and finally into words with music, and finally into words with a vague adumbration of music, words suggestive of music, words measured, or words in a rhythm that preserves some accurate trait of the emotive impression, or of the sheer character of the fostering or parental emotion.

When this rhythm, or when the vowel and consonantal melody or sequence seems truly to bear the trace of emotion which the poem (for we have come at last to the poem) is intended to communicate, we say that this part of the work is good. And "this part of the work" is by now "technique." That "dry, dull, pedantic" technique, that all bad artists rail against. It is only a part of technique, it is rhythm, cadence, and the arrangement of sounds.

Also the "prose," the words and their sense must be such as fit the emotion. Or, from the other side, ideas, or fragments of ideas, the emotion and concomitant emotions of this "Intellectual and Emotional Complex"[15] (for we have come to the intellectual and emotional complex) must be in harmony, they must form an organism, they must be an oak sprung from an acorn.

When you have words of a lament set to the rhythm and tempo of *There'll be a Hot Time in the Old Town to-night* you have either an intentional burlesque or you have rotten art. Shelley's *Sensitive Plant* is one of the rottenest poems ever written, at least one of the worst ascribable to a recognized author. It jiggles to the same tune as *A little peach in the orchard grew*. Yet Shelley recovered and wrote the fifth act of the Cenci.[16]

IV

It is occasionally suggested by the wise that poets should acquire the graces of prose. That is an extension of what has been said above anent control. Prose does not need emotion. It may, but it need not, attempt to portray emotion.

Poetry is a centaur. The thinking, word-arranging, clarifying faculty must move and leap with the energizing, sentient, musical faculties. It is precisely the difficulty of this amphibious existence that keeps down the census record of good poets. The accomplished prose author will tell you that he "can only write poetry when he has a bellyache" and thence he will argue that poetry just isn't an art.

I dare say there are very good marksmen who just can't shoot from a horse.

---

[14] Henry James (1843–1916), American novelist, one of Pound's favorites, often cited for the delicacy and precision of his nuances.

[15] In an "Imagist" manifesto of 1913, Pound had written, "An 'Image' is that which presents an intellectual and emotional complex in an instant of time."

[16] *The Cenci*, a tragedy, published in 1819.

Likewise if a good marksman only mounted a few times he might never acquire any proficiency in shooting from the saddle. Or leaving metaphor, I suppose that what, in the long run, makes the poet is a sort of persistence of the emotional nature, and, joined with this, a peculiar sort of control.

The saying that "a lyric poet might as well die at thirty" is simply saying that the emotional nature seldom survives this age, or that it becomes, at any rate, subjected and incapable of moving the whole man. Of course this is a generality, and, as such, inaccurate.

It is true that most people poetize more or less, between the ages of seventeen and twenty-three. The emotions are new, and, to their possessor, interesting, and there is not much mind or personality to be moved. As the man, as his mind, becomes a heavier and heavier machine, a constantly more complicated structure, it requires a constantly greater voltage of emotional energy to set it in harmonious motion. It is certain that the emotions increase in vigour as a vigorous man matures. In the case of Guido[17] we have his strongest work at fifty. Most important poetry has been written by men over thirty.

"En l'an trentiesme de mon eage,"[18] begins Villon and considering the nature of his life thirty would have seen him more spent than forty years of more orderly living.

Aristotle will tell you that "The apt use of metaphor, being as it is, the swift perception of relations, is the true hall-mark of genius." That abundance, that readiness of the figure is indeed one of the surest proofs that the mind is upborne upon the emotional surge.

By "apt use," I should say it were well to understand, a swiftness, almost a violence, and certainly a vividness. This does not mean elaboration and complication.

There is another poignancy which I do not care to analyse into component parts, if, indeed, such vivisection is possible. It is not the formal phrasing of Flaubert much as such formality is desirable and noble. It is such phrasing as we find in

> Era gìa l'ora che volge il disio
> Ai naviganti. . . .[19]

Or the opening of the ballata which begins:

> Perch 'io non spero di tornar già mai
> Ballatetta, in Toscana.[20]

Or:

---

[17] Pound almost surely means Guido Cavalcanti, who, Pound estimates, lived from 1250 to 1300 (in *Ezra Pound: Translations*, New Directions, 1963, p. 20). Most scholars place Cavalcanti's birthdate between 1255 and 1259.

[18] "In the thirtieth year of my age," from Villon's *Testament*. Villon was a vagabond, rogue, murderer, and thief.

[19] "It was now the hour that turns back the longing of seafarers, . . ." from Dante's *Purgatorio*, VIII, 1–2.

[20] "Because I do not hope ever to return again/Ballatetta, to Tuscany," from Cavalcanti's ballata "In Exile at Sarzana."

> S'ils n 'ayment fors que pour l'argent,
> On ne les ayme que pour l'heure.[21]

Or, in its context:

> The fire that stirs about her, when she stirs,[22]

or, in its so different setting,

> Ne maeg werigmod wryde withstondan
> ne se hreo hyge helpe gefremman:
> for thon domgeorne dreorigne oft
> in hyra breostcofan bindath faeste.[23]

These things have in them that passionate simplicity which is beyond the precisions of the intellect. Truly they are perfect as fine prose is perfect, but they are in some way different from that so masterly ending of the Herodias: "Comme elle était très lourde ils la portaient alternativement"[24] or from the constatation in St. Julian Hospitalier: "Et l'idée lui vient d'employer son existence au service des autres."[25]

The prose author has shown the triumph of his intellect and one knows that such triumph is not without its sufferings by the way, but by the verses one is brought upon the passionate moment. This moment has brought with it nothing that violates the prose simplicities. The intellect has not found it but the intellect has been moved.

There is little but folly in seeking the lines of division, yet if the two arts must be divided we may as well use that line as any other. In the verse something has come upon the intelligence. In the prose the intelligence has found a subject for its observations. The poetic fact pre-exists.

In a different way, of course, the subject of the prose pre-exists. Perhaps the difference is undemonstrable, perhaps it is not even communicable to any save those of good will. Yet I think this orderliness in the greatest poetic passages, this quiet statement that partakes of the nature of prose and is yet floated and tossed in the emotional surges, is perhaps as true a test as that mentioned by the Greek theorician.

---

[21] "If they do not love except for money, they are loved for only an hour." From Villon.

[22] From a poem by William Butler Yeats, "The Folly of Being Comforted."

[23] First four lines of the Anglo-Saxon poem, "The Seafarer." Pound's own free translation runs,
   May I for my own self song's truth reckon,
   Journey's jargon, how I in harsh days
   Hardship endured oft.
   Bitter breast-cares have I abided. . . .

[24] "Since she was very heavy, they took turns carrying her," from Flaubert's story "Herodias."

[25] "And the idea came to him of devoting his life to the existence of others," from Flaubert's story, "The Legend of St. Julian the Hospitaler."

V

La poésie, avec ses comparaisons obligées, sa mythologie que ne croit pas, le poète, sa dignité de style à la Louis XIV, et tout l'attirail de ses ornements appelés poétiques, est bien audessous de la prose dès qu'il s'agit de donner une idée claire et précise des mouvements du coeur; or, dans ce genre, on n'émeut que par la clarté.—*Stendhal*[26]

And that is precisely why one employs oneself in seeking precisely the poetry that shall be without this flummery, this fustian *à la Louis XIV*, "*farcie de comme.*"[27] The above critique of Stendhal's does not apply to the Poema del Cid,[28] nor to the parting of Odysseus and Calypso.[29] In the writers of the duo-cento and early tre-cento[30] we find a precise psychology, embedded in a now almost unintelligible jargon, but there nevertheless. If we cannot get back to these things; if the serious artist cannot attain this precision in verse, then he must either take to prose or give up his claim to being a serious artist.

It is precisely because of this fustian that the Parnassiads[31] and epics of the eighteenth century and most of the present-day works of most of our contemporary versifiers are pests and abominations.

As the most efficient way to say nothing is to keep quiet, and as technique consists precisely in doing the thing that one sets out to do, in the most efficient manner, no man who takes three pages to say nothing can expect to be seriously considered as a technician. To take three pages to say nothing is not style, in the serious sense of that word.

There are several kinds of honest work. There is the thing that will out. There is the conscientious formulation, a thing of infinitely greater labour, for the first is not labour at all, though the efficient doing of it may depend on a deal of labour foregoing.

There is the "labour foregoing," the patient testing of media, the patient experiment which shall avail perhaps the artist himself, but is as likely to avail some successor.

The first sort of work may be poetry.

---

[26] In *ABC of Reading* (New Directions, 1951), p. 97, Pound translates the passage from Stendhal as follows: "Poetry with its obligatory comparisons, the mythology the poet doesn't believe in, his so-called dignity of style, à la Louis XIV, and all that trail of what they call poetic ornament, is vastly inferior to prose if you are trying to give a clear and exact idea of the '*mouvements du coeur*' ['movements of the heart']; if you are trying to show what a man feels, you can only do it by clarity."

[27] "Stuffed with similitudes" in the manner of French neo-classical poetry.

[28] A twelfth-century Spanish epic poem.

[29] In Book V of the *Odyssey*.

[30] Pound is referring to the troubadour poets of the twelfth and thirteenth centuries.

[31] "Parnassus" was the ancient Greek name for the mountain now called Liakoura. It was sacred to the Muses. "Parnassiad" is formed on the analogy of such titles as *Iliad* and would mean something like "verse that is epically fatuous in its neo-classicism."

The second sort, the conscientious formulation, is more than likely to be prose.

The third sort of work savours of the laboratory, it concerns the specialist, and the dilettante, if that word retains any trace of its finer and original sense.[32] A dilettante proper is a person who takes delight in the art, not a person who tries to interpose his inferior productions between masterwork and the public.

I reject the term connoisseurship, for "connoisseurship" is so associated in our minds with a desire for acquisition. The person possessed of connoisseurship is so apt to want to buy the rare at one price and sell it at another. I do not believe that a person with this spirit has ever *seen* a work of art. Let me restore the foppish term dilettante, the synonym for folly, to its place near the word *diletto*.

The dilettante has no axe to grind for himself. If he be artist as well, he will be none the less eager to preserve the best precedent work. He will drag out "sources" that prove him less original than his public would have him.

As for Stendhal's stricture, if we can have a poetry that comes as close as prose, *pour donner une idée claire et précise*,[33] let us have it, "*E di venire a ciò io studio quanto posso . . . che la mia vita per alquanti anni duri.*" . . .[34] And if we cannot attain to such a poetry, *noi altri poeti*,[35] for God's sake let us shut up. Let us "Give up, go down," etcetera; let us acknowledge that our art, like the art of dancing in armour, is out of date and out of fashion. Or let us go to our ignominious ends knowing that we have strained at the cords, that we have spent our strength in trying to pave the way for a new sort of poetic art—it is not a new sort but an old sort—but let us know that we have tried to make it more nearly possible for our successors to recapture this art. To write a poetry that can be carried as a communication between intelligent men.

To this end *io studio quanto posso*. I have tried to establish a clear demarcation. I have been challenged on my use of the phrase "great art" in an earlier article. It is about as useless to search for a definition of "great art" as it is to search for a scientific definition of life. One knows fairly well what one means. One means something more or less proportionate to one's experience. One means something quite different at different periods of one's life.

It is for some such reason that all criticism should be professedly personal criticism. In the end the critic can only say "I like it," or "I am moved," or something of that sort. When he has shown us himself we are able to understand him.

Thus, in painting, I mean something or other vaguely associated in my mind with work labelled Dürer, and Rembrandt, and Velasquez, etc., and with the painters whom I scarcely know, possibly of T'ang and Sung—though I dare say I've got the wrong labels—and with some Egyptian designs that should probably be thought of as sculpture.

And in poetry I mean something or other associated in my mind with the names of a dozen or more writers.

[32] That is, "one who delights in the arts."
[33] "In order to present a clear and precise idea."
[34] "And to come to that, I study as much as possible . . . that my life may endure for a few years."
[35] "We poets."

On closer analysis I find that I mean something like "maximum efficiency of expression"; I mean that the writer has expressed something interesting in such a way that one cannot re-say it more effectively. I also mean something associated with discovery. The artist must have discovered something—either of life itself or of the means of expression.

Great art must of necessity be a part of good art. I attempted to define good art in an earlier chapter. It must bear true witness. Obviously great art must be an exceptional thing. It cannot be the sort of thing anyone can do after a few hours' practice. It must be the result of some exceptional faculty, strength, or perception. It must almost be that strength of perception working with the connivance of fate, or chance, or whatever you choose to call it.

And who is to judge? The critic, the receiver, however stupid or ignorant, must judge for himself. The only really vicious criticism is the academic criticism of those who make the grand abnegation, who refuse to say what they think, if they do think, and who quote accepted opinion; these men are the vermin, their treachery to the great work of the past is as great as that of the false artist to the present. If they do not care enough for the heritage to have a personal conviction then they have no licence to write.

Every critic should give indication of the sources and limits of his knowledge. The criticism of English poetry by men who knew no language but English, or who knew little but English and school-classics, has been a marasmus.[36]

When we know to what extent each sort of expression has been driven, in, say, half a dozen great literatures, we begin to be able to tell whether a given work has the excess of great art. We would not think of letting a man judge pictures if he knew only English pictures, or music if he knew only English music—or only French or German music for that matter.

The stupid or provincial judgment of art bases itself on the belief that great art must be like the art that it has been reared to respect.

---

[36] A progressive emaciation because of malnutrition and enfeebled constitution.

Sigmund Freud

THE THEME OF THE
THREE CASKETS

It is often said, and with entire truth, that no man of his time has had
an influence on the cultural life of Europe and America equal to that
of Sigmund Freud (1856–1936). It is felt not only in therapeutic psychology, where it has been decisive, but also in many of the humanistic
disciplines and the social sciences; even theology has been affected by it.
Freud's intellectual authority—against which, it should be said, a certain
antagonism has developed in recent years—was won against great opposition. The importance in the mental life that Freud gave to the sexual
instincts was thought to be a scandal, made the more outrageous because
sexuality was imputed even to children and infants. Another reason for
discounting psychoanalysis was that it assumed that there are operations
of the mind which are not present to the consciousness—the idea of an
unconscious part of the mind seemed a contradiction in terms. A response
that Freud made to the latter objection has become famous. On an
occasion when he was being honored as "the discoverer of the unconscious," he said, "Not I but the poets discovered the unconscious." By
this he chiefly meant that the dramatists and story tellers had long
taken it for granted that their characters often spoke and acted out of
motives of which they were not aware, sometimes in contradiction to
their conscious purpose. He also meant that literary artists, however
conscious they may be in their overarching intentions for a work, put
a very considerable reliance on what will be contributed to it by
faculties not wholly under their control. Freud did not, of course, derive
the theory of the unconscious from literature but from his efforts as a
physician to understand the painful states or aberrant behavior of his
patients. But having developed his theory, he turned it to the understanding of literary works, or at least to certain of their elements. This
was the more material because, although priding himself on the strictness of his scientific training and method, Freud had a deep feeling for
literature. His schooling, in the fashion of his day, had grounded him
thoroughly in the humanities and he had responded to his instruction
with enthusiasm. He read Greek with ease—as a boy he wrote his diary
in Greek—and his feeling for the ancient classical literature was intense.
For some years he read nothing but English books, especially Dickens,

From *The Complete Psychological Works of Sigmund Freud* (Standard Edition, Volume
12). By permission of Sigmund Freud Copyrights Ltd., The Institute of Psycho-Analysis,
and The Hogarth Press. Chapter XV of *The Collected Papers of Sigmund Freud*, Volume
4, edited by Ernest Jones. New York: Basic Books, Inc., Publishers, 1959. By permission
of Basic Books, Inc., Publishers.

Milton, and Shakespeare. And he had, of course, an easy familiarity with German and Austrian literature. A summary account of his speculations about literature and of the effect of these on criticism is given in the Introduction to the present volume (pp. 26 f.). "The Theme of the Three Caskets" was first published in 1913 in *Imago*, the journal that Freud founded for the discussion of the non-medical applications of psychoanalysis.

I

Two scenes from Shakespeare, one from a comedy and the other from a tragedy, have lately given me occasion for posing and solving a small problem.

The first of these scenes is the suitors' choice between the three caskets in *The Merchant of Venice*. The fair and wise Portia is bound at her father's bidding to take as her husband only that one of her suitors who chooses the right casket from among the three before him. The three caskets are of gold, silver and lead: the right casket is the one that contains her portrait. Two suitors have already departed unsuccessful: they have chosen gold and silver. Bassanio, the third, decides in favour of lead; thereby he wins the bride, whose affection was already his before the trial of fortune. Each of the suitors gives reasons for his choice in a speech in which he praises the metal he prefers and depreciates the other two. The most difficult task thus falls to the share of the fortunate third suitor; what he finds to say in glorification of lead as against gold and silver is little and has a forced ring. If in psycho-analytic practice we were confronted with such a speech, we should suspect that there were concealed motives behind the unsatisfying reasons produced.

Shakespeare did not himself invent this oracle of the choice of a casket; he took it from a tale in the *Gesta Romanorum*,[1] in which a girl has to make the same choice to win the Emperor's son.[*] Here too the third metal, lead, is the bringer of fortune. It is not hard to guess that we have here an ancient theme, which requires to be interpreted, accounted for and traced back to its origin. A first conjecture as to the meaning of this choice between gold, silver and lead is quickly confirmed by a statement of Stucken's,[†] who has made a study of the same material over a wide field. He writes: "The identity of Portia's three suitors is clear from their choice: the Prince of Morocco chooses the gold casket—he is the sun; the Prince of Arragon chooses the silver casket—he is the moon; Bassanio chooses the leaden casket—he is the star youth." In support of this explanation he cites an episode from the Estonian folk-epic "Kalewipoeg," in which the three suitors appear undisguisedly as the sun, moon and star youths (the last being "the Pole-star's eldest boy") and once again the bride falls to the lot of the third.

Thus our little problem has led us to an astral myth! The only pity is that

[1] A medieval collection of Latin stories of unknown authorship.

[*] Brandes (1896). [Georg Brandes, *William Shakespeare*, Paris (1896).] [Freud's note.]

[†] Stucken (1907, 655). [E. Stucken, *Astralmythen der Herbraeer, Babylonier und Agypter*, Leipsig (1907).] [Freud's note.]

with this explanation we are not at the end of the matter. The question is not exhausted, for we do not share the belief of some investigators that myths were read in the heavens and brought down to earth; we are more inclined to judge with Otto Rank* that they were projected on to the heavens after having arisen elsewhere under purely human conditions. It is in this human content that our interest lies.

Let us look once more at our material. In the Estonian epic, just as in the tale from the *Gesta Romanorum,* the subject is a girl choosing between three suitors; in the scene from *The Merchant of Venice* the subject is apparently the same, but at the same time something appears in it that is in the nature of an inversion of the theme: a *man* chooses between three—caskets. If what we were concerned with were a dream, it would occur to us at once that caskets are also women, symbols of what is essential in woman, and therefore of a woman herself—like coffers, boxes, cases, baskets, and so on.[2] If we boldly assume that there are symbolic substitutions of the same kind in myths as well, then the casket scene in *The Merchant of Venice* really becomes the inversion we suspected. With a wave of the wand, as though we were in a fairy tale, we have stripped the astral garment from our theme; and now we see that the theme is a human one, *a man's choice between three women.*

This same content, however, is to be found in another scene of Shakespeare's, in one of his most powerfully moving dramas; not the choice of a bride this time, yet linked by many hidden similarities to the choice of the casket in *The Merchant of Venice.* The old King Lear resolves to divide his kingdom while he is still alive among his three daughters, in proportion to the amount of love that each of them expresses for him. The two elder ones, Goneril and Regan, exhaust themselves in asseverations and laudations of their love for him; the third, Cordelia, refuses to do so. He should have recognized the unassuming, speechless love of his third daughter and rewarded it, but he does not recognize it. He disowns Cordelia, and divides the kingdom between the other two, to his own and the general ruin. Is not this once more the scene of a choice between three women, of whom the youngest is the best, the most excellent one?

There will at once occur to us other scenes from myths, fairy tales and literature, with the same situation as their content. The shepherd Paris has to choose between three goddesses, of whom he declares the third to be the most beautiful.[3] Cinderella, again, is a youngest daughter, who is preferred by the prince to her two elder sisters. Psyche, in Apuleius's story,[4] is the youngest and fairest of three sisters. Psyche is, on the one hand, revered as Aphrodite in human form; on the other, she is treated by that goddess as Cinderella was treated by her stepmother and is set the task of sorting a heap of mixed seeds, which she accomplishes with the help of small creatures (doves in the case of

---

* Rank (1909, 8 ff.). [O. Rank, *Der Mythos von der Geburt des Helden,* Leipsig and Vienna (1909).] [Freud's note.]

[2] See "The Interpretation of Dreams" (1900), *The Complete Psychological Works of Sigmund Freud* (Standard Edition, Volume 5, page 364).

[3] In Greek myth Paris had to decide among Hera, Athene, and Aphrodite. He chose Aphrodite.

[4] *The Golden Ass,* by Lucius Apuleius, second-century Latin writer.

Cinderella, ants in the case of Psyche).* Anyone who cared to make a wider survey of the material would undoubtedly discover other versions of the same theme preserving the same essential features.

Let us be content with Cordelia, Aphrodite, Cinderella and Psyche. In all the stories the three women, of whom the third is the most excellent one, must surely be regarded as in some way alike if they are represented as sisters. (We must not be led astray by the fact that Lear's choice is between three *daughters*; this may mean nothing more than that he has to be represented as an old man. An old man cannot very well choose between three women in any other way. Thus they become his daughters.)

But who are these three sisters and why must the choice fall on the third? If we could answer this question, we should be in possession of the interpretation we are seeking. We have once already made use of an application of psycho-analytic technique, when we explained the three caskets symbolically as three women. If we have the courage to proceed in the same way, we shall be setting foot on a path which will lead us first to something unexpected and incomprehensible, but which will perhaps, by a devious route, bring us to a goal.

It must strike us that this excellent third woman has in several instances certain peculiar qualities besides her beauty. They are qualities that seem to be tending towards some kind of unity; we must certainly not expect to find them equally well marked in every example. Cordelia makes herself unrecognizable, inconspicuous like lead, she remains dumb, she "loves and is silent." Cinderella hides so that she cannot be found. We may perhaps be allowed to equate concealment and dumbness. These would of course be only two instances out of the five we have picked out. But there is an intimation of the same thing to be found, curiously enough, in two other cases. We have decided to compare Cordelia, with her obstinate refusal, to lead. In Bassanio's short speech while he is choosing the casket, he says of lead (without in any way leading up to the remark):

> Thy paleness† moves me more than eloquence.

That is to say: "Thy plainness moves me more than the blatant nature of the other two." Gold and silver are "loud"; lead is dumb—in fact like Cordelia, who "loves and is silent."‡

In the ancient Greek accounts of the Judgement of Paris, nothing is said of any such reticence on the part of Aphrodite. Each of the three goddesses speaks to the youth and tries to win him by promises. But, oddly enough, in a quite modern handling of the same scene this characteristic of the third one which has struck us makes its appearance again. In the libretto of Offenbach's *La Belle Hélène,* Paris, after telling of the solicitations of the other two goddesses, describes Aphrodite's behaviour in this competition for the beauty-prize:

---

* I have to thank Dr. Otto Rank for calling my attention to these similarities. [Freud's note.]

† "Plainness" according to another reading. [Freud's note.]

‡ In Schlegel's translation this allusion is quite lost; indeed, it is given the opposite meaning: "Dein schlichtes Wesen spricht beredt mich an." ["Thy plainness speaks to me with eloquence."] [Freud's note.]

La troisième, ah! la troisième . . .
La troisième ne dit rien.
Elle eut le prix tout de même . . .[5]

If we decide to regard the peculiarities of our "third one" as concentrated in her "dumbness," then psycho-analysis will tell us that in dreams dumbness is a common representation of death.[*]

More than ten years ago a highly intelligent man told me a dream which he wanted to use as evidence of the telepathic nature of dreams. In it he saw an absent friend from whom he had received no news for a very long time, and reproached him energetically for his silence. The friend made no reply. It afterwards turned out that he had met his death by suicide at about the time of the dream. Let us leave the problem of telepathy on one side: there seems, however, not to be any doubt that here the dumbness in the dream represented death. Hiding and being unfindable—a thing which confronts the prince in the fairy tale of Cinderella three times, is another unmistakable symbol of death in dreams; so, too, is a marked pallor, of which the "paleness" of the lead in one reading of Shakespeare's text is a reminder.[6] It would be very much easier for us to transpose these interpretations from the language of dreams to the mode of expression used in the myth that is now under consideration if we could make it seem probable that dumbness must be interpreted as a sign of being dead in productions other than dreams.

At this point I will single out the ninth story in Grimm's *Fairy Tales*, which bears the title "The Twelve Brothers." A king and a queen have twelve children, all boys. The king declares that if the thirteenth child is a girl, the boys will have to die. In expectation of her birth he has twelve coffins made. With their mother's help the twelve sons take refuge in a hidden wood, and swear death to any girl they may meet. A girl is born, grows up, and learns one day from her mother that she has had twelve brothers. She decides to seek them out, and in the wood she finds the youngest; he recognizes her, but is anxious to hide her on account of the brothers' oath. The sister says: "I will gladly die, if by so doing I can save my twelve brothers." The brothers welcome her affectionately, however, and she stays with them and looks after their house for them. In a little garden beside the house grow twelve lilies. The girl picks them and gives one to each brother. At that moment the brothers are changed into ravens, and disappear, together with the house and garden. (Ravens are spirit-birds; the killing of the twelve brothers by their sister is represented by the picking of the flowers, just as it is at the beginning of the story by the coffins and the disappearance of the brothers.) The girl, who is once more ready to save her brothers from death, is now told that as a condition she must be dumb for seven years, and not speak a single word. She submits to the test, which brings her herself into mortal danger. She herself, that is, dies for her brothers,

---

[5] Literally: "The third one, ah! the third one . . . the third one said nothing. She won the prize all the same." The quotation is from Act I, Scene 7, of Meilhac and Halévy's libretto. In the German version used by Freud, "the third one" *"blieb stumm"*—"remained dumb."

[*] In Stekel's *Sprache des Traumes* [Weisbaden (1911)], too, dumbness is mentioned among the "death" symbols. [Freud's note.]

[6] Stekel, loc. cit. [Freud's note.]

as she promised to do before she met them. By remaining dumb she succeeds at last in setting the ravens free.

In the story of "The Six Swans"[7] the brothers who are changed into birds are set free in exactly the same way—they are restored to life by their sister's dumbness. The girl has made a firm resolve to free her brothers, "even if it should cost her her life"; and once again (being the wife of the king) she risks her own life because she refuses to give up her dumbness in order to defend herself against evil accusations.

It would certainly be possible to collect further evidence from fairy tales that dumbness is to be understood as representing death. These indications would lead us to conclude that the third one of the sisters between whom the choice is made is a dead woman. But she may be something else as well— namely, Death itself, the Goddess of Death. Thanks to a displacement that is far from infrequent, the qualities that a deity imparts to men are ascribed to the deity himself. Such a displacement will surprise us least of all in relation to the Goddess of Death, since in modern versions and representations, which these stories would thus be forestalling, Death itself is nothing other than a dead man.

But if the third of the sisters is the Goddess of Death, the sisters are known to us. They are the Fates, the Moerae, the Parcae or the Norns,[8] the third of whom is called Atropos, the inexorable.

II

We will for the time being put aside the task of inserting the interpretation that we have found into our myth, and listen to what the mythologists have to teach us about the role and origin of the Fates.[9]

The earliest Greek mythology (in Homer) only knew a single Μοῖρα, personifying inevitable fate. The further development of this one Moera into a company of three (or less often two) sister-goddesses probably came about on the basis of other divine figures to which the Moerae were closely related—the Graces and the Horae [the Seasons].

The Horae were originally goddesses of the waters of the sky, dispensing rain and dew, and of the clouds from which rain falls; and, since the clouds were conceived of as something that has been spun, it came about that these goddesses were looked upon as spinners, an attribute that then became attached to the Moerae. In the sun-favoured Mediterranean lands it is the rain on which the fertility of the soil depends, and thus the Horae became vegetation goddesses. The beauty of flowers and the abundance of fruit was their doing, and they were accredited with a wealth of agreeable and charming traits. They became the divine representatives of the Seasons, and it is possibly owing to

[7] Another tale from the famous collection of *märchen*—fairy tales—put together by Jakob and Wilhelm Grimm in 1812–1815.

[8] Freud uses the Greek, Latin, Norse names, successively, for the three Fates, always represented as women.

[9] What follows is taken from Roscher's lexicon [*Ausführliches Lexikon der griechischen und römischen Mythologie*, Leipzig (1884–1937)], under the relevant headings. [Freud's note.]

this connection that there were three of them, if the sacred nature of the number three is not a sufficient explanation. For the peoples of antiquity at first distinguished only three seasons: winter, spring and summer. Autumn was only added in late Graeco-Roman times, after which the Horae were often represented in art as four in number.

The Horae retained their relation to time. Later they presided over the times of day, as they did at first over the times of the year; and at last their name came to be merely a designation of the hours (*heure, ora*). The Norns of German mythology are akin to the Horae and the Moerae and exhibit this time-signification in their names.[10] It was inevitable, however, that a deeper view should come to be taken of the essential nature of these deities, and that their essence should be transposed on to the regularity with which the seasons change. The Horae thus became the guardians of natural law and of the divine Order which causes the same thing to recur in Nature in an unalterable sequence.

This discovery of Nature reacted on the conception of human life. The nature-myth changed into a human myth: the weather-goddesses became goddesses of Fate. But this aspect of the Horae found expression only in the Moerae, who watch over the necessary ordering of human life as inexorably as do the Horae over the regular order of nature. The ineluctable severity of Law and its relation to death and dissolution, which had been avoided in the charming figures of the Horae, were now stamped upon the Moerae, as though men had only perceived the full seriousness of natural law when they had to submit their own selves to it.

The names of the three spinners, too, have been significantly explained by mythologists. Lachesis, the name of the second, seems to denote "the accidental that is included in the regularity of destiny"[11]—or, as we should say, "experience"; just as Atropos stands for "the ineluctable"—Death. Clotho would then be left to mean the innate disposition with its fateful implications.

But now it is time to return to the theme which we are trying to interpret—the theme of the choice between three sisters. We shall be deeply disappointed to discover how unintelligible the situations under review become and what contradictions of their apparent content result, if we apply to them the interpretation that we have found. On our supposition the third of the sisters is the Goddess of Death, Death itself. But in the Judgement of Paris she is the Goddess of Love, in the tale of Apuleius she is someone comparable to the goddess for her beauty, in *The Merchant of Venice* she is the fairest and wisest of women, in *King Lear* she is the one loyal daughter. We may ask whether there can be a more complete contradiction. Perhaps, improbable though it may seem, there is a still more complete one lying close at hand. Indeed, there certainly is; since, whenever our theme occurs, the choice between the women is free, and yet it falls on death. For, after all, no one chooses death, and it is only by a fatality that one falls a victim to it.

However, contradictions of a certain kind—replacements by the precise opposite—offer no serious difficulty to the work of analytic interpretation. We

[10] Their names may be rendered: "What was," "What is," "What shall be."

[11] Roscher [ibid.], quoting L. Preller [*Griechische Mythologie*, Berlin], ed. C. Robert (1894). [Freud's note.]

shall not appeal here to the fact that contraries are so often represented by one and the same element in the modes of expression used by the unconscious, as for instance in dreams. But we shall remember that there are motive forces in mental life which bring about replacement by the opposite in the form of what is known as reaction-formation; and it is precisely in the revelation of such hidden forces as these that we look for the reward of this enquiry. The Moerae were created as a result of a discovery that warned man that he too is a part of nature and therefore subject to the immutable law of death. Something in man was bound to struggle against this subjection, for it is only with extreme unwillingness that he gives up his claim to an exceptional position. Man, as we know, makes use of his imaginative activity in order to satisfy the wishes that reality does not satisfy. So his imagination rebelled against the recognition of the truth embodied in the myth of the Moerae, and constructed instead the myth derived from it, in which the Goddess of Death was replaced by the Goddess of Love and by what was equivalent to her in human shape. The third of the sisters was no longer Death; she was the fairest, best, most desirable and most lovable of women. Nor was this substitution in any way technically difficult: it was prepared for by an ancient ambivalence, it was carried out along a primaeval line of connection which could not long have been forgotten. The Goddess of Love herself, who now took the place of the Goddess of Death, had once been identical with her. Even the Greek Aphrodite had not wholly relinquished her connection with the underworld, although she had long surrendered her chthonic role to other divine figures, to Persephone, or to the tri-form Artemis-Hecate. The great Mother-goddesses of the oriental peoples, however, all seem to have been both creators and destroyers—both goddesses of life and fertility and goddesses of death. Thus the replacement by a wishful opposite in our theme harks back to a primaeval identity.

The same consideration answers the question how the feature of a choice came into the myth of the three sisters. Here again there has been a wishful reversal. Choice stands in the place of necessity, of destiny. In this way man overcomes death, which he has recognized intellectually. No greater triumph of wishfulfilment is conceivable. A choice is made where in reality there is obedience to a compulsion; and what is chosen is not a figure of terror, but the fairest and most desirable of women.

On closer inspection we observe, to be sure, that the original myth is not so thoroughly distorted that traces of it do not show through and betray its presence. The free choice between the three sisters is, properly speaking, no free choice, for it must necessarily fall on the third if every kind of evil is not to come about, as it does in *King Lear*. The fairest and best of women, who has taken the place of the Death-goddess, has kept certain characteristics that border on the uncanny, so that from them we have been able to guess at what lies beneath.*

---

* The Psyche of Apuleius's story has kept many traits that remind us of her relation with death. Her wedding is celebrated like a funeral, she has to descend into the underworld, and afterwards she sinks into a death-like sleep (Otto Rank).—On the significance of Psyche as goddess of the spring and as "Bride of Death," cf. A. Zinzow, *Psyche und Eros,* Halle (1881).—In another of Grimm's Tales ("The Goose-girl at the Fountain") there is, as in "Cinderella," an alternation between the

So far we have been following out the myth and its transformation, and it is to be hoped that we have correctly indicated the hidden causes of the transformation. We may now turn our interest to the way in which the dramatist has made use of the theme. We get an impression that a reduction of the theme to the original myth is being carried out in his work, so that we once more have a sense of the moving significance which had been weakened by the distortion. It is by means of this reduction of the distortion, this partial return to the original, that the dramatist achieves his more profound effect upon us.

To avoid misunderstandings, I should like to say that it is not my purpose to deny that King Lear's dramatic story is intended to inculcate two wise lessons: that one should not give up one's possessions and rights during one's life-time, and that one must guard against accepting flattery at its face value. These and similar warnings are undoubtedly brought out by the play; but it seems to me quite impossible to explain the overpowering effect of *King Lear* from the impression that such a train of thought would produce, or to suppose that the dramatist's personal motives did not go beyond the intention of teaching these lessons. It is suggested, too, that his purpose was to present the tragedy of ingratitude, the sting of which he may well have felt in his own heart, and that the effect of the play rests on the purely formal element of its artistic presentation; but this cannot, so it seems to me, take the place of the understanding brought to us by the explanation we have reached of the theme of the choice between the three sisters.

Lear is an old man. It is for this reason, as we have already said, that the three sisters appear as his daughters. The relationship of a father to his children, which might be a fruitful source of many dramatic situations, is not turned to further account in the play. But Lear is not only an old man: he is a dying man. In this way the extraordinary premiss of the division of his inheritance loses all its strangeness. But the doomed man is not willing to renounce the love of women; he insists on hearing how much he is loved. Let us now recall the moving final scene, one of the culminating points of tragedy in modern drama. Lear carries Cordelia's dead body on to the stage. Cordelia is Death. If we reverse the situation it becomes intelligible and familiar to us. She is the Death-goddess who, like the Valkyrie in German mythology, carries away the dead hero from the battlefield. Eternal wisdom, clothed in the primaeval myth, bids the old man renounce love, choose death and make friends with the necessity of dying.

The dramatist brings us nearer to the ancient theme by representing the man who makes the choice between the three sisters as aged and dying. The regressive revision which he has thus applied to the myth, distorted as it was by wishful transformation, allows us enough glimpses of its original meaning to enable us perhaps to reach as well a superficial allegorical interpretation of the three female figures in the theme. We might argue that what is represented

---

beautiful and the ugly aspect of the third sister, in which one may no doubt see an indication of her double nature—before and after the substitution. This third daughter is repudiated by her father, after a test which is almost the same as the one in *King Lear*. Like her sisters, she has to declare how fond she is of their father, but can find no expression for her love but a comparison with salt. (Kindly communicated by Dr. Hanns Sachs.) [Freud's note.]

here are the three inevitable relations that a man has with a woman—the woman
who bears him, the woman who is his mate and the woman who destroys him;
or that they are the three forms taken by the figure of the mother in the course
of a man's life—the mother herself, the beloved one who is chosen after her
pattern, and lastly the Mother Earth who receives him once more. But it is
in vain that an old man yearns for the love of woman as he had it first from his
mother; the third of the Fates alone, the silent Goddess of Death, will take him
into her arms.

James Joyce

STEPHEN'S DISCOURSE

Stephen Dedalus is the hero of *A Portrait of the Artist as a Young Man,*
the novel that James Joyce (1882–1941) began in 1904, completed in
1914, and published in 1916. At the time of his discourse with—or,
rather, to—his friend Lynch, he is some twenty years old and at a crisis
in his life. The son of a middle-class Dublin family whose fortunes had
declined to the point of poverty, he had, in better days, attended a
fashionable Jesuit boarding school, then a good Jesuit day school in
Dublin, and is now an undergraduate at University College, a Catholic
institution. Earlier in his college career he had experienced what seemed
a vocation for the priesthood; not only did this prove illusory but his
religious faith itself, nurtured by a pious mother, is now rapidly moving
towards dissolution. Having from earliest childhood been enthralled by
the power and mystery of language, he has been pressing closer and
closer to the decision that he must live as an artist—as he puts it, "a
priest of the eternal imagination." To that end, he believes, he must cut
all ties, to his family, even though it will need his help, to religion, and
to his native land in its aspiration to throw off English rule and become
an independent nation. This statement of his intention of personal
liberty is famous: "I will not serve that in which I no longer believe,
whether it call itself my home, my fatherland or my Church: and I
will try to express myself in some mode of life and art as freely as I
can, using for my defense the only arms I allow myself to use—silence,
exile, and cunning." Not long after his walk with Lynch he goes into
exile, leaving Dublin for Paris. As did his creator, for of course all that
has been said of Stephen Dedalus's early life applies as well to Joyce's:
critics warn us that *A Portrait of the Artist as a Young Man* is an autobiographical novel, not an autobiography, and that we must not assume
that Stephen Dedalus "is" James Joyce; perhaps not, but the two young
men are like enough to be mistaken for each other. The "cunning" with
which Dedalus arms himself is appropriate to his name, the strangeness
of which for an Irish family is often remarked in the novel, for in
ancient Greek legend, Dedalus was—and his name means—the cunning artificer; it was he who built the labyrinth of Crete and who,
when he was imprisoned in it, fashioned wings to escape. Dedalus-Joyce
has in mind, we presume, not only personal craftiness in dealing with
persons but also craftsmanly ingenuity in his art. And although the

"silence" with which he arms himself is a way of dealing with his associates that is conformable to his personal temperament, it is also the
quality he desires for his art; it is to exist in itself as an aesthetic object,
detached from the personality of its maker. This is an intention that
Joyce carried out in *Ulysses* and *Finnegans Wake* and it is an instructive
irony that Joyce, who stood in the vanguard of modern "experimental"
art should have based his theory on Aristotle and St. Thomas Aquinas.

. . . They passed back through the garden and out through the hall where
the doddering porter was pinning up a notice in the frame. At the foot of the
steps they halted and Stephen took a packet of cigarettes from his pocket and
offered it to his companion.

—I know you are poor, he said.

—Damn your yellow insolence, answered Lynch.

This second proof of Lynch's culture made Stephen smile again.

—It was a great day for European culture, he said, when you made up your
mind to swear in yellow.

They lit their cigarettes and turned to the right. After a pause Stephen
began:

—Aristotle has not defined pity and terror. I have. I say . . .

Lynch halted and said bluntly:

—Stop! I won't listen! I am sick. I was out last night on a yellow drunk
with Horan and Goggins.

Stephen went on:

—Pity is the feeling which arrests the mind in the presence of whatsoever
is grave and constant in human sufferings and unites it with the human sufferer.
Terror is the feeling which arrests the mind in the presence of whatsoever is
grave and constant in human sufferings and unites it with the secret cause.

Repeat, said Lynch.

Stephen repeated the definitions slowly.

—A girl got into a hansom a few days ago, he went on, in London. She
was on her way to meet her mother whom she had not seen for many years.
At the corner of a street the shaft of a lorry shivered the window of the hansom
in the shape of a star. A long fine needle of the shivered glass pierced her
heart. She died on the instant. The reporter called it a tragic death. It is not.
It is remote from terror and pity according to the terms of my definitions.

—The tragic emotion, in fact, is a face looking two ways, towards terror
and towards pity, both of which are phases of it. You see I use the word *arrest*.
I mean that the tragic emotion is static. Or rather the dramatic emotion is. The
feelings excited by improper art are kinetic, desire or loathing. Desire urges
us to possess, to go to something; loathing urges us to abandon, to go from
something. These are kinetic emotions. The arts which excite them, porno-
graphical or didactic, are therefore improper arts. The esthetic emotion (I use
the general term) is therefore static. The mind is arrested and raised above
desire and loathing.

—You say that art must not excite desire, said Lynch. I told you that one day I wrote my name in pencil on the backside of the Venus of Praxiteles in the Museum.[1] Was that not desire?

—I speak of normal natures, said Stephen. You also told me that when you were a boy in that charming carmelite[2] school you ate pieces of dried cowdung.

Lynch broke again into a whinny of laughter and again rubbed both his hands over his groins but without taking them from his pockets.

—O I did! I did! he cried.

Stephen turned towards his companion and looked at him for a moment boldly in the eyes. Lynch, recovering from his laughter, answered his look from his humbled eyes. The long slender flattened skull beneath the long pointed cap brought before Stephen's mind the image of a hooded reptile. The eyes, too, were reptilelike in glint and gaze. Yet at that instant, humbled and alert in their look, they were lit by one tiny human point, the window of a shrivelled soul, poignant and selfembittered.

—As for that, Stephen said in polite parenthesis, we are all animals. I also am an animal.

—You are, said Lynch.

—But we are just now in a mental world, Stephen continued. The desire and loathing excited by improper esthetic means are really unesthetic emotions not only because they are kinetic in character but also because they are not more than physical. Our flesh shrinks from what it dreads and responds to the stimulus of what it desires by a purely reflex action of the nervous system. Our eyelid closes before we are aware that the fly is about to enter our eye.

Not always, said Lynch critically.

In the same way, said Stephen, your flesh responded to the stimulus of a naked statue but it was, I say, simply a reflex action of the nerves. Beauty expressed by the artist cannot awaken in us an emotion which is kinetic or a sensation which is purely physical. It awakens, or ought to awaken, or induces, or ought to induce, an esthetic stasis, an ideal pity or an ideal terror, a stasis called forth, prolonged and at last dissolved by what I call the rhythm of beauty.

—What is that exactly? asked Lynch.

—Rhythm, said Stephen, is the first formal esthetic relation of part to part in any esthetic whole or of an esthetic whole to its part or parts or of any part to the esthetic whole of which it is a part.

—If that is rhythm, said Lynch, let me hear what you call beauty: and please remember, though I did eat a cake of cowdung once, that I admire only beauty.

Stephen raised his cap as if in greeting. Then, blushing slightly, he laid his hand on Lynch's thick tweed sleeve.

—We are right, he said, and the others are wrong. To speak of these things and to try to understand their nature and, having understood it, to try slowly and humbly and constantly to express, to press out again, from the gross earth or what it brings forth, from sound and shape and colour which

[1] A plaster cast of the Cnidian Venus of Praxiteles (fourth-century Greek sculptor) stood in the National Museum in Dublin.
[2] Roman Catholic Order of Our Lady of Mount Carmel.

are the prison gates of our soul, an image of the beauty we have come to understand—that is art.

They had reached the canal bridge and, turning from their course, went on by the trees. A crude grey light, mirrored in the sluggish water, and a smell of wet branches over their heads seemed to war against the course of Stephen's thought.

—But you have not answered my question, said Lynch. What is art? What is the beauty it expresses?

—That was the first definition I gave you, you sleepyheaded wretch, said Stephen, when I began to try to think out the matter for myself. Do you remember the night? Cranly lost his temper and began to talk about Wicklow bacon.

—I remember, said Lynch. He told us about them flaming fat devils of pigs.

—Art, said Stephen, is the human disposition of sensible or intelligible matter for an esthetic end. You remember the pigs and forget that. You are a distressing pair, you and Cranly.

Lynch made a grimace at the raw grey sky and said:

—If I am to listen to your esthetic philosophy give me at least another cigarette. I don't care about it. I don't even care about women. Damn you and damn everything. I want a job of five hundred a year.[3] You can't get me one.

Stephen handed him the packet of cigarettes. Lynch took the last one that remained, saying simply:

—Proceed!

—Aquinas, said Stephen, says that is beautiful the apprehension of which pleases.

Lynch nodded.

I remember that, he said. *Pulcra sunt quæ visa placent.*[4]

—He uses the word *visa,* said Stephen, to cover esthetic apprehensions of all kinds, whether through sight or hearing or through any other avenue of apprehension. This word, though it is vague, is clear enough to keep away good and evil which excite desire and loathing. It means certainly a stasis and not a kinesis. How about the true? It produces also a stasis of the mind. You would not write your name in pencil across the hypothenuse of a right-angled triangle.

—No, said Lynch, give me the hypothenuse of the Venus of Praxiteles.

—Static therefore, said Stephen. Plato, I belive, said that beauty is the splendour of truth. I don't think that it has a meaning but the true and the beautiful are akin. Truth is beheld by the intellect which is appeased by the most satisfying relations of the intelligible: beauty is beheld by the imagination which is appeased by the most satisfying relations of the sensible. The first step in the direction of truth is to understand the frame and scope of the intellect itself, to comprehend the act itself of intellection. Aristotle's entire

[3] Five hundred pounds per year was a figure often given as what it took to live like a gentleman in the pre-World War I Britain.

[4] The actual phrase from the *Summa Theologica* of St. Thomas Aquinas is *pulchra enim dicunter quae visa placent*—"beauty is that which gives pleasure to the sight."

system of philosophy rests upon his book of psychology and that, I think, rests on his statement that the same attribute cannot at the same time and in the same connection belong to and not belong to the same subject. The first step in the direction of beauty is to understand the frame and scope of the imagination, to comprehend the act itself of esthetic apprehension. Is that clear?

—But what is beauty? asked Lynch impatiently. Out with another definition. Something we see and like! Is that the best you and Aquinas can do?

—Let us take woman, said Stephen.

—Let us take her! said Lynch fervently.

—The Greek, the Turk, the Chinese, the Copt, the Hottentot, said Stephen, all admire a different type of female beauty. That seems to be a maze out of which we cannot escape. I see however two ways out. One is this hypothesis: that every physical quality admired by men in women is in direct connection with the manifold functions of women for the propagation of the species. It may be so. The world, it seems, is drearier than even you, Lynch, imagined. For my part I dislike that way out. It leads to eugenics rather than to esthetic. It leads you out of the maze into a new gaudy lecture-room where MacCann, with one hand on *The Origin of Species* and the other hand on the new testament, tells you that you admired the great flanks of Venus because you felt that she would bear you burly offspring and admired her great breasts because you felt that she would give good milk to her children and yours.

—Then MacCann is a sulphuryellow liar, said Lynch energetically.

—There remains another way out, said Stephen, laughing.

—To wit? said Lynch.

—This hypothesis, Stephen began.

A long dray laden with old iron came round the corner of Sir Patrick Dun's hospital covering the end of Stephen's speech with the harsh roar of jangled and rattling metal. Lynch closed his ears and gave out oath after oath till the dray had passed. Then he turned on his heel rudely. Stephen turned also and waited for a few moments till his companion's illhumour had had its vent.

—This hypothesis, Stephen repeated, is the other way out: that, though the same object may not seem beautiful to all people, all people who admire a beautiful object find in it certain relations which satisfy and coincide with the stages themselves of all esthetic apprehension. These relations of the sensible, visible to you through one form and to me through another, must be therefore the necessary qualities of beauty. Now, we can return to our old friend saint Thomas for another pennyworth of wisdom.

Lynch laughed.

—It amuses me vastly, he said, to hear you quoting him time after time like a jolly round friar. Are you laughing in your sleeve?

—MacAlister, answered Stephen, would call my esthetic theory applied Aquinas. So far as this side of esthetic philosophy extends Aquinas will carry me all along the line. When we come to the phenomena of artistic conception, artistic gestation and artistic reproduction I require a new terminology and a new personal experience.

—Of course, said Lynch. After all Aquinas, in spite of his intellect, was exactly a good round friar. But you will tell me about the new personal experience and new terminology some other day. Hurry up and finish the first part.

—Who knows? said Stephen, smiling. Perhaps Aquinas would understand me better than you. He was a poet himself. He wrote a hymn for Maundy Thursday. It begins with the words *Pange lingua gloriosi*.[5] They say it is the highest glory of the hymnal. It is an intricate and soothing hymn. I like it: but there is no hymn that can be put beside that mournful and majestic processional song, the *Vexilla Regis* of Venantius Fortunatus.

Lynch began to sing softly and solemnly in a deep bass voice:

> *Impleta sunt quæ concinit*
> *David fideli carmine*
> *Dicendo nationibus*
> *Regnavit a ligno Deus*.[6]

—That's great! he said, well pleased. Great music!

They turned into Lower Mount Street. A few steps from the corner a fat young man, wearing a silk neckcloth, saluted them and stopped

—Did you hear the results of the exams? he asked. Griffin was plucked. Halpin and O'Flynn are through the home civil.[7] Moonan got fifth place in the Indian.[8] O'Shaughnesssy got fourteenth. The Irish fellows in Clarke's gave them a feed last night. They all ate curry.

His pallid bloated face expressed benevolent malice and, as he had advanced through his tidings of success, his small fatencircled eyes vanished out of sight and his weak wheezing voice out of hearing.

In a reply to a question of Stephen's his eyes and his voice came forth again from their lurkingplaces.

—Yes, MacCullagh and I, he said. He's taking pure mathematics and I'm taking constitutional history. There are twenty subjects. I'm taking botany too. You know I'm a member of the field club.

He drew back from the other two in a stately fashion and placed a plump woollengloved hand on his breast, from which muttered wheezing laughter at once broke forth.

—Bring us a few turnips and onions the next time you go out, said Stephen drily, to make a stew.

The fat student laughed indulgently and said:

---

[5] St. Thomas' hymn celebrating Christ's triumph on the cross begins, *"Tell, my tongue* of the victory gained in *glorious* conflict."* Maundy Thursday is the day before Good Friday.

[6] From "The Banners of the King Advance," by Venantius Fortunatus (c. 530–600), Bishop of Poitiers:
> Fulfilled is all that David told
> In true prophetic song of old:
> Amidst the nations, God, saith he,
> Hath reigned and triumphed from the Tree.

[7] Examinations for domestic civil service positions.

[8] That is, examinations for civil service positions in India.

—We are all highly respectable people in the field club. Last Saturday we went out to Glenmalure, seven of us.

—With women, Donovan? said Lynch.

Donovan again laid his hand on his chest and said:

—Our end is the acquisition of knowledge.

Then he said quickly:

—I hear you are writing some essay about esthetics.

Stephen made a vague gesture of denial.

—Goethe and Lessing, said Donovan, have written a lot on that subject, the classical school and the romantic school and all that. The *Laocoon* interested me very much when I read it. Of course it is idealistic, German, ultraprofound.

Neither of the others spoke. Donovan took leave of them urbanely.

—I must go, he said softly and benevolently. I have a strong suspicion, amounting almost to a conviction, that my sister intended to make pancakes today for the dinner of the Donovan family.

—Goodbye, Stephen said in his wake. Don't forget the turnips for me and my mate.

Lynch gazed after him, his lip curling in slow scorn till his face resembled a devil's mask:

—To think that that yellow pancakeeating excrement can get a good job, he said at length, and I have to smoke cheap cigarettes!

They turned their faces towards Merrion Square and went on for a little in silence.

—To finish what I was saying about beauty, said Stephen, the most satisfying relations of the sensible must therefore correspond to the necessary phases of artistic apprehension. Find these and you find the qualities of universal beauty. Aquinas says:: *ad pulcritudinem tria requiruntur, integritas, consonantia, claritas.* I translate it so: *Three things are needed for beauty, wholeness, harmony and radiance.* Do these correspond to the phases of apprehension? Are you following?

—Of course, I am, said Lynch. If you think I have an excrementitious intelligence run after Donovan and ask him to listen to you.

Stephen pointed to a basket which a butcher's boy had slung inverted on his head.

—Look at that basket, he said.

—I see it, said Lynch.

—In order to see that basket, said Stephen, your mind first of all separates the basket from the rest of the visible universe which is not the basket. The first phase of apprehension is a bounding line drawn about the object to be apprehended. An esthetic image is presented to us either in space or in time. What is audible is presented in time, what is visible is presented in space. But, temporal or spatial, the esthetic image is first luminously apprehended as selfbounded and selfcontained upon the immeasurable background of space or time which is not it. You apprehend it as *one* thing. You see it as one whole. You apprehend its wholeness. That is *integritas.*

Bull's eye! said Lynch, laughing. Go on.

—Then, said Stephen, you pass from point to point, led by its formal lines; you apprehend it as balanced part against part within its limits; you feel the rhythm of its structure. In other words the synthesis of immediate perception is followed by the analysis of apprehension. Having first felt that it is *one* thing you feel now that it is a *thing*. You apprehend it as complex, multiple, divisible, separable, made up of its parts, the result of its parts and their sum, harmonious. That is *consonantia*.

—Bull's eye again! said Lynch wittily. Tell me now what is *claritas* and you win the cigar.

—The connotation of the word, Stephen said, is rather vague. Aquinas uses a term which seems to be inexact. It baffled me for a long time. It would lead you to believe that he had in mind symbolism or idealism, the supreme quality of beauty being a light from some other world, the idea of which the matter is but the shadow, the reality of which it is but the symbol. I thought he might mean that *claritas* is the artistic discovery and representation of the divine purpose in anything or a force of generalisation which would make the esthetic image a universal one, make it outshine its proper conditions. But that is literary talk. I understand it so. When you have apprehended that basket as one thing and have then analysed it according to its form and apprehended it as a thing you make the only synthesis which is logically and esthetically permissible. You see that it is that thing which it is and no other thing. The radiance of which he speaks is the scholastic *quidditas,* the *whatness* of a thing. This supreme quality is felt by the artist when the esthetic image is first conceived in his imagination. The mind in that mysterious instant Shelley likened beautifully to a fading coal.[9] The instant wherein that supreme quality of beauty, the clear radiance of the esthetic image, is apprehended luminously by the mind which has been arrested by its wholeness and fascinated by its harmony is the luminous silent stasis of esthetic pleasure, a spiritual state very like to that cardiac condition which the Italian physiologist Luigi Galvani, using a phrase almost as beautiful as Shelley's, called the enchantment of the heart.

Stephen paused and, though his companion did not speak, felt that his words had called up around them a thoughtenchanted silence.

—What I have said, he began again, refers to beauty in the wider sense of the word, in the sense which the word has in the literary tradition. In the marketplace it has another sense. When we speak of beauty in the second sense of the term our judgment is influenced in the first place by the art itself and by the form of that art. The image, it is clear, must be set between the mind or senses of the artist himself and the mind or senses of others. If you bear this in memory you will see that art necessarily divides itself into three forms progressing from one to the next. These forms are: the lyrical form, the form wherein the artist presents his image in immediate relation to himself; the epical form, the form wherein he presents his image in mediate relation to himself and to others; the dramatic form, the form wherein he presents his image in immediate relation to others.

—That you told me a few nights ago, said Lynch, and we began the famous discussion.

—I have a book at home, said Stephen, in which I have written down

[9] Shelley used the simile in his "A Defence of Poetry," 1821.

questions which are more amusing than yours were. In finding the answers to them I found the theory of esthetic which I am trying to explain. Here are some questions I set myself: *Is a chair finely made tragic or comic? Is the portrait of Mona Lisa good if I desire to see it? Is the bust of Sir Philip Crampton[10] lyrical, epical or dramatic? Can excrement or a child or a louse be a work of art? If not, why not?*

—Why not, indeed? said Lynch, laughing.

—*If a man hacking in fury at a block of wood*, Stephen continued, *make there an image of a cow, is that image a work of art? If not, why not?*

—That's a lovely one, said Lynch, laughing again. That has the true scholastic stink.

—Lessing,[11] said Stephen, should not have taken a group of statutes to write of. The art, being inferior, does not present the forms I spoke of distinguished clearly one from another. Even in literature, the highest and most spiritual art, the forms are often confused. The lyrical form is in fact the simplest verbal vesture of an instant of emotion, a rhythmical cry such as ages ago cheered on the man who pulled at the oar or dragged stones up a slope. He who utters it is more conscious of the instant of emotion than of himself as feeling emotion. The simplest epical form is seen emerging out of lyrical literature when the artist prolongs and broods upon himself as the centre of an epical event and this form progresses till the centre of emotional gravity is equidistant from the artist himself and from others. The narrative is no longer purely personal. The personality of the artist passes into the narration itself, flowing round and round the persons and the action like a vital sea. This progress you will see easily in that old English ballad *Turpin Hero* which begins in the first person and ends in the third person. The dramatic form is reached when the vitality which has flowed and eddied round each person fills every person with such vital force that he or she assumes a proper and intangible esthetic life. The personality of the artist, at first a cry or a cadence or a mood and then a fluid and lambent narrative, finally refines itself out of existence, impersonalises itself, so to speak. The esthetic image in the dramatic form is life purified in and reprojected from the human imagination. The mystery of esthetic like that of material creation is accomplished. The artist, like the God of the creation, remains within or behind or beyond or above his handiwork, invisible, refined out of existence, indifferent, paring his fingernails.

—Trying to refine them also out of existence, said Lynch.

A fine rain began to fall from the high veiled sky and they turned into the duke's lawn, to reach the national library before the shower came.

—What do you mean, Lynch asked surlily, by prating about beauty and the imagination in this miserable God-forsaken island? No wonder the artist retired within or behind his handiwork after having perpetrated this country.

The rain fell faster. When they passed through the passage beside the

[10] Sir Philip Crampton (1777–1852) was a Dublin surgeon whose bust stood in St. Stephen's Green near University College, Dublin.

[11] Lessing's *Laocoon* takes its name from a famous statue-group depicting the strangling of Laocoon and his two sons by two giant snakes. The story is told by Virgil in Book II of the Aeneid. The statue-group, of perhaps the second century A.D., was discovered in 1506 among the ruins of the house of the Roman Emperor Titus.

royal Irish academy they found many students sheltering under the arcade of the library. Cranly, leaning against a pillar, was picking his teeth with a sharpened match, listening to some companions. Some girls stood near the entrance door. Lynch whispered to Stephen:

—Your beloved is here.

Stephen took his place silently on the step below the group of students, heedless of the rain which fell fast, turning his eyes towards her from time to time. She too stood silently among her companions. She has no priest to flirt with, he thought with conscious bitterness, remembering how he had seen her last. Lynch was right. His mind, emptied of theory and courage, lapsed back into a listless peace.

*   *   *

D. H. Lawrence

NATHANIEL HAWTHORNE AND
THE SCARLET LETTER

D[avid] H[erbert] Lawrence stands with James Joyce as one of the two greatest novelists writing in English in the twentieth century. He was born in Nottingham in 1885 to parents of quite ill-assorted backgrounds. His father was a coal-miner, virtually illiterate, his mother a woman of some education who had brought to the increasingly unhappy marriage the habits and aspirations of her middle-class rearing. Lawrence gave early evidence of his intellectual and artistic bent, which his mother encouraged. He attended University College in Nottingham, qualified as a schoolteacher, and for some years taught school—grudgingly but, it is said, effectively—while making his first steps toward the fulfilment of his literary ambitions.

The disparity between his parents' temperaments and cultural standards and the tension it caused in the life of the family are superbly described by Lawrence in his first mature novel, *Sons and Lovers* (1913), and are generally recognized to have been definitive in determining the nature of his genius. His early loyalty had been given to his mother and to her ideals of amenity, enlightenment, and achievement, but as the years passed he came increasingly to believe that his father embodied principles that were more authentic, that his "darkness" was, in its instinctuality, more "life-giving." Although the best of his novels—*The Rainbow* (1915) and *Women in Love* (1920) may be mentioned in this category—transcend the limitations of a systematic dialectic, Lawrence committed his thought, and his creative powers as well, to his conception of the conflict between the conscious and the instinctual aspects of the soul. His quarrel with modern culture for giving the preference to the "higher" as against the "lower" faculties informs all his novels as well as his overtly polemical works, of which *The Fantasia of the Unconscious* (1922) may be taken as typical, and his literary criticism.

The discussion of Hawthorne forms part of *Studies in Classic American Literature* (1923). This work was undertaken when Lawrence was planning to come to America to settle in Taos, New Mexico, where the climate, it was hoped, would benefit his health—he suffered from tuberculosis and died of the disease in 1930. For many years the *Studies* won but little regard, in part, no doubt, because the book's unconventional manner and jeering tone proved alienating. It is now thought by many students of American literature to be one of the most illuminating works on the subject ever written.

Nathaniel Hawthorne writes romance.

And what's romance? Usually, a nice little tale where you have everything As You Like It, where rain never wets your jacket and gnats never bite your nose and its always daisy-time. *As You Like It* and *Forest Lovers*,[1] etc. *Morte D'Arthur*.

Hawthorne obviously isn't this kind of romanticist: though nobody has muddy boots in the *Scarlet Letter* either.

But there is more to it. *The Scarlet Letter* isn't a pleasant, pretty romance. It is a sort of parable, an earthly story with a hellish meaning.

All the time there is this split in the American art and art-consciousness. On the top it is as nice as pie, goody-goody and lovey-dovey. Like Hawthorne being such a blue-eyed darling, in life, and Longfellow and the rest such sucking doves. Hawthorne's wife said she "never saw him in time," which doesn't mean she saw him too late. But always in the "frail effulgence of eternity."

Serpents they were. Look at the inner meaning of their art and see what demons they were.

You *must* look through the surface of American art, and see the inner diabolism of the symbolic meaning. Otherwise it is all mere childishness.

That blue-eyed darling Nathaniel knew disagreeable things in his inner soul. He was careful to send them out in disguise.

Always the same. The deliberate consciousness of Americans so fair and smooth-spoken, and the under-consciousness so devilish. *Destroy! destroy! destroy!* hums the under-consciousness. *Love and produce! Love and produce!* cackles the upper consciousness. And the world hears only the Love-and-produce cackle. Refuses to hear the hum of destruction underneath. Until such time as it will *have* to hear.

The American has got to destroy. It is his destiny. It is his destiny to destroy the whole corpus of the white psyche, the white consciousness. And he's got to do it secretly. As the growing of a dragon-fly inside a chrysalis or cocoon destroys the larva grub, secretly.

Though many a dragon-fly never gets out of the chrysalis case: dies inside. As America might.

So the secret chrysalis of *The Scarlet Letter*, diabolically destroying the old psyche inside.

Be good! Be good! warbles Nathaniel. *Be good, and never sin! Be sure your sins will find you out.*

---

[1] *Forest Lovers* (1898), by Maurice Hewlett (1861–1923) is a softly voluptuous tale of the Middle Ages modeled on the *Morte D'Arthur* (by Thomas Malory, d. 1471), which gathers together the main body of legends about King Arthur and his knights into one comprehensive narrative.

So convincingly that his wife never saw him "as in time."

Then listen to the diabolic undertone of *The Scarlet Letter*.

Man ate of the tree of knowledge, and became ashamed of himself.

Do you imagine Adam had never lived with Eve before that apple episode? Yes, he had. As a wild animal with his mate.

It didn't become "sin" till the knowledge-poison entered. That apple of Sodom.

We are divided in ourselves, against ourselves. And that is the meaning of the cross symbol.

In the first place, Adam knew Eve as a wild animal knows its mate, momentaneously, but vitally, in blood-knowledge. Blood-knowledge, not mind-knowledge. Blood-knowledge, that seems utterly to forget, but doesn't. Blood-knowledge, instinct, intuition, all the vast vital flux of knowing that goes on in the dark, antecedent to the mind.

Then came that beastly apple, and the other sort of knowledge started.

Adam began to look at himself. "My hat!" he said. "What's this? My Lord! What the deuce!—And Eve! I wonder about Eve."

Thus starts KNOWING. Which shortly runs to UNDERSTANDING, when the devil gets his own.

When Adam went and took Eve, *after* the apple, he didn't do any more than he had done many a time before, in act. But in consciousness he did something very different. So did Eve. Each of them kept an eye on what they were doing, they watched what was happening to them. They wanted to KNOW. And that was the birth of sin. Not *doing* it, but KNOWING about it. Before the apple, they had shut their eyes and their minds had gone dark. Now, they peeped and pried and imagined. They watched themselves. And they felt uncomfortable after. They felt self-conscious. So they said, "The *act* is sin. Let's hide. We've sinned."

No wonder the Lord kicked them out of the Garden. Dirty hypocrites.

The sin was the self-watching, self-consciousness. The sin and the doom. Dirty understanding.

Nowadays men do hate the idea of dualism. It's no good, dual we are. The Cross. If we accept the symbol, then, virtually, we accept the fact. We are divided against ourselves.

For instance, the blood *hates* being KNOWN by the mind. It feels itself destroyed when it is KNOWN. Hence the profound instinct of privacy.

And on the other hand, the mind and the spiritual consciousness of man simply *hates* the dark potency of blood-acts: hates the genuine dark sensual orgasms, which do, for the time being, actually obliterate the mind and the spiritual consciousness, plunge them in a suffocating flood of darkness.

You can't get away from this.

Blood-consciousness overwhelms, obliterates, and annuls mind-consciousness.

Mind-consciousness extinguishes blood-consciousness, and consumes the blood.

We are all of us conscious in both ways. And the two ways are antagonistic in us.

They will always remain so.

That is our cross.

The antagonism is so obvious, and so far-reaching, that it extends to the smallest thing. The cultured, highly-conscious person of to-day *loathes* any form of physical, "menial" work: such as washing dishes or sweeping a floor or chopping wood. This menial work is an insult to the spirit. "When I see men carrying heavy loads, doing brutal work, it always makes me want to cry," said a beautiful, cultured woman to me.

"When you say that, it makes me want to beat you," said I, in reply. "When I see you with your beautiful head pondering heavy thoughts, I just want to hit you. It outrages me."

My father hated books, hated the sight of anyone reading or writing.

My mother hated the thought that any of her sons should be condemned to manual labour. Her sons must have something higher than that.

She won. But she died first.

He laughs longest who laughs last.

There is a basic hostility in all of us between the physical and the mental, the blood and the spirit. The mind is "ashamed" of the blood. And the blood is destroyed by the mind, actually. Hence pale-faces.

At present the mind-consciousness and the so-called spirit triumphs. In America supremely. In America, nobody does anything from the blood. Always from the nerves, if not from the mind. The blood is chemically reduced by the nerves, in American activity.

When an Italian labourer labours, his mind and nerves sleep, his blood acts ponderously.

Americans, when they are *doing* things, never seem really to be doing them. They are "busy about" it. They are always busy "about" something. But truly *immersed* in *doing* something, with the deep blood-consciousness active, that they never are.

They *admire* the blood-consciousness spontaneity. And they want to get it in their heads. "Live from the body," they shriek. It is their last mental shriek. *Co-ordinate.*

It is a further attempt still to rationalize the body and blood. "Think about such and such a muscle," they say, "and relax there."

And every time you "conquer" the body with the mind (you can say "heal" it, if you like) you cause a deeper, more dangerous complex or tension somewhere else.

Ghastly Americans, with their blood no longer blood. A yellow spiritual fluid.

The Fall.

There have been lots of Falls.

We *fell* into *knowledge* when Eve bit the apple. Self-conscious knowledge. For the first time the mind put up a fight against the blood. Wanting to UNDERSTAND. That is to intellectualize the blood.

The blood must be *shed*, says Jesus.

Shed on the cross of our own divided psyche.

Shed the blood, and you become mind-conscious. Eat the body and drink the blood, self-cannibalizing, and you become extremely conscious, like Americans and some Hindus. Devour yourself, and God knows what a lot you'll know, what a lot you'll be conscious of.

Mind you don't choke yourself.

For a long time men *believed* that they could be perfected through the mind, through the spirit. They believed, passionately. They had their ecstasy in pure consciousness. They *believed* in purity, chastity, and the wings of the spirit.

America soon plucked the bird of the spirit. America soon killed the *belief* in the spirit. But not the practice. The practice continued with a sarcastic vehemence. America, with a perfect inner contempt for the spirit and the consciousness of man, practises the same spirituality and universal love and KNOWING all the time, incessantly, like a drug habit. And inwardly gives not a fig for it. Only for the *sensation*. The pretty-pretty *sensation* of love, loving all the world. And the nice fluttering aeroplane *sensation* of knowing, knowing, knowing. Then the prettiest of all sensations, the sensation of UNDERSTANDING. Oh, what a lot they understand, the darlings! *So* good at the trick, they are. Just a trick of self-conceit.

The Scarlet Letter gives the show away.

You have your pure-pure young parson Dimmesdale.

You have the beautiful Puritan Hester at his feet.

And the first thing she does is to seduce him.

And the first thing he does is to be seduced.

And the second thing they do is to hug their sin in secret, and gloat over it, and try to understand.

Which is the myth of New England.

Deerslayer[2] refused to be seduced by Judith Hutter. At least the Sodom apple of sin didn't fetch him.

But Dimmesdale was seduced gloatingly. Oh, luscious Sin!

He was such a pure young man.

That he had to make a fool of purity.

The American psyche.

Of course the best part of the game lay in keeping up pure appearances.

The greatest triumph a woman can have, especially an American woman, is the triumph of seducing a man: especially if he is pure.

And he gets the greatest thrill of all, in falling.—"Seduce me, Mrs. Hercules."

And the pair of them share the subtlest delight in keeping up pure appearances, when everybody knows all the while. But the power of pure appearances is something to exult in. All America gives in to it. *Look* pure!

To seduce a man. To have everybody know. To keep up appearances of purity. Pure!

This is the great triumph of woman.

A. The Scarlet Letter. Adulteress! The great Alpha. Alpha! Adulteress! The new Adam and Adama! American!

A. Adulteress! Stitched with gold thread, glittering upon the bosom. The proudest insignia.

Put her upon the scaffold and worship her there. Worship her there. The Woman, the Magna Mater. *A.* Adulteress! Abel!

---

[2] Deerslayer is Natty Bumppo, hero of the Leatherstocking novels of James Fenimore Cooper (1789–1851). Judith Hutter is the heroine of *Deerslayer* (1841).

Abel! Abel! Abel! Admirable!

It becomes a farce.

The fiery heart. A. Mary of the Bleeding Heart. Mater Adolerata! A. Capital A. Adulteress. Glittering with gold thread. Abel! Adultery. Admirable!

It is, perhaps, the most colossal satire ever penned. *The Scarlet Letter.* And by a blue-eyed darling of a Nathaniel.

Not Bumppo, however.

The human spirit, fixed in a lie, adhering to a lie, giving itself perpetually the lie.

All begins with A.

Adulteress. Alpha. Abel, Adam. A. America.

The Scarlet Letter.

"Had there been a Papist among the crowd of Puritans, he might have seen in this beautiful woman, so picturesque in her attire and mien, and with the infant at her bosom, an object to remind him of the image of Divine Maternity, which so many illustrious painters have vied with one another to represent; something which should remind him, indeed, but only by contrast, of that sacred image of sinless Motherhood, whose infant was to redeem the world."

Whose infant was to redeem the world indeed! It will be a startling redemption the world will get from the American infant.

"Here was a taint of deepest sin in the most sacred quality of human life, working such effect that the world was only the darker for this woman's beauty, and more lost for the infant she had borne."

Just listen to the darling. Isn't he a master of apology?

Of symbols, too.

His pious blame is a chuckle of praise all the while.

Oh, Hester, you are a demon. A man *must* be pure, just that you can seduce him to a fall. Because the greatest thrill in life is to bring down the Sacred Saint with a flop into the mud. Then when you've brought him down, humbly wipe off the mud with your hair, another Magdalen. And then go home and dance a witch's jig of triumph, and stitch yourself a Scarlet Letter with gold thread, as duchesses used to stitch themselves coronets. And then stand meek on the scaffold and fool the world. Who will all be envying you your sin, and beating you because you've stolen an advantage over them.

Hester Prynne is the great nemesis of woman. She is the KNOWING Ligeia[3] risen diabolic from the grave. Having her own back. UNDERSTANDING.

This time it is Mr. Dimmesdale who dies. She lives on and is Abel.

His spiritual love was a lie. And prostituting the woman to his spiritual love, as popular clergymen do, in his preachings and loftiness, was a tall white lie. Which came flop.

We are so pure in spirit. Hi-tiddly-i-ty!

Till she tickled him in the right place, and he fell.

Flop.

[3] Ligeia, in a story by Poe that takes her name for its title, comes from the grave to usurp the body and soul of her former husband's new wife, Rowena.

Flop goes spiritual love.

But keep up the game. Keep up appearances. Pure are the pure. To the pure all things, etc.

Look out, Mister, for the Female Devotee. Whatever you do, don't let her start tickling you. She knows your weak spot. Mind your Purity.

When Hester Prynne seduced Arthur Dimmesdale it was the beginning of the end. But from the beginning of the end to the end of the end is a hundred years or two.

Mr. Dimmesdale also wasn't at the end of his resources. Previously, he had lived by governing his body, ruling it, in the interests of his spirit. Now he has a good time all by himself torturing his body, whipping it, piercing it with thorns, macerating himself. It's a form of masturbation. He wants to get a mental grip on his body. And since he can't quite manage it with the mind, witness his fall—he will give it what for, with whips. His will shall *lash* his body. And he enjoys his pains. Wallows in them. To the pure all things are pure.

It is the old self-mutilation process, gone rotten. The mind wanting to get its teeth in the blood and flesh. The ego exulting in the tortures of the mutinous flesh. I, the ego, I *will* triumph over my own flesh. Lash! Lash! I am a grand free spirit. *Lash!* I am the master of my soul! *Lash! Lash!* I am the captain of my soul. *Lash!* Hurray! "In the fell clutch of circumstance," etc., etc.

Good-bye Arthur. He depended on women for his Spiritual Devotees, spiritual brides. So, the woman just touched him in his weak spot, his Achilles Heel of the flesh. Look out for the spiritual bride. She's after the weak spot.

It is the battle of wills.

"For the will therein lieth, which dieth not—"[4]

The Scarlet Woman becomes a Sister of Mercy. Didn't she just, in the late war. Oh, Prophet Nathaniel!

Hester urges Dimmesdale to go away with her, to a new country, to a new life. He isn't having any.

He knows there is no new country, no new life on the globe to-day. It is the same old thing, in different degrees, everywhere. *Plus ça change, plus c'est la même chose.*[5]

Hester thinks, with Dimmesdale for her husband, and Pearl for her child, in Australia, maybe, she'd have been perfect.

But she wouldn't. Dimmesdale had already fallen from his integrity as a minister of the Gospel of the Spirit. He had lost his manliness. He didn't see the point of just leaving himself between the hands of a woman, and going away to a "new country," to be her thing entirely. She'd only have despised him more, as every woman despises a man who has "fallen" to her: despises him with her tenderest lust.

---

[4] The epigraph to Poe's "Ligeia" is "And the will therein lieth, which dieth not. Who knoweth the mysteries of the will, with its vigor? For God is but a great will pervading all things by nature of its intentness. Man doth not yield himself to the angels, nor unto death utterly, save only through the weakness of his feeble will." Poe assigns these remarks to Joseph Glanvill, but no one has ever been able to find the remarks in that man's works.

[5] "The greater the change, the more it is the same thing."

He stood for nothing any more. So let him stay where he was and dree out his weird.

She had dished him and his spirituality, so he hated her. As Angel Clare was dished, and hated Tess. As Jude in the end hated Sue:[6] or should have done. The women make fools of them, the spiritual men. And when, as men, they've gone flop in their spirituality, they can't pick themselves up whole any more. So they just crawl, and die detesting the female, or the females, who made them fall.

The saintly minister gets a bit of his own back, at the last minute, by making public confession from the very scaffold where she was exposed. Then he dodges into death. But he's had a bit of his own back, on everybody.

" 'Shall we not meet again?' whispered she, bending her face down close to him. 'Shall we not spend our immortal life together? Surely, surely we have ransomed one another with all this woe! Thou lookest far into eternity with those bright dying eyes. Tell me what thou seeest!' "

" 'Hush, Hester—hush,' said he, with tremulous solemnity. 'The law we broke!—the sin here so awfully revealed! Let these alone be in thy thoughts. I fear! I fear!' "

So he dies, throwing the "sin" in her teeth, and escaping into death.

The law we broke, indeed. You bet!

Whose law?

But it is truly a law, that man must either stick to the belief he has grounded himself on, and obey the laws of that belief. Or he must admit the belief itself to be inadequate, and prepare himself for a new thing.

There was no change in belief, either in Hester or in Dimmesdale or in Hawthorne or in America. The same old treacherous belief, which was really cunning disbelief, in the Spirit, in Purity, in Selfless Love, and in Pure Consciousness. They would go on following this belief, for the sake of the sensationalism of it. But they would make a fool of it all the time. Like Woodrow Wilson, and the rest of modern Believers. The rest of modern Saviours.

If you meet a Saviour, to-day, be sure he is trying to make an innermost fool of you. Especially if the saviour be an UNDERSTANDING WOMAN, offering her love.

Hester lives on, pious as pie, being a public nurse. She becomes at last an acknowledged saint, Abel of the Scarlet Letter.

She would, being a woman. She has had her triumph over the individual man, so she quite loves subscribing to the whole spiritual life of society. She will make herself as false as hell, for society's sake, once she's had her real triumph over Saint Arthur.

Blossoms out into a Sister-of-Mercy Saint.

But it's a long time before she really takes anybody in. People kept on thinking her a witch, which she was.

As a matter of fact, unless a woman is held, by man, safe within the bounds of belief, she becomes inevitably a destructive force. She can't help herself. A woman is almost always vulnerable to pity. She can't bear to see

---

[6] Angel Clare and Tess are hero and heroine of *Tess of the D'Urbervilles* (1891); Jude and Sue are the major male and female characters of *Jude the Obscure* (1896), both novels by Thomas Hardy (1840–1928).

anything *physically* hurt. But let a woman loose from the bounds and restraints of man's fierce belief, in his gods and in himself, and she becomes a gentle devil. She becomes subtly diabolic. The colossal evil of the united spirit of Woman. WOMAN, German woman or American woman, or every other sort of woman, in the last war, was something frightening. As every *man* knows.

Woman becomes a helpless, would-be-loving demon. She is helpless. Her very love is a subtle poison.

Unless a man believes in himself and his gods, *genuinely*: unless he fiercely obeys his own Holy Ghost; his woman will destroy him. Woman is the nemesis of doubting man. She can't help it.

And with Hester, after Ligeia, woman becomes a nemesis to man. She bolsters him up from the outside, she destroys him from the inside. And he dies hating her, as Dimmesdale did.

Dimmesdale's spirituality had gone on too long, too far. It had become a false thing. He found his nemesis in woman. And he was done for.

Woman is a strange and rather terrible phenomenon, to man. When the subconscious soul of woman recoils from its creative union with man, it becomes a destructive force. It exerts, willy-nilly, an invisible destructive influence. The woman herself may be as nice as milk, to all appearance, like Ligeia. But she is sending out waves of silent destruction of the faltering spirit in men, all the same. She doesn't know it. She can't even help it. But she does it. The devil is in her.

The very women who are most busy saving the bodies of men, and saving the children: these women-doctors, these nurses, these educationalists, these public-spirited women, these female saviours: they are all, from the inside, sending out waves of destructive malevolence which eat out the inner life of a man, like a cancer. It is so, it will be so, till men realize it and react to save themselves.

God won't save us. The women are so devilish godly. Men must save themselves in this strait, and by no sugary means either.

A woman can use her sex in sheer malevolence and poison, while she is *behaving* as meek and good as gold. Dear darling, she is really snow-white in her blamelessness. And all the while she is using her sex as a she-devil, for the endless hurt of her man. She doesn't know it. She will never believe it if you tell her. And if you give her a slap in the face for her fiendishness, she will rush to the first magistrate, in indignation. She is so *absolutely* blameless, the she-devil, the dear, dutiful creature.

Give her the great slap, just the same, just when she is being most angelic. Just when she is bearing her cross most meekly.

Oh, woman out of bounds is a devil. But it is man's fault. Woman never *asked*, in the first place, to be cast out of her bit of an Eden of belief and trust. It is man's business to bear the responsibility of belief. If he becomes a spiritual fornicator and liar, like Ligeia's husband and Arthur Dimmesdale, how *can* a woman believe in him? Belief doesn't go by choice. And if a woman doesn't believe in a *man*, she believes, essentially, in nothing. She becomes, willy-nilly, a devil.

A devil she is, and a devil she will be. And most men will succumb to her devilishness.

Hester Prynne was a devil. Even when she was so meekly going round as a sick-nurse. Poor Hester. Part of her wanted to be saved from her own devilishness. And another part wanted to go on and on in devilishness, for revenge. Revenge! REVENGE! It is this that fills the unconscious spirit of woman to-day. Revenge against man, and against the spirit of man, which has betrayed her into unbelief. Even when she is most sweet and a salvationist, she is her most devilish, is woman. She gives her man the sugar-plum of her own submissive sweetness. And when he's taken this sugar-plum in his mouth, a scorpion comes out of it. After he's taken this Eve to his bosom, oh, so loving, she destroys him inch by inch. Woman and her revenge! She will have it, and go on having it, for decades and decades, unless she's stopped. And to stop her you've got to believe in yourself and your gods, your own Holy Ghost, Sir Man; and then you've got to fight her, and never give in. She's a devil. But in the long run she is conquerable. And just a tiny bit of her wants to be conquered. You've got to fight three-quarters of her, in absolute hell, to get at the final quarter of her that wants a release, at last, from the hell of her own revenge. But it's a long last. And not yet.

"She had in her nature a rich, voluptuous, oriental characteristic—a taste for the gorgeously beautiful." This is Hester. This is American. But she repressed her nature in the above direction. She would not even allow herself the luxury of labouring at fine, delicate stitching. Only she dressed her little sin-child Pearl vividly, and the scarlet letter was gorgeously embroidered. Her Hecate[7] and Astarte[8] insignia.

"A voluptuous, oriental characteristic—" That lies waiting in American women. It is probable that the Mormons are the forerunners of the coming real America. It is probable that men will have more than one wife, in the coming America. That you will have again a half-oriental womanhood, and a polygamy.

The grey nurse, Hester. The Hecate, the hellcat. The slowly-evolving voluptuous female of the new era, with a whole new submissiveness to the dark, phallic principle.

But it takes time. Generation after generation of nurses and political women and salvationists. And in the end, the dark erection of the images of sex-worship once more, and the newly submissive women. That kind of depth. Deep women in that respect. When we have at last broken this insanity of mental-spiritual consciousness. And the women *choose* to experience again the great submission.

"The poor, whom she thought out to be the objects of her bounty, often reviled the hand that was stretched to succour them."

Naturally. The poor hate a salvationist. They smell the devil underneath.

"She was patient—a martyr indeed—but she forbore to pray for her enemies, lest, in spite of her forgiving aspirations, the words of the blessing should stubbornly twist themselves into a curse."

So much honesty, at least. No wonder the old witch-lady Mistress Hibbins claimed her for another witch.

"She grew to have a dread of children; for they had imbibed from their parents a vague idea of something horrible in this dreary woman gliding

---

[7] In Greek mythology, goddess of ghosts and witchcraft.
[8] Phoenician and Babylonian goddess of fertility and love.

silently through the town, with never any companion but only one child."

"A vague idea!" Can't you see her "gliding silently?" It's not a question of a vague idea imbibed, but a definite feeling directly received.

"But sometimes, once in many days, or perchance in many months, she felt an eye—a human eye—upon the ignominious brand, that seemed to give a momentary relief, as if half her agony were shared. The next instant, back it all rushed again, with a still deeper throb of pain; for in that brief interval she had sinned again. Had Hester sinned alone?"

Of course not. As for sinning again, she would go on all her life silently, changelessly "sinning." She never repented. Not she. Why should she? She had brought down Arthur Dimmesdale, that too-too snow-white bird, and that was her life-work.

As for sinning again when she met two dark eyes in a crowd, why of course. Somebody who understood as she understood.

I always remember meeting the eyes of a gypsy woman, for one moment, in a crowd, in England. She knew, and I knew. What did we know? I was not able to make out. But we knew.

Probably the same fathomless hate of this spiritual-conscious society in which the outcast woman and I both roamed like meek-looking wolves. Tame wolves waiting to shake off their tameness. Never able to.

And again, that "voluptuous, oriental" characteristic that knows the mystery of the ithyphallic[9] gods. She would not betray the ithyphallic gods to this white, leprous-white society of "lovers." Neither will I, if I can help it. These leprous-white, seducing, spiritual women, who "understand" so much. One has been too often seduced, and "understood." "I can read him like a book," said my first lover of me. The book is in several volumes, dear. And more and more comes back to me the gulf of dark hate and *other* understanding, in the eyes of the gypsy woman. So different from the hateful white light of understanding which floats like scum on the eyes of white, oh, so white English and American women, with their understanding voices and their deep, sad words, and their profound, *good* spirits. Pfui!

Hester was scared only of one result of her sin: Pearl. Pearl, the scarlet letter incarnate. The little girl. When women bear children, they produce either devils or sons with gods in them. And it is an evolutionary process. The devil in Hester produced a purer devil in Pearl. And the devil in Pearl will produce—she married an Italian Count—a piece of purer devilishness still.

> And so from hour to hour we ripe and ripe.
> And then from hour to hour we rot and rot.[10]

There was that in the child "which often impelled Hester to ask in bitterness of heart, whether it were for good or ill that the poor little creature had been born at all."

[9] From the Greek *ithys,* straight + *phallos,* phallus.

[10] In Shakespeare's *As You Like It,* Jacques reports Touchstone as saying,
   And so from hour to hour we ripe and ripe
   And then from hour to hour we rot and rot.
   And thereby hangs a tale.
                                                    II, vii, 26–28.
There are quibbles on hour/whore, ripe/reap, rot/root, and "tale" was a slang term for penis.

For ill, Hester. But don't worry. Ill is as necessary as good. Malevolence is as necessary as benevolence. If you have brought forth, spawned, a young malevolence, be sure there is a rampant falseness in the world against which this malevolence must be turned. Falseness has to be bitten and bitten, till it is bitten to death. Hence Pearl.

Pearl. Her own mother compares her to the demon of plague, or scarlet fever, in her red dress. But then plague is necessary to destroy a rotten, false humanity.

Pearl, the devilish girl-child, who can be so tender and loving and *understanding,* and then, when she has understood, will give you a hit across the mouth, and turn on you with a grin of sheer diabolic jeering.

Serves you right, you shouldn't be *understood.* That is your vice. You shouldn't want to be loved, and then you'd not get hit across the mouth. Pearl will love you: marvellously. And she'll hit you across the mouth: oh, so neatly. And serves you right.

Pearl is perhaps the most modern child in all literature.

Old-fashioned Nathaniel, with his little-boy charm, he'll tell you what's what. But he'll cover it with smarm.

Hester simply *hates* her child, from one part of herself. And from another, she cherishes her child as her one precious treasure. For Pearl is the continuing of her female revenge on life. But female revenge hits both ways. Hits back at its own mother. The female revenge in Pearl hits back at Hester, the mother, and Hester is simply livid with fury and "sadness," which is rather amusing.

"The child could not be made amenable to rules. In giving her existence a great law had been broken; and the result was a being whose elements were perhaps beautiful and brilliant, but all in disorder, or with an order peculiar to themselves, amidst which the point of variety and arrangement was difficult or impossible to discover."

Of course the order is peculiar to themselves. But the point of variety is this: "Draw out the loving, sweet soul, draw it out with marvellous understanding; and then spit in its eye."

Hester, of course, didn't at all like it when her sweet child drew out her motherly soul, with yearning and deep understanding: and then spit in the motherly eye, with a grin. But it was a process the mother had started.

Pearl had a peculiar look in her eyes: "a look so intelligent, yet so inexplicable, so perverse, sometimes so malicious, but generally accompanied by a wild flow of spirits, that Hester could not help questioning at such moments whether Pearl was a human child."

A little demon! But her mother, and the saintly Dimmesdale, had borne her. And Pearl, by the very openness of her perversity, was more straightforward than her parents. She flatly refuses any Heavenly Father, seeing the earthly one such a fraud. And she has the pietistic Dimmesdale on toast, spits right in his eye: in both his eyes.

Poor, brave, tormented little soul, always in a state of recoil, she'll be a devil to men when she grows up. But the men deserve it. If they'll let themselves be "drawn," by her loving understanding, they deserve that she shall slap them across the mouth the moment they *are* drawn. The chickens! Drawn and trussed.

Poor little phenomenon of a modern child, she'll grow up into the devil of a modern woman. The nemesis of weak-kneed modern men, craving to be love-drawn.

The third person in the diabolic trinity, or triangle, of the Scarlet Letter, is Hester's first husband, Roger Chillingworth. He is an old Elizabethan physician with a grey beard and a long-furred coat and a twisted shoulder. Another healer. But something of an alchemist, a magician. He is a magician on the verge of modern science, like Francis Bacon.[11]

Roger Chillingworth is of the old order of intellect, in direct line from the mediæval Roger Bacon[12] alchemists. He has an old, intellectual belief in the dark sciences, the Hermetic philosophies.[13] He is no Christian, no selfless aspirer. He is not an aspirer. He is the old authoritarian in man. But without passional belief. Only intellectual belief in himself and his male authority.

Shakespeare's whole tragic wail is because of the downfall of the true male authority, the ithyphallic authority and masterhood. It fell with Elizabeth.[14] It was trodden underfoot with Victoria.[15]

But Chillingworth keeps on the *intellectual* tradition. He hates the new spiritual aspirers, like Dimmesdale, with a black, crippled hate. He is the old male authority, in intellectual tradition.

You can't keep a wife by force of an intellectual tradition. So Hester took to seducing Dimmesdale.

Yet her only marriage, and her last oath, is with the old Roger. He and she are accomplices in pulling down the spiritual saint.

"Why dost thou smile so at me—" she says to her old, vengeful husband. "Art thou not like the Black Man that haunts the forest around us? Hast thou not enticed me into a bond which will prove the ruin of my soul?"

"Not thy soul!" he answered with another smile. "Not, not thy soul!"

It is the soul of the pure preacher, that false thing, which they are after. And the crippled physician—this other healer—blackly vengeful in his old, distorted male authority, and the "loving" woman, they bring down the saint between them.

A black and complementary hatred, akin to love, is what Chillingworth feels for the young, saintly parson. And Dimmesdale responds, in a hideous kind of love. Slowly the saint's life is poisoned. But the black old physician smiles, and tries to keep him alive. Dimmesdale goes in for self-torture, self-lashing, lashing his own white, thin, spiritual saviour's body. The dark old Chillingworth listens outside the door and laughs, and prepares another medicine, so that the game can go on longer. And the saint's very soul goes rotten. Which is the supreme triumph. Yet he keeps up appearances still.

[11] Francis Bacon (1561–1626), English philosopher, essayist, and statesman, who advocated the inductive method, fact-gathering, and experiment, as opposed to scholastic *a priori* reasoning.

[12] Roger Bacon (c. 1214–1294), Franciscan monk, scholastic philosopher, also had an interest in what we would now call science.

[13] A mixture of metaphysics, astrology, magic, and alchemy, from books attributed to Hermes Trismegistus ("thrice-greatest Hermes"), who by Hellenistic Greeks was identified with Thoth, Egyptian god of writing, wisdom, and the underworld.

[14] Queen Elizabeth I (1533–1603).

[15] Queen Victoria (1819–1901).

The black, vengeful soul of the crippled, masterful male, still dark in his authority: and the white ghastliness of the fallen saint! The two halves of manhood mutually destroying one another.

Dimmesdale has a "coup" in the very end. He gives the whole show away by confessing publicly on the scaffold, and dodging into death, leaving Hester dished, and Roger as it were, doubly cuckolded. It is a neat last revenge.

Down comes the curtain, as in Ligeia's poem.

But the child Pearl will be on in the next act, with her Italian Count and a new brood of vipers. And Hester greyly Abelling, in the shadows, after her rebelling.

It is a marvellous allegory. It is to me one of the greatest allegories in all literature, *The Scarlet Letter*. Its marvellous under-meaning! And its perfect duplicity.

The absolute duplicity of that blue-eyed *Wunderkind* of a Nathaniel. The American wonderchild, with his magical allegorical insight.

But even wonder-children have to grow up in a generation or two.

And even SIN becomes stale.

I. A. Richards

PRINCIPLES OF LITERARY CRITICISM

I. A. Richards was born in Sandbach, Cheshire, in 1893. He was educated at Clinton College and at Magdalene College, Cambridge, taking his degree in 1915. In 1922 he became lecturer in English and Moral Sciences at Cambridge, and four years later was elected fellow of Magdalene College. During the Thirties he held visiting professorships in various parts of the world, including China, and in 1939 he joined the Harvard faculty; in 1944 he was appointed to a University Professorship. Since his retirement in 1963 he has published two volumes of poems and a verse drama.

Richards has exerted a direct and pervasive influence on the study of literature for nearly fifty years. His early works—*Foundations of Aesthetics,* written with C. K. Ogden (1921); *The Meaning of Meaning,* also written with Ogden (1923); *Principles of Literary Criticism* (1924); *Science and Poetry* (1925); and *Practical Criticism* (1929)—not only laid the theoretical foundations for what came to be called New Criticism, but also generated the principles of the revolution in the teaching of literature that took place in English and American universities during the second quarter of this century. Stanley Edgar Hyman flatly states that "what we have been calling modern criticism began in 1924, with the publication of *Principles of Literary Criticism,*" and he is probably right.

Richards' early criticism seemed to be what was needed at the time in part because it displayed a sound classical education, a sensitive mind, a genuine feeling for literature, but especially because it was informed by a careful study of the rapidly growing social sciences, of linguistics and semantics, and by a tough-minded anti-metaphysical bias that seemed to ally it with the characteristic tendencies of contemporary philosophy. After Richards' first half-dozen books, critics found it very difficult to speak in a naive way of Beauty, of the "aesthetic response," of absolute criteria of poetic value, but found it natural and profitable to study with care the relations among the actual words of actual poems.

Other books by Richards of special interest to the student of criticism are *Mencius on the Mind* (1932), *The Philosophy of Rhetoric* (1936), *Speculative Instruments* (1955), and above all, *Coleridge on Imagination* (1935).

From *Principles of Literary Criticism,* by I. A. Richards. London: Routledge & Kegan Paul Ltd., New York: Harcourt, Brace & World, Inc. Reprinted by permission of the publishers.

IV. Communication and the Artist

Poetry is the record of the best and happiest moments of the happiest and best minds.—The Defence of Poetry.

The two pillars upon which a theory of criticism must rest are an account of value and an account of communication. We do not sufficiently realise how great a part of our experience takes the form it does, because we are social beings and accustomed to communication from infancy. That we acquire many of our ways of thinking and feeling from parents and others is, of course, a commonplace. But the effects of communication go much deeper than this. The very structure of our minds is largely determined by the fact that man has been engaged in communicating for so many hundreds of thousands of years, throughout the course of his human development and beyond even that. A large part of the distinctive features of the mind are due to its being an in-strument for communication. An experience has to be formed, no doubt, before it is communicated, but it takes the form it does largely because it may have to be communicated. The emphasis which natural selection has put upon com-municative ability is overwhelming.

There are very many problems of psychology, from those with which some of the exponents of *Gestalt theorie*[1] are grappling to those by which psycho-analysts are bewildered, for which this neglected, this almost overlooked aspect of the mind may provide a key, but it is pre-eminently in regard to the arts that it is of service. For the arts are the supreme form of the communicative activity. As we shall see, most of the difficult and obscure points about the structures of the arts, for example the priority of formal elements to content, or the imperson-ality and detachment so much stressed by æstheticians, become easily intelligible as soon as we consider them from this angle. But a possible misunderstanding must be guarded against. Although it is as a communicator that it is most profitable to consider the artist, it is by no means true that he commonly looks upon himself in this light. In the course of his work he is not as a rule deliberately and consciously engaged in a communicative endeavour. When asked, he is more likely than not to reply that communication is an irrelevant or at best a minor issue, and that what he is making is something which is beautiful in itself, or satisfying to him personally, or something expressive, in a more or less vague sense, of his emotions, or of himself, something personal and individual. That other people are going to study it, and to receive ex-periences from it may seem to him a merely accidental, inessential circum-stance. More modestly still, he may say that when he works he is merely amus-ing himself.

---

[1] *Gestalt* means "form" or "shape," and Gestalt psychologists are concerned with the way human perception apprehends phenomena in shapes, forms, configurations, patterns. The term *Gestalt* was first used in this context in 1890, but the psycho-logical school did not begin to define itself until around 1912.

That the artist is not as a rule consciously concerned with communication, but with getting the work, the poem or play or statue or painting or whatever it is, "right," apparently regardless of its communicative efficacy, is easily explained. To make the work "embody," accord with, and represent the precise experience upon which its value depends is his major preoccupation, in difficult cases an overmastering preoccupation, and the dissipation of attention which would be involved if he considered the communicative side as a separate issue would be fatal in most serious work. He cannot stop to consider how the public or even how especially well qualified sections of the public may like it or respond to it. He is wise, therefore, to keep all such considerations out of mind altogether. Those artists and poets who can be suspected of close separate attention to the communicative aspect tend (there are exceptions to this, of which Shakespeare might be one) to fall into a subordinate rank.

But this conscious neglect of communication does not in the least diminish the importance of the communicative aspect. It would only do so if we were prepared to admit that only our conscious activities matter. The very process of getting the work "right" has itself, so far as the artist is normal, immense communicative consequences. Apart from certain special cases, to be discussed later, it will, when "right," have much greater communicative power than it would have had if "wrong." The degree to which it accords with the relevant experience of the artist is a measure of the degree to which it will arouse similar experiences in others.

But more narrowly the reluctance of the artist to consider communication as one of his main aims, and his denial that he is at all influenced in his work by a desire to affect other people, is no evidence that communication is not actually his principal object. On a simple view of psychology, which overlooked unconscious motives, it would be, but not on any view of human behaviour which is in the least adequate. When we find the artist constantly struggling towards impersonality, towards a structure for his work which excludes his private, eccentric, momentary idiosyncrasies, and using always as its basis those elements which are most uniform in their effects upon impulses; when we find private works of art, works which satisfy the artist,* but are incomprehensible to everybody else, so rare, and the publicity of the work so constantly and so intimately bound up with its appeal to the artist himself, it is difficult to believe that efficacy for communication is not a main part of the "rightness"† which the artist may suppose to be something quite different.

How far desire actually to communicate, as distinguished from desire to produce something with communicative efficacy (however disguised), is an "unconscious motive" in the artist is a question to which we need not hazard an answer. Doubtless individual artists vary enormously. To some the lure of "immortality" of enduring fame, of a permanent place in the influences which govern the human mind, appears to be very strong. To others it is often negligible. The degree to which such notions are avowed certainly varies with current

---

* Again the normality of the artist has to be considered. [Richards' note.]

† As will be seen, I am not going to identify "beauty" with "communicative efficacy." This is a trap which it is easy to fall into. A number of the exoteric followers of Croce may be found in it, though not Croce hiself. [Richards' note. Richards refers to Benedetto Croce (1866–1952), Italian philosopher and critic.]

social and intellectual fashions. At present the appeal to posterity, the "nurslings of immortality" attitude to works of art appears to be much out of favour. "How do we know what posterity will be like? They may be awful people!" a contemporary is likely to remark, thus confusing the issue. For the appeal is not to posterity merely as living at a certain date, but as especially qualified to judge, a qualification most posterities have lacked.

What concerns criticism is not the avowed or unavowed motives of the artist, however interesting these may be to psychology, but the fact that his procedure does, in the majority of instances, make the communicative efficacy of his work correspond with his own satisfaction and sense of its rightness. This may be due merely to his normality, or it may be due to unavowed motives. The first suggestion is the more plausible. In any case it is certain that no mere careful study of communicative possibilities, together with any desire to communicate, however intense, is ever sufficient without close natural correspondence between the poet's impulses and possible impulses in his reader. All supremely successful communication involves this correspondence, and no planning can take its place. Nor is the deliberate conscious attempt directed to communication so successful as the unconscious indirect method.

Thus the artist is entirely justified in his apparent neglect of the main purpose of his work. And when in what follows he is alluded to without qualification as being primarily concerned with communication, the reservations here made should be recalled.

Since the poet's unconscious motives have been alluded to, it may be well at this point to make a few additional remarks. Whatever psycho-analysts may aver, the mental processes of the poet are not a very profitable field for investigation. They offer far too happy a hunting-ground for uncontrollable conjecture. Much that goes to produce a poem is, of course, unconscious. Very likely the unconscious processes are more important than the conscious, but even if we knew far more than we do about how the mind works, the attempt to display the inner working of the artist's mind by the evidence of his work alone must be subject to the gravest dangers. And to judge by the published work of Freud upon Leonardo da Vinci or of Jung upon Goethe (e.g. *The Psychology of the Unconscious,* p. 305),[2] psycho-analysts tend to be peculiarly inept as critics.

The difficulty is that nearly all speculations as to what went on in the artist's mind are unverifiable, even more unverifiable than the similar speculations as to the dreamer's mind. The most plausible explanations are apt to depend upon features whose actual causation is otherwise. I do not know whether anyone but Mr. Graves[3] has attempted to analyse *Kubla Khan*, a poem which by its mode of composition and by its subject suggests itself as well fitted for analysis. The reader acquainted with current methods of analysis can imagine the results of a thoroughgoing Freudian onslaught.

[2] Sigmund Freud's study of Leonardo was first published in 1910; the work by C. G. Jung translated as *The Psychology of the Unconscious* was first published in 1912 as *Wandlungen und Symbole der Libido.*

[3] The first attempt by Robert Graves, English poet and critic, to analyse "Kubla Khan" was in *On English Poetry,* 1922. There have been numerous attempts, by Graves and others, since to interpret the poem psychoanalytically.

If he will then open *Paradise Lost,* Book IV, at line 223, and read onwards for sixty lines, he will encounter the actual sources of not a few of the images and phrases of the poem. In spite of—

> Southward through *Eden* went a River large,
> Nor changed his course, but through the shaggie hill
> Pass'd underneath ingulft . . .

in spite of—

> Rose a fresh Fountain, and with many a rill
> Waterd the Garden; thence united fell
> Down the steep glade, and met the neather Flood . . .

in spite of—

> Rowling on Orient Pearl and sands of Gold
> With mazie error under pendant shades
> Ran Nectar . . .

in spite of—

> Meanwhile murmuring waters fall
> Down the slope hills, disperst . . .

his doubts may still linger until he reaches

> Nor where *Abassin* Kings thir issue Guard,
> Mount Amara.

and one of the most cryptic points in Coleridge's poem, the Abyssinian maid, singing of Mount Abora, finds its simple explanation. The closing line of the poem perhaps hardly needs this kind of derivation.

From one source or another almost all the matter of *Kubla Khan* came to Coleridge in a similar fashion. I do not know whether this particular indebtedness has been remarked before, but *Purchas his Pilgrimage,* Bartram's *Travels in North and South Carolina,* and Maurice's *History of Hindostan* are well-known sources, some of them indicated by Coleridge himself.

This very representative instance of the unconscious working of a poet's mind may serve as a not inapposite warning against one kind at least of possible applications of psychology in criticism.

The extent to which the arts and their place in the whole scheme of human affairs have been misunderstood, by Critics, Moralists, Educators, Æstheticians . . . is somewhat difficult to explain. Often those who most misunderstood have been perfect in their taste and ability to respond, Ruskin[4] for example. Those who both knew what to do with a work of art and also understood what they were doing, have been for the most part artists and little inclined for, or capable of, the rather special task of explaining. It may have seemed to them too obvious to need explanation. Those who have tried have as a rule been foiled by language. For the difficulty which has always prevented the arts from being explained as well as "enjoyed" (to use an inadequate word in default of an adequate) is language.

---

[4] John Ruskin (1819–1900), critic and social theorist.

> Happy who can
> Appease this virtuous enemy of man!

It was perhaps never so necessary as now that we should know why the arts are important and avoid inadequate answers. It will probably become increasingly more important in the future. Remarks such as these, it is true, are often uttered by enthusiastic persons, and are apt to be greeted with the same smile as the assertion that the future of England is bound up with Hunting. Yet their full substantiation will be found to involve issues which are nowhere lightly regarded.

The arts are our storehouse of recorded values. They spring from and perpetuate hours in the lives of exceptional people, when their control and command of experience is at its highest, hours when the varying possibilities of existence are most clearly seen and the different activities which may arise are most exquisitely reconciled, hours when habitual narrowness of interests or confused bewilderment are replaced by an intricately wrought composure. Both in the genesis of a work of art, in the creative moment, and in its aspect as a vehicle of communication, reasons can be found for giving to the arts a very important place in the theory of Value. They record the most important judgments we possess as to the values of experience. They form a body of evidence which, for lack of a serviceable psychology by which to interpret it, and through the desiccating influence of abstract Ethics, has been left almost untouched by professed students of value. An odd omission, for without the assistance of the arts we could compare very few of our experiences, and without such comparison we could hardly hope to agree as to which are to be preferred. Very simple experiences—a cold bath in an enamelled tin, or running for a train—may to some extent be compared without elaborate vehicles; and friends exceptionally well acquainted with one another may manage some rough comparisons in ordinary conversation. But subtle or recondite experiences are for most men incommunicable and indescribable, though social conventions or terror of the loneliness of the human situation may make us pretend the contrary. In the arts we find the record in the only form in which these things can be recorded of the experiences which have seemed worth having to the most sensitive and discriminating persons. Through the obscure perception of this fact the poet has been regarded as a seer and the artist as a priest, suffering from usurpations. The arts, if rightly approached, supply the best data available for deciding what experiences are more valuable than others. The qualifying clause is all-important however. Happily there is no lack of glaring examples to remind us of the difficulty of approaching them rightly.

V. The Critic's Concern with Value

What hinders? Are you beam-blind, yet to a fault
In a neighbour deft-handed? Are you that liar?
And cast by conscience out, spendsavour salt?

—Gerard Hopkins.

Between the general inquiry into the nature of the good and the appreciation of particular works of art, there may seem to be a wide gap, and the discussion upon which we are about to embark may appear a roundabout way of approaching our subject. Morals have often been treated, especially in recent times, as a side-issue for criticism, from which the special concern of the critic must be carefully separated. His business, so it has been said, is with the work of art in itself, not with any consequences which lie outside it. These may be left, it has been supposed, to others for attention, to the clergy perhaps or to the police.

That these authorities are sadly incompetent is a minor disadvantage. Their blunderings are as a rule so ridiculous that the effects are brief. They often serve a useful purpose in calling attention to work which might be overlooked. What is more serious is that these indiscretions, vulgarities and absurdities encourage the view that morals have little or nothing to do with the arts, and the even more unfortunate opinion that the arts have no connection with morality. The ineptitudes of censors, their choice of censorable objects, ignoble blasphemy, such as that which declared *Esther Waters*[5] an impure book, displays of such intelligence as considered *Madame Bovary*[6] an apology for adulterous wrong, innumerable comic, stupefying, enraging interferences fully explain this attitude, but they do not justify it.

The common avoidance of all discussion of the wider social and moral aspects of the arts by people of steady judgment and strong heads is a misfortune, for it leaves the field free for folly, and cramps the scope of good critics unduly. So loath have they been to be thought at large with the wild asses that they have virtually shut themselves up in a paddock. If the competent are to refrain because of the antics of the unqualified, an evil and a loss which are neither temporary nor trivial increase continually. It is as though medical men were all to retire because of the impudence of quacks. For the critic is as closely occupied with the health of the mind as the doctor with the health of the body. In a different way, it is true, and with a wider and subtler definition of health, by which the healthiest mind is that capable of securing the greatest amount of value.

The critic cannot possibly avoid using some ideas about value. His whole occupation is an application and exercise of his ideas on the subject, and an avoidance of moral preoccupations on his part can only be either an abdication or a rejection under the title of "morality" of what he considers to be mistaken or dishonest ideas and methods. The term has a dubious odour, it has been

---

[5] A novel of 1894 by George Moore (1952–1933), Anglo-Irish novelist, dramatist, autobiographer.
[6] A novel of 1857 by Gustave Flaubert (1821–1880).

handled by many objectionable as well as admirable people, and we may agree to avoid it. But the errors exemplified by censorship exploits are too common, and misconceptions as to the nature of value too easy to fall into and too wide-spread, for useful criticism to remain without a general theory and an explicit set of principles.

What is needed is a defensible position for those who believe that the arts are of value. Only a general theory of value which will show the place and function of the arts in the whole system of values will provide such a strong-hold. At the same time we need weapons with which to repel and overthrow misconceptions. With the increase of population the problem presented by the gulf between what is preferred by the majority and what is accepted as excellent by the most qualified opinion has become infinitely more serious and appears likely to become threatening in the near future. For many reasons standards are much more in need of defence than they used to be. It is perhaps premature to envisage a collapse of values, a transvaluation by which popular taste replaces trained discrimination. Yet commercialism has done stranger things: we have not yet fathomed the more sinister potentialities of the cinema and the loud-speaker, and there is some evidence, uncertain and slight no doubt, that such things as "best-sellers" (compare *Tarzan* with *She*),[7] maga-zine verses, mantelpiece pottery, Academy pictures, Music Hall songs, County Council buildings, War Memorials . . . are decreasing in merit. Notable excep-tions, in which the multitude are better advised than the experts, of course occur sometimes, but not often.

To bridge the gulf, to bring the level of popular appreciation nearer to the consensus of best qualified opinion, and to defend this opinion against damag-ing attacks (Tolstoy's is a typical example),[8] a much clearer account than has yet been produced, of why this opinion is right, is essential. These attacks are dangerous, because they appeal to a natural instinct, hatred of "superior per-sons." The expert in matters of taste is in an awkward position when he differs from the majority. He is forced to say in effect, "I am better than you. My taste is more refined, my nature more cultured, you will do well to become more like me than you are." It is not his fault that he has to be so arrogant. He may, and usually does, disguise the fact as far as possible, but his claim to be heard as an expert depends upon the truth of these assumptions. He ought then to be ready with reasons of a clear and convincing kind as to why his preferences are worth attention, and until these reasons are forthcoming, the accusations that he is a charlatan and a prig are embarrassing. He may indeed point to years of pre-occupation with his subject, he may remark like the wiseacre Longinus, sixteen hundred years ago, "The judgment of literature is the final outcome of much endeavour," but with him are many Professors to prove that years of endeavour may lead to nothing very remarkable in the end.

To habilitate the critic, to defend accepted standards against Tolstoyan at-tacks, to narrow the interval between these standards and popular taste, to pro-tect the arts against the crude moralities of Puritans and perverts, a general theory of value, which will not leave the statement "This is good, that bad,"

---

[7] *Tarzan of the Apes,* by Edgar Rice Burroughs (1875–1950), was first published in 1914. Many other Tarzan novels followed. *She,* by (Sir Henry) Rider Haggard, an adventure novel laced with mysticism, was published in 1887.

[8] Tolstoy defended popular, as against expert, taste in *What Is Art?* (1898).

either vague or arbitrary, must be provided. There is no alternative open. Nor is it such an excursus from the inquiry into the nature of the arts as may be supposed. For if a well-grounded theory of value is a necessity for criticism, it is no less true that an understanding of what happens in the arts is needed for the theory. The two problems "What is good?" and "What are the arts?" reflect light upon one another. Neither in fact can be fully answered without the other. To the unravelling of the first we may now proceed.

VI. Value As An Ultimate Idea

Some lovely glorious nothing I did see.—Aire and Angels.

It has always been found far more easy to divide experiences* into good and bad, valuable and the reverse, than to discover what we are doing when we make the division. The history of opinions as to what constitutes value, as to why and when anything is rightly called good, shows a bewildering variety. But in modern times the controversy narrows itself down to two questions. The first of these is whether the difference between experiences which are valuable and those which are not can be fully described in psychological terms; whether some additional distinctive "ethical" or "moral" idea of a non-psychological nature is or is not required. The second question concerns the exact psychological analysis needed in order to explain value if no further "ethical" idea is shown to be necessary.

The first question will not detain us long. It has been ably maintained† and widely accepted that when we say that an experience is good we are simply saying that it is endowed with a certain ethical property or attribute not to be reduced to any psychological properties or attributes such as being desired or approved, and that no further elucidation of this special ethical property by way of analysis is possible. "Good" on this view is in no way a shorthand term for some more explicit account. The things which are good, it is held, are just good, possess a property which can be recognised by immediate intuition, and here, since good is unanalysable, the matter must rest. All that the study of value can do is to point out the things which possess this property, classify them, and remove certain confusions between ends which are good in themselves and means which are only called good, because they are instrumental in the attainment of intrinsically good ends. Usually those who maintain this view also hold that the only things which are good for their own sakes and not merely as

---

* Throughout this discussion "experience" will be used in a wide sense to stand for any occurrence in the mind. It is equivalent to "mental state, or process." The term has often unfortunate suggestions of passiveness and of consciousness, but many of the "experiences" here referred to would ordinarily be called "actions" and have parts which are not conscious and not accessible to introspection as important as those which are. [Richards' note.]

† A chief advocate of this view is Dr. G. E. Moore, whose *Principia Ethica* and *Ethics* contain brilliant statements of the position. [Richards' note.]

a means are certain conscious experiences, for example, knowledge, admiring contemplation of beauty, and feelings of affection and veneration under some circumstances. Other things, such as mountains, books, railways, courageous actions, are good instrumentally because, and in so far as, they cause or make possible states of mind which are valuable intrinsically. Thus the occurrence of states of mind which are recognised as good is regarded as an isolated fact of experience, not capable of being accounted for, or linked up with the rest of human peculiarities as a product of development in the way made familiar by the biological sciences.

The plausibility of this view derives principally from the metaphysical assumption that there are properties, in the sense of subsistent entities, which attach to existent particulars, but which might without absurdity be supposed to attach to nothing. These metaphysical entities, variously named Ideas, Notions, Concepts or Universals, may be divided into two kinds, sensuous and supersensuous.* The sensuous are those which may be apprehended by the senses, such as "red," "cold," "round," "swift," "painful," and the supersensuous, those apprehended not in sensuous perception but otherwise. Logical relations, "necessity" or "impossibility," and such ideas as "willing," "end," "cause," and "being three in number," have in this way been supposed to be directly apprehensible by the mind. Amongst these supersensuous Ideas good is to be found.

Nothing could be simpler than such a view, and to many people the subsistence of such a property of goodness appears not surprising. But to others the suggestion seems merely a curious survival of abstractionism, if such a term may be defended by its close parallel with obstructionism. A blind man in a dark room chasing a black cat which is not there would seem to them well employed in comparison with a philosopher apprehending such "Concepts." While ready for convenience of discourse to talk and even to think as though Concepts and Particulars were separable and distinct kinds of entities, they refuse to believe that the structure of the world actually contains such a cleavage. The point is perhaps undiscussable, and is probably unimportant, except in so far as the habit of regarding the world as actually so cloven is a fruitful source of bogus entities, usually hypostatised words. The temptation to introduce premature ultimates—Beauty in Æsthetics, the Mind and its faculties in psychology, Life in physiology, are representative examples—is especially great for believers in Abstract Entities. The objection to such Ultimates is that they bring an investigation to a dead end too suddenly. An ultimate Good is, in this instance, just such an arbitrary full stop.

It will be agreed that a less cryptic account of good, if one can be given, which is in accordance with verifiable facts, would be preferable, even though no means were available for refuting the simpler theory. Upholders of this theory, however, have produced certain arguments to show that no other view of good is possible, and these must first be briefly examined. They provide, in addition, an excellent example of the misuse of psychological assumptions in research, for although a psychological approach is often of the utmost service, it can also be a source of obscurantism and over-confidence. The arguments against any naturalistic account depend upon the alleged results of directly

---

* Cf. F. Brentano, *The Origin of the Knowledge of Right and Wrong*, pp. 12, 46. [Richards' note.]

inspecting what is before our minds when we judge that anything is good. If we substitute, it is maintained, any account of good whatever for "good" in the assertion, "This is good"—for example, "This is desired" or "This is approved"— we can detect that what is substituted is different from "good," and that we are not then making the same judgment. This result, it is claimed, is confirmed by the fact that we can always ask, "Is what is desired, or what is approved, good?" however we may elaborate the account provided, and that this is always a genuine question which would be impossible were the substituted account actually the analysis of good.

The persuasiveness of this refutation is found to vary enormously from individual to individual, for the results of the experiments upon which it relies differ. Those who have accustomed themselves to the belief that good is a supersensuous simple Idea readily discover the fraudulent character of any offered substitute, while those who hold some psychological theory of value, with equal ease identify their account with "good." The further question, "When and under what conditions can judgments be distinguished?" arises, a question so difficult to answer that any argument becomes suspect which depends upon assuming that they can be infallibly recognised as different. If for any reason we wish to distinguish two judgments, we can persuade ourselves, in any case in which they are differently formulated, that they are different. Thus it has been thought that "*a* exceeds *b*" and "*a* is greater than *b*" are distinguishable, the first being supposed to state simply that *a* has the relation "exceeds" to *b*, while the second is supposed to state that *a* has the relation "is" to *greater* which again has the relation "than" to *b*.* The conclusion to be drawn from the application of such methods to the problem of the meaning of Good would seem to be that they are not competent to decide anything about it—by no means a valueless result.

Since nothing can be concluded from a comparison of "This is good" with, let us say, "This is sought by an impulse belonging to a dominant group," let us see whether light can be gained by considering analogous instances in which special distinct ideas have for a time been thought indispensable only to yield later to analysis and substitution. The case of Beauty is perhaps too closely related to that of Good for our purpose. Those who can persuade themselves that Good is an unique irreducible entity might believe the same of Beauty. An episode in the theory of the tides is more instructive. It was once thought that the moon must have a peculiar Affinity with water. When the moon is full the tides are higher. Clearly the seas swell in sympathy with the increase of the moon. The history of science is full of mysterious unique entities which have gradually evaporated as explanation advanced.

The struggles of economists with "utility," of mathematical philosophers

---

* Cf. Russell, *The Principles of Mathematics*, p. 100. "On this principle, from which I can see no escape, that every genuine word must have some meaning, the *is* and *than* must form part of '*a* is greater than *b*,' which thus contains more than two terms and a relation. The *is* seems to state that *a* has to *greater* the relation of referent, while the *than* states similarly that *b* has to *greater* the relation of relatum. But '*a* exceeds *b*' may be held to express solely the relation of *a* to *b*, without including any of the implications of further relations." On the introspective comparison of judgments *The Meaning of Meaning*, by C. K. Ogden and the writer, may be consulted. [Richards' note.]

with "points" and "instants," of biologists with "entelechies," and the adventures of psycho-analysts with "the libido" and "the collective unconscious" are instances in point. At present theoretical psychology in particular is largely made up of the manipulation of similar suspects. The Act of Judgment, the relation of Presentation, Immediate Awareness, Direct Inspection, the Will, Feeling, Assumption, Acceptance, are only a few of the provisional ultimates introduced for convenience of discussion. Some of them may in the end prove to be indispensable, but meanwhile they are not, to prudent people, more than symbolic conveniences; theories dependent upon them must not be allowed to shut off from investigation fields which may be fruitful.

VII. A Psychological Theory of Value

Hands that can grasp, eyes
that can dilate, hair that can rise
    if it must, these things are important not because a
high-sounding interpretation can be put upon them, but because they are
useful.—Marianne Moore.[9]

The method then by which any attempt to analyse "good" has been condemned is itself objectionable, and yields no sound reason why a purely psychological account of the differences between good, bad, and indifferent experiences should not be given. The data for the inquiry are in part supplied by anthropology. It has become clear that the disparity among the states of mind recognised as good by persons of different races, habits and civilisations is overwhelming. Any observant child, it is true, might discover in the home circle how widely people disagree, but the effect of education is to suppress these scientific efforts. It has needed the vast accumulations of anthropological evidence now available to establish the fact that as the organisation of life and affairs alters very different experiences are perceived to be good or bad, are favoured or condemned. The Bakairi of Central Brazil and the Tahitians, among others, are reported, for example, to look upon eating with the same feelings which we reserve for quite different physiological performances, and to regard the public consumption of food as a grave breach of decency. In many parts of the world feelings of forgiveness towards enemies, for example, are looked upon as low and ignoble. The experiences which one person values are thought vicious by another. We must allow, it is true, for widespread confusion between intrinsic and instrumental values, and for the difficulty of identifying experiences. Many states of mind in other people which we judge to be bad or indifferent are no doubt unlike what we imagine them to be, or contain elements which we overlook, so that with fuller knowledge we might discover them to be good. In this manner it may be possible to reduce the reported disparity of value intuitions,

[9] Reprinted with permission of The Macmillan Company from *Collected Poems* by Marianne Moore. Copyright 1935 The Macmillan Company, renewed 1963 Marianne Moore and T. S. Eliot.

but few people acquainted with the varying moral judgments of mankind will doubt that circumstances and necessities, present and past, explain our approval and disapproval. We start, then, with a hearty scepticism of all immediate intuitions, and inquire how it is that individuals in different conditions, and at different stages of their development, esteem things so differently.

With the exception of some parents and nursemaids we have lately all been aghast at revelations of the value judgments of infants. Their impulses, their desires, their preferences, the things which they esteem, as displayed by the psycho-analysts, strike even those whose attitude towards humanity is not idealistic with some dismay. Even when the stories are duly discounted, enough which is verifiable remains for *infans polypervers* to present a truly impressive figure dominating all future psychological inquiry into value.

There is no need here to examine in detail how these early impulses are diverted and disguised by social pressures. The rough outlines are familiar of the ways in which by growth, by the appearance of fresh instinctive tendencies, by increase of knowledge and of command over the world, under the control of custom, magical beliefs, public opinion, inculcation and example, the primitive new-born animal may be gradually transformed into a bishop. At every stage in the astonishing metamorphosis, the impulses, desires, and propensities of the individual take on a new form, or, it may be, a further degree of systematisation. This systematisation is never complete. Always some impulse, or set of impulses, can be found which in one way or another interferes, or conflicts, with others. It may do so in two ways, directly or indirectly. Some impulses are in themselves psychologically incompatible, some are incompatible only indirectly, through producing contrary effects in the world outside. The difficulty some people have in smoking and writing at the same time is a typical instance of the first kind of incompatibility; the two activities get in each other's way by a psychological accident as it were. Interference of this kind can be overcome by practice to an unexpected degree, as the feats of jugglers show; some, however, are insurmountable; and these incompatibilities are often, as we shall see, of supreme consequence in moral development. Indirect incompatibilities arising through the consequences of our acts are more easy to find. Our whole existence is one long study of them, from the infant's first choice whether he shall use his mouth for screaming or for sucking, to the last codicil to his Will.

These are simple instances, but the conduct of life is throughout an attempt to organize impulses so that success is obtained for the greater number or mass of them, for the most important and the weightiest set. And here we come face to face again with the problem of value. How shall we decide which among these are more important than others, and how shall we distinguish different organisations as yielding more or less value one than another? At this point we need to be on our guard not to smuggle in any peculiar ethical, non-psychological, idea under some disguise, under "important" or "fundamental," for example.

Among those who reject any metaphysical view of value it has become usual to define value as capacity for satisfying feeling and desire in various intricate ways.* For the purpose of tracing in detail the very subtle and varied

---

* E.g., "The value of the object is its capacity of becoming the object of feeling and desire through actualisation of dispositional tendencies by acts of presumption, judgment, and assumption." Urban, *Valuation,* p. 53. [Richards' note.]

modes in which people actually value things, a highly intricate treatment is indispensable, but here a simpler definition will suffice.

We may start from the fact that impulses may be divided into appetencies and aversions, and begin by saying that anything is valuable which satisfies an appetency or "seeking after." The term "desire" would do as well if we could avoid the implication of accompanying conscious beliefs as to what is sought and a further restriction to felt and recognised longings. The term "want" used so much by economists has the same disadvantages. Appetencies may be, and for the most part are, unconscious, and to leave out those which we cannot discover by introspection would involve extensive errors. For the same reason it is wiser not to start from feeling. Appetencies then, rather than felt appetencies or desires, shall be our starting-point.

The next step is to agree that apart from consequences anyone *will actually prefer* to satisfy a greater number of equal appetencies rather than a less. Observation of people's behaviour, including our own, is probably sufficient to establish this agreement. If now we look to see what consequences can intervene to upset this simple principle, we shall find that only interferences, immediate or remote, direct or indirect, with other appetencies, need to be considered. The only *psychological* restraints upon appetencies are other appetencies.*

We can now extend our definition. Anything is valuable which will satisfy an appetency without involving the frustration of some equal or *more important* appetency; in other words, the only reason which can be given for not satisfying a desire is that more important desires will thereby be thwarted. Thus morals become purely prudential, and ethical codes merely the expression of the most general scheme of expediency† to which an individual or a race has attained. But we have still to say what "important" stands for in this formulation.

There are certain evident priorities among impulses, some of which have been studied in various ways by economists under the headings of primary wants and secondary wants. Some needs or impulses must be satisfied in order that others may be possible. We must eat, drink, sleep, breathe, protect ourselves and carry on an immense physiological business as a condition for any further activities. Some of these impulses, breathing, for example, can be satisfied directly, but most of them involve us in complicated cycles of instrumental labour. Man for the most part must exert himself half his life to satisfy even the primitive needs, and these activities, failing other means of

---

* Or, of course, aversions. In what follows we shall take no further note of aversions. To do so would introduce inessential complications. The omission in no way affects the argument, since for our present purposes they may be counted in with appetencies. [Richards' note.]

† This view plainly has close connections with Utilitarianism. In fact if Bentham's editor is to be trusted in his interpretation of his master's doctrine, it would be what Bentham intended to teach. "The term nearest to being synonymous with pleasure is *volition:* what it pleases a man to do is simply what he wills to do. . . . What a man wills to do, or what he pleases to do, may be far from giving him enjoyment; yet shall we say that in doing it, he is not following his own pleasure? . . . A native of Japan, when he is offended, stabs himself to prove the intensity of his feelings. It is difficult to prove enjoyment in this case: yet the man obeyed his impulses." John Hill Burton, *Jeremy Bentham's Works,* vol. I, p. 22. [Richards' note.]

reaching the same ends, share their priority. In their turn they involve as conditions a group of impulses, whose satisfaction becomes only second in importance to physiological necessities, those, namely, upon which communication and the ability to co-operate depend. But these, since man is a social creature, also become more directly necessary to his well-being. The very impulses which enable him to co-operate in gaining his dinner would themselves, if not satisfied, wreck by their mere frustration all his activities. This happens all through the hierarchy. Impulses, whose exercise may have been originally only important as means, and which might once have been replaced by quite different sets, become in time necessary conditions for innumerable quite different performances. Objects, again, originally valued because they satisfy one need, are found later to be also capable of satisfying others. Dress, for example, appears to have originated in magical, "life-giving," ornaments,* but so many other interests derive satisfaction from it that controversy can still arise as to its primitive uses.

The instances of priorities given must only be taken as examples. It is hardly necessary to remind the reader that for a civilised man, activities originally valuable as means only, often become so important through their connections with the rest of his activities, that life without them is regarded as intolerable. Thus acts which will debar him from his normal relations with his fellows are often avoided, even at the cost of death. Total cessation of all activities is preferred to the dreadful thwarting and privation which would ensue. The case of the soldier, or of the conscientious objector, is thus no exception to the principle. Life deprived of all but the barest physiological necessities, for example, prison life, is for many people worse than non-existence. Those who even so incur it in defence of some "moral ideal" do so because they are so organised, either permanently or temporarily, that only in this way can their dominant impulses secure satisfaction. The self-regarding impulses form only a part of the total activities of social man, and the impulse of the martyr to bear witness at any cost to what he regards as truth, is only one extreme instance of the degree to which other impulses often assume supremacy.

For another reason any priorities mentioned must be taken only as illustrations. We do not know enough yet about the precedences, the hierarchies, the modes of systematisation, actual and possible, in that unimaginable organisation, the mind, to say what order in any case actually exists, or between what the order holds. We only know that a growing order is the principle of the mind, that its function is to co-ordinate, and we can detect that in some of its forms the precedence is different from that in others. This we could do by observation, by comparing the drunken man with the sober, but from our own experience of our own activity we can go much further. We can feel differences between clear coherent thinking and confusion or stupidity, between free, controlled emotional response and dull or clogged impassivity, between moments when we do with our bodies more delicate and dexterous things than seem possible, and moments of clumsiness, when we are "all thumbs," have no "balance" or "timing," and nothing "comes off." These differences are differences in momentary organisation, differences in precedence between rival possible system-

* Cf. W. J. Perry, *The Origin of Magic and Religion*, p. 15. [Richards' note.]

atisations. The more permanent and more specifically "moral" differences between individuals grow out of differences such as these and correspond to similar precedences between larger systems.

The complications possible in the systematisation of impulses might be illustrated indefinitely. The plasticity of special appetencies and activities varies enormously. Some impulses can be diverted more easily than others. Sex has a wider range of satisfactions than hunger, for example; some are weaker than others; some (not the same necessarily) can be suppressed in the long run with less difficulty. Some can be modified; some obey the "all or none" rule—they must either be satisfied specifically or completely inhibited—well-established habits may have this peculiarity. In judging the importance of any impulse all these considerations must be taken into account. The affiliations of impulses, at present often inexplicable, need especially to be considered. Within the whole partially systematised organisation, numerous sub-systems can be found, and what would be expected to be quite trivial impulses are often discovered to be important, because they belong to powerful groups. Thus there are reasonable persons who, without a high polish on their shoes, are almost incapacitated.

The importance of an impulse, it will be seen, can be defined for our purposes as *the extent of the disturbance of other impulses in the individual's activities which the thwarting of the impulse involves*. A vague definition, it is true, but therefore suitable to our at present incomplete and hazy knowledge of how impulses are related. It will be observed that no special ethical idea is introduced. We can now take our next step forward and inquire into the relative merits of different systematisations.

No individual can live one minute without a very intricate and, so far as it goes, very perfect co-ordination of impulses. It is only when we pass from the activities which from second to second maintain life to those which from hour to hour determine what kind of life it shall be, that we find wide differences. Fortunately for psychology we can each find wide enough differences in ourselves from hour to hour. Most people in the same day are Bonaparte and Oblomov[10] by turns. Before breakfast Diogenes,[11] after dinner Petronius[12] or Bishop Usher.[13] But throughout these mutations certain dispositions usually remain much the same, those which govern public behaviour in a limited number of affairs varying very greatly from one society or civilisation to another. Every systematisation in the degree to which it is stable involves a degree of sacrifice, but for some the price to be paid in opportunities foregone is greater than for others. By the extent of the loss, the range of impulses thwarted or starved, and their degree of importance, the merit of a systematisation is judged. That organisation which is least wasteful of human possibilities is, in short, the best. Some individuals, hag-ridden by their vices, or their virtues, to a point at which the law of diminishing returns has deprived even these of their appropriate

[10] The lazy and self-defeating hero of *Oblomov* (1858), by Ivan Goncharov (1812–1891).

[11] The Greek Cynic philosopher (c. 412–323 B.C.)

[12] Petronius Arbiter, Roman satirist, profligate lover of luxury, director of the emperor Nero's entertainments.

[13] James Usher (or Ussher, 1581–1656), Irish Bishop of Maeth, noted for his scholarship. He set the date for the creation of the world at 4004 B.C.

satisfactions, are still unable to reorganise; they go through life incapacitated for most of its possible enjoyments.* Others, paralysed with their conflicts, are unable to do anything freely; whatever they attempt some implicated but baffled impulse is still fitfully and fretfully stirring. The debauchee and the victim of conscience alike have achieved organisations whose price in sacrifice is excessive. Both their individual satisfactions, and those for which they are dependent upon sympathetic relations with their fellows, an almost equal group, are unduly restricted. Upon grounds of prudence alone they have been injudicious, and they may be condemned without any appeal to peculiarly "ethical" standards. The muddle in which they are forced to live is itself sufficient ground for reprobation.

At the other extreme are those fortunate people who have achieved an ordered life, whose systems have developed clearing-houses by which the varying claims of different impulses are adjusted. Their free, untrammelled activity gains for them a maximum of varied satisfactions and involves a minimum of suppression and sacrifice. Particularly is this so with regard to those satisfactions which require humane, sympathetic, and friendly relations between individuals. The charge of egoism, or selfishness, can be brought against a naturalistic or utilitarian morality such as this only by overlooking the importance of these satisfactions in any well-balanced life. Unfair or aggressive behaviour, and preoccupation with self-regarding interests to the exclusion of due sensitiveness to the reciprocal claims of human intercourse, lead to a form of organisation which deprives the person so organised of whole ranges of important values. No mere loss of social pleasures is in question, but a twist or restriction of impulses, whose normal satisfaction is involved in almost all the greatest goods of life. The two senses in which a man may "take advantage" of his fellows can be observed in practice to conflict. Swindling and bullying, whether in business matters or in personal relations, have their cost; which the best judges agree to be excessive. And the greater part of the cost lies *not* in the consequences of being found out, in the loss of social esteem and so forth, but in actual systematic disability to attain important values.

Although the person who habitually disregards the claims of his fellows to fair treatment and sympathetic understanding may be condemned, in most cases, upon the ground of his own actual loss of values in such behaviour, this of course is not the reason for the steps which may have to be taken against him. It may very well be the case that a person's own interests are such that, *if he understood them*, were well organised in other words, he would be a useful and charming member of his community; but, so long as people are about who are not well organised, communities must protect themselves. They can defend their action on the ground that the general loss of value which would follow if they did not protect themselves far outweighs such losses as are incurred by the people whom they suppress or deport.

---

* Both "enjoyment" and "satisfaction" are unsuitable terms in this connection. An unfortunate linguistic gap must be recognised. The full exercise of an activity is commonly its own "satisfaction," and, as we shall see later, what pleasure may accompany it is derivative and incidental.

"Beatitudo non est virtutis præmium, sed ipsa virtus." [Happiness is not the first virtue, but virtue itself.] [Richards' note.]

To extend this individual morality to communal affairs is not difficult. Probably the best brief statement upon the point is the following note by Bentham, if we interpret "happiness" in his formula not as pleasure but as the satisfaction of impulses.

June 29, 1827.

1. Constantly actual end of action on the part of every individual at the moment of action, his greatest happiness, according to his view of it at that moment.

2. Constantly proper end of action on the part of every individual at the moment of action, his real greatest happiness from that moment to the end of life.

3. Constantly proper end of action on the part of every individual considered as trustee for the community, of which he is considered as a member, the greatest happiness of that same community, in so far as it depends upon the interest which forms the bond of union between its members.*

But communities, as is well known, tend to behave in the same way to people who are better organised as well as to people who are worse organised than the standard of the group. They deal with Socrates or Bruno[14] as severely as with Turpin[15] or Bottomley.[16] Thus mere interference with ordinary activities is not by itself a sufficient justification for excluding from the group people who are different and therefore nuisances. The precise nature of the difference must be considered, and whether and to what degree it is the group, not the exceptional member, which ought to be condemned. The extent to which alteration is practicable is also relevant, and the problem in particular cases becomes very intricate.

But the final court of appeal concerns itself in such cases with questions, not of the wishes of majorities, but of the actual range and degree of satisfaction which different possible systematisations of impulse yield. Resentment at interference and gratitude for support and assistance are to be distinguished from disapproval and approval. The esteem and respect accorded to persons with the social† virtues well developed is only in a small degree due to the use which we find we can make of them. It is much more a sense that their lives are rich and full.

When any desire is denied for the sake of another, the approved and accepted activity takes on additional value; it is coveted and pursued all the more for what it has cost. Thus the spectacle of other people enjoying both activities without difficulty, thanks to some not very obvious adjustment, is peculiarly distressing, and such people are usually regarded as especially

---

* *Works,* vol. X, p. 560 [Richards' note.]

[14] Giordano Bruno (1548–1600), Italian philosopher, who was burned to death by the Inquisition.

[15] Richard Turpin (1706–1739), horse thief and all-around robber.

[16] Horatio William Bottomley (1860–1933), English businessman, editor, publisher, Member of Parliament. In 1922 he was found guilty of fraudulent practices and sentenced to prison. He died a pauper.

† Not necessarily "social workers." Only personal communication can show who have the virtues here referred to. [Richards' note.]

depraved. In different circumstances this view may or may not be justified. The element of sacrifice exacted by any stable system explains to a large extent the tenacity with which custom is clung to, the intolerance directed against innovations, the fanaticism of converts, the hypocrisy of teachers, and many other lamentable phenomena of the moral attitudes. However much an individual may privately find his personality varying from hour to hour, he is compelled to join in maintaining a public façade of some rigidity and buttressed with every contrivance which can be invented. The Wills of Gods, the Conscience, the Catechism, Taboos, Immediate Intuitions, Penal Laws, Public Opinion, Good Form, are all more or less ingenious and efficient devices with the same aim—to secure the uniformity which social life requires. By their means and by Custom, Convention, and Superstition, the underlying basis of morality, the effort to attain maximum satisfaction through coherent systematisation, is veiled and disguised to an extraordinary degree. Whence arise great difficulties and many disasters. It is so necessary and so difficult to secure a stable and general system of public behaviour that any means whatever are justifiable, failing the discovery of better. All societies hitherto achieved, however, involve waste and misery of appalling extent.

Any public code of behaviour must, it is generally agreed, represent a cruder and more costly systematisation than those attained to by many of the individuals who live under the code, a point obviously to be remembered in connection with censorship problems. Customs change more slowly than conditions, and every change in conditions brings with it new possibilities of systematisation. None of the afflictions of humanity are worse than its obsolete moral principles. Consider the effects of the obsolete virtues of nationalism under modern conditions, or the absurdity of the religious attitude to birth control. The present lack of plasticity in such things involves a growing danger. Human conditions and possibilities have altered more in a hundred years than they had in the previous ten thousand, and the next fifty may overwhelm us, unless we can devise a more adaptable morality. The view that what we need in this tempestuous turmoil of change is a Rock to shelter under or to cling to, rather than an efficient aeroplane in which to ride it, is comprehensible but mistaken.

To guard against a possible misunderstanding it may be added that the organisation and systematisation of which I have been speaking in this chapter are not primarily an affair of conscious planning or arrangement, as this is understood, for example, by a great business house or by a railway. We pass as a rule from a chaotic to a better organised state by ways which we know nothing about. Typically through the influence of other minds. Literature and the arts are the chief means by which these influences are diffused. It should be unnecessary to insist upon the degree to which high civilisation, in other words, free, varied and unwasteful life, depends upon them in a numerous society.

T. S. Eliot

TRADITION AND THE INDIVIDUAL TALENT

Few poets have influenced the poetical practice of their age so decisively as T[homas] S[tearns] Eliot, and few critics have had so great an effect upon criticism as he. His work, together with that of I. A. Richards (see pp. 341 ff.), is commonly said to have provided the impetus for the notable concern with criticism that developed in England and even more in the United States in the mid-1930s. Eliot was not a systematic theorist like Richards. His influence was achieved as much through his manner as through his doctrine. John Gross puts the matter well in his account of Eliot's career in *The Rise and Fall of the Man of Letters*: "What makes [Eliot's] poetry so memorable (literally memorable) is that each line seems to have been looked at for six months and the same is true of his best essays. Every effect has been carefully scrutinized, every aside has been pondered. There is no slack in his criticism. And this tension is intimidating—it convicts the reader of lazy-mindedness, as the Edwardians [that is, the critics of the preceding period] never did. The most glancing opinion is charged with significance, every topic he touches on demands to be explored. Undoubtedly his impact is heightened by the fact that he expresses himself through self-contained essays. The hierarchy of values behind his work involves us all the more deeply because it is never made fully explicit, because we have to piece it together for ourselves from hints and suggestions." In addition to instituting what in its day was a new attitude in writing about literature, an exigent seriousness that had not prevailed since Matthew Arnold wrote, Eliot introduced certain specific considerations which were novel in their time. One had to do with the particularity of literature and the consequently necessary particularity of criticism; as Eliot put it in a striking witticism, in literature "the spirit killeth, but the letter giveth life," which is in effect a paraphrase of Mallarmé's no less celebrated dictum that poetry is made not with thoughts but with words. Of equal importance was Eliot's insistence on the continuous tradition of literature and on the necessity of constantly re-evaluating the literature of the past. Himself a radical innovator in poetic method, he championed the modern in its divergence from the past, but firmly maintained his connection with the past and especially admired those of his contemporaries —Joyce for example—who did the same.

Eliot was born in St. Louis in 1888. He entered Harvard in 1906 and after his graduation stayed on at the university to pursue the study of philosophy. In 1913 he went abroad to study in Germany and at Oxford and thereafter made England his home; in 1927 he became a British subject. By the publication of *Prufrock and Other Observations* (1917) and *Poems* (1920) Eliot had gained a considerable reputation as a poet; in 1922 *The Waste Land* brought him world-wide fame. It was followed by *The Hollow Men* (1925) and *Ash Wednesday* (1930). The great work of his late period, *Four Quartets,* appeared in 1943. Of his verse plays, *Murder in the Cathedral* (1935) is the best known and the most successful. Eliot's reputation as a critic was established by the publication of *The Sacred Wood* (1920) and consolidated by *Selected Essays* (1932). His other critical works include *The Use of Poetry and the Use of Criticism* (1933), *Notes Toward the Definition of Culture* (1948), and *On Poetry and Poets* (1957).

I

In English writing we seldom speak of tradition, though we occasionally apply its name in deploring its absence. We cannot refer to "the tradition" or to "a tradition"; at most, we employ the adjective in saying that the poetry of So-and-so is "traditional" or even "too traditional." Seldom, perhaps, does the word appear except in a phrase of censure. If otherwise, it is vaguely approbative, with the implication, as to the work approved, of some pleasing archaeological reconstruction. You can hardly make the word agreeable to English ears without this comfortable reference to the reassuring science of archaeology.

Certainly the word is not likely to appear in our appreciations of living or dead writers. Every nation, every race, has not only its own creative, but its own critical turn of mind; and is even more oblivious of the shortcomings and limitations of its critical habits than of those of its creative genius. We know, or think we know, from the enormous mass of critical writing that has appeared in the French language the critical method or habit of the French; we only conclude (we are such unconscious people) that the French are "more critical" than we, and sometimes even plume ourselves a little with the fact, as if the French were the less spontaneous. Perhaps they are; but we might remind ourselves that criticism is as inevitable as breathing, and that we should be none the worse for articulating what passes in our minds when we read a book and feel an emotion about it, for criticizing our own minds in their work of criticism. One of the facts that might come to light in this process is our tendency to insist, when we praise a poet, upon those aspects of his work in which he least resembles any one else. In these aspects or parts of his work we pretend to find what is individual, what is the peculiar essence of the man. We dwell with satisfaction upon the poet's difference from his predecessors, especially his immediate predecessors; we endeavour to find something that can be isolated in order to be enjoyed. Whereas if we approach a poet without this prejudice we shall often find that not only the best, but the most individual parts of his work may be those in which the dead poets, his ancestors, assert their immortality most vigorously. And I do not mean the impressionable period of adolescence, but the period of full maturity.

Yet if the only form of tradition, of handing down, consisted in following the ways of the immediate generation before us in a blind or timid adherence to its successes, "tradition" should positively be discouraged. We have seen many such simple currents soon lost in the sand; and novelty is better than repetition. Tradition is a matter of much wider significance. It cannot be inherited, and if you want it you must obtain it by great labour. It involves, in the first place, the historical sense, which we may call nearly indispensable to any one who would continue to be a poet beyond his twenty-fifth year; and the historical sense involves a perception, not only of the pastness of the past, but of its presence; the historical sense compels a man to write not merely with his own generation in his bones, but with a feeling that the whole of the literature of Europe from Homer and within it the whole of the literature of his own country has a simultaneous existence and composes a simultaneous order. This historical sense, which is a sense of the timeless as well as of the temporal and of the timeless and of the temporal together, is what makes a writer traditional. And it is at the same time what makes a writer most acutely conscious of his place in time, of his own contemporaneity.

No poet, no artist of any art, has his complete meaning alone. His significance, his appreciation is the appreciation of his relation to the dead poets and artists. You cannot value him alone; you must set him, for contrast and comparison, among the dead. I mean this as a principle of aesthetic, not merely historical, criticism. The necessity that he shall conform, that he shall cohere, is not onesided; what happens when a new work of art is created is something that happens simultaneously to all the works of art which preceded it. The existing monuments form an ideal order among themselves, which is modified by the introduction of the new (the really new) work of art among them. The existing order is complete before the new work arrives; for order to persist after the supervention of novelty, the *whole* existing order must be, if ever so slightly, altered; and so the relations, proportions, values of each work of art toward the whole are readjusted; and this is conformity between the old and the new. Whoever has approved this idea of order, of the form of European, of English literature will not find it preposterous that the past should be altered by the present as much as the present is directed by the past. And the poet who is aware of this will be aware of great difficulties and responsibilities.

In a peculiar sense he will be aware also that he must inevitably be judged by the standards of the past. I say judged, not amputated, by them; not judged to be as good as, or worse or better than, the dead; and certainly not judged by the canons of dead critics. It is a judgment, a comparison, in which two things are measured by each other. To conform merely would be for the new work not really to conform at all; it would not be new, and would therefore not be a work of art. And we do not quite say that the new is more valuable because it fits in; but its fitting in is a test of its value—a test, it is true, which can only be slowly and cautiously applied, for we are none of us infallible judges of conformity. We say: it appears to conform, and is perhaps individual, or it appears individual, and may conform; but we are hardly likely to find that it is one and not the other.

To proceed to a more intelligible exposition of the relation of the poet to the past: he can neither take the past as a lump, an indiscriminate bolus, nor can he form himself wholly on one or two private admirations, nor can he form himself wholly upon one preferred period. The first course is inadmissible, the second is an important experience of youth, and the third is a pleasant and highly desirable supplement. The poet must be very conscious of the main current, which does not at all flow invariably through the most distinguished reputations. He must be quite aware of the obvious fact that art never improves, but that the material of art is never quite the same. He must be aware that the mind of Europe—the mind of his own country—a mind which he learns in time to be much more important than his own private mind—is a mind which changes, and that this change is a development which abandons nothing *en route,* which does not superannuate either Shakespeare, or Homer, or the rock drawing of the Magdalenian[1] draughtsmen. That this development, refinement perhaps, complication certainly, is not, from the point of view of the artist, any improvement. Perhaps not even an improvement from the point of view of the psychologist or not to the extent which we imagine; perhaps only in the end based upon a complication in economics and machinery. But the difference between the present and the past is that the conscious present is an awareness of the past in a way and to an extent which the past's awareness of itself cannot show.

Some one said: "The dead writers are remote from us because we *know* so much more than they did." Precisely, and they are that which we know.

I am alive to a usual objection to what is clearly part of my programme for the *métier*[2] of poetry. The objection is that the doctrine requires a ridiculous amount of erudition (pedantry), a claim which can be rejected by appeal to the lives of poets in any pantheon. It will even be affirmed that much learning deadens or perverts poetic sensibility. While, however, we persist in believing that a poet ought to know as much as will not encroach upon his necessary receptivity and necessary laziness, it is not desirable to confine knowledge to whatever can be put into a useful shape for examinations, drawing-rooms, or the still more pretentious modes of publicity. Some can absorb knowledge, the more tardy must sweat for it. Shakespeare acquired more essential history from Plutarch[3] than most men could from the whole British Museum. What is to be insisted upon is that the poet must develop or procure the consciousness of the past and that he should continue to develop this consciousness throughout his career.

What happens is a continual surrender of himself as he is at the moment to something which is more valuable. The progress of an artist is a continual self-sacrifice, a continual extinction of personality.

There remains to define this process of depersonalization and its relation to the sense of tradition. It is in this depersonalization that art may be said to approach the condition of science. I, therefore, invite you to consider, as

[1] The final, and most advanced, culture of the European Paleolithic period, known best from Cro-Magnon cave paintings.

[2] Trade, occupation.

[3] Greek essayist and biographer (c. 46–120 A.D.), author of *The Parallel Lives,* from which Shakespeare took much of the material for his Roman plays.

a suggestive analogy, the action which takes place when a bit of finely filiated platinum is introduced into a chamber containing oxygen and sulphur dioxide.

II

Honest criticism and sensitive appreciation are directed not upon the poet but upon the poetry. If we attend to the confused cries of the newspaper critics and the *susurrus*[4] of popular repetition that follows, we shall hear the names of poets in great numbers; if we seek not Blue-book[5] knowledge but the enjoyment of poetry, and ask for a poem, we shall seldom find it. I have tried to point out the importance of the relation of the poem to other poems by other authors, and suggested the conception of poetry as a living whole of all the poetry that has ever been written. The other aspect of this Impersonal theory of poetry is the relation of the poem to its author. And I hinted, by an analogy, that the mind of the mature poet differs from that of the immature one not precisely in any valuation of "personality," not being necessarily more interesting, or having "more to say," but rather by being a more finely perfected medium in which special, or very varied, feelings are at liberty to enter into new combinations.

The analogy was that of the catalyst. When the two gases previously mentioned are mixed in the presence of a filament of platinum, they form sulphurous acid. This combination takes place only if the platinum is present; nevertheless the newly formed acid contains no trace of platinum, and the platinum itself is apparently unaffected; has remained inert, neutral, and unchanged. The mind of the poet is the shred of platinum. It may partly or exclusively operate upon the experience of the man himself; but, the more perfect the artist, the more completely separate in him will be the man who suffers and the mind which creates; the more perfectly will the mind digest and transmute the passions which are its material.

The experience, you will notice, the elements which enter the presence of the transforming catalyst, are of two kinds: emotions and feelings. The effect of a work of art upon the person who enjoys it is an experience different in kind from any experience not of art. It may be formed out of one emotion, or may be a combination of several; and various feelings, inhering for the writer in particular words or phrases or images, may be added to compose the final result. Or great poetry may be made without the direct use of any emotion whatever: composed out of feelings solely. Canto XV of the *Inferno* (Brunetto Latini)[6] is a working up of the emotion evident in the situation; but the effect, though single as that of any work of art, is obtained by considerable complexity of detail. The last quatrain gives an image, a feeling attaching to an image, which "came," which did not develop simply out of what precedes, but which was probably in suspension in the poet's mind until the proper com-

---

[4] Murmur, rustle.

[5] British official government publications.

[6] In the *Inferno*, Dante meets his old master Brunetto Latini on a burning desert, suffering eternal punishment for sodomy, yet still loved and admired by Dante. Brunetto's present situation, his sin, the old friendship between the two men underlie the courteous and restrained words they speak to each other.

bination arrived for it to add itself to.[7] The poet's mind is in fact a receptacle for seizing and storing up numberless feelings, phrases, images, which remain there until all the particles which can unite to form a new compound are present together.

If you compare several representative passages of the greatest poetry you see how great is the variety of types of combination, and also how completely any semi-ethical criterion of "sublimity" misses the mark. For it is not the "greatness," the intensity, of the emotions, the components, but the intensity of the artistic process, the pressure, so to speak, under which the fusion takes place, that counts. The episode of Paolo and Francesca[8] employs a definite emotion, but the intensity of the poetry is something quite different from whatever intensity in the supposed experience it may give the impression of. It is no more intense, furthermore, than Canto XXVI, the voyage of Ulysses,[9] which has not the direct dependence upon an emotion. Great variety is possible in the process of transmutation of emotion: the murder of Agamemnon,[10] or the agony of Othello, gives an artistic effect apparently closer to a possible original than the scenes from Dante. In the *Agamemnon*, the artistic emotion approximates to the emotion of an actual spectator; in *Othello* to the emotion of the protagonist himself. But the difference between art and the event is always absolute; the combination which is the murder of Agamemnon is probably as complex as that which is the voyage of Ulysses. In either case there has been a fusion of elements. The ode of Keats contains a number of feelings which have nothing particular to do with the nightingale, but which the nightingale, partly, perhaps, because of its attractive name, and partly because of its reputation, served to bring together.

The point of view which I am struggling to attack is perhaps related to the metaphysical theory of the substantial unity of the soul: for my meaning is, that the poet has, not a "personality" to express, but a particular medium, which is only a medium and not a personality, in which impressions and experiences combine in peculiar and unexpected ways. Impressions and experiences which are important for the man may take no place in the poetry, and those which become important in the poetry may play quite a negligible part in the man, the personality.

I will quote a passage which is unfamiliar enough to be regarded with fresh attention in the light—or darkness—of these observations:

> And now methinks I could e'en chide myself
> For doating on her beauty, though her death
> Shall be revenged after no common action.
> Does the silkworm expend her yellow labours

---

[7] The interview over, Brunetto (in John D. Sinclair's translation) "turned about and seemed like one of those that run [in a foot-race] for the green cloth in the field at Verona, and he seemed not the loser among them, but the winner."

[8] Who, in the second circle of hell, are eternally buffeted around by winds in punishment for their illicit love. Dante swoons with pity.

[9] Ulysses, in the eighth circle for giving false counsel, tells Dante of his final voyage.

[10] By his wife Clytemnestra, with the aid of her lover Aigisthus, in Aeschylus' tragedy, the *Agamemnon*.

> For thee? For thee does she undo herself?
> Are lordships sold to maintain ladyships
> For the poor benefit of a bewildering minute?
> Why does yon fellow falsify highways,
> And put his life between the judge's lips,
> To refine such a thing—keeps horse and men
> To beat their valours for her? . . . [11]

In this passage (as is evident if it is taken in its context) there is a combination of positive and negative emotions: an intensely strong attraction toward beauty and an equally intense fascination by the ugliness which is contrasted with it and which destroys it. This balance of contrasted emotion is in the dramatic situation to which the speech is pertinent, but that situation alone is inadequate to it. This is, so to speak, the structural emotion, provided by the drama. But the whole effect, the dominant tone, is due to the fact that a number of floating feelings, having an affinity to this emotion by no means superficially evident, have combined with it to give us a new art emotion.

It is not in his personal emotions, the emotions provoked by particular events in his life, that the poet is in any way remarkable or interesting. His particular emotions may be simple, or crude, or flat. The emotion in his poetry will be a very complex thing, but not with the complexity of the emotions of people who have very complex or unusual emotions in life. One error, in fact, of eccentricity in poetry is to seek for new human emotions to express; and in this search for novelty in the wrong place it discovers the perverse. The business of the poet is not to find new emotions, but to use the ordinary ones and, in working them up into poetry, to express feelings which are not in actual emotions at all. And emotions which he has never experienced will serve his turn as well as those familiar to him. Consequently, we must believe that "emotion recollected in tranquillity"[12] is an inexact formula. For it is neither emotion, nor recollection, nor, without distortion of meaning, tranquillity. It is a concentration, and a new thing resulting from the concentration, of a very great number of experiences which to the practical and active person would not seem to be experiences at all; it is a concentration which does not happen consciously or of deliberation. These experiences are not "recollected," and they finally unite in an atmosphere which is "tranquil" only in that it is a passive attending upon the event. Of course this is not quite the whole story. There is a great deal, in the writing of poetry, which must be conscious and deliberate. In fact, the bad poet is usually unconscious where he ought to be conscious, and conscious where he ought to be unconscious. Both errors tend to make him "personal." Poetry is not a turning loose of emotion, but an escape from emotion; it is not the expression of personality, but an escape from personality. But, of course, only those who have personality and emotions know what it means to want to escape from these things.

---

[11] From Cyril Tourneur's *The Revenger's Tragedy* (1607), III, iv.
[12] See Wordsworth's "Preface" to the *Lyrical Ballads*, p. 154 of this volume.

III

ὁ δὲ νοῦς ἴσως θειότερόν τι χαὶ ἀπαθές ἐστιν.[13]

This essay proposes to halt at the frontier of metaphysics or mysticism, and confine itself to such practical conclusions as can be applied by the responsible person interested in poetry. To divert interest from the poet to the poetry is a laudable aim: for it would conduce to a juster estimation of actual poetry, good and bad. There are many people who appreciate the expression of sincere emotion in verse, and there is a smaller number of people who can appreciate technical excellence. But very few know when there is an expression of *significant* emotion, emotion which has its life in the poem and not in the history of the poet. The emotion of art is impersonal. And the poet cannot reach this impersonality without surrendering himself wholly to the work to be done. And he is not likely to know what is to be done unless he lives in what is not merely the present, but the present moment of the past, unless he is conscious, not of what is dead, but of what is already living.

[13] "The mind is doubtless something more divine and unimpressionable," from Aristotle's *De Anima* ("On the Soul").

T. S. Eliot

THE METAPHYSICAL POETS

A reading of this essay of Eliot's in connection with Dr. Johnson's on the same subject (pp. 122 ff.) will provide a classic instance of how the taste of one age is revised and even inverted by a succeeding age. Although it is not quite the case, as it is sometimes said to be, that the metaphysical poets fell wholly into oblivion or disrepute during the eighteenth and nineteenth centuries, they were, as Eliot suggests, thought to be chiefly quaint and curious and not in the main current of the tradition of English poetry; Arnold, in "The Study of Poetry," does not even raise the question of their being in that current, does not mention them at all. The brief article on them in *The Oxford Companion to English Literature* concludes by saying that "modern opinion does not wholly endorse Johnson's condemnation of these poets," which is surely one of the most remarkable understatements of all time in view of the enthusiastic admiration for them which developed in the early twentieth century and which still continues. The new opinion was signalized in 1912 by Herbert J. C. Grierson's famous edition of John Donne's poems, by his anthology which Eliot considers in his essay, and not least by the essay itself, which became the point of departure for much of the great body of critical comment on the metaphysical poets produced in the intervening years since its first publication in *The Times Literary Supplement* in 1921; it is included in Eliot's *Selected Essays* (1932).

By collecting these poems* from the work of a generation more often named than read, and more often read than profitably studied, Professor Grierson has rendered a service of some importance. Certainly the reader will meet with many poems already preserved in other anthologies, at the same time that he discovers poems such as those of Aurelian Townshend or Lord Herbert of Cherbury here included. But the function of such an anthology as this is neither that of Professor Saintsbury's admirable edition of Caroline poets[1]

---

* *Metaphysical Lyrics and Poems of the Seventeenth Century*: Donne to Butler. Selected and edited, with an Essay, by Herbert J. C. Grierson (Oxford: Clarendon Press. London: Milford). [Eliot's note.]

[1] George Saintsbury, *Minor Poets of the Caroline Period* (Oxford; 1905–1921).

nor that of the *Oxford Book of English Verse*. Mr. Grierson's book is in itself
a piece of criticism and a provocation of criticism; and we think that he was
right in including so many poems of Donne, elsewhere (though not in many
editions) accessible, as documents in the case of "metaphysical poetry." The
phrase has long done duty as a term of abuse or as the label of a quaint and
pleasant taste. The question is to what extent the so-called metaphysicals formed
a school (in our own time we should say a "movement"), and how far this so-
called school or movement is a digression from the main current.

Not only is it extremely difficult to define metaphysical poetry, but difficult
to decide what poets practise it and in which of their verses. The poetry of
Donne (to whom Marvell and Bishop King are sometimes nearer than any
of the other authors) is late Elizabethan, its feeling often very close to that
of Chapman. The "courtly" poetry is derivative from Jonson, who borrowed
liberally from the Latin; it expires in the next century with the sentiment and
witticism of Prior. There is finally the devotional verse of Herbert, Vaughan,
and Crashaw (echoed long after by Christina Rossetti and Francis Thompson);
Crashaw, sometimes more profound and less sectarian than the others, has a
quality which returns through the Elizabethan period to the early Italians. It
is difficult to find any precise use of metaphor, simile, or other conceit, which
is common to all the poets and at the same time important enough as an
element of style to isolate these poets as a group. Donne, and often Cowley,
employ a device which is sometimes considered characteristically "metaphysical";
the elaboration (contrasted with the condensation) of a figure of speech to the
farthest stage to which ingenuity can carry it. Thus Cowley develops the commonplace comparison of the world to a chess-board through long stanzas (*To
Destiny*), and Donne, with more grace, in *A Valediction*, the comparison of
two lovers to a pair of compasses. But elsewhere we find, instead of the mere
explication of the content of a comparison, a development by rapid association
of thought which requires considerable agility on the part of the reader.

> On a round ball
> A workman that hath copies by, can lay
> An Europe, Afrique, and an Asia,
> And quickly make that, which was nothing, All,
>   So doth each teare,
> Which thee doth weare,
> A globe, yea, world by that impression grow,
> Till thy tears mixt with mine doe overflow
> This world, by waters sent from thee, my heaven dissolved so.[2]

Here we find at least two connexions which are not implicit in the first figure,
but are forced upon it by the poet: from the geographer's globe to the tear,
and the tear to the deluge. On the other hand, some of Donne's most successful
and characteristic effects are secured by brief words and sudden contrasts:

> A bracelet of bright hair about the bone,[3]

where the most powerful effect is produced by the sudden contrast of associations of "bright hair" and of "bone." This telescoping of images and mul-

[2] John Donne: "A Valediction: Of Weeping."
[3] "The Relique."

tiplied associations is characteristic of the phrase of some of the dramatists of
the period which Donne knew: not to mention Shakespeare, it is frequent
in Middleton, Webster, and Tourneur, and is one of the sources of the vitality
of their language.

Johnson, who employed the term "metaphysical poets," apparently having
Donne, Cleveland, and Cowley chiefly in mind, remarks of them that "the
most heterogeneous ideas are yoked by violence together."[4] The force of this
impeachment lies in the failure of the conjunction, the fact that often the
ideas are yoked but not united; and if we are to judge of styles of poetry
by their abuse, enough examples may be found in Cleveland to justify Johnson's condemnation. But a degree of heterogeneity of material compelled into
unity by the operation of the poet's mind is omnipresent in poetry. We need not
select for illustration such a line as:

> Notre âme est un trois-mâts cherchant son Icarie;[5]

we may find it in some of the best lines of Johnson himself (*The Vanity of
Human Wishes*):

> His fate was destined to a barren strand,
> A petty fortress, and a dubious hand;
> He left a name at which the world grew pale,
> To point a moral, or adorn a tale.

where the effect is due to a contrast of ideas, different in degree but the same
in principle, as that which Johnson mildly reprehended. And in one of the
finest poems of the age (a poem which could not have been written in any other
age), the *Exequy* of Bishop King, the extended comparison is used with perfect
success: the idea and the simile become one, in the passage in which the
Bishop illustrates his impatience to see his dead wife, under the figure of a
journey:

> Stay for me there; I will not faile
> To meet thee in that hollow Vale.
> And think not much of my delay;
> I am already on the way,
> And follow thee with all the speed
> Desire can make, or sorrows breed.
> Each minute is a short degree,
> And ev'ry houre a step towards thee.
> At night when I betake to rest,
> Next morn I rise nearer my West
> Of life, almost by eight houres sail,
> Than when sleep breath'd his drowsy gale. . . .
> But heark! My Pulse, like a soft Drum

---

[4] See Johnson's Life of Cowley, included in this volume, pp. 122 ff.

[5] "Our soul is a three-master searching for her Icarie," from "Le Voyage," by
Charles Baudelaire (1821–1867), often considered the father of the French Sym-
bolist movement. ("Icarie" is a utopia in the novel *Voyage en Icarie*, by Étienne
Cabet.)

> Beats my approach, tells *Thee* I come;
> And slow howere my marches be,
> I shall at last sit down by *Thee*.

(In the last few lines there is that effect of terror which is several times attained by one of Bishop King's admirers, Edgar Poe.) Again, we may justly take these quatrains from Lord Herbert's Ode,[6] stanzas which would, we think, be immediately pronounced to be of the metaphysical school:

> So when from hence we shall be gone,
> And be no more, nor you, nor I,
> As one another's mystery,
> Each shall be both, yet both but one.

> This said, in her up-lifted face,
> Her eyes, which did that beauty crown,
> Were like two starrs, that having faln down,
> Look up again to find their place:

> While such a moveless silent peace
> Did seize on their becalmed sense,
> One would have thought some influence
> Their ravished spirits did possess.

There is nothing in these lines (with the possible exception of the stars, a simile not at once grasped, but lovely and justified) which fits Johnson's general observations on the metaphysical poets in his essay on Cowley. A good deal resides in the richness of association which is at the same time borrowed from and given to the word "becalmed"; but the meaning is clear, the language simple and elegant. It is to be observed that the language of these poets is as a rule simple and pure; in the verse of George Herbert this simplicity is carried as far as it can go—a simplicity emulated without success by numerous modern poets. The *structure* of the sentences, on the other hand, is sometimes far from simple, but this is not a vice; it is a fidelity to thought and feeling. The effect, at its best, is far less artificial than that of an ode by Gray.[7] And as this fidelity induces variety of thought and feeling, so it induces variety of music. We doubt whether, in the eighteenth century, could be found two poems in nominally the same metre, so dissimilar as Marvell's *Coy Mistress* and Crashaw's *Saint Teresa*; the one producing an effect of great speed by the use of short syllables, and the other an ecclesiastical solemnity by the use of long ones:

> Love, thou art absolute sole lord
> Of life and death.

If so shrewd and sensitive (though so limited) a critic as Johnson failed to define metaphysical poetry by its faults, it is worth while to inquire whether we may not have more success by adopting the opposite method: by assuming that the poets of the seventeenth century (up to the Revolution)[8] were the

[6] That is, Lord Herbert of Cherbury (1583–1684), brother of George Herbert.
[7] Thomas Gray (1716–1771), author of "Elegy in a Country Churchyard."
[8] Of 1688.

direct and normal development of the precedent age; and, without prejudicing their case by the adjective "metaphysical," consider whether their virtue was not something permanently valuable, which subsequently disappeared, but ought not to have disappeared. Johnson has hit, perhaps by accident, on one of their peculiarities, when he observes that "their attempts were always analytic"; he would not agree that, after the dissociation, they put the material together again in a new unity.

It is certain that the dramatic verse of the later Elizabethan and early Jacobean poets expresses a degree of development of sensibility which is not found in any of the prose, good as it often is. If we except Marlowe, a man of prodigious intelligence, these dramatists were directly or indirectly (it is at least a tenable theory) affected by Montaigne. Even if we except also Jonson and Chapman, these two were notably erudite, and were notably men who incorporated their erudition into their sensibility: their mode of feeling was directly and freshly altered by their reading and thought. In Chapman especially there is a direct sensuous apprehension of thought, or a recreation of thought into feeling, which is exactly what we find in Donne:

> in this one thing, all the discipline
> Of manners and of manhood is contained;
> A man to join himself with th' Universe
> In his main sway, and make in all things fit
> One with that All, and go on, round as it;
> Not plucking from the whole his wretched part,
> And into straits, or into nought revert,
> Wishing the complete Universe might be
> Subject to such a rag of it as he;
> But to consider great Necessity.[9]

We compare this with some modern passage:

> No, when the fight begins within himself,
> A man's worth something. God stoops o'er his head,
> Satan looks up between his feet—both tug—
> He's left, himself, i' the middle; the soul wakes
> And grows. Prolong that battle through his life![10]

It is perhaps somewhat less fair, though very tempting (as both poets are concerned with the perpetuation of love by offspring), to compare with the stanzas already quoted from Lord Herbert's Ode the following from Tennyson:

> One walked between his wife and child,
> With measured footfall firm and mild,
> And now and then he gravely smiled.
>   The prudent partner of his blood
>   Leaned on him, faithful, gentle, good,
>   Wearing the rose of womanhood.
>   And in their double love secure,

[9] From *The Revenge of Bussy d'Ambois*, IV, i, 37–46.
[10] Robert Browning's *Bishop Blougram's Apology*.

> The little maiden walked demure,
> Pacing with downward eyelids pure.
> These three made unity so sweet,
> My frozen heart began to beat,
> Remembering its ancient heat.[11]

The difference is not a simple difference of degree between poets. It is something which had happened to the mind of England between the time of Donne or Lord Herbert of Cherbury and the time of Tennyson and Browning; it is the difference between the intellectual poet and the reflective poet. Tennyson and Browning are poets, and they think; but they do not feel their thought as immediately as the odour of a rose. A thought to Donne was an experience; it modified his sensibility. When a poet's mind is perfectly equipped for its work, it is constantly amalgamating disparate experience; the ordinary man's experience is chaotic, irregular, fragmentary. The latter falls in love, or reads Spinoza,[12] and these two experiences have nothing to do with each other, or with the noise of the typewriter or the smell of cooking; in the mind of the poet these experiences are always forming new wholes.

We may express the difference by the following theory: The poets of the seventeenth century, the successors of the dramatists of the sixteenth, possessed a mechanism of sensibility which could devour any kind of experience. They are simple, artificial, difficult, or fantastic, as their predecessors were; no less nor more than Dante, Guido Cavalcanti, Guinizelli, or Cino.[13] In the seventeenth century a dissociation of sensibility set in, from which we have never recovered; and this dissociation, as is natural, was aggravated by the influence of the two most powerful poets of the century, Milton and Dryden. Each of these men performed certain poetic functions so magnificently well that the magnitude of the effect concealed the absence of others. The language went on and in some respects improved; the best verse of Collins, Gray, Johnson, and even Goldsmith satisfies some of our fastidious demands better than that of Donne or Marvell or King. But while the language became more refined, the feeling became more crude. The feeling, the sensibility, expressed in the *Country Churchyard* (to say nothing of Tennyson and Browning) is cruder than that in the *Coy Mistress.*

The second effect of the influence of Milton and Dryden followed from the first, and was therefore slow in manifestation. The sentimental age began early in the eighteenth century, and continued. The poets revolted against the ratiocinative, the descriptive; they thought and felt by fits, unbalanced; they reflected. In one or two passages of Shelley's *Triumph of Life,* in the second *Hyperion,*[14] there are traces of a struggle toward unification of sensibility. But Keats and Shelley died, and Tennyson and Browning ruminated.

After this brief exposition of a theory—too brief, perhaps, to carry con-

[11] "The Two Voices."

[12] Baruch Spinoza (1632–1677), Dutch philosopher.

[13] Guido Cavalcanti (c. 1259–1300); Guido Guinizelli (c. 1235–c. 1276); Cino da Pistoia (c. 1270–c. 1337); Italian poets, all of Dante's milieu, members of the Tuscan school of lyric love poets.

[14] The second of Keats' two attempts to finish a poem on the subject of the mythological figure, Hyperion, is usually called *The Fall of Hyperion.*

viction—we may ask, what would have been the fate of the "metaphysical" had the current of poetry descended in a direct line from them, as it descended in a direct line to them? They would not, certainly, be classified as metaphysical. The possible interests of a poet are unlimited; the more intelligent he is the better; the more intelligent he is the more likely that he will have interests: our only condition is that he turn them into poetry, and not merely meditate on them poetically. A philosophical theory which has entered into poetry is established, for its truth or falsity in one sense ceases to matter, and its truth in another sense is proved. The poets in question have, like other poets, various faults. But they were, at best, engaged in the task of trying to find the verbal equivalent for states of mind and feeling. And this means both that they are more mature, and that they wear better, than later poets of certainly not less literary ability.

It is not a permanent necessity that poets should be interested in philosophy, or in any other subject. We can only say that it appears likely that poets in our civilization, as it exists at present, must be *difficult*. Our civilization comprehends great variety and complexity, and this variety and complexity, playing upon a refined sensibility, must produce various and complex results. The poet must become more and more comprehensive, more allusive, more indirect, in order to force, to dislocate if necessary, language into his meaning. (A brilliant and extreme statement of this view, with which it is not requisite to associate oneself, is that of M. Jean Epstein, *La Poésie d' aujourd-hui.*)[15] Hence we get something which looks very much like the conceit—we get, in fact, a method curiously similar to that of the "metaphysical poets," similar also in its use of obscure words and of simple phrasing.

> O géraniums diaphanes, guerroyeurs sortilèges,
> Sacrilèges monomanes!
> Emballages, dévergondages, douches! O pressoirs
> Des vendanges des grands soirs!
> Layettes aux abois,
> Thyrses au fond des bois!
> Transfusions, représailles,
> Relevailles, compresses et l'éternal potion,
> Angélus! n'en pouvoir plus
> De débâcles nuptiales! de débâcles nuptiales![16]

The same poet could write also simply:

> Elle est bien loin, elle pleure,
> Le grand vent se lamente aussi . . .[17]

[15] "The Poetry of Today."

[16] "O transparent geraniums, bellicose sorceries,/Monomaniac sacrileges!/Packings, shamelessnesses, showers! O wine presses/Of vintages of great evenings!/Baby clothes at bay/Thyrsis in the depths of the woods!/Transfusions, reprisals,/Churchings, compresses and the eternal potion,/Angelus! no longer shall we bear/Disastrous marriages! disastrous marriages!" From *Dernier Vers X* (1890, "Last Poems"), by Jules Laforgue (1860–1887).

[17] "She is far away, she weeps,/The great wind mourns also. . . ." From *Dernier Vers XI, Sur une défunte* ("On a Dead Woman").

Jules Laforgue, and Tristan Corbière[18] in many of his poems, are nearer to the "school of Donne" than any modern English poet. But poets more classical than they have the same essential quality of transmuting ideas into sensations, of transforming an observation into a state of mind.

> Pour l'enfant, amoureux de cartes et d'estampes,
> L'univers est égal à son vaste appétit.
> Ah, que le monde est grand à la clarté des lampes!
> Aux yeux du souvenir que le monde est petit![19]

In French literature the great master of the seventeenth century—Racine—and the great master of the nineteenth—Baudelaire—are in some ways more like each other than they are like any one else. The greatest two masters of diction are also the greatest two psychologists, the most curious explorers of the soul. It is interesting to speculate whether it is not a misfortune that two of the greatest masters of diction in our language, Milton and Dryden, triumph with a dazzling disregard of the soul. If we continued to produce Miltons and Drydens it might not so much matter, but as things are it is a pity that English poetry has remained so incomplete. Those who object to the "artificiality" of Milton or Dryden sometimes tell us to "look into our hearts and write." But that is not looking deep enough; Racine or Donne looked into a good deal more than the heart. One must look into the cerebral cortex, the nervous system, and the digestive tracts.

May we not conclude, then, that Donne, Crashaw, Vaughan, Herbert and Lord Herbert, Marvell, King, Cowley at his best, are in the direct current of English poetry, and that their faults should be reprimanded by this standard rather than coddled by antiquarian affection? They have been enough praised in terms which are implicit limitations because they are "metaphysical" or "witty," "quaint" or "obscure," though at their best they have not these attributes more than other serious poets. On the other hand, we must not reject the criticism of Johnson (a dangerous person to disagree with) without having mastered it, without having assimilated the Johnsonian canons of taste. In reading the celebrated passage in his essay on Cowley we must remember that by wit he clearly means something more serious than we usually mean today; in his criticism of their versification we must remember in what a narrow discipline he was trained, but also how well trained; we must remember that Johnson tortures chiefly the chief offenders, Cowley and Cleveland. It would be a fruitful work, and one requiring a substantial book, to break up the classification of Johnson (for there has been none since) and exhibit these poets in all their difference of kind and of degree, from the massive music of Donne to the faint, pleasing tinkle of Aurelian Townshend—whose *Dialogue between a Pilgrim and Time* is one of the few regrettable omissions from the excellent anthology of Professor Grierson.

---

[18] Another member of the French Symbolist movement (1845–1875).

[19] "For the child, lover of maps and prints,/The earth is equal to his vast appetite./Ah, how large the world is by the light of lamps!/To the eyes of memory, how small is the world!" From Baudelaire's "Le Voyage."

Edmund Wilson

IS VERSE A DYING TECHNIQUE?

Over recent decades in England and even more in America, criticism
has established itself in the universities and it has become virtually the
rule for the notable critic to be a university teacher. The career of
Edmund Wilson (1895–   ) makes the striking American exception.
Such regular employment as Mr. Wilson has had has been journalistic.
After his graduation from Princeton in 1916, he worked for a year on
the *New York Evening Sun;* following a period of service in the First
World War, he became the managing editor of *Vanity Fair;* from 1926
to 1931 he was associate editor of the *The New Republic,* and from
1944 to 1948 the regular reviewer of books for *The New Yorker.* But
for the greater part of his life he has worked without institutional ties
of any kind. His experience in journalism may be supposed to have confirmed his natural talent for dealing seriously with literature in a way
calculated to engage the interest of the general educated public, and it
is beyond question that, of all American critics of our time, he is the
most widely read. But the word journalism almost inevitably carries
connotations of superficiality, whereas Mr. Wilson's criticism is based in
an erudition that is at once profound and wide-ranging and that might
well be the envy of university scholars. Perhaps the most remarkable
example of his scholarly bent is his study of the newly discovered Hebrew and Aramaic manuscripts, *The Scrolls from the Dead Sea* (1955).

Mr. Wilson established his critical reputation with the publication,
in 1931, of *Axel's Castle,* a series of essays on the writers—Yeats, Eliot,
Proust, Joyce, and Gertrude Stein—who make the classic tradition of
modern literature. Other collections of his essays are *The Triple Thinkers* (1935; revised and enlarged 1948), *The Wound and the Bow*
(1941), *Classics and Commercials* (1950), and *The Shores of Light*
(1952). *To the Finland Station* (1940) is an account of the revolutionary tradition of Europe from Michelet to Lenin and Trotsky; *Patriotic
Gore* (1962) is a series of studies in the literature of the American
Civil War. Mr. Wilson has also written fiction—*I Thought of Daisy*
(1929), a novel, and *Memoirs of Hecate County* (1947), a volume of
stories—as well as plays and a number of books on public questions.

From *The Triple Thinkers: Twelve Essays on Literary Subjects,* revised edition, by
Edmund Wilson. New York: Oxford University Press, Inc., 1948. By permission of the
author.

The more one reads the current criticism of poetry by poets and their reviewers, the more one becomes convinced that the discussion is proceeding on false assumptions. The writers may belong to different schools, but they all seem to share a basic confusion.

This confusion is the result of a failure to think clearly about what is meant by the words "prose," "verse," and "poetry"—a question which is some-times debated but which never gets straightened out. Yet are not the obvious facts as follows?

What we mean by the words "prose" and "verse" are simply two different techniques of literary expression. Verse is written in lines with a certain num-ber of metrical feet each; prose is written in paragraphs and has what we call rhythm. But what is "poetry," then? What I want to suggest is that "poetry" formerly meant one kind of thing but that it now means something different, and that one ought not to generalize about "poetry" by taking all the writers of verse, ancient, medieval and modern, away from their various periods and throwing them together in one's mind, but to consider both verse and prose in relation to their functions at different times.

The important thing to recognize, it seems to me, is that the literary technique of verse was once made to serve many purposes for which we now, as a rule, use prose. Solon,[1] the Athenian statesman, expounded his political ideas in verse; the *Works and Days* of Hesiod are a shepherd's calendar in verse; his *Theogony* is versified mythology; and almost everything that in contemporary writing would be put into prose plays and novels was versified by the Greeks in epics or plays.

It is true that Aristotle tried to discriminate. "We have no common name," he wrote, "for a mime of Sophron or Xenarchus and a Socratic conversation; and we should still be without one even if the imitation in the two instances were in trimeters or elegiacs or some other kind of verse—though it is the way with people to tack on 'poet' to the name of a meter, and talk of elegiac-poets and epic-poets, thinking that they call them poets not by reason of the imitative nature of their work, but indiscriminately by reason of the meter they write in. Even if a theory of medicine or physical philosophy be put forth in a metrical form, it is usual to describe the writer in this way; Homer and Empedocles, however, have really nothing in common apart from their meter; so that, if the one is to be called a poet, the other should be termed a physicist rather than a poet."

But he admitted that there was no accepted name for the creative—what he calls the "imitative"—art which had for its mediums both prose and verse; and his posterity followed the custom of which he had pointed out the im-propriety by calling anything in meter a "poem." The Romans wrote treatises in verse on philosophy and astronomy and farming. The "poetic" of Horace's *Ars Poetica*[2] applies to the whole range of ancient verse—though Horace did think it just as well to mingle the "agreeable" with the "useful"—and this essay in literary criticism is itself written in meter. "Poetry" remained identified with

---

[1] Solon (c. 639–559 B.C.) is best known as a giver of laws and as a reformer, but some of his patriotic verse survives.

[2] "The Art of Poetry," by Quintus Horatius Flaccus (65–8 B.C.), was finished by 13 B.C.

verse; and since for centuries both dramas and narratives continued largely to be written in verse, the term of which Aristotle had noticed the need—a term for imaginative literature itself, irrespective of literary techniques—never came into common use.

But when we arrive at the nineteenth century, a new conception of "poetry" appears. The change is seen very clearly in the doubts which began to be felt as to whether Pope were really a poet. Now, it is true that a critic like Johnson would hardly have assigned to Pope the position of pre-eminence he does at any other period than Johnson's own; but it is *not* true that only a critic of the latter part of the eighteenth century, a critic of an "age of prose," would have considered Pope a poet. Would not Pope have been considered a poet in any age before the age of Coleridge?

But the romantics were to redefine "poetry." Coleridge, in the *Biographia Literaria,* denies that any excellent work in meter may be properly called a "poem." "The final definition . . ." he says, "may be thus worded. A poem is that species of composition which is opposed to works of science by proposing for its *immediate* object pleasure, not truth; and from all other species—(having *this* object in common with it)—it is discriminated by proposing to itself such delight from the *whole* as is compatible with a distinct gratification from each component part.[3] This would evidently exclude the *Ars Poetica* and the *De Rerum Natura,*[4] whose immediate objects are as much truth as pleasure. What is really happening here is that for Coleridge the function of "poetry" is becoming more specialized. Why? Coleridge answers this question in formulating an objection which may be brought against the first part of his definition: "But the communication of pleasure may be the immediate object of a work not metrically composed; and that object may have been in a high degree attained, as in novels and romances." Precisely; and the novels and romances were formerly written in verse, whereas they are now usually written in prose. In Coleridge's time, tales in verse were more and more giving place to prose novels. Before long, novels in verse such as *Aurora Leigh* and *The Ring and the Book*[5] were to seem more or less literary oddities. "Poetry," then, for Coleridge, has become something which, unless he amends his definition, may equally well be written in prose: Isaiah and Plato and Jeremy Taylor will, as he admits, be describable as "poetry." Thereafter, he seems to become somewhat muddled; but he finally arrives at the conclusion that the "peculiar property of poetry" is "the property of exciting a more continuous and equal attention than the language of prose aims at, whether colloquial or written."

The truth is that Coleridge is having difficulties in attempting to derive his new conception of poetry from the literature of the past, which has been based on the old conception. Poe, writing thirty years later, was able to get a good deal further. Coleridge had said—and it seems to have been really what he was principally trying to say—that "a poem of any length neither can be, nor ought to

---

[3] For the context of Coleridge's discussion, see p. 166 of this volume.

[4] "On the Nature of Things," a long poem in Latin by the Roman poet Lucretius (c. 99–55 B.C.) setting forth the ideas of the Greek philosophers Democritus and Epicurus.

[5] *Aurora Leigh* (1857) was written by Elizabeth Barrett Browning (1806–1861), and *The Ring and the Book* (1865–1869) was written by Robert Browning (1812–1889).

be, all poetry." (Yet are not the *Divine Comedy* and Shakespeare's tragedies "all poetry"? Or rather, in the case of these masterpieces, is not the work as a whole really a "poem," maintained, as it is, at a consistently high level of intensity and style and with the effects of the different parts dependent on one another?) Poe predicted that "no very long poem would ever be popular again,"[6] and made "poetry" mean something even more special by insisting that it should approach the indefiniteness of music. The reason why no very long poem was ever to be popular again was simply that verse as a technique was then passing out of fashion in every department of literature except those of lyric poetry and the short idyl. The long poems of the past—Shakespeare's plays, the *Divine Comedy*, the Greek dramatists and Homer—were going to continue to be popular; but writers of that caliber in the immediate future were not going to write in verse.

Matthew Arnold was to keep on in Coleridge's direction, though by a route somewhat different from Poe's. He said, as we have heard so repeatedly, that poetry was at bottom a criticism of life; but, though one of the characteristics which true poetry might possess was "moral profundity," another was "natural magic," and "eminent manifestations of this magical power of poetry" were "very rare and very precious."[7] "Poetry" is thus, it will be seen, steadily becoming rarer. Arnold loved quoting passages of natural magic and he suggested that the lover of literature should carry around in his mind as touchstones a handful of such topnotch passages to test any new verse he encountered. His method of presenting the poets makes poetry seem fleeting and quintessential. Arnold was not happy till he had edited Byron and Wordsworth in such a way as to make it appear that their "poetry" was a kind of elixir which had to be distilled from the mass of their work—rather difficult in Byron's case: a production like *Don Juan* does not really give up its essence in the sequences excerpted by Arnold.

There was, to be sure, some point in what Arnold was trying to do for these writers: Wordsworth and Byron both often wrote badly and flatly. But they would not have lent themselves at all to this high-handed kind of anthologizing if it had not been that, by this time, it had finally become almost impossible to handle large subjects successfully in verse. Matthew Arnold could have done nothing for Dante by reducing him to a little book of extracts—nor, with all Shakespeare's carelessness, for Shakespeare. The new specialized idea of poetry appears very plainly and oddly when Arnold writes about Homer: the *Iliad* and the *Odyssey*, which had been for the Greeks fiction and scripture, have come to appear to this critic long stretches of ancient legend from which we may pick out little crystals of moral profundity and natural magic.

And in the meantime the ideas of Poe, developed by the Symbolists in France, had given rise to the *Art poétique*[8] of Verlaine, so different from that

[6] In his essay, "The Poetic Principle," first published in 1850, a year after Poe's death, although he had delivered it as a lecture many times during the last years of his life.

[7] Wilson here and throughout the course of his argument refers to a number of essays by Matthew Arnold, but especially to "The Study of Poetry," included in this volume.

[8] "The Art of Poetry." Wilson proceeds to quote this poem by Paul Verlaine (1844–1896), French symbolist poet.

of Horace: "Music first of all . . . no Color, only the *nuance*! . . . Shun Point, the murderer, cruel Wit and Laughter the impure. . . Take eloquence and wring its neck! . . . Let your verse be the luck of adventure flung to the crisp morning wind that brings us a fragrance of thyme and mint—and all the rest is literature."

Eliot and Valéry followed. Paul Valéry, still in the tradition of Poe, regarded a poem as a specialized machine for producing a certain kind of "state."[9] Eliot called poetry a "superior amusement," and he anthologized, in both his poems and his essays, even more fastidiously than Arnold. He, too, has his favorite collection of magical and quintessential passages; and he possesses an uncanny gift for transmitting to them a personal accent and imbuing them with a personal significance. And as even those passages of Eliot's poems which have not been imitated or quoted often seemed to have been pieced together out of separate lines and fragments, so his imitators came to work in broken mosaics and "pinches of glory"—to use E. M. Forster's[10] phrase about Eliot— rather than with conventional stanzas.

The result has been an optical illusion. The critic, when he read the classic, epic, eclogue, tale or play, may have grasped it and enjoyed it as a whole; yet when the reader reads the comment of the critic, he gets the impression, looking back on the poem, that the *Divine Comedy*, say, so extraordinarily sustained and so beautifully integrated, is remarkable mainly for Eliot-like fragments. Once we know Matthew Arnold's essay, we find that the ἀνήριθμον γέλασμα[11] of Aeschylus and the "daffodils that come before the swallow dares" of Shakespeare tend to stick out from their contexts in a way that they hardly deserve to. Matthew Arnold, unintentionally and unconsciously, has had the effect of making the poet's "poetry" seem to be concentrated in the phrase or the line.

Finally, Mr. A. E. Housman, in his lecture on *The Name and Nature of Poetry*, has declared that he cannot define poetry. He can only become aware of its presence by the symptoms he finds it producing: "Experience has taught me, when I am shaving of a morning, to keep watch over my thought, because if a line of poetry strays into my memory, my skin bristles so that the razor ceases to act. This particular symptom is accompanied by a shiver down the spine; there is another which consists in a constriction of the throat and a precipitation of water to the eyes; and there is a third which I can only describe by borrowing a phrase from one of Keats's last latters, where he says, speaking of Fanny Brawne, 'everything that reminds me of her goes through me like a spear.' The seat of this sensation is the pit of the stomach."

One recognizes these symptoms; but there are other things, too, which produce these peculiar sensations: scenes from prose plays, for example (the final curtain of *The Playboy of the Western World*[12] could make one's hair stand on end when it was first done by the Abbey Theater), passages from prose

---

[9] See Valéry's "Poetry and Abstract Thought," pp. 451 ff. of this volume.
[10] Edward Morgan Forster (b. 1879), English novelist.
[11] "Limitless laughter."
[12] A play by John Millington Synge (1871–1909), first performed in 1907. The play pokes sharp fun at Irish character, and when it opened in the Abbey Theatre, in Dublin, the audience rioted.

novels (Stephen Daedalus' broodings over his mother's death in the opening episode of *Ulysses*[13] and the end of Mrs. Bloom's soliloquy), even scenes from certain historians, such as Mirabeau's arrival in Aix at the end of Michelet's *Louis XVI*,[14] even passages in a philosophical dialogue: the conclusion of Plato's *Symposium*. Though Housman does praise a few long English poems, he has the effect, like these other critics, of creating the impression that "poetry" means primarily lyric verse, and this only at its most poignant or most musical moments.

Now all that has been said here is, of course, not intended to belittle the value of what such people as Coleridge and Poe, Arnold and Eliot have written on the subject of poetry. These men are all themselves first-class poets; and their criticism is very important because it constitutes an attempt to explain what they have aimed at in their own verse, of what they have conceived, in their age, to be possible or impossible for their medium.

Yet one feels that in the minds of all of them a certain confusion persists between the new idea of poetry and the old—between Coleridge's conception, on the one hand, and Horace's, on the other; that the technique of prose is inevitably tending more and more to take over the material which had formerly provided the subjects for compositions in verse, and that, as the two techniques of writing are beginning to appear, side by side or combined, in a single work, it is becoming more and more impossible to conduct any comparative discussion of literature on a basis of this misleading division of it into the departments of "poetry" and of "prose."

One result of discussion on this basis, especially if carried on by verse-writers, is the creation of an illusion that contemporary "poets" of relatively small stature (though of however authentic gifts) are the true inheritors of the genius and carriers-on of the tradition of Aeschylus, Sophocles and Virgil, Dante, Shakespeare and Milton. Is it not time to discard the word "poetry" or to define it in such a way as to take account of the fact that the most intense, the most profound, the most beautifully composed and the most comprehensive of the great works of literary art (which for these reasons are also the most thrilling and give us most prickly sensations while shaving) have been written sometimes in verse technique, sometimes in prose technique, depending partly on the taste of the author, partly on the mere current fashion. It is only when we argue these matters that we become involved in absurdities. When we are reading, we appraise correctly. Matthew Arnold cites examples of that "natural magic" which he regards as one of the properties of "poetry" from Chateaubriand[15] and Maurice de Guérin,[16] who did not write verse but prose, as well as from Shakespeare and Keats; and he rashly includes Molière[17] among the "larger and more splendid luminaries in the poetical heaven," though

---

[13] A novel (1922) by James Joyce (1882–1941).

[14] Jules Michelet (1798–1874), French historian. Honoré-Gabriel Riquetti, Comte de Mirabeau (1749–1791), French revolutionist, who in 1789 was elected a delegate for the third estate for Aix-en-Provence in the States-General.

[15] Francois René, Vicomte de Chateaubriand (1768–1848), French writer and statesman.

[16] Maurice de Guérin (1810–1839), French writer, best known for his prose poems.

[17] Jean Baptiste Poquelin Molière (1622–1673), the greatest French writer of comedies.

Molière was scarcely more "poetic" in any sense except perhaps that of "moral profundity" when he wrote verse than when he wrote prose and would certainly not have versified at all if the conventions of his time had not demanded it. One who has first come to Flaubert at a sensitive age when he is also reading Dante may have the experience of finding that the paragraphs of the former remain in his mind and continue to sing just as the lines of the latter do. He has got the prose by heart unconsciously just as he has done with favorite passages of verse; he repeats them, admiring the form, studying the choice of words, seeing more and more significance in them. He realizes that, though Dante may be greater than Flaubert, Flaubert belongs in Dante's class. It is simply that by Flaubert's time the Dantes present their visions in terms of prose drama or fiction rather than of epics in verse. At any other period, certainly, *La Tentation de Saint Antoine*[18] would have been written in verse instead of prose.

And if one happens to read Virgil's *Georgics* not long after having read Flaubert, the shift from verse to prose technique gets the plainest demonstration possible. If you think of Virgil with Tennyson, you have the illusion that the Virgilian poets are shrinking; but if you think of Virgil with Flaubert, you can see how a great modern prose-writer has grown out of the great classical poets. Flaubert somewhere—I think, in the Goncourt[19] journal—expresses his admiration for Virgil; and, in method as well as in mood, the two writers are often akin. Flaubert is no less accomplished in his use of words and rhythms than Virgil; and the poet is as successful as the novelist in conveying emotion through objective statement. The *Georgics* were seven years in the writing, as *Madame Bovary* was six. And the fact that—in *Madame Bovary* especially— Flaubert's elegiac feeling as well as his rural settings run so close to the characteristic vein of Virgil makes the comparison particularly interesting. Put the bees of the *Georgics,* for example, whose swarming Virgil thus describes:

> aethere in alto
> Fit sonitus, magnum mixtae glomerantur in orbem
> Praecipitesque cadunt[20]

beside the bees seen and heard by Emma Bovary on an April afternoon: "quelquefois les abeilles, tournoyant dans la lumière, frappaient contre les carreaux comme des balles d'or rebondissantes."[21] Put

> Et iam summa procul villarum culmina fumant,
> Maioresque cadunt altis de montibus umbrae[22]

beside: "La tendresse des anciens jours leur revenait au cœur, abondante et silencieuse comme la rivière qui coulait, avec autant de mollesse qu'en apportait le parfum des seringas, et projetait dans leurs souvenirs des ombres

[18] *The Temptation of St. Anthony* (1874) by Flaubert.
[19] Edmond (1822–1896) and Jules (1830–1870) Goncourt collaborated on numerous writings, the most famous of which is the Journal, a first-hand account of Parisian life from 1851 to 1895.
[20] "High in the heavens a sound arises; they cluster, mingled, in a large ball and fall headlong." *Georgics,* IV, 78–80.
[21] "Sometimes the bees, jousting in the light, struck against the flagstones, like bouncing golden balls."
[22] "And now the highest tops of the farmhouses smoke from afar and shadows growing larger fall from the tops of mountains." *Eclogues* I, 82–83.

plus dèmesurées et plus mélancoliques que celles des saules immobiles qui s'allongeaient sur l'herbe."[23] And compare Virgil's sadness and wistfulness with the sadness and nostalgia of Flaubert: the melancholy of the mountainous pastures laid waste by the cattle plague:

> desertaque regna
> Pastorum, et longe saltus lateque vacantes[24]

with the modern desolations of Paris in *L'Education sentimentale*: "Les rues étaient désertes. Quelquefois une charrette lourde passait, en ébranlant les pavés,"[25] etc.; or Palinurus, fallen into the sea, swimming with effort to the coast of Italy, but only to be murdered and left there "naked on the unknown sand," while his soul, since his corpse lies unburied, must forever be excluded from Hades, or Orpheus still calling Eurydice when his head has been torn from his body, till his tongue has grown cold and the echo of his love has been lost among the river banks[26]—compare these with Charles Bovary, a schoolboy, looking out on fine summer evenings at the sordid streets of Rouen and sniffing for the good country odors "qui ne venaient pas jusqu'a lui"—(tendebantque manus ripae ulterioris amore")[27]—or with the scene in which Emma Bovary receives her father's letter and remembers the summers of her girlhood, with the galloping colts and the bumping bees, and knows that she has spent all her illusions in maidenhood, in marriage, in adultery, as a traveler leaves something of his money at each of the inns of the road.

We find, in this connection, in Flaubert's letters the most explicit statements. "To desire to give verse-rhythm to prose, yet to leave it prose and very much prose," he wrote to Louise Colet (March 27, 1853), "and to write about ordinary life as histories and epics are written, yet without falsifying the subject, is perhaps an absurd idea. Sometimes I almost think it is. But it may also be a great experiment and very original." The truth is that Flaubert is a crucial figure. He is the first great writer in prose deliberately to try to take over for the treatment of ambitious subjects the delicacy, the precision and the intensity that have hitherto been identified with verse. Henrik Ibsen, for the poetic drama, played a role hardly less important. Ibsen began as a writer of verse and composed many short and non-dramatic poems as well as *Peer Gynt* and *Brand* and his other plays in verse, but eventually changed over to prose for the concentrated Sophoclean tragedies that affected the whole dramatic tradition. Thereafter the dramatic "poets"—the Chekhovs,[28] the Synges and the

---

[23] "The tenderness of former days was recalled to the heart, abundant and silent, like the river that flowed, with as much softness as the perfume of the syringa brought, and projected into their memories shadows more shapeless and melancholy than those of the immobile willows stretched out along the grass."

[24] "And the deserted realms of the shepherds and meadows empty far and wide." *Georgics* III, 476–477.

[25] "The streets were empty. Sometimes a heavy cart passed, shaking the paving stones."

[26] Episodes from Book VI of Virgil's *Aeneid*.

[27] "Which never reached them"—("they reached out their hands with a yearning for the far shore"). *Aeneid* VI, 314.

[28] Anton Pavlovich Chekhov (1860–1904), Russian fiction writer and dramatist, whose best-known play is *The Cherry Orchard* (1904).

Shaws (Hauptmann[29] had occasional relapses)—wrote almost invariably in prose. It was by such that the soul of the time was given its dramatic expression: there was nothing left for Rostand's[30] alexandrines but fireworks and declamation.

In the later generation, James Joyce, who had studied Flaubert and Ibsen as well as the great classical verse-masters, set out to merge the two techniques. Dickens and Herman Melville had occasionally resorted to blank verse for passages which they meant to be elevated, but these flights had not matched their context, and the effect had not been happy. Joyce, however, now, in *Ulysses,* has worked out a new medium of his own which enables him to exploit verse metrics in a texture which is basically prose; and he has created in *Finnegans Wake* a work of which we cannot say whether it ought, in the old-fashioned phraseology, to be described as prose or verse. A good deal of *Finnegans Wake* is written in regular meter and might perfectly well be printed as verse, but, except for the interpolated songs, the whole thing is printed as prose. As one reads it, one wonders, in any case, how anything could be demanded of "poetry" by Coleridge with his "sense of novelty and freshness with old and familiar objects," by Poe with his indefiniteness of music, by Arnold with his natural magic, by Verlaine with his nuance, by Eliot with his unearthliness, or by Housman with his bristling of the beard, which the *Anna Livia Plurabelle* chapter (or canto)[31] does not fully supply.

If, then, we take literature as a whole for our field, we put an end to many futile controversies—the controversies, for example, as to whether or not Pope is a poet, as to whether or not Whitman is a poet. If you are prepared to admit that Pope is one of the great English writers, it is less interesting to compare him with Shakespeare—which will tell you something about the development of English verse but not bring out Pope's peculiar excellence—than to compare him with Thackeray, say, with whom he has his principal theme— the vanity of the world—in common and who throws into relief the more passionate pulse and the solider art of Pope. And so the effort to apply to Whitman the ordinary standards of verse has hindered the appreciation of his careful and exquisite art.

If, in writing about "poetry," one limits oneself to "poets" who compose in verse, one excludes too much of modern literature, and with it too much of life. The best modern work in verse has been mostly in the shorter forms, and it may be that our lyric poets are comparable to any who have ever lived, but we have had no imaginations of the stature of Shakespeare or Dante who have done their major work in verse. The horizon and even the ambition of the contemporary writer of verse has narrowed with the specialization of the

---

[29] Gerhart Hauptmann (1862–1946), German dramatist, novelist, and poet, who became famous with his naturalistic play *Before Dawn* (1889).

[30] Edmond Rostand (1868–1918), French poet and dramatist, best known for *Cyrano de Bergerac* (1897).

[31] Here is a sample from the Anna Livia Plurabelle episode of *Finnegans Wake* (1939): "Or whatever it was they threed to make out he thried to two in the Fiendish park. He's an awful old reppe. Look at the shirt of him! Look at the dirt of it! He has all my water black on me. And it steeping and stuping since this time last wik."

function of verse itself. (Though the novelists Proust[32] and Joyce are both masters of what used to be called "numbers," the verses of the first are negligible and those of the second minor.)

Would not D. H. Lawrence, for example, if he had lived a century earlier, probably have told his tales, as Byron and Crabbe[33] did: in verse? Is it not just as correct to consider him the last of the great English romantic poets as one of the most original of modern English novelists? Must we not, to appreciate Virginia Woolf, be aware that she is trying to do the kind of thing that the writers of verse have done even more than she is trying to do what Jane Austen or George Eliot were doing?[34]

Recently the techniques of prose and verse have been getting mixed up at a bewildering rate—with the prose technique steadily gaining. You have had the verse technique of Ezra Pound[35] gradually changing into prose technique. You have had William Faulkner,[36] who began by writing verse, doing his major work in prose fiction without ever quite mastering prose, so that he may at any moment upset us by interpolating a patch of verse. You have had Robinson Jeffers,[37] in narrative "poems" which are as much novels as some of Lawrence's, reeling out yards of what are really prose dithyrambs with a loose hexametric base; and you have had Carl Sandburg, of *The People, Yes*,[38] producing a queer kind of literature which oscillates between something like verse and something like the paragraphs of a newspaper "column."

Sandburg and Pound have, of course, come out of the old *vers libre*, which, though prose-like, was either epigrammatic or had the rhythms of the Whitmanesque chant. But since the Sandburg-Pound generation, a new development in verse has taken place. The sharpness and the energy disappear; the beat gives way to a demoralized weariness. Here the "sprung-rhythm" of Gerard Manley Hopkins[39] has sometimes set the example. But the difference is that Hopkins' rhythms convey agitation and tension, whereas the rhythms of MacNeice and Auden[40] let down the taut traditions of lyric verse with an effect that is often comic and probably intended to be so—these poets are not far at moments from the humorous rhymed prose of Ogden Nash.[41] And finally—what is very strange to see—Miss Edna St. Vincent Millay in *Conversation at Mid-*

---

[32] Marcel Proust (1871–1922), French novelist, chiefly known for *The Remembrance of Things Past* (1913–1927), which first appeared in 16 volumes.

[33] George Crabbe (1754–1832), English poet. For his stories in verse, see *Tales* (1812) and *Tales of the Hall* (1819).

[34] For an example of poetic prose by Virginia Woolf (1882–1941) see *The Waves* (1931) especially.

[35] Wilson is thinking of the *Cantos* of Ezra Pound (b. 1885), still in progress.

[36] William Faulkner (1897–1962), American novelist, whose youthful book of poems, *The Marble Faun*, appeared in 1924.

[37] Robinson Jeffers (1887–1962), American poet. For the verse narratives that first brought him renown, see *Roan Stallion, Tamar and Other Poems* (1925).

[38] Carl Sandburg (1878–1967) published *The People, Yes* in 1936.

[39] Gerard Manley Hopkins (1844–1889), known for his experiments in poetic metre and rhythms.

[40] The verse of the English poets Louis MacNeice (1907–1963) and W. H. Auden (b. 1907) shows the influence of Hopkins.

[41] Ogden Nash (b. 1902), American writer of light verse.

night,[42] slackening her old urgent pace, dimming the ring of her numbers, has given us a curious example of metrics in full dissolution, with the stress almost entirely neglected, the lines running on for paragraphs and even the rhymes sometimes fading out. In some specimens of this recent work, the beat of verse has been so slurred and muted that it might almost as well have been abandoned. We have at last lived to see the day when the ballads of Gilbert and Hood,[43] written without meter for comic effect in long lines that look and sound like paragraphs, have actually become the type of a certain amount of serious poetry.

You have also the paradox of Eliot attempting to revive the verse-drama with rhythms which, adapting themselves to the rhythms of colloquial speech, run sometimes closer to prose. And you have Mr. Maxwell Anderson[44] trying to renovate the modern theater by bringing back blank verse again—with the result that, once a writer of prose dialogue distinguished by some color and wit, he has become, as a dramatic poet, banal and insipid beyond belief. The trouble is that no verse technique is more obsolete today than blank verse. The old iambic pentameters have no longer any relation whatever to the tempo and language of our lives. Yeats was the last who could write them, and he only because he inhabited, in Ireland and in imagination, a grandiose anachronistic world. You cannot deal with contemporary events in an idiom which was already growing trite in Tennyson's and Arnold's day; and if you try to combine the rhythm of blank verse with the idiom of ordinary talk, you get something—as in Anderson's *Winterset*—which lacks the merits of either. Nor can you try to exploit the worked-out rhythm without also finding yourself let in for the antiquated point of view. The comments on the action in *Winterset* are never the expression of sentiments which we ourselves could conceivably feel in connection with the events depicted: they are the echoes of Greek choruses and Elizabethan soliloquies reflecting upon happenings of a different kind.

Thus if the poets of the Auden-MacNeice school find verse turning to prose in their hands, like the neck of the flamingo in Lewis Carroll with which Alice tried to play croquet, Mr. Anderson, returning to blank verse, finds himself in the more awkward predicament of the girl in the fairy tale who could never open her mouth without having a toad jump out.

But what has happened? What, then, is the cause of this disuse into which verse technique has been falling for at least the last two hundred years? And what are we to expect in the future? Is verse to be limited now to increasingly specialized functions and finally to go out altogether? Or will it recover the domains it has lost?

To find out, if it is possible to do so, we should be forced to approach this change from the anthropological and sociological points of view. Is verse a more

[42] *Conversations at Midnight* by Edna St. Vincent Millay (1892–1950) was published in 1937.

[43] Sir William Schwenck Gilbert (1836–1911) of the famous team of Gilbert and Sullivan; Thomas Hood (1799–1845), known chiefly for his comic prose and verse.

[44] Maxwell Anderson (1888–1959), American dramatist, is known chiefly for *Winterset* (1935); his first play in blank verse was *Elizabeth the Queen* (1930).

primitive technique than prose? Are its fixed rules like the syntax of languages, which are found to have been stiffer and more complicated the further back one goes? Aside from the question of the requirements of taste and the self-imposed difficulties of form which have always, in any period, been involved in the production of great works of art, does the easy flexibility, say, of modern English prose bear to the versification of Horace the same relation that English syntax bears to Horace's syntax, or that Horace's bears to that of the Eskimos?

It seems obvious that one of the important factors in the history of the development of verse must have been its relations with music. Greek verse grew up in fusion with music: verse and music were learned together. It was not till after Alexander the Great that prosody was detached from harmony. The Greek name for "prose" was "bare words"—that is, words divorced from music. But what the Romans took over and developed was a prosody that was purely literary. This, I believe, accounts for the fact that we seem to find in Greek poetry, if we compare it with Latin poetry, so little exact visual observation. Greek poetry is mainly for the ear. Compare a landscape in one of the choruses of Sophocles or Aristophanes with a landscape of Virgil or Horace: the Greeks are *singing* about the landscape, the Romans are fixing it for the eye of the mind; and it is Virgil and Horace who lead the way to all the later picture poetry down to our own Imagists. Again, in the Elizabethan age, the English were extremely musical: the lyrics of Campion[45] could hardly have been composed apart from their musical settings; and Shakespeare is permeated with music. When Shakespeare wants to make us see something, he is always compelling and brilliant; but the effect has been liquefied by music so that it sometimes gives a little the impression of objects seen under water. The main stream of English poetry continues to keep fairly close to music through Milton, the musician's son, and even through the less organ-voiced Dryden. What has really happened with Pope is that the musical background is no longer there and that the ocular sense has grown sharp again. After this, the real music of verse is largely confined to lyrics—songs—and it becomes more and more of a trick to write them so that they seem authentic—that is, so that they sound like something sung. It was the aim of the late-nineteenth-century Symbolists, who derived their theory from Poe, to bring verse closer to music again, in opposition to the school of the Parnassians,[46] who cultivated an opaque objectivity. And the excellence of Miss Millay's lyrics is obviously connected with her musical training, as the metrical parts of Joyce—such as the Sirens episode in *Ulysses,* which attempts to render music, the response to a song of its hearer—are obviously associated with his vocal gifts. (There is of course a kind of poetry which produces plastic effects not merely by picture-making through explicit descriptions or images, but by giving the language itself—as Allen Tate is able to do—a plastic quality rather than a musical one.)

[45] Thomas Campion (1567–1620), English poet and musician, who set his own poems to music and who tried to adapt English verse to classical metres.
[46] The French poets Théophile Gautier (1811–1872) and Charles Baudelaire are among those included in three collections edited by a certain Lemerne and called *Le Parnasse Contemporain* (1866, 1871, 1876). Among later symbolists, Wilson seems to have in mind Paul Valéry, Paul Verlaine (1844–1896), and Stéphane Mallarmé (1842–1898).

We might perhaps see a revival of verse in a period and in a society in which music played a leading role. It has long played a great role in Russia; and in the Soviet Union at the present time you find people declaiming poetry at drinking parties or while traveling on boats and trains almost as readily as they burst into song to the accordion or the balalaika, and flocking to poetry-readings just as they do to concerts. It is possible that the Russians at the present time show more of an appetite for "poetry," if not always for the best grade of literature, than any of the Western peoples. Their language, half-chanted and strongly stressed, in many ways extremely primitive, provides by itself, as Italian does, a constant stimulus to the writing of verse.

Here in the United States, we have produced some of our truest poetry in the folk-songs that are inseparable from their tunes. One is surprised, in going through the collections of American popular songs (of Abbé Niles and W. C. Handy, of Carl Sandburg, of the various students trained by Professor Kittredge),[47] which have appeared during the last ten or fifteen years, to discover that the peopling of the continent has had as a by-product a body of folk-verse not unworthy of comparison with the similar material that went to make Percy's *Reliques*.[48] The air of the popular song will no doubt be carrying the words that go with it into the "poetry" anthologies of the future when many of the set-pieces of "poetry," which strain to catch a music gone with Shakespeare, will have come to seem words on the page, incapable of reverberation or of flight from between the covers.

Another pressure that has helped to discourage verse has undoubtedly been the increased demand for reading matter which has been stimulated by the invention of the printing press and which, because ordinary prose is easier to write than verse, has been largely supplied by prose. Modern journalism has brought forth new art-forms; and you have had not only the masterpieces of fiction of such novelists as Flaubert and Joyce, who are also consummate artists in the sense that the great classical poets were, but also the work of men like Balzac and Dickens which lacks the tight organization and the careful attention to detail of the classical epic or drama, and which has to be read rapidly in bulk. The novels of such writers are the epics of societies: they have neither the concision of the folk-song nor the elegance of the forms of the court; they sprawl and swarm over enormous areas like the city populations they deal with. Their authors, no longer schooled in the literary tradition of the Renaissance, speak the practical everyday language of the dominant middle class, which has destroyed the Renaissance world. Even a writer like Dostoevsky rises out of this weltering literature. You cannot say that his insight is less deep, that his vision is less noble or narrower, or that his mastery of his art is less complete than that of the great poets of the past. You can say only that what he achieves he achieves by somewhat different methods.

[47] John Jacob "Abbé" Niles (b. 1892) collected southern folk songs; W. C. Handy (1873–1958), orchestra leader and composer, author of such songs as "St. Louis Blues," "Memphis Blues," "Beale Street Blues"; Professor George Lyman Kittredge (1860–1941), best known as an editor of Shakespeare and scholar of folklore, trained students to collect popular rural and urban songs.
[48] Thomas Percy (1729–1811), Bishop of Dromore, who collected ballads, songs, and metrical romances in *Reliques of Ancient English Poetry* (1765).

The technique of prose today seems thus to be absorbing the technique of verse; but it is showing itself quite equal to that work of the imagination which caused men to call Homer "divine": that re-creation, in the harmony and logic of words, of the cruel confusion of life. Not, of course, that we shall have Dante and Shakespeare redone in some prose form any more than we shall have Homer in prose. In art, the same things are not done again or not done again except as copies. The point is that literary techniques are tools, which the masters of the craft have to alter in adapting them to fresh uses. To be too much attached to the traditional tools may be sometimes to ignore the new masters.

. . .

1948. The recent work of W. H. Auden has not shown a running-to-seed of the tendencies mentioned above, but has on the contrary taken the direction of returning to the older tradition of serviceable and vigorous English verse. His *New Year Letter* must be the best specimen of purely didactic verse since the end of the eighteenth century, and the alliterative Anglo-Saxon meter exploited in *The Age of Anxiety*[49] has nothing in common with prose. It may, however, be pointed out, for the sake of my argument above, that in the speech of the girl over the sleeping boy in the fifth section of the latter poem, the poet has found it easy to slip into the rhythms and accents of Mrs. Earwicker's half-prose soliloquy at the end of *Finnegans Wake*.

---

[49] These two works were published by Auden in 1941 and 1948, respectively.

Archibald MacLeish

ARS POETICA

It is a not uncommon assumption that a poem is necessarily a communication which the poet makes to the reader. And the assumption must be thought natural enough in view of the predominant practice of poetry for many centuries and of all that poets and critics have said about what poetry should communicate, and how. At the end of the eighteenth century changes in poetical practice and critical theory—on this development, see the Introduction to this volume, pp. 10–11—weakened the idea that the poet directed his utterance to a reader, and by the end of the nineteenth century many poets rejected the idea that a reader was being addressed at all: if it so chanced that he came upon the poem and found pleasure or significance in it, that was wholly his affair. The poet in making the poem did not have him in mind, only the perfecting of the poem; most certainly the poet was not using the poem as an intermediary between him and the reader; he had no intention of *telling* the reader anything about anything. This attitude was, of course, a way of asserting the autonomy of the poem, of making it discontinuous with discourse or conversation, and of protecting it from the consequences of the belief that it is susceptible to paraphrase or summary. A poem most fulfilled itself when it was a self-existent object, like an object in nature aesthetically considered. This view came to prevail among many English and American poets in the Twenties and Thirties of this century and was given memorable expression in Archibald MacLeish's poem prescribing how the poetic art should be practiced. The concluding distich of the poem is one of the most frequently quoted tags of modern criticism. Mr. MacLeish (1892–   ) was graduated from Yale in 1915, served in the First World War, took the degree of LL.B. at Harvard in 1919 and practiced law until 1923, when he went to live in Europe and devoted himself to poetry. His *Collected Poems 1917–1952* was published in 1952 and won the Pulitzer Prize. He has also written verse drama. He has held important posts in government, serving as Librarian of Congress (1939–1944) and Assistant Secretary of State (1944–1945), and he has been Boylston Professor at Harvard (1949–1962).

A POEM should be palpable and mute
As a globed fruit

From *Collected Poems of Archibald MacLeish*. Boston: Houghton Mifflin Company, 1963. By permission of Houghton Mifflin Company.

Dumb
As old medallions to the thumb

Silent as the sleeve-worn stone
Of casement ledges where the moss has grown—

A poem should be wordless
As the flight of birds

                    .   .   .

A poem should be motionless in time
As the moon climbs

Leaving, as the moon releases
Twig by twig the night-entangled trees,

Leaving, as the moon behind the winter leaves,
Memory by memory the mind—

A poem should be motionless in time
As the moon climbs

                    .   .   .

A poem should be equal to:
Not true

For all the history of grief
An empty doorway and a maple leaf

For love
The leaning grasses and two lights above the sea—

A poem should not mean
But be

Cleanth Brooks

LITERARY CRITICISM: POET, POEM, AND READER

Cleanth Brooks was born in Murray, Kentucky in 1906. He was graduated from Vanderbilt University in 1928, took the degree of M.A. from Tulane in 1928 and the B. Litt. degree from Oxford in 1932. He taught English at Louisiana State University from 1932 until 1947. Since then he has taught at Yale University, where in 1960 he became Gray Professor of Rhetoric.

From 1935 to 1942 Brooks edited with Robert Penn Warren the *Southern Review,* "a literary journal," which, says Louise Cowan (in *The Fugitive Group,* 1959), "has set the pattern for excellence in America." Certainly that journal, along with Brooks's writings, especially *Understanding Poetry* (1938; written with Robert Penn Warren) and *The Well-Wrought Urn* (1947), were important in disseminating the ideas about literature and the methods of investigating it that together make up what came to be called New Criticism. Brooks also collaborated with Warren in writing *Understanding Fiction* (1943) and *Modern Rhetoric* (1950); with Robert Heilman in writing *Understanding Drama* (1947); and with W. K. Wimsatt, Jr., in writing *Literary Criticism: A Short History* (1957). Among his other critical works are *Modern Poetry and the Tradition* (1939) and *William Faulkner: The Yoknapatawpha Country* (1963). The essay reprinted here was first published in 1962.

The critical activity of the last forty years has created a sufficient stir. It has developed new methods for teaching literature; it has generated a new critical vocabulary, and, as might have been predicted, it has aroused a vigorous reaction. Undoubtedly there has been faddishness connected with some of its critical ideas and, like other kinds of faddishness, what is mere fad will die and will eventually be replaced, one supposes, by a newer fad. I dare say that aspects of recent criticism have been overpraised; but it is plain that other aspects have been overblamed. In any case the recent trend in criticism has been only partially understood even by some of its converts. The fact of misunderstanding helps account for the mechanization of certain of its critical

From *Varieties of Literary Experience,* edited by Stanley Burnshaw. New York: New York University Press, 1962. By permission of the author.

"methods"—for example, heavy-handed and witless analyses of literary works, often pushed to absurd limits and sometimes becoming an extravagant "symbol-mongering."

These are general remarks. To become more specific: a typical misunderstanding interprets modern criticism as mere aestheticism. Our renewed interest in poetic form, in the eyes of some viewers, approaches dangerously near to a doctrine of art-for-art's sake in its apparent neglect of the great moral problems with which it is assumed that art ought to concern itself.

A few years ago, Professor Douglas Bush, in his presidential address to the Modern Language Association, put this case very forcibly. He scolded what he called the "new criticism" for its "preoccupation with technique, its aloof intellectuality, its fear of emotion and action, its avoidance of moral values, its dislike of 'impure' poetry (which includes," he went on to argue, "the greatest poetry we have)." He summed up the indictment of what he regards as "a timid aestheticism" by saying: "The common reader might go so far as to think that poetry deals with life, that for the serious poet life embraces morality and religion, and that it seems very strange for a serious critic to retreat into technical problems."

It may be amusing to reconsider, in the light of these strictures, the first great critical document of our Western tradition. Aristotle was certainly no timid aesthete. As a many-sided and healthy Greek of the great period, he took all knowledge to be his province. He was very much concerned with politics and morality as his *Nicomachean Ethics* and his treatise on politics testify. And what does he say about Greek tragedy? Does he praise Aeschylus for his profound insight into the human soul? Does he call attention to Sophocles' deep concern for moral problems? Well, hardly. Here is the sort of thing that Aristotle singles out for a comment in Sophocles' masterpiece, *Oedipus Rex:*

> A Peripety is the change of the kind described from one state of things within the play to its opposite . . . as it is for instance in *Oedipus*. . . . A Discovery is, as the very word implies, a change from ignorance to knowledge, and thus to either love or hate, in the personages marked for good or evil fortune. The finest form of Discovery is one attended by Peripeties, like that which goes with the Discovery in *Oedipus*.

Aristotle made plot the soul of the drama, and since plot is concerned with action, his discussion of plot might seem to promise a consideration of moral problems. But when we turn to the text of the *Poetics*, we find that Aristotle is again back to technicalities, writing: "We assume that, for the finest form of Tragedy, the Plot must be not simple but complex. . . ." If the author were other than Aristotle, the moralistic critic might be tempted to argue that the sentence was written for the delectation of a coterie of aesthetes and that the critic had forgotten that the great Greek tragedies were presented before flesh-and-blood auditors, interested in and oppressed by, grave moral problems and the issues of life and death.

The *Poetics*, in sum, does not discuss the lives of the dramatists, nor their deep human experiences, nor the way in which their plays reveal their personalities. Even when Aristotle addresses himself directly to the moral issues encountered in a work of art, he scarcely writes in a fashion to satisfy the determined moralist. When he faces the specific question of whether something said in a poem is "morally right or not," the critic hot for certainties might find him evasive, for Aristotle counsels us to consider "not only the intrinsic quality of the actual word or deed, but also the person who says or does it, the time, the means, and the motive of the agent." Instead of making a strict interpretation of a given code, Aristotle seems to appeal to something like a principle of dramatic propriety. In asking us to judge a statement or action in terms of the total dramatic context he sounds suspiciously like the so-called (and badly named) "new critics."

Now my purpose in dragging Aristotle into this discussion is not to claim that the *Poetics* is the be-all and end-all of criticism. It is not even to claim that recent criticism is markedly Aristotelian. My point is a more modest one: I invoke Aristotle's example simply to suggest that a man who has a proper interest in politics, history, and morals may still find it useful to concern himself with the structure of literary works and with defining the nature and limits of aesthetic judgment.

In view of such considerations, it is possible to restate the history of criticism in our time thus: We have been witnessing a strenuous attempt to focus attention upon the poem rather than upon the poet or upon the reader. Along with this stress upon the poem as a structure in its own right, has come the attempt to fix the boundaries and limits of poetry. Modern critics have tried to see what was meant when one considered the poem as an artistic document.

I. A. Richards, some thirty years ago, argued that for the sake of the health of literature, we needed a spell of purer poetry and of purer criticism.[1] The attempt at a purer criticism has been made. But in my more pessimistic moments, I wonder whether there has been much real clarification of the critical problem. The popular critics—in *Time* magazine, for example, or in the great metropolitan newspapers—continue to print their literary chitchat, their gossip, and their human interest notes on the author of the latest best-seller. And often out of the other side of their mouths, they go on to talk about the novelist's politics, his moral asseverations, and his affirmation or lack of affirmation of "life." To such people, the discussion of literary *form* is bound to seem empty. Ingrained habits of thinking make it hard for them to conceive of form as anything other than an empty container. On the other hand, when a critic like Allen Tate makes the point that form is *meaning,* he deliberately rejects any notion of form as a mere envelope for some valuable ethical or psychological content. Indeed, he rejects the whole implied dualism of a form-content poetics. To understand modern criticism, it is necessary to grasp this point. Some typical misunderstandings of this point may be avoided by remembering the example of Aristotle. A universal thinker, not a mere aesthete, a man who believed that art "imitated" reality and that art could exert ethical and political pressure, could nevertheless find it profitable to deal with literature in formal terms on the assumption that it possessed a structure of a characteristic kind.

Poetry has a characteristic structure and yields a characteristic knowledge. It does not compete with, but exists alongside of, and complements scientific

---

[1] In *Principles of Literary Criticism* (1924). See pp. 341 ff. of this volume.

knowledge and historical knowledge. Since poetic knowledge is made available through poetic form, the attempt to assimilate poetic knowledge too directly and abruptly to other kinds of knowledge has its risks. We lose the value of poetic knowledge in losing the perspective that poetic form gives. It is surely quite proper to deal with Milton's *Paradise Lost,* for instance, as a reflection of a Puritan ethic. But we may learn more about its ethical content if we respect its own characteristic mode of statement as a poem and do not, in our anxiety to extract the ethical content, violate that mode.

My argument is not an esoteric one: it involves no mystical view of poetry. Rather it rests upon the evident fact that poetry does make use of certain characteristic devices and that if we ignore these devices we shall have badly misread the special kind of document that is the poem.

One of the simplest but surely the most essential of these devices is metaphor. (Robert Frost has made the point that poetry *is* fundamentally metaphor.)[2] But the function of metaphor is often misconceived. Many readers still take its function to be that of mere illustration or decoration, with term A being "compared" to term B, or term B to term A. This misconception of metaphor as a kind of rhetorical glossing of the "facts" is one aspect of the form-content dualism which sees the poetic form as simply a superficial gilding of the content—not as something by which it is transformed. If, under the impression that we are somehow being "scientific" and thus more directly grasping reality, we do write off metaphor as mere decoration, we shall certainly lose what poetry has to give us. After all, we must not forget how much of our discovery of the truth—scientific as well as poetic—is gained through metaphor.

I confess that I once thought that the imagery in the second stanza of Wordsworth's "Solitary Reaper" was meant to be merely decorative, vaguely ennobling. Hence it is small wonder that I found the poem rather flat and dull. It was only when I stumbled upon the fact that the thinking of the poem was really being done through these images—that the poet had implicated a whole manifold of relations in associating the natural spontaneous songs of the nightingale and the cuckoo with the natural and spontaneous singing of the girl—it was only then that the poem came to be deeply meaningful to me. The Highland girl was not simply being complimented for the beauty of her song. Hers was presumably not a great voice; it was evidently an untrained voice—as "natural" as that of a bird. In effect, her song was wordless, for the girl was singing in an unknown tongue, Gaelic, as the nightingale sang in another unknown tongue, "nightingale." Like the birds, the girl was conscious of no audience and was singing for none, the song simply welling up out of the daily round of her activities, as the birds' welled up out of theirs. And like the birds, the girl sang "As if her song could have no ending." A work of art, Aristotle has told us, has a beginning, a middle, and an end; and the concert singer had better sing *her* song with a concern for its beginning, its middle, and its end. But the songs of the birds (and of the girl) are not the music of art, but of nature—they properly have no ending. In sum, through the two bird images— and only through these images—the hearer indicates the special significance of

[2] Robert Frost (1874–1963) made this point in talks and in "The Figure a Poem Makes," introduction to *Collected Poems* (1939).

the solitary reaper's song. It is as if the traveler had been allowed, through the utterly unself-conscious song of the solitary girl bending to her task, to overhear the "still, sad music of humanity" rising from hidden depths, plaintive, sweet, artless. Thus, the bird comparisons cannot be dismissed as mere decoration: what the poem "says" is said primarily through the imagery.

To recur to a point made earlier: the attempt to assimilate poetic knowledge too directly to other kinds of knowledge is dangerous. If we ignore the poetic form, we may hopelessly distort the meaning. One can illustrate the danger from another lyric by Wordsworth, one of the celebrated Lucy poems.

> She dwelt among the untrodden ways
>   Beside the springs of Dove,
> A Maid whom there were none to praise
>   And very few to love:
>
> A violet by a mossy stone
>   Half hidden from the eye!
> —Fair as a star, when only one
>   Is shining in the sky.
>
> She lived unknown, and few could know
>   When Lucy ceased to be:
> But she is in her grave, and, oh,
>   The difference to me!

A few years ago a critic and literary scholar insisted upon using the poem to make a sociological point. Knowing that the young Wordsworth sympathized with the common man and had been strongly affected by the French Revolution, our scholar was bent on showing how much this simple love poem actually reflected a transitional age and foreshadowed the modern age to come. Indeed, he found in the poem a number of remarkable reflections of the changing nineteenth-century social scheme. For one thing, the speaker was revealed to be conscious of his moral isolation in his choice of a love object—someone who "dwelt among the untrodden ways." Moreover, Lucy herself turned out to be a young woman of neurotic personality—and the speaker "modern" in choosing a neurotic. You may wonder how our scholar detected Lucy's neurosis. The answer is simple. He interpreted the lines "A Maid whom there were none to praise/And very few to love" with painful literalness. One had always assumed that the lines meant that in her remote, rural situation, none of the few simple people who knew the maiden and loved her was capable of singing her praises; that is, Lucy lacked the poet that her loveliness deserved. One had also supposed that the second stanza praised Lucy's modesty ("A violet by a mossy stone") and her sweet serenity ("Fair as a star, when only one/Is shining in the sky"). But our critic was convinced that her shyness concealed what he called "an unpleasant rejection of other people." Few loved her, and of those that did, none could honestly say a good word for her! Granted that the example just cited is an extreme case, there are plenty of misreadings conducted under the same auspices which are only somewhat less absurd.

I once knew a sociologist who delivered his judgment to the effect that

Shakespeare's Cleopatra was simply a maladjusted girl. I dare say that in some sense she was. But his remark makes sufficiently plain the fact that he had missed the meaning of the play. One can, to be sure, treat *Antony and Cleopatra* sociologically, psychologically, historically, morally, etc., but the play is, after all, a work of art, and if we consider it to be a work of art we shall find ourselves talking about it necessarily in terms appropriate to aesthetic structure —whether terms like Aristotle's *peripeteia* and *anagnōrisis,*[3] or those of recent criticism like *tension* and *ironic reversal,* or in still other terms. To treat the play in terms of aesthetic structure does *not* mean that we are denying ethical problems. There can certainly be no objection to making use of terms that have to do with human interests, human motives, and human emotions. Indeed, how can we avoid such references if we are to talk about the play in terms of its pattern of tensions, complications, and resolutions? For these are the things that are patterned, balanced, and resolved. But whatever the terminology we use, we will do well to keep the ethical problems at one remove, seeing them, that is, in the perspective which aesthetic structure affords and which the fictional nature of the play actually enjoins. Otherwise we shall find that our study of this play with its "maladjusted girl" and its adultery and double suicide threatens to turn into a clinical study or a police court inquest.

One could illustrate nearly everything about poetic structure and its relation to politics and morality from this complex and brilliant play. But present purposes call for an example that is smaller and more readily manageable. For that, one might go back to "The Solitary Reaper," which in spite of its apparent simplicity can tell us a great deal about poetic form. But it may be better to illustrate from a longer and more complicated poem, "The Grassehopper," by Richard Lovelace, one of the Cavalier poets of the seventeenth century.

THE GRASSE-HOPPER

To my Noble Friend, Mr. Charles Cotton

ODE

I.

Oh thou that swing'st upon the waving haire
    Of some well-filled Oaten Beard,
Drunke ev'ry night with a Delicious teare
    Dropt thee from Heav'n, where now th'art reard.

II.

The Joyes of Earth and Ayre are thine intire,
    That with thy feet and wings dost hop and flye;
And when thy Poppy workes thou dost retire
    To thy Carv'd Acron-bed to lye.

III.

Up with the Day, the Sun thou welcomst then,
    Sportst in the guilt-plats of his Beames,

---

[3] Terms usually translated "reversal" and "recognition."

And all these merry dayes mak'st merry men,
   Thy selfe, and Melancholy streames.

IV.

But ah the Sickle! Golden Eares are Cropt;
   Ceres and *Bacchus* bid good night;
Sharpe frosty fingers all your Flowr's have topt,
   And what sithes spar'd, Winds shave off quite.

V.

Poore verdant foole! and now green Ice! thy Joys
   Large and as lasting, as thy Peirch of Grasse,
Bid us lay in 'gainst Winter Raine, and poize
   Their flouds, with an o'reflowing glasse.

VI.

Thou best of *Men* and *Friends!* we will create
   A Genuine Summer in each others breast;
And spite of this cold Time and frosen Fate
   Thaw us a warme seate to our rest.

VII.

Our sacred harthes shall burne eternally
   As Vestal Flames, the North-wind, he
Shall strike his frost-stretch'd Winges, dissolve and flye
   This *Ætna* in Epitome.

VIII.

Dropping *December* shall come weeping in,
   Bewayle th'usurping of his Raigne;
But when in show'rs of old Greeke we beginne,
   Shall crie, he hath his Crowne againe!

IX.

Night as cleare *Hesper* shall our Tapers whip
   From the light Casements where we play,
And the darke Hagge from her black mantle strip,
   And sticke there everlasting Day.

X.

Thus richer then untempted Kings are we,
   That asking nothing, nothing need:
Though Lord of all what Seas imbrace; yet he
   That wants himselfe, is poore indeed.

          —*The Poems of Richard Lovelace,*
        ed. C. H. Wilkinson (Oxford, 1925)

The poem is addressed by the poet "To my noble friend, Mr. Charles Cotton." It would be interesting to know more than we do about Lovelace's noble friend. The scholars do not agree as to his identity. C. H. Wilkinson thinks it was Charles Cotton, the son; C. H. Hartmann, Charles Cotton, the father.[4] But even if we do not know the identity of the noble friend we still can enjoy the poem and understand it.

There are, I grant, poems which do depend for their basic meaning upon some knowledge of the historical characters mentioned in them. Marvell's "Horatian Ode upon Cromwell's Return from Ireland" would be hopelessly obscure to a reader who knew absolutely nothing about Oliver Cromwell.[5] Yet we can and must make a distinction between a poem as a personal document and as a poetic structure. For example, it is conceivable, though highly improbable, that some day a scholar may come upon a set of seventeenth-century letters which would tell us that Mr. Charles Cotton had performed several great services for our poet, and that this little poem had been written by Lovelace in grave apprehension as he received news that his friend had been stricken with a serious illness. While we are using our imagination, let us suppose further that the letters showed that this poem was written in the hope of cheering his friend by suggesting that they had many more years of fine companionship before them. Such letters might very well enhance for us the meaning of the poem as a personal document of Lovelace's life. But if we may thus enhance a poem at will by importing into it all sorts of associations and meaning, then we can theoretically turn an obscure poem into a clear poem—and a poor poem into a good poem. Even the verse from the newspaper agony column beginning "It is now a year and a day/Since little Willie went away" might move us deeply if we actually knew little Willie and his sorrowing mother. But only the unwary would take the triggering of such an emotional response as proof of the goodness of the poem. In the hypothetical case just cited, the response comes not from the poem as poem but as personal document. What references and allusions are legitimate parts of a poem and what are merely adventitious associations? The distinction is not always obvious, and I do not care to try to fix here a doctrinaire limitation. But I think that we shall have to agree that some limits must exist.

The first part of Lovelace's poem derives from the Anacreontic poem "The Grasshopper." (I use Abraham Cowley's translation.)[6]

> Happy *Insect* what can be
> In happiness compar'd to thee?
> Fed with nourishment divine,

---

[4] C. H. Wilkinson is the editor of the standard edition of Lovelace's works. C. H. Hartmann is author of *The Cavalier Spirit and its Influence on the Life and Work of Richard Lovelace* (1925).

[5] Chief ruler of England and Lord Protector under the Commonwealth and the Protectorate from the beheading of Charles I in 1649 until Cromwell's death in 1658. The "Horatian Ode" by Andrew Marvell (1621–1678) celebrates Cromwell's return in May 1650 from subjugating Ireland and looks forward to his campaign against the Scots.

[6] For Cowley, see pp. 122 ff. of this volume. An Anacreontic is a poem written in the manner of Anacreon, Greek poet of the sixth century B.C.

The dewy *Mornings* gentle *Wine!*
Nature waits upon thee still,
And thy verdant Cup does fill;
'Tis fill'd where ever thou does tread,
Natures selfe's thy Ganimed.
Thou does drink, and dance, and sing;
Happier than the happiest King! . . .

Lovelace evidently began his poem as a free translation of the Greek poem; but he went on to develop out of it a thoroughly different poem—different in theme and different in tone. The little Anacreontic poem becomes merely a starting point of the poem that Lovelace actually writes. Whereas the Greek poet contents himself with giving a charming account of the insect's life, Lovelace uses the account of the grasshopper's life to set up the contrast between the spurious summer of nature and the genuine summer to which men have access. If we are interested in the way in which the poem was composed, we shall certainly want to know what sources Lovelace used, and there may be a special delight in seeing how he has reshaped his sources to his own purpose. But a mere round-up of the sources will never in itself tell us what the poet has done with them. A bad poem may assimilate Anacreon as well as a good poem. The value of a poem as a work of art is not to be determined by an account of its sources.

In the same way, the history of ideas might tell us a great deal about this poem. The historian can trace the development of such concepts as that of the actual considered to be a dim and limited reflection of the ideal—specifically, the summer of the grasshopper in the natural world of the seasons viewed as a mere shadow of the genuine summer which transcends the seasonal world of nature. The historians of ideas can trace for us the development of the concept of richness based not upon the possession of goods but upon one's freedom from wants—that is, the notion of richness as completeness. The ideas that Lovelace is using here are familiar to most readers and can be taken for granted; but I concede that the reader who is not familiar with these concepts might have serious trouble with the poem. Even so, criticism has to be distinguished from the scholarship of the history of ideas, for the obvious reason that the historian of ideas may find just as much to explain in a poor and unsuccessful poem as in a good poem.

It is the critic of moralistic bias, as we have already noted, who is most likely to object sharply to modern critical procedure. The serious moralist finds it hard not to become impatient with a critic who seems to ignore the moral problems, and to concern himself merely with "form" and technique. Nor will he necessarily be satisfied with the critic's concession that wisdom is certainly to be found in poetry. Lovelace's poem, for example, says, among other things, that happiness is not dependent upon external circumstances but is an inward quality. But the moralist argues that this is surely the doctrine that ought to be emphasized in any critical account of the poem. For it may appear to him that it is this moral truth that gives the poem its value.

But the sternest moralist will have to concede that many poems that contain admirable doctrine—Longfellow's "Psalm of Life," for example—are very poor poems. Furthermore, if one tries to save the case by stipulating that the doctrine must not only be true, but must be rendered clearly, acceptably, and persuasively, he will have come perilously close to reducing the poet's art to that of the mere rhetorician.

Moralists as diverse as Marxists and the later Van Wyck Brooks[7] are all for making the Muse a rewrite girl. But the Muse is willful and stubborn: a thesis presented eloquently and persuasively is not necessarily the same thing as a poem. "The Grasshopper" is, among other things, a document in the personal history of Lovelace, testifying to his relation with Charles Cotton. It is an instance of Lovelace's regard for the classics; it incorporates an amalgam of ideas inherited from the Christian-classical tradition of Western thought; it is an admonition to find happiness within oneself. The point is that it could be all of these things and yet be a very poor poem. It could be all of these things and not be a poem at all. It could be, for example, a letter from Lovelace to Charles Cotton, or an entry in Lovelace's commonplace book.

It happens to be a poem and a rather fine one. But defense of this judgment, if it were questioned, would involve an examination of the structure of the poem as poem. And with this kind of examination the so-called "new criticism" is concerned. I should be happy to drop the adjective "new" and simply say: with this kind of judgment, literary criticism is concerned.

Lovelace's poem is a little masterpiece in the management of tone. Lovelace makes the life of the insect thoroughly Lucullan.[8] The grasshopper is "drunk ev'ry night": Lovelace provides him with a carved bed in which to sleep off his debauch. But actually the grasshopper is up with the dawn, for his tipple is a natural distillation, the free gift of heaven. The joys to which he abandons himself are all innocent and natural, and his merrymaking makes men merry too.

The grasshopper's life, then, though described in terms that hint at the human world, is not used to symbolize a type of human experience to be avoided. We have here no fable of the ant and the grasshopper. Lovelace would not reform the little wastrel, but delights in him, so joyously and thoughtlessly at home in his world.

Stanzas V and VI define very delicately and precisely this attitude, one of humor and amusement, touched with the merest trace of pity. The grasshopper is happy because he cannot possibly foresee the harvest or the biting blasts of winter. "But ah the Sickle! Golden Eares are Cropt." Everything in the line conspires to place the emphasis upon the word *golden,* a word rich in every sort of association: wealth, ripeness, luxury, the Saturnian age of gold. But the full force of *golden* is perhaps not realized until we come to line 13: "Poore verdant foole! and now green Ice!" The clash of gold and green absorbs and carries within it the whole plight of the grasshopper. Green suggests not only the little insect's color but all that is growing, immature, unripe, and innocently simple. The oaten ears on which the grasshopper loves to swing change, by natural process, from green to gold; the grasshopper cannot change with them. The

[7] American critic and biographer (1886–1963), known especially for his studies of American literature and American writers.

[8] Like L. Licinius Lucullus (c. 110–56 B.C.), wealthy Roman consul and general famous for his banquets.

mature oaten ears may resemble the precious metal—one remembers Milton's "vegetable gold"—but greenness turned to something hard and stiff and cold— the sliver of green ice—is a pathetic absurdity.

I should not press the contrast so hard, had Lovelace not insisted on the color, and emphasized its connection with springing verdure by his phrase "Poore verdant foole!" And here it becomes proper to acknowledge the critic's debt to the lexicographer and to concede that my suggestion that *verdant* here means *gullible* has no specific dictionary warrant. The Oxford Dictionary's first entry for this sense of *verdant* is as late as 1824; the same dictionary, however, does indicate that *green* could carry these connotations as early as 1548. In the context of this poem, *verdant,* followed by the phrase "green ice," and associated as it is with "fool," must surely carry the meaning of inexperienced, thoughtless innocence.

The gentle and amused irony that suffuses "Poore verdant foole" continues through the lines that follow: the grasshopper's joys are measured by the instability of the insect's precarious perch—"Large and as lasting, as thy Peirch of Grasse." But the speaker soon turns from his contemplation of these ephemeral joys to man's perdurable joys—from the specious summer of nature to the genuine summer which he and his noble friend can create, each in the other's breast.

The poem pivots sharply in the fifth stanza, and the management of tone is so dextrous that we may be tempted to pass over the last half of the poem too easily. But these latter stanzas have their difficulties and if we want to understand the poem I think we shall want to find precisely what goes on. Moreover, these stanzas present their problem of tone also. The poem must not seem smug and sanctimonious; man's happiness must not seem too easily achieved. For if man rises superior to the animal kingdom, he is not, for all of that, a disembodied spirit. He is animal too, and he has to reckon with the "frost-stretch'd winges" of the North Wind and with the blackness of the winter night. Moreover, as man, he has his peculiar bugbears of a sort that the grasshopper does not have to contend with. There is at least a hint of this in the reference to "untempted kings."

As a general comment, suffice it to say that in this poem the flesh is given its due: the warm hearth, the lighted casements, and showers of old Greek wine fortify the friends against the winter night and give a sense of real gaiety and mirth. If there is high thinking, the living is not so plain as to be unconvincing. And the sentiment on which the poem closes is none the less serious because it comes out of festivity and has been warmed by wine. He who "wants himselfe"—who owns things but has not mastered himself—is poor indeed. It is this full possession of himself, this lack of dependence upon things, which makes him richer than "untempted Kings."

The last phrase, however, is curious. In this context, Lovelace ought to be writing to his friend: "since we are untempted by material possessions, we are actually richer than kings." The force of the contrast depends upon the fact that kings are more than most men tempted by material possessions. Why then *untempted* kings? The solution is probably to be sought in the source of the poem. In the Anacreontic "Grasshopper" the insect is referred to as a king—the

Greek text has Βασιλεύς[9]—and Abraham Cowley, Lovelace's contemporary, uses the word *king* in his translation. Lovelace, then, for his fit audience who knew the Greek poem, is saying: we are like the grasshopper, that rare specimen, an untempted king; but we are richer than he, since our joys do not end with the natural summer, but last on through the genuine (and unending) summer of the heart.

But it is Stanzas VIII and IX that cause the real trouble. As C. H. Hartmann remarks: "Lovelace himself could on occasion become so involved as to be utterly incomprehensible even without the assistance of an eccentric printer." To deal first with Stanza IX: the drift of the argument is plain enough, but Lovelace's editor, Wilkinson, also confesses to difficulties here: the friends will whip night away from their casements. But what are we to make of the phrase "as clear Hesper"? Wilkinson writes "The meaning would seem to be that "just as Hesperus shines clearer as the day draws to a close, so will our tapers whip night from the lighted casements of the room where we amuse ourselves. . . .' " But I fail to see the relevance of his argument that Hesper shines the brighter as the skies darken. Why not simply read "as clear Hesper" as an ellipsis for "as clear Hesper does"? Our tapers will whip away night as clear Hesper whips it away. Moreover, the poet chooses as the dispeller of gloom the modest light of the star just because it is modest. He is not claiming that he and his friend can abolish winter. "Dropping *December*" *shall* come weeping in. The friendly association with Cotton will not do away with the wintry night. What the human being can do is to rid the night of its horror—exorcise the hag—maintain a small circle of light amid the enveloping darkness. This is precisely what the evening star, clear Hesper, does, and all that he and his friend with their gleaming tapers propose to do. As with light, so with heat. Their hearth will be an Aetna, but an Aetna as epitome—a tiny volcano of heat. The poet is very careful not to claim too much.

Stanza VIII contains the most difficult passage in the poem, and Lovelace's editors have not supplied a note. "Dropping *December*" means *dripping*, or *rainy* December. But why will December lament the usurping of his reign? Does the warm fire and pleasant company maintained by the two friends constitute the usurpation against which he will protest? We may at first be inclined to think so, but the lines that follow make it plain that December is not crying out against, but rejoicing in, the two friends' festivities. Seeing them at their wine, December exclaims that he has "his Crowne againe." But what is December's crown? One looks for it throughout Greek and Roman mythology in vain.

We have here, I am convinced, a topical allusion. The crown of December is evidently the Christmas festivities, festivities actually more ancient than Christianity—the age-old feast of the winter solstice of which the Roman Saturnalia is an instance. December's crown is indeed a venerable one. And who has stolen December's crown—who has usurped his reign? The Puritans, by abolishing the celebration of Christmas. We remember that it is a Cavalier poet writing, and I suspect, if we care to venture at dating the poem, we shall

[9] "Basileus," king.

have to put it at some time between the Puritan abolition of Christmas in 1642 and the publication of Lovelace's volume, *Lucasta,* in 1649. Line 23, then, "And spite of this cold Time and frosen Fate," is seen to refer to more than the mere winter season. It must allude to the Puritan domination—for Lovelace, a cold time and frozen fate indeed. I would not press the historical allusion. The poem is certainly not primarily an anti-Puritan poem. The basic contrast is made between animal life and the higher and more enduring joys to which man can attain. But a casual allusion to the troubled state of England would be a thoroughly natural one for the poet of "To Althea from Prison" to have written, and nowhere more appropriately than here, in a poem to a close friend.

The reader may not be convinced by this interpretation of the eighth stanza. Very frankly, my basic concern has been to read the poem, not to seek out historical allusions. But an honest concern with the text characterizes, or ought to characterize, the work of both scholar and critic. In view of the much advertised quarrel between scholarship and criticism, the point is worth stressing. The critic selects from scholarship those things which will help him understand the poem *qua* poem; in some matters the contribution of the scholar may be indispensable. Literary criticism and literary scholarship are therefore natural allies in their concern to understand the poem; they may at points coalesce. But if, because of unavoidable specialization, the scholar and critic cannot always be one and the same man, I think it a pity if, with short-sighted jealousy, they elbow each other as rivals and combatants.

Earlier in this paper, I said that recent criticism had attempted to focus attention on the poem rather than upon the poet or upon the reader. But there is no danger that people will cease to talk about the poet and his reader. Our basic human interest is most readily served when we talk about the reader's reactions—our own responses to the poem or the novel—the chill down our spine or perhaps it is the special sensation in the pit of the stomach that A. E. Housman claimed to experience when he encountered a genuine poem.[10] Human interest may be almost as readily served if we talk about the personality of the author. Such talk may include everything from Lord Byron's amours to the possible effects of Keats's tuberculosis upon his personality—everything from Shakespeare's alleged Oedipus complex to Robert Frost's love for New Hampshire.

No one wants to forbid either the study of the author or the study of the reader. Both kinds of study are legitimate and have their own interest. In view of the present state of criticism, it may be somewhat more to the point to say a final word in justification of recent stress upon the poem as such.

A study of the reader's reactions may be most interesting and illuminating. But concentration on the reader's reactions tends to take us away from the work of art into the domain of reader-psychology. We ask why Keats's "Ode on a Grecian Urn" provokes the different responses that it does, and we find the answer in the differing psychological make-up of the various readers. Or we may ask why certain aspects of Shakespeare were praised in the eighteenth century and others in the nineteenth, and typically find our answer in the

---

[10] A. E. Housman (1859–1936) made this claim in *The Name and Nature of Poetry* (1933). And see p. 380 of this volume.

differing cultural climates of the two centuries. But even though a poem can be realized only through some reader's response to it, the proper study of the poem is the study of the poem.

A study of the poet's personality and intellectual background will almost certainly be rewarding. After all, the poem is an expression of the mind and sensibility of the man who wrote it, and may well reflect his cultural background and the time spirit of his age. Yet concentration upon these matters can also take us away from the poem—into author psychology or the history of ideas or cultural history. In any case, it is valuable to ponder the fact that we often know very little about the author's experience beyond what he has been able to catch and make permanent within the poem. We know, for example, very little about Richard Lovelace. About the greatest of our poets, Shakespeare, we know even less—if we exclude what we may surmise from the works themselves. Even where we know a great deal about the author's personality and ideas, *we rarely know as much as the poem itself can tell us about itself*; for the poem is no mere effusion of a personality. It is a construct—an articulation of ideas and emotions—a dramatization. It is not a slice of raw experience but a product of the poet's imagination—not merely something suffered by him but the result of his creative activity. As a work of art, it calls for a reciprocal imaginative activity on our part; and that involves seeing it for what it *is*.

Harry Levin

LITERATURE AS AN INSTITUTION

When, in 1960, Harvard University established a professorial chair named in honor of one of its celebrated teachers, Irving Babbitt (1865–1933), it was generally felt to be appropriate that Harry Levin should be its first incumbent. In point of intellectual temperament and critical doctrine there is no similarity between the two men, for Babbitt was polemical in the extreme and saw as the corruption of a great tradition those tendencies of modern culture to which Mr. Levin has been hospitable. But on the occasion of his inaugural lecture as Irving Babbitt Professor of Comparative Literature Mr. Levin said of Babbitt, "Scholarship was the precondition of criticism for him, as criticism was the consummation of scholarship," and this can as truly be said of Mr. Levin as of his former teacher. Born in Minneapolis in 1912, Mr. Levin was graduated from Harvard in 1933. He came to prominence as a critic in 1941 with *James Joyce: A Critical Introduction,* still one of the best helps to the reading of a still difficult author. His other works include *The Overreacher: A Study of Christopher Marlowe* (1952), *Symbolism and Fiction* (1956), *The Question of Hamlet* (1959), *The Power of Blackness: Hawthorne, Poe, Melville* (1958), *The Gates of Horn: Five French Realists* (1963), *Refractions: Essays in Comparative Literature* (1966), and *The Myth of the Golden Age in the Renaissance* (1969). "Literature as an Institution" was first published in *Accent,* Spring, 1946; in a somewhat revised version it constitutes the second and third sections of the first chapter of *The Gates of Horn.*

1. THE CONTRIBUTION OF TAINE

"Literature is the expression of society, as speech is the expression of man." In this aphorism the Vicomte de Bonald* summed up one of the bitter lessons that the French Revolution had taught the world. With the opening years of the nineteenth century, and the return of the Emigration, coincided a two-volume study by Madame de Staël: *De la Littérature considérée dans ses rap-*

* *Législation primitive* (1817), II, 228. [Levin's note.]

From *Accent,* Vol. VI (Spring 1946). Reprinted by permission of the author and Oxford University Press.

ports avec les institutions sociales.[1] This was not the first time, of course, that some relationship had been glimpsed. Renaissance humanism, fighting out the invidious quarrel between ancient and modern literatures, had concluded that each was the unique creation of its period, and had adumbrated a historical point of view. Romantic nationalism, seeking to undermine the prestige of the neo-classic school and to revive the native traditions of various countries, was now elaborating a series of geographical comparisons. It was left for Hippolyte Taine—in the vanguard of a third intellectual movement, scientific positivism—to formulate a sociological approach. To the historical and geographical factors, the occasional efforts of earlier critics to discuss literature in terms of "moment"[*] and "race," he added a third conception, which completed and finally eclipsed them. "Milieu,"[†] as he conceived it, is the link between literary criticism and the social sciences. Thus Taine raised a host of new problems by settling an old one.

When Taine's history of English literature appeared, it smelled—to a contemporary reader, Amiel[2]—like the exhalations from a laboratory. To that sensitive Swiss idealist, it conveyed a whiff of "the literature of the future in the American style," of "the death of poetry flayed and anatomized by science." This "intrusion of technology into literature," as Amiel was shrewd enough to observe, is a responsibility which Taine shares with Balzac and Stendhal. As Taine self-consciously remarked, "From the novel to criticism and from criticism to the novel, the distance at present is not very great." Taine's critical theory is grounded upon the practice of the realists, while their novels are nothing if not critical. His recognition of the social forces behind literature coincides with their resolution to embody those forces in their works. The first to acknowledge Stendhal as a master, he welcomed Flaubert as a colleague and lived to find Zola[3] among his disciples. "When M. Taine studies Balzac," Zola acknowledged, "he does exactly what Balzac himself does when he studies Père Grandet."[4] There is no better way to bridge the distance between criticism and the novel, or to scrutinize the presuppositions of modern literature, than by a brief reconsideration of Taine's critical method.

A tougher-minded reader than Amiel, Flaubert, noted in 1864[‡] that—whatever the *Histoire de la littérature anglaise* left unsettled—it got rid of the uncritical notion that books dropped like meteorites from the sky. The social basis of art might thereafter be overlooked, but it could hardly be disputed.

[1] Anne-Louise-Germaine Necker, Mme. de Staël (1766–1817), French-Swiss novelist, woman of letters. The book cited is on the relations of literature to social institutions.

[*] See W. H. Ree, "The Meaning of Taine's Moment," *Romanic Review* (1939), xxx, 273 ff. [Levin's note.]

[†] See Leo Spitzer, "Milieu and Ambience," *Essays in Historical Semantics* (New York, 1948), pp. 179 ff. [Levin's note.]

[2] Henri-Frédéric Amiel (1821–1881). The remark is in his diary, *Fragments d'un journal intime.*

[3] Émile Zola (1840–1902), French novelist, whose work is the chief monument of the French Naturalist movement.

[4] Père Grandet is a character in Zola's fiction.

[‡] *Correspondance* (1929), V, 160. [Levin's note.]

Any lingering belief in poetic inspiration could hardly withstand the higher criticism that had disposed of spontaneous generation and was disposing of divine revelation. When Renan,[5] proclaiming his disbelief in mysteries, depicted Jesus as the son of man and analyzed the origins of Christianity, then Taine could depict genius as the outgrowth of environment and analyze the origins of literature. On the whole, though critics have deplored the crudity of his analyses and scholars have challenged the accuracy of his facts, his working hypothesis has won acceptance. He has become the stock example of a rigorous determinist—especially for those who think determinism is a modern version of fatalism. Taine's determinism, however, is simply an intensive application of the intellectual curiosity of his age. It is no philosopher's attempt to encroach upon the freedom of the artist's will; it is simply a historian's consciousness of what the past has already determined.

As for Taine's rigor, a more thoroughgoing historical materialist, George Plekhanov,* has gone so far as to accuse him of arrant idealism. A recent artist-philosopher, Jean-Paul Sartre,† describes Taine's empiricism as an unsuccessful effort to set up a realistic system of metaphysics. Actually his position is that of most realists, so outrageous to their early readers and so tame to later critics. His method explained too much to satisfy his contemporaries; it has not explained enough to satisfy ours. Confronted with the provocative statement, "Vice and virtue are products like vitriol and sugar,"‡ we are not shocked by the audacity that reduces moral issues to chemical formulae; we are amused at the naïveté that undertakes to solve them both by a single equation. Taine's introduction to his history of English literature, which abounds in dogmas of this sort, is rather a manifesto than a methodology. If, reading on, we expect the history to practice what the introduction preaches, we are amiably disappointed. Each successive author is more freely individualized. How does Taine's all-determining scheme meet its severest test? With Shakespeare,§ he explains, after canvassing the material factors, "all comes from within—I mean from his soul and his genius; circumstances and externals have contributed but little to his development."

The loophole that enables Taine to avoid the strict consequences of his three determinants is a fourth—a loose system of psychology. Psychology takes over where sociology has given up, and the sociologist has shown surprisingly little interest in classes or institutions. He has viewed history as a parade of influential individuals, themselves the creatures of historical influences. To understand their achievements is "a problem in psychological mechanics."|| The psychologist must disclose their ruling passions; he must hit upon that magnificent obsession, that "master faculty" which conditions have created within the soul of every great man. Let us not be put off by the

---

[5] Ernest Renan (1823–1892), French Orientalist and writer on Biblical subjects. Levin refers to Renan's *Life of Jesus* (1863).
* *Essays in the History of Materialism* (London, 1934), p. 235. [Levin's note.]
† *L'Imagination* (1936), p. 27. [Levin's note.]
‡ Taine, *Histoire de la littérature anglaise* (1866), I, xv. [Levin's note.]
§ *Littérature anglaise*, II, 164. [Levin's note.]
|| *Littérature anglaise*, I, xxxii. [Levin's note.]

circular logic, the mechanical apparatus, and the scientific jargon: Taine, conscientious child of his temperament and time, was an ardent individualist. His theory of character owes quite as much to Balzac as his theory of environment owes to Stendhal. Had it been the other way around, had he combined Stendhal's psychological insight with Balzac's sociological outlook, he might have been a better critic. His portrait of Balzac, for better or worse, is as monomaniacal as Balzac's portrait of Grandet.

Psychology is a knife, Dostoevsky, warns us,* which cuts two ways. We may look for a man in his books, or we may look to the man for the explanation of his books. Taine's is the more dangerous way: to deduce the qualities of a work from a presupposition about the author. The whole *Comédie humaine*[6] follows from the consideration that Balzac was a business man, and Livy's history is what you might expect from a writer who was really an orator. This mode of critical characterization must perforce be limited to a few broad strokes, much too exaggerated and impressionistic to be compared with the detailed nuances of Sainte-Beuve's portraiture. Most of Taine's figures bear a strong family likeness. He is most adroit at bringing out the generic traits of English literature: the response to nature, the puritan strain, the fact—in short—that it was written by Englishmen. He himself, true to his theories, remains an intransigent Frenchman, and his history—to the point where he abandons Tennyson for Musset and recrosses the channel—remains a traveler's survey of a foreign culture. Why, in spite of all temptations to interpret other cultures, should Taine have been attracted to England?

Taine's critical faculties were conditioned not by science but by romanticism, and who was Taine to repudiate his own conditioning? Madame de Staël had been drawn to Germany, and Melchior de Vogüé[7] would soon be seeking the Russian soul, but English was for most Frenchmen the typically romantic literature. France had been the Bastille of classicism, while Britain had never been enslaved to the rules; untamed nature, in Saxon garb, resisted the shackles of Norman constraint. It took very little perception of the technique of English poetry for Taine to prefer blank verse to Alexandrines. Form, as he construed it, was a body of artificial restrictions which inhibited free expression, and which English men of letters had somehow succeeded in doing without. One might almost say that they had developed a literature of pure content. "Not in Greece, nor in Italy, nor in Spain, nor in France," said Taine, "has an art been seen which tried so boldly to express the soul and the most intimate depths of the soul, the reality and the whole reality."† What seemed to him so unprecedented is, on closer scrutiny, a complex tradition. Elizabethan drama is so much more baroque than the succinct tragedies of Racine that Taine missed its pattern altogether, and believed he was facing a chaos of first-hand and unconstrained realities. His impressions were those

* *The Brothers Karamazov,* tr. Constance Garnett (New York, 1916), p. 785. [Levin's note.]

[6] The name Balzac gave to his vast series of interconnected novels and stories.

[7] Eugéne Marie Melchior, Vicomte de Vogüé (1848–1910), French critic, author of a book on the Russian novel (1886).

† *Littérature anglaise,* II, 52. [Levin's note.]

of Fielding's barber Partridge at the play, wholly taken in by theatrical make-believe, naïvely mistaking the actors for the characters they represent, quixotically confusing literature with life.[8]

2. SOCIOLOGICAL CRITICISM AND SOCIAL CRITICS

Remembering Lamb's essay[9] on the artificiality of Restoration comedy, we cannot share Taine's facile assumption that the English stage received and retained "the exact imprint of the century and the nation."* We cannot accept this free translation of Hamlet's impulse to give "the very age and body of the time his form and pressure."† We can admit that Taine was less of a critic than a historian, but we cannot forgive him for being such an uncritical historian. His professed willingness to trade quantities of charters for the letters of Saint Paul or the memoirs of Cellini‡ does not indicate a literary taste; it merely states a preference for human documents as against constitutional documents. In exploiting literature for purposes of historical documentation, Taine uncovered a new mine of priceless source material. But he never learned the difference between ore and craftsmanship. In his *Philosophie de l'art,* to be sure, he could no longer sidestep esthetic and technical discussion. He was forced to concede that art could be idealistic as well as realistic, and to place Greek sculpture at a farther remove from reality than Flemish painting. This concession allowed him to turn his back on the sculpture, and to reconstruct, with a freer hand than ever, the moment, the race, and the milieu of ancient Greece.

The serious objection to environmentalism is that it failed to distinguish, not between one personality and another, but between personality and art. It encouraged scholars to write literary histories which, as Ferdinand Brunetière§ pointed out, were nothing but chronological dictionaries of literary biography. It discouraged the realization, which Brunetière called the evolution of *genres,* that literary technique had a history of its own. It advanced a brilliant generalization, and established—as first-rate ideas will do in second-rate minds—a rule of thumb. The incidental and qualified extent to which books epitomize their epoch may vary from one example to the next. Taine's successors made no allowances for the permutations of form; rather they industrialized his process for extracting the contents of the books. The prevailing aim of literary historiography, under the sponsorship of Gustave Lanson[10] in France and other professors elsewhere, has been a kind of illustrated supplement to

---

[8] The episode takes place in Book XVI, Chap. V. of *Tom Jones* (1749), by Henry Fielding.

[9] "On the Artificial Comedy of the Last Century," by Charles Lamb.

* *Littérature anglaise,* II, 3 [Levin's note.]

† *Hamlet,* III, ii, 27. [Levin's note.]

‡ *Littérature anglaise,* I, xlvi. [Levin's note.]

§ *L'Evolution des genres dans l'histoire de la littérature* (1891), p. xii. [Levin's note.]

[10] Gustave Lanson (1857–1934), author of *Histoire de la littérature française* (1894).

history. Academic research has concentrated so heavily on the backgrounds of literature that the foreground has been almost obliterated.

Meanwhile Taine's influence has been felt in the wider areas of criticism, and here it has been subordinated to political ends. Taine himself was bitterly anti-political. He did not realize the importance of ideas until he had lost faith in his own: originally he had been a proponent of the doctrines of the *philosophes*,[11] which he blamed in his later studies, *Les Origines de la France contemporaine*,[12] for instigating the revolution of 1789. It was a Danish critic, closely associated with Ibsen, Nietzsche, and the controversies of the eighties, who broadened the range and narrowed the tendency of literary history. For politics, and for literature too, Georg Brandes[13] had more feeling than Taine. A cosmopolitan liberal, deeply suspicious of the ascendancy of Prussia, he found a touchstone for the romanticists in their struggles or compromises with clerical reaction and the authority of the state. Byron and Heine were his urbane prophets, the Schlegels[14] were renegades, and the revolution of 1848 was the anticlimax toward which his *Main Currents of Nineteeth Century Literature* moved. Where a book had been an end-product to Taine, to Brandes it was continuing force, and the critic's function was to chart its repercussions.

Both aspects have been duly stressed in the critical interpretation of American writers—their reactions to their environment and their contributions to the liberal tradition. Our foremost literary historian, V. L. Parrington,[15] extended and modified Taine's formula to fit our problems, dramatizing New England puritanism from the standpoint of western populism, and pitting a heroic Jefferson against a sinister Hamilton. His title, *Main Currents in American Thought*, conveyed a fraternal salute to Brandes, and denoted an additional qualification. Parrington got around Taine's difficulty—the difficulty of using imaginative writers as historical sources—by drawing upon the moralists and the publicists. His chapters on Roger Williams and John Marshall[16] are ample and rewarding; his accounts of Poe and Henry James are so trivial that they might better have been omitted. The latest period is inevitably the hardest and his last volume is posthumous and fragmentary, but it seems to mark an increasing conflict between artistic and political standards. Granville Hicks, going over the same ground, was able to resolve that conflict by the simple device of discarding artistic standards.*

Mr. Hicks, if he still adheres to his somewhat elusive conception of *The Great Tradition*, is a Marxist critic in the sense that Parrington was a Jeffer-

---

[11] A term used for scientists, literary men, and philosophers of the eighteenth century who were noted for their belief in reason and their dislike for what they considered outmoded institutions.

[12] "The Origins of Contemporary France."

[13] Georg Morris Cohen Brandes (1842–1927), Danish critic.

[14] August Wilhelm (1767–1845) and Friedrich von Schlegel (1772–1829), German writers, who engaged in criticism, translation, classical scholarship, and philosophy.

[15] Vernon Louis Parrington (1871–1929). *Main Currents* (1927–1930) was left unfinished at Parrington's death.

[16] Roger Williams (c. 1603–1683), clergyman, colonist, and writer; John Marshall (1755–1835), lawyer, public official, jurist, biographer.

* Granville Hicks, *The Great Tradition* (New York, 1933); cf. *Harper's*, CXCII, 1153 (June, 1946), unnumbered last pages. [Levin's note.]

sonian critic. The choice between them is largely a matter of political standards. Jeffersonianism, naturally the most favorable climate in which to discuss American literature, has been taken in vain so often that it has begun to resist definition. Marxism, by redefining milieu in economic terms, has presented a more rigorous theory of historical causation than Taine's and a more ruthless canon of political allegiance than Brandes'. It has introduced criticism to a sociological system which is highly illuminating and a social doctrine which is highly controversial. It has tightened the relations between literature and life by oversimplifying them beyond recognition. In this respect Karl Marx, as he occasionally confessed, was no Marxist: he repeatedly cautioned his followers against expecting the arts to show a neat conformity with his views.* Perhaps if he had written his projected study of Balzac, he would have bequeathed them a critical method. For lack of one, they took what was available. Marxist criticism superimposed its socialistic doctrine on the deterministic method, and judged according to Marx what it had interpreted according to Taine.

Extension and modification have added their corollary to Taine's method: the relations between literature and society are reciprocal. Literature is not only the effect of social causes; it is also the cause of social effects. The critic may investigate its causes, as Taine tried to do; or he may, like Brandes and others, be more interested in its effects. So long as he is correlating works of art with trends of history, his function is relatively clear. It becomes less clear as he encounters his contemporaries, and as the issues become more immediate. He is then concerned, no longer with a secure past, but with a problematic future. An insecure present may commit him to some special partisanship, Marxist or otherwise, and incline him to judge each new work by its possible effect—whether it will advance or hinder his party's program. Since art can be a weapon, among other things, it will be judged in the heat of the battle by its polemical possibilities. We need not deny the relevance or significance of such judgments; we need only recognize that they carry us beyond the limits of esthetic questions into the field of moral values. There are times when criticism cannot conveniently stop at the border. Whenever there are boundary disputes, questions involving propaganda or regulation, we may be called upon to go afield. We shall be safe while we are aware that virtue and beauty are as intimately related as beauty and truth, and as eternally distinct.

3. THE RÔLE OF CONVENTION

It was as if Taine had discovered that the earth was round, without realizing that another continent lay between Europe and Asia. The distance was longer, the route more devious, than sociological criticism had anticipated. Not that the intervening territory was unexplored; but those who had explored it most thoroughly were isolationists. Those who were most familiar with the techniques and traditions of literature were least conscious of its social responsibilities. Most of them were writers themselves, lacking in critical method perhaps,

* Karl Marx and Friedrich Engels, *Sur la littérature et l'art*, ed. and tr. Jean Freville (1936), p. 59. [Levin's note.]

yet possessing the very skills and insights that the methodologists lacked. A few were philosophers, striving—on the high plane of idealism—toward a historical synthesis of the arts. Their concept of expressive form, inherited by the esthetic of Croce from the literary history of Francesco de Sanctis,[17] resembles the "organic principle"* that Anglo-American criticism inherits from the theory of Coleridge, the preaching of Emerson, and the practice of Thoreau. By whichever name, it is too sensitive an instrument to be used effectively, except by acute critics on acknowledged masterpieces. With cruder material, in unskilled hands, its insistence on the uniqueness of each work of art and its acceptance of the artist at his own evaluation dissolve into esthetic impressionism and romantic hero-worship.

While this school is responsible for many admirable critiques, it has never produced that "new criticism" which the late J. E. Spingarn[18] tried vainly to define. Conceiving art as the fullest expression of individuality, it has disregarded the more analytic approaches. Taine's school, though less discriminating, has been more influential, because it conceives art as a collective expression of society. The fallacy in this conception—we have already seen—is to equate art with society, to assume a one-to-one correspondence between a book and its subject-matter, to accept the literature of an age as a complete and exact replica of the age itself. One way or another, literature is bound to tell the truth; but it has told the whole truth very seldom, and nothing but the truth hardly ever; some things are bound to be left out, and others to be exaggerated in the telling. Sins of omission can usually be traced to some restriction in the artist's freedom of speech, his range of experience, or his control of his medium. Sins of commission are inherent in the nature of his materials. The literary historian must reckon with these changing degrees of restriction and exaggeration. Literary history, if it is to be accurate, must be always correcting its aim.

To mention one conspicuous case, the relations between the sexes have received a vast—possibly a disproportionate—amount of attention from writers. From their miscellaneous and contradictory testimony it would be rash to infer very much, without allowing for the artistic taboos of one period or the exhibitionism of another. An enterprising sociologist, by measuring the exposed portions of the human figure in various paintings, has arrived at a quantitative historical index of comparative sensuality. What inference could not be drawn, by some future sciolist, from the preponderance of detective stories on the shelves of our circulating libraries? Those volumes testify, for us, to the colorless comfort of their readers' lives. We are aware, because we are not dependent on literary evidence, that ours is no unparalleled epoch of domestic crime—of utterly ineffectual police, of criminals who bear all the earmarks of innocence, and of detectives whose nonchalance is only equalled by their erudition. These, we are smugly aware, have not much more sig-

---

[17] Francesco de Sanctis (1817–1883), author of *Storia della letteratura italiana* (1870–1871; tr. J. Redfern, *History of Italian Literature*).

* See F. O. Matthiessen, *American Renaissance* (New York, 1941), p. 133 [Levin's note.]

[18] Joel Elias Spingarn (1875–1939), American critic and teacher, who delivered an address at Columbia University in 1910 entitled "The New Criticism."

nificance than the counters of a complicated game. Nevertheless, it is disturbing to imagine what literal-minded critics may deduce when the rules of the game have been forgotten. It suggests that we ourselves may be misreading other books through our ignorance of the lost conventions on which they hinge.

Convention may be described as a necessary difference between art and life. Some differences, strictly speaking, may be quite unnecessary: deliberate sallies of the imagination, unconscious effects of miscalculation or misunderstanding. But art must also differ from life for technical reasons: limitations of form, difficulties of expression. The artist, powerless to overcome these obstacles by himself, must have the assistance of his audience. They must agree to take certain formalities and assumptions for granted, to take the word for the deed or the shading for the shadow. The result of their unspoken agreement is a compromise between the possibilities of life and the exigencies of art. Goethe might have been speaking of convention when he said, *"In der Beschränkung zeigt sich erst der Meister."*[19] Limitation has often been a source of new forms, and difficulty—as the defenders of rhyme have argued, from Samuel Daniel[20] to Paul Valéry—has prompted poets to their most felicitous expressions. Without some sort of conventionalization art could hardly exist. It exists by making virtues of necessities; after the necessities disappear, we forget the conventions. After perspective is invented, we misjudge the primitives; after the scenery is set up, we challenge the unities. And Taine, forgetting that feminine roles were played by boys, is appalled at finding masculine traits* in Elizabethan heroines.

His former classmate. Francisque Sarcey, who became—through forty years of playgoing—the most practical of critics, might have supplied the needed correction for Taine's theories. "It is inadequate to repeat that the theater is a representation of human life," Sarcey had learned. "It would be a more precise definition to say that dramatic art is the sum of conventions, universal or local, eternal or temporary, which help—when human life is represented on the stage—to give a public the illusion of truth."† This illusion may be sustained in the novel more easily than on the stage; but it is still an illusion, as Maupassant frankly admitted.‡ Although drama may be the most conventional of literary forms, and fiction the least, even fiction is not entirely free. Even Proust, the most unconventional of novelists, must resort to the convention of eavesdropping in order to sustain the needs of first-person narrative. We need not condone such melodramatic stratagems; we can observe that the modern novel has endeavored to get along without them; upon fuller consideration we may even conclude that the whole modern movement of realism, technically considered, is an endeavor to emancipate literature from the sway of conventions.

[19] "It is under restrictions that the master first reveals himself." From Goethe's "Natur und Kunst" ("Nature and Art").
[20] Samuel Daniel (1562–1619), English poet, author of *Defence of Rhyme* (1602?).
* Taine, *Littérature anglaise*, pp. 496 ff. [Levin's note.]
† Francisque Sarcey, "Essai d'une esthétique de théâtre," *Quarante ans du théâtre* (1900), I, 132. [Levin's note.]
‡ Guy de Maupassant, *Pierre et Jean* (1892), pp. xvii f. [Levin's note.]

4. TOWARD AN INSTITUTIONAL METHOD

This provisional conclusion would explain why literary historians, under the influence of realism, have slighted literary form. In their impatience to lay bare the so-called content of a work, they have missed a more revealing characteristic: the way the artist handles the appropriate conventions. Whether it is possible, or even desirable, to eliminate artifice from art—that is one of the largest questions that criticism must face. But realistic novelists who declare their intentions of transcribing life have an obvious advantage over realistic critics who expect every book to be a literal transcript. Stendhal, when he declares that "a novel is a mirror riding along a highway,"* is in a position to fulfil his picaresque intention. When Taine echoes this precept, defining the novel as "a kind of portable mirror which can be conveyed everywhere, and which is most convenient for reflecting all aspects of nature and life,"† he puts the mirror before the horse. He is then embarrassed to discover so few reflections of the *ancien régime* in French novels of the eighteenth century. His revulsion from neo-classical generalities and his preference for descriptive details carry him back across the channel, from Marmontel and Crébillon *fils* to Fielding and Smollett.[21] Some mirrors, Taine finally discovered, are less reliable than others.

The metaphor of the mirror held up to nature, the idea that literature reflects life, was mentioned by Plato‡ only to be rejected. By the time of Cicero§ it was already a commonplace of criticism. It was applied by the ancients to comedy, the original vehicle of realism; later it became a byword for artistic didacticism, for the medieval zeal to see vice exposed and virtue emulated. When Shakespeare invoked it, he had a definite purpose which those who quote him commonly ignore. Hamlet is not merely describing a play, he is exhorting the players. His advice is a critique of bad acting as well as an apology for the theater, a protest against unnatural conventions as well as a plea for realism. Like modern critics who derive their metaphors from photography, he implies a further comparision with more conventionalized modes of art—particularly with painting. To hold up a photograph or a mirror, as it were, is to compare the "abstract and brief chronicles of the time"|| with the distorted journeywork that "imitated humanity so abominably."# Art should be a reflection of life, we are advised, not a distortion—as it has all too frequently been. Criticism, in assuming that art invariably reflects and forgetting that it fre-

* Stendhal, *Le Rouge et le Noir,* ed. Henri Martineau (1927), I, 132. [Levin's note.]

† *Les Origines de la France contemporaine: l'Ancien Régime* (1909), I, 312. [Levin's note.]

21 Jean-François Marmontel (1723–1799), French man of letters; Claud-Prosper Jolyot de Crébillon *fils* (1707–1777) French novelist; Tobias Smollett (1721–1771), English novelist.

‡ See Richard McKeon, "Literary Criticism and the Concept of Imitation in Antiquity," *Modern Philology* (1936), XXXIV, 12. [Levin's note.]

§ Aelius Donatus, *Excerpta de comoeda.* [Levin's note.]

|| *Hamlet,* II, ii, 547 ff. [Levin's note.]

Hamlet, III, ii. 39 f. [Levin's note.]

quently distorts, wafts us through the looking-glass into a sphere of its own, where everything is clear and cool, logical and literal, and more surrealistic than real.

In questioning the attempts of scholars to utilize Shakespeare as the mirror of his time, Professor Stoll* has reminded them that their business is to separate historical fact from literary illusion, to distinguish the object from its reflected image. Literature, instead of reflecting life, refracts it. Our task, in any given case, is to determine the angle of refraction. Since the angle depends upon the density of the medium, it is always shifting, and the task is never easy. We are aided today, however, by a more flexible and accurate kind of critical apparatus than Taine was able to employ. An acquaintance with artistic conventions, which can best be acquired through comparative studies in technique, should complement an awareness of social backgrounds. "Literature is complementary to life." This formula of Lanson's† is broad enough to include the important proviso that there is room in the world of art for ideals and projects, fantasies and anxieties, which do not ordinarily find a habitation in the world of reality. But, in recognizing that literature adds something to life or that it subtracts something from life, we must not overlook the most important consideration of all—that literature is at all times an intrinsic part of life. It is, if we can work out the implications of Leslie Stephen's phrase, "a particular function of the whole social organism."‡

The organic character of this relationship has been most explicitly formulated by a statesman and historian, Prosper de Barante.§ Writing of the ideas behind the French revolution while they were still fresh in men's minds, his comprehension of their political interplay was broader than Taine's. "In the absence of regular institutions," wrote Barante, "literature became one." The truth, though it has long been obscured by a welter of personalities and technicalities, is that literature has always been an institution. Like other institutions, the church or the law, it cherishes a unique phase of human experience and controls a special body of precedents and devices: it tends to incorporate a self-perpetuating discipline, while responding to the main currents of each succeeding period; it is continually accessible to all the impulses of life at large, but it must translate them into its own terms and adapt them to its peculiar forms. Once we have grasped this fact, we begin to perceive how art may belong to society and yet be autonomous within its own limits, and are no longer puzzled by the apparent polarity of social and formal criticism. These, in the last analysis, are complementary frames of reference whereby we may discriminate the complexities of a work of art. In multiplying these discriminations between external impulses and internal peculiarities—in other words, between the effects of environment and convention—our ultimate justification is to understand the vital process to which they are both indispensable.

* E. E. Stoll, *From Shakespeare to Joyce* (New York, 1949), p. 28. [Levin's note.]
† Gustave Lanson, "L'Histoire littéraire et la sociologie." *Revue de métaphysique et de morale* (1904), XII, 635. [Levin's note.]
‡ *English Literature and Society in the Eighteenth Century* (London, 1907), p. 13. [Levin's note.]
§ Prosper de Barante, *De la littérature française pendant le dix-huitième siècle* (1854), p. 5; cf. Max Lerner and Edwin Mims, Jr., "Literature," *Encyclopedia of the Social Sciences* (New York, 1933), IX, 523. [Levin's note.]

To consider the novel as an institution, then, imposes no dogma, exacts no sacrifice, and excludes none of the critical methods that have proved illuminating in the past. If it tends to subordinate the writer's personality to his achievement, it requires no further apology, for criticism has long been unduly subordinated to biography. The tendency of the romanticists to live their writings and write their lives, and the consequent success of their critics as biographers, did much to justify this subordination; but even Sainte-Beuve's "natural history of souls,"* though it unified and clarified an author's works by fitting them into the pattern of his career, was too ready to dismiss their purely artistic qualities as "rhetoric." More recently the doctrines of Freud, while imposing a topheavy vocabulary upon the discussion of art, have been used to corroborate and systematize the sporadic intuitions of artists; but the psychologists, like the sociologists, have been more interested in utilizing books for documentary purposes than in exploring their intrinsic nature. Meanwhile, on the popular level, the confusion between a novelist and his novels has been consciously exploited. A series of novelized biographies, calling itself *Le Roman des grandes existences*,[22] invites the common reader to proceed from "the prodigious life of Balzac" through "the mournful life of Baudelaire" to "the wise and merry life of Montaigne."

If fiction has seldom been discussed on a plane commensurate with its achievements, it is because we are too often sidetracked by personalities. If, with Henry James, we recognize the novelist's intention as a figure in a carpet, we must recognize that he is guided by his material, his training, his commission, by the size and shape of his loom, and by his imagination to the extent that it accepts and masters those elements. Psychology—illuminating as it has been—has treated literature too often as a record of personal idiosyncrasies, too seldom as the basis of a collective consciousness. Yet it is on that basis that the greatest writers have functioned. Their originality has been an ability to "seize on the public mind," in Bagehot's opinion; conventions have changed and styles have developed as lesser writers caught "the traditional rhythm of an age." The irreducible element of individual talent would seem to play the same role in the evolution of *genres* that natural selection plays in the origin of species. Amid the mutations of modern individualism, we may very conceivably have overstressed the private aspects of writing. One convenience of the institutional method is that it gives due credit to the never-ending collaboration between writer and public. It sees no reason to ignore what is relevant in the psychological prepossessions of the craftsman, and it knows that he is ultimately to be judged by the technical resources of his craftsmanship; but it attains its clearest and most comprehensive scope by centering on his craft—on his social status and his historical function as participant in a skilled group and a living tradition.

When Edgar Quinet announced a course at the Collège de France in *La Littérature et les institutions comparées de l'Europe méridionelle*, he was requested by Guizot's ministry to omit the word "institutions" and to limit himself to purely literary discussion. When he replied that this would be impossi-

---

* Sainte-Beuve, *Portraits littéraires*, III, 546. [Levin's note.]
22 "The Romance of Great Lives."

ble, his course was suspended, and his further efforts went directly into those reform agitations which culminated in the democratic revolution of the following year, 1848.* Thereby proceeding from sociological to social criticism, he demonstrated anew what French critics and novelists have understood particularly well—the dynamic interaction between ideas and events. In a time which has seen that demonstration repeated on so vast a scale, the institutional forces that impinge upon literature are self-evident. The responsibilities that literature owes to itself, and the special allegiance it exacts from us, should also become apparent when we conceive it as an institution in its own right. The misleading dichotomy between substance and form, which permits literary historians, like Parrington, to dismiss "belletristic philandering," and esthetic impressionists, like Mr. R. P. Blackmur,[23] to dispose of "separable content," should disappear as soon as abstract categories are dropped and concrete relations are taken up. And the jurisdictional conflict between truth and beauty should dissolve when esthetics discovers the truth about beauty; when criticism becomes—as Bacon[24] intended, and Renan and Sainte-Beuve remembered, and all too many other critics have forgotten—the science of art.

---

* C. L. Chassin, *Edgar Quinet: sa vie et son oeuvre* (1859), pp. 57 ff. [Levin's note.]
[23] Richard Palmer Blackmur (1904–1968), American teacher and critic.
[24] Francis Bacon, English philosopher, statesman, and essayist.

Allen Tate

IS LITERARY
CRITICISM POSSIBLE?

Allen Tate was born in 1899 in Winchester, Kentucky. He attended
Vanderbilt University, where he became one of a notable group of
young men brought together by their interest in poetry, their dissatisfaction with the quality of American life, and their commitment to the
traditional Christian-humanist values that, as they believed, characterized
the old South at its best. From 1922 to 1925 this group published a
journal, *The Fugitive,* which was not the less tendentious for being
devoted exclusively to poetry. The views that informed the poems of
The Fugitive were developed and made more explicit when Tate and
three other distinguished members of the group—John Crowe Ransom,
David Davidson, and Robert Penn Warren—with eight other like-
minded scholars in various fields formed a loose association, referring
to themselves as "Agrarians." In 1930 the Agrarians published a collection of essays whose title, *I'll Take My Stand,* will be recognized as a
phrase from "Dixie." As the introduction to the volume says, the essays
"all tend to support a Southern way of life against what may be called
the American or prevailing way; and all as much as agree that the best
terms in which to represent the distinction are contained in the phrase
Agrarian *versus* Industrial." Although the cultural program the essays
proposed never gained practical influence even in the South and although many of its proponents ceased to adhere to it, the volume is still
thought of as a landmark in American social criticism.

Mr. Tate, who has taught in many universities in America, in
England, and on the continent, is currently a Professor of English at
the University of Minnesota. From 1943 to 1944 he held the post of
Fellow in American Letters at the Library of Congress. He is the author
of biographies of Stonewall Jackson (1928) and of Jefferson Davis
(1929) and of a novel, *The Fathers* (1938), which is widely and de-
servedly admired. It is, however, upon his achievement as a poet and
as a critic that Mr. Tate's reputation is chiefly based. From the many
single volumes of his poetry that have been published, *Poems* (1960)
has collected much of his later work. The Bollingen Poetry Prize, won
in 1956, is among the many awards which the poems have earned. The
greater part of his criticism has been brought together in two collections,
The Man of Letters in the Modern World (1955) and *Essays of Four
Decades* (1968).

From Allen Tate, *Essays of Four Decades,* Swallow Press, Chicago: Copyright 1968.

The questions that I propose to discuss in this essay will fall into two main divisions. I shall undertake to discuss, first, the teaching of literary criticism in the university. Since I am not able to *define* literary criticism I shall be chiefly concerned with the idea of a formal relation; that is to say, supposing we knew what criticism is, what relation would it have to the humanities, of which it seems to be a constituent part? In the second division I shall try to push the discussion a little further, towards a question that has been acute in our time: Is literary criticism possible at all? The answer to this question ought logically to precede the discussion of a formal relation, for we ought to know what it is that we are trying to relate to something else. But we shall never know this; we shall only find that in teaching criticism we do not know what we are teaching, even though criticism daily talks about a vast material that we are in the habit of calling the humanities. The mere fact of this witnesses our sense of a formal relation that ought to exist between two things of the nature of which we are ignorant.

I

Literary criticism as a member of the humanities I take to be a problem of academic statesmanship inviting what we hopefully call "solutions" of both the theoretical and the practical sort. Is literary criticism properly a branch of humanistic study? That is the theoretical question, to which I shall avoid the responsibility of giving the answer. Without this answer, we cannot hope to understand the practical question: What is the place of criticism in the humanities program; on what grounds should it be there (if it should be there at all), given the kind of education that the present teachers of the humanities bring to their work?

The two questions, the theoretical and the practical, together constitute the formal question; that is to say, whatever criticism and the humanities may be, we should have to discuss their relation in some such terms as I am suggesting. But before we follow this clue we must address ourselves more candidly to the fact of our almost total ignorance.

The three grand divisions of higher education in the United States are, I believe, the Natural Sciences, the Social Sciences, and the Humanities. Of the first, I am entirely too ignorant to speak. Of the social sciences I know little, and I am not entitled to suspect that they do not really exist; I believe this in the long run because I want to believe it, the actuality of a science of human societies being repellent to me, apart from its dubious scientific credentials. Of the humanities, the division with which as poet and critic I am presumably most concerned, one must speak with melancholy as well as in ignorance. For into the humanistic bag we throw everything that cannot qualify as a science, natural or social. This discrete mixture of hot and cold, moist and dry, creates in the bag a vortex, which emits a powerful wind of ineffectual heroics, somewhat as follows: We humanists bring within the scope of the humanities all the great records—sometimes we call them the

remains: poetry, drama, pre-scientific history (Herodotus, Joinville, Bede)[1]—
of the experience of man *as* man; we are not concerned with him as vertebrate,
biped, mathematician, or priest. Precisely, reply the social scientists; that is just
what is wrong with you; you don't see that man is not man, that he is
merely a *function;* and your records (or remains) are so full of error that
we are glad to relegate them to professors of English, poets, and other dilettanti,
those "'former people" who live in the Past. The Past, which we can neither
smell, see, taste, nor touch, was well labeled by our apostle, Mr. Carl Sandburg,[2] as a bucket of ashes . . . No first-rate scientific mind is guilty of
this vulgarity. Yet as academic statesmen, the humanists must also be practical politicians who know that they cannot stay in office unless they have
an invigorating awareness of the power, and of the superior foot-work, of the
third-rate mind.

As for literary criticism, we here encounter a stench and murk not unlike
that of a battlefield three days after the fighting is over and the armies have
departed. Yet in this war nobody has suggested that criticism is one of the
social sciences, except a few Marxists, who tried fifteen years ago to make it
a branch of sociology. History not long ago became a social science, and
saved its life by losing it; and there is no reason why sociology "oriented"
toward literature should not be likewise promoted, to the relief of everybody
concerned. And whatever criticism may be, we should perhaps do well to
keep it with the humanities, where it can profit by the sad example of
Hilaire Belloc's[3] Jim, who failed "To keep ahold of Nurse/For fear of
getting something worse."

It may not be necessary to know what criticism is; it may be quite enough
to see that it is now being written, that a great deal of it was written in the
past, that it is concerned with one of the chief objects of humanistic study:
literature. And we therefore study it either as an "area" in itself—that is, we
offer courses in its history; or as a human interest in some past age—that is,
we use criticism as one way of understanding the age of Johnson or the high
Renaissance. Guided by the happy theory of spontaneous understanding resulting from the collision of pure intelligence with its object—a theory injected
into American education by Charles W. Eliot[4]—we expose the student mind
to "areas" of humanistic material, in the confident belief that if it is exposed to
enough "areas" it will learn something. If we expose it to enough "areas" in
all three grand divisions, the spontaneous intelligence will automatically become
educated without thought.

[1] Herodotus (c. 484–425 B.C.), Greek historian, often called the Father of History;
Jean, Sire de Joinville (c. 1224–1317), French chronicler, biographer of Louis IX;
Bede (c. 673–735), English monk and historian, called the Venerable.

[2] Carl Sandburg (1878–1967), American poet, journalist, and biographer of
Lincoln.

[3] Hilaire Belloc (1870–1953), though born in France, wrote novels, verse, travel
books, history, and biography in English. He also wrote verse for children, from
which Tate quotes.

[4] Charles W. Eliot (1834–1926), President of Harvard (1869–1909), editor of
The Harvard Classics (1910), a 50-volume selection from world literature.

The natural sciences have a high-powered rationale of their daily conquests of nature. The social sciences have a slippery analogical* metaphor to sustain their self-confidence. The humanities modestly offer the vision of the historical lump. This lump is tossed at the student mind, which is conceived as the miraculous combination of the *tabula rasa*[5] and innate powers of understanding. In short, the humanities have no rationale. We suppose that it is sufficient to show that a given work—a poem, a play, a critical "document"—came before or after some other poem, play, or critical "document," or was written when something else was happening, like Alexander's invasion of India or the defeat of the Armada.[6] When these and other correlations are perceived, the result is understanding. But the result of correlation is merely the possibility of further correlation. Our modest capacity for true understanding is frustrated. For the true rationale of humanistic study is now what it has always been, even though now it is not only in decay, but dead. I allude to the arts of rhetoric.

By rhetoric I mean the study and the use of the figurative language of experience as the discipline by means of which men govern their relations with one another in the light of truth. Rhetoric presupposes the study of two prior disciplines, grammar and logic, neither of which is much pursued today, except by specialists.

These disciplines are no longer prerequisite even to the study of philosophy. An Eastern university offers a grandiose course in Greek philosophical ideas to sophomores who will never know a syllogism from a handsaw. A graduate student who, I was told, was very brilliant in nuclear physics, decided that he wanted to take a course in *The Divine Comedy*. (Why he wanted to study Dante I do not know, but his humility was impressive.) I was assured by the academic grapevine that he understood difficult mathematical formulae, but one day in class he revealed the fact that he could neither define nor recognize a past participle. At the end of the term he confessed that nobody had ever told him that the strategies of language, or the arts of rhetoric, could be as important and exacting a discipline as the theory of equations. He had thought courses in English a little sissified; he had not been told that it might be possible, after severe application, to learn how to read. He had learned to talk without effort in infancy, in a decadent democracy, and no doubt supposed that grammar came of conditioning, and that he would get it free.

Back of this homely exemplum stands a formidable specter whose name is Cultural Decay—at a time when men are more conscious of cultures than ever before, and stock their universities and museums with lumps of cultures, like inert geological specimens in a glass case. I am far from believing that a revival of the trivium, or the three primary liberal arts, would bring the dead bodies to life: revivals have a fatal incapacity to revive anything. But unless we can create and develop a hierarchy of studies that can lead not merely to further studies but to truth, one may doubt that the accelerating decline of modern culture will be checked.

* Analogous to the natural sciences. [Tate's note.]
[5] A smoothed tablet, a blank slate.
[6] The Spanish Armada, a fleet launched by Philip of Spain for the invasion of England; defeated by calms, storms, English might and cunning, bad luck.

Without quite knowing what literary criticism is, let us assume again that we are teaching it within the humanities division, usually in the English Department, either because it ought to be there or because nobody else wants it. For convenience we may think of the common relations between the work of the imagination and the teaching activity under four heads, which I shall put in the form of rhetorical questions:

(1) Can a given work, say *Clarissa Harlowe*[7] or *Kublai Khan*,[8] be "taught," in such a way as to make it understood, without criticism?

(2) Can the work be taught first, and the criticism then applied as a mode of understanding?

(3) Can the criticism be presented first and held in readiness for the act of understanding which could thus be simultaneous with the act of reading the novel or the poem?

(4) Is the purpose of teaching imaginative works to provide materials upon which the critical faculty may exercise itself in its drive toward the making of critical systems, which then perpetuate themselves without much reference to literature?

These four versions of the relation by no means exhaust its possible variations. The slippery ambiguity of the word criticism itself ought by now to be plain. But for the purposes of this localized discussion, which I am limiting for the moment to the question of how to teach, we may think of criticism as three familiar kinds of discourse about works of literature. (We must bear in mind not only our failure to know what criticism is, but another, more difficult failure resulting from it: the failure to know what literature is.) The three kinds of critical discourse are as follows: (1) acts of evaluation of literature (whatever these may be); (2) the communication of insights; and (3) the rhetorical study of the language of the imaginative work.

I am not assuming, I am merely pretending that any one of the three activities is to be found in its purity. To the extent that they may be separated, we must conclude that the two first, acts of evaluation and the communication of insights, cannot be taught, and that the third, rhetorical analysis, has not been taught effectively in this country since the rise of the historical method in literary studies.

When I first taught a college class, about eighteen years ago, I thought that anything was possible; but with every year since it has seemed a little more absurd to try to teach students to "evaluate" works of literature, and perhaps not less absurd to try to evaluate them oneself. The assumption that we are capable of just evaluation (a word that seems to have got into criticism by way of Adam Smith)[9] is one of the subtler, if crude, abuses of democratic doctrine, as follows: all men ought to exercise independent judgment, and all men being equal, all are equally capable of it, even in literature and the arts. I have observed that when my own opinions seem most original and independent

---

[7] A novel by Samuel Richardson (1689–1761) of 1747–1748.

[8] The poem by Coleridge is meant.

[9] Adam Smith (1723–1790), Scottish economist, professor of philosophy at the University of Glasgow, whose book *The Wealth of Nations* (1776) is the classic statement of laissez-faire economics. Whether or not Tate is correct about the source of the word "evaluation," his tone is ironic.

they turn out to be almost wholly conventional. An absolutely independent judgment (if such a thing were possible) would be an absolutely ignorant judgment.

Shall the instructor, then, set before the class his own "evaluations"? He will do so at the risk of disseminating a hierarchy that he may not have intended to create, and thus may be aborted, or at least stultified, the student's own reading. It is inevitable that the instructor shall say to the class that one poem is "better" than another. The student, in the degree of his intelligence, will form clear preferences or rejections that will do little harm if he understands what they are. But the teaching of literature through the assertion of preference will end up either as mere impressionism, or as the more sinister variety of impressionism that Irving Babbitt[10] detected in the absorption of the literary work into its historical setting.

As to the communication of "insights," it would perhaps be an inquiry without benefit to anybody to ask how this elusive maid-of-all-work got into modern criticism. She is here, and perhaps we ought to be grateful, because she is obviously willing to do all the work. Insight could mean two things, separately or taken together: the perception of meanings ordinarily or hitherto undetected, and/or the synthetic awareness that brings to the text similar or contrasting qualities from other works. These awarenesses are the critical or receiving end of the Longinian "flash" proceeding from varying degrees of information and knowledge, unpredictable and largely unviable. They are doubtless a good thing for a teacher to have, but they cannot be taught to others; they can be only exhibited. If insight is like faith, a gift by the grace of God, there is no use in teaching at all—if insight-teaching is our only way of going about it. But if it is partly a gift and partly the result of labor (as Longinus thought), perhaps the teacher could find a discipline of language to expound to the class, with the hope that a latent gift of insight may be liberated.

Rhetoric is an unpopular word today, and it deserves to be, if we understand it as the "pragmatic dimension" of discourse as this has been defined by Charles W. Morris,[11] and other semanticists and positivists. In this view rhetoric is semantically irresponsible; its use is to move people to action which is at best morally neutral; or if it is good action, this result was no necessary part of the rhetorician's purpose. The doctrine is not new; it is only a pleasantly complex and double-talking revival of Greek sophistry. But if we think of rhetoric in another tradition, that of Aristotle and of later, Christian rhetoricians, we shall be able to see it as the study of the full language of experience, not the specialized languages of method.* Through this full language of experience Dante and Shakespeare could arrive at truth.

[10] Irving Babbitt (1865–1933), Professor of French at Harvard (1894–1933) and leader of the New Humanist movement. The impressionism that Babbitt detected is revealed in *Rousseau and Romanticism* (1919) especially.

[11] Charles W. Morris makes this definition in *Foundations of the Theory of Signs*, Vol. I, no. 2 of *The Encyclopedia of Unified Science*, Chicago, 1938.

* I hope it is plain by this time that by "rhetorical analysis" and the "study of rhetoric" I do not mean the prevailing *explication of texts*. If rhetoric is the *full* language of experience, its study must be informed by a peculiar talent, not wholly

This responsible use implies the previous study of the two lower, but not inferior, disciplines that I have already mentioned. One of these was once quaintly known as "grammar," the art that seems to be best learned at the elementary stage in a paradigmatic language like Latin. I think of a homely exemplum that will illustrate one of the things that have happened since the decay of grammar. I had a student at the University of Chicago who wrote a paper on T. S. Eliot's religious symbolism, in which he failed to observe that certain sequences of words in "Ash Wednesday" are without verbs: he had no understanding of the relation of the particulars to the universals in Eliot's diction. The symbols floated, in this student's mind, in a void of abstraction; the language of the poem was beyond his reach. Is the domination of historical scholarship responsible for the decline of the grammatical arts? I think that it may be; but it would not follow from its rejection that these arts or their equivalent would rise again. (One must always be prepared for the rise of nothing.) My Chicago student was laudably trying to read the text of the poem; he had nothing but a good mind and good intentions to read it with. What he had done, of course, was to abstract Eliot's symbols out of their full rhetorical context, so that they had become neither Eliot's nor anybody else's symbols. They were thus either critically useless, or potentially useful in a *pragmatic dimension* of discourse where ideas may be *power*: as the fullback is said to "bull" through the opposing line. The rhetorical disciplines, which alone seem to yield something like the full import of the work of imagination, are by-passed; and we by-pass these fundamentals of understanding no less when we read our own language. All reading is translation, even in the native tongue; for translation may be described as the act of mediation between universals and particulars in the complex of metaphor. As qualified translators we are inevitably rhetoricians. One scarcely sees how the student (like the Chicago student, who is also the Minnesota, the Harvard, and the Cornell student) can be expected to begin the study of rhetoric at the top, particularly if below it there is no bottom. If he begins at the top, as a "critic," he may become the victim of "insights" and "evaluations" that he has not earned, or he may parrot critical systems that his instructors have expounded or perhaps merely alluded to, in class. In any case, man being by nature, or by the nature of his language, a rhetorician, the student becomes a bad rhetorician. It is futile to expect him to be a critic when he has not yet learned how to read.

How can rhetoric, or the arts of language, be taught today? We are not likely to begin teaching something in which we do not believe: we do not believe in the uses of rhetoric because we do not believe that the full language of the human situation can be the vehicle of truth. We are not facing the problem when we circumvent it by asking the student to study the special languages of "criticism," in which we should like to believe. Can we believe in the language of humane truth without believing in the possibility of a

---

reducible to method, which I have in the past called the "historical imagination," a power that has little to do with the academic routine of "historical method." For a brilliant recent statement of this difference, see "Art and the Sixth Sense" by Philip Rahv, *Partisan Review,* vol. IX, no. 2 (March–April, 1952), pp. 225–233. The "sixth sense" is the historical imagination. [Tate's note.]

higher unity of truth, which we must posit as *there*, even if it must remain
beyond our powers of understanding? Without such a belief are we not
committed to the assumption that literature has nothing to do with truth, that
it is only illusion, froth on the historical current, the Platonic *gignomenon*?[12] We
languish, then, in the pragmatic vortex where ideas are disembodied into power;
but power for what it is not necessary here to try to say. I turn now to literary
criticism as it seems to be in itself, apart from any question of teaching it.

II

We have reached the stage of activity in individual criticism at which we
begin to ask whether what we severally do has, or ought to have, a common
end. What has a common end may be better reached, or at any rate more effi-
ciently pursued, if the long ways to it are by-passed for the short ways—if
happily we can agree on a common methodology, or at worst a few cooperating
methodologies. The image that this enticing delusion brings to mind is that
of the cheerful, patient bulldozer leveling off an uncharted landscape. The
treeless plain thus made could be used as a desert—by those who can use
deserts—or as an airfield from which to fly somewhere else.

The notes that follow I have put in the form of propositions, or theses,
which either I or some imaginable person might be presumed to uphold at
the present time. Some will be found to contradict others; but this is to be
expected when we try to distinguish the aims and habits of literary critics over
a period so long as a quarter of a century. The ten theses will affirm, deny,
or question a belief or a practice.

I. Literary criticism is in at least one respect (perhaps more than one)
like a mule: it cannot reproduce itself, though, like a mule, it is capable of
trying. Its end is outside itself. If the great formal works of literature are not
wholly autonomous, criticism, however theoretical it may become, is necessarily even less so. It cannot in the long run be practiced apart from what it
confronts, that gives rise to it. It has no formal substance: it is always *about*
something else. If it tries to be about itself, and sets up on its own, it initiates
the infinite series: one criticism within another leading to another criticism
progressively more formal-looking and abstract; or it is progressively more irrelevant to its external end as it attends to the periphery, the historical buzz in the
ear of literature.

II. The more systematic and methodical, the "purer," criticism becomes,
the less one is able to feel in it the presence of its immediate occasion. It tends
more and more to *sound* like philosophical discourse. There are countless degrees, variations, and overlappings of method, but everyone knows that there
are three typical directions that method may take: (1) Aesthetics, which aims
at the ordering of criticism within a large synthesis of either experimental
psychology or ontology; from the point of view of which it is difficult to say
anything about literature that is not merely pretentious. For example: Goethe's

---

[12] A discrete and sharply experienced "happening" that is not susceptible of integration into a system of cause and effect.

Concrete Universal,[13] Coleridge's Esemplastic Power,[14] Croce's Expression.[15] (2) Analysis of literary language, or "stylistics" (commonly supposed to be the orbit of the New Criticism). Without the correction of a total rhetoric, this *techné*[16] must find its limit, if it is not at length to become only a habit, in the extreme "purity" of nominalism ("positivism") or of metaphysics. (3) Historical scholarship, the "purest" because the most methodical criticism of all, offers the historical reconstruction as the general possibility of literature, without accounting for the unique, miraculous superiority of *The Tempest* or of *Paradise Lost*.

III. When we find criticism appealing to phrases like "frame of reference," "intellectual discipline," or even "philosophical basis," it is not improper to suspect that the critic is asking us to accept his "criticism" on the authority of something in which he does not believe. The two first phrases contain perhaps hidden analogies to mathematics; the third, a metaphor of underpinning. This is nothing against them; all language is necessarily figurative. But used as I have indicated, the phrases have no ontological, or substantive, meaning. The critic is only avoiding the simple word truth, and begging the question. Suppose we acknowledge that the critic, as he begs this question, gives us at the same moment a new and just insight into a scene in *The Idiot*[17] or *King Lear*. Yet the philosophical language in which he visibly expounds the insight may seem to reflect an authority that he has not visibly earned. The language of criticism had better not, then, try to be univocal. It is neither fish nor fowl, yet both, with that unpleasant taste that we get from fishing ducks.

IV. Literary criticism may become prescriptive and dogmatic when the critic achieves a coherence in the logical and rhetorical orders which exceeds the coherence of the imaginative work itself in those orders. We substitute with the critic a dialectical order for the elusive, and perhaps quite different, order of the imagination. We fall into the trap of the logicalization of parts discretely attended. This sleight of hand imposed upon the reader's good faith invites him to share the critic's own intellectual pride. Dazzled by the refractions of the critic's spectrum, the reader accepts as his own the critic's dubious superiority to the work as a whole. He is only attending serially to the separated parts in which he worships his own image. This is critical idolatry; the idols of its three great sects are the techniques of purity described in Thesis II.

V. If criticism undertakes the responsibility and the privilege of a strict theory of knowledge, the critic will need all the humility that human nature is capable of, almost the self-abnegation of the saint. Is the critic willing to test his epistemology against a selfless reading of *The Rape of the Lock, War and*

---

[13] A particular image, character, object, or event in literature that represents the class of which it is a member; that is, a sharply individualized character who is representative of all humanity.

[14] The power of the imagination that fuses and coalesces heterogeneous elements.

[15] Benedetto Croce (1866–1952), Italian philosopher, argued in *Aesthetics* (1902) the identity of intuition and expression. He argued that there is no knowledge of a thing until it is expressed, even if one only expresses what he knows to himself.

[16] Art, skill.

[17] A novel by the Russian author Feodor Dostoevski (1821–1881) published in 1869.

Peace, or a lyric by Thomas Nashe?[18] Or is his criticism merely the report of a quarrel between the imagined life of the work and his own "philosophy"? Has possession of the critic by a severe theory of knowledge interfered with the primary office of criticism? What is the primary office of criticism? Is it to expound and to elucidate, with as little distortion as possible, the knowledge of life contained by the novel or the poem or the play? What critic has ever done this?

VI. A work of the imagination differs from a work of the logical intellect in some radical sense that seems to lie beyond our comprehension. But this much may be said: the imaginative work admits of neither progressive correction nor substitution or rearrangement of parts; it is never obsolete, it is always up-to-date. Dryden does not "improve" Shakespeare; Shakespeare does not replace Dante, in the way that Einstein's physics seems to have "corrected" Newton's. There is no competition among poems. A good poem suggests the possibility of other poems equally good. But criticism is perpetually obsolescent and replaceable.

VII. The very terms of elucidation—the present ones, like any others—carry with them, concealed, an implicated judgment. The critic's rhetoric, laid out in his particular grammar, is the critic's mind. This enables him to see much that is there, a little that is there, nothing that is there, or something that is not there; but none of these with perfect consistency. We may ask again: to what extent is the critic obligated to dredge the bottom of his mind and to exhibit to an incredulous eye his own skeleton? We might answer the question rhetorically by saying: We are constantly trying to smoke out the critic's "position." This is criticism of criticism. Should we succeed in this game to our perfect satisfaction, we must be on guard lest our assent to or dissent from a critic's "position" mislead us into supposing that his gift of elucidation is correspondingly impressive or no good. If absolutely just elucidation were possible, it would also be philosophically sound, even though the critic might elsewhere announce his adherence to a philosophy that we should want to question.

VIII. If the implicated judgment is made overt, is there not in it an invitation to the reader to dismiss or to accept the work before he has read it? Even though he "read" the work first? (Part of this question is dealt with in Thesis V.) Is *a priori* judgment in the long run inevitable? What unformulated assumption lurks, as in the thicket, back of T. S. Eliot's unfavorable comparison of "Ripeness is all" with *"E'n la sua voluntade è nostra pace"?*[19] Is Shakespeare's summation of life naturalistic, pagan, and immature? J. V. Cunningham has shown that "Ripeness is all" is a statement within the natural law, quite as Christian as Dante's statement within the divine law.[20] The beacon of con-

18 *The Rape of the Lock* (1712), a mock-epic poem by Alexander Pope (1688–1744); *War and Peace* (1865–1869), an epic novel by Leo Tolstoy (1825–1910); Thomas Nashe (1567–1601), English poet and satirist.

19 Eliot makes the unfavorable comparison in "Shakespeare," "Hamlet," and "Dante," three essays in *Selected Essays* (1950; see pp. 116–117; p. 226, for example); and in his introduction to *The Wheel of Fire* (1930) by G. Wilson Knight. The Italian phrase, from Dante's *Purgatorio,* III. 85, means "And in his will is our peace." "Ripeness is all" comes from *King Lear,* V. ii. 11.

20 Cunningham makes this point in *Woe or Wonder,* 1951.

ceptual thought as end rather than means in criticism is a standing menace to critical order because it is inevitable, human nature being what it is. One thing that human nature is, is "fallen."

IX. In certain past ages there was no distinct activity of the mind conscious of itself as literary criticism; for example, the age of Sophocles and the age of Dante. In the age of Dante the schoolmen held that poetry differed from scriptural revelation in its *historia,* or fable, at which, in poetry, the literal event could be part or even all fiction. But the other, higher meanings of poetry might well be true, in spite of the fictional plot, if the poet had the gift of anagogical, or spiritual, insight. Who was capable of knowing when the poet had achieved this insight? Is literary criticism possible without a criterion of absolute truth? Would a criterion of absolute truth make literary criticism as we know it unnecessary? Can it have a relevant criterion of truth without acknowledging an emergent order of truth in its great subject matter, literature itself?

X. Literary criticism, like the Kingdom of God on earth, is perpetually necessary and, in the very nature of its middle position between imagination and philosophy, perpetually impossible. Like a man, literary criticism is nothing in itself; criticism, like man, embraces pure experience or exalts pure rationality at the price of abdication from its dual nature. It is of the nature of man and of criticism to occupy the intolerable position. Like man's, the intolerable position of criticism has its own glory. It is the only position that it is ever likely to have.

W. K. Wimsatt, Jr., and Monroe C. Beardsley

THE INTENTIONAL FALLACY

W. K. Wimsatt, Jr., was born in Washington, D.C., in 1907. He received the degrees of B.A. and M.A. from Georgetown University in 1928 and 1929. After taking his Ph.D. at Yale in 1939 he began teaching in that university, where he is now Professor of English Literature. He is the author of *The Prose Style of Samuel Johnson* (1941), *Philosophic Words* (1948), *The Verbal Icon: Studies in the Meaning of Poetry* (1954), and, with Cleanth Brooks, *Literary Criticism: A Short History* (1957).

Monroe C. Beardsley was born in Connecticut in 1917 and received his graduate and undergraduate degrees from Yale. Since 1947 he has taught at Swarthmore College, where he is now Professor of Philosophy. He is the author of *Practical Logic* (1950), *Thinking Straight* (rev. ed., 1966), *Aesthetics: Problems in the Philosophy of Criticism* (1958), *Aesthetics from Ancient Greece to the Present: A Short History* (1966), and, with Elizabeth Beardsley, *Philosophical Thinking: An Introduction* (1965).

The special quality of authority that characterizes Professor Wimsatt's critical writings has long been recognized; it is the product of a lucid intelligence, analytic rigor, and impeccable scholarship. Critics who are unsympathetic to the contextual approach to literature—an approach based on the notion that the proper business of criticism is to study the relations of part to part within a literary work, rather than the work's relations to the man who wrote it or to the historical moment in which it was written—have found that above all it was Wimsatt's arguments for contextual criticism that they had to counter. Three essays on which he contextual criticism that they had to counter. The three essays written in collaboration with Professor Beardsley, "The Affective Fallacy," "The Concept of Meter: An Exercise in Abstraction," and "The Intentional Fallacy," reprinted below, have especially occasioned much debate.

The claim of the author's "intention" upon the critic's judgment has been challenged in a number of recent discussions, notably in the debate entitled

The Personal Heresy, between Professors Lewis and Tillyard.[1] But it seems doubtful if this claim and most of its romantic corollaries are as yet subject to any widespread questioning. The present writers, in a short article entitled "Intention" for a *Dictionary** of literary criticism, raised the issue but were unable to pursue its implications at any length. We argued that the design or intention of the author is neither available nor desirable as a standard for judging the success of a work of literary art, and it seems to us that this is a principle which goes deep into some differences in the history of critical attitudes. It is a principle which accepted or rejected points to the polar opposites of classical "imitation" and romantic expression. It entails many specific truths about inspiration, authenticity, biography, literary history and scholarship, and about some trends of contemporary poetry, especially its allusiveness. There is hardly a problem of literary criticism in which the critic's approach will not be qualified by his view of "intention."

"Intention," as we shall use the term, corresponds to *what he intended* in a formula which more or less explicitly has had wide acceptance. "In order to judge the poet's performance, we must know *what he intended.*" Intention is design or plan in the author's mind. Intention has obvious affinities for the author's attitude toward his work, the way he felt, what made him write.

We begin our discussion with a series of propositions summarized and abstracted to a degree where they seem to us axiomatic.

1. A poem does not come into existence by accident. The words of a poem, as Professor Stoll[2] has remarked, come out of a head, not out of a hat. Yet to insist on the designing intellect as a *cause* of a poem is not to grant the design or intention as a *standard* by which the critic is to judge the worth of the poet's performance.

2. One must ask how a critic expects to get an answer to the question about intention. How is he to find out what the poet tried to do? If the poet succeeded in doing it, then the poem itself shows what he was trying to do. And if the poet did not succeed, then the poem is not adequate evidence, and the critic must go outside the poem—for evidence of an intention that did not become effective in the poem. "Only one *caveat* must be borne in mind," says an eminent intentionalist† in a moment when his theory repudiates itself; "the poet's aim must be judged at the moment of the creative act, that is to say, by the art of the poem itself."

3. Judging a poem is like judging a pudding or a machine. One demands that it work. It is only because an artifact works that we infer the intention of an artificer. "A poem should not mean but be." A poem can *be* only through its *meaning*—since its medium is words—yet it *is,* simply *is,* in the sense that we have no excuse for inquiring what part is intended or meant. Poetry

---

[1] *The Personal Heresy* (Magnolia, Mass.: Smith, 1939).

* *Dictionary of World Literature,* Joseph T. Shipley, ed. (New York, 1942), 216–29. [Authors' note.]

[2] Elmer Edgar Stoll (1874–1959), American critic, for many years professor of English at the University of Minnesota, author of numerous books on Shakespeare, the most influential of which is *Art and Artifice in Shakespeare,* (Cambridge University Press, 1933).

† J. E. Spingarn, "The New Criticism," in *Criticism in America* (New York, 1924), 24–25. [Authors' note.]

is a feat of style by which a complex of meaning is handled all at once. Poetry suceeds because all or most of what is said or implied is relevant; what is irrelevant has been excluded, like lumps from pudding and "bugs" from machinery. In this respect poetry differs from practical messages, which are sucessful if and only if we correctly infer the intention. They are more abstract than poetry.

4. The meaning of a poem may certainly be a personal one, in the sense that a poem expresses a personality or state of soul rather than a physical object like an apple. But even a short lyric poem is dramatic, the response of a speaker (no matter how abstractly conceived) to a situation (no matter how universalized). We ought to impute the thoughts and attitudes of the poem immediately to the dramatic *speaker,* and if to the author at all, only by an act of biographical inference.

5. There is a sense in which an author, by revision, may better achieve his original intention. But it is a very abstract sense. He intended to write a better work, or a better work of a certain kind, and now has done it. But it follows that his former concrete intention was not his intention. "He's the man we were in search of, that's true," says Hardy's rustic constable, "and yet he's not the man we were in search of. For the man we were in search of was not the man we wanted."[3]

"Is not a critic," asks Professor Stoll, "a judge, who does not explore his own consciousness, but determines the author's meaning or intention, as if the poem were a will, a contract, or the constitution? The poem is not the critic's own." He has accurately diagnosed two forms of irresponsibility, one of which he prefers. Our view is yet different. The poem is not the critic's own and not the author's (it is detached from the author at birth and goes about the world beyond his power to intend about it or control it). The poem belongs to the public. It is embodied in language, the peculiar possession of the public, and it is about the human being, an object of public knowledge. What is said about the poem is subject to the same scrutiny as any statement in linguistics or in the general science of psychology.

A critic of our *Dictionary* article, Ananda K. Coomaraswamy, has argued* that there are two kinds of inquiry about a work of art: (1) whether the artist achieved his intentions; (2) whether the work of art "ought ever to have been undertaken at all" and so "whether it is worth preserving." Number (2), Coomaraswamy maintains, is not "criticism of any work of art *qua* work of art," but is rather moral criticism; number (1) is artistic criticism. But we maintain that (2) need not be moral criticism: that there is another way of deciding whether works of art are worth preserving and whether, in a sense, they "ought" to have been undertaken, and this is the way of objective criticism of works of art as such, the way which enables us to distinguish between a skillful murder and a skillful poem. A skillful murder is an example which Coomaraswamy uses, and in his system the difference between the murder and the poem is simply a "moral" one, not an "artistic" one, since each if carried out according to plan is "artistically" successful. We maintain that (2)

---

[3] The rustic constable is in *The Three Strangers,* by Thomas Hardy (1840–1928).
* Ananda K. Coomaraswamy, "Intention," in *American Bookman,* I (1944), 41–48. [Authors' note.]

is an inquiry of more worth than (1), and since (2) and not (1) is capable of distinguishing poetry from murder, the name "artistic criticism" is properly given to (2).

II

It is not so much a historical statement as a definition to say that the intentional fallacy is a romantic one. When a rhetorician of the first century A.D writes: "Sublimity is the echo of a great soul," or when he tells us that "Homer enters into the sublime actions of his heroes" and "shares the full inspiration of the combat," we shall not be surprised to find this rhetorician considered as a distant harbinger of romanticism and greeted in the warmest terms by Saintsbury. One may wish to argue whether Longinus should be called romantic, but there can hardly be a doubt that in one important way he is.

Goethe's three questions for "constructive criticism" are "What did the author set out to do? Was his plan reasonable and sensible, and how far did he succeed in carrying it out?" If one leaves out the middle question, one has in effect the system of Croce—the culmination and crowning philosophic expression of romanticism. The beautiful is the successful intuition-expression, and the ugly is the unsuccessful; the intuition or private part of art is *the* aesthetic fact, and the medium or public part is not the subject of aesthetic at all.

> The Madonna of Cimabue is still in the Church of Santa Maria Novella; but does she speak to the visitor of to-day as to the Florentines of the thirteenth century?
>
> *Historical interpretation* labours . . . to reintegrate in us the psychological conditions which have changed in the course of history. It . . . enables us to see a work of art (a physical object) as its *author saw it* in the moment of production.*

The first italics are Croce's, the second ours. The upshot of Croce's system is an ambiguous emphasis on history. With such passages as a point of departure a critic may write a nice analysis of the meaning or "spirit" of a play by Shakespeare or Corneille—a process that involves close historical study but remains aesthetic criticism—or he may, with equal plausibility, produce an essay in sociology, biography, or other kinds of non-aesthetic history.

III

> I went to the poets; tragic, dithyrambic, and all sorts. . . . I took them some of the most elaborate passages in their own writings, and asked what was the meaning of them. . . . Will you believe me? . . . there is

* It is true that Croce himself in his *Ariosto, Shakespeare and Corneille* (London, 1920), chap. VII, "The Practical Personality and the Poetical Personality," and in his *Defence of Poetry* (Oxford, 1933), 24, and elsewhere, early and late, has delivered telling attacks on emotive geneticism, but the main drive of the *Aesthetic* is surely toward a kind of cognitive intentionalism. [Authors' note.]

hardly a person present who would not have talked better about their poetry than they did themselves. Then I knew that not by wisdom do poets write poetry, but by a sort of genius and inspiration.[4]

That reiterated mistrust of the poets which we hear from Socrates may have been part of a rigorously ascetic view in which we hardly wish to participate, yet Plato's Socrates saw a truth about the poetic mind which the world no longer commonly sees—so much criticism, and that the most inspirational and most affectionately remembered, has proceeded from the poets themselves.

Certainly the poets have had something to say that the critic and professor could not say; their message has been more exciting: that poetry should come as naturally as leaves to a tree, that poetry is the lava of the imagination, or that it is emotion recollected in tranquillity.[5] But it is necessary that we realize the character and authority of such testimony. There is only a fine shade of difference between such expressions and a kind of earnest advice that authors often give. Thus Edward Young,[6] Carlyle, Walter Pater:

> I know two golden rules from *ethics,* which are no less golden in *Composition,* than in life. 1. *Know thyself;* 2dly, *Reverence thyself.*

> This is the grand secret for finding readers and retaining them: let him who would move and convince others, be first moved and convinced himself. Horace's rule, *Si vis me flere,*[7] is applicable in a wider sense than the literal one. To every poet, to every writer, we might say: Be true, if you would be believed.

> Truth! there can be no merit, no craft at all, without that. And further, all beauty is in the long run only *fineness* of truth, or what we call expression, the finer accommodation of speech to that vision within.

And Housman's little handbook to the poetic mind[8] yields this illustration:

> Having drunk a pint of beer at luncheon—beer is a sedative to the brain, and my afternoons are the least intellectual portion of my life—I would go out for a walk of two or three hours. As I went along, thinking of nothing in particular, only looking at things around me and following the progress of the seasons, there would flow into my mind, with sudden and unaccountable emotion, sometimes a line or two of verse, sometimes a whole stanza at once.

This is the logical terminus of the series already quoted. Here is a confession of how poems were written which would do as a definition of poetry just as well as "emotion recollected in tranquillity"—and which the young poet might equally well take to heart as a practical rule. Drink a pint of beer, relax, go walking, think on nothing in particular, look at things, surrender

[4] Socrates speaking in the *Apology* by Plato.
[5] Statements by Keats, Shelley, and Wordsworth, respectively.
[6] Edward Young (1683–1765), English poet, playwright, satirist.
[7] "If force compels me."
[8] *The Name and Nature of Poetry* (1933), by A. E. Housman (1859–1936).

yourself to yourself, search for the truth in your own soul, listen to the sound of your own inside voice, discover and express the *vraie vérité*.[9]

It is probably true that all this is excellent advice for poets. The young imagination fired by Wordsworth and Carlyle is probably closer to the verge of producing a poem than the mind of the student who has been sobered by Aristotle or Richards.[10] The art of inspiring poets, or at least of inciting something like poetry in young persons, has probably gone further in our day than ever before. Books of creative writing such as those issued from the Lincoln School are interesting evidence of what a child can do* All this, however, would appear to belong to an art separate from criticism—to a psychological discipline, a system of self-development, a yoga, which the young poet perhaps does well to notice, but which is something different from the public art of evaluating poems.

Coleridge and Arnold were better critics than most poets have been, and if the critical tendency dried up the poetry in Arnold and perhaps in Coleridge, it is not inconsistent with our argument, which is that judgment of poems is different from the art of producing them. Coleridge has given us the classic "anodyne" story, and tells what he can about the genesis of a poem which he calls a "psychological curiosity,"[11] but his definitions of poetry and of the poetic quality "imagination" are to be found elsewhere[12] and in quite other terms.

It would be convenient if the passwords of the intentional school, "sincerity," "fidelity," "spontaneity," "authenticity," "genuineness," "originality," could be equated with terms such as "integrity," "relevance," "unity," "function," "maturity," "subtlety," "adequacy," and other more precise terms of evaluation—in short, if "expression" always meant aesthetic achievement. But this is not so.

"Aesthetic" art, says Professor Curt Ducasse, an ingenious theorist of expression, is the conscious objectification of feelings, in which an intrinsic part is the critical moment. The artist corrects the objectification when it is not adequate. But this may mean that the earlier attempt was not successful in objectifying the self, or "it may also mean that it was a successful objectification of a self which, when it confronted us clearly, we disowned and repudiated in favor of another."† What is the standard by which we disown or accept the self? Professor Ducasse does not say. Whatever it may be, however, this

[9] The real truth.
[10] I. A. Richards, that is.
* See Hughes Mearns, *Creative Youth* (Garden City, 1925), esp. 10, 27–29. The technique of inspiring poems has apparently been outdone more recently by the study of inspiration in successful poets and other artists. See, for instance, Rosamond E. M. Harding, *An Anatomy of Inspiration* (Cambridge, 1940); Julius Portnoy, *A Psychology of Art Creation* (Philadelphia, 1942); Rudolf Arnheim and others, *Poets at Work* (New York, 1947); Phyllis Bartlett, *Poems in Process* (New York, 1951); Brewster Ghiselin (ed.), *The Creative Process: A Symposium* (Berkeley and Los Angeles, 1952). [Authors' note.]
[11] In a note to "Kubla Khan," Coleridge describes the poem as a "psychological curiosity," which he had dreamed after having taken an "anodyne," probably laudanum.
[12] Especially in *Biographia Literaria*.
† Curt Ducasse, *The Philosophy of Art* (New York, 1929), 116. [Authors' note.]

standard is an element in the definition of art which will not reduce to terms of objectification. The evaluation of the work of art remains public; the work is measured against something outside the author.

IV

There is criticism of poetry and there is author psychology, which when applied to the present or future takes the form of inspirational promotion; but author psychology can be historical too, and then we have literary biography, a legitimate and attractive study in itself, one approach, as Professor Tillyard would argue, to personality, the poem being only a parallel approach. Certainly it need not be with a derogatory purpose that one points out personal studies, as distinct from poetic studies, in the realm of literary scholarship. Yet there is danger of confusing personal and poetic studies; and there is the fault of writing the personal as if it were poetic.

There is a difference between internal and external evidence for the meaning of a poem. And the paradox is only verbal and superficial that what is (1) internal is also public: it is discovered through the semantics and syntax of a poem, through our habitual knowledge of the language, through grammars, dictionaries, and all the literature which is the source of dictionaries, in general through all that makes a language and culture; while what is (2) external is private or idiosyncratic; not a part of the work as a linguistic fact: it consists of revelations (in journals, for example, or letters or reported conversations) about how or why the poet wrote the poem—to what lady, while sitting on what lawn, or at the death of what friend or brother. There is (3) an intermediate kind of evidence about the character of the author or about private or semiprivate meanings attached to words or topics by an author or by a coterie of which he is a member. The meaning of words is the history of words, and the biography of an author, his use of a word, and the associations which the word had for *him*, are part of the word's history and meaning.* But the three types of evidence, especially (2) and (3), shade into one another so subtly that it is not always easy to draw a line between examples, and hence arises the difficulty for criticism. The use of biographical evidence need not involve intentionalism, because while it may be evidence of what the author intended, it may also be evidence of the meaning of his words and the dramatic character of his utterance. On the other hand, it may not be all this. And a critic who is concerned with evidence of type (1) and moderately with that of type (3) will in the long run produce a different sort of comment from that of the critic who is concerned with (2) and with (3) where it shades into (2).

The whole glittering parade of Professor Lowes' *Road to Xanadu*,[13] for instance, runs along the border between types (2) and (3) or boldly traverses the romantic region of (2). " 'Kubla Khan,' " says Professor Lowes, "is the fabric

---

*And the history of words *after* a poem is written may contribute meanings which if relevant to the original pattern should not be ruled out by a scruple about intention. [Authors' note.]

13 In *The Road to Xanadu, A Study of the Ways of the Imagination* (1927), John Livingston Lowes shows how much of Coleridge's reading was transformed by his imagination into the poems "Kubla Khan" and "The Ancient Mariner."

of a vision, but every image that rose up in its weaving had passed that way before. And it would seem that there is nothing haphazard or fortuitous in their return." This is not quite clear—not even when Professor Lowes explains that there were clusters of associations, like hooked atoms, which were drawn into complex relation with other clusters in the deep well of Coleridge's memory, and which then coalesced and issued forth as poems. If there was nothing "haphazard or fortuitous" in the way the images returned to the surface, that may mean (1) that Coleridge could not produce what he did not have, that he was limited in his creation by what he had read or otherwise experienced, or (2) that having received certain clusters of associations, he was bound to return them in just the way he did, and that the value of the poem may be described in terms of the experiences on which he had to draw. The latter pair of propositions (a sort of Hartleyan[14] associationism which Coleridge himself repudiated in the *Biographia*) may not be assented to. There were certainly other combinations, other poems, worse or better, that might have been written by men who had read Bartram and Purchas and Bruce and Milton.[15] And this will be true no matter how many times we are able to add to the brilliant complex of Coleridge's reading. In certain flourishes (such as the sentence we have quoted) and in chapter headings like "The Shaping Spirit," "The Magical Synthesis," "Imagination Creatix," it may be that Professor Lowes pretends to say more about the actual poems than he does. There is a certain deceptive variation in these fancy chapter titles; one expects to pass on to a new stage in the argument, and one finds—more and more sources, more and more about "the streamy nature of association.*

"Wohin der Weg?" quotes Professor Lowes for the motto of his book. "Kein Weg! Ins Unbetretene."[16] Precisely because the way is *unbetreten,* we should say, it leads away from the poem. Bartram's *Travels* contains a good deal of the history of certain words and of certain romantic Floridian conceptions that appear in "Kubla Khan." And a good deal of that history has passed and was then passing into the very stuff of our language. Perhaps a person who has read Bartram appreciates the poem more than one who has not. Or, by looking up the vocabulary of "Kubla Khan" in the *Oxford English Dictionary,* or by reading some of the other books there quoted, a person may know the poem better. But it would seem to pertain little to the poem to know that *Coleridge* had read Bartram. There is a gross body of life, of sensory and mental experience, which lies behind and in some sense causes every poem, but can never be and need not be known in the verbal and hence intellectual composition which is the poem. For all the objects of our manifold experience, for every unity, there is an action of the mind which cuts off roots, melts away context— or indeed we should never have objects or ideas or anything to talk about.

---

[14] David Hartley (1705–1757), English physician and philosopher, is the founder of associationist psychology, which holds that all consciousness is the result of the combination, according to a few laws of association, of simple and irreducible elements given from sense experience.

[15] Authors of works, phrases from which reappear in the two poems by Coleridge.

* Chaps. VIII, "The Pattern," and XVI, "The Known and Familiar Landscape," will be found of most help to the student of the poem. [Authors' note.]

[16] "Whither the way?" "No way. Upon the untrodden [way]."

It is probable that there is nothing in Professor Lowes' vast book which could detract from anyone's appreciation of either *The Ancient Mariner* or "Kubla Khan." We next present a case where preoccupation with evidence of type (3) has gone so far as to distort a critic's view of a poem (yet a case not so obvious as those that abound in our critical journals).

In a well known poem by John Donne appears this quatrain:

> Moving of th' earth brings harmes and feares,
>   Men reckon what it did and meant,
> But trepidation of the spheares,
>   Though greater farre, is innocent.[17]

A recent critic in an elaborate treatment of Donne's learning has written of this quatrain as follows:

> He touches the emotional pulse of the situation by a skillful allusion to the new and the old astronomy. . . . Of the new astronomy, the "moving of the earth" is the most radical principle; of the old, the "trepidation of the spheres" is the motion of the greatest complexity. . . . The poet must exhort his love to quietness and calm upon his departure; and for this purpose the figure based upon the latter motion (trepidation), long absorbed into the traditional astronomy, fittingly suggests the tension of the moment without arousing the "harmes and feares" implicit in the figure of the moving earth.[*]

The argument is plausible and rests on a well substantiated thesis that Donne was deeply interested in the new astronomy and its repercussions in the theological realm. In various works Donne shows his familiarity with Kepler's *De Stella Nova*, with Galileo's *Siderius Nuncius*, with William Gilbert's *De Magnete*, and with Clavius' commentary on the *De Sphaera* of Sacrobosco. He refers to the new science in his Sermon at Paul's Cross and in a letter to Sir Henry Goodyer. In *The First Anniversary* he says the "new philosophy calls all in doubt." In the *Elegy on Prince Henry* he says that the "least moving of the center" makes "the world to shake."

It is difficult to answer argument like this, and impossible to answer it with evidence of like nature. There is no reason why Donne might not have written a stanza in which the two kinds of celestial motion stood for two sorts of emotion at parting. And if we become full of astronomical ideas and see Donne only against the background of the new science, we may believe that he did. But the text itself remains to be dealt with, the analyzable vehicle of a complicated metaphor. And one may observe: (1) that the movement of the earth according to the Copernican theory is a celestial motion, smooth and regular, and while it might cause religious or philosophic fears, it could not be associated with the crudity and earthiness of the kind of commotion which the speaker in the poem wishes to discourage; (2) that there is another moving of the earth, an earthquake, which has just these qualities and is to be associated with the tear-floods and sigh-tempests of the second stanza of the poem;

---

[17] Third stanza of "A Valediction: Forbidding Mourning."

[*] Charles M. Coffin, *John Donne and the New Philosophy* (New York, 1927), 97–98. [Authors' note.]

(3) that "trepidation" is an appropriate opposite of earthquake, because each is a shaking or vibratory motion; and "trepidation of the spheres" is "greater far" than an earthquake, but not much greater (if two such motions can be compared as to greatness) than the annual motion of the earth; (4) that reckoning what it "did and meant" shows that the event has passed, like an earthquake, not like the incessant celestial movement of the earth. Perhaps a knowledge of Donne's interest in the new science may add another shade of meaning, an overtone to the stanza in question, though to say even this runs against the words. To make the geocentric and heliocentric antithesis the core of the metaphor is to disregard the English language, to prefer private evidence to public, external to internal.

V

If the distinction between kinds of evidence has implications for the historical critic, it has them no less for the contemporary poet and his critic. Or, since every rule for a poet is but another side of a judgment by a critic, and since the past is the realm of the scholar and critic, and the future and present that of the poet and the critical leaders of taste, we may say that the problems arising in literary scholarship from the intentional fallacy are matched by others which arise in the world of progressive experiment.

The question of "allusiveness," for example, as acutely posed by the poetry of Eliot, is certainly one where a false judgment is likely to involve the intentional fallacy. The frequency and depth of literary allusion in the poetry of Eliot and others has driven so many in pursuit of full meanings to the *Golden Bough* and the Elizabethan drama[18] that it has become a kind of commonplace to suppose that we do not know what a poet means unless we have traced him in his reading—a supposition redolent with intentional implications. The stand taken by F. O. Matthiessen is a sound one and partially forestalls the difficulty.

> If one reads these lines with an attentive ear and is sensitive to their sudden shifts in movement, the contrast between the actual Thames and the idealized vision of it during an age before it flowed through a megalopolis is sharply conveyed by that movement itself, whether or not one recognizes the refrain to be from Spenser.[19]

Eliot's allusions work when we know them—and to a great extent even when we do not know them, through their suggestive power.

But sometimes we find allusions supported by notes, and it is a nice question whether the notes function more as guides to send us where we

---

[18] T. S. Eliot, in footnotes to *The Waste Land,* refers to a number of seventeenth-century English plays and to *The Golden Bough* (published in its first, shorter version in 1890), by Sir James George Frazer (1854–1941), as containing material used by Eliot in *The Waste Land.* The main concern of *The Golden Bough* is the relations among primitive myth, magic, and ritual.

[19] See F. O. Matthiessen, *The Achievement of T. S. Eliot* (with a chapter on Eliot's later work by C. L. Barber) third edition, Oxford University Press, 1958, p. 47. All the quotations from Matthiessen occur between pages 47 and 53 of this edition.

may be educated, or more as indications in themselves about the character of the allusions. "Nearly everything of importance . . . that is apposite to an appreciation of 'The Waste Land,' " writes Matthiessen of Miss Weston's book, "has been incorporated into the structure of the poem itself, or into Eliot's Notes." And with such an admission it may begin to appear that it would not much matter if Eliot invented his sources (as Sir Walter Scott invented chapter epigraphs from "old plays" and "anonymous" authors, or as Coleridge wrote marginal glosses for *The Ancient Mariner*). Allusions to Dante, Webster, Marvell, or Baudelaire doubtless gain something because these writers existed, but it is doubtful whether the same can be said for an allusion to an obscure Elizabethan:

> The sound of horns and motors, which shall bring
> Sweeney to Mrs. Porter in the spring.

"Cf. Day, *Parliament of Bees:*" says Eliot,

> When of a sudden, listening, you shall hear,
> A noise of horns and hunting, which shall bring
> Actaeon to Diana in the spring,
> Where all shall see her naked skin.[20]

The irony is completed by the quotation itself; had Eliot, as is quite conceivable, composed these lines to furnish his own background, there would be no loss of validity. The conviction may grow as one reads Eliot's next note: "I do not know the origin of the ballad from which these lines are taken: it was reported to me from Sydney, Australia." The important word in this note—on Mrs. Porter and her daughter who washed their feet in soda water— is "ballad." And if one should feel from the lines themselves their "ballad" quality, there would be little need for the note. Ultimately, the inquiry must focus on the integrity of such notes as parts of the poem, for where they constitute special information about the meaning of phrases in the poem, they ought to be subject to the same scrutiny as any of the other words in which it is written. Matthiessen believes the notes were the price Eliot "had to pay in order to avoid what he would have considered muffling the energy of his poem by extended connecting links in the text itself." But it may be questioned whether the notes and the need for them are not equally muffling. F. W. Bateson has plausibly argued that Tennyson's "The Sailor Boy" would be better if half the stanzas were omitted,[21] and the best versions of ballads like "Sir Patrick Spens" owe their power to the very audacity with which the minstrel has taken for granted the story upon which he comments. What then if a poet finds he cannot take so much for granted in a more recondite context and rather than write informatively, supplies notes? It can be said in favor of this plan that at least the notes do not pretend to be dramatic, as they would if written in verse. On the other hand, the notes may look like unassimilated material

[20] The first two lines quoted are lines 197–198 of *The Waste Land*; the second quotation is from Eliot's footnote to line 197. Reprinted by permission of the publishers: Harcourt, Brace & World, Inc., New York; and Faber and Faber Limited, London.

[21] In *English Poetry and the English Language* (Oxford, 1934).

lying loose beside the poem, necessary for the meaning of the verbal symbol, but not integrated, so that the symbol stands incomplete.

We mean to suggest by the above analysis that whereas notes tend to seem to justify themselves as external indexes to the author's *intention,* yet they ought to be judged like any other parts of a composition (verbal arrangement special to a particular context), and when so judged their reality as parts of the poem, or their imaginative integration with the rest of the poem, may come into question. Matthiessen, for instance, sees that Eliot's titles for poems and his epigraphs are informative apparatus, like the notes. But while he is worried by some of the notes and thinks that Eliot "appears to be mocking himself for writing the note at the same time that wants to convey something by it," Matthiessen believes that the "device" of epigraphs "is not at all open to the objection of not being sufficiently structural." "The *intention,*" he says, "is to enable the poet to secure a condensed expression in the poem itself." "In each case the epigraph is *designed* to form an integral part of the effect of the poem." And Eliot himself, in his notes, has justified his poetic practice in terms of intention.

> The Hanged Man, a member of the traditional pack, fits my purpose in two ways: because he is associated in my mind with the Hanged God of Frazer, and because I associate him with the hooded figure in the passage of the disciples to Emmaus in Part V. . . . The man with Three Staves (an authentic member of the Tarot pack) I associate, quite arbitrarily, with the Fisher King himself.[22]

And perhaps he is to be taken more seriously here, when off guard in a note, than when in his Norton Lectures he comments on the difficulty of saying what a poem means and adds playfully that he thinks of prefixing to a second edition of *Ash Wednesday* some lines from *Don Juan:*

> I don't pretend that I quite understand
> My own meaning when I would be *very* fine;
> But the fact is that I have nothing planned
> Unless it were to be a moment merry.[23]

If Eliot and other contemporary poets have any characteristic fault, it may be in *planning* too much.

Allusiveness in poetry is one of several critical issues by which we have illustrated the more abstract issue of intentionalism, but it may be for today the most important illustration. As a poetic practice allusiveness would appear to be in some recent poems an extreme corollary of the romantic intentionalist assumption, and as a critical issue it challenges and brings to light in a special way the basic premise of intentionalism. The following instance from the poetry of Eliot may serve to epitomize the practical implications of what we have been saying. In Eliot's "Love Song of J. Alfred Prufrock," toward the end, occurs the line: "I have heard the mermaids singing, each to each," and this bears a certain resemblance to a line in a Song by John Donne, "Teach me to

[22] Note to line 4 of *The Waste Land.*
[23] See T. S. Eliot, *The Use of Poetry and the Use of Criticism* (the Charles Eliot Norton Lectures for 1932–1933), ed. 2 (London: Faber and Faber, 1964), p. 31.

heare Mermaids singing," so that for the reader acquainted to a certain degree
with Donne's poetry, the critical question arises: Is Eliot's line an allusion to
Donne's? Is Prufrock thinking about Donne? Is Eliot thinking about Donne?
We suggest that there are two radically different ways of looking for an answer
to this question. There is (1) the way of poetic analysis and exegesis, which
inquires whether it makes any sense if Eliot-Prufrock *is* thinking about Donne.
In an earlier part of the poem, when Prufrock asks, "Would it have been worth
while, . . . To have squeezed the universe into a ball," his words take half their
sadness and irony from certain energetic and passionate lines of Marvell "To his
Coy Mistress." But the exegetical inquirer may wonder whether mermaids
considered as "strange sights" (to hear them is in Donne's poem analogous to
getting with child a mandrake root) have much to do with Prufrock's mermaids, which seem to be symbols of romance and dynamism, and which incidentally have literary authentication, if they need it, in a line of a sonnet
by Gérard de Nerval.[24] This method of inquiry may lead to the conclusion
that the given resemblance between Eliot and Donne is without significance
and is better not thought of, or the method may have the disadvantage of
providing no certain conclusion. Nevertheless, we submit that this is the true
and objective way of criticism, as contrasted to what the very uncertainty of
exegesis might tempt a second kind of critic to undertake: (2) the way of biographical or genetic inquiry, in which, taking advantage of the fact that Eliot
is still alive, and in the spirit of a man who would settle a bet, the critic
writes to Eliot and asks what he meant, or if he had Donne in mind. We shall
not here weigh the probabilities—whether Eliot would answer that he meant
nothing at all, had nothing at all in mind—a sufficiently good answer to such
a question—or in an unguarded moment might furnish a clear and, within its
limit, irrefutable answer. Our point is that such an answer to such an inquiry
would have nothing to do with the poem "Prufrock"; it would not be a critical
inquiry. Critical inquiries, unlike bets, are not settled in this way. Critical inquiries are not settled by consulting the oracle.

[24] Pseudonym of Gérard Labrunie (1808–1885). The sonnet is "El Desdichado"
("The Disinherited"), in which Nerval writes, "I have/Dreamed where the siren
swims in her sea-cave."

René Wellek and Austin Warren

LITERARY THEORY, CRITICISM, AND HISTORY

René Wellek was born in Vienna in 1903. After receiving his doctorate in 1926 from the Charles University in Prague, he came to the United States, where he taught at Princeton University and Smith College until 1930. He then taught at Prague until 1935, at the University of London until 1939, and at the State University of Iowa until 1946, when he came to Yale University, where in 1951 he became Sterling Professor of Comparative Literature. One of America's most distinguished literary scholars, he has been awarded honorary degrees by Oxford, Harvard, and Columbia Universities, and by the University of Rome. His encyclopedic *History of Modern Criticism* (five vols., four of which have been published, 1955–1965) is the indispensable work on its subject. Professor Wellek is also the author of *Kant in England* (1931), *The Rise of English Literary History* (1941), *Concepts of Criticism* (1963), and *Confrontations* (1965).

Austin Warren was born in Waltham, Massachusetts, in 1899. He received his B.A. from Wesleyan University, his M.A. from Harvard, and his Ph.D. from Princeton. He has taught at the universities of Kentucky and Minnesota, at Boston University, and at the State University of Iowa; in 1948 he joined the faculty of the University of Michigan as Professor of English and American Literature. He has been associate editor of the *New England Quarterly, American Literature,* and *Comparative Literature.* He is the author of *Alexander Pope as Critic and Humanist* (1929), *The Elder Henry James* (1934), *Richard Crashaw, a Study in Baroque Sensibility* (1939), *Rage for Order: Essays in Criticism* (1948), *New England Saints* (1956), and *The New England Conscience* (1966).

In the preface to their *Theory of Literature* (1942), from which Chapter IV, "Literary Theory, Criticism, History," has been reproduced below, Warren and Wellek explain that they have "sought to unite 'poetics' (or literary theory) and 'criticism' (evaluation of literature) with 'scholarship' ('research') and 'literary history' (the 'dynamics' of literature, in contrast to the 'statics' of theory and criticism)." They insist that "scholarship" and criticism are compatible, and this insistence distinguishes them from a number of writers who are thought of as exemplary New Critics. On the other hand, their pointed refusal "to distinguish between 'contemporary' and past literature," and their championing of the intrinsic study of literature (which considers each work as "a structure of norms") over "the extrinsic approach" (which considers works in their relations to biography, psychology, society, ideas, or the other arts) place them firmly in the New Critical school.

As we have envisaged a rationale for the study of literature, we must conclude the possibility of a systematic and integrated study of literature. English affords no very satisfactory name for this. The most common terms for it are "literary scholarship" and "philology." The former term is objectionable only because it seems to exclude "criticism" and to stress the academic nature of the study; it is acceptable, doubtless, if one interprets the term "scholar" as inclusively as did Emerson.[1] The latter term, "philology," is open to many misunderstandings. Historically, it has been used to include not only all literary and linguistic studies but studies of all products of the human mind. Though its greatest vogue was in nineteenth-century Germany, it still survives in the titles of such reviews as *Modern Philology, Philological Quarterly,* and *Studies in Philology.* Boeckh, who wrote a fundamental *Encyklopädie und Methodologie der philologischen Wissenschaften* (1877, but based on lectures partly dating back to 1809),* defined "philology" as the "knowledge of the known" and hence the study of language and literatures, arts and politics, religion and social customs. Practically identical with Greenlaw's "literary history,"[2] Boeckh's philology is obviously motivated by the needs of classical studies, for which the help of history and archaeology seems particularly necessary. With Boeckh, literary study is only one branch of philology, understood as a total science of civilization, particularly a science of what he, with German Romanticism, called the "National Spirit." Today, because of its etymology and much of the actual work of specialists, philology is frequently understood to mean linguistics, especially historical grammar and the study of past forms of languages. Since the term has so many and such divergent meanings, it is best to abandon it.

Another alternative term for the work of the literary scholar is "research." But this seems particularly unfortunate, for it stresses the merely preliminary search for materials and draws, or seems to draw, an untenable distinction between materials which have to be "searched for" and those which are easily available. For example, it is "research" when one visits the British Museum to read a rare book, while it apparently involves a different mental process to sit at home in an arm-chair and read a reprint of the same book. At most, the term "research" suggests certain preliminary operations, the extent and nature of which will vary greatly with the nature of the problem. But it ill suggests

---

[1] Ralph Waldo Emerson (1803–1882), in his Phi Beta Kappa oration, "The American Scholar," defines the scholar as "man thinking."
* Philip August Boeckh, *Encyklopädie und Methodologie der philologischen Wissenschaften,* Leipzig, 1877 (Second ed. 1886). [Authors' note.]
[2] In Edwin Greenlaw, *The Province of Literary History* (Baltimore, 1931).

those subtle concerns with interpretation, characterization, and evaluation which are peculiarly characteristic of literary studies.

Within our "proper study," the distinctions between literary theory, criticism, and history are clearly the most important. There is, first, the distinction between a view of literature as a simultaneous order and a view of literature which sees it primarily as a series of works arranged in a chronological order and as integral parts of the historical process. There is, then, the further distinction between the study of the principles and criteria of literature and the study of the concrete literary works of art, whether we study them in isolation or in a chronological series. It seems best to draw attention to these distinctions by describing as "literary theory" the study of the principles of literature, its categories, criteria, and the like, and by differentiating studies of concrete works of art as either "literary criticism" (primarily static in approach) or "literary history." Of course, "literary criticism" is frequently used in such a way as to include all literary theory; but such usage ignores a useful distinction. Aristotle was a theorist; Sainte-Beuve, primarily a critic. Kenneth Burke is largely a literary theorist, while R. P. Blackmur is a literary critic.[3] The term "theory of literature" might well include—as this book does— the necessary "theory of literary criticism" and "theory of literary history."

These distinctions are fairly obvious and rather widely accepted. But less common is a realization that the methods so designated cannot be used in isolation, that they implicate each other so thoroughly as to make inconceivable literary theory without criticism or history, or criticism without theory and history, or history without theory and criticism. Obviously, literary theory is impossible except on the basis of a study of concrete literary works. Criteria, categories, and schemes cannot be arrived at *in vacuo*.[4] But, conversely, no criticism or history is possible without some set of questions, some system of concepts, some points of reference, some generalizations. There is here, of course, no unsurmountable dilemma: we always read with some preconceptions, and we always change and modify these preconceptions upon further experience of literary works. The process is dialectical: a mutual interpenetration of theory and practice.

There have been attempts to isolate literary history from theory and criticism. For example, F. W. Bateson† argued that literary history shows A to derive from B, while criticism pronounces A to be better than B. The first type, according to this view, deals with verifiable facts; the second, with matters of opinion and faith. But this distinction is quite untenable. There are simply no data in literary history which are completely neutral "facts". Value judgements are implied in the very choice of materials: in the simple preliminary distinction between books and literature, in the mere allocation of space to this or that author. Even the ascertaining of a date or a title presupposes

[3] Charles Augustin Sainte-Beuve (1804–1869), French literary historian and critic; Kenneth Burke (b. 1897), who as well as being an author of numerous books of criticism and literary theory, writes poetry and fiction; R. P. Blackmur (1904– 1968), American educator, critic, and poet.

[4] In a vacuum.

† F. W. Bateson, "Correspondence," *Scrutiny*, IV (1935), pp. 181–85. [Authors' note.]

some kind of judgement, one which selects this particular book or event from the millions of other books and events. Even if we grant that there are facts comparatively neutral, facts such as dates, titles, biographical events, we merely grant the possibility of compiling the annals of literature. But any question a little more advanced, even a question of textual criticism or of sources and influences, requires constant acts of judgement. Such a statement, for example, as "Pope derives from Dryden" not only presupposes the act of selecting Dryden and Pope out of the innumerable versifiers of their times, but requires a knowledge of the characteristics of Dryden and Pope and then a constant activity of weighing, comparing, and selecting which is essentially critical. The question of the collaboration of Beaumont and Fletcher[5] is insoluble unless we accept such an important principle as that certain stylistic traits (or devices) are related to one rather than to the other of the two writers; otherwise we have to accept the stylistic differences merely as matter of fact.

But usually the case for the isolation of literary history from literary criticism is put on different grounds. It is not denied that acts of judgement are necessary, but it is argued that literary history has its own peculiar standards and criteria, i.e. those of the other ages. We must, these literary reconstructionists argue, enter into the mind and attitudes of past periods and accept their standards, deliberately excluding the intrusions of our own preconceptions. This view, called "historicism," was elaborated consistently in Germany during the nineteenth century, though even there it has been criticized by historical theorists of such eminence as Ernst Troeltsch.* It seems now to have penetrated directly or indirectly to England and the United States, and to it many of our "literary historians" more or less clearly profess allegiance. Hardin Craig, for instance, said that the newest and best phase of recent scholarship is the "avoidance of anachronistic thinking."† E. E. Stoll, studying the conventions of the Elizabethan stage and the expectations of its audience, works on the theory that the reconstruction of the author's intention is the central purpose of literary history.‡ Some such theory is implied in the many attempts to study Elizabethan psychological theories, such as the doctrine of humours, or of the scientific or pseudo-scientific conceptions of poets.§ Rosemond Tuve has tried to explain

[5] Francis Beaumont (c. 1584–1616) and John Fletcher (1579–1625) collaborated in the writing of over thirty plays.

* Ernst Troeltsch, *Der Historismus und seine Probleme,* Tübingen, 1922; *Der Historismus und seine Überwindung,* Berlin, 1924. [Authors' note.]

† Hardin Craig, *Literary Study and the Scholarly Profession,* Seattle, Wash., 1944, p. 70. *Cf.* also: "The last generation has rather unexpectedly decided that it will discover the meaning and values of old authors themselves and has pinned its faith to the idea, for example, that Shakespeare's own meaning is the greatest of Shakespearean meanings." Pp. 126–7. [Authors' note.]

‡ E.g., in *Poets and Playwrights,* Minneapolis, 1930, p. 217; and *From Shakespeare to Joyce,* New York, 1944, p. ix. [Authors' note.]

§ E.g., in Lily Campbell, *Shakespeare's Tragic Heroes: Slaves of Passion,* Cambridge, 1930; also Oscar J. Campbell, "What is the Matter with Hamlet?" *Yale Review,* XXXII (1942), pp. 309–22. Stoll holds to a different variety of historicism which insists on reconstructing stage conventions but attacks the reconstruction of psychological theories. See "Jacques and the Antiquaries," *From Shakespeare to Joyce,* pp. 138–45. [Authors' note.]

the origin and meaning of metaphysical imagery by reference to the training in Ramist logic received by Donne and his contemporaries.*

As such studies cannot but convince us that different periods have entertained different critical conceptions and conventions, it has been concluded that each age is a self-contained unity expressed through its own type of poetry, incommensurate with any other. This view has been candidly and persuasively expounded by Frederick A. Pottle in his *Idiom of Poetry*.† He calls his position that of "critical relativism," and speaks of profound "shifts of sensibility," of a "total discontinuity" in the history of poetry. His exposition is the more valuable as he combines it with an acceptance of absolute standards in ethics and religion.

At its finest, this conception of "literary history" requires an effort of imagination, of "empathy," of deep congeniality with a past age or a vanished taste. Successful efforts have been made to reconstruct the general outlook on life, the attitudes, conceptions, prejudices, and underlying assumptions of many civilizations. We know a great deal about the Greek attitude towards the gods, women, and slaves; we can describe the cosmology of the Middle Ages in great detail; and we have attempts to show the very different manner of seeing, or at least the very different artistic traditions and conventions, implied by Byzantine and Chinese art. Especially in Germany there is a plethora of studies, many of them influenced by Spengler,[6] on the Gothic man, the Baroque man—all supposed to be sharply set off from our time, living in a world of their own.

In the study of literature, this attempt at historical reconstruction has led to great stress on the intention of the author, which, it is supposed, can be studied in the history of criticism and literary taste. It is usually assumed that if we can ascertain this intention and can see that the author has fulfilled it, we can also dispose of the problem of criticism. The author has served a contemporary purpose, and there is no need or even possibility of further criticizing his work. The method thus leads to the recognition of a single critical standard, that of contemporary success. There are then not only one or two but literally hundreds of independent, diverse, and mutually exclusive conceptions of literature, each of which is in some way "right." The ideal of poetry is broken up in so many splinters that nothing remains of it: a general anarchy or, rather a levelling of all values must be the result. The history of literature is reduced to a series of discrete and hence finally incomprehensible fragments. A more moderate form is the view that there are polar poetical ideals which are so different that there is no common denominator between them: Classicism and Romanticism, the ideal of Pope and of Wordsworth, the poetry of statement and the poetry of implication.

The whole idea that the "intention" of the author is the proper subject

---

* "Imagery and Logic: Ramus and Metaphysical Poetics," *Journal of the History of Ideas,* III (1942), pp. 365–400. [Authors' note.]

† F. A. Pottle, *The Idiom of Poetry,* Ithaca, N. Y., 1941 (Second ed., 1946). [Authors' note.]

6 Oswald Spengler (1880–1936), German philosopher; author of *The Decline of the West.*

of literary history seems, however, quite mistaken. The meaning of a work of art is not exhausted by, or even equivalent to, its intention. As a system of values, it leads an independent life. The total meaning of a work of art cannot be defined merely in terms of its meaning for the author and his contemporaries. It is rather the result of a process of accretion, i.e. the history of its criticism by its many readers in many ages. It seems unnecessary and actually impossible to declare, as the historical reconstructionists do, that this whole process is irrelevant and that we must return only to its beginning. It is simply not possible to stop being men of the twentieth century while we engage in a judgement of the past: we cannot forget the associations of our own language, the newly acquired attitudes, the impact and import of the last centuries. We cannot become contemporary readers of Homer or Chaucer or members of the audience of the theatre of Dionysus in Athens[7] or of the Globe in London.[8] There will always be a decisive difference between an act of imaginative reconstruction and actual participation in a past point of view. We cannot really believe in Dionysus and laugh at him at the same time, as the audience of Euripides' *Bacchae* may have done;* and few of us can accept Dante's circles of Hell and mountain of Purgatory as literal truth. If we should really be able to reconstruct the meaning which *Hamlet* held for its contemporary audience, we would merely impoverish it. We would suppress the legitimate meanings which later generations found in *Hamlet*. We would bar the possibility of a new interpretation. This is not a plea for arbitrary subjective misreadings: the problem of a distinction between "correct" and wrong-headed readings will remain, and will need a solution in every specific case. The historical scholar will not be satisfied to judge a work of art merely from the point of view of our own time—a privilege of the practising critic, who will re-evaluate the past in terms of the needs of a present-day style or movement. It may be even instructive for him to look at a work of art from the point of view of a third time, contemporaneous neither with him nor with the author, or to survey the whole history of the interpretation and criticism of a work which will serve as a guide to the total meaning.

In practice, such clear-cut choices between the historical and the present-day point of view are scarcely feasible. We must beware of both false relativism and false absolutism. Values grow out of the historical process of valuation, which they in turn help us to understand. The answer to historical relativism is not a doctrinaire absolutism which appeals to "unchanging human nature" or the "universality of art." We must rather adopt a view for which the term "Perspectivism" seems suitable. We must be able to refer a work of art to the values of its own time and of all the periods subsequent to its own. A work of art is both "eternal" (i.e. preserves a certain identity) and "historical" (i.e. passes through a process of traceable development). Relativism reduces the history of literature to a series of discrete and hence discontinuous fragments, while most absolutisms serve either only a passing present-day situation or are based (like the standards

---

[7] Where the tragedies of Aeschylus, Sophocles, and Euripides were played.

[8] Built in 1598, and thereafter the home of Shakespeare's company of players.

* Cf. the exposition by Hoyt Trowbridge, "Aristotle and the New Criticism," *Sewanee Review*, LII (1944), pp. 537–55. [Authors' note.]

of the New Humanists,[9] the Marxists, and the Neo-Thomists[10]) on some abstract non-literary ideal unjust to the historical variety of literature. "Perspectivism" means that we recognize that there is one poetry, one literature, comparable in all ages, developing, changing, full of possibilities. Literature is neither a series of unique works with nothing in common nor a series of works enclosed in time-cycles of Romanticism or Classicism, the age of Pope and the age of Wordsworth. Nor is it, of course, the "block-universe" of sameness and immutability which an older Classicism conceived as ideal. Both absolutism and relativism are false; but the more insidious danger today, at least in England and the United States, is a relativism equivalent to an anarchy of values, a surrender of the task of criticism.

In practice, no literary history has ever been written without some principles of selection and some attempt at characterization and evaluation. Literary historians who deny the importance of criticism are themselves unconscious critics, usually derivative critics, who have merely taken over traditional standards and reputations. Usually, today, they are belated Romanticists who have closed their minds to all other types of art and especially to modern literature. But, as R. G. Collingwood has said very pertinently, a man "who claims to know what makes Shakespeare a poet is tacitly claiming to know whether Miss Stein[11] is a poet, and if not, why not."*

The exclusion of recent literature from serious study has been an especially bad consequence of this "scholarly" attitude. The term "modern" literature used to be interpreted so widely by academics that scarcely any work after Milton's was considered a quite respectable object of study. Since then, the eighteenth century has been accepted into good and regular standing as conventional literary history and has even become fashionable, since it appears to offer an escape into a more gracious, more stable, and more hierarchic world. The Romantic period and the later nineteenth century are also beginning to receive the attention of the scholars, and there are even a few hardy men in academic positions who defend and practise the scholarly study of contemporary literature.

The only possible argument against the study of living authors is the point that the student forgoes the perspective of the completed work, of the explication which later works may give to the implications of the earlier. But this disadvantage, valid only for developing authors, seems small compared to the advantages we have in knowing the setting and the time and in the opportunities for personal acquaintance and interrogation or at least correspondence. If many second-rate or even tenth-rate authors of the past are worth study, a first-rate or even second-rate author of our time is worth studying, too. It is usually lack of perception or timidity which makes academics reluctant

---

[9] Irving Babbitt (1865–1933) and Paul Elmer More (1864–1937) are prominent examples.

[10] Such as Jacques Maritain (b. 1882); professor of philosophy at Princeton.

[11] Gertrude Stein (1874–1946), American author, critic, patron of the arts.

* The example comes from Harold Cherniss, "The Biographical Fashion in Literary Criticism," *University of California Publications in Classical Philology*, XII (1943), pp. 179–93. [Authors' note.]

to judge for themselves. They profess to await the "verdict of the ages," not realizing that this is but the verdict of other critics and readers, including other professors. The whole supposed immunity of the literary historian to criticism and theory is thoroughly false, and that for a simple reason: every work of art is existing now, is directly accessible to observation, and is a solution of certain artistic problems whether it was composed yesterday or a thousand years ago. It cannot be analysed, characterized, or evaluated without a constant recourse to critical principles. "The literary historian must be a critic even in order to be an historian."*

Conversely, literary history is also highly important for literary criticism as soon as the latter goes beyond the most subjective pronouncement of likes and dislikes. A critic who is content to be ignorant of all historical relationships would constantly go astray in his judgements. He could not know which work is original and which derivative; and, through his ignorance of historical conditions, he would constantly blunder in his understanding of specific works of art. The critic possessed of little or no history is inclined to make slipshod guesses, or to indulge in autobiographical "adventures among masterpieces," and, on the whole, will avoid concern with the more remote past, content to hand that over to the antiquarian and the "philologist."

A case in point is medieval literature, especially English medieval literature, which—with the possible exception of Chaucer—has scarcely been approached from any aesthetic and critical point of view. The application of modern sensibility would give a different perspective to much Anglo-Saxon poetry or to the rich medieval lyric, just as, conversely, an introduction of historical points of view and a systematic examination of genetic problems could throw much light on contemporary literature. The common divorce between literary criticism and literary history has been detrimental to both.

---

* R. G. Collingwood, *Principles of Art,* Oxford, 1938, p. 4. As Allen Tate observes, "The scholar who tells us that he understands Dryden but makes nothing of Hopkins or Yeats is telling us that he does not understand Dryden," in "Miss Emily and the Bibliographer" (*Reason in Madness,* New York, 1941, p. 115). [Authors' note.]

Paul Valéry

POETRY AND
ABSTRACT THOUGHT

Paul Valéry (1871–1945) was born in Cette (now Sète) of a French father and an Italian mother. He went to school and to the university, where he studied law, at Montpellier; in 1892 he came to Paris. He soon began to publish, in small literary reviews, poems much influenced by the Symbolist writers, especially Mallarmé. But two short prose works, *Introduction à la méthode de Léonard de Vinci* (1895) and *La soirée avec Monsieur Teste* (1895), indicated that Valéry's interests were already turning from the writing of poetry to abstract speculation and to study. For fifteen years or so, in the leisure left him by his work in the War Office (beginning in 1897) and in the secretariat of the Havas News Agency (from 1900 until 1922) he wrote almost no poetry, but filled his famous *Cahiers* or notebooks with precise and rigorous analyses of problems in physics, mathematics, philosophy, linguistics, art, poetry, religion, politics, dreams, consciousness itself. These notebooks appeared posthumously in 29 volumes of 900 pages or so each.

In 1913 he was persuaded to put together a volume of his early poems; the reconsideration of these stimulated him into once more turning his attention to the serious writing of verse. The result was *La jeune parque* (1917) and *Charmes* (1922), which, together with the publication of works in prose, brought him such renown that after 1923 he was able to depend on writing alone for a livelihood. He became, indeed, not only a favorite of the most exclusive Parisian salons, but also in 1925 a member of the Académie française and in 1937 Professor of Poetry (a chair created especially for him) at the Collège de France. During the last twenty years of his life, through lectures at home and abroad, he became thought of as a pre-eminent representative of the contemporary French literary culture.

The idea of Poetry is often contrasted with that of Thought, and particularly "Abstract Thought." People say "Poetry and Abstract Thought" as they say Good and Evil, Vice and Virtue, Hot and Cold. Most people, without

From *The Collected Works of Paul Valéry*, edited by Jackson Mathews, Bollingen Series XIV, Volume 7, *The Art of Poetry*, translated by Denise Folliot (Copyright © 1958 by Bollingen Foundation, New York, N. Y.): "Poetry and Abstract Thought," pp. 52–81. Reprinted by permission of Princeton University Press and Routledge & Kegan Paul Ltd.

thinking any further, believe that the analytical work of the intellect, the efforts of will and precision in which it implicates the mind, are incompatible with that freshness of inspiration, that flow of expression, that grace and fancy which are the signs of poetry and which reveal it at its very first words. If a poet's work is judged profound, its profundity seems to be of a quite different order from that of a philosopher or a scientist. Some people go so far as to think that even meditation on his art, the kind of exact reasoning applied to the cultivation of roses, can only harm a poet, since the principal and most charming object of his desire must be to communicate the impression of a newly and happily born state of creative emotion which, through surprise and pleasure, has the power to remove the poem once and for all from any further criticism.

This opinion may possibly contain a grain of truth, though its simplicity makes me suspect it to be of scholarly origin. I feel we have learned and adopted this antithesis without reflection, and that we now find it firmly fixed in our mind, as a verbal contrast, as though it represented a clear and real relationship between two well-defined notions. It must be admitted that that character always in a hurry to have done, whom we call *our mind,* has a weakness for this kind of simplification, which freely enables him to form all kinds of combinations and judgments, to display his logic, and to develop his rhetorical resources—in short, to carry out as brilliantly as possible his business of being a mind.

At all events, this classic contrast, crystallized, as it were, by language, has always seemed to me too abrupt, and at the same time too facile, not to provoke me to examine the things themselves more closely.

Poetry, Abstract Thought. That is soon said, and we immediately assume that we have said something sufficiently clear and sufficiently precise for us to proceed, without having to go back over our experiences; and to build a theory or begin a discussion using this contrast (so attractive in its simplicity) as pretext, argument, and substance. One could even fashion a whole metaphysics—or at the least a "psychology"—on this basis, and evolve for oneself a system of mental life, of knowledge, and of the invention and production of works of the mind, whose consequence would inevitably be the same terminological dissonance that had served as its starting point. . . .[1]

For my part I have the strange and dangerous habit, in every subject, of wanting to begin at the beginning (that is, at my *own* beginning), which entails beginning again, going back over the whole road, just as though many others had not already mapped and traveled it. . . .

This is the road offered to us, or imposed on us, by *language.*

With every question, before making any deep examination of the content, I take a look at the language; I generally proceed like a surgeon who sterilizes his hands and prepares the area to be operated on. This is what I call *cleaning up the verbal situation.* You must excuse this expression equating the words and forms of speech with the hands and instruments of a surgeon.

I maintain that we must be careful of a problem's first contact with our

---

[1] The occasional dots at the end of paragraphs do not indicate omissions from the text. They are a part of the author's original punctuation.

minds. We should be careful of the first words a question utters in our mind. A new question arising in us is in a state of infancy; it stammers; it finds only strange terms, loaded with adventitious values and associations; it is forced to borrow these. But it thereby insensibly deflects our true need. Without realizing it we desert our original problem, and in the end we shall come to believe that we have chosen an opinion wholly our own, forgetting that our choice was exercised only on a mass of opinions that are the more or less blind work of other men and of chance. This is what happens with the programs of political parties, no one of which is (or can be) the one that would exactly match our temperament and our interests. If we choose one among them, we gradually become the man suited to that party and to that program.

Philosophical and aesthetic questions are so richly obscured by the quantity, diversity, and antiquity of researches, arguments, and solutions, all produced within the orbit of a very restricted vocabulary, of which each author uses the words according to his own inclinations, that taken as a whole such works give me the impression of a district in the classical Underworld especially reserved for deep thinkers. Here, are the Danaïdes, Ixions, and Sisyphuses,[2] eternally laboring to fill bottomless casks and to push back the falling rock, that is, to redefine the same dozen words whose combinations form the treasure of Speculative Knowledge.

Allow me to add to these preliminary considerations one last remark and one illustration. Here is the remark: you have surely noticed the curious fact that a certain *word*, which is perfectly clear when you hear or use it in *everyday* speech, and which presents no difficulty when caught up in the rapidity of an ordinary sentence, becomes mysteriously cumbersome, offers a strange resistance, defeats all efforts at definition, the moment you withdraw it from circulation for separate study and try to find its meaning after taking away its temporary function. It is almost comic to inquire the exact meaning of a term that one uses constantly with complete satisfaction. For example: I stop the word *Time* in its flight. This word was utterly limpid, precise, honest, and faithful in its service as long as it was part of a remark and was uttered by someone who wished to say something. But here it is, isolated, caught on the wing. It takes its revenge. It makes us believe that it has more meanings than uses. It was only a *means,* and it has become an *end,* the object of a terrible philosophical desire. It turns into an enigma, an abyss, a torment of thought. . . .

It is the same with the word *Life* and all the rest.

This readily observed phenomenon has taken on great critical value for me. Moreover, I have drawn from it an illustration that, for me, nicely conveys this strange property of our verbal material.

Each and every word that enables us to leap so rapidly across the chasm of thought, and to follow the prompting of an idea that constructs its own expression, appears to me like one of those light planks which one throws across a ditch or a mountain crevasse and which will bear a man crossing it

---

[2] The Danaïdes, 49 of the 50 daughters of Danaus, had to pour water into a vessel with holes in the bottom. Ixion was forever bound to a turning wheel. Sisyphus had to push up a hill a rock that rolled back down each time it reached the top.

rapidly. But he must pass without weighing on it, without stopping—above all, he must not take it into his head to dance on the slender plank to test its resistance! . . . Otherwise the fragile bridge tips or breaks immediately, and all is hurled into the depths. Consult your own experience; and you will find that we understand each other, and ourselves, only thanks to our *rapid passage over words*. We must not lay stress upon them, or we shall see the clearest discourse dissolve into enigmas and more or less learned illusions.

But how are we to think—I should say *rethink*, study deeply whatever seems to merit deep study—if we hold language to be something essentially provisional, as a banknote or a check is provisional, what we call its "value" requiring us to forget its true nature, which is that of a piece of paper, generally dirty? The paper has passed through so many hands. . . . But words have passed through so many mouths, so many phrases, so many uses and abuses, that the most delicate precautions must be taken to avoid too much confusion in our minds between what we think and are trying to think, and what dictionaries, authors, and, for that matter, the whole human race since the beginning of language, want us to think. . . .

I shall therefore take care not to accept what the words *Poetry* and *Abstract Thought* suggest to me the moment they are pronounced. But I shall look into myself. There I shall seek my real difficulties and my actual observations of my real states; there I shall find my own sense of the rational and the irrational; I shall see whether the alleged antithesis exists and how it exists in a living condition. I confess that it is my habit, when dealing with problems of the mind, to distinguish between those which I might have invented and which represent a need truly felt by my mind, and the rest, which are other people's problems. Of the latter, more than one (say forty per cent) seem to me to be nonexistent, to be no more than apparent problems: *I do not feel them.* And as for the rest, more than one seem to me to be badly stated. . . . I do not say I am right. I say that I observe what occurs within myself when I attempt to replace the verbal formulas by values and meanings that are nonverbal, that are independent of the language used. I discover naïve impulses and images, raw products of my needs and of my personal experiences. *It is my life itself that is surprised,* and my life must, if it can, provide my answers, for it is only in the reactions of our life that the full force, and as it were the necessity, of our truth can reside. The thought proceeding from that life never uses for its own account certain words which seem to it fit only for external consumption; nor certain others whose depths are obscure and which may only deceive thought as to its real strength and value.

I have, then, noticed in myself certain states which I may well call *poetic,* since some of them were finally realized in poems. They came about from no apparent cause, arising from some accident or other; they developed according to their own nature, and consequently I found myself for a time jolted out of my habitual state of mind. Then, the cycle completed, I returned to the rule of ordinary exchanges between my life and my thought. But meanwhile *a poem had been made,* and in completing itself the cycle left something behind. This closed cycle is the cycle of an act which has, as it were, aroused and given external form to a poetic power. . . .

On other occasions I have noticed that some no less insignificant incident caused—or seemed to cause—a quite different excursion, a digression of another nature and with another result. For example, a sudden concatenation of ideas, an analogy, would strike me in much the way the sound of a horn in the heart of a forest makes one prick up one's ears, and virtually directs the co-ordinated attention of all one's muscles toward some point in the distance, among the leafy depths. But this time, instead of a poem, it was an analysis of the sudden intellectual sensation that was taking hold of me. It was not verses that were being formed more or less easily during this phase, but some proposition or other that was destined to be incorporated among my habits of thought, some formula that would henceforward serve as an instrument for further researches. . . .

I apologize for thus revealing myself to you; but in my opinion it is more useful to speak of what one has experienced than to pretend to a knowledge that is entirely impersonal, an observation with no observer. In fact there is no theory that is not a fragment, carefully prepared, of some autobiography.

I do not pretend to be teaching you anything at all. I will say nothing you do not already know; but I will, perhaps, say it in a different order. You do not need to be told that a poet is not always incapable of solving a *rule of three;*[3] or that a logician is not always incapable of seeing in words something other than concepts, categories, and mere pretexts for syllogisms.

On this point I would add this paradoxical remark: if the logician could never be other than a logician, he would not, and could not, be a logician; and if the poet were never anything but a poet, without the slightest hope of being able to reason abstractly, he would leave no poetic traces behind him. I believe in all sincerity that if each man were not able to live a number of other lives besides his own, he would not be able to live his own life.

My experience has thus shown me that the same *self* can take very different forms, can become an abstract thinker or a poet, by successive specializations, each of which is a deviation from that entirely unattached state which is superficially in accord with exterior surroundings and which is the average state of our existence, the state of undifferentiated exchanges.

Let us first see in what may consist that initial and *invariably accidental* shock which will construct the poetic instrument within us, and above all, what are its effects. The problem can be put in this way: Poetry is an art of Language; certain combinations of words can produce an emotion that others do not produce, and which we shall call *poetic.* What kind of emotion is this?

I recognize it in myself by this: that all possible objects of the ordinary world, external or internal, beings, events, feelings, and actions, while keeping their usual appearance, are suddenly placed in an indefinable but wonderfully fitting relationship with the modes of our general sensibility. That is to say that these well-known things and beings—or rather the ideas that represent them— somehow change in value. They attract one another, they are connected in ways quite different from the ordinary; they become (if you will permit the expres-

---

[3] In mathematics, the rule for finding the fourth term of a proportion when three are given.

sion) *musicalized*, resonant, and, as it were, harmonically related. The poetic universe, thus defined, offers extensive analogies with what we can postulate of the dream world.

Since the word *dream* has found its way into this talk, I shall say in passing that in modern times, beginning with Romanticism, there has arisen a fairly understandable confusion between the notion of the dream and that of poetry. Neither the dream nor the daydream is necessarily poetic; it may be so: but figures formed *by chance* are only *by chance* harmonious figures.

In any case, our memories of dreams teach us, by frequent and common experience, that our consciousness can be invaded, filled, entirely absorbed by the production of an *existence* in which objects and beings seem the same as those in the waking state; but their meanings, relationships, modes of variation and of substitution are quite different and doubtless represent, like symbols or allegories, the immediate fluctuations of our *general* sensibility uncontrolled by the sensitivities of our *specialized* senses. In very much the same way the *poetic state* takes hold of us, develops, and finally disintegrates.

This is to say that the *state of poetry* is completely irregular, inconstant, involuntary, and fragile, and that we lose it, as we find it, *by accident*. But this state is not enough to make a poet, any more than it is enough to see a treasure in a dream to find it, on waking, sparkling at the foot of one's bed.

A poet's function—do not be startled by this remark—is not to experience the poetic state: that is a private affair. His function is to create it in others. The poet is recognized—or at least everyone recognizes his own poet—by the simple fact that he causes his reader to become "inspired." Positively speaking, inspiration is a graceful attribute with which the reader endows his poet: the reader sees in us the transcendent merits of virtues and graces that develop in him. He seeks and finds in us the wondrous cause of his own wonder.

But poetic feeling and the artificial synthesis of this state in some work are two quite distinct things, as different as sensation and action. A sustained action is much more complex than any spontaneous production, particularly when it has to be carried out in a sphere as conventional as that of language. Here you see emerging through my explanations the famous ABSTRACT THOUGHT which custom opposes to POETRY. We shall come back to that in a moment. Meanwhile I should like to tell you a true story, so that you may feel as I felt, and in a curiously clear way, the whole difference that exists between the poetic state or emotion, even creative and original, and the production of a work. It is a rather remarkable observation of myself that I made about a year ago.

I had left my house to relax from some tedious piece of work by walking and by a consequent change of scene. As I went along the street where I live, I was suddenly *gripped* by a rhythm which took possession of me and soon gave me the impression of some force outside myself. It was as though someone else were making use of my *living-machine*. Then another rhythm overtook and combined with the first, and certain strange *transverse* relations were set up between these two principles (I am explaining myself as best I can). They combined the movement of my walking legs and some kind of song I was murmuring, or rather which was being murmured *through me*. This composition became more and more complicated and soon in its complexity went far beyond anything I could reasonably produce with my ordinary, usable rhythmic faculties. The sense of strangeness that I mentioned became almost painful, almost disquieting. I am no musician; I am completely ignorant of musical technique; yet here I was, prey to a development in several parts more complicated than any poet could dream. I argued that there had been an error of person, that this grace had descended on the wrong head, since I could make no use of a gift which for a musician would doubtless have assumed value, form, and duration, while these parts that mingled and separated offered me in vain a composition whose cunningly organized sequence amazed my ignorance and reduced it to despair.

After about twenty minutes the magic suddenly vanished, leaving me on the bank of the Seine, as perplexed as the duck in the fable, that saw a swan emerge from the egg she had hatched. As the swan flew away, my surprise changed to reflection. I knew that walking often induces in me a quickened flow of ideas and that there is a certain reciprocity between my pace and my thoughts —my thoughts modify my pace; my pace provokes my thoughts—which after all is remarkable enough, but is fairly understandable. Our various "reaction periods" are doubtless synchronized, and it is interesting to have to admit that a reciprocal modification is possible between a form of action which is purely muscular and a varied production of images, judgments, and reasonings.

But in the case I am speaking of, my movement in walking became in my consciousness a very subtle system of rhythms, instead of instigating those images, interior words, and potential actions which one calls *ideas*. As for ideas, they are things of a species familiar to me; they are things that I can note, provoke, and handle. . . . *But I cannot say the same of my unexpected rhythms.*

What was I to think? I supposed that mental activity while walking must correspond with a general excitement exerting itself in the region of my brain; this excitement satisfied and relieved itself as best it could, and so long as its energy was expended, it mattered little whether this was on ideas, memories, or rhythms unconsciously hummed. On that day, the energy was expended in a rhythmical intuition that developed before the awakening in my consciousness of *the person who knows that he does not know music.* I imagine it is the same as when *the person who knows he cannot fly* has not yet become active in the man who dreams he is flying.

I apologize for this long and true story—as true, that is, as a story of this kind can be. Notice that everything I have said, or tried to say, happened in relation to what we call the *External World,* what we call *Our Body,* and what we call *Our Mind,* and requires a kind of vague collaboration between these three great powers.

Why have I told you this? In order to bring out the profound difference existing between spontaneous production by the mind—or rather by our *sensibility as a whole*—and the fabrication of works. In my story, the substance of a musical composition was freely given to me, but the organization which would have seized, fixed, and reshaped it was lacking. The great painter Degas often repeated to me a very true and simple remark by Mallarmé. Degas occasionally wrote verses, and some of those he left were delightful. But he often found great difficulty in this work accessory to his painting. (He was, by the way, the kind of man who would bring all possible difficulty to any art whatever.) One day he said to Mallarmé: "Yours is a hellish craft. I can't manage to say what I want, and yet I'm full of ideas. . . ." And Mallarmé answered: "My dear Degas, one does not make poetry with ideas, but with *words.*"

Mallarmé was right. But when Degas spoke of ideas, he was, after all, thinking of inner speech or of images, which might have been expressed in *words*. But these words, these secret phrases which he called ideas, all these intentions and perceptions of the mind, do not make verses. There is something else, then, a modification, or a transformation, sudden or not, spontaneous or not, laborious or not, which must necessarily intervene between the thought that produces ideas—that activity and multiplicity of inner questions and solutions— and, on the other hand, that discourse, so different from ordinary speech, which is verse, which is so curiously ordered, which answers no need *unless it be the need it must itself create,* which never speaks but of absent things or of things profoundly and secretly felt; strange discourse, as though made by someone *other* than the speaker and addressed to someone *other* than the listener. In short, it is a *language within a language.*

Let us look into these mysteries.

Poetry is an art of language. But language is a practical creation. It may be observed that in all communication between men, certainty comes only from practical acts and from the verification which practical acts give us. *I ask you for a light. You give me a light:* you have understood me.

But in asking me for a light, you were able to speak those few unimportant words with a certain intonation, a certain tone of voice, a certain inflection, a certain languor or briskness perceptible to me. I have understood your words, since without even thinking I handed you what you asked for—a light. But the matter does not end there. The strange thing: the sound and as it were the features of your little sentence come back to me, echo within me, as though they were pleased to be there; I, too, like to hear myself repeat this little phrase, which has almost lost its meaning, which has stopped being of use, and which can yet go on living, though with quite another life. It has acquired a value; and has acquired it *at the expense of its finite significance.* It has created the need to be heard again. . . . Here we are on the very threshold of the poetic state. This tiny experience will help us to the discovery of more than one truth.

It has shown us that language can produce effects of two quite different kinds. One of them tends to bring about the complete negation of language it-self. I speak to you, and if you have understood my words, those very words are abolished. If you have understood, it means that the words have vanished from your minds and are replaced by their counterpart, by images, relationships, impulses; so that you have within you the means to retransmit these ideas and images in a language that may be very different from the one you received. *Understanding* consists in the more or less rapid replacement of a system of sounds, intervals, and signs by something quite different, which is, in short, a modification or interior reorganization of the person to whom one is speaking. And here is the counterproof of this proposition: the person who does not understand *repeats* the words, or *has them repeated* to him.

Consequently, the perfection of a discourse whose sole aim is comprehen-sion obviously consists in the ease with which the words forming it are trans-formed into something quite different: the *language* is transformed first into *non-language* and then, if we wish, into a form of language differing from the original form.

In other terms, in practical or abstract uses of language, the form—that is the physical, the concrete part, the very act of speech—does not last; it does not outlive understanding; it dissolves in the light; it has acted; it has done its work; it has brought about understanding; it has lived.

But on the other hand, the moment this concrete form takes on, by an effect of its own, such importance that it asserts itself and makes itself, as it were, respected; and not only remarked and respected, but desired and therefore repeated—then something new happens: we are insensibly transformed and ready to live, breathe, and think in accordance with a rule and under laws which are no longer of the practical order—that is, nothing that may occur in this state will be resolved, finished, or abolished by a specific act. We are entering the poetic universe.

Permit me to support this notion of a *poetic universe* by referring to a similar notion that, being much simpler, is easier to explain: the notion of a *musical universe*. I would ask you to make a small sacrifice: limit yourselves for a moment to your faculty of hearing. One simple sense, like that of hearing, will offer us all we need for our definition and will absolve us from entering into all the difficulties and subtleties to which the conventional structure and historical complexities of ordinary language would lead us. We live by ear in the world of noises. Taken as a whole, it is generally incoherent and irregularly supplied by all the mechanical incidents which the ear may interpret as it can. But the same ear isolates from this chaos a group of noises particularly remarkable and simple—that is, easily recognizable by our sense of hearing and furnishing it with points of reference. These elements have relations with one another which we sense as we do the elements themselves. The interval between two of these privileged noises is as clear to us as each of them. These are the *sounds,* and these units of sonority tend to form clear combinations, successive or simultaneous implications, series, and intersections which one may term *intelligible:* this is why abstract possibilities exist in music. But I must return to my subject.

I will confine myself to saying that the contrast between noise and sound is the contrast between pure and impure, order and disorder; that this differentiation between pure sensations and others has permitted the constitution of music; that it has been possible to control, unify, and codify this constitution, thanks to the intervention of physical science, which knows how to adjust measure to sensation so as to obtain the important result of teaching us to produce this sonorous sensation consistently, and in a continuous and identical fashion, by instruments that are, in reality, *measuring instruments.*

The musician is thus in possession of a perfect system of well-defined means which exactly match sensations with acts. From this it results that music has formed a domain absolutely its own. The world of the art of music, a world of sounds, is distinct from the world of noises. Whereas a *noise* merely rouses in us some isolated event—a dog, a door, a motor car—*a sound evokes, of itself, the musical universe.* If, in this hall where I am speaking to you and where you hear the noise of my voice, a tuning fork or a well-tempered instrument began to vibrate, you would at once, as soon as you were affected by this pure and exceptional noise that cannot be confused with others, have the feeling of a beginning, the beginning of a world; a quite different atmosphere would immediately be created, a new order would arise, and you yourselves would unconsciously *organize* yourselves to receive it. The musical universe, therefore, was within you, with all its associations and proportions—as in a saturated salt solution a crystalline universe awaits the molecular shock of a minute crystal in order *to declare itself.* I dare not say: the crystalline idea of such a system awaits. . . .

And here is the counter proof of our little experiment: if, in a concert hall dominated by a resounding symphony, a chair happens to fall, someone coughs, or a door shuts, we immediately have the impression of a kind of rupture. Something indefinable, something like a spell or a Venetian glass, has been broken or cracked. . . .

The poetic universe is not created so powerfully or so easily. It exists, but the poet is deprived of the immense advantages possessed by the musician. He does not have before him, ready for the uses of beauty, a body of resources expressly made for his art. He has to borrow *language*—the voice of the public, that collection of traditional and irrational terms and rules, oddly created and transformed, oddly codified, and very variedly understood and pronounced. Here there is no physicist who has determined the relations between these elements; no tuning forks, no metronomes, no inventors of scales or theoreticians of harmony. Rather, on the contrary, the phonetic and semantic fluctuations of vocabulary. Nothing pure; but a mixture of completely incoherent auditive and psychic stimuli. Each word is an instantaneous coupling of a *sound* and a *sense* that have no connection with each other. Each sentence is an act so complex that I doubt whether anyone has yet been able to provide a tolerable definition of it. As for the use of the resources of language and the modes of this action, you know what diversity there is, and what confusion sometimes results. A discourse can be logical, packed with sense, but devoid of rhythm and measure. It can be pleasing to the ear, yet completely absurd or insignificant; it can be clear, yet useless; vague, yet delightful. But to grasp its strange multiplicity, which is no more than the multiplicity of life itself, it suffices to name all the sciences which have been created to deal with this diversity, each to study one of its aspects. One can analyze a text in many different ways, for it falls successively under the jurisdiction of phonetics, semantics, syntax, logic, rhetoric, philology, not to mention metrics, prosody, and etymology. . . .

So the poet is at grips with this verbal matter, obliged to speculate on sound and sense at once, and to satisfy not only harmony and musical timing but all the various intellectual and aesthetic conditions, not to mention the conventional rules. . . .

You can see what an effort the poet's undertaking would require if he had *consciously* to solve all these problems. . . .

It is always interesting to try to reconstruct one of our complex activities, one of those complete actions which demand a specialization at once mental, sensuous, and motor, supposing that in order to accomplish this act we were obliged to understand and organize all the functions that we know play their part in it. Even if this attempt, at once imaginative and analytical, is clumsy, it will always teach us something. As for myself, who am, I admit, much more attentive to the formation or fabrication of works than to the works themselves, I have a habit, or obsession, of appreciating works only as actions. In my eyes a poet is a man who, as a result of a certain incident, undergoes a hidden transformation. He leaves his ordinary condition of general disposability, and I see taking shape in him an agent, a living system for producing verses. As among animals one suddenly sees emerging a capable hunter, a nest maker, a bridge builder, a digger of tunnels and galleries, so in a man one sees a composite organization declare itself, bending its functions to a specific piece of work. Think of a very small child: the child we have all been bore many possibilities within him. After a few months of life he has learned, at the same or almost the same time, to speak and to walk. He has acquired two types of action. That is to say that he now possesses two kinds of potentiality from which the accidental circumstances of each moment will draw what they can, in answer to his varying needs and imaginings.

Having learned to use his legs, he will discover that he can not only walk, but run; and not only walk and run, but dance. This is a great event. He has at that moment both invented and discovered a kind of *secondary use* for his limbs, a generalization of his formula of movement. In fact, whereas walking is after all a rather dull and not easily perfectible action, this new form of action, the Dance, admits of an infinite number of creations and variations or *figures.*

But will he not find an analogous development in speech? He will explore the possibilities of his faculty of speech; he will discover that more can be done with it than to ask for jam and deny his little sins. He will grasp the power of reasoning; he will invent stories to amuse himself when he is alone; he will repeat to himself words that he loves for their strangeness and mystery.

So, parallel with *Walking* and *Dancing,* he will acquire and distinguish the divergent types, *Prose and Poetry.*

This parallel has long struck and attracted me; but someone saw it before I did. According to Racan, Malherbe[4] made use of it. In my opinion it is more than a simple comparison. I see in it an analogy as substantial and pregnant as those found in physics when one observes the identity of formulas that represent the measurement of seemingly very different phenomena. Here is how our comparison develops.

Walking, like prose, has a definite aim. It is an act directed at something we wish to reach. Actual circumstances, such as the need for some object, the impulse of my desire, the state of my body, my sight, the terrain, etc., which order the manner of walking, prescribe its direction and its speed, and give it a *definite end.* All the characteristics of walking derive from those instantaneous conditions, which combine *in a novel way* each time. There are no movements in walking that are not special adaptations, but, each time, they are abolished and, as it were, absorbed by the accomplishment of the act, by the attainment of the goal.

The dance is quite another matter. It is, of course, a system of actions; but of actions whose end is in themselves. It goes nowhere. If it pursues an object, it is only an ideal object, a state, an enchantment, the phantom of a flower, an

---

[4] François de Malherbe (1555–1628), French poet and critic. Honoré de Bueil, Marquis de Racan (1584–1670), edited a selection of Malherbe's poems.

extreme of life, a smile—which forms at last on the face of the one who summoned it from empty space.

It is therefore not a question of carrying out a limited operation whose end is situated somewhere in our surroundings, but rather of creating, maintaining, and exalting a certain *state,* by a periodic movement that can be executed on the spot; a movement which is almost entirely dissociated from sight, but which is stimulated and regulated by auditive rhythms.

But please note this very simple observation, that however different the dance may be from walking and utilitarian movements, it uses the same organs, the same bones, the same muscles, only differently co-ordinated and aroused.

Here we come again to the contrast between prose and poetry. Prose and poetry use the same words, the same syntax, the same forms, and the same sounds or tones, but differently co-ordinated and differently aroused. Prose and poetry are therefore distinguished by the difference between certain links and associations which form and dissolve in our psychic and nervous organism, whereas the components of these modes of functioning are identical. This is why one should guard against reasoning about poetry as one does about prose. What is true of one very often has no meaning when it is sought in the other. But here is the great and decisive difference. When the man who is walking has reached his goal—as I said—when he has reached the place, book, fruit, the object of his desire (which desire drew him from his repose), this possession at once entirely annuls his whole act; the effect swallows up the cause, the end absorbs the means; and, whatever the act, only the result remains. It is the same with utilitarian language: the language I use to express my design, my desire, my command, my opinion; this language, when it has served its purpose, evaporates almost as it is heard. I have given it forth to perish, to be radically transformed into something else in your mind; and I shall know that I was *understood* by the remarkable fact that my speech no longer exists: it has been completely replaced by its *meaning*—that is, by images, impulses, reactions, or acts that belong to you: in short, by an interior modification in you.

As a result the perfection of this kind of language, whose sole end is to be understood, obviously consists in the ease with which it is transformed into something altogether different.

The poem, on the other hand, does not die for having lived: it is expressly designed to be born again from its ashes and to become endlessly what it has just been. Poetry can be recognized by this property, that it tends to get itself reproduced in its own form: it stimulates us to reconstruct it identically.

That is an admirable and uniquely characteristic property.

I should like to give you a simple illustration. Think of a pendulum oscillating between two symmetrical points. Suppose that one of these extremes represents *form:* the concrete characteristics of the language, sound, rhythm, accent, tone, movement—in a word, the *Voice* in action. Then associate with the other point, the acnode of the first, all significant values, images and ideas, stimuli of feeling and memory, virtual impulses and structures of understanding—in short, everything that makes the *content,* the meaning of a discourse. Now observe the effect of poetry on yourselves. You will find that at each line the meaning produced within you, far from destroying the musical form communicated to you, recalls it. The living pendulum that has swung from *sound* to *sense* swings back to its felt point of departure, as though the very sense which is present to your mind can find no other outlet or expression, no other answer, than the very music which gave it birth.

So between the form and the content, between the sound and the sense, between the poem and the state of poetry, a symmetry is revealed, an equality between importance, value, and power, which does not exist in prose; which is contrary to the law of prose—the law which ordains the inequality of the two constitutents of language. The essential principle of the mechanics of poetry— that is, of the conditions for producing the poetic state by words—seems to me to be this harmonious exchange between expression and impression.

I introduce here a slight observation which I shall call "philosophical," meaning simply that we could do without it.

Our poetic pendulum travels from our sensation toward some idea or some sentiment, and returns toward some memory of the sensation and toward the potential act which could reproduce the sensation. Now, whatever is sensation is essentially *present*. There is no other definition of the present except sensation itself, which includes, perhaps, the impulse to action that would modify that sensation. On the other hand, whatever is properly thought, image, sentiment, is always, in some way, *a production of absent things*. Memory is the substance of all thought. Anticipation and its gropings, desire, planning, the projection of our hopes, of our fears, are the main interior activity of our being.

Thought is, in short, the activity which causes what does not exist to come alive in us, lending to it, whether we will or no, our present powers, making us take the part for the whole, the image for reality, and giving us the illusion of seeing, acting, suffering, and possessing independently of our dear old body, which we leave with its cigarette in an armchair until we suddenly retrieve it when the telephone rings or, no less strangely, when our stomach demands provender. . . .

Between Voice and Thought, between Thought and Voice, between Presence and Absence, oscillates the poetic pendulum.

The result of this analysis is to show that the value of a poem resides in the indissolubility of sound and sense. Now this is a condition that seems to demand the impossible. There is no relation between the sound and the meaning of a word. The same thing is called HORSE in English, HIPPOS in Greek, EQUUS in Latin, and CHEVAL in French; but no manipulation of any of these terms will give me an idea of the animal in question; and no manipulation of the idea will yield me any of these words—otherwise, we should easily know all languages, beginning with our own.

Yet it is the poet's business to give us the feeling of an intimate union between the word and the mind.

This must be considered, strictly speaking, a marvelous result. I say *marvelous,* although it is not exceptionally rare. I use *marvelous* in the sense we give that word when we think of the miracles and prodigies of ancient magic. It must not be forgotten that for centuries poetry was used for purposes of enchantment. Those who took part in these strange operations had to believe in the power of the word, and far more in the efficacy of its sound than in its significance. Magic formulas are often without meaning; but it was never thought that their power depended on their intellectual content.

Let us listen to lines like these:

Mère des souvenirs, maîtresse des maîtresses. . . .[5]

or

Sois sage, ô ma Douleur, et tiens-toi plus tranquille. . . .[6]

These words work on us (or at least on some of us) without telling us very much. They tell us, perhaps, that they have nothing to tell us; that, by the very means which usually tell us something, they are exercising a quite different function. They act on us like a chord of music. The impression produced depends largely on resonance, rhythm, and the number of syllables; but it is also the result of the simple bringing together of meanings. In the second of these lines the accord between the vague ideas of Wisdom and Grief, and the tender solemnity of the tone produce the inestimable value of a spell: the *momentary being* who made that line could not have done so had he been in a state where the form and the content occurred separately to his mind. On the contrary, he was in a special phase in the domain of his psychic existence, a phase in which the sound and the meaning of the word acquire or keep an equal importance— which is excluded from the habits of practical language, as from the needs of abstract language. The state in which the inseparability of sound and sense, in which the desire, the expectation, the possibility of their intimate and indissoluble fusion are required and sought or given, and sometimes anxiously awaited, is a comparatively rare state. It is rare, firstly because all the exigencies of life are against it; secondly because it is opposed to the crude simplifying and specializing of verbal notations.

But this state of inner modification, in which all the properties of our language are indistinctly but harmoniously summoned, is not enough to produce that complete object, that compound of beauties, that collection of happy chances for the mind which a noble poem offers us.

From this state we obtain only fragments. All the precious things that are found in the earth, gold, diamonds, uncut stones, are there scattered, strewn, grudgingly hidden in a quantity of rock or sand, where chance may sometimes uncover them. These riches would be nothing without the human labor that draws them from the massive night where they were sleeping, assembles them, alters and organizes them into ornaments. These fragments of metal embedded in formless matter, these oddly shaped crystals, must owe all their luster to intelligent labor. It is a labor of this kind that the true poet accomplishes. Faced with a beautiful poem, one can indeed feel that it is most unlikely that any man, however gifted, could have improvised without a backward glance, with no other effort than that of writing or dictating, such a simultaneous and complete system of lucky finds. Since the traces of effort, the second thoughts, the changes, the amount of time, the bad days, and the distaste have now vanished, effaced by the supreme return of a mind over its work, some people, seeing only the perfection of the result, will look on it as due to a sort of magic that they

---

[5] "Mother of memories, mistress of mistresses," the first line of "Le Balcon," by Charles Baudelaire.

[6] "Be quiet, O my sorrow, and lie still," from Baudelaire's "Recueillement."

call INSPIRATION. They thus make of the poet a kind of temporary *medium*. If one were strictly to develop this doctrine of pure inspiration, one would arrive at some very strange results. For example, one would conclude that the poet, since he merely transmits what he receives, merely delivers to unknown people what he has taken from the unknown, has no need to understand what he writes, which is dictated by a mysterious voice. He could write poems in a language he did not know. . . .

In fact, the poet has indeed a kind of spiritual energy of a special nature: it is manifested in him and reveals him to himself in certain moments of infinite worth. Infinite for him. . . . I say, *infinite for him,* for, alas, experience shows us that these moments which seem to us to have a universal value are sometimes without a future, and in the end make us ponder on this maxim: *what is of value for one person only has no value.* This is the iron law of Literature.

But every true poet is necessarily a first-rate critic. If one doubts this, one can have no idea of what the work of the mind is: that struggle with the inequality of moments, with chance associations, lapses of attention, external distractions. The mind is terribly variable, deceptive and self-deceiving, fertile in insoluble problems and illusory solutions. How could a remarkable work emerge from this chaos if this chaos that contains everything did not also contain some serious chances to know oneself and to choose within oneself whatever is worth taking from each moment and using carefully?

That is not all. Every true poet is much more capable than is generally known of right reasoning and abstract thought.

But one must not look for his real philosophy in his more or less philosophical utterances. In my opinion, the most authentic philosophy lies not so much in the objects of our reflection as in the very act of thought and in its handling. Take from metaphysics all its pet or special terms, all its traditional vocabulary, and you may realize that you have not impoverished the thought. Indeed, you may perhaps have eased and freshened it, and you will have got rid of other people's problems, so as to deal only with your own difficulties, your surprises that owe nothing to anyone, and whose intellectual spur you feel actually and directly.

It has often happened, however, as literary history tells us, that poetry has been made to enunciate theses or hypotheses and that the *complete* language which is its own—the language whose *form*, that is to say the action and sensation of the *Voice*, is of the same power as the *content*, that is to say the eventual modification of a *mind*—has been used to communicate "abstract" ideas, which are on the contrary independent of their form, or so we believe. Some very great poets have occasionally attempted this. But whatever may be the talent which exerts itself in this very noble undertaking, it cannot prevent the attention given to following the ideas from competing with the attention that follows the song. The DE RERUM NATURA[7] is here in conflict with the nature of things. The state of mind of the reader of poems is not the state of mind of the reader of pure thought. The state of mind of a man dancing

---

[7] "On the Nature of Things," a long poem in Latin by the Roman poet Lucretius (c. 99–55 B.C.), setting forth the ideas of the Greek philosophers Democritus and Epicurus.

is not that of a man advancing through difficult country of which he is making a topographical survey or a geological prospectus.

I have said, nevertheless, that the poet has his abstract thought and, if you like, his philosophy; and I have said that it is at work in his very activity as a poet. I said this because I have observed it, in myself and in several others. Here, as elsewhere, I have no other reference, no other claim or excuse, than recourse to my own experience or to the most common observation.

Well, every time I have worked as a poet, I have noticed that my work exacted of me not only that presence of the poetic universe I have spoken of, but many reflections, decisions, choices, and combinations, without which all possible gifts of the Muses, or of Chance, would have remained like precious materials in a workshop without an architect. Now an architect is not himself necessarily built of precious materials. In so far as he is an architect of poems, a poet is quite different from what he is as a producer of those precious elements of which all poetry should be composed, but whose composition is separate and requires an entirely different mental effort.

One day someone told me that lyricism is enthusiasm, and that the odes of the great lyricists were written at a single stroke, at the speed of the voice of delirium, and with the wind of inspiration blowing a gale. . . .

I replied that he was quite right; but that this was not a privilege of poetry alone, and that everyone knew that in building a locomotive it is indispensable for the builder to work at eighty miles an hour in order to do his job.

A poem is really a kind of machine for producing the poetic state of mind by means of words. The effect of this machine is uncertain, for nothing is certain about action on other minds. But whatever may be the result, in its uncertainty, the construction of the machine demands the solution of many problems. If the term *machine* shocks you, if my mechanical comparison seems crude, please notice that while the composition of even a very short poem may absorb years, the action of the poem on the reader will take only a few minutes. In a few minutes the reader will receive his shock from discoveries, connections, glimmers of expression that have been accumulated during months of research, waiting, patience, and impatience. He may attribute much more to inspiration than it can give. He will imagine the kind of person it would take to create, without pause, hesitation, or revision, this powerful and perfect work which transports him into a world where things and people, passions and thoughts, sonorities and meanings proceed from the same energy, are transformed one into another, and correspond according to exceptional laws of harmony, for it can only be an exceptional form of stimulus that simultaneously produces the exaltation of our sensibility, our intellect, our memory, and our powers of verbal action, so rarely granted to us in the ordinary course of life.

Perhaps I should remark here that the execution of a poetic work—if one considers it as the engineer just mentioned would consider the conception and construction of his locomotive, that is, making explicit the problems to be solved —would appear impossible. In no other art is the number of conditions and independent functions to be co-ordinated so large. I will not inflict on you a detailed demonstration of this proposition. It is enough for me to remind you of what I said regarding sound and sense, which are linked only by pure convention, but which must be made to collaborate as effectively as possible. From their double nature words often make me think of those complex quantities which geometricians take such pleasure in manipulating.

Fortunately, some strange virtue resides in certain moments in certain people's lives which simplifies things and reduces the insurmountable difficulties I spoke of to the scale of human energies.

The poet awakes within man at an unexpected event, an outward or inward incident: a tree, a face, a "subject," an emotion, a word. Sometimes it is the will to expression that starts the game, a need to translate what one feels; another time, on the contrary, it is an element of form, the outline of an expression which seeks its origin, seeks a meaning within the space of my mind. . . . Note this possible duality in ways of getting started: either something wants to express itself, or some means of expression wants to be used.

My poem *Le Cimetière marin*[8] began in me by a rhythm, that of a French line . . . of ten syllables, divided into four and six. I had as yet no idea with which to fill out this form. Gradually a few hovering words settled in it, little by little determining the subject, and my labor (a very long labor) was before me. Another poem, *La Pythie,*[9] first appeared as an eight-syllable line whose sound came of its own accord. But this line implied a sentence, of which it was part, and this sentence, if it existed, implied many other sentences. A problem of this kind has an infinite number of solutions. But with poetry the musical and metrical conditions greatly restrict the indefiniteness. Here is what happened: my fragment acted like a living fragment, since, plunged in the (no doubt nourishing) surroundings of my desire and waiting thought, it proliferated, and engendered all that was lacking: several lines before and a great many lines after.

I apologize for having chosen my examples from my own little story: but I could hardly have taken them elsewhere.

Perhaps you think my conception of the poet and the poem rather singular. Try to imagine, however, what the least of our acts implies. Think of everything that must go on inside a man who utters the smallest intelligible sentence, and then calculate all that is needed for a poem by Keats or Baudelaire to be formed on an empty page in front of the poet.

Think, too, that of all the arts, ours is perhaps that which co-ordinates the greatest number of independent parts or factors: sound, sense, the real and the imaginary, logic, syntax, and the double invention of content and form . . . and all this by means of a medium essentially practical, perpetually changing, soiled, a maid of all work, *everyday language,* from which we must draw a pure, ideal Voice, capable of communicating without weakness, without apparent effort, without offense to the ear, and without breaking the ephemeral sphere of the poetic universe, an idea of some *self* miraculously superior to Myself.

[8] "The Cemetery by the Sea."
[9] "The Pythoness."

Georg Lukács

BALZAC:
LOST ILLUSIONS

The reputation of Georg Lukács is of a strangely ambiguous kind. His early works, none of them available in English, would seem to entitle him to be thought of as the greatest of Marxist cultural theorists. On the basis of his later works he must be judged to be an orthodox Marxist critic of more than usual cogency and force but of no special originality. Born in 1885 in Hungary as Georg von Lukács (he later dropped the aristocratic *von*), the son of a wealthy Jewish banking family which had recently been raised to the nobility, he showed an astonishing intellectual power at an early age. At the University of Berlin and at the University of Heidelberg his precocity amazed and delighted his famous teachers, themselves men of genius, the sociologists Max Weber and Georg Simmel. His first work, *The Metaphysics of Tragedy,* was published when he was twenty-two. Other works followed in fairly rapid succession, including the influential *Theory of the Novel* (1916). In 1918 he joined the Communist Party of Hungary and when, in 1919, the party staged a briefly successful revolution, he served as Minister of Education. Upon the overthrow of the revolutionary government, Lukács fled to Vienna where he lived for some years and wrote the work that is generally considered his masterpiece, *History and Class Consciousness* (1923). This work was judged to diverge in important ways from the line of official Marxist thought and it was basically condemned by the leading Russian theorists of the day, including Lenin. As a result, Lukács was expelled from the Central Committee of the Hungarian Communist Party. He held to his views for a decade in the face of the Party's hostility, but in 1933, when he was living in Moscow after Hitler came to power in Germany, he abjured the book and all his previous writings and his work came into closer conformity with accepted Communist doctrine. After the war he returned to Hungary, now under Communist control, and taught at the University of Budapest. In 1956 the Hungarians, including many Communists, revolted against the Russian domination of their land. Lukács joined the uprising and was made a minister in the government that was briefly established. When the Russians invaded to suppress the revolution in ruthless fashion, Lukács' life was spared, although many of his political colleagues were sentenced to death; after a brief exile, he was allowed to return and take up his teaching and writing again. His literary sensibility had been formed chiefly by the great masters of the nineteenth century novel and to them his taste has remained committed—and limited. Such writers of a later time as are in accord with older methods and values win his praise; others he sees and denounces as exemplifying in one way or another the decadence of the bourgeoisie. The essay on Balzac's *Lost Illusions* appeared in *Studies in European Realism,* first published in 1938 and reissued in 1948. It gives but little evidence of the subtlety and complexity of mind that makes the chapter on the romanticism of disillusionment in *The Theory of the Novel* so engaging; it is, nevertheless, a sturdy and useful piece of work and serves to exemplify the enlightenment that the Marxist investigation of social process can bring to literature.

Balzac wrote this novel in the fullness of his maturity as a writer; with it he created a new type of novel which was destined to influence decisively the literary development of the nineteenth century. This new type of novel was the novel of disillusionment, which shows how the conception of life of those living in a *bourgeois* society—a conception which although false, is yet necessarily what it is—is shattered by the brute forces of capitalism.

It was not, of course, in the works of Balzac that the shipwreck of illusions made its first appearance in the modern novel.

The first great novel, Cervantes' *Don Quixote* is also a story of lost illusions. But in *Don Quixote* it is the nascent *bourgeois* world which destroys the still lingering feudal illusions; in Balzac's novel it is the conceptions of mankind, human society, art, etc., necessarily engendered by *bourgeois* development itself —i.e. the highest ideological products of the revolutionary development of the *bourgeoisie*—which are shown to be empty illusions when measured by the standards set by the realities of capitalist economy.

The eighteenth-century novel also dealt with the destruction of certain illusions, but these illusions were feudal survivals still lingering in the sphere of thoughts and emotions; or else certain groundless, pedestrian conceptions imperfectly anchored in reality were dispelled by another more complete conception of the same reality viewed from the same angle.

But it is in this novel of Balzac that the bitter laughter of derision at the highest ideological products of *bourgeois* development itself is heard for the first time—it is here that we see for the first time, shown in its totality, the tragic self-dissolution of *bourgeois* ideals by their own economic basis, by the forces of capitalism. Diderot's immortal masterpiece *The Nephew of Rameau*[1] is the only work that can be regarded as the ideological precursor of this Balzac novel.

Of course Balzac was by no means the only writer of the time who chose this theme. Stendhal's *Scarlet And Black*[2] and Musset's *Confessions Of A Child Of The Century*[3] even preceded *Lost Illusions* in time. The theme was in the air, not because of some literary fashion but because it was thrown up by social evolution in France, the country that provided the pattern for the

[1] Written by Denis Diderot (1713–1784) some time between 1761 and 1774.
[2] Stendhal published *Le Rouge et le Noir* in 1827.
[3] Alfred de Musset published *Confessions of a Child of the Century* in 1836.

political growth of the *bourgeoisie* everywhere. The heroic epochs of the French revolution and the First Empire had awakened, mobilized and developed all the dormant energies of the *bourgeois* class. This heroic epoch gave the best elements of the *bourgeoisie* the opportunity for the immediate translation into reality of their heroic ideals, the opportunity to live and to die heroically in accordance with those ideals. This heroic period came to an end with the fall of Napoleon, the return of the Bourbons and the July revolution. The ideals became superfluous ornaments and frills on the sober reality of everyday life and the path of capitalism, opened up by the revolution and by Napoleon, broadened into a convenient, universally accessible highway of development. The heroic pioneers had to disappear and make way for the humanly inferior exploiters of the new development, the speculators and racketeers.

"*Bourgeois* society in its sober reality had produced its true interpreters and spokesmen in the Says, the Cousins, the Royer-Collards, the Benjamin Constants, the Guizots; its real generals sat at the counting-house desks and their political head was the fat-head Louis XVIII." (Marx.)

The drive of ideals, a necessary product of the previous necessarily heroic period was now no longer wanted; its representatives, the young generation schooled in the traditions of the heroic period, was inevitably doomed to deteriorate.

This inevitable degradation and frustration of the energies born of the revolution and the Napoleonic era was a theme common to all novels of disillusionment of the period, an indictment common to them all of the prosaic scurviness of the Bourbon restoration and the July monarchy. Balzac, although politically a royalist and legitimist, yet saw this character of the restoration with merciless clarity. He writes in *Lost Illusions*:

"Nothing is such a condemnation of the slavery to which the restoration has condemned our youth. The young men who did not know what to do with their strength, have harnessed only to journalism, political conspiracies and the arts, but in strange excesses as well . . . If they worked, they demanded power and pleasure; as artists, they desired treasures; as idlers, passionate excitement— but be that as it may, they demanded a place for themselves and politics refused it to them . . ."

It was the tragedy of a whole generation and the recognition of this fact and the portrayal of it is common to Balzac and his contemporaries both great and small; but in spite of this common trait, *Lost Illusions* in its portrayal of the time rises to a solitary height far above any other French literary work of the period. For Balzac did not content himself with the recognition and description of this tragic or tragi-comic social situation. He saw farther and delved deeper.

He saw that the end of the heroic period of French *bourgeois* evolution was at the same time the beginning of the rapid development of French capitalism. In almost every one of his novels Balzac depicts this capitalist development, the transformation of traditional handicrafts into modern capitalist production; he shows how stormily accumulating money-capital usuriously exploits town and countryside and how the old social formations and ideologies must yield before its triumphant onslaught.

Lost Illusions is a tragi-comic epic showing how, within this general process, the spirit of man is drawn into the orbit of capitalism. The theme of the novel is the transformation of literature (and with it of every ideology) into a commodity and this complete "capitalization" of every sphere of intellectual, literary and artistic activity fits the general tragedy of the post-Napoleonic generation into a much more profoundly conceived social pattern than can be found in the writings even of Stendhal, Balzac's greatest contemporary.

The transformation of literature into a commodity is painted by Balzac in great detail. From the writer's ideas, emotions and convictions to the paper on which he writes them down, everything is turned into a commodity that can be bought and sold. Nor is Balzac content merely to register in general terms the ideological consequences of the rule of capitalism—he uncovers every stage in the concrete process of "capitalization" in every sphere (the periodical press, the theatre, the publishing business, etc.) together with all the factors governing the process.

"What is fame?" asks Dauriat, the publisher, and answers himself: "Twelve thousand francs' worth of newspaper articles and three thousand francs' worth of dinners . . ." Then he expounds: "I haven't the slightest intention of risking two thousand francs on a book merely in order to make the same amount by it. I speculate in literature; I publish forty volumes in an edition of ten thousand copies each.—My power and the newspaper articles which I get published thus, bring me in business to the value of three hundred thousand francs, instead of a measly two thousand. A manuscript which I buy for a hundred thousand francs is cheaper than the manuscript of an unknown author which I can get for a mere 600 francs."

The writers think as the publishers do.

"Do you really believe what you write?" Vernon asks sarcastically. "But surely we are word-merchants and are talking shop . . . The articles that the public reads today and has forgotten by tomorrow have no other meaning for us save that we get paid for them."

With all this, the writers and journalists are exploited, their talent has become a commodity, an object of profiteering by the capitalist speculators who deal in literature. They are exploited but they are also prostitutes; their ambition is to become exploiters themselves or at least overseers over other exploited colleagues. Before Lucien de Rubempré turns journalist, his colleague and mentor Lousteau explains the situation to him in these terms:

"Mark this, my boy: in literature the secret of success is not work, but the exploitation of the work done by others. The newspaper-owners are the building contractors and we are the bricklayers. The more mediocre a man is, the sooner he will reach his goal, for he will at need be willing to swallow a frog, and do anything else to flatter the passions of the little literary sultans. Today you are still severe and have a conscience, but to-morrow your conscience will bow to the ground before those who can tear success from your grasp and those who could give you life by a single word and yet refuse to speak that word, for believe me, a fashionable author is haughtier and harsher towards the new generation than the most leech-like of publishers. Where the publisher sees only a loss of money, the fashionable author fears a rival: the publisher merely rejects the beginner, the fashionable author annihilates him."

This breadth of the theme—the capitalization of literature, embracing everything from the manufacturing of paper to the lyrical sensibility of a poet, determines the artistic form of the composition in this as in all other works of Balzac. The friendship between David Séchard and Lucien de Rubempré, the shattered illusions of their enthusiastic youth and their mutually complementary contrasting characters are the elements that provide the general outline of the story. Balzac's genius manifests itself even in this basic lay-out of the composition. The objective tensions inherent in the theme are expressed through the human passions and individual aspirations of the characters: David Séchard, the inventor who discovers a cheaper method of making paper but is swindled by the capitalists, and Lucien de Rubempré, the poet who carries the purest and most delicate lyrical poems to the capitalist market of Paris. On the other hand, the contrast between the two characters demonstrates the extremely different ways in which men can react to the abominations accompanying the transition to capitalism. David Séchard is a puritan stoic while Lucien de Rubempré incarnates perfectly the sensual love of pleasure and the rootless, over-refined epicureanism of the post-revolutionary generation.

Balzac's composition is never pedantic; unlike his later successors he never affects a dry "scientific" attitude. In his writings the unfolding of material problems is always indissolubly bound up with the consequences arising from the personal passions of his characters. This method of composition—although it seems to take the individual alone for its starting-point—contains a deeper understanding of social interconnections and implications, a more correct evaluation of the trends of social development than does the pedantic, "scientific" method of the later realists.

In *Lost Illusions* Balzac focuses his story on Lucien de Rubempré's fate and with it the transformation of literature into a commodity; the capitalization of the material basis of literature, the capitalist exploitation of technical progress is only an episodic final chord. This method of composition, which apparently reverses the logical and objective connection between the material basis and the superstructure, is extremely skilful both from the artistic point of view and from the angle of social criticism. It is artistically skilful because the rich diversity of Lucien's changing destinies, unfolded before our eyes in the course of his struggle for fame, provides a much more colourful, lively and complete picture than the pettily infamous intrigues of the provincial capitalists out to swindle David Séchard. It is skilful from the point of view of social criticism because Lucien's fate involves in its entirety the question of the destruction of culture by capitalism. Séchard in resigning himself to his fate, quite correctly feels that what is really essential is that his invention should be put to good use; the fact that he has been swindled is merely his personal bad luck. But Lucien's catastrophe represents at the same time the capitalist debasement and prostitution of literature itself.

The contrast between the two principal characters illustrates most vividly the two main types of personal reaction to the transformation of ideology into a commodity. Séchard's reaction is to resign himself to the inevitable.

Resignation plays a very important part in the *bourgeois* literature of the nineteenth century. The aged Goethe was one of the first to strike this note of resignation. It was the symptom of a new period in the evolution of the *bourgeoisie*. Balzac in his utopian novels follows in Goethe's footsteps: only those who have given up or who must give up their personal happiness can pursue social, non-selfish aims. Séchard's resignation is, of course, of a somewhat different nature. He gives up the struggle, abandons the pursuit of any aim and wants only to live for his personal happiness in peace and seclusion. Those who wish to remain pure must withdraw from all capitalist business—it is in this, not ironical, not in the least Voltairean sense that David Séchard withdraws to "cultivate his own garden.[4]

Lucien for his part plunges into life in Paris; he is determined to win through and establish the rights and power of "pure poetry." This struggle makes him one of those post-Napoleonic young men who either perished with polluted souls during the restoration or adapted themselves to the filth of an age turned unheroic and in it carved a career for themselves, like Julien Sorel,[5] Rastignac, de Marsay, Blondet[6] and others of the same kidney. Lucien belongs to the latter group but occupies an entirely independent position in this company. With admirable daring and sensitivity Balzac created a new, specifically *bourgeois* type of poet: the poet as an Aeolian harp sounding to the veering winds and tempests of society, the poet as a rootless, aimlessly drifting, oversensitive bundle of nerves,—a type of poet as yet very rare in this period, but most characteristic for the subsequent evolution of *bourgeois* poetry from Verlaine[7] to Rilke.[8] This type is diametrically opposed to what Balzac himself wanted the poet to be; he portrayed his ideal poet in the person of Daniel D'Arthez, a character in this novel who is intended for a self-portrait.

The characterization of Lucien is not only true to type, it also provides the opportunity for unfolding all the contradictions engendered by the penetration of capitalism into literature. The intrinsic contradiction between Lucien's poetic talent and his human weakness and rootlessness makes him a plaything of the political and literary trends exploited by the capitalists. It is this mixture of instability and ambition, the combination of a hankering for a pure and honourable life with a boundless but erratic ambition, which make possible the brilliant rise of Lucien, his rapid prostitution and his final ignominious disaster. Balzac never serves up his heroes with a sauce of morality; he shows the objective dialectic of their rise or fall, always motivating both by the total sum of their own natures and the mutual interaction of this their nature with the total sum of objective circumstances, never by any isolated value-judgment of their "good" and "bad" qualities.

Rastignac, the climber, is no worse than Lucien, but in him a different mixture of talent and demoralization is at work, which enables him adroitly to turn to his own advantage the same reality on which Lucien, for all his naive Machiavellianism, is shipwrecked both materially and morally.

Balzac's sour remark in *Melmoth Reconciled* that men are either cashiers or embezzlers, i.e. either honest fools or clever rogues, is proved true in endless variety in this tragi-comic epic of the capitalization of the spirit.

[4] The main characters in *Candide* (1759), by Voltaire, after many tribulations, decide that each man should stay home and "cultivate his own garden."
[5] Hero of Stendhal's *Scarlet and Black.*
[6] Characters who re-occur throughout Balzac's *Comédie humaine,* a series of interrelated novels and stories.
[7] Paul Verlaine (1844–1896), French poet.
[8] Rainer Maria Rilke (1875–1926), German poet.

Thus the ultimate integrating principle of this novel is the social process itself and its real subject is the advance and victory of capitalism. Lucien's personal catastrophe is the typical fate of the poet and of true poetic talent in the world of fully developed capitalism.

Nevertheless Balzac's composition is not abstractly objective and this novel is not a novel with a theme, not a novel relating, in the manner of the later novelists, to one sphere of society alone, although Balzac by a most subtle weaving of his story introduces every feature of the capitalization of literature and brings onto the scene none but these features of capitalism. But here as in all other works of Balzac the general social fabric is never directly shown on the surface. His characters are never mere lay figures expressing certain aspects of the social reality he wants to present. The aggregate of social determinants is expressed in an uneven, intricate, confused and contradictory pattern, in a labyrinth of personal passions and chance happenings. The characters and situations are always determined by the totality of the socially decisive forces, but never simply and never directly. For this reason this so completely universal novel is at the same time the story of one particular individual, an individual different from all others. Lucien de Rubempré, on the stage, seems to react independently to the internal and external forces which hamper his rise and which help or hinder him as a result of apparently fortuitous personal circumstances or passions, but which, whatever form they take, always spring from the same social environment which determines his aspirations and ambition.

This unity of the multifarious is a feature peculiar to Balzac; it is the poetic form in which he expresses his conception of the working of social forces. Unlike many other great novelists he does not resort to any machinery such as, for instance, the tower in *Wilhelm Meister's Apprenticeship;*[9] every cog in the mechanism of a Balzacian plot is a complete, living human being with specific personal interests, passions, tragedies and comedies. The bond which links each character with the whole of the story is provided by some element in the make-up of the character itself, always in full accordance with the tendencies inherent to it. As this link always develops organically out of the interests, passions etc. of the character, it appears necessary and vital. But it is the broader inner urges and compulsions of the characters themselves which give them fulness of life and render them non-mechanical, no mere components of the plot. Such a conception of the characters necessarily causes them to burst out of the story. Broad and spacious as Balzac's plots are, the stage is crowded by so many actors living such richly varied lives that only a few of them can be fully developed within one story.

This seems a deficiency of Balzac's method of composition; in reality it is what gives his novels their full-blooded vitality and it is also what made the cyclic form a necessity for him. His remarkable and nevertheless typical characters cannot unfold their personality fully within a single novel, but only certain features of it and that only episodically; they protrude beyond the framework of one novel and demand another, the plot and theme of which permit them to occupy the centre of the stage and develop to the full all their qualities and possibilities. The characters who remain in the background in *Lost Illusions*,

[9] By Goethe, published in 1796.

Blondet, Rastignac, Nathan, Michel Chrestien, play leading parts in other novels. The cyclical interdependence of Balzac's novels derives from his urge to develop every one of his characters to the full and hence is never dry and pedantic as cyclic novels of other, even very good writers, so often are. For the several parts of the cycle are never determined by circumstances external to the characters, i.e. by chronological or objective limits.

The general is thus always concrete and real because it is based on a profound understanding of what is typical in each of the characters figuring in it—an understanding so deep that the particular is not eclipsed but on the contrary emphasized and concretized by the typical, and on the other hand the relationship between the individual and the social setting of which it is the product and in which—or against which—it acts, is always clearly discernible, however intricate this relationship may be. The Balzac characters, complete within themselves, live and act within a concrete, complexly stratified social reality and it is always the totality of the social process that is linked with the totality of the character. The power of Balzac's imagination manifests itself in his ability to select and manipulate his characters in such a way that the centre of the stage is always occupied by the figure whose personal, individual qualities are the most suitable for the demonstration, as extensively as possible and in transparent connection with the whole, of some important single aspect of the social process. The several parts of a Balzacian cycle have their own independent life because each of them deals with individual destinies. But these individual destinies are always a radiation of the socially typical, of the socially universal, which can be separated from the individual only by an analysis *a posteriori*. In the novels themselves the individual and the general are inseparably united, like a fire with the heat it radiates. Thus, in *Lost Illusions* the development of Lucien's character is inseparably bound up with the capitalist penetration of literature.

Such a method of composition demands an extremely broad basis for characterization and plot. Breadth is also required to exclude the element of chance from that accidental intertwinement of persons and events which Balzac, like every other great epic poet, uses with such sovereign superiority. Only a great wealth of multiple interconnections affords sufficient elbow-room in which chance can become artistically productive and ultimately lose its fortuitous character.

"In Paris only people who have many connections can count on chance to favour them; the more connections one has, the greater the prospect of success; for chance, too, is on the side of the bigger battalions."

Balzac's method of sublimating chance is thus still "old-fashioned" and differs in principle from the method used by modern authors. In his review of John Dos Passos' *Manhattan Transfer* Sinclair Lewis[10] criticizes the "old" method of plot-building. Although he talks mostly of Dickens, the gist of his criticism applies to Balzac just as much. He says that the classical method was clumsily contrived; by an unhappy chance Mr. Jones had to travel in the same mail coach as Mr. Smith, in order that something very unpleasant and very entertaining might happen. He points out that there is nothing of this in *Manhattan Transfer*, where the characters either do not meet at all, or do so in a perfectly natural way.

[10] In the *Saturday Review of Literature,* Dec. 5, 1925.

What lies at the core of this modern conception is a non-dialectical approach to causality and chance, although of course most writers are entirely unaware of this. They contrast chance with causality and believe that chance ceases to be chance if its immediate cause is revealed. But poetic motivation gains little, if anything, by such a device. Introduce an accident, however well-founded causally, into any tragic conflict and it is merely grotesque; no chain of cause and effect could ever turn such an accident into a necessity. The most thorough and accurate description of the state of the ground which would cause Achilles to sprain his ankle while pursuing Hector or the most brilliant medico-pathological explanation why Antony lost his voice through a throat infection just before he was due to make his great speech over Caesar's body in the forum could never make such things appear as anything but grotesque accidents; on the other hand, in the catastrophe of Romeo and Juliet the rough-hewn, scarcely motivated accidents do not appear as mere chance.

Why?

For no other reason, of course, than that the necessity which nullifies chance consists of an intricate network of causal connections and because only the aggregate necessity of an entire trend of developments constitutes a *poetic* necessity. Romeo's and Juliet's love *must* end in tragedy and only this necessity nullifies the accidental character of all the happenings which are the immediate causes that bring about, stage by stage, this inevitable development of the plot. It is of secondary importance whether such happenings taken by themselves, are motivated or not, and if the former, to what extent. One happening is not more a matter of chance than another and the poet has a perfect right to choose, among several equally accidental occurrences, the one he regards as best suited to his purpose. Balzac makes sovereign use of this freedom, and so did Shakespeare.

The poetic presentation of necessity by Balzac rests on his profound grasp of the line of development concretely incarnated in the theme in hand. By means of a broad and deep conception of his characters, a broad and deep portrayal of society and of the subtle and multiple interconnections between his characters and the social basis and setting of their actions, Balzac creates a wide space within which hundreds of accidents may intersect each other and yet in their aggregate produce fateful necessities.

The true necessity in *Lost Illusions* is that Lucien must perish in Paris. Every step, every phase in the rise and decline of his fortunes provide ever more profound social and psychological links in this chain of necessity. The novel is so conceived that every incident is a step towards the same end, although each single happening, while helping to reveal the underlying necessity, is in itself accidental. The uncovering of such deep-seated social necessities is always effected by means of some action, by the forceful concentration of events all moving towards the catastrophe. The extensive and sometimes most circumstantial descriptions of a town, a dwelling or an inn are never mere descriptions; by means of them Balzac creates again and again the wide and varied space required for the explosion of the catastrophe. The catastrophe itself is mostly sudden, but its suddenness is only apparent, for the traits brightly illuminated by the catastrophe are the same traits we have long been able to observe, even though at a much lower intensity.

It is most characteristic of Balzac's methods that in *Lost Illusions* two great turning-points in the story occur within a few days or even within a few hours of each other. A few days suffice for Lucien de Rubempré and Louise Bargeton to discover of each other that they are both provincials—a discovery that causes each of them to turn from the other. The catastrophe occurs during an evening spent together at the theatre. Even more sudden is Lucien's journalistic success. One afternoon, in despair, he reads his poem to the journalist Lousteau; Lousteau invites him to his office, introduces him to his publisher, takes him to the theatre; Lucien writes his first review as a dramatic critic and awakes next morning to find himself a famous journalist. The truth of such catastrophes is of a social nature; it lies in the truth of the social categories which in the final count determine such sudden turns of fortune. The catastrophe produces a concentration of essential determinants and prevents the intrusion of inessential details.

The problem of the essential and inessential is another aspect of the problem of chance. From the point of view of the writer every quality of every human being is an accident and every object merely a piece of stage property, until their decisive interconnections are expressed in poetic form, by means of some action. Hence there is no contradiction between the broad foundations on which Balzac's novels are built up and their pointed, explosive action which moves from catastrophe to catastrophe. On the contrary, the Balzacian plots require just such broad foundations, because their intricacy and tension, while revealing ever new traits in each character, never introduce anything radically new, but merely give explicit expression in action to things already implicitly contained in the broad foundation. Hence Balzac's characters never possess any traits which are in this sense accidental. For the characters have not a single quality, not even a single external attribute which does not acquire a decisive significance at some point in the plot. Precisely for this reason Balzac's descriptions never create a setting in the sense in which the word was later used in positivist sociology and it is for the same reason that for instance Balzac's very detailed descriptions of people's houses never appear as mere stage settings.

Consider for instance, the part played in Lucien's first disaster in Paris by his four suits of clothes. Two of these he has brought with him from Angoulême and even the better of the two proves quite impossible during the very first walk Lucien takes in Paris. His first Paris-made suit also turns out to be an armour with too many chinks in the first battle with Parisian society which he has to fight in Madame d'Espard's box at the Opera. The second Parisian suit is delivered too late to play a part in this first phase of the story and is put away in a cupboard during the ascetic, poetic period—to emerge again later for a short time in connection with the journalistic episode. All other objects described by Balzac play a similar dramatic part and embody similar essential factors.

Balzac builds his plots on broader foundations than any other author before or after him, but nevertheless there is nothing in them not germane to the story. The many-sided influence of multifariously determined factors in them is in perfect conformity with the structure of objective reality whose wealth we can never adequately grasp and reflect with our ever all too abstract, all too rigid, all too direct, all too unilateral thinking.

Balzac's many-sided, many tiered world approaches reality much more closely than any other method of presentation.

But the more closely the Balzacian method approaches objective reality, the more it diverges from the accustomed, the average, the direct and immediate manner of reflecting this objective reality. Balzac's method transcends the narrow, habitual, accepted limits of this immediacy and because it thus runs counter to the comfortable, familiar, usual way of looking at things, it is regarded by many as "exaggerated" or "cumbersome." It is the wide sweep, the greatness itself of Balzac's realism which forms the sharpest contrast to the habits of thought and the experience of an age which is to an increasing degree turning away from objective reality and is content to regard either immediate experience, or experience inflated into a myth as the utmost that we can grasp of reality.

But it is, of course, not only in the breadth, depth and multifariousness of his reproduction of reality that Balzac transcends the immediate. He goes beyond the boundaries of average reality in his mode of expression as well. D'Arthez (who is meant for a portrait of Balzac himself) says in this novel: "And what is art? Nothing more than concentrated nature. But this concentration is never formal; on the contrary, it is the greatest possible intensification of the content, the social and human essence of a situation."

Balzac is one of the wittiest writers who ever lived. But his wit is not confined to brilliant and striking formulations; it consists rather in his ability strikingly to present some essential point at the maximum tension of its inner contradictions. At the outset of his career as a journalist, Lucien de Rubempré must write an unfavourable review of Nathan's novel which he greatly admires. A few days later he has to write a second article refuting his own unfavourable review. Lucien, the novice journalist, is at first completely at a loss when faced with such a task. But first Lousteau and then Blondet enlighten him. In both cases Balzac gives us a brilliant discourse, perfect in its reasoning. Lucien is amazed and dismayed by Lousteau's arguments. "But what you are saying now," he exclaims, "is perfectly correct and reasonable." "Well, could you tear Nathan's book to pieces, if it were not?" asks Lousteau. Many writers after Balzac have described the unprincipled nature of journalism and shown how men wrote articles against their own convictions and better knowledge; but only Balzac penetrated to the very core of the journalistic sophism when he made his journalists playfully and brilliantly marshal the arguments for and against any issue according to the requirements of those who paid them and turn the ability to do this into a trade in which they are highly skilled, quite without relation to their own convictions.

On this level of expression the Balzacian "stock-exchange of the spirit" is revealed as a profound tragi-comedy of the spirit of the *bourgeois* class. Later realist writers described the already completed capitalist corruption of bourgeois ethics; but Balzac paints its earlier stage, its primitive accumulation in all the sombre splendour of its atrocity. In *Lost Illusions* the fact that the spirit has become a commodity to be bought and sold is not yet accepted as a matter of course and the spirit is not yet reduced to the dreary greyness of a machine-made article. The spirit turns into a commodity here before our eyes; it is something just happening, a new event loaded with dramatic tension. Lousteau and

Blondet were yesterday what Lucien turns into in the course of the novel: writers who have been forced to allow their gifts and convictions to become a commodity. It is the cream of the post-war *intelligentsia* which is here driven to take the best of their thoughts and feelings to market, offering for sale the finest, if belated, flowering of the ideas and emotions produced by the *bourgeois intellectuals* since the days of the Renaissance. And this late flowering is not merely an aftermath of epigones. Balzac endows his characters with an agility, scope and depth of mind, with a freedom from all provincial narrowmindedness, such as had never before been seen in France in this form, even though its dialectic is constantly twisted into a sophistic toying with the contradictions of existence. It is because this fine flowering of the spirit is at the same time a swamp of self-prostitution, corruption and depravity that the tragi-comedy enacted before us in this novel achieves a depth never before attained in *bourgeois* literature.

Thus it is the very depth of Balzac's realism which removes his art so completely beyond the photographic reproduction of "average" reality. For the great concentration of the content lends the picture, even without the addition of any romantic ingredients, a sombre, gruesome and fantastic quality. Only in this sense does Balzac at his best submit to some extent to romantic influences, without himself becoming a romanticist. The fantastic element in Balzac derives merely from the fact that he radically thinks through to the end the necessities of social reality, beyond their normal limits, beyond even their feasibility. An instance of this is the story *Melmoth Reconciled,* in which Balzac turns the soul's salvation into a commodity which is quoted on the produce exchange and the price of which begins to fall rapidly from its initial height owing to excessive supplies.

The figure of Vautrin is the incarnation of this fantastic quality in Balzac. It is certainly not by chance that this "Cromwell of the hulks" figures in those novels of Balzac in which the typical figures of the young post-war revolutionary generation turn from ideals to reality. Thus Vautrin appears in the shabby little boarding-house in which Rastignac experiences his personal ideological crisis: thus he turns up again at the end of *Lost Illusions* when Lucien de Rubempré, hopelessly ruined both materially and morally, is about to commit suicide. Vautrin takes the stage with the same motivated-unmotivated suddenness as Mephistopheles in Goethe's *Faust* or Lucifer in Byron's *Cain.* Vautrin's function in Balzac's *Human Comedy* is the same as that of Mephistopheles and Lucifer in Goethe's and Byron's mystery-plays. But the changed times have not only deprived the devil—the principle of negation—of his superhuman greatness and glory, have not only sobered him and brought him down to earth—the nature and method of his temptation have also changed. Although Goethe's old age reached well into the post-revolutionary epoch and although he gave the most profound expression to its deepest problems, he still regarded the great transformation of the world since the Renaissance as something positive and valuable and his Mephistopheles was "a part of the force that ever wills the evil but ever creates the good." In Balzac this "good" no longer exists save in the shape of fantastic dreams. Vautrin's Mephistophelian criticism of the world is only the brutal and cynical expression of what everyone does in this world and of what everyone who wants to survive *must* do. Vautrin says to Lucien: "You have nothing. You are in the position in which the Medicis, Richelieu, Napoleon were at the outset of their careers. They all bought their future with ingratitude, betrayals and sharp contradictions. He who wants everything must risk all. Consider: when you sit down to the gaming-table, do you argue about the rules of the game? The rules are cut and dried. You accept them." In this conception of society it is not only the content that is cynical. Such conceptions had already been put forward long before Balzac. But the point in the words of temptation spoken by Vautrin is that they express nakedly, without illusions and without spiritual frills, the worldly wisdom which is common to all intelligent men. The "temptation" lies in the fact that Vautrin's wisdom is identical with the wisdom of the purest, saintliest characters of Balzac's world.

In the famous letter which the "saintly" Mme. de Mortsauf writes to Felix de Vandenesse, she says about society:

"For me the existence of society is not in question. As soon as you accept society instead of living outside it, you must accept as excellent its basic principles and tomorrow you will, in a manner of speaking, sign a contract with it."

This is expressed in a rather vague and poetic form, but the naked meaning of the words is the same as what Vautrin tells Lucien—just as Rastignac noted with amazement that Vautrin's cynical wisdom was identical in its content with the dazzlingly witty aphorisms of the Vicomtesse de Beauséant . . . This profound conformity in the assessment of what is essential in capitalist reality, this conformity of opinion between the escaped convict and the flower of the aristocratic *intelligentsia* takes the place of the theatrically mystic appearance of a Mephistopheles. Not for nothing is Vautrin nicknamed "Cheat-Death" in the language of the hulks and of the police narks. Vautrin stands in truth in the graveyard of all illusions developed during several centuries, on his face the satanic grin of the bitter Balzacian wisdom that all men are either fools or knaves.

But this sombre picture does not signify pessimism in the later-nineteenth-century sense of the word. The great poets and thinkers of this phase of *bourgeois* development fearlessly rejected the dull apologetics of capitalist progress, the myth of a contradictionless, smoothly evolutionary advance. It was precisely this depth and many-sidedness that forced them into a contradictory position: their proud, critical recognition, their intellectual and poetic grasp of the contradictions of capitalist development is necessarily coupled with groundless illusions. In *Lost Illusions* the circle around Daniel D'Arthez is the poetic manifestation of these illusions, just as in *The Nephew of Rameau* Diderot himself is the incarnation of these illusions. In all these cases the existence of another and a better truth is poetically opposed to the squalid reality. In his analysis of Diderot's masterpiece Hegel already pointed out the weakness of this poetic argumentation.[11] Hegel already pointed out the weakness of this poetic argumentation. Hegel saw clearly, in connection with Diderot, that the voice of historical evolution is heard, not in the isolated portrayal of what is good, but in the negative, in what is evil and perverse. According to Hegel, the perverse consciousness sees the connection—or at least the contradictory nature of the connection—while the illusory good has to be content with

[11] Hegel's analysis occurs in the *Phenomenology of Mind*.

incidental and isolated details. "The content of what the spirit says of and about itself is thus a complete inversion of all concepts and realities, a general deception of itself and all others and hence the shamelessness with which the deception is proclaimed is the greatest truth."

But in spite of all illusions, the Diderot of the Rameau dialogue or the D'Arthez-Balzac of *Lost Illusions* should not, of course, be rigidly set against the poetically represented negative world. The basic contradiction lies precisely in the fact that in spite of all the illusions of D'Arthez, Balzac did write *Lost Illusions*. Diderot's and Balzac's consciousness did embrace both the positive and the negative of the worlds they described, both the illusions and their refutation by capitalist reality. By thus creatively expressing the true nature of the capitalist world, these writers rose not only above the illusory opinions put forward in their writings by the characters who are their mouthpieces, but also above the sophistic cynicism of the genuine representatives of capitalism which they portray. To express "that-which-is" is the highest level of cognizance which a *bourgeois* thinker or poet can attain before social evolution has reached the stage at which he can altogether jettison the *bourgeois* class basis. Naturally a core of idealist illusions inevitably still persists even in such expressions of "that-which-is." Hegel, at the end of his analysis of Diderot, sums up these illusions by saying that the clear recognition of these contradictions signifies that the spirit has in reality already overcome them.

It is of course an obvious and typical illusion when Hegel believes that the perfect intellectual grasp of the contradictions of reality is equivalent to overcoming them in fact; for even this intellectual grasp of contradictions which cannot as yet be overcome in fact, will itself always prove illusory. The form is different but the essence of the illusion remains the same.

Nevertheless these illusions contributed to the continuation of the great struggle of mankind for freedom, however mistaken a motivation may have been Balzac's desperately earnest searching for truth and justice is an important and tragic phase in the history of humanism. In the twilight of a traditional period when the sun of the revolutionary humanism of the *bourgeoisie* had already set and the light of the rising new democratic and proletarian humanism was not yet visible over the horizon, such a criticism of capitalism as Balzac's was the surest way to preserve the great heritage of *bourgeois* humanism and save what was best in it for the future benefit of mankind.

In *Lost Illusions* Balzac created a new type of novel of disillusionment, but his novel far outgrew the forms which this type of novel took later in the nineteenth century. The difference between the latter and the former, which makes this novel and Balzac's whole *oeuvre* unique in the literature of the world, is a historical difference. Balzac depicted the original accumulation of capital in the ideological sphere, while his successors, even Flaubert, the greatest of them, already accepted as an accomplished fact that all human values were included in the commodity structure of capitalism. In Balzac we see the tumultuous tragedy of birth; his successors give us the lifeless fact of consummation and lyrically or ironically mourn the dead. Balzac depicts the last great struggle against the capitalist degradation of man, while his successors paint an already degraded capitalist world. Romanticism—which for Balzac was only one feature of his total conception, a feature which he overcame and developed further—was not overcome by his successors, but lyrically and ironically transmuted into reality which it overgrew, blanketing the great motive forces of evolution and providing only elegiac or ironical moods and impressions instead of an active and objective presentation of things in themselves. The militant participation in the great human struggle for liberation slackens into mourning over the slavery that capitalism has brought on mankind and the militant anger at this degradation dies down to an impotently arrogant passive irony. Thus Balzac not only created the novel of disillusionment but also exhausted the highest possibilities of this type of novel. His successors who continued in his footsteps, moved on a downward slope, however great their literary achievements may have been. Their artistic decline was socially and historically unavoidable.

G. Wilson Knight

ON THE PRINCIPLES
OF SHAKESPEARE
INTERPRETATION

Of the scarcely numerable critical essays on the plays of Shakespeare that have been published in the twentieth century, it may well be that G. Wilson Knight's "On the Principles of Shakespeare Interpretation" is the one that has had the greatest influence. There are now few critics of Shakespeare who do not accept Professor Knight's method of dealing with "each play as a visionary unit based upon a self-consistent pattern of words, imagery, and events." This summary description of Knight's procedure is quoted from Richard Harrier's article on Shakespeare's imagery in *A Shakespeare Encyclopedia* (ed. O. M. Campbell); Professor Harrier, after taking note of the positive response to the principles of interpretation that the essay sets forth, goes on to speak of the resistance offered to Knight's own use of them to develop the view that the plays which Shakespeare wrote between 1599 and 1611 constitute a single unified work which gives expression to a coherent "vision" of life that is at once humanistic and transcendant, or, as might be said, both naturalistic and Christian. But the critics' dissent from Knight's doctrinal conclusions does not diminish their respect for the method by which he reached them.

G[eorge] Wilson Knight was born in 1897 and was educated at Dulwich College and at St. Edmund's Hall, Oxford. In addition to holding several distinguished academic posts, of which the last was the Professorship of English Literature at Leeds University, he has been a producer of Shakespeare's plays and an actor in them. His many books include *Myth and Miracle* (1929), *The Wheel of Fire* (1930), *The Imperial Theme* (1931), *The Shakespearean Tempest* (1932), *The Principles of Shakespearean Production* (1936), *The Burning Oracle* (1939), *The Starlit Dome* (1941), *Christ and Nietzsche* (1941), *Lord Byron: Christian Virtues* (1952), *The Sovereign Flower* (1958), and *The Golden Labyrinth* (1962). "On the Principles of Shakespeare Interpretation" is the first chapter of *The Wheel of Fire*. It is a revised and expanded version of an essay that appeared in the September 1928 number of *The Shakespeare Review;* this original version has been reprinted in an appendix to *The Sovereign Flower*.

From *The Wheel of Fire,* by G. Wilson Knight. Reprinted by permission of the publishers, Methuen & Co., Ltd., London.

The following essays present an interpretation of Shakespeare's work which may tend at first to confuse and perhaps even repel the reader: therefore I here try to clarify the points at issue. In this essay I outline what I believe to be the main hindrances to a proper understanding of Shakespeare; I also suggest the path which I think a sound interpretation should pursue. My remarks are, however, to be read as a counsel of perfection. Yet, though I cannot claim to follow them throughout in practice, this preliminary discussion, in showing what I have been at pains to do and to avoid, will serve to indicate the direction of my attempt.

At the start, I would draw a distinction between the terms "criticism" and "interpretation." It will be as well to define, purely for my immediate purpose, my personal uses of the words. "Criticism" to me suggests a certain process of deliberately objectifying the work under consideration; the comparison of it with other similar works in order especially to show in what respects it surpasses, or falls short of, those works; the dividing its "good" from its "bad"; and, finally, a formal judgement as to its lasting validity. "Interpretation," on the contrary, tends to merge into the work it analyses; it attempts, as far as possible, to understand its subject in the light of its own nature, employing external reference, if at all, only as a preliminary to understanding; it avoids discussion of merits, and, since its existence depends entirely on its original acceptance of the validity of the poetic unit which it claims, in some measure, to translate into discursive reasoning, it can recognize no division of "good" from "bad." Thus criticism is active and looks ahead, often treating past work as material on which to base future standards and canons of art; interpretation is passive, and looks back, regarding only the imperative challenge of a poetic vision. Criticism is a judgement of vision; interpretation a reconstruction of vision. In practice, it is probable that neither can exist, or at least has yet on any comprehensive scale existed, quite divorced from the other. The greater part of poetic commentary pursues a middle course between criticism and interpretation. But sometimes work is created of so resplendent a quality, so massive a solidity of imagination, that adverse criticism beats against it idly as the wind that flings its ineffectual force against a mountain-rock. Any profitable commentary on such work must necessarily tend towards a pure interpretation.

The work of Shakespeare is of this transcendent order. Though much has already been writtten on it, only that profitably survives which in its total effect tends to interpretation rather than criticism. Coleridge, repelled by one of the horrors in *King Lear*, admitted that the author's judgement, being so consistently faultless, was here probably superior to his own: and he was right.[1] That is the interpretative approach. Hazlitt and A. C. Bradley[2] both developed that approach: their work is primarily interpretative. But to-day there is a strong tendency to "criticize" Shakespeare, to select certain aspects of his mature works and point out faults. These faults are accounted for in various ways: it

---

[1] Of Gloucester's blinding and subsequent suffering, Coleridge said, "I will not disguise my conviction that in this one point the tragic has been urged beyond the outermost mark and *ne plus ultra* of the dramatic." See *Coleridge's Writings on Shakespeare*, ed. Terence Hawks (New York, 1959), p. 180.

[2] William Hazlitt, *Characters of Shakespeare's Plays* (1817–1818), see pp. 186 ff. of this volume; A. C. Bradley, *Shakespearian Tragedy* (1904).

is said that Shakespeare, though a great genius, was yet a far from perfect artist; that certain elements were introduced solely to please a vulgar audience; or even, if the difficulty be extreme, that they are the work of another hand. Now it will generally be found that when a play is understood in its totality, these faults automatically vanish. For instance, Hamlet's slowness to avenge his father, the forgiveness of Angelo, Macbeth's vagueness of motive, Timon's universal hate—all these, which have continually baffled commentators, instead of projecting as ugly curiosities, will, when once we find the true focus demanded by the poet's work, appear not merely as relevant and even necessary, but as crucial, and themselves the very essence of the play concerned. It is, then, a matter of correct focal length; nor is it the poet's fault if our focus is wrong. For our imaginative focus is generally right enough. In reading, watching, or acting Shakespeare for pure enjoyment we accept everything. But when we think "critically" we see faults which are not implicit in the play nor our enjoyment of it, but merely figments of our own minds. We should not, in fact, think critically at all: we should interpret our original imaginative experience into the slower consciousness of logic and intellect, preserving something of that childlike faith which we possess, or should possess, in the theatre. It is exactly this translation from one order of consciousness to another that interpretation claims to perform. Uncritically, and passively, it receives the whole of the poet's vision; it then proceeds to re-express this experience in its own terms.

But to receive the whole Shakespearian vision into the intellectual consciousness demands a certain and very definite act of mind. One must be prepared to see the whole play in space as well as in time. It is natural in analysis to pursue the steps of the tale in sequence, noticing the logic that connects them, regarding those essentials that Aristotle noted; the beginning, middle, and end. But by giving supreme attention to this temporal nature of drama we omit what, in Shakespeare, is at least of equivalent importance. A Shakespearian tragedy is set spatially as well as temporally in the mind. By this I mean that there are throughout the play a set of correspondences which relate to each other independently of the time-sequence which is the story: such are the intuition-intelligence opposition active within and across *Troilus and Cressida,* the death-theme in *Hamlet,* the nightmare evil of *Macbeth.* This I have sometimes called the play's "atmosphere." In interpretation of *Othello* it has to take the form of an essential relation, abstracted from the story, existing between the Othello, Desdemona, and Iago conceptions. Generally, however, there is unity, not diversity. Perhaps it is what Aristotle meant by "unity of idea." Now if we are prepared to see the whole play laid out, so to speak, as an area, being simultaneously aware of these thickly-scattered correspondences in a single view of the whole, we possess the unique quality of the play in a new sense. "Faults" begin to vanish into thin air. Immediately we begin to realize necessity where before we saw irrelevance and beauty dethroning ugliness. For the Shakespearian person is intimately fused with this atmospheric quality; he obeys a spatial as well as a temporal necessity. Gloucester's mock-suicide, Malcolm's detailed confession of crimes, Ulysses' long speech on order, are cases in point. But because we, in our own lives and those of our friends, see events most strongly as a time-sequence—thereby blurring our vision of other significances—we next, quite arbitrarily and unjustly, abstract from the Shakespearian drama that element which the intellect most easily assimilates; and, finding it not to correspond with our own life as we see it, begin to observe "faults." This, however, is apparent only after we try to rationalize our impressions; what I have called the "spatial" approach is implicit in our imaginative pleasure to a greater or a less degree always. It is, probably, the ability to see larger and still larger areas of a great work spatially with a continual widening of vision that causes us to appreciate it more deeply, to own it with our minds more surely, on every reading; whereas at first, knowing it only as a story, much of it may have seemed sterile, and much of it irrelevant. A vivid analogy to this Shakespearian quality is provided by a fine modern play, *Journey's End.*[3] Everything in the play gains tremendous significance from war. The story, which is slight, moves across a stationary background: if we forget that background for one instant parts of the dialogue fall limp; remember it, and the most ordinary remark is tense, poignant—often of shattering power. To study *Measure for Measure* or *Macbeth* without reference to their especial "atmospheres" is rather like forgetting the war as we read or witness *Journey's End;* or the cherry orchard in Tchehov's famous play.[4] There is, however, a difference. In *Journey's End* the two elements, the dynamic and static, action and background, are each firmly actualized and separated except in so far as Stanhope, rather like Hamlet, bridges the two. In *The Cherry Orchard* there is the same division. But with Shakespeare a purely spiritual atmosphere interpenetrates the action, there is a fusing rather than a contrast; and where a direct personal symbol growing out of the dominating atmosphere is actualized, it may be a supernatural being, as the Ghost, symbol of the death-theme in *Hamlet,* or the Weird Sisters, symbols of the evil in *Macbeth.*

Since in Shakespeare there is this close fusion of the temporal, that is, the plot-chain of event following event, with the spatial, that is, the omnipresent and mysterious reality brooding motionless over and within the play's movement, it is evident that my two principles thus firmly divided in analysis are no more than provisional abstractions from the poetic unity. But since to make the first abstraction with especial crudity, that is, to analyse the sequence of events, the "causes" linking dramatic motive to action and action to result in time, is a blunder instinctive to the human intellect, I make no apology for restoring balance by insistence on the other. My emphasis is justified, in that it will be seen to clarify many difficulties. It throws neglected beauties into strong relief, and often resolves the whole play with a sudden revelation. For example, the ardour of Troilus in battle against the Greeks at the close of *Troilus and Cressida,* Mariana's lovely prayer for Angelo's life, the birth of love in Edmund at the close of *King Lear,* and the stately theme of Alcibiades' revenge in *Timon of Athens*—all these cannot be properly understood without a clear knowledge of the general themes which vitalize the action of those plays.

These dual elements seem perfectly harmonized in *Troilus and Cressida, Measure for Measure, Macbeth,* and *King Lear.* In *Hamlet* the spatial element is mainly confined to the theme of Hamlet and the Ghost, both sharply contrasted with their environment: thus the play offers a less unified statement

[3] *Journey's End* (1929), by Robert Cedric Sherriff (b. 1896).
[4] *The Cherry Orchard* (1904) by Anton Pavlovich Tchekov, or Chekhov (1860–1904).

as a whole, and interpretation is rendered difficult and not wholly satisfactory. With *Othello,* too, there is difficulty. Unless the play is to be considered as purely a sequence of events, if we are to find a spatial reality, we must view the qualities of the three chief persons together and in their essential relation to each other expect to find the core of the metaphysical significance: for the primary fact of the play is not, as in *Macbeth* and *King Lear,* a blending, but rather a differentiating, a demarcation, and separation, of essence from essence. In *Timon of Athens* both elements appear, but the temporal predominates in that the imaginative atmosphere itself changes with the play's progress: which fact here seems to reflect the peculiar clarity and conscious mastery of the poet's mind. With the poet, as with the reader, the time-sequence will be uppermost in consciousness, the pervading atmosphere or static background tending to be unconsciously apprehended or created, a half-realized significance, a vague all-inclusive deity of the dramatic universe. In respect of this atmospheric suggestion we find a sense of mystery in *King Lear* which cannot be found in *Othello;* and, in so far as the Shakespearian play lacks mystery, it seems, as a rule, to lack profundity. But in *Timon of Athens* the mystery of *King Lear* is, as it were, mastered, and yet re-expressed with the clarity of *Othello.* Here the poet explicates the atmospheric quality of former plays in a philosophic tragedy whose dominant temporal quality thus mirrors the clarity, in no sense the sterility, of the poet's vision. The spatial, that is, the spiritual, quality uses the temporal, that is, the story, lending it dominance in order to express itself the more clearly: *Timon of Athens* is essentially an allegory or parable. My suggestion as to the poet's "consciousness" must, however, be considered as either pure hazard or useful metaphor, illuminating the play's nature and perhaps hitting the truth of Shakespeare's mind in composition. Certainly Hazlitt thought that in *Timon of Athens* the poet was of all his plays the most "in earnest." But elsewhere I am not concerned with the poet's "consciousness," or "intentions." Nor need the question arise; but, since a strong feeling exists that no subtlety or profundity can be born from a mind itself partly unconscious of such things, and since Shakespeare's life appears not to have been mainly concerned with transcendental realities—except in that he was born, loved, was ambitious, and died—it will be as well to refer briefly to the matter of "intentions." This I shall do next, and will afterwards deal with two other critical concepts which, with "intentions," have helped to work chaos with our understanding of poetry.

There is a maxim that a work of art should be criticized according to the artist's "intentions": than which no maxim could be more false. The intentions of the artist are but clouded forms which, if he attempt to crystallize them in consciousness, may prefigure a quite different reality from that which eventually emerges in his work,

> not answering the aim
> And that unbodied figure of the thought
> That gave't surmised shape.[5]

In those soliloquies where Brutus and Macbeth try to clarify their own motives into clean-cut concepts, we may see good examples of the irrelevance born by

[5] *Troilus and Cressida,* I, iii, 15–17.

"intentions" to the instinctive power which is bearing the man towards his fate: it is the same with the poet. Milton's puritanical "intentions" bear little relevance to his Satan. "Intentions" belong to the plane of intellect and memory: the swifter consciousness that awakens in poetic composition touches subtleties and heights and depths unknowable by intellect and intractable to memory. That consciousness we can enjoy at will when we submit ourselves with utmost passivity to the poet's work; but when the intellectual mode returns it often brings with it a troop of concepts irrelevant to the nature of the work it thinks to analyse, and, with its army of "intentions," "causes," "sources," and "characters," and its essentially ethical outlook, works havoc with our minds, since it is trying to impose on the vivid reality of art a logic totally alien to its nature. In interpretation we must remember not the facts but the quality of the original poetic experience; and, in translating this into whatever concepts appear suitable, we find that the facts too fall into place automatically when once the qualitative focus is correct. Reference to the artist's "intentions" is usually a sign that the commentator—in so far as he is a commentator rather than a biographer—has lost touch with the essentials of the poetic work. He is thinking in terms of the time-sequence and causality, instead of allowing his mind to be purely receptive. It will be clear, then, that the following essays say nothing new as to Shakespeare's "intentions," attempt to shed no light directly on Shakespeare the man; but claim rather to illuminate our own poetic experiences enjoyed whilst reading, or watching, the plays. In this sense, they are concerned only with realties, since they claim to interpret what is generally admitted to exist: the supreme quality of Shakespeare's work.

Next as to "sources." This concept is closely involved with that of "intentions." Both try to explain art in terms of causality, the most natural implement of intellect. Both fail empirically to explain any essential whatsoever. There is, clearly, a relation between Shakespeare's plays and the work of Plutarch, Holinshed, Vergil, Ovid,[6] and the Bible; but not one of these, nor any number of them, can be considered a cause of Shakespeare's poetry and therefore the word "source," that is, the origin whence the poetic reality flows, is a false metaphor. In Shakespeare's best known passage of aesthetic philosophy we hear that the poet's eye glances "from heaven to earth, from earth to heaven," and that the poet's pen turns to "shapes" the "forms of things unknown." It "gives to airy nothing a local habitation and a name."[7] That is, the source of poetry

---

[6] Plutarch (c. A.D. 46–120), Greek essayist and biographer, author of the *Parallel Lives,* from which Shakespeare took much information for his Roman plays. Raphael Holinshed (d. 1580), English chronicler, from whose *Chronicles of England, Scotland, and Ireland* Shakespeare took material for his history plays and his legendary tragedies. Ovid (Publius Ovidius Naso, 43 B.C.–A.D. 18), Latin poet, from whose *Ars Amatoria* ("Art of Love") and *Metamorphoses* Shakespeare used various themes and images for a number of plays and poems.

[7] The poet's eye, in a fine frenzy rolling,
Doth glance from heaven to earth, from earth to heaven;
And as imagination bodies forth
The forms of things unknown, the poet's pen
Turns them to shapes and gives to airy nothing
A local habitation and a name.

A Midsummer-Night's Dream, V, i, 12–17.

is rooted in the otherness of mental or spiritual realities; these, however, are a "nothing" until mated with earthly shapes. Creation is thus born of a union between "earth" and "heaven," the material and the spiritual. Without "shapes" the poet is speechless; he needs words, puppets of the drama, tales. But the unknown "forms" come first. In another profound but less known passage (*Richard II*, v. v. 6) we hear that in creation the brain is "the female to the soul." The spiritual then is the masculine, the material the feminine, agent in creation. The "source" of *Antony and Cleopatra,* if we must indeed have a "source" at all, is the transcendent erotic imagination of the poet which finds its worthy bride in an old world romance. It seems, indeed, that the great poet must, if he is to forgo nothing of concreteness and humanity, lose himself in contemplation of an actual tale or an actual event in order to find himself in supreme vision; otherwise he will tend to philosophy, to the divine element unmated to the earthly. Therefore "sources," as usually understood, have their use for the poet: they have little value for the interpreter. The tale of Cleopatra married to a Hardy's[8] imagination would have given birth to a novel very different from Shakespeare's play: the final poetic result is always a mystery. That result, and not vague hazards as to its "source," must be the primary object of our attention. It should further be observed that, although the purely "temporal" element of Shakespearian drama may sometimes bear a close relation to a tale probably known by Shakespeare, what I have called the "spatial" reality is ever the unique child of his mind; therefore interpretation, concerned, as in the following essays, so largely with that reality, is clearly working outside and beyond the story alone. Now, whereas the spatial quality of these greater plays is different in each, they nearly all turn on the same plot. It is therefore reasonable to conclude that the poet has chosen a series of tales to whose life-rhythm he is spontaneously attracted, and has developed them in each instance according to his vision.

And finally, as to "character." In the following essays the term is refused, since it is so constantly entwined with a false and unduly ethical criticism. So often we hear that "in *Timon of Athens* it was Shakespeare's intention to show how a generous but weak character may come to ruin through an unwise use of his wealth"; that "Shakespeare wished in *Macbeth* to show how crime inevitably brings retribution"; that, "in *Antony and Cleopatra* Shakespeare has given us a lesson concerning the dangers of an uncontrolled passion." These are purely imaginary examples, coloured for my purpose, to indicate the type of ethical criticism to which I refer. It continually brings in the intention-concept, which our moral-philosophy, rightly or wrongly, involves. Hence, too, the constant and fruitless search for "motives" sufficient to account for Macbeth's and Iago's actions: since the moral critic feels he cannot blame a "character" until he understands his "intentions," and without the opportunity of praising and blaming he is dumb. It is not, indeed, possible to avoid ethical considerations; nor is it advisable. Where one person within the drama is immediately apparent as morally good and another as bad, we will note the difference; but we should follow our dramatic intuitions. A person in the drama may act in such a way that we are in no sense antagonized but are aware of beauty and supreme

---

[8] Thomas Hardy (1840–1928), English poet and novelist.

interest only; yet the analogy to that same action may well be intolerable to us in actual life. When such a divergence occurs the commentator must be true to his artistic, not his normal, ethic. Large quantities of Shakespeare criticism have wrecked themselves on the teeth of this dualism. In so far as moral values enter into our appreciation of the poetic work, they will tend to be instinctive to us: Shakespeare here, as in his other symbols, speaks our own language. I mean, it is as natural to us to like Cordelia better than Goneril with a liking which may be said to depend partly on moral values as it is for us to recognize the power of Shakespeare's tempest-symbol as suggesting human tragedy, or his use of jewel-metaphors to embody the costly riches of love. In ages hence, when perhaps tempests are controlled by science and communism has replaced wealth, then the point of Shakespeare's symbolism may need explanation; and then it may, from a new ethical view-point, be necessary to analyse at length the moral values implicit in the Cordelia and Edmund conceptions. But in these matters Shakespeare speaks almost the same language as we, and ethical terms, though they must frequently occur in interpretation, must only be allowed in so far as they are used in absolute obedience to the dramatic and aesthetic significance: in which case they cease to be ethical in the usual sense.

This false criticism is implied by the very use of the word "character." It is impossible to use the term without any tinge of a morality which blurs vision. The term, which in ordinary speech often denotes the degree of moral control exercised by the individual over his instinctive passions, is altogether unsuited to those persons of poetic drama whose life consists largely of passion unveiled. *Macbeth* and *King Lear* are created in a soul-dimension of primal feeling, of which in real life we may be only partly conscious or may be urged to control by a sense of right and wrong. In fact, it may well seem that the more we tend away from the passionate and curbless life of poetic drama, the stronger we shall be as "characters." And yet, in reading *Macbeth* or *King Lear* we are aware of strength, not weakness. We are not aware of failure: rather we "let determined things to destiny hold unbewailed their way." We must observe, then, this paradox: the strong protagonist of poetic drama would probably appear a weakling if he were a real man; and, indeed, the critic who notes primarily Macbeth's weakness is criticizing him as a man rather than a dramatic person. Ethics are essentially critical when applied to life; but if they hold any place at all in art, they will need to be modified into a new artistic ethic which obeys the peculiar nature of art as surely as a sound morality is based on the nature of man. From a true interpretation centred on the imaginative qualities of Shakespeare, certain facts will certainly emerge which bear relevance to human life, to human morals: but interpretation must come first. And interpretation must be metaphysical rather than ethical. We shall gain nothing by applying to the delicate symbols of the poet's imagination the rough machinery of an ethical philosophy created to control the turbulences of actual life. Thus when a critic adopts the ethical attitude, we shall generally find that he is unconsciously lifting the object of his attention from his setting and regarding him as actually alive. By noting "faults" in Timon's "character" we are in effect saying that he would not be a success in real life: which is beside the point, since he, and Macbeth, and Lear, are evidently dramatic successes. Now, whereas the moral attitude to life is positive and dynamic and tells us what we ought to do, that attitude applied to literature is invariably negative and destructive. It is continually thrusting on our attention a number of "failures," "mistakes," and "follies" in connexion with those dramatic persons from whom we have consistently derived delight and a sense of exultation. Even when terms of negation, such as "evil," necessarily appear—as with *Hamlet* and *Macbeth*—we should so employ them that the essence they express is felt to be something powerful, autonomous, and grand. Our reaction to great literature is a positive and dynamic experience. Crudely, sometimes ineffectually, interpretation will attempt to translate that experience in a spirit also positive and dynamic.

To do this we should regard each play as a visionary whole, close-knit in personification, atmospheric suggestion, and direct poetic-symbolism: three modes of transmission, equal in their importance. Too often the first of these alone receives attention: whereas, in truth, we should not be content even with all three, however clearly we have them in our minds, unless we can work back through them to the original vision they express. Each incident, each turn of thought, each suggestive symbol throughout *Macbeth* or *King Lear* radiates inwards from the play's circumference to the burning central core without knowledge of which we shall miss their relevance and necessity: they relate primarily, not directly to each other, nor to the normal appearances of human life, but to this central reality alone. The persons of Shakespeare have been analysed carefully in point of psychological realism. But in giving detailed and prolix attention to any one element of the poet's expression, the commentator, starting indeed from a point on the circumference, instead of working into the heart of the play, pursues a tangential course, riding, as it were, on his own life-experiences farther and farther from his proper goal. Such is the criticism that finds fault with the Duke's decisions at the close of *Measure for Measure*: if we are to understand the persons of Shakespeare we should consider always what they do rather than what they might have done. Each person, event, scene, is integral to the poetic statement: the removing, or blurring, of a single stone in the mosaic will clearly lessen our chance of visualizing the whole design.

Too often the commentator discusses Shakespeare's work without the requisite emotional sympathy and agility of intellect. Then the process of false criticism sets in: whatever elements lend themselves most readily to analysis on the analogy of actual life, these he selects, roots out, distorting their natural growth; he then praises or blames according to their measure of correspondence with his own life-experiences, and, creating the plaster figures of "character," searches everywhere for "causes" on the analogy of human affairs, noting that Iago has no sufficient reason for his villainy, executing some strange transference such as the statement that Lady Macbeth would have done this or that in Cordelia's position; observing that there appears to have been dull weather on the occasion of Duncan's murder. But what he will not do is recapture for analysis his own original experience, concerned, as it was, purely with a dramatic and artistic reality: with Iago the person of motiveless and instinctive villainy, with Cordelia known only with reference to the *Lear* universe, with the vivid extravagant symbolism of abnormal phenomena in beast and element and the sun's eclipse which accompanies the unnatural act of murder. These, the true, the poetic, realities, the commentator too often passes over. He does not look straight at the work he would interpret, is not true to his own imaginative reaction. My complaint is, not that such a commentator cannot appreciate the imaginative nature of Shakespeare—that would be absurd and unjustifiable—but that he falsifies his own experience when he begins to criticize. Part of the play—and that the less important element of story—he tears out ruthlessly for detailed analysis on the analogy of human life: with a word or two about "the magic of poetry" or "the breath of genius" he dismisses the rest. Hence the rich gems of Shakespeare's poetic symbolism have been left untouched and unwanted, whilst Hamlet was being treated in Harley Street.[9] Hence arises the criticism discovering faults in Shakespeare. But when a right interpretation is offered it will generally be seen that both the fault and the criticism which discovered it are without meaning. The older critics drove psychological analysis to unnecessary lengths: the new school of "realistic" criticism, in finding faults and explaining them with regard to Shakespeare's purely practical and financial "intentions," is thus in reality following the wrong vision of its predecessors. Both together trace the process of my imaginary critic, who, thinking to have found an extreme degree of realism in one place, ends by complaining that he finds too little in another. Neither touch the heart of the Shakespearian play.

Nor will a sound knowledge of the stage and the especial theatrical technique of Shakespeare's work render up its imaginative secret. True, the plays were written as plays, and meant to be acted. But that tells us nothing relevant to our purpose. It explains why certain things cannot be found in Shakespeare: it does not explain why the finest things, the fascination of *Hamlet,* the rich music of *Othello,* the gripping evil of *Macbeth,* the pathos of *King Lear,* and the gigantic architecture of *Timon of Athens* came to birth. Shakespeare wrote in terms of drama, as he wrote in English. In the grammar of dramatic structure he expresses his vision: without that, or some other, structure he could not have expressed himself. But the dramatic nature of a play's origin cannot be adduced to disprove a quality implicit in the work itself. True, when there are any faults to be explained, this particular pursuit and aim of Shakespeare's poetry may well be noted to account for their presence. Interpretation, however, tends to resolve all but minor difficulties in connexion with the greater plays: therefore it is not necessary in the following essays to remember, or comment on, the dramatic structure of their expression, though from another point of view such comment and analysis may well be interesting. It illuminates one facet of their surface: but a true philosophic and imaginative interpretation will aim at cutting below the surface to reveal that burning core of mental or spiritual reality from which each play derives its nature and meaning.

That soul-life of the Shakespearian play is, indeed, a thing of divine worth. Its perennial fire is as mysterious, as near and yet as far, as that of the sun, and, like the sun, it burns on while generations pass. If interpretation attempts to split the original beam into different colours for inspection and analysis it does not claim, any more than will the scientist, that its spectroscope reveals the

[9] Street in London where many eminent doctors have their offices.

whole reality of its attention. It discovers something: exactly what it discovers, and whether that discovery be of ultimate value, cannot easily be demonstrated. But, though we know the sun better in the spring fields than in the laboratory, yet we might remember that the spectroscope discovered Helium first in the solar ray, which chemical was after sought and found on earth. So, too, the interpretation of poetic vision may have its use. And if it seems sometimes to bear little relevance to its original, if its mechanical joints creak and its philosophy lumber clumsily in attempt to follow the swift arrow-flight of poetry, it is, at least, no less rational a pursuit than that of the mathematician who writes a rhythmic curve in the stiff symbols of an algebraic equation.

I shall now shortly formulate what I take to be the main principles of right Shakespearian interpretation:

(i) Before noticing the presence of faults we should first regard each play as a visionary unit bound to obey none but its own self-imposed laws. To do this we should attempt to preserve absolute truth to our own imaginative reaction, whithersoever it may lead us in the way of paradox and unreason. We should at all costs avoid selecting what is easy to understand and forgetting the superlogical.

(ii) We should thus be prepared to recognize what I have called the "temporal" and the "spatial" elements: that is, to relate any given incident or speech either to the time-sequence of story or the peculiar atmosphere, intellectual or imaginative, which binds the play. Being aware of this new element we should not look for perfect verisimilitude to life, but rather see each play as an expanded metaphor, by means of which the original vision has been projected into forms roughly correspondent with actuality, conforming thereto with greater or less exactitude according to the demands of its own nature. It will then usually appear that many difficult actions and events become coherent and, within the scope of their universe, natural.

(iii) We should analyse the use and meaning of direct poetic symbolism— that is, events whose significance can hardly be related to the normal processes of actual life. Also the minor symbolic imagery of Shakespeare, which is extremely consistent, should receive careful attention. Where certain images continually recur in the same associative connexion, we can, if we have reason to believe that this associative force is strong enough, be ready to see the presence of the associative value when the images occur alone. Nor should we neglect the symbolic value of aural effects such as the discharge of cannon in *Hamlet* and *Othello* or the sound of trumpets in *Measure for Measure* and *King Lear*.

(iv) The plays from *Julius Caesar* (about 1599) to *The Tempest* (about 1611) when properly understood fall into a significant sequence. This I have called "the Shakespeare Progress." Therefore in detailed analysis of any one play it may sometimes be helpful to have regard to its place in the sequence, provided always that thought of this sequence be used to illuminate, and in no sense be allowed to distort, the view of the play under analysis. Particular notice should be given to what I have called the "hate-theme," which is turbulent throughout most of these plays: an especial mode of cynicism toward love, disgust at the physical body, and dismay at the thought of death; a revulsion from human life caused by a clear sight of its limitations—more especially limitations imposed by time. This progress I have outlined in *Myth and Miracle*,[10] being concerned there especially with the Final Plays. The following essays are ordered according to the probable place in the Shakespeare Progress of the plays concerned. The order is that given by the late Professor Henry Norman Hudson in *The New Hudson Shakespeare*. Though I here compare one theme in *Julius Caesar* with *Macbeth,* I postpone a comprehensive analysis of the play, since its peculiar quality relates it more directly to the later tragedies than to those noticed in this treatment.

These arguments I have pursued at some length, since my interpretation reaches certain conclusions which may seem somewhat revolutionary. Especially will this be apparent in my reading of the Final Plays as mystical representations of a mystic vision. A first sketch of this reading I have already published in *Myth and Miracle*. Since the publication of my essay, my attention has been drawn to Mr. Colin Still's remarkable book *Shakespeare's Mystery Play: A Study of The Tempest* (Cecil Palmer, 1921). Mr. Still's interpretation of *The Tempest* is very similar to mine. His conclusions were reached by a detailed comparison of the play in its totality with other creations of literature, myth, and ritual throughout the ages; mine are reached solely through seeing *The Tempest* as the conclusion to the Shakespeare Progress. *The Tempest* is thus exactly located as a work of mystic insight with reference to the cross-axes of universal and Shakespearian vision. It would seem, therefore, that my method of interpretation as outlined in this essay has already met with some degree of empirical proof.

In conclusion, I would emphasize that I here lay down certain principles and make certain objections for my immediate purpose only. I would not be thought to level complaint against the value of "criticism" in general. My private and personal distinction between "criticism" and "interpretation" aims at no universal validity. It can hardly be absolute. No doubt I have narrowed the term "criticism" unjustly. Much of the critical work of to-day is, according to my distinction, work of a high interpretative order. Nor do I suggest that true "criticism" in the narrow sense I apply to it is of any lesser order than true interpretation: it may well be a higher pursuit, since it is, in a sense, the more creative and endures a greater burden of responsibility. The relative value of the two modes must vary in exact proportion to the greatness of the literature they analyse: that is why I believe the most profitable approach to Shakespeare to be interpretation rather than criticism.

[10] Knight's first book; published in 1929.

Jean-Paul Sartre

WHY WRITE?

Jean-Paul Sartre, unquestionably the pre-eminent figure in French letters since the Second World War, was born in Paris in 1905. He attended the intellectually elite and exigent École Normale Supérieure, which for generations has supplied France not only with her most distinguished scholars and teachers but also with some of her most notable writers. He was graduated in 1929 and for the next ten years served as a teacher of philosophy in *lycées* in the provinces and in Paris, with the exception of 1933–1934, which he spent in Berlin studying modern German philosophy. He was in active service during the war and was taken prisoner in 1940; upon his release after nine months he returned to Paris and teaching. He had already achieved a considerable place in the intellectual life of Paris by the publication of two philosophical works and especially by his novel *La Nausée* (1938; translated in America as *Nausea* and in England as *The Diary of Antoine Roquentin*), and after the war, with the success of his first two plays *The Flies* (1943) and *No Exit* (1944), he gave up teaching and devoted himself wholly to writing. His production has been impressive even in mere size; it includes three novels in addition to *La Nausée* and a volume of short stories, seven plays following the two already mentioned, several film scripts, many volumes of literary and political essays, and an auto-biography. And this is not to mention the philosophical works which provide the ideational ground on which the rest of his work stands; of these *L'Être et le Néant* (1943; translated as *Being and Nothingness*) is the best known.

Sartre is identified with the philosophical movement known as exis-tentialism. Limitations of space prevent anything like an adequate ac-count of the existential position in general and of Sartre's particular version of it, and in any case such an account is not needed for an ade-quate reading of Sartre's essay. But perhaps reference should be made to the distinction that philosophers draw between existence and essence. Both words mean "being," but essence denotes what defines the being of a thing conceptually and as it belongs to a class of things, while existence signifies the being of a thing in its particularity, actuality, and activity. The "thing" that Sartre has in mind is, of course, man, who realizes the potentials of his being through his consciousness of his particularity, through the actual and particular choices he makes. The implications of the position so far as they are political have led Sartre to the advocacy of a radical activism which expresses itself as an uneasy and still-developing connection with Marxism. "Why Write?" is a section of the long essay *What Is Literature?* (1949).

From *What Is Literature,* by Jean-Paul Sartre, translated by Bernard Frechtman. New York: Harper & Row, 1965 (A Colophon Book). Reprinted by permission of Literary Masterworks, Inc.

Each one has his reasons: for one, art is a flight; for another, a means of conquering. But one can flee into a hermitage, into madness, into death. One can conquer by arms. Why does it have to be *writing*, why does one have to manage his escapes and conquests by *writing*? Because, behind the various aims of authors, there is a deeper and more immediate choice which is common to all of us. We shall try to elucidate this choice, and we shall see whether it is not in the name of this very choice of writing that the engagement of writers must be required.

Each of our perceptions is accompanied by the consciousness that human reality is a "revealer," that is, it is through human reality that "there is" being, or, to put it differently, that man is the means by which things are manifested. It is our presence in the world which multiplies relations. It is we who set up a relationship between this tree and that bit of sky. Thanks to us, that star which has been dead for millennia, that quarter moon, and that dark river are disclosed in the unity of a landscape. It is the speed of our auto and our airplane which organizes the great masses of the earth. With each of our acts, the world reveals to us a new face. But, if we know that we are directors of being, we also know that we are not its producers. If we turn away from this landscape, it will sink back into its dark permanence. At least, it will sink back; there is no one mad enough to think that it is going to be annihilated. It is we who shall be annihilated, and the earth will remain in its lethargy until another consciousness comes along to awaken it. Thus, to our inner certainty of being "revealers" is added that of being inessential in relation to the thing revealed.

One of the chief motives of artistic creation is certainly the need of feeling that we are essential in relationship to the world. If I fix on canvas or in writing a certain aspect of the fields or the sea or a look on someone's face which I have disclosed, I am conscious of having produced them by condensing relationships, by introducing order where there was none, by imposing the unity of mind on the diversity of things. That is, I feel myself essential in relation to my creation. But this time it is the created object which escapes me; I can not reveal and produce at the same time. The creation becomes inessential in relation to the creative activity. First of all, even if it appears to others as definitive, the created object always seems to us in a state of suspension; we can always change this line, that shade, that word. Thus, it never *forces itself*. A novice painter asked his teacher, "When should I consider my painting finished?" And the teacher answered, "When you can look at it in amazement and say to yourself 'I'm the one who did *that!*' "

Which amounts to saying "never." For it is virtually considering one's work with someone else's eyes and revealing what one has created. But it is self-evident that we are proportionally less conscious of the thing produced and more conscious of our productive activity. When it is a matter of pottery or carpentry, we work according to traditional norms, with tools whose usage is codified; it is Heidegger's famous "they"[1] who are working with our hands. In this case, the result can seem to us sufficiently strange to preserve its ob-

---

[1] Heidegger's "they," that is, "The whole past one inherits," from *Sein und Zeit* (1927; trans., *Being and Times,* 1962), by Martin Heidegger.

jectivity in our eyes. But if we ourselves produce the rules of production, the measures, the criteria, and if our creative drive comes from the very depths of our heart, then we never find anything but ourselves in our work. It is we who have invented the laws by which we judge it. It is our history, our love, our gaiety that we recognize in it. Even if we should regard it without touching it any further, we never *receive* from it that gaiety or love. We put them into it. The results which we have obtained on canvas or paper never seem to us *objective*. We are too familiar with the processes of which they are the effects. These processes remain a subjective discovery; they are ourselves, our inspiration, our ruse, and when we seek to *perceive* our work, we create it again, we repeat mentally the operations which produced it; each of its aspects appears as a result. Thus, in the perception, the object is given as the essential thing and the subject as the inessential. The latter seeks essentiality in the creation and obtains it, but then it is the object which becomes the inessential.

This dialectic is nowhere more apparent than in the art of writing, for the literary object is a peculiar top which exists only in movement. To make it come into view a concrete act called reading is necessary, and it lasts only as long as this act can last. Beyond that, there are only black marks on paper. Now, the writer can not read what he writes, whereas the shoemaker can put on the shoes he has just made if they are his size, and the architect can live in the house he has built. In reading, one foresees; one waits. He foresees the end of the sentence, the following sentence, the next page. He waits for them to confirm or disappoint his foresights. The reading is composed of a host of hypotheses, of dreams followed by awakenings, of hopes and deceptions. Readers are always ahead of the sentence they are reading in a merely probable future which partly collapses and partly comes together in proportion as they progress, which withdraws from one page to the next and forms the moving horizon of the literary object. Without waiting, without a future, without ignorance, there is no objectivity.

Now the operation of writing involves an implicit quasi-reading which makes real reading impossible. When the words form under his pen, the author doubtless sees them, but he does not see them as the reader does, since he knows them before writing them down. The function of his gaze is not to reveal, by stroking them, the sleeping words which are waiting to be read, but to control the sketching of the signs. In short, it is a purely regulating mission, and the view before him reveals nothing except for slight slips of the pen. The writer neither foresees nor conjectures; he *projects*. It often happens that he awaits, as they say, the inspiration. But one does not wait for himself the way he waits for others. If he hesitates, he knows that the future is not made, that he himself is going to make it, and if he still does not know what is going to happen to his hero, that simply means that he has not thought about it, that he has not decided upon anything. The future is then a blank page, whereas the future of the reader is two hundred pages filled with words which separate him from the end. Thus, the writer meets everywhere only *his* knowledge, *his* will, *his* plans, in short, himself. He touches only his own subjectivity; the object he creates is out of reach; he does not create it *for himself*. If he rereads himself, it is already too late. The sentence will never quite be a thing in his eyes. He goes to the very limits of the subjective but without crossing it. He appreciates the effect of a touch, of an epigram, of a well-placed adjective, but it is the effect they will have on others. He can judge it, not feel it. Proust never discovered the homosexuality of Charlus,[2] since he had decided upon it even before starting on his book. And if a day comes when the book takes on for its author a semblance of objectivity, it is that years have passed, that he has forgotten it, that its spirit is quite foreign to him, and doubtless he is no longer capable of writing it. This was the case with Rousseau when he reread the *Social Contract*[3] at the end of his life.

Thus, it is not true that one writes for himself. That would be the worst blow. In projecting his emotions on paper, one barely manages to give them a languishing extension. The creative act is only an incomplete and abstract moment in the production of a work. If the author existed alone he would be able to write as much as he liked; the work as *object* would never see the light of day and he would either have to put down his pen or despair. But the operation of writing implies that of reading as its dialectical correlative and these two connected acts necessitate two distinct agents. It is the conjoint effort of author and reader which brings upon the scene that concrete and imaginary object which is the work of the mind. There is no art except for and by others.

Reading seems, in fact, to be the synthesis of perception and creation.* It supposes the essentiality of both the subject and the object. The object is essential because it is strictly transcendent, because it imposes its own structures, and because one must wait for it and observe it; but the subject is also essential because it is required not only to disclose the object (that is, to make *there be* an object) but also so that this object might *be* (that is, to produce it). In a word, the reader is conscious of disclosing in creating, of creating by disclosing. In reality, it is not necessary to believe that reading is a mechanical operation and that signs make an impression upon him as light does on a photographic plate. If he is inattentive, tired, stupid, or thoughtless, most of the relations will escape him. He will never manage to "catch on" to the object (in the sense in which we see that fire "catches" or "doesn't catch"). He will draw some phrases out of the shadow, but they will seem to appear as random strokes. If he is at his best, he will project beyond the words a synthetic form, each phrase of which will be no more than a partial function: the "theme," the "subject," or the "meaning." Thus, from the very beginning, the meaning is no longer contained in the words, since it is he, on the contrary, who allows the signification of each of them to be understood; and the literary object, though realized *through* language, is never given *in* language. On the contrary, it is by nature a silence and an opponent of the word. In addition, the hundred thousand words aligned in a book can be read one by one so that the meaning of the work does not emerge. Nothing is accomplished if the reader does not put himself from the very beginning and almost without a guide at the height of this silence; if, in short, he

[2] Charlus is a character in *The Remembrance of Things Past* (1913–1927) by Marcel Proust (1871–1922).

[3] The *Social Contract*, by Jean Jacques Rousseau (1712–1788), was published in 1762.

* The same is true in different degrees regarding the spectator's attitude before other works of art (paintings, symphonies, statues, etc). [Sartre's note.]

does not invent it and does not then place there, and hold on to, the words and sentences which he awakens. And if I am told that it would be more fitting to call this operation a re-invention or a discovery, I shall answer that, first, such a re-invention would be as new and as original an act as the first invention. And, especially, when an object has never existed before, there can be no question of re-inventing it or discovering it. For if the silence about which I am speaking is really the goal at which the author is aiming, he has, at least, never been familiar with it; his silence is subjective and anterior to language. It is the absence of words, the undifferentiated and lived silence of inspiration, which the word will then particularize, whereas the silence produced by the reader is an object. And at the very interior of this object there are more silences—which the author does not tell. It is a question of silences which are so particular that they could not retain any meaning outside of the object which the reading causes to appear. However, it is these which give it its density and its particular face.

To say that they are unexpressed is hardly the word; for they are precisely the inexpressible. And that is why one does not come upon them at any definite moment in the reading; they are everywhere and nowhere. The quality of the marvelous in *The Wanderer* (*Le Grand Meaulnes*),[4] the grandiosity of *Armance*,[5] the degree of realism and truth of Kafka's[6] mythology, these are never given. The reader must invent them all in a continual exceeding of the written thing. To be sure, the author guides him, but all he does is guide him. The landmarks he sets up are separated by the void. The reader must unite them; he must go beyond them. In short, reading is directed creation.

On the one hand, the literary object has no other substance than the reader's subjectivity; Raskolnikov's[7] waiting is *my* waiting which I lend him. Without this impatience of the reader he would remain only a collection of signs. His hatred of the police magistrate who questions him is my hatred which has been solicited and wheedled out of me by signs, and the police magistrate himself would not exist without the hatred I have for him via Raskolnikov. That is what animates him, it is his very flesh.

But on the other hand, the words are there like traps to arouse our feelings and to reflect them toward us. Each word is a path of transcendence; it shapes our feelings, names them, and attributes them to an imaginary personage who takes it upon himself to live them for us and who has no other substance than these borrowed passions; he confers objects, perspectives, and a horizon upon them.

Thus, for the reader, all is to do and all is already done; the work exists only at the exact level of his capacities; while he reads and creates, he knows that he can always go further in his reading, can always create more profoundly, and thus the work seems to him as inexhaustible and opaque as things.

[4] A novel by Alain-Fournier (pseudonym of Henri-Alban Fournier, 1886–1914), published in 1913.
[5] The first novel (1827) by Stendhal.
[6] Franz Kafka (1883–1924), Austrian writer of fiction.
[7] Raskolnikov is the chief character in *Crime and Punishment* (1886), by Feodor Mikhailovich Dostoevski (1821–1881).

We would readily reconcile that "rational intuition" which Kant[8] reserved to divine Reason with this absolute production of qualities, which, to the extent that they emanate from our subjectivity, congeal before our eyes into impermeable objectivities.

Since the creation can find its fulfillment only in reading, since the artist must entrust to another the job of carrying out what he has begun, since it is only through the consciousness of the reader that he can regard himself as essential to his work, all literary work is an appeal. To write is to make an appeal to the reader that he lead into objective existence the revelation which I have undertaken by means of language. And if it should be asked *to what* the writer is appealing, the answer is simple. As the sufficient reason for the appearance of the aesthetic object is never found either in the book (where we find merely solicitations to produce the object) or in the author's mind, and as his subjectivity, which he cannot get away from, cannot give a reason for the act of leading into objectivity, the appearance of the work of art is a new event which cannot *be explained* by anterior data. And since this directed creation is an absolute beginning, it is therefore brought about by the freedom of the reader, and by what is purest in that freedom. Thus, the writer appeals to the reader's freedom to collaborate in the production of his work.

It will doubtless be said that all tools address themselves to our freedom since they are the instruments of a possible action, and that the work of art is not unique in that. And it is true that the tool is the congealed outline of an operation. But it remains on the level of the hypothetical imperative. I may use a hammer to nail up a case or to hit my neighbor over the head. Insofar as I consider it in itself, it is not an appeal to my freedom; it does not put me face to face with it; rather, it aims at using it by substituting a set succession of traditional procedures for the free invention of means. The book does not serve my freedom; it requires it. Indeed, one cannot address himself to freedom as such by means of constraint, fascination, or entreaties. There is only one way of attaining it; first, by recognizing it, then, having confidence in it, and finally, requiring of it an act, an act in its own name, that is, in the name of the confidence that one brings to it.

Thus, the book is not, like the tool, a means for any end whatever; the end to which it offers itself is the reader's freedom. And the Kantian expression "finality without end"[9] seems to me quite inappropriate for designating the work of art. In fact, it implies that the aesthetic object presents only the appearance of a finality and is limited to soliciting the free and ordered play of the imagination. It forgets that the imagination of the spectator has not only a regulating function, but a constitutive one. It does not play; it is called upon to recompose the beautiful object beyond the traces left by the artist. The imagination can not revel in itself any more than can the other functions of the mind; it is always on the outside, always engaged in an enterprise. There would be finality without end if some object offered such a set ordering that it would lead us to

---

[8] Immanuel Kant (1724–1804), German philosopher.

[9] This expression and the ideas Sartre goes on to discuss come from Kant's *Critique of Judgment* (1790).

suppose that it has one even though we can not ascribe one to it. By defining the beautiful in this way one can—and this is Kant's aim—liken the beauty of art to natural beauty, since a flower, for example, presents so much symmetry, such harmonious colors, and such regular curves, that one is immediately tempted to seek a finalist explanation for all these properties and to see them as just so many means at the disposal of an unknown end. But that is exactly the error. The beauty of nature is in no way comparable to that of art. The work of art *does not have* an end; there we agree with Kant. But the reason is that it is an end. The Kantian formula does not account for the appeal which resounds at the basis of each painting, each statue, each book. Kant believes that the work of art first exists as fact and that it is then seen. Whereas, it exists only if one *looks* at it and if it is first pure appeal, pure exigence to exist. It is not an instrument whose existence is manifest and whose end is undetermined. It presents itself as a task to be discharged; from the very beginning it places itself on the level of the categorical imperative. You are perfectly free to leave that book on the table. But if you open it, you assume responsibility for it. For freedom is not experienced by its enjoying its free subjective functioning, but in a creative act required by an imperative. This absolute end, this imperative which is transcendent yet acquiesced in, which freedom itself adopts as its own, is what we call a value. The work of art is a value because it is an appeal.

If I appeal to my readers so that we may carry the enterprise which I have begun to a successful conclusion, it is self-evident that I consider him as a pure freedom, as an unconditioned activity; thus, in no case can I address myself to his passivity, that is, try to *affect* him, to communicate to him, from the very first, emotions of fear, desire, or anger. There are, doubtless, authors who concern themselves solely with arousing these emotions because they are foreseeable, manageable, and because they have at their disposal sure-fire means for provoking them. But it is also true that they are reproached for this kind of thing, as Euripides has been since antiquity because he had children appear on the stage. Freedom is alienated in the state of passion; it is abruptly engaged in partial enterprises; it loses sight of its task which is to produce an absolute end. And the book is no longer anything but a means for feeding hate or desire. The writer should not seek to *overwhelm*; otherwise he is in contradiction with himself; if he wishes to *make demands* he must propose only the task to be fulfilled. Hence, the character of pure presentation which appears essential to the work of art. The reader must be able to make a certain aesthetic withdrawal. This is what Gautier[10] foolishly confused with "art for art's sake" and the Parnassians[11] with the imperturbability of the artist. It is simply a matter of precaution, and Genet[12] more justly calls it the author's politeness toward the reader. But that does not mean that the writer makes an appeal to some sort of abstract and conceptual freedom. One certainly creates the aesthetic object with

[10] Théophile Gautier (1811–1872), French poet, novelist, and critic. Gautier advocated the doctrine of art for art's sake in his poetry, novels, and criticism.
[11] The French poets Théophile Gautier and Charles Baudelaire are among those included in three collections edited by a certain Lemerne and called *Le Parnasse Contemporain* (1866, 1871, 1876).
[12] Jean Genet (b. 1910), French novelist and dramatist.

feelings; if it is touching, it appears through our tears; if it is comic, it will be recognized by laughter. However, these feelings are of a particular kind. They have their origin in freedom; they are loaned. The belief which I accord the tale is freely assented to. It is a Passion, in the Christian sense of the word, that is, a freedom which resolutely puts itself into a state of passivity to obtain a certain transcendent effect by this sacrifice. The reader renders himself credulous; he descends into credulity which, though it ends by enclosing him like a dream, is at every moment conscious of being free. An effort is sometimes made to force the writer into this dilemma: "Either one believes in your story, and it is intolerable, or one does not believe in it, and it is ridiculous." But the argument is absurd because the characteristic of aesthetic consciousness is to be a belief by means of engagement, by oath, a belief sustained by fidelity to one's self and to the author, a perpetually renewed choice to believe. I can awaken at every moment, and I know it; but I do not want to; reading is a free dream. So that all feelings which are exacted on the basis of this imaginary belief are like particular modulations of my freedom. Far from absorbing or masking it, they are so many different ways it has chosen to reveal itself to itself. Raskolnikov, as I have said, would only be a shadow, without the mixture of repulsion and friendship which I feel for him and which makes him live. But, by a reversal which is the characteristic of the imaginary object, it is not his behavior which excites my indignation or esteem, but my indignation and esteem which give consistency and objectivity to his behavior. Thus, the reader's feelings are never dominated by the object, and as no external reality can condition them, they have their permanent source in freedom; that is, they are all generous— for I call a feeling generous which has its origin and its end in freedom. Thus, reading is an exercise in generosity, and what the writer requires of the reader is not the application of an abstract freedom but the gift of his whole person, with his passions, his prepossessions, his sympathies, his sexual temperament, and his scale of values. Only this person will give himself generously; freedom goes through and through him and comes to transform the darkest masses of his sensibility. And as activity has rendered itself passive in order for it better to create the object, vice-versa, passivity becomes an act; the man who is reading has raised himself to the highest degree. That is why we see people who are known for their toughness shed tears at the recital of imaginary misfortunes; for the moment they have become what they would have been if they had not spent their lives hiding their freedom from themselves.

Thus, the author writes in order to address himself to the freedom of readers, and he requires it in order to make his work exist. But he does not stop there; he also requires that they return this confidence which he has given them, that they recognize his creative freedom, and that they in turn solicit it by a symmetrical and inverse appeal. Here there appears the other dialectical paradox of reading; the more we experience our freedom, the more we recognize that of the other; the more he demands of us, the more we demand of him.

When I am enchanted with a landscape, I know very well that it is not I who create it, but I also know that without me the relations which are established before my eyes among the trees, the foliage, the earth, and the grass would not exist at all. I know that I can give no reason for the appearance of finality which I discover in the assortment of hues and in the harmony of the forms and movements created by the wind. Yet, it exists; there it is before my eyes, and I can make *there be* being only if being already *is*. But even if I believe in God, I can not establish any passage, unless it be purely verbal, between the divine, universal solicitude and the particular spectacle which I am considering. To say that He made the landscape in order to charm me or that He made me the kind of person who is pleased by it is to take a question for an answer. Is the marriage of this blue and that green deliberate? How can I know? The idea of a universal providence is no guarantee of any particular intention, especially in the case under consideration, since the green of the grass is explained by biological laws, specific constants, and geographical determinism, while the reason for the blue of the water is accounted for by the depth of the river, the nature of the soil and the swiftness of the current. The assorting of the shades, if it is willed, can only be something *thrown into the bargain;* it is the meeting of two causal series, that is to say, at first sight, a fact of chance. At best, the finality remains problematic. All the relations we establish remain hypotheses; no end is proposed to us in the manner of an imperative, since none is expressly revealed as having been willed by a creator. Thus, our freedom is never *called forth* by natural beauty. Or rather, there is an appearance of order in the ensemble of the foliage, the forms, and the movements, hence, the illusion of a calling forth which seems to solicit this freedom and which disappears immediately when one regards it. Hardly have we begun to run our eyes over this arrangement, than the call disappears; we remain alone, free to tie up one color with another or with a third, to set up a relationship between the tree and the water or the tree and the sky, or the tree, the water and the sky. My freedom becomes caprice. To the extent that I establish new relationships, I remove myself further from the illusory objectivity which solicits me. I *muse* about certain motifs which are vaguely outlined by the things; the natural reality is no longer anything but a pretext for musing. Or, in that case, because I have deeply regretted that this arrangement which was momentarily perceived was not offered to me by somebody and consequently is not *real,* the result is that I fix my dream, that I transpose it to canvas or in writing. Thus, I interpose myself between the finality without end which appears in the natural spectacles and the gaze of other men. I transmit it to them. It becomes human by this transmission. Art here is a ceremony of the *gift* and the gift alone brings about the metamorphosis. It is something like the transmission of titles and powers in the matriarchate where the mother does not possess the names, but is the indispensable intermediary between uncle and nephew. Since I have captured this illusion in flight, since I lay it out for other men and have disengaged it and rethought it for them, they can consider it with confidence. It has become intentional. As for me, I remain, to be sure, at the border of the subjective and the objective without ever being able to contemplate the objective ordonnance which I transmit.

The reader, on the contrary, progresses in security. However far he may go, the author has gone farther. Whatever connections he may establish among the different parts of the book—among the chapters or the words—he has a guarantee, namely, that they have been expressly willed. As Descartes says, he can even pretend that there is a secret order among parts which seem to have no connection.[13] The creator has preceded him along the way, and the most beautiful disorders are effects of art, that is, again order. Reading is induction, interpolation, extrapolation, and the basis of these activities rests on the reader's will, as for a long time it was believed that that of scientific induction rested on the divine will. A gentle force accompanies us and supports us from the first page to the last. That does not mean that we fathom the artist's intentions easily. They constitute, as we have said, the object of conjectures, and there is an *experience* of the reader; but these conjectures are supported by the great certainty we have that the beauties which appear in the book are never accidental. In nature, the tree and the sky harmonize only by chance; if, on the contrary, in the novel, the protagonists find themselves in a *certain* tower, in a *certain* prison, if they stroll in a *certain* garden, it is a matter both of the restitution of independent causal series (the character had a certain state of mind which was due to a succession of psychological and social events; on the other hand, he betook himself to a determined place and the layout of the city required him to cross a certain park) and of the expression of a deeper finality, for the park came into existence only *in order to* harmonize with a certain state of mind, to express it by means of things or to put it into relief by a vivid contrast, and the state of mind itself was conceived in connection with the landscape. Here it is causality which is appearance and which might be called "causality without cause," and it is the finality which is the profound reality. But if I can thus in all confidence put the order of ends under the order of causes, it is because by opening the book I am asserting that the object has its source in human freedom.

If I were to suspect the artist of having written out of passion and in passion, my confidence would immediately vanish, for it would serve no purpose to have supported the order of causes by the order of ends. The latter would be supported in its turn by a psychic causality and the work of art would end by re-entering the chain of determinism. Certainly I do not deny when I am reading that the author may be impassioned, nor even that he might have conceived the first plan of his work under the sway of passion. But his decision to write supposes that he withdraws somewhat from his feelings, in short, that he has transformed his emotions into free emotions as I do mine while reading him; that is, that he is in an attitude of generosity.

Thus, reading is a pact of generosity between author and reader. Each one trusts the other; each one counts on the other, demands of the other as much as he demands of himself. For this confidence is itself generosity. Nothing can force the author to believe that his reader will use his freedom; nothing can force the reader to believe that the author has used his. Both of them make a free decision. There is then established a dialectical going-and-coming; when I read, I make demands; if my demands are met, what I am then reading provokes me to demand more of the author, which means to demand of the author that he demand more of me. And, vice-versa, the author's demand is that I carry my demands to the highest pitch. Thus, my freedom, by revealing itself, reveals the freedom of the other.

[13] René Descartes (1596–1650) makes this remark in *Discourse on Method* (1637).

It matters little whether the aesthetic object is the product of "realistic" art (or supposedly such) or "formal" art. At any rate, the natural relations are inverted; that tree on the first plane of the Cézanne[14] painting first appears as the product of a causal chain. But the causality is an illusion; it will doubtless remain as a proposition as long as we look at the painting, but it will be supported by a deep finality; if the tree is placed in such a way, it is because the rest of the painting *requires* that this form and those colors be placed on the first plane. Thus, through the phenomenal causality, our gaze attains finality as the deep structure of the object, and, beyond finality, it attains human freedom as its source and original basis. Vermeer's[15] realism is carried so far that at first it might be thought to be photographic. But if one considers the splendor of his texture, the pink and velvety glory of his little brick walls, the blue thickness of a branch of woodbine, the glazed darkness of his vestibules, the orange-colored flesh of his faces which are as polished as the stone of holy-water basins, one suddenly feels, in the pleasure that he experiences, that the finality is not so much in the forms or colors as in his material imagination. It is the very substance and temper of the things which here give the forms their reason for being. With this realist we are perhaps closest to absolute creation, since it is in the very passivity of the matter that we meet the unfathomable freedom of man.

The work is never limited to the painted, sculpted, or narrated object. Just as one perceives things only against the background of the world, so the objects represented by art appear against the background of the universe. On the background of the adventures of Fabrice are the Italy of 1820, Austria, France, the sky and stars which the Abbé Blanis[16] consults, and finally the whole earth. If the painter presents us with a field or a vase of flowers, his paintings are windows which are open on the whole world. We follow the red path which is buried among the wheat much farther than Van Gogh[17] has painted it, among other wheat fields, under other clouds, to the river which empties into the sea, and we extend to infinity, to the other end of the world, the deep finality which supports the existence of the field and the earth. So that, through the various objects which it produces or reproduces, the creative act aims at a total renewal of the world. Each painting, each book, is a recovery of the totality of being. Each of them presents this totality to the freedom of the spectator. For this is quite the final goal of art: to recover this world by giving it to be seen as it is, but as if it had its source in human freedom. But, since what the author creates takes on objective reality only in the eyes of the spectator, this recovery is consecrated by the ceremony of the spectacle—and particularly of reading. We are already in a better position to answer the question we raised a while ago: the writer chooses to appeal to the freedom of other men so that, by the reciprocal implications of their demands, they may re-adapt the totality of being to man and may again enclose the universe within man.

If we wish to go still further, we must bear in mind that the writer, like

---

[14] Paul Cézanne (1839–1906), French painter, a profound influence on modern art.
[15] Jan Vermeer (1632–1675), Dutch painter.
[16] Fabrice and Abbé Blanis, an amateur astronomer, are characters in *The Charterhouse of Parma* (1839), by Stendhal.
[17] Vincent van Gogh (1853–1890), Dutch painter.

all other artists, aims at giving his reader a certain feeling that is customarily
called aesthetic pleasure, and which I would very much rather call aesthetic
joy, and that this feeling, when it appears, is a sign that the work is achieved.
It is therefore fitting to examine it in the light of the preceding considerations.
In effect, this joy, which is denied to the creator, insofar as he creates, becomes
one with the aesthetic consciousness of the spectator, that is, in the case under
consideration, of the reader. It is a complex feeling but one whose structures and
condition are inseparable from one another. It is identical, at first, with the
recognition of a transcendent and absolute end which, for a moment, suspends
the utilitarian round of ends-means and means-ends,* that is, of an appeal or,
what amounts to the same thing, of a value. And the positional consciousness
which I take of this value is necessarily accompanied by the non-positional consciousness of my freedom, since my freedom is manifested to itself by a transcendent exigency. The recognition of freedom by itself is joy, but this structure
of non-thetical[18] consciousness implies another: since, in effect, reading is creation, my freedom does not only appear to itself as pure autonomy but as creative
activity, that is, it is not limited to giving itself its own law but perceives itself
as being constitutive of the object. It is on this level that the phenomenon
specifically is manifested, that is, a creation wherein the created object is given
as object to its creator. It is the sole case in which the creator gets any enjoyment out of the object he creates. And the word enjoyment which is applied to
the positional consciousness of the work read indicates sufficiently that we are
in the presence of an essential structure of aesthetic joy. This positional enjoyment is accompanied by the non-positional consciousness of being essential in
relation to an object perceived as essential. I shall call this aspect of aesthetic
consciousness the feeling of security; it is this which stamps the strongest
aesthetic emotions with a sovereign calm. It has its origin in the authentication
of a strict harmony between subjectivity and objectivity. As, on the other hand,
the aesthetic object is properly the world insofar as it is aimed at through the
imaginary, aesthetic joy accompanies the positional consciousness that the
world is a value, that is, a task proposed to human freedom. I shall call this the
aesthetic modification of the human project, for, as usual, the world appears as
the horizon of our situation, as the infinite distance which separates us from
ourselves, as the synthetic totality of the given, as the undifferentiated ensemble
of obstacles and implements—but never as a demand addressed to our freedom.
Thus, aesthetic joy proceeds to this level of the consciousness which I take of
recovering and internalizing that which is non-ego par excellence, since I transform the given into an imperative and the fact into a value. The world is *my
task,* that is, the essential and freely accepted function of my freedom is to make
that unique and absolute object which is the universe come into being in an
unconditioned movement. And, thirdly, the preceding structures imply a pact
between human freedoms, for, on the one hand, reading is a confident and
exacting recognition of the freedom of the writer, and, on the other hand,
aesthetic pleasure, as it is itself experienced in the form of a value, involves an
absolute exigence in regard to others; every man, insofar as he is a freedom,

---

* In *practical life* a means may be taken for an end as soon as one searches for it,
and each end is revealed as a means of attaining another end. [Sartre's note.]
[18] Unprescribed, free.

feels the same pleasure in reading the same work. Thus, all mankind is present in its highest freedom; it sustains the being of a world which is both *its* world and the "external" world. In aesthetic joy the positional consciousness is an *image-making* consciousness of the world in its totality both as being and having to be, both as totally ours and totally foreign, and the more ours as it is the more foreign. The non-positional consciousness *really* envelops the harmonious totality of human freedoms insofar as it makes the object of a universal confidence and exigency.

To write is thus both to disclose the world and to offer it as a task to the generosity of the reader. It is to have recourse to the consciousness of others in order to make one's self be recognized as *essential* to the totality of being; it is to wish to live this essentiality by means of interposed persons; but, on the other hand, as the real world is revealed only by action, as one can feel himself in it only by exceeding it in order to change it, the novelist's universe would lack thickness if it were not discovered in a movement to transcend it. It has often been observed that an object in a story does not derive its density of existence from the number and length of the descriptions devoted to it, but from the complexity of its connections with the different characters. The more often the characters handle it, take it up, and put it down, in short, go beyond it toward their own ends, the more real will it appear. Thus, of the world of the novel, that is, the totality of men and things, we may say that in order for it to offer its maximum density the disclosure-creation by which the reader discovers it must also be an imaginary engagement in the action; in other words, the more disposed one is to change it, the more alive it will be. The error of realism has been to believe that the real reveals itself to contemplation, and that consequently one could draw an impartial picture of it. How could that be possible, since the very perception is partial, since by itself the naming is already a modification of the object? And how could the writer, who wants himself to be essential to this universe, want to be essential to the injustice which this universe comprehends? Yet, he must be; but if he accepts being the creator of injustices, it is in a movement which goes beyond them toward their abolition. As for me who read, if I create and keep alive an unjust world, I can not help making myself responsible for it. And the author's whole art is bent on obliging me to *create* what he *discloses,* therefore to compromise myself. So both of us bear the responsibility for the universe. And precisely because this universe is supported by the joint effort of our two freedoms, and because the author, with me as medium, has attempted to integrate it into the human, it must appear truly *in itself,* in its very marrow, as being shot through and through with a freedom which has taken human freedom as its end, and if it is not really the city of ends that it ought to be, it must at least be a stage along the way; in a word, it must be a becoming and it must always be considered and presented not as a crushing mass which weighs us down, but from the point of view of its going beyond toward that city of ends. However bad and hopeless the humanity which it paints may be, the work must have an air of generosity. Not, of course, that this generosity is to be expressed by means of edifying discourses and virtuous characters; it must not even be premeditated, and it is quite true that fine sentiments do not make fine books. But it must be the very warp and woof of the book, the stuff out of which the people and things are cut; whatever the subject, a sort of essential lightness must appear everywhere and remind us that the work is never a natural datum, but an *exigence* and a *gift*. And if I am given this world with its injustices, it is not so that I might contemplate them coldly, but that I might animate them with my indignation, that I might disclose them and create them with their nature as injustices, that is, as abuses to be suppressed. Thus, the writer's universe will only reveal itself in all its depth to the examination, the admiration, and the indignation of the reader; and the generous love is a promise to maintain, and the generous indignation is a promise to change, and the admiration a promise to imitate; although literature is one thing and morality a quite different one, at the heart of the aesthetic imperative we discern the moral imperative. For, since the one who writes recognizes, by the very fact that he takes the trouble to write, the freedom of his readers, and since the one who reads, by the mere fact of his opening the book, recognizes the freedom of the writer, the work of art, from whichever side you approach it, is an act of confidence in the freedom of men. And since readers, like the author, recognize this freedom only to demand that it manifest itself, the work can be defined as an imaginary presentation of the world insofar as it demands human freedom. The result of which is that there is no "gloomy literature," since, however dark may be the colors in which one paints the world, he paints it only so that free men may feel their freedom as they face it. Thus, there are only good and bad novels. The bad novel aims to please by flattering, whereas the good one is an exigence and an act of faith. But above all, the unique point of view from which the author can present the world to those freedoms whose concurrence he wishes to bring about is that of a world to be impregnated always with more freedom. It would be inconceivable that this unleashing of generosity provoked by the writer could be used to authorize an injustice, and that the reader could enjoy his freedom while reading a work which approves or accepts or simply abstains from condemning the subjection of man by man. One can imagine a good novel being written by an American Negro even if hatred of the whites were spread all over it, because it is the freedom of his race that he demands through this hatred. And, as he invites me to assume the attitude of generosity, the moment I feel myself a pure freedom I can not bear to identify myself with a race of oppressors. Thus, I require of all freedoms that they demand the liberation of colored people against the white race and against myself insofar as I am a part of it, but nobody can suppose for a moment that it is possible to write a good novel in praise of anti-Semitism.* For, the moment I feel that my freedom is indissolubly linked with that of all other men, it can not be demanded of me that I use it to approve the enslavement of a part of these men. Thus, whether he is an essayist, a pamphleteer, a satirist, or a novelist, whether he speaks only of individual passions or

---

* This last remark may arouse some readers. If so, I'd like to know a single good novel whose express purpose was to serve oppression, a single good novel which has been written against Jews, Negroes, workers, or colonial people. "But if there isn't any, that's no reason why someone may not write one some day." But you then admit that you are an abstract theoretician. You, not I. For it is in the name of your abstract conception of art that you assert the possibility of a fact which has never come into being, whereas I limit myself to proposing an explanation for a recognized fact. [Sartre's note.]

whether he attacks the social order, the writer, a free man addressing free men, has only one subject—freedom.

Hence, any attempt to enslave his readers threatens him in his very art. A blacksmith can be affected by fascism in his life as a man, but not necessarily in his craft; a writer will be affected in both, and even more in his craft than in his life. I have seen writers, who before the war, called for fascism with all their hearts, smitten with sterility at the very moment when the Nazis were loading them with honors. I am thinking of Drieu la Rochelle[19] in particular; he was mistaken, but he was sincere. He proved it. He had agreed to direct a Nazi-inspired review. The first few months he reprimanded, rebuked, and lectured his countrymen. No one answered him because no one was free to do so. He became irritated; he no longer *felt* his readers. He became more insistent, but no sign appeared to prove that he had been understood. No sign of hatred, nor of anger either; nothing. He seemed disoriented, the victim of a growing distress. He complained bitterly to the Germans. His articles had been superb; they became shrill. The moment arrived when he struck his breast; no echo, except among the bought journalists whom he despised. He handed in his resignation, withdrew it, again spoke, still in the desert. Finally, he kept still, gagged by the silence of others. He had demanded the enslavement of others, but in his crazy mind he must have imagined that it was voluntary, that it was still free. It came; the man in him congratulated himself mightily, but the writer could not bear it. While this was going on, others, who, happily, were in the majority, understood that the freedom of writing implies the freedom of the citizen. One does not write for slaves. The art of prose is bound up with the only regime in which prose has meaning, democracy. When one is threatened, the other is too. And it is not enough to defend them with the pen. A day comes when the pen is forced to stop, and the writer must then take up arms. Thus, however you might have come to it, whatever the opinions you might have professed, literature throws you into battle. Writing is a certain way of wanting freedom; once you have begun, you are engaged, willy-nilly.

Engaged in what? Defending freedom? That's easy to say. Is it a matter of acting as guardian of ideal values like Benda's clerk before the betrayal,[20] or is it concrete, everyday freedom which must be protected by our taking sides in political and social struggles? The question is tied up with another one, one very simple in appearance but which nobody ever asks himself: "For whom does one write?"

[19] Pierre Drieu la Rochelle (1893–1945), French writer of fiction, journalist, and essayist, who was editor of *Nouvelle Revue Française* during the German occupation and committed suicide at the end of the war.
[20] See Julian Benda (1867–1956), *La Trahison des clercs* (1927; translated as *The Treason of the Intellectuals*).

F. R. Leavis

LITERATURE
AND SOCIETY*

Since 1932, when he published *New Bearings in English Poetry,*
F[rank] R[aymond] Leavis (1895–   ) has been in some ways the
most influential and certainly the most controversial of English critics.
Educated at Cambridge, he taught for many years at Downing College
of that university (he retired in 1962) where his exigent and usually
censorious view of the English cultural situation attracted to his lectures
many students who gave him their deep allegiance. Although for Matthew Arnold's urbane and often ironic manner Dr. Leavis substitutes a
combative directness, he shares Arnold's characteristic assumption that
literature has an important relation to the health of a society and he
has set his face and raised his voice against the mediocre and the merely
fashionable, and even more, against the critical judgment that tolerates
it. Dr. Leavis's essays usually appeared first in *Scrutiny,* the magazine
which he founded and edited with his wife, Q. D. Leavis, a critic of
note in her own right; it ceased publication in 1953. The many controversies in which his evangelical feeling for literature involved him have
had the unhappy effect of obscuring for some readers the often striking
accuracy of Dr. Leavis's literary perceptivity and judgment. His works
include *Revaluations* (1932), *The Great Tradition: George Eliot,
James, and Conrad* (1948), *The Common Pursuit* (1952), *D. H. Lawrence, Novelist* (1955), *Anna Karenina and Other Essays* (1968) and,
with Q. D. Leavis, *Lectures in America* (1969).

Two or three years back, or at any time in the Marxizing decade, having
been invited to discourse on "Literature and Society," I should have known
what was expected of me—and what to expect. I should have been expected to
discuss, or to give opportunities for discussing, the duty of the writer to identify
himself with the working-class, the duty of the critic to evaluate works of literature in terms of the degree in which they seemed calculated to further (or
otherwise) the proper and pre-destined outcome of the class-struggle, and the
duty of the literary historian to explain literary history as the reflection of chang-

* This is the substance of an address given to the Students' Union of the London
School of Economics and Politics. [Leavis's note.]

From *The Common Pursuit*, by F. R. Leavis. London: Chatto and Windus Ltd.; New
York: New York University Press, 1964. Reprinted by permission of Chatto and Windus,
Ltd. and New York University Press.

ing economic and material realities (the third adjective, "social," which I almost added here, would be otiose). I should have been braced for such challenges as the proposition that D. H. Lawrence, though he

> was unquestionably aware of and tried to describe the outside forces that were undermining the bourgeois society into which he made his way . . . saw those forces from a bourgeois viewpoint, as destroyers to be combated. Consequently he misrepresented reality.*

What was wrong with his work was that he "shared the life of a social class which has passed its prime."

I assume that the expectation I should have had to address myself to in those not so very remote days isn't entertained at all generally on the present occasion, and I assume it gladly. But that does leave me with a large undirected formula on my hands: "Literature and Society" might, in fact, seem to be daunting and embarrassing in the wealth of possibilities it covers. However, certain major interests of my own respond to it quite comfortably and I had no difficulty in concluding that I should be expected to do what, in accordance with those interests, it would suit me to do: that is, to try and define on what grounds and in what ways the study of literature—literature as it concerns me, who am avowedly in the first place a literary critic—should, I think, be seen as intimately relevant to what may be presumed to be the major interest of students at the London School of Economics.

For if the Marxist approach to literature seems to me unprofitable, that is not because I think of literature as a matter of isolated works of art, belonging to a realm of pure literary values (whatever they might be); works regarding the production of which it is enough to say that individuals of specific creative gifts were born and created them. No one interested in literature who began to read and think immediately after the 1914 war—at a time, that is, co-incident with the early critical work of T. S. Eliot—can fail to have taken stock, for conscious rejection, of the Romantic critical tradition (if it can be called that): the set of ideas and attitudes about literary creation coming down through the nineteenth century. That tradition laid all the stress on inspiration and the individual genius. How do masterpieces arrive? Gifted individuals occur, inspiration sets in, creation results. Mr. Eliot, all of whose early prose may be said to have been directed against the Romantic tradition, which till then had not been effectively challenged, lays the stress on the other things (or some of them) besides individual talent and originative impulse from within that have to be taken account of when we try to understand any significant achievement in art. Of course, it was no discovery that there are these things to be taken account of: criticism and literary history had for generations dealt in influences, environments and the extra-literary conditions of literary production. But we are apt to be peculiarly under the influence of ideas and attitudes of which we are not fully conscious, they prevail until rejected, and the Romantic set—an atmosphere of the unformulated and vague—may be said to have prevailed until Mr. Eliot's criticism, co-operating with his poetry, made unconsciousness impossible and rejection inevitable.

* *The Mind in Chains*, edited by C. Day Lewis. [Leavis's note.]

Something like the idea of Tradition so incisively and provocatively formulated by him plays, I think, an essential part in the thinking of everyone to-day who is seriously interested in literature. If I say that idea represents a new emphasis on the social nature of artistic achievement, I ought to add at once that the word "social" probably doesn't occur in the classical essay, *Tradition and the Individual Talent* (the word that takes Mr. Eliot's stress is "impersonal"). The "society" implied in this "social"—and (which is, of course, my point) in the idea of Tradition—is not the Marxist concept; and the difference is what I have my eye on. But let me first remind you of the idea as Mr. Eliot formulates it. The individual writer is to be aware that his work is of the Literature to which it belongs and not merely added externally to it. A literature, that is, must be thought of as essentially something more than an accumulation of separate works: it has an organic form, or constitutes an organic order, in relation to which the individual writer has his significance and his being. "Mind" is the analogy (if this is the right word) used:

> He must be aware that the mind of Europe—the mind of his own country—a mind which he learns in time to be much more important than his own private mind—is a mind which changes . . .

and so on.

Something, I said, in the nature of this way of thinking seems to me inevitable for anyone who thinks about literature at all. The ways in which it is at odds with Marxist theories of culture are obvious. It stresses, not economic and material determinants, but intellectual and spiritual, so implying a different conception from the Marxist of the relation between the present of society and the past, and a different conception of society. It assumes that, enormously—no one will deny it—as material conditions count, there is a certain measure of spiritual autonomy in human affairs, and that human intelligence, choice and will do really and effectively operate, expressing an inherent human nature. There is a human nature—that is how, from the present point of view, we may take the stress as falling; a human nature, of which an understanding is of primary importance to students of society and politics. And here is the first way that presents itself of indicating the kind of importance literature—the literary critic's literature—should be recognized to have for such students: the study of it is, or should be, an intimate study of the complexities, potentialities and essential conditions of human nature.

But that by itself is too large a proposition to take us anywhere. Let me, by way of moving towards more discussible particularity, make another obvious note on the difference between the Marxist kind of attitude toward literature and that represented by the idea of Tradition I've invoked. It's true that this latter stresses the social aspect of creative achievement as the Romantic attitude didn't: but it allows for the individual aspect more than the Marxist does. This is inevitably a crude way of putting it—as you'll see, that "inevitably" is my point. But to postpone that for a moment: you can't be interested in literature and forget that the creative individual is indispensable. Without the individual talent there is no creation. While you are in intimate touch with literature no amount of dialectic, or of materialistic interpretation, will obscure for long the truth that human life lives only in individuals: I might have said, the truth that it is only in individuals that society lives.

The point I wanted to make is this: you can't contemplate the nature of literature without acquiring some inhibition in respect of that antithesis, "the individual and society," and losing any innocent freedom you may have enjoyed in handling it; without, that is, acquiring some inhibiting apprehensions of the subtleties that lie behind the antithesis.

An illustration presents itself readily. I have spoken of the "Romantic" attitude, and the phrase might be called misleading, since the actual poets of the Romantic period—Wordsworth, Coleridge, Byron, Shelley, Keats—differ widely among themselves. No general description worth offering will cover them. Though as influences they merge later in a Romantic tradition, they themselves do not exemplify any common Romanticism. What they have in common is that they belong to the same age; and in belonging to the same age they have in common something negative: the absence of anything to replace the very positive tradition (literary, and more than literary—hence its strength) that had prevailed till towards the end of the eighteenth century. It is this tradition, the Augustan, that I want to consider briefly first.

It originated in the great changes in civilization that make the second part of the seventeenth century look so unlike the first, and its early phase may be studied in the works of John Dryden. The conventions, standards and idiom of its confident maturity offer themselves for contemplation in *The Tatler* and *The Spectator*.[1] The relevant point to be made about it for the present purpose is that it laid a heavy stress on the social. Its insistence that man is a social being was such as to mean in effect that all his activities, inner as well as outer, that literature took cognizance of, were to belong to an overtly social context. Even the finest expressions of the spirit were to be in resonance with a code of Good Form—for with such a code the essential modes and idioms of Augustan culture were intimately associated. The characteristic movements and dictions of the eighteenth century, in verse as well as prose, convey a suggestion of social deportment and company manners.

An age in which such a tradition gets itself established is clearly an age in which the writer feels himself very much at one with society. And the Augustan heyday, the Queen Anne period,[2] was a period very confident of its flourishing cultural health. But we should expect such an insistence on the social to have in time a discouraging effect on the deeper sources of originality, the creative springs in the individually experiencing mind. We should expect to find evidence of this in the field of poetry, and we find it. This is no place to pretend to give a fair account of the Augustan decline, which was a complex affair: I'm merely stressing an aspect that is relevant to my present purpose. Where, then, a tradition like that I have adumbrated prevails, there is bound before long to be a movement of protest in minds of the kind that ought to be creative. They will feel that conventional expression—that which, nevertheless, seems natural and inevitable to the age—imposes a conventional experience, and that this, suppressing, obtruding, muffling, and misrepresenting, is at odds with their own. There will be a malaise, a sense of blunted vitality, that would ex-

---

[1] Popular and influential journals of the eighteenth century. The *Tatler*, edited by Richard Steele (1672–1729), appeared twice weekly from April 1709 until January 1711. The *Spectator*, edited by Steele and Joseph Addison (1672–1719), appeared daily from March 1711 until December 1712.

[2] Queen Anne reigned from 1702 to 1714.

press itself to this effect if it were fully conscious. Full consciousness is genius, and manifests itself in technical achievement, the new use of words. In the seventeen-eighties it is William Blake.[3]

Blake in his successful work says implicitly: "It is I who see and feel. I see only what I see and feel only what I feel. My experience is mine, and in its specific quality lies its significance." He may be said to have reversed for himself the shift of stress that occurred at the Restoration.[4] But to such a reversal there is clearly a limit. Blake uses the English language, and not one of his own invention; and to say that he uses it is not to say that it is for him a mere instrument. His individuality has developed in terms of the language, with the ways of experiencing, as well as of handling experience, that it involves. The mind and sensibility that he has to express are of the language.

I may seem here to be handling a truism of the kind that there's no point in recalling. But I believe that the familiar truths that we contemplate when we contemplate the nature of language—in the way, that is, in which we have to when we take a critical interest in literature—have the familiarity of the familiar things that we tend to lose sight of when we begin to think. And what I have just been touching on is perhaps the most radical of the ways in which the literary critic's interest in literature leads to a new recognition of the essentially social nature of the individual—and (I may add) of the "reality" he takes for granted.

In any case, I want to pass at once to an order of consideration that will probably seem to have more discussible bearings on the normal pre-occupations of the student of society. The measure of social collaboration and support represented by the English language didn't make Blake prosperously self-sufficient: he needed something more—something that he didn't get. This is apparent in a peculiar kind of difficulty that his work offers to the critic. I am thinking of the difficulty one so often has in deciding what kind of thing it is one has before one.

> A petty sneaking knave I knew—
> O! Mr. Cromek, how do ye do?[5]

—that is clearly a private blow-off. *The Tyger* is clearly a poem (in spite of the bluffed-out defeat in the third stanza).* But again and again one comes on the thing that seems to be neither wholly private nor wholly a poem. It seems not to know what it is or where it belongs, and one suspects that Blake didn't know.

[3] The earliest collection of poems by William Blake (1757–1827) is *Poetical Sketches* (1783).

[4] That is, the restoration of monarchical government in England upon the accession in 1660 of Charles II, following the collapse of the Commonwealth and the Protectorate, both led by Oliver Cromwell.

[5] From Blake's "Mr. Cromek to Mr. Stothard."

* The second interrogative sentence of the stanza Blake made a number of attempts at completing before he threw up the problem. [Leavis's note.]

> The third stanza of Blake's famous poem is
> And what shoulder, and what art,
> Could twist the sinews of thy heart?
> And when thy heart began to beat,
> What dread hand? and what dread feet?

Blake appears to have tried "formed thy" and "forged thy" as alternatives to "and what" in the last line quoted.

What he did know—and know deep down in himself—was that he had no public: he very early gave up publishing in any serious sense. One obvious consequence, or aspect, of this knowledge is the carelessness that is so apparent in the later prophetic books. Blake had ceased to be capable of taking enough trouble. The uncertainty I have just referred to is a more radical and significant form of the same kind of disability. In the absence, we may put it, of adequate social collaboration (the sense, or confident prospect, of a responsive community of minds was the minimum he needed) his powers of attaining in achieved creation to that peculiar impersonal realm to which the work of art belongs and in which minds can meet—it is as little a world of purely private experience as it is the public world of the laboratory—failed to develop as, his native endowment being what it was, they ought to have done.*

The inevitable way in which serious literary interest develops towards the sociological is suggested well enough here. What better conditions, one asks, can one imagine for a Blake? Can one imagine him in a tradition that should have nurtured his genius rather than have been something it had to escape from, and in a society that should have provided him with the best conceivable public? But what is the best conceivable public? And so one is led on to inquire into the nature and conditions of cultural health and prosperity.

I will illustrate with a line of reflection that has occupied me a good deal. Harking back from Blake one notes that the establishment of the Augustan tradition was associated with—indeed, it involved—a separation, new and abrupt, between sophisticated culture and popular. Anticipating the problem of bringing home as convincingly and vividly as possible to (say) students of modern social and political questions what is meant by saying that there was, in the seventeenth century, a real culture of the people, one thinks first of Dryden's contemporary, Bunyan. If *The Pilgrim's Progress*[6] is a humane masterpiece, that is in spite of the bigoted sectarian creed that Bunyan's allegory, in detail as in sum, directs itself to enforcing. In spite of his aim, a humane masterpiece resulted because he belonged to the civilization of his time, and that meant, for a small-town "mechanick,"[7] participating in a rich traditional culture.

It is on the reader approaching as a literary critic that this truth compels

---

* The following, both in its curiously striking qualities—it clearly comes from a remarkable poet—and in what I take to be its lack of self-sufficiency as a poem, seems to me a representatively suggestive document of the case I have been trying to describe:

> Truly, my Satan, thou art but a dunce,
> And dost not know the garment from the man;
> Every harlot was a virgin once,
> Nor canst thou ever change Kate into Nan.
>
> Tho' thou art worship'd by the names divine
> Of Jesus and Jehovah, thou art still
> The Son of Morn in weary night's decline,
> The lost traveller's dream under the hill.

[Leavis's note. Actually, the lines Leavis quotes are the epilogue (entitled "To the Accuser Who is the God of this World") to Blake's *For the Sexes: The Gates of Paradise*; it was never printed as a "self-sufficient" poem.]

6 *The Pilgrim's Progress*, by John Bunyan (1628–1688), was first published in 1678.

7 That is, an artisan. Bunyan had worked as a tinsmith before turning to writing and preaching.

itself (others seem to miss it).* Consider, not one of the most striking illustrations of Bunyan's art, such as the apologia and self-characterization of By-Ends, but a passage representative in a routine kind of way:

> *Christian:* Did you hear no talk of neighbour Pliable?
>
> *Faithful:* Yes, Christian, I heard that he followed you till he came at the Slough of Despond, where, as some said, he fell in; but he would not be known to have so done; but I am sure he was soundly bedabbled with that kind of dirt.
>
> *Christian:* And what said the neighbours to him?
>
> *Faithful:* He hath, since his going back, been had greatly in derision, and that among all sorts of people; some do mock and despise him; and scarce will any set him on work. He is now seven times worse than if he had never gone out of the city.
>
> *Christian:* But why should they be so set against him, since they also despise the way that he forsook?
>
> *Faithful:* Oh, they say, hang him, he is a turncoat! he was not true to his profession. I think God has stirred up even his enemies to hiss at him, and make him a proverb, because he hath forsaken the way.
>
> *Christian:* Had you no talk with him before you came out?
>
> *Faithful:* I met him once in the streets, but he leered away on the other side, as one ashamed of what he had done; so I spoke not to him.
>
> *Christian:* Well, at my first setting out, I had hopes of that man; but now I fear he will perish in the over-throw of the city; for it is happened to him according to the true proverb, *The dog is turned to his own vomit again; and the sow that was washed, to her wallowing in the mire.*

The relation of this to the consummate art of the By-Ends passage is plain; we have the idiomatic life that runs to saw and proverb, and runs also to what is closely akin to these, the kind of pungently characterizing epitome represented by "turncoat" (which, with a capital letter, might have appeared in By-Ends' list of his kindred). The vitality here is not merely one of raciness; an art of civilized living is implicit, with its habits and standards of serious moral valuation.

This then is what the literary critic has to deduce from his reading. If he finds that others, interested primarily in social reform and social history, do not seem properly impressed by such evidence, he can, by way of bringing home to them in how full a sense there is, behind the literature, a social culture and an art of living, call attention to Cecil Sharp's introduction to *English Folk-Songs from the Southern Appalachians.*[8] Hearing that the English folk-song still persisted in the remoter valleys of those mountains Sharp, during the war of 1914, went over to investigate, and brought back a fabulous haul. More than that, he discovered that the tradition of song and dance (and a reminder is in place at this point of the singing and dancing with which the

---

* See, e.g., two books discussed below [in a later essay by F. R. Leavis]. *John Bunyan: Maker of Myths,* by Jack Lindsay, and *John Bunyan: Mechanick Preacher,* by William York Tindall. [Leavis's note.]

8 Cecil Sharp (1859–1924), edited numerous collections of folk songs; the collection Leavis refers to appeared in 1917.

pilgrims punctuate their progress in the second part of Bunyan's Calvinistic allegory) had persisted so vigorously because the whole context to which folk-song and folk-dance belong was there too: he discovered, in fact, a civilization or "way of life" (in our democratic parlance) that was truly an art of social living.

The mountaineers were descended from settlers who had left this country in the eighteenth century.

> The region is from its inaccessibility a very secluded one . . . the inhabitants have for a hundred years or more been completely isolated and shut off from all traffic with the rest of the world. Their speech is English, not American, and, from the number of expressions they use that have long been obsolete elsewhere, and the old-fashioned way in which they pronounce many of their words, it is clear that they are talking the language of a past day. They are a leisurely, cheery people in their quiet way, in whom the social instinct is very highly developed . . . They know their Bible intimately and subscribe to an austere creed, charged with Calvinism and the unrelenting doctrines of determinism or fatalism . . . They have an easy unaffected bearing and the unself-conscious manners of the well-bred . . . A few of those we met were able to read and write, but the majority were illiterate. They are however good talkers, using an abundant vocabulary racily and picturesquely.
>
> That the illiterate may nevertheless reach a high level of culture will surprise only those who imagine that education and cultivation are convertible terms. The reason, I take it, why these mountain people, albeit unlettered, have acquired so many of the essentials of culture, is partly to be attributed to the large amount of leisure they enjoy, without which, of course, no cultural development is possible, but chiefly to the fact that they have one and all entered at birth into the full enjoyment of their racial inheritance. Their language, wisdom, manners and the many graces of life that are theirs, are merely racial attributes, which have been gradually acquired and accumulated in past centuries and handed down generation by generation, each generation adding its quota to what it received . . .
>
> . . . Of the supreme value of an inherited tradition, even when unenforced by any formal school education, our mountain community in the Southern Highlands is an outstanding example.[9]

Correlation of Cecil Sharp's introduction with Bunyan should sufficiently confirm and enforce the significance attributed to Bunyan above. And Bunyan himself shows how the popular culture to which he bears witness could merge with literary culture at the level of great literature. The converse, regarding the advantages enjoyed by the literary writer, the "intellectual," need not be stated: they are apparent in English literature from Shakespeare to Marvell.[10] We see Marvell—it is, of course, for this reason I name him—as pre-eminently refined, European in sophistication, and intimately related to a tradition of courtly

[9] From *English Folk-Songs from the Southern Appalachians,* edited by Cecil Sharp. London: Oxford University Press. Reprinted by permission of Oxford University Press.

[10] Andrew Marvell (1621–1678).

urbanity; but his refinement involves no insulation from the popular—the force of which judgment is brought out by contrast with Pope. In prose, compare Halifax with Dryden. Halifax (the Trimmer)[11] is "easy," "natural" and urbane, a master of the spoken tone and movement; in short he is unmistakably of the Restoration; but his raciness and idiomatic life relate him as unmistakably to Bunyan. I don't think I am being fanciful when I say that when Dryden gets lively, as in the Preface to *All for Love,* he tends towards the Cockney; he assimilates, in fact, with L'Estrange.[12] At least, his polite idiomatic ease is wholly of the coffee-house, that new organ of metropolitan culture the vibration of which seems essentially to exclude any intimate relations with Bunyan's world. The exclusive, or insulating, efficacy of the politeness of Augustan verse, even in Pope, whose greatness manifests itself in his power of transcending the Augustan, is at any rate obvious; and Pope's politeness belongs to the same world as the politeness of Addison's prose. Where, in short, Augustan convention and idiom, with their social suggestion, prevail, sophisticated culture cuts itself off from the traditional culture of the people.

The eighteenth century, significantly, had a habit of attempting the naïve, and, characteristically, evoked its touching simplicities of low life in modes that, Augustan tone and movement being inescapable, evoked at the same time the elegant and polite. It is one of the manifestations of Blake's genius that he, unique in this, can—the evidence is apparent here and there in *Poetical Sketches* (1783)—be genuinely, in verse that has nothing Augustan about it, of the people (popular London in his time was clearly still something of a "folk"). The mention of this aspect of Blake serves to bring out by contrast the significance of Wordsworth's kind of interest in rustic life. It is essentially—in so far as it is more than nominal—an interest in something felt as external to the world to which he himself belongs, and very remote from it: the reaction that Wordsworth represents against the Augustan century doesn't mean any movement towards re-establishing the old organic relations between literary culture and the sources of vitality in the general life. By Wordsworth's death, the Industrial Revolution had done its work, and the traditional culture of the people was no longer there, except vestigially.

No one, then, seriously interested in modern literature can feel that it represents a satisfactory cultural order. But if any one should conclude that it ought therefore—the literature that the literary critic finds significant—to be contemned, and that a really significant contemporary literature would have the Marxizing or Wellsian[13] kind of relation to social, political and economic problems, he may be reminded that, but for the persisting literary tradition, the history I have so inadequately sketched would have been lost, and our notions of what a popular culture might be, and what relations might exist between it

[11] George Savile, Marquess of Halifax (1633–1675), writer of political pamphlets, is chiefly known for his "character of a Trimmer" (1688).

[12] Sir Roger L'Estrange (1616–1704), an active Royalist, who wrote political pamphlets attacking the Puritans and defending the monarchy. Leavis is saying that writers who reached full maturity before the Restoration (1660), writers like Bunyan, Marvell, and Halifax, have something in common, no matter what their politics, that separates them from writers a generation or two younger.

[13] H. G. Wells (1866–1946) was for a while a socialist, but he moved to a utopianism of his own, a peculiar blend of mysticism and scientism.

and a "highbrow" culture, would have been very different. And it needs stressing that where there isn't, in the literary critic's sense, a significant contemporary literature, the literary tradition—the "mind" (and mind includes memory)—is not fully alive. To have a vital literary culture we must have a literature that is a going concern; and that will be what, under present conditions of civilization, it has to be. Where it is can be determined only by the literary critic's kind of judgment.

What one has to suggest in general by way of urging on students of politics and society the claims of literary studies (I don't mean the ordinary academic kind) to be regarded as relevant and important is that thinking about political and social matters ought to be done by minds of some real literary education, and done in an intellectual climate informed by a vital literary culture. More particularly, of course, there are, capable of endless development and illustration, the hints for the social historian and the sociologist I have thrown out in the course of my argument. These all involve the principle that literature will yield to the sociologist, or anyone else, what it has to give only if it is approached as literature. For what I have in mind is no mere industrious searching for "evidence," and collecting of examples, in whatever happens to have been printed and preserved. The "literature" in question is something in the definition of which terms of value-judgment figure essentially, and something accessible only to the reader capable of intelligent and sensitive criticism.

I am thinking, in this insistence, not of the actual business of explicit valuation, but of the ability to respond appropriately and appreciatively to the subtleties of the artist's use of language and to the complexities of his organizations. And I am not thinking merely of poetry. It is to poetry, mainly, that I have made my illustrative references, but if one were enumerating the more obvious kinds of interest that literature has to offer the sociologist, prose fiction, it is plain, would figure very largely. There seems to be a general view that anyone can read a novel; and the uses commonly made of novels as evidence, sociological or other, would seem to illustrate that view. Actually, to use as evidence or illustration the kinds of novel that are most significant and have most to offer requires an uncommon skill, the product of a kind of training that few readers submit themselves to. For instance, the sociologist can't learn what D. H. Lawrence has to teach about the problems of modern civilized man without being a more intelligent critic than any professional literary guide he is likely to find. Nor, without being an original critic, adverted and sensitized by experience and the habit of critical analysis, can the social psychologist learn what Conrad[14] has to teach about the social nature of the individual's "reality."

Then there are kinds of inquiry where the literary-critical control cannot be so delicate and full, but where, at the same time, the critic's experience and understanding have their essential rôle. Hints are to be found in Gilbert Murray's *Rise of the Greek Epic*—a book that has a still greater value when pondered along with Dame Bertha Phillpotts' *Edda and Saga*.[15] She, towards the end of chapter viii, throws out some peculiarly good incitements to inquiry. Observing that the Saga literature was democratic ("it had to interest all classes, because all classes listened to it") she says:

[14] That is, Joseph Conrad (1857–1924), English novelist of Polish birth.
[15] Murray's book was published in 1907 and Dame Bertha's in 1931.

But though it was democratic in the sense that it appealed to the whole people, [it] was mainly the creation of the intellectual classes, and it obviously brought about a general levelling-up of interests and culture. This is an effect of oral literature which it is easy to overlook. Printing . . . makes knowledge very easy to avoid.

And she makes—is it acceptable? (and if not, why not?)—an optimistic suggestion about broadcasting.

These instances must suffice—I choose them for their suggestive diversity. Instead of offering any further, I will end by making a general contention in other terms. Without the sensitizing familiarity with the subtleties of language, and the insight into the relations between abstract or generalizing thought and the concrete of human experience, that the trained frequentation of literature alone can bring, the thinking that attends social and political studies will not have the edge and force it should.

Erich Auerbach

ODYSSEUS' SCAR

Erich Auerbach (1892–1957) was born in Berlin, Germany. He studied law, Romance philology, and art history at a number of German universities; he received the Ph.D. in philology from Griefswald University in 1921 and the degree of Doctor of Laws from Heidelberg in 1930. In 1929 he was appointed Professor of Romance Philology at Marburg University; in 1935 he was dismissed from the post by order of the Nazi government. After teaching at the Turkish State University at Istanbul until 1947, he came to the United States. He was a visiting professor at Pennsylvania State University during the academic year 1948–1949 and a member of the Institute for Advanced Study at Princeton in 1949–1950. From 1950 until his death he taught at Yale University, where in 1956 he had been made Sterling Professor of Romance Languages.

Auerbach's magisterial *Mimesis: The Representation of Reality in Western Literature,* the first chapter of which is reprinted here, has had a steady and pervasive effect upon our understanding of its subject since the original German edition of 1946 and its subsequent translation into a half-dozen languages—but for all that, *Mimesis* remains unique, unclassifiable, without imitation even. It is as though Auerbach had exhausted the subject in the very process of bringing it into existence. Certain traditions that went into the making of *Mimesis* can, of course, be isolated. There is the concern with *Weltliteratur,* a term coined by Wolfgang von Goethe to mean "universal literature" in the sense of all the literature that works in concert not only to describe man but to bring him into consciousness of his nature, and not only to reveal but also to create his idea of himself. There is the German tradition of philology, which was essentially concerned with the study of human verbal activity in nearly all its varieties and in all its historical contingency. And there is the tradition of German idealist historiography, which viewed the representation of human thought and action as a problem arising out of the differences between the world-views of the historical moment in which the historian wrote and of the one he was trying to fix in words. But although these and other traditions can be identified as informing *Mimesis,* the work remains unique in the combined delicacy and rigor of its analysis of rhetoric, in its scope, and in its precision with which it traces the evolution of the realities that have been distilled into words by Western writers from Homer to the modernists of this century.

From *Mimesis: The Representation of Reality in Western Literature,* by Erich Auerbach, translated by Willard R. Trask. Princeton, N.J.; Princeton University Press, 1953; Princeton Paperback, 1968. Reprinted by permission of Princeton University Press.

Of Auerbach's many works, the following are available in English: *Scenes from the Drama of European Literature* (1959), *Introduction to Romance Languages and Literature* (1961), *Dante, Poet of the Secular World* (1961), and *Literary Language and Its Public in Late Latin Antiquity* (1965).

Readers of the *Odyssey* will remember the well-prepared and touching scene in book 19, when Odysseus has at last come home, the scene in which the old housekeeper Euryclea, who had been his nurse, recognizes him by a scar on his thigh. The stranger has won Penelope's good will; at his request she tells the housekeeper to wash his feet, which, in old stories, is the first duty of hospitality toward a tired traveler. Euryclea busies herself fetching water and mixing cold with hot, meanwhile speaking sadly of her absent master, who is probably of the same age as the guest, and who perhaps, like the guest, is even now wandering somewhere, a stranger; and she remarks how astonishingly like him the guest looks. Meanwhile Odysseus, remembering his scar, moves back out of the light; he knows that, despite his efforts to hide his identity, Euryclea will now recognize him, but he wants at least to keep Penelope in ignorance. No sooner has the old woman touched the scar than, in her joyous surprise, she lets Odysseus' foot drop into the basin; the water spills over, she is about to cry out her joy; Odysseus restrains her with whispered threats and endearments; she recovers herself and conceals her emotion. Penelope, whose attention Athena's foresight had diverted from the incident, has observed nothing.

All this is scrupulously externalized and narrated in leisurely fashion. The two women express their feelings in copious direct discourse. Feelings though they are, with only a slight admixture of the most general considerations upon human destiny, the syntactical connection between part and part is perfectly clear, no contour is blurred. There is also room and time for orderly, perfectly well-articulated, uniformly illuminated descriptions of implements, ministrations, and gestures; even in the dramatic moment of recognition, Homer does not omit to tell the reader that it is with his right hand that Odysseus takes the old woman by the throat to keep her from speaking, at the same time that he draws her closer to him with his left. Clearly outlined, brightly and uniformly illuminated, men and things stand out in a realm where everything is visible; and not less clear—wholly expressed, orderly even in their ardor —are the feelings and thoughts of the persons involved.

In my account of the incident I have so far passed over a whole series of verses which interrupt it in the middle. There are more than seventy of these verses—while to the incident itself some forty are devoted before the interruption and some forty after it. The interruption, which comes just at the point when the housekeeper recognizes the scar—that is, at the moment of crisis— describes the origin of the scar, a hunting accident which occurred in Odysseus' boyhood, at a boar hunt, during the time of his visit to his grandfather Autolycus. This first affords an opportunity to inform the reader about Autolycus, his house, the precise degree of the kinship, his character, and, no less exhaustively than touchingly, his behavior after the birth of his grandson; then follows the visit of Odysseus, now grown to be a youth; the exchange of greetings, the banquet with which he is welcomed, sleep and waking, the early start for the hunt, the tracking of the beast, the struggle, Odysseus' being wounded by the boar's tusk, his recovery, his return to Ithaca, his parents' anxious questions—all is narrated, again with such a complete externalization of all the elements of the story and of their interconnections as to leave nothing in obscurity. Not until then does the narrator return to Penelope's chamber, not until then, the digression having run its course, does Euryclea, who had recognized the scar before the digression began, let Odysseus' foot fall back into the basin.

The first thought of a modern reader—that this is a device to increase suspense—is, if not wholly wrong, at least not the essential explanation of this Homeric procedure. For the element of suspense is very slight in the Homeric poems; nothing in their entire style is calculated to keep the reader or hearer breathless. The digressions are not meant to keep the reader in suspense, but rather to relax the tension. And this frequently occurs, as in the passage before us. The broadly narrated, charming, and subtly fashioned story of the hunt, with all its elegance and self-sufficiency, its wealth of idyllic pictures, seeks to win the reader over wholly to itself as long as he is hearing it, to make him forget what had just taken place during the foot-washing. But an episode that will increase suspense by retarding the action must be so constructed that it will not fill the present entirely, will not put the crisis, whose resolution is being awaited, entirely out of the reader's mind, and thereby destroy the mood of suspense; the crisis and the suspense must continue, must remain vibrant in the background. But Homer—and to this we shall have to return later—knows no background. What he narrates is for the time being the only present, and fills both the stage and the reader's mind completely. So it is with the passage before us. When the young Euryclea (vv. 401 ff.) sets the infant Odysseus on his grandfather Autolycus' lap after the banquet, the aged Euryclea, who a few lines earlier had touched the wanderer's foot, has entirely vanished from the stage and from the reader's mind.

Goethe and Schiller, who, though not referring to this particular episode, exchanged letters in April 1797 on the subject of "the retarding element" in the Homeric poems in general, put it in direct opposition to the element of suspense—the latter word is not used, but is clearly implied when the "retarding" procedure is opposed, as something proper to epic, to tragic procedure (letters of April 19, 21 and 22). The "retarding element," the "going back and forth" by means of episodes, seems to me, too, in the Homeric poems, to be opposed to any tensional and suspensive striving toward a goal, and doubtless Schiller is right in regard to Homer when he says that what he gives us is "simply the quiet existence and operation of things in accordance with their natures"; Homer's goal is "already present in every point of his progress." But both Schiller and Goethe raise Homer's procedure to the level of a law for epic poetry in general, and Schiller's words quoted above are meant to be universally binding upon the epic poet, in contradistinction from the tragic. Yet in both modern and ancient times, there are important epic works which are composed throughout with no "retarding element" in this sense but, on the contrary, with suspense throughout, and which perpetually "rob us of our emotional freedom"—which power Schiller will grant only to the tragic poet. And besides it seems to me undemonstrable and improbable that this procedure of Homeric poetry was directed by aesthetic considerations or even by an aesthetic feeling of the sort postulated by Goethe and Schiller. The effect, to be sure, is precisely that which they describe, and is, furthermore, the actual source of the conception of epic which they themselves hold, and with them all writers decisively influenced by classical antiquity. But the true cause of the impression of "retardation" appears to me to lie elsewhere—namely, in the need of the Homeric style to leave nothing which it mentions half in darkness and unexternalized.

The excursus upon the origin of Odysseus' scar is not basically different from the many passages in which a newly introduced character, or even a newly appearing object or implement, though it be in the thick of a battle, is described as to its nature and origin; or in which, upon the appearance of a god, we are told where he last was, what he was doing there, and by what road he reached the scene; indeed, even the Homeric epithets seem to me in the final analysis to be traceable to the same need for an externalization of phenomena in terms perceptible to the senses. Here is the scar, which comes up in the course of the narrative; and Homer's feeling simply will not permit him to see it appear out of the darkness of an unilluminated past; it must be set in full light, and with it a portion of the hero's boyhood—just as, in the *Iliad*, when the first ship is already burning and the Myrmidons finally arm that they may hasten to help, there is still time not only for the wonderful simile of the wolf, not only for the order of the Myrmidon host, but also for a detailed account of the ancestry of several subordinate leaders (16, vv. 155ff.). To be sure, the aesthetic effect thus produced was soon noticed and thereafter consciously sought; but the more original cause must have lain in the basic impulse of the Homeric style: to represent phenomena in a fully externalized form, visible and palpable in all their parts, and completely fixed in their spatial and temporal relations. Nor do psychological processes receive any other treatment: here too nothing must remain hidden and unexpressed. With the utmost fullness, with an orderliness which even passion does not disturb, Homer's personages vent their inmost hearts in speech; what they do not say to others, they speak in their own minds, so that the reader is informed of it. Much that is terrible takes place in the Homeric poems, but it seldom takes place wordlessly: Polyphemus talks to Odysseus; Odysseus talks to the suitors when he begins to kill them; Hector and Achilles talk at length, before battle and after; and no speech is so filled with anger or scorn that the particles which express logical and grammatical connections are lacking or out of place. This last observation is true, of course, not only of speeches but of the presentation in general. The separate elements of a phenomenon are most clearly placed in relation to one another; a large number of conjunctions, adverbs, particles, and other syntactical tools, all clearly circumscribed and delicately differentiated in meaning, delimit persons, things, and portions of incidents in respect to one another, and at the same time bring them together in a continuous and ever flexible connection; like the separate phenomena themselves, their relationships —their temporal, local, causal, final, consecutive, comparative, concessive, antithetical, and conditional limitations—are brought to light in perfect fullness; so that a continuous rhythmic procession of phenomena passes by, and never is there a form left fragmentary or half-illuminated, never a lacuna, never a gap, never a glimpse of unplumbed depths.

And this procession of phenomena takes place in the foreground—that is, in a local and temporal present which is absolute. One might think that the many interpolations, the frequent moving back and forth, would create a sort of perspective in time and place; but the Homeric style never gives any such impression. The way in which any impression of perspective is avoided can be clearly observed in the procedure for introducing episodes, a syntactical construction with which every reader of Homer is familiar; it is used in the passage we are considering, but can also be found in cases when the episodes are much shorter. To the word scar (v. 393) there is first attached a relative clause ("which once long ago a boar . . ."), which enlarges into a voluminous syntactical parenthesis; into this an independent sentence unexpectedly intrudes (v. 396: "A god himself gave him . . ."), which quietly disentangles itself from syntactical subordination, until, with verse 399, an equally free syntactical treatment of the new content begins a new present which continues unchallenged until, with verse 467 ("The old woman now touched it . . ."), the scene which had been broken off is resumed. To be sure, in the case of such long episodes as the one we are considering, a purely syntactical connection with the principal theme would hardly have been possible; but a connection with it through perspective would have been all the easier had the content been arranged with that end in view; if, that is, the entire story of the scar had been presented as a recollection which awakens in Odysseus' mind at this particular moment. It would have been perfectly easy to do; the story of the scar had only to be inserted two verses earlier, at the first mention of the word scar, where the motifs "Odysseus" and "recollection" were already at hand. But any such subjectivistic-perspectivistic procedure, creating a foreground and background, resulting in the present lying open to the depths of the past, is entirely foreign to the Homeric style; the Homeric style knows only a foreground, only a uniformly illuminated, uniformly objective present. And so the excursus does not begin until two lines later, when Euryclea has discovered the scar—the possibility for a perspectivistic connection no longer exists, and the story of the wound becomes an independent and exclusive present.

The genius of the Homeric style becomes even more apparent when it is compared with an equally ancient and equally epic style from a different world of forms. I shall attempt this comparison with the account of the sacrifice of Isaac, a homogeneous narrative produced by the so-called Elohist. The King James version translates the opening as follows (Genesis 22:1): "And it came to pass after these things, that God did tempt Abraham, and said to him, Abraham! and he said, Behold, here I am." Even this opening startles us when we come to it from Homer. Where are the two speakers? We are not told. The reader, however, knows that they are not normally to be found together in one place on earth, that one of them, God, in order to speak to Abraham, must come from somewhere, must enter the earthly realm from some unknown heights or depths. Whence does he come, whence does he call to Abraham? We are not told. He does not come, like Zeus or Poseidon, from the Aethiopians, where he has been enjoying a sacrificial feast. Nor are we told anything of his reasons for tempting Abraham so terribly. He has not, like Zeus, discussed them in set speeches with other gods gathered in council; nor have the deliberations in his own heart been presented to us; unexpected and mysterious, he enters the scene from some unknown height or depth and calls: Abraham! It will at once be said that this is to be explained by the particular concept of God which the Jews held and which was wholly different from that of the Greeks. True enough—but this constitutes no objection. For how is the Jewish concept of God to be explained? Even their earlier God of the desert was not fixed in form and content, and was alone; his lack of form, his lack of local habitation, his singleness, was in the end not only maintained but developed even further in competition with the comparatively far more manifest gods of the surrounding Near Eastern world. The concept of God held by the Jews is less a cause than a symptom of their manner of comprehending and representing things.

This becomes still clearer if we now turn to the other person in the dialogue, to Abraham. Where is he? We do not know. He says, indeed: Here I am—but the Hebrew word means only something like "behold me," and in any case is not meant to indicate the actual place where Abraham is, but a moral position in respect to God, who has called to him—Here am I awaiting thy command. Where he is actually, whether in Beersheba or elsewhere, whether indoors or in the open air, is not stated; it does not interest the narrator, the reader is not informed; and what Abraham was doing when God called to him is left in the same obscurity. To realize the difference, consider Hermes' visit to Calypso, for example, where command, journey, arrival and reception of the visitor, situation and occupation of the person visited, are set forth in many verses; and even on occasions when gods appear suddenly and briefly, whether to help one of their favorites or to deceive or destroy some mortal whom they hate, their bodily forms, and usually the manner of their coming and going, are given in detail. Here, however, God appears without bodily form (yet he "appears"), coming from some unspecified place—we only hear his voice, and that utters nothing but a name, a name without an adjective, without a descriptive epithet for the person spoken to, such as is the rule in every Homeric address; and of Abraham too nothing is made perceptible except the words in which he answers God: *Hinne-ni*, Behold me here—with which, to be sure, a most touching gesture expressive of obedience and readiness is suggested, but it is left to the reader to visualize it. Moreover the two speakers are not on the same level: if we conceive of Abraham in the foreground, where it might be possible to picture him as prostrate or kneeling or bowing with outspread arms or gazing upward, God is not there too: Abraham's words and gestures are directed toward the depths of the picture or upward, but in any case the undetermined, dark place from which the voice comes to him is not in the foreground.

After this opening, God gives his command, and the story itself begins: everyone knows it; it unrolls with no episodes in a few independent sentences whose syntactical connection is of the most rudimentary sort. In this atmosphere it is unthinkable that an implement, a landscape through which the travelers passed, the serving-men, or the ass, should be described, that their origin or descent or material or appearance or usefulness should be set forth in terms of praise; they do not even admit an adjective: they are serving-men, ass, wood, and knife, and nothing else, without an epithet; they are there to serve the end which God has commanded; what in other respects they were, are, or will be, remains in darkness. A journey is made, because God has designated the place where the sacrifice is to be performed; but we are told nothing about the journey except that it took three days, and even that we are told in a mysterious way: Abraham and his followers rose "early in the morning" and "went unto" the place of which God had told him; on the third day he lifted up his eyes and saw the place from afar. That gesture is the only gesture, is indeed the only occurrence during the whole journey, of which we are told; and though its motivation lies in the fact that the place is elevated, its uniqueness still heightens the impression that the journey took place through a vacuum; it is as if, while he traveled on, Abraham had looked neither to the right nor to the left, had suppressed any sign of life in his followers and himself save only their footfalls.

Thus the journey is like a silent progress through the indeterminate and the contingent, a holding of the breath, a process which has no present, which is inserted, like a blank duration, between what has passed and what lies ahead, and which yet is measured: three days! Three such days positively demand the symbolic interpretation which they later received. They began "early in the morning." But at what time on the third day did Abraham lift up his eyes and see his goal? The text says nothing on the subject. Obviously not "late in the evening," for it seems that there was still time enough to climb the mountain and make the sacrifice. So "early in the morning" is given, not as an indication of time, but for the sake of its ethical significance; it is intended to express the resolution, the promptness, the punctual obedience of the sorely tried Abraham. Bitter to him is the early morning in which he saddles his ass, calls his serving-men and his son Isaac, and sets out; but he obeys, he walks on until the third day, then lifts up his eyes and sees the place. Whence he comes, we do not know, but the goal is clearly stated: Jeruel in the land of Moriah. What place this is meant to indicate is not clear—"Moriah" especially may be a later correction of some other word. But in any case the goal was given, and in any case it is a matter of some sacred spot which was to receive a particular consecration by being connected with Abraham's sacrifice. Just as little as "early in the morning" serves as a temporal indication does "Jeruel in the land of Moriah" serve as a geographical indication; and in both cases alike, the complementary indication is not given, for we know as little of the hour at which Abraham lifted up his eyes as we do of the place from which he set forth—Jeruel is significant not so much as the goal of an earthly journey, in its geographical relation to other places, as through its special election, through its relation to God, who designated it as the scene of the act, and therefore it must be named.

In the narrative itself, a third chief character appears: Isaac. While God and Abraham, the serving-men, the ass, and the implements are simply named, without mention of any qualities or any other sort of definition, Isaac once receives an appositive; God says, "Take Isaac, thine only son, whom thou lovest." But this is not a characterization of Isaac as a person, apart from his relation to his father and apart from the story; he may be handsome or ugly, intelligent or stupid, tall or short, pleasant or unpleasant—we are not told. Only what we need to know about him as a personage in the action, here and now, is illuminated, so that it may become apparent how terrible Abraham's temptation is, and that God is fully aware of it. By this example of the contrary, we see the significance of the descriptive adjectives and digressions of the Homeric poems; with their indications of the earlier and as it were absolute existence of the persons described, they prevent the reader from concentrating exclusively on a present crisis; even when the most terrible things are occurring, they prevent the establishment of an overwhelming suspense. But here, in the story of Abraham's sacrifice, the overwhelming suspense is present; what Schiller makes the goal of the tragic poet—to rob us of our emotional freedom, to turn our intellectual and spiritual powers (Schiller says "our activity") in one direction, to concentrate them there—is effected in this Biblical narrative, which certainly deserves the epithet epic.

We find the same contrast if we compare the two uses of direct discourse. The personages speak in the Bible story too; but their speech does not serve, as does speech in Homer, to manifest, to externalize thoughts—on the contrary, it serves to indicate thoughts which remain unexpressed. God gives his command in direct discourse, but he leaves his motives and his purpose unexpressed; Abraham, receiving the command, says nothing and does what he has been told to do. The conversation between Abraham and Isaac on the way to the place of sacrifice is only an interruption of the heavy silence and makes it all the more burdensome. The two of them, Isaac carrying the wood and Abraham with fire and a knife, "went together." Hesitantly, Isaac ventures to ask about the ram, and Abraham gives the well-known answer. Then the text repeats: "So they went both of them together." Everything remains unexpressed.

It would be difficult, then, to imagine styles more contrasted than those of these two equally ancient and equally epic texts. On the one hand, externalized, uniformly illuminated phenomena, at a definite time and in a definite place, connected together without lacunae in a perpetual foreground; thoughts and feeling completely expressed; events taking place in leisurely fashion and with very little of suspense. On the other hand, the externalization of only so much of the phenomena as is necessary for the purpose of the narrative, all else left in obscurity; the decisive points of the narrative alone are emphasized, what lies between is nonexistent; time and place are undefined and call for interpretation; thoughts and feeling remain unexpressed, are only suggested by the silence and the fragmentary speeches; the whole, permeated with the most unrelieved suspense and directed toward a single goal (and to that extent far more of a unity), remains mysterious and "fraught with background."

I will discuss this term in some detail, lest it be misunderstood. I said above that the Homeric style was "of the foreground" because, despite much going back and forth, it yet causes what is momentarily being narrated to give the impression that it is the only present, pure and without perspective. A consideration of the Elohistic text teaches us that our term is capable of a broader and deeper application. It shows that even the separate personages can be represented as possessing "background"; God is always so represented in the Bible, for he is not comprehensible in his presence, as is Zeus; it is always only "something" of him that appears, he always extends into depths. But even the human beings in the Biblical stories have greater depths of time, fate, and consciousness than do the human beings in Homer; although they are nearly always caught up in an event engaging all their faculties, they are not so entirely immersed in its present that they do not remain continually conscious of what has happened to them earlier and elsewhere; their thoughts and feelings have more layers, are more entangled. Abraham's actions are explained not only by what is happening to him at the moment, nor yet only by his character (as Achilles' actions by his courage and his pride, and Odysseus' by his versatility and foresightedness), but by his previous history; he remembers, he is constantly conscious of, what God has promised him and what God has already accomplished for him—his soul is torn between desperate rebellion and hopeful expectation; his silent obedience is multilayered, has background. Such a problematic psychological situation as this is impossible for any of the Homeric heroes, whose destiny is clearly defined and who wake every morning as if it were the first day of their lives: their emotions, though strong, are simple and find expression instantly.

How fraught with background, in comparison, are characters like Saul and David! How entangled and stratified are such human relations as those between David and Absalom, between David and Joab![1] Any such "background" quality of the psychological situation as that which the story of Absalom's death and its sequel (II Samuel 18 and 19, by the so-called Jahvist) rather suggests than expresses, is unthinkable in Homer. Here we are confronted not merely with the psychological processes of characters whose depth of background is veritably abysmal, but with a purely geographical background too. For David is absent from the battlefield; but the influence of his will and his feelings continues to operate, they affect even Joab in his rebellion and disregard for the consequences of his actions; in the magnificent scene with the two messengers, both the physical and psychological background is fully manifest, though the latter is never expressed. With this, compare, for example, how Achilles, who sends Patroclus first to scout and then into battle, loses almost all "presentness" so long as he is not physically present. But the most important thing is the "multilayeredness" of the individual character; this is hardly to be met with in Homer, or at most in the form of a conscious hesitation between two possible courses of action; otherwise, in Homer, the complexity of the psychological life is shown only in the succession and alternation of emotions; whereas the Jewish writers are able to express the simultaneous existence of various layers of consciousness and the conflict between them.

The Homeric poems, then, though their intellectual, linguistic, and above all syntactical culture appears to be so much more highly developed, are yet comparatively simple in their picture of human beings; and no less so in their relation to the real life which they describe in general. Delight in physical existence is everything to them, and their highest aim is to make that delight perceptible to us. Between battles and passions, adventures and perils, they show us hunts, banquets, palaces and shepherds' cots, athletic contests and washing days—in order that we may see the heroes in their ordinary life, and seeing them so, may take pleasure in their manner of enjoying their savory present, a present which sends strong roots down into social usages, landscape, and daily life. And thus they bewitch us and ingratiate themselves to us until we live

---

[1] The story of David extends from I Samuel 17:12 through II Samuel to I Kings 2:11.

with them in the reality of their lives; so long as we are reading or hearing the poems, it does not matter whether we know that all this is only legend, "make-believe." The oft-repeated reproach that Homer is a liar takes nothing from his effectiveness, he does not need to base his story on historical reality, his reality is powerful enough in itself; it ensnares us, weaving its web around us, and that suffices him. And this "real" world into which we are lured, exists for itself, contains nothing but itself; the Homeric poems conceal nothing, they contain no teaching and no secret second meaning. Homer can be analyzed, as we have essayed to do here, but he cannot be interpreted. Later allegorizing trends have tried their arts of interpretation upon him, but to no avail. He resists any such treatment; the interpretations are forced and foreign, they do not crystallize into a unified doctrine. The general considerations which occasionally occur (in our episode, for example, v. 360: that in misfortune men age quickly) reveal a calm acceptance of the basic facts of human existence, but with no compulsion to brood over them, still less any passionate impulse either to rebel against them or to embrace them in an ecstasy of submission.

It is all very different in the Biblical stories. Their aim is not to bewitch the senses, and if nevertheless they produce lively sensory effects, it is only because the moral, religious, and psychological phenomena which are their sole concern are made concrete in the sensible matter of life. But their religious intent involves an absolute claim to historical truth. The story of Abraham and Isaac is not better established than the story of Odysseus, Penelope, and Eury-clea; both are legendary. But the Biblical narrator, the Elohist, had to believe in the objective truth of the story of Abraham's sacrifice—the existence of the sacred ordinances of life rested upon the truth of this and similar stories. He had to believe in it passionately; or else (as many rationalistic interpreters believed and perhaps still believe) he had to be a conscious liar—no harmless liar like Homer, who lied to give pleasure, but a political liar with a definite end in view, lying in the interest of a claim to absolute authority.

To me, the rationalistic interpretation seems psychologically absurd; but even if we take it into consideration, the relation of the Elohist to the truth of his story still remains a far more passionate and definite one than is Homer's relation. The Biblical narrator was obliged to write exactly what his belief in the truth of the tradition (or, from the rationalistic standpoint, his interest in the truth of it) demanded of him—in either case, his freedom in creative or representative imagination was severely limited; his activity was per-force reduced to composing an effective version of the pious tradition. What he produced, then, was not primarily oriented toward "realism" (if he succeeded in being realistic, it was merely a means, not an end); it was oriented toward truth. Woe to the man who did not believe it! One can perfectly well entertain historical doubts on the subject of the Trojan War or of Odysseus' wanderings, and still, when reading Homer, feel precisely the effects he sought to produce; but without believing in Abraham's sacrifice, it is impossible to put the nar-rative of it to the use for which it was written. Indeed, we must go even further. The Bible's claim to truth is not only far more urgent than Homer's, it is tyrannical—it excludes all other claims. The world of the Scripture stories is not satisfied with claiming to be a historically true reality—it insists that it is the only real world, is destined for autocracy. All other scenes, issues, and ordinances have no right to appear independently of it, and it is promised that all of them, the history of all mankind, will be given their due place within its frame, will be subordinated to it. The Scripture stories do not, like Homer's, court our favor, they do not flatter us that they may please us and enchant us—they seek to subject us, and if we refuse to be subjected we are rebels.

Let no one object that this goes too far, that not the stories, but the religious doctrine, raises the claim to absolute authority; because the stories are not, like Homer's, simply narrated "reality." Doctrine and promise are incarnate in them and inseparable from them; for that very reason they are fraught with "background" and mysterious, containing a second, concealed meaning. In the story of Isaac, it is not only God's intervention at the beginning and the end, but even the factual and psychological elements which come between, that are mysterious, merely touched upon, fraught with background; and therefore they require subtle investigation and interpretation, they demand them. Since so much in the story is dark and incomplete, and since the reader knows that God is a hidden God, his effort to interpret it constantly finds something new to feed upon. Doctrine and the search for enlightenment are inextricably connected with the physical side of the narrative—the latter being more than simple "reality"; indeed they are in constant danger of losing their own reality, as very soon happened when interpretation reached such proportions that the real vanished.

If the text of the Biblical narrative, then, is so greatly in need of interpretation on the basis of its own content, its claim to absolute authority forces it still further in the same direction. Far from seeking, like Homer, merely to make us forget our own reality for a few hours, it seeks to overcome our reality: we are to fit our own life into its world, feel ourselves to be elements in its structure of universal history. This becomes increasingly difficult the further our historical environment is removed from that of the Biblical books; and if these nevertheless maintain their claim to absolute authority, it is inevitable that they themselves be adapted through interpretative transformation. This was for a long time comparatively easy; as late as the European Middle Ages it was possible to represent Biblical events as ordinary phenomena of contemporary life, the methods of interpretation themselves forming the basis for such a treatment. But when, through too great a change in environment and through the awakening of a critical consciousness, this becomes impossible, the Biblical claim to absolute authority is jeopardized; the method of interpretation is scorned and rejected, the Biblical stories become ancient legends, and the doctrine they had contained, now dissevered from them, becomes a disembodied image.

As a result of this claim to absolute authority, the method of interpretation spread to traditions other than the Jewish. The Homeric poems present a definite complex of events whose boundaries in space and time are clearly delimited; before it, beside it, and after it, other complexes of events, which do not depend upon it, can be conceived without conflict and without difficulty. The Old Testament, on the other hand, presents universal history: it begins with the beginning of time, with the creation of the world, and will end with the Last Days, the fulfilling of the Covenant, with which the world will come to an end. Everything else that happens in the world can only be conceived as an element in this sequence; into it everything that is known about the world, or at least everything that touches upon the history of the Jews, must be fitted as an ingredient of the divine plan; and as this too became possible only by interpreting the new material as it poured in, the need for interpretation reaches out beyond the original Jewish-Israelitish realm of reality—for example to Assyrian, Babylonian, Persian, and Roman history; interpretation in a determined direction becomes a general method of comprehending reality; the new and strange world which now comes into view and which, in the form in which it presents itself, proves to be wholly unutilizable within the Jewish religious frame, must be so interpreted that it can find a place there. But this process nearly always also reacts upon the frame, which requires enlarging and modifying. The most striking piece of interpretation of this sort occurred in the first century of the Christian era, in consequence of Paul's mission to the Gentiles: Paul and the Church Fathers reinterpreted the entire Jewish tradition as a succession of figures prognosticating the appearance of Christ, and assigned the Roman Empire its proper place in the divine plan of salvation. Thus while, on the one hand, the reality of the Old Testament presents itself as complete truth with a claim to sole authority, on the other hand that very claim forces it to a constant interpretative change in its own content; for millennia it undergoes an incessant and active development with the life of man in Europe.

The claim of the Old Testament stories to represent universal history, their insistent relation—a relation constantly redefined by conflicts—to a single and hidden God, who yet shows himself and who guides universal history by promise and exaction, gives these stories an entirely different perspective from any the Homeric poems can possess. As a composition, the Old Testament is incomparably less unified than the Homeric poems, it is more obviously pieced together—but the various components all belong to one concept of universal history and its interpretation. If certain elements survived which did not immediately fit in, interpretation took care of them; and so the reader is at every moment aware of the universal religio-historical perspective which gives the individual stories their general meaning and purpose. The greater the separateness and horizontal disconnection of the stories and groups of stories in relation to one another, compared with the *Iliad* and the *Odyssey*, the stronger is their general vertical connection, which holds them all together and which is entirely lacking in Homer. Each of the great figures of the Old Testament, from Adam to the prophets, embodies a moment of this vertical connection. God chose and formed these men to the end of embodying his essence and will—yet choice and formation do not coincide, for the latter proceeds gradually, historically, during the earthly life of him upon whom the choice has fallen. How the process is accomplished, what terrible trials such a formation inflicts, can be seen from our story of Abraham's sacrifice. Herein lies the reason why the great figures of the Old Testament are so much more fully developed, so much more fraught with their own biographical past, so much more distinct as individuals, than are the Homeric heroes. Achilles and Odysseus are splendidly described in many well-ordered words, epithets cling to them, their emotions are constantly displayed in their words and deeds—but they have no development, and their life-histories are clearly set forth once and for all. So little are the Homeric heroes presented as developing or having developed, that most of them—Nestor, Agamemnon, Achilles—appear to be of an age fixed from the very first. Even Odysseus, in whose case the long lapse of time and the many events which occurred offer so much opportunity for biographical development, shows almost nothing of it. Odysseus on his return is exactly the same as he was when he left Ithaca two decades earlier. But what a road, what a fate, lie between the Jacob who cheated his father out of his blessing and the old man whose favorite son has been torn to pieces by a wild beast!—between David the harp player, persecuted by his lord's jealousy, and the old king, surrounded by violent intrigues, whom Abishag the Shunnamite warmed in his bed, and he knew her not! The old man, of whom we know how he has become what he is, is more of an individual than the young man; for it is only during the course of an eventful life that men are differentiated into full individuality; and it is this history of a personality which the Old Testament presents to us as the formation undergone by those whom God has chosen to be examples. Fraught with their development, sometimes even aged to the verge of dissolution, they show a distinct stamp of individuality entirely foreign to the Homeric heroes. Time can touch the latter only outwardly, and even that change is brought to our observation as little as possible; whereas the stern hand of God is ever upon the Old Testament figures; he has not only made them once and for all and chosen them, but he continues to work upon them, bends them and kneads them, and, without destroying them in essence, produces from them forms which their youth gave no grounds for anticipating. The objection that the biographical element of the Old Testament often springs from the combination of several legendary personages does not apply; for this combination is a part of the development of the text. And how much wider is the pendulum swing of their lives than that of the Homeric heroes! For they are bearers of the divine will, and yet they are fallible, subject to misfortune and humiliation—and in the midst of misfortune and in their humiliation their acts and words reveal the transcendent majesty of God. There is hardly one of them who does not, like Adam, undergo the deepest humiliation—and hardly one who is not deemed worthy of God's personal intervention and personal inspiration. Humiliation and elevation go far deeper and far higher than in Homer, and they belong basically together. The poor beggar Odysseus is only masquerading, but Adam is really cast down, Jacob really a refugee, Joseph really in the pit and then a slave to be bought and sold. But their greatness, rising out of humiliation, is almost superhuman and an image of God's greatness. The reader clearly feels how the extent of the pendulum's swing is connected with the intensity of the personal history—precisely the most extreme circumstances, in which we are immeasurably forsaken and in despair, or immeasurably joyous and exalted, give us, if we survive them, a personal stamp which is recognized as the product of a rich existence, a rich development. And very often, indeed generally, this element of development gives the Old Testament stories a historical character, even when the subject is purely legendary and traditional.

Homer remains within the legendary with all his material, whereas the material of the Old Testament comes closer and closer to history as the narrative proceeds; in the stories of David the historical report predominates. Here too, much that is legendary still remains, as for example the story of David and Goliath; but much—and the most essential—consists in things which the narrators knew from their own experience or from firsthand testimony. Now the difference between legend and history is in most cases easily perceived by a reasonably experienced reader. It is a difficult matter, requiring careful historical and philological training, to distinguish the true from the synthetic or the biased in a historical presentation; but it is easy to separate the historical from the legendary in general. Their structure is different. Even where the legendary does not immediately betray itself by elements of the miraculous, by the repetition of well-known standard motives, typical patterns and themes, through neglect of clear details of time and place, and the like, it is generally quickly recognizable by its composition. It runs far too smoothly. All crosscurrents, all friction, all that is casual, secondary to the main events and themes, everything unresolved, truncated, and uncertain, which confuses the clear progress of the action and the simple orientation of the actors, has disappeared. The historical event which we witness, or learn from the testimony of those who witnessed it, runs much more variously, contradictorily, and confusedly; not until it has produced results in a definite domain are we able, with their help, to classify it to a certain extent; and how often the order to which we think we have attained becomes doubtful again, how often we ask ourselves if the data before us have not led us to a far too simple classification of the original events! Legend arranges its material in a simple and straightforward way; it detaches it from its contemporary historical context, so that the latter will not confuse it; it knows only clearly outlined men who act from few and simple motives and the continuity of whose feelings and actions remains uninterrupted. In the legends of martyrs, for example, a stiff-necked and fanatical persecutor stands over against an equally stiff-necked and fanatical victim; and a situation so complicated—that is to say, so real and historical—as that in which the "persecutor" Pliny finds himself in his celebrated letter to Trajan on the subject of the Christians,[2] is unfit for legend. And that is still a comparatively simple case. Let the reader think of the history which we are ourselves witnessing; anyone who, for example, evaluates the behavior of individual men and groups of men at the time of the rise of National Socialism in Germany, or the behavior of individual peoples and states before and during the last war, will feel how difficult it is to represent historical themes in general, and how unfit they are for legend; the historical comprises a great number of contradictory motives in each individual, a hesitation and ambiguous groping on the part of groups; only seldom (as in the last war) does a more or less plain situation, comparatively simple to describe, arise, and even such a situation is subject to division below the surface, is indeed almost constantly in danger of losing its simplicity; and the motives of all the interested parties are so

---

[2] Pliny the Younger (c. 62–113 A.D.) was sent by the emperor Trajan (c. 53–117 A.D.) to govern the proconsular province of Pontus-Bithynia. He suddenly found himself forced to prosecute people accused of Christianity, a capital crime. He knew nothing about Christians; there were few precedents in Roman law for dealing with them; the pagan populace, blaming the Christians for natural calamities and hating their exclusiveness, howled for their blood; some of the Christians were anxious to become martyrs; but Pliny, a civilized and humane, if complacent, man, though amazed at the intransigence of the Christians, was not happy about executing them. He sought loopholes in the law and token avowals to the pagan gods from the Christians. He wrote to Trajan for advice.

complex that the slogans of propaganda can be composed only through the crudest simplification—with the result that friend and foe alike can often employ the same ones. To write history is so difficult that most historians are forced to make concessions to the technique of legend.

It is clear that a large part of the life of David as given in the Bible contains history and not legend. In Absalom's rebellion, for example, or in the scenes from David's last days, the contradictions and crossing of motives both in individuals and in the general action have become so concrete that it is impossible to doubt the historicity of the information conveyed. Now the men who composed the historical parts are often the same who edited the older legends too; their peculiar religious concept of man in history, which we have attempted to describe above, in no way led them to a legendary simplification of events; and so it is only natural that, in the legendary passages of the Old Testament, historical structure is frequently discernible—of course, not in the sense that the traditions are examined as to their credibility according to the methods of scientific criticism; but simply to the extent that the tendency to a smoothing down and harmonizing of events, to a simplification of motives, to a static definition of characters which avoids conflict, vacillation, and development, such as are natural to legendary structure, does not predominate in the Old Testament world of legend. Abraham, Jacob, or even Moses produces a more concrete, direct, and historical impression than the figures of the Homeric world—not because they are better described in terms of sense (the contrary is the case) but because the confused, contradictory multiplicity of events, the psychological and factual cross-purposes, which true history reveals, have not disappeared in the representation but still remain clearly perceptible. In the stories of David, the legendary, which only later scientific criticism makes recognizable as such, imperceptibly passes into the historical; and even in the legendary, the problem of the classification and interpretation of human history is already passionately apprehended—a problem which later shatters the framework of historical composition and completely overruns it with prophecy; thus the Old Testament, in so far as it is concerned with human events, ranges through all three domains: legend, historical reporting, and interpretative historical theology.

Connected with the matters just discussed is the fact that the Greek text seems more limited and more static in respect to the circle of personages involved in the action and to their political activity. In the recognition scene with which we began, there appears, aside from Odysseus and Penelope, the housekeeper Euryclea, a slave whom Odysseus' father Laertes had bought long before. She, like the swineherd Eumaeus, has spent her life in the service of Laertes' family; like Eumaeus, she is closely connected with their fate, she loves them and shares their interests and feelings. But she has no life of her own, no feelings of her own; she has only the life and feelings of her master. Eumaeus too, though he still remembers that he was born a freeman and indeed of a noble house (he was stolen as a boy), has, not only in fact but also in his own feeling, no longer a life of his own, he is entirely involved in the life of his masters. Yet these two characters are the only ones Homer brings to life who do not belong to the ruling class. Thus we become conscious of the fact that in the Homeric poems life is enacted only among the ruling class—others appear only in the role of servants to that class. The ruling class is still so strongly patriarchal, and still itself so involved in the daily activities of domestic life, that one is sometimes likely to forget their rank. But they are unmistakably a sort of feudal aristocracy, whose men divide their lives between war, hunting, marketplace councils, and feasting, while the women supervise the maids in the house. As a social picture, this world is completely stable; wars take place only between different groups of the ruling class; nothing ever pushes up from below. In the early stories of the Old Testament the patriarchal condition is dominant too, but since the people involved are individual nomadic or half-nomadic tribal leaders, the social picture gives a much less stable impression; class distinctions are not felt. As soon as the people completely emerges—that is, after the exodus from Egypt—its activity is always discernible, it is often in ferment, it frequently intervenes in events not only as a whole but also in separate groups and through the medium of separate individuals who come forward; the origins of prophecy seem to lie in the irrepressible politico-religious spontaneity of the people. We receive the impression that the movements emerging from the depths of the people of Israel-Judah must have been of a wholly different nature from those even of the later ancient democracies—of a different nature and far more elemental.

With the more profound historicity and the more profound social activity of the Old Testament text, there is connected yet another important distinction from Homer: namely, that a different conception of the elevated style and of the sublime is to be found here. Homer, of course, is not afraid to let the realism of daily life enter into the sublime and tragic; our episode of the scar is an example, we see how the quietly depicted, domestic scene of the foot-washing is incorporated into the pathetic and sublime action of Odysseus' homecoming. From the rule of the separation of styles which was later almost universally accepted and which specified that the realistic depiction of daily life was incompatible with the sublime and had a place only in comedy or, carefully stylized, in idyl—from any such rule Homer is still far removed. And yet he is closer to it than is the Old Testament. For the great and sublime events in the Homeric poems take place far more exclusively and unmistakably among the members of a ruling class; and these are far more untouched in their heroic elevation than are the Old Testament figures, who can fall much lower in dignity (consider, for example, Adam, Noah, David, Job); and finally, domestic realism, the representation of daily life, remains in Homer in the peaceful realm of the idyllic, whereas, from the very first, in the Old Testament stories, the sublime, tragic, and problematic take shape precisely in the domestic and commonplace: scenes such as those between Cain and Abel, between Noah and his sons, between Abraham, Sarah, and Hagar, between Rebekah, Jacob, and Esau, and so on, are inconceivable in the Homeric style. The entirely different ways of developing conflicts are enough to account for this. In the Old Testament stories the peace of daily life in the house, in the fields, and among the flocks, is undermined by jealousy over election and the promise of a blessing, and complications arise which would be utterly incomprehensible to the Homeric heroes. The latter must have palpable and clearly expressible reasons for their conflicts and enmities, and these work themselves out in free battles; whereas, with the former, the perpetually smouldering jealousy and the connection between the domestic and the spiritual, between the paternal blessing and the divine blessing, lead to daily life being permeated with the stuff of conflict, often with poison. The sublime influence of God here reaches so deeply into the everyday that the two realms of the sublime and the everyday are not only actually unseparated but basically inseparable.

We have compared these two texts, and, with them, the two kinds of style they embody, in order to reach a starting point for an investigation into the literary representation of reality in European culture. The two styles, in their opposition, represent basic types: on the one hand fully externalized description, uniform illumination, uninterrupted connection, free expression, all events in the foreground, displaying unmistakable meanings, few elements of historical development and of psychological perspective; on the other hand, certain parts brought into high relief, others left obscure, abruptness, suggestive influence of the unexpressed, "background" quality, multiplicity of meanings and the need for interpretation, universal-historical claims, development of the concept of the historically becoming, and preoccupation with the problematic.

Homer's realism is, of course, not to be equated with classical-antique realism in general; for the separation of styles, which did not develop until later, permitted no such leisurely and externalized description of everyday happenings; in tragedy especially there was no room for it; furthermore, Greek culture very soon encountered the phenomena of historical becoming and of the "multilayeredness" of the human problem, and dealt with them in its fashion; in Roman realism, finally, new and native concepts are added. We shall go into these later changes in the antique representation of reality when the occasion arises; on the whole, despite them, the basic tendencies of the Homeric style, which we have attempted to work out, remained effective and determinant down into late antiquity.

Since we are using the two styles, the Homeric and the Old Testament, as starting points, we have taken them as finished products, as they appear in the texts; we have disregarded everything that pertains to their origins, and thus have left untouched the question whether their peculiarities were theirs from the beginning or are to be referred wholly or in part to foreign influences. Within the limits of our purpose, a consideration of this question is not necessary; for it is in their full development, which they reached in early times, that the two styles exercised their determining influence upon the representation of reality in European literature.

Ronald Crane

PHILOSOPHY, LITERATURE, AND THE HISTORY OF IDEAS*

Ronald Crane (1886–1967) was born in Tecumseh, Michigan. He was graduated from the University of Michigan in 1908 and took his doctorate at the University of Pennsylvania in 1911. After teaching at Northwestern University from 1911 to 1924, Crane moved to the University of Chicago, where he remained until his retirement as Distinguished Service Professor Emeritus of English.

At Chicago Crane became a leader of a group of neo-Aristotelian critics distinguished by their formidable erudition and rigorous theorizing. As part of their program for establishing literary criticism as a regular academic discipline, Crane and his colleagues called for a philosophic criticism, one based on "a special framework of concepts and distinctions," a criticism more pragmatic in the Aristotelian manner than that practiced by the "Platonist" New Critics, a criticism that emphasizes the formal cause of a literary work, its plot-architecture, rather than "the poet's mind" (the efficient cause) or "his medium," words (the material cause) or "the psychology of his audience" (the final cause). What a poet does distinctively as a poet, says Crane, is "by means of his art, to build materials of language and experience into wholes of various kinds to which, as we experience them, we tend to attribute final rather than merely instrumental value. The criticism of poetry (in the large sense that includes prose fiction and drama) is, according to this view, pri-

* A paper read before a conference on the history of ideas in relation to literature and the arts held at Reed College, Portland, Oregon, April 23–24, 1954, under the auspices of the Pacific Coast Council on the Humanities. The committee in charge of the conference had proposed as a theme for consideration the issues raised by Lionel Trilling's discussion (*The Liberal Imagination* [New York, 1950], pp. 281 ff.) of "the meaning of a literary idea" and especially by his criticism (*ibid.,* p. 190) of Professor Arthur O. Lovejoy's views on the relation between ideas in literature and ideas in philosophy. My assignment was primarily the literary bearings of the question; the philosophical bearings were treated in a paper by Professor Arthur E. Murphy, then of the University of Washington. [Crane's note.]
From *The Idea of the Humanities and Other Essays,* by Ronald Crane. © 1967 by The University of Chicago. Chicago: University of Chicago Press. Reprinted by permission of the University of Chicago Press.

marily an inquiry into the specific characters and powers, and the necessary constituent elements, of possible kinds of poetic wholes, leading to an appreciation, in individual works, of how well their writers have accomplished the particular sorts of poetic tasks which the natures of the wholes they have attempted to construct imposed on them."

These remarks come from the preface to *Critics and Criticism; Ancient and Modern* (1954), the major group effort of the Chicago Aristotelians, a volume edited by Crane and to which he contributed four essays. He is the author of a bibliography of Thomas Gray (1918); *The Vogue of Medieval Chivalric Romance during the English Renaissance* (1919); with F. B. Kaye, *A Census of British Newspapers and Periodicals, 1620–1800* (1927); *The Language of Criticism and the Structure of Poetry* (1953); and *The Idea of the Humanities and other Essays Critical and Historical* (1967).

My subject is stated so ambiguously in my title that I must begin by saying how I understand it. I propose to discuss "literary ideas," or rather ideas in literature, in the context both of ideas in philosophy and of ideas in the history of ideas; and in doing so I want to lay the final emphasis on the distinctively literary characteristics and functions of literary ideas. I shall use, accordingly, what Jung[1] calls a "constructive" as opposed to a "reductive" method of procedure. I shall look, that is, for both likenesses and differences among the three classes or embodiments of ideas I speak of; but I shall not move from differences to likenesses—as in the many attempts to interpret poetry as a kind of philosophy or philosophy as a kind of poetry or to identify the study of either poetry or philosophy with the history of ideas—but rather in the contrary direction, from the common characteristics of ideas in all three fields to the more or less sharply differentiated characteristics that distinguish ideas as they function in literature from ideas as they function in philosophy and in the history of ideas. I want, furthermore, to be as matter of fact as possible and hence to start with a minimum of commitment as to the essential natures and interrelationships of my three fields. I shall assume at the outset, therefore, only very rough discriminations of meaning among the three terms in my title—such discriminations as we all make when we classify *Othello, Tom Jones,* and the "Ode to a Nightingale," for example, as works of literary art primarily rather than of philosophy or intellectual history; Spinoza's *Ethics,* Hume's *Enquiry concerning the Principles of Morals,* and Kant's *Critique of Judgment*[2] as works of philosophy primarily rather than of literary art or intellectual history; and *The Great Chain of Being* and *Essays in the History of Ideas* as works of intellectual history primarily rather than of philosophy or literary art. There is no need, to begin with at least, for any greater refinement of definition than this: literature is simply what men do when they

[1] Carl Gustav Jung (1875–1961), Swiss psychiatrist, a disciple of Freud who broke with the master to become founder of analytic psychology.
[2] The *Ethics* (published posthumously in 1677) by Baruch Spinoza (1632–1677), Dutch philosopher; *Enquiry concerning the Principles of Morals* (1751), by David Hume (1711–1776), Scottish philosopher; the *Critique of Judgment* (1790) by Immanuel Kant (1724–1804), German philosopher.

write works, whatever their special themes, that resemble more closely, in struc-ture, method, and intent, the works in the first group than those in either of the other two; and so, similarly, for philosophy and the history of ideas.

I have singled out Lovejoy's[3] *The Great Chain of Being* and his *Essays in the History of Ideas* for two reasons. These books embody, for one thing, a clearly defined conception of the history of ideas as an independent discipline, a distinctive way of dealing with ideas, from which much instruction can be drawn with respect to our problem. And, for another thing—and by virtue of the peculiar character of this conception—they afford as good a starting point as could well be found for discussing ideas themselves, considered apart from what happens to them when they become ingredients in the constructions of intellectual history, philosophy, and literature.

I refer here to Lovejoy's notion of "unit-ideas" or "individual ideas"—a notion which, so far as I am aware, he was the first, if not to entertain, at least to erect into a principle of historical method. The history of ideas, he says, is "something at once more specific and less restricted than the history of philoso-phy." It is less restricted in that it takes as its documents not merely the writings of accredited philosophers but any writings in which ideas may be discerned, whether their authors be philosophers, theologians, scientists, historians, scholars, critics, essayists, preachers, orators, journalists, novelists, dramatists, or poets. And it is more specific than the history of philosophy or, presumably, of any other mode of discursive thought, in that it applies to its documents an initial procedure "somewhat analogous," as he remarks, "to that of analytic chemistry." The procedure is one of separating out from particular systems of thought, viewed as more or less unstable "compounds," the basic conceptual and meth-odological elements of which they are composed; and the results of this analysis —the "unit-ideas" it fixes our attention on—become the essential data of the history of ideas.[*] Examples will occur to all readers of Lovejoy's books and papers: the themes of continuity, plenitude, and gradation; the metaphor of the chain of being; the reference of values to the ambiguous norm of Nature; the antitheses of nature and art, the simple and the complex, the regular and the irregular, the uniform and the diverse, the notions of progress, decline, and cyclical change; and so on. These are all, in varying degrees of complexity, "unit-ideas."

So far, it seems to me, this is a wholly sound procedure, reflecting an insight into the nature of intellectual constructions which everyone can easily verify. Considered as individual wholes, such constructions are unique things, and they are unique also, in another sense, when viewed as aggregates of particular statements about their subjects. Yet we can always discover in any work, however original, that involves thought a large number of minor forms or schemes of subject matter and reasoning which, if we are at all widely read, will have for us a familiar ring. We have met with the same things before—the same sets of general terms, the same questions, the same, or ap-parently the same, distinctions, the same analogies, the same bits of doctrine,

---

[3] Arthur Oncken Lovejoy (1873–1962), for many years Professor of Philosophy at Johns Hopkins University, who is best known for his work on the history of ideas.

[*] *The Great Chain of Being* (Cambridge, Mass., 1936), pp. 3 ff. [Crane's note.]

the same modes or lines of proof, the same myths—in many other writers, in the same or different departments of writing, earlier or later.

The more broadly learned we are, indeed, the more correspondences of this kind, linking together parts or brief passages in writings of the most diverse sorts, we shall be likely to note in the margins of our books or in scholarly papers. And what we thus note will be "unit-ideas" in Lovejoy's meaning of the word. I should prefer to call them "commonplaces," partly to suggest their affinity with the *topoi*[4] and places of argument of the ancient, medieval, and early modern writers on rhetoric and logic, and partly to emphasize their character as more or less crystallized and discrete conceptual materials or devices of method that are capable, as their history shows, of being put to a great variety of uses in all or many fields of discussion and literary art. Some, though by no means all, of them are *disjecta membra*[5] of philosophic or scientific systems that have survived, independently, as parts of a common stock of usable notions and patterns of reasoning upon which all educated men can draw: for example, the divided line of Plato,[6] the four causes of Aristotle,[7] the atoms of Democritus,[8] the Ciceronian division of the virtues,[9] the moral sense of Shaftesbury,[10] the Kantian distinction of reason and understanding,[11] the various fragments of doctrine and method torn loose, in our day, from the psychologies of Freud and Jung. The question of origin, however, is less important here than the question of intellectual status; and of ideas in this elementary sense, including those discussed so learnedly and trenchantly by Lovejoy, I think we must say that, wherever they occur, they represent not so much what the writers in whose treatises, essays, poems, or novels we find

---

[4] Topics, commonplaces.

[5] Scattered parts.

[6] In Book VI of the *Republic*, Socrates says, "take a line cut in two unequal segments, one for the class that is seen, the other for the class that is intellected—and go on and cut each segment in the same proportion." The first class, then, will have two subdivisions—one of the pure ideas, the Platonic forms, the other of concepts, thought-images. The second class will also have two subdivisions—one of objects, natural and manufactured, the other of reflections of these objects, as in water, mirrors, shadows.

[7] In his book on natural science Aristotle says that there are four causes, or determining factors, for the existence or occurrence of anything: the *material* cause—e.g., the statue is to be made of marble; the *formal* cause—the statue is to be in the shape of an heroic male; the *efficient* cause—a sculptor chips away at the marble; the *final* cause—the statue is to make Apollo kindly disposed toward those who commissioned the statue.

[8] Democritus (c. 460–370 B.C.) held that all matter was made of particles too small for the eye to see, indivisible and indestructible, called atoms.

[9] Marcus Tullius Cicero (106–43 B.C.), in *De officiis* ("On Moral Duty") divided the virtues into those that are *honestum,* morally right, and those that are *utile,* useful, and further divided those that are morally right into wisdom, courage, justice, and self-control.

[10] Anthony Ashley Cooper, third Earl of Shaftesbury (1671–1713), argued that men are innately equipped with a moral sense that leads to a harmony between the general welfare and individual happiness.

[11] The Kantian distinction is between *Vernunft* (reason), the highest faculty of the mind, the one capable of framing general propositions and of directly apprehending universals; and *Verstand* (understanding), the conceptual faculty, the one capable of rendering experience intelligible by subsuming perceived particulars under appropriate concepts.

them are thinking *about* as what they are thinking with. In this paper of mine, for instance, you will find the commonplaces, among others, of a "constructive" as distinct from a "reductive" method and of the difference between materials and synthesis. These enter into the paper, however, not as controlling problems in the discussion but as means of formulating and conducting it. To the extent that my paper is philosophical in form, they can doubtless be called "philosophical ideas"; but they clearly have no definite philosophical meaning or value apart from the uses, good or bad, I put them to or the uses, rather different from mine, they were put to in the philosophers who first conceived them. And the same thing would have to be said about them as literary ideas, should we encounter them, as we easily might, in works of literary art. In themselves, in short—and this is true of all ideas when isolated as unit-conceptions—they are only materials or devices and hence only potentially either philosophical or literary.

Now it is obvious that if ideas in this sense can be abstracted from the constructions in which they have served as elements, they can be made the subject matter of historical study, and this in several different ways. One of these would involve taking as one's point of departure an important philosophical or literary text and building up around it a rich body of scholarly annotation designed to show in detail the extent of its author's reliance on the commonplaces available to him in earlier writings; this has been done with notable success in such editions as Gilson's of the *Discours de la méthode*,[12] André Morize's of *Candide*,[13] Daniel Mornet's of the *Nouvelle Héloïse*,[14] and Maynard Mack's of the *Essay on Man*.[15] Another way would be that which Lovejoy himself exemplifies in *Primitivism and Related Ideas in Antiquity* and (in a more tightly organized fashion) in *The Great Chain of Being*: here one proceeds by first isolating some idea or closely connected group of ideas; then bringing together from different fields and for an extended period of time as many texts expressive of it as one can find; and, finally, so correlating one's materials as to exhibit the stages of its dissemination and use, in writings of all kinds, for as long as it remained current. Lastly, one might concentrate, not on a text or author or on an idea, but on a period, such as the English Renaissance or the Enlightenment, and set oneself the problem of discovering and describing the various sets of ideas that operate as recurrent commonplaces in some or all of its provinces of thought and artistic expression, and such shifts in the character or sources of these as the texts may disclose: Lovejoy has attempted something like this in his essay on the meaning of "Romanticism" for the historian of ideas,* and there are approximations to it in the discussions by Hardin Craig

---

[12] René Descartes, *Discours de la méthode* ("Discourse on Method"), ed. Étienne Gilson (Paris: Librarie Philosophique, 1925).

[13] François Marie Arouet de Voltaire, *Candide*, ed. André Morize (Paris: Hachette, 1913).

[14] Jean Jacques Rousseau, *La Nouvelle Héloïse*, ed. Daniel Mornet (Paris: Hachette, 1925).

[15] Alexander Pope, *The Essay on Man*, ed. Maynard Mack, Vol. 3, Part 1 of the Twickingham Edition of the Poems of Alexander Pope (New Haven: Yale University Press, 1950).

* *Journal of the History of Ideas*, 2 (1941): 257–78. [Crane's note.]

and E. M. W. Tillyard[16] of the so-called "world view" of the Elizabethans. We have not made yet, in any of these three branches of study, more than a few beginnings; but what has been done is enough to suggest the immense value of the history of ideas, as thus conceived, for philosophical interpretation and the criticism and history of literature. The things men say in philosophy and literature are conditioned, in every age, by the means available to them, in the ever-changing common storehouse of intellectual materials and devices, for saying these things; and it is well to know, as fully and exactly as possible, for any of the philosophers or literary artists we may wish to study, what the means accessible to them were and from what sources—philosophical, literary, or popular—they were derived.

This is the sphere of the history of ideas in the now commonly accepted sense of that word; and its value for the interpretation of philosophical and literary works is likely to be all the greater in proportion as we recognize what it necessarily leaves out. For the history of "individual ideas" can give us at best, to use another venerable commonplace, only some of the material causes of what philosophers and literary artists think and say, abstracted from the particular forms by virtue of which the writings it investigates become significant as philosophy or literature. It is like the history of language as written by grammarians innocent of philosophy or literary criticism. It can tell us much about the conceptual vocabularies and idioms of method that philosophers and literary men at different times have used, but little or nothing about how they have used these, or why in this manner rather than in some other, or with what consequences for the vocabularies and idioms themselves. For such understanding we must look beyond the idea-materials which the history of ideas, as so defined, undertakes to study.

It must be said that Lovejoy is aware of this, with the result that the history he writes—especially, though not exclusively, in *The Great Chain of Being*—is much more than a merely descriptive account of the intellectual phenomena with which it deals. These phenomena are basically, as we have seen, unit-ideas or the distinguishable parts of idea-complexes such as the chain of being or the cluster of significations attached to the sacred word "Nature"; and concerning such elements it is sufficient for him to give descriptive definitions, as in a dictionary, in terms of their respective conceptual contents, and to apply these directly to shorter or longer passages in writings of all kinds, philosophical or literary. The ideas or idea elements he deals with are thus, in a sense, irreducible atoms that are assumed to be constant in meaning throughout the history. The problem of the history itself, however, is what happens to the ideas, once they are, so to speak, set in motion. It is the problem, first, of showing how they coalesce to form the particular "unstable compounds" of unit-ideas—the conception is highly significant—which we call "philosophic systems" or "bodies of doctrine" in philosophy or literature and, second, and in a larger perspective, of making intelligible the major historical shifts in attitude and belief that have occurred from time to time, as when the Enlightenment gave place to Romanticism. And for these purposes Lovejoy introduces what I can only call a "philosophy" of ideas and their history.

[16] Hardin Craig, *The Enchanted Glass* (New York, 1936), E. M. W. Tillyard, *The Elizabethan World Picture* (London, 1943).

He does this by positing, as general principles of explanation in any history of ideas, certain basic motor forces, as they may be termed, that operate as determining factors in the thought of both individual writers and ages. They appear to be of three kinds, corresponding to three levels of human thought— the semantic, the doctrinal or dialectical, and the psychological. The first force is that inherent in the ambiguity of words, and especially of those large and peculiarly multivocal catchwords, like "Nature," that have dotted the pages of philosophers, essayists, and poets in all periods. This very multivocality, he says —and illustrates in many pages—is a potent cause of confusion in our thinking and "sometimes facilitates or promotes (though it doubtless seldom or never solely causes) changes—some of them revolutionary changes—in the reigning fashions in ideas."* The second force is again one inherent in the materials: it is the capacity of particular unit-ideas to attract or repel one another, often without the author's being aware of what is going on. The assumption here is that ideas themselves, apart from their particular uses in philosophical or literary discourse, are connected with other ideas by logical relations of "simple congruity or mutual implication or mutual incongruity"† and that this fact often gives rise to latent discords or conflicts among the ideas compounded in a given system or piece of writing. The third force, which influences profoundly but never wholly dominates the operation of the other two, is the force, or rather, more often, the internally conflicting forces, of temperamental predilection. What a writer thinks is determined in considerable part by his frequently "incongruous propensities of feeling or taste," the "underlying affective factors in his personality";‡ and the history of ideas in general, Lovejoy tells us in *The Great Chain of Being*, reflects the working of two fundamental and opposing biases of temperament, which have competed with each other for domination throughout the evolution of Western thought, as "the primary antithesis in philosophical or religious tendencies." These are the two basic moods (reminiscent of William James's division of all men into the "tender-minded" and the "tough-minded")[17] which Lovejoy calls "other-worldliness" and "this-worldliness."§

All the causes in Lovejoy's history can, I think, be reduced to the interplay of these three forces, each with a distinctive efficacy of its own, in the formation and exposition of thought alike by individual writers and by traditions or ages of writers. The result—unless I have missed the point entirely—is an interesting species of historical determinism, in which individual ideas are treated as solid particles, with the same thought content wherever they appear, and in which the different syntheses they enter into are describable in terms of the never wholly harmonious impulses, inherent in human nature, in the ideas themselves, and in the words that express them, by which writers are moved, often in spite of what they consciously intend, in one direction or another or in two directions at once. It is inevitable, on this view, that even great thinkers and literary artists should be frequently at odds with themselves and that fundamental inconsistency, in assumptions and doctrines, should be the rule rather

* *Essays in the History of Ideas* (Baltimore, 1948). pp. xiv–xv. [Crane's note.]
† *Ibid.*, pp. xv–xvii. [Crane's note.]
‡ *Ibid.*, pp. xvi, 254. [Crane's note.]
[17] In *Varieties of Religious Experience* (1902).
§ *The Great Chain of Being*, pp. 24 ff. [Crane's note.]

than the exception. To see how this follows from the method, you have only to read Lovejoy's discussions of Plato, Aristotle, Aquinas, Spinoza, Milton, Pope, Rousseau, Herder, Schiller, Coleridge.

The Great Chain of Being is one of the distinguished books of our time, and it can be read in several ways: as a scholarly history, marked by fresh and impressive erudition; as a moving ironic epic of human failure in a foredoomed quest that has yet had, incidentally, some happy outcomes; finally—and this is the aspect I now want to stress—as a piece of sustained dialectic in historical guise, in which the Democritean tradition in philosophic method is given a modern and evolutionary turn.

I emphasize this last aspect because it seems to me to have a direct bearing on our central question of the nature of ideas not only in the history of ideas but in philosophy and literature. I shall leave ideas in philosophy, for the most part, to better hands, but it is necessary to say one or two things, and, in the first place, to point out the inadequacy of Lovejoy's concept of "unit-ideas," taken as irreducible elements of philosophic "compounds," for the understanding even of that concept itself. If I have at all succeeded in making clear the meaning and value of the notion of "unit-ideas" in Lovejoy, it is because I have gone beyond the notion as such and inquired into the place it has, the uses it serves, and the method by which it is defined in the over-all dialectic concerning ideas and their history that informs and organizes his discussion. Looked at apart from such considerations, it is merely a piece of ambiguous language that might be used in a different dialectic to signify a concept quite distinct from Lovejoy's. Its actual content and significance as a particular concept in his writings, in short, is relative to what he does with it in the construction of his argument as a whole.

And what is true of this idea of Lovejoy's is true of all the so-called "individual" concepts, distinctions, analogies, doctrines, etc., we meet with in philosophic works. They become meaningful, as ideas of the philosopher in question, only when we view them as parts of a dialectical whole that determines their peculiar contents and functions and is itself determined by the special problem the philosopher has set himself to solve, as *he* conceives it, and by his distinctive assumptions and principles of method. To talk about them in separation from the particular activity of reasoning by which they are ordered and defined in philosophic discourse is to talk about them merely as floating commonplaces or themes, as indeterminate in meaning as the hundred or so "great ideas" that Mortimer Adler[18] has assembled, with illustrative quotations from poets and rhetoricians as well as philosophers, in his *Syntopicon*. Here, then, are necessities of a much more immediately compelling sort than the very general and, so to speak, collective necessities that alone are recognized in Lovejoy's theory; and it is these—the necessities of the particular argument as a whole—that give individual life and being to the commonplaces of human thought or of the age and that, when the argument is of one of the kinds we agree to call philosophical, confer the character of philosophical, rather than of,

[18] Mortimer J[erome] Adler (1902–   ), editor, with Robert Hutchins, then president of The University of Chicago, of the "Great Books of the Western World" (1952). The *Syntopicon* is an index of these books, in relation to 102 great ideas and 3000 subordinate ones.

say, rhetorical or literary, ideas upon the various concepts and distinctions it brings into play.

The nature of literary ideas, or of ideas in literature, has to be approached in similar terms. Trilling is surely right in taking exception to Lovejoy's assertion that "the ideas in serious reflective literature are, of course, in great part philosophical ideas in dilution."* From one point of view and up to a certain stage of analysis, indeed, the assertion makes sense. If you concentrate on those literary productions in which the thought has an evident genetic relationship to the thought expressed in earlier works by competent philosophers, and take the kind of integration and elaboration of ideas to be found in the latter as your standard, you will almost invariably observe a falling-off in rigor of statement and connection and be tempted to view the ratio of literature to philosophy, in this aspect, as equivalent to the ratio of the "easy philosophy" to the "abstruse philosophy" described by David Hume. In all such cases the metaphor of "dilution" is forced upon you: for example, by what has happened to the dialectic of the *Phaedrus*[19] in the many lyrics that turn on the theme of earthly and spiritual love, or to the Aristotelian analysis of the virtues in the second book of *The Faerie Queene*, or to the psychology of Hartley[20] in the early poems of Wordsworth. What you generally find in the poets and other literary artists who have drawn upon philosophers for ideas—when you judge them by criteria of philosophic construction—is a kind of borrowing that leaves behind the distinctive wholes philosophers have created and, in doing so, inevitably reduces the component parts of these which it seizes upon to a lower level of *philosophic* interest and value.

But not necessarily—and this is where Trilling is right—of *literary* interest and value. Would the *Divine Comedy* be better or worse, as a poem with philosophic implications, if it had more of the philosophic completeness and sophistication of the *Summa theologica*?[21] Or is the obvious "dilution" of the "philosophical ideas" of King and Bolingbroke[22] in the first epistle of the *Essay on Man* a merit or defect when the *Essay* is considered, as I think it must be considered if full justice is to be done to it, as a work of literary art? Or is the relative simplicity of the moral ideas that underlie *Tom Jones*, when these are viewed, abstractly, in comparison with the arguments on similar themes in (say) Hume's *Enquiry concerning the Principles of Morals,* to be counted an advantage or a disadvantage in Fielding's making of that masterpiece of comic fiction? The very fact that we can sensibly ask such questions, and not always

* *Ibid.*, pp. 16–17; cf. Trilling [*The Liberal Imagination*], p. 190. [Crane's note].

[19] The dialogue by Plato is meant.

[20] David Hartley (1705–1757), English physician and philosopher, founder of associational psychology.

[21] The *Summa theologica* (1267–1273), a systematic exposition of theology based on Aristotle's philosophy, and the most important work of St. Thomas Aquinas (1225–1274). It provided much of the conceptual structure of Dante's *Divine Comedy*.

[22] William King (1650–1729), Archbishop of Dublin, author of *De Origine Mali* ("The Origin of Evil"; 1702). Henry St. John, Viscount of Bolingbroke (1678–1751), Secretary of State during the Tory ministry of 1710–1714, was "deep in metaphysics" with Alexander Pope while the latter was writing *Essay on Man* (1732–1734). Pope and Bolingbroke were probably reading a new translation (1730) of King's book. The *Essay on Man* is dedicated to Bolingbroke.

answer them to the discredit of the poets or novelists, suggests that the problem of the uses and judgment of ideas in literature is, in some significant respects at least, quite different from the problem of the uses and judgment of ideas, even the same ideas, in philosophy. It could hardly, indeed, be otherwise. For though both philosophers and literary artists are engaged in constructing wholes, the principles that determine wholeness, completeness, integrity[23] in philosophy and in literature are not the same—at any rate in those instances of philosophic and literary construction that we normally regard as most typical of the two fields; and it follows that the conceptual parts in each kind of whole, however similar these may appear to be when taken as "individual ideas," will have, as parts, a different nature and significance, depending on the uses to which they are put and the relationships into which they are made to enter.

In order to talk about ideas in literature as "literary," therefore, we must consider them in the light of the literary syntheses they help to make possible and of their various functions relative to these. And here we are confronted with the fact that the principles of literary synthesis, even within what we are wont to call "poetic" literature, have been of a good many different kinds and that the line between some of these and the distinctive forms of philosophy is often hard to draw. What is the difference, if any, between the character and functioning of the ideas in Lucretius' poem[24] and the character and functioning of the ideas, of a generally similar philosophic order, in the treatises of Gassendi and Boyle?[25] I suppose the best answer is that, whereas the shaping of the particular thoughts is determined immediately, in both the poem and the treatises, by the exigencies of a controlling and explicitly stated line of argument, with respect to which they are logical parts, the ideas in the *De rerum natura* are also conditioned by a further set of necessities, deriving from the poet's choice of verse as his medium and, more especially, from his intention of using his argument to inculcate certain emotional states, such as freedom from superstitious fear, in his audience. It is thus a composite work, both philosophical and literary, and whether we emphasize the one or the other aspect as more essential will depend upon our scholarly preoccupations.

There are many other works of discursive or "philosophical" poetry, in all languages, for which the line separating literature from philosophy is much easier to draw. Consider, for instance, Pope's *Essay on Man* and Thomson's *Seasons*.[26] In both poems a dialectical structure of sorts can be discerned, but this is only part of the subsuming form that determines, in each, the selection, expression, and concatenation of particular ideas and arguments, and hence their meanings and values. The ideas and arguments are not in any important sense parts of a demonstration but simply materials and devices, modified by the

[23] For the source of these terms see p. 323 f. of this volume.
[24] *On the Nature of Things,* by Titus Lucretius Carus (c. 99–55 B.C.), a long poem setting forth the ideas of Democritus and Epicurus.
[25] Pierre Gassendi (1592–1655), French philosopher and scientist, wrote treatises in 1647 and 1649 in exposition of the ideas of Democritus and Epicurus. Robert Boyle (1627–1691), Anglo-Irish natural philosopher and chemist, after whom Boyle's Law is named, author of numerous treatises in exposition of "Corpuscular Philosophy," that is, the atomic theories of Democritus and Epicurus. His best-known work is *The Skeptical Chymist* (1661).
[26] James Thomson (1700–1748), Scottish poet. *The Seasons* is a poem in blank verse, in four books, one for each season (1726–1730).

stylistic principles of the two authors, for achieving the predominantly rhetorical ends of the two poems: in the *Essay*, that of inducing men, as Pope said, to "look upon this life with comfort and pleasure" and of putting morality "in good humour"; in the *Seasons*, that of evoking sentiments of benevolence and deistic piety in a world which, for all its shortcomings, is yet governed by an Almighty Hand.

But let us leave discursive poetry, philosophical or rhetorical, for that large and much more central class of literary forms that is exemplified—to recur to my original instances—by *Othello, Tom Jones,* and the "Ode to a Nightingale." These may be called "representational" forms, in the sense that in them the principle of continuity—what we are invited to attend to successively and to respond to—is not the stages of an explicit argument but the moments of an imagined human activity, external or internal, long or short. They are of two main varieties, according as the depicted action is used as a means of developing, indirectly, a thesis of some sort, as in Ibsen's *Doll's House*[27] and George Orwell's *1984*,[28] or is invented and embodied in words for the sake of its intrinsic human and emotional interest, as is the case, I think, in my three examples. In what follows I shall have in mind chiefly forms of the second kind, in dramas, novels, and lyric poems.

What is the role of ideas—and especially of ideas that are either borrowed from, or have some analogy to, ideas in philosophy—in literary works of this type, and how are they to be judged? The answer to the first question must be as complex as are the literary structures themselves that are here in question. They are structures built out of language, and especially of language in which metaphors and analogies play an important part; and we all know how often the bases of particular metaphors or analogies involve general or even technical ideas, and this not merely in the metaphysical poets. They are structures, secondly, in which the dramatis personae are frequently made to state universal propositions or to develop generalized arguments in order that their estimates of the situation, their motives in the action, their plans and deliberations may be clear. They are structures, thirdly, that very often depend on the depiction of character and disposition as an essential source of their emotional power; and here the function of ideas and arguments is to serve as external signs or manifestations of inner moral habits and states of mind, as, for example, in Hamlet's great speeches on the nature of man. Many of them, fourthly, are structures in which the organizing activity is itself primarily an activity of thought—that is to say, of men thinking, or debating with one another, on issues of universal import as well as of personal concern, as in some of Ibsen's plays or in the innumerable lyrics in the tradition exemplified by Milton's "Lycidas," Gray's "Elegy," Wordsworth's "Intimations" ode, Arnold's "The Scholar Gypsy," Dylan Thomas' "Altarwise by owl-light" sonnets, and so on. And, finally, there is the problem in all such structures of helping the reader or spectator to interpret, and so to feel, properly, what is taking place; and here again we see an important role for ideas, whether they are given the form of discursive commentary by chorus or choral character or narrator or messenger or are signified

---

[27] *The Doll's House* by Henrik Ibsen (1828–1906) was first produced in 1879.
[28] George Orwell is the pen-name of Eric Blair (1903–1950), whose *1984* appeared in 1949.

indirectly through complex metaphors or symbols, parallel lines of action, or sequences of implicative imagery.

In all these cases the ideas we become aware of, more or less insistently, in literary works of this kind, may be regarded as functional parts or devices serving various uses, of an artistic rather than a philosophical order, in the working out of the form. But there is also something else, and it is equally important. We often speak of the "vision of life," the "world view," the "philosophy" of particular dramatists, novelists, or lyric poets, and in doing so what we usually have in mind is some scheme of general propositions that are implied by, rather than directly asserted in, their individual works. They are what the writer has assumed, in the way of more or less coherent basic presuppositions, in his acts of artistic creation. There are no representational works that do not rest upon universally intelligible postulates of some kind concerning both the moral, social, political, or religious values involved in their actions and the laws of probability that operate at least within the artist's imagined world. Without them, indeed, no convincing or emotionally unified representational forms would be possible. We may say, in fact, that they are to these forms as the primary and often buried principles of a philosopher are to the particular arguments he constructs; and it is sometimes possible to trace in them the reflection of some characteristic philosophical or theological system—Stoic,[29] Pascalian,[30] Positivist,[31] Kierkegaardian,[32] Existentialist, or the like. Whether philosophic in this sense or not, they are the elements in literary works that justify us most completely in using philosophic language to talk about and discriminate what writers have thought or believed; witness such excellent recent studies as George Orwell's essays on Dickens and boys' magazines,* John Holloway's chapters on George Eliot and Thomas Hardy in *The Victorian Sage*,† Elder Olson's analysis of the moral universe of Dylan Thomas' poems,‡ and Eliseo Vivas' pages on Céline's *Journey to the End of the Night* in his paper on "Literature and Knowledge."§ This underlying and philosophically meaningful universality of literary works—though at a still broader level of significance—is also, I think, what those modern critics who have talked so much about myths and psychological "archetypes," often somewhat confusedly, have really been getting at.

Ideas, then, are involved in literary works of the kind we are now considering in two principal ways: as moral and intellectual bases of their forms and as parts or devices necessitated or made appropriate by their forms. And the criteria for judging the significance and value of ideas in literature will naturally

[29] Stoicism is a school of philosophy founded by Zeno of Citium about the beginning of the third century B.C.

[30] From Blaise Pascal (1623–1662), French scientist and religious philosopher.

[31] A philosophical position implicit in David Hume, but usually thought of as deriving from Auguste Comte, who coined the name; it denies validity to metaphysics and takes the position that philosophy must describe rather than explain.

[32] From Soren Kierkegaard (1813–1855), Danish philosopher.

* *Dickens, Dali & Others: Studies in Popular Culture* (New York, 1946), pp. 1–75, 76–114. [Crane's note.]

† (London, 1953), chaps. v, viii. [Crane's note.]

‡ *The Poetry of Dylan Thomas* (Chicago, 1954), pp. 1–18. [Crane's note.]

§ *Sewanee Review,* 60 (1952): 574–80. [Crane's note.]

differ according as we attend primarily to the first or the second of these two functions. Both entail a use of ideas for artistic rather than philosophical purposes; but the systems of moral, physical, and psychological ideas implied by literary works appear to lend themselves more easily than do the thoughts and reasonings such works explicitly contain to modes of interpretation and judgment that are at least analogous to those we use in speaking of philosophic arguments. The difference between a tragedy or an artistically serious comedy or novel or lyric poem and a merely sensational, melodramatic, sentimental, or fanciful work is more than a difference in form and technique. It is a difference we cannot very well state without bringing in distinctions between true, comprehensive, or at least mature conceptions of things and false, partial, arbitrary, or simple-minded conceptions; and it is in terms of precisely such distinctions, of course, that we tend to differentiate among metaphysical, ethical, political, and esthetic constructions in philosophy, distinct as these are from literary constructions in method and intent.

The peculiarly literary value of literary works, however, is a function not of their presuppositions or of their materials of ideas and images as such but of these as formed into fully realized and beautiful individual wholes. We can indeed say of such wholes, with Trilling, that they give us a kind of pleasure that is hard to distinguish psychologically from the pleasure of "cogency" we experience in reading successfully a philosophic argument;[*] in both cases our delight is dependent on our perception of certain things following, necessarily or probably, from certain things laid down. I shall not pursue this point; but it is essential to remark that the cogency achieved in an excellent literary work is not, as in philosophy, a matter of adequate proof but rather of the sustained efficiency of what is done in the component parts of a novel, drama, or poem relative to the special quality of the imagined human activity that is being represented. Whatever ideas or arguments are good for this—whether as parts of the activity itself, or as signs of character or thought and emotion, or as choral commentary, or as congruous embellishment—are good ideas or arguments, regardless of what might be said of them as elements in a philosophic demonstration; and their meanings, as "literary ideas," are bound up with that fact. A merely referential or logical or "philosophical" consideration of them is never sufficient to tell us what they are, and it is likely, besides, to lead to irrelevant judgments of value. For it is clearly not true in literature, as it presumably is in philosophy, that ambiguities and non sequiturs are always bad; they may be, in fact, precisely what the writer requires if he is to achieve his literary ends; and it is not a weakness in "Lycidas," for example, that the final stage of the meditation is connected with the beginning by no intrinsic dialectical necessity but only by the poetic inevitability of such an outcome, in the situation depicted in the poem, for the special kind of man the lyric speaker is conceived to be.

---

[*] *The Liberal Imagination*, pp. 289–91; cf. pp. 295–99. [Crane's note.]

Jacques Barzun

BYRON AND THE
BYRONIC IN HISTORY

Jacques Barzun was born in France in 1907 and came to the United
States when he was twelve. He was educated at Columbia University,
both as an undergraduate and as a graduate student, and has taught
history at the university since 1929, his special field being the cultural
history of modern Europe. For some years he served as the Dean of
Columbia's Graduate Faculties and also as Provost of the University and
Dean of Faculties. He has written widely on many aspects of the intellectual and cultural life. His books include *Darwin, Marx, Wagner:
Critique of a Heritage* (1941), *Romanticism and the Modern Ego*
(1943), which was revised and expanded as *Classic, Romantic, and
Modern* (1961), *Teacher in America* (1943), a study of American
higher education, *The House of Intellect* (1959), *Science: The Glorious
Entertainment* (1964), and *The American University* (1968). His
Berlioz and the Romantic Century (2 vols., 1950; reissued 1969) is the
definitive life of the composer and one of the notable biographies of our
time. "Byron and the Byronic in History" was first published as an
introduction to a selection of Byron's letters and is included in Mr.
Barzun's collection of essays, *The Energies of Art* (1956).

The great men of the past whose names have given an adjective to the lan-
gauge are by that very fact most vulnerable to the reductive treatment. Everybody knows what Machiavellian means, and Rabelaisian; everybody uses the
terms "Platonic" and "Byronic" and relies on them to express certain commonplace notions in frequent use. Unfortunately, this common application of proper
names stamps but a detached fragment of the truth, and sometimes less than a
fragment—a mere shadow of it. With regard to "Byronic," the reduction is truly
ad absurdum, for the adjective points to the man exclusively and to a single
one of his moods only. In fact, one of the poet's fictional types has engrossed
his name. But Byron's thought, work, and character as a whole cannot be adequately summed up in the popular figure of the headlong lover in an open
collar, whose fits of melancholy are a pose. A review of Byron's life might, it is
true, enlarge the definition of Byronism, were not biography too often inspired
by relish for scandal. Tradition thus perpetuates error, until the poet's words

themselves are read in a moralizing frame of mind not far removed from that of the "Sweet Singer of Michigan":[1]

> The character of Lord Byron
>   Was of a low degree,
> Caused by his reckless conduct
>   And bad company.
> He sprung from an ancient home,
>   Noble but poor indeed,
> His career on earth was marred
>   By his own misdeeds.

This was written half a century after Byron's death. In a later generation, a thinker as independent as John Jay Chapman[2] had to confess that he "closed the door for years on Byron with the single phrase 'Byron was a blackguard.' " And still today, in the middle of the twentieth century, the public mind mirrors itself in a British film entitled *The Bad Lord Byron*, which manhandles history and challenges the spectator to decide: How bad was he?

One thing should be clear: Byron was either bad and truthful or affected and not bad; he could not be both. In any event, he should not be condemned on the record of fictional heroes whose great popularity implied in every reader a secret wish to re-enact their crimes. To put it more generally, Byron and the Byronic are two distinct things, though in part overlapping. The Byronic is found in Byron's early works and in those of his large literary progeny. Byron himself is to be found in the usual first-hand sources of biography, and especially in his letters. For unlike the popular narratives—whether novel or biography— the letters enable us to feel directly the "fascination" the books speak of, the power that Byron exerted over his contemporaries, men as well as women. We then understand and can even explain the attraction Byron has always had for posterity, including the circulating-library readers of *Glorious Apollo* and *Her Demon Lover*.[3]

The corrective effect of Byron's letters comes not only from their abundant and various merits but also from their power to carry, as few letters do, the current of the writer's energy; they bring us within his magnetic field of force, which was not, as the Byronic stereotype might suggest, mere agitation and recklessness. It was concentrated mind and high spirits, wit, daylight good sense, and a passion for truth—a unique discharge of intellectual vitality. When with the aid of the letters one has discovered the genius behind the matinée idol, one can gauge the enormous loss incurred in forming any judgment of Byron on the basis of tradition, even the academic tradition which professes, for the sake of our education, to decant the muddied stream of history.

Even the Byronic in its narrowest meaning begins to look different when it is removed from the neighborhood of other clichés and replaced in its his-

---

[1] Julia A. Moore (1847–1920), about whom Max Herzberg has said, "She had an unfailing instinct for the banal phrase and the irrelevant detail."

[2] John Jay Chapman (1862–1933), American critic, essayist, poet, playwright.

[3] *Glorious Apollo* by Mrs. L. Adams Beck (pseudonym of E. Barrington; London, 1926). Perhaps Barzun means "The Demon Lover," title story of a collection by Elizabeth Bowen (London, 1946).

torical setting. As everybody knows, after bringing out in early youth two volumes of imitative verse, Byron spent a couple of years touring the Mediterranean and the Levant, returned with the first cantos of *Childe Harold*, published them, and "awoke to find himself famous." The date was 1812. During the next four years, that is to say before his twenty-eighth year, when he left England forever, he poured forth half a dozen more verse narratives of kindred strain, and thereby established throughout Europe and the Americas a reputation that has varied in strength but never died.

On this showing alone, which leaves his mature work out of account, Byron would hold his place in history. Read or unread, he still would mark a moment in the consciousness of Western man—a moment to which it would be impossible to refuse the name of "Byronic." We may like to think of that epoch as done with, its mood irrecoverable; and yet in certain ways we are today well equipped to understand it. By 1812 England and the Continent had been deadlocked in warfare, both "hot" and "cold," for three decades. The French Revolution seemed as ever-present a threat to the countries surrounding its birthplace as the Russian Revolution does to the West, for then as now revolution united fanatic faith to imperialism: in the very year of *Childe Harold* Napoleon would invade Russia in hopes of mastering all Europe: it was the fifth time the French had assaulted their neighbors in twenty years. Every country, moreover, had to cope with those of its subjects who secretly or openly sided with the enemy, convinced as many were by the revolutionary program of popular liberties. From his school-days at Harrow, Byron himself had been a liberal and a Bonapartist, and he was not the first among Englishmen: for thirty years the embittering struggle of democrat and reactionary had infected every branch of literature and public life.

Into the superheated atmosphere of factional strife, *Childe Harold* came like a breeze from the open sea. The poem, as the preface told the reader, had been written "amidst the scenes which it attempts to describe," and these scenes began with departure from the beleaguered British Isles. The reader was taken through Gibraltar to the Near East and shown its picturesque ambiguity, now classic Greek, now oriental Turk. Forgetting claustrophobia, the Western imagination could slacken its tension and enlarge its sympathies without breach of patriotism or principle, could recuperate on novelty that was both safe and real.

Only a young poet who was his own hero and pilgrim could have supplied this relief from war news and politics, for the needed salve required fresh feelings and new scenery; and the verse, while recalling familiar objects of reverence, must purge (without naming it) the long guilt and anxiety of hate. For this reason the prevailing tone must be that of melancholy self-accusation and erotic self-pity:

> Worse than Adversity the Childe befell;
> He felt the fulness of Satiety:
> Then loathed he in his native land to dwell,
> Which seemed to him more lone than Eremite's sad cell.

> For he through Sin's long labyrinth had run,
> Nor made atonement when he did amiss,
> Had sighed to many though he loved but one,
> And that loved one, alas! could ne'er be his.

Once he had exorcised these blue devils by writing of them, Byron could truthfully say: "I would not be such a fellow as I have made my hero for all the world." But in the longing for freedom there was a second element which still wanted outlet, the impulse to action. Byronic melancholy, which is to say almost all nineteenth-century melancholy, had its roots in energy repressed. Ennui, as bored young men have always discovered, is the product of enforced inaction or curbed desire. Byronic heroism is its antidote or vicarious fulfillment. In the Eastern tales that follow *Childe Harold* (for the author had naturally become specialized on the Orient), the hero is no longer a pensive but an active wanderer, a Corsair or chieftain, still crime-laden, but redeemed by some daring act of revenge that condemns the corrupt society he has abjured—in a word, the Byronic hero in action is a noble outlaw.

By the beginning of our century, when Shaw satirized it in the brigand of *Man and Superman*,[4] this figure had become stagy and ridiculous through repetition, but what it first symbolized is valid enough to survive its successive embodiments in diverse costumes. Long before Byron's Corsair with his turban and cutlass, the same popular hero-worship and the same connotations of social justice inspired the tales of Robin Hood. After the Corsair (who, incidentally, was actual, not fanciful, in nineteenth-century waters), we have the historic Garibaldi[5] and the legend of his invincible thousand; and still later, in spite of Shaw's ineffectual bandit, we have in modern dress the Existentialist hero of novels about the *maquis*.[6] As long as situations occur, public or private, in which deliberately antisocial behavior proves worthier of regard than abiding by the law, so long will the bold brigand aspect of Byronism find expression and justification in art.

Had fact and reason not supported the Byronic idea, it would be impossible to understand its lasting influence on the strongest, ablest minds of Byron's time. From Goethe, Pushkin, Stendhal, Heine, Balzac, Scott, Carlyle, Mazzini, Leopardi, Berlioz, George Sand, and Delacroix down to Flaubert, Tennyson, Ruskin, George Eliot, the Brontës, Baudelaire, Becque, Nietzsche, Wilde, and Strindberg, one can scarcely name a writer who did not come under the spell of Byronism and turn it to some use in his own life or work. Goethe may be said to have been obsessed by the power of Byronism to the end. Balzac, whether in exalting his will-full young men or in fashioning his Vautrin,[7] the hero-criminal whose deeds form a critique of bourgeois society, owes and acknowledges a debt to Byron. Delacroix,[8] soon after learning the truth of bright color in Morocco, paints with sympathetic fury the fight between the Giaour and the Pasha. About the same time, the young Berlioz and the young Victor Hugo[9] alike give vent to their impatient energy in brigand songs that transcend the

[4] *Man and Superman*, by George Bernard Shaw (1856–1950), was first published in 1903.

[5] Giuseppe Garibaldi (1807–1882), Italian patriot, soldier, and popular hero.

[6] French partisan or guerrilla forces during the German occupation of World War II.

[7] A master criminal who figures in a number of the novels that make up the *Comédie humaine* written by Honoré de Balzac (1799–1850).

[8] Ferdinand Victor Eugène Delacroix (1798–1863), French painter.

[9] Louis Hector Berlioz (1803–1869), French composer. Victor Marie, Vicomte de Hugo (1802–1885), French poet, dramatist, and novelist.

picturesque. And Stendhal invents the career of Julien Sorel[10] to show that a man who dies on the scaffold may represent genius and will power succumbing to mediocrity. In all these fictions, as in Byron's own, one readily discerns the shadow of Napoleon and the revolutionary ideal of genius paramount. Byron was simply the first, or the most successful among the first, to dramatize the attitude of the new man, the mysterious unknown who has experienced Faustian longings but who, not finding a constructive social task, risks life for the glory of avenging mankind upon society.

Encouraged by success, Byron went on to analyze within himself the sensations of this representative temperament, but the traits he singled out were not inventions of his own; they were part of the human nature of his time, which was being reflected here and there in unexpected places. Rousseau[11] had already pointed out that men who would accomplish great things in a stubborn world must possess "souls of fire," and it was to Rousseau that one such man, the nerve-ridden but irrepressible Boswell,[12] described himself Byronically, years before Byron: "I with my melancholy, I who often look on myself as a despicable being, as a good-for-nothing creature who should make his escape from life. . . ."

A little later, and by means of other traits, the professed dandies whose vogue preceded Byron's foreshadowed his poetic heroes in real life. After the unforgettable advent of Childe Harold, the type dominates literature and develops there independently of his creator. Even in the quiet work of Jane Austen one can see that the hero of *Pride and Prejudice,* Mr. Darcy, owes something of his charm to superior rudeness wrapped in mystery, and like a Byronic figure he holds equally in contempt common womanhood and the opinion of society. Darcyism turns sinister in Charlotte Brontë's Rochester and demonic in the hero of her sister's *Wuthering Heights.*[13] The combination of all these traits recurs, deliberate, pathetically foiled and misplaced on the urban scene, in Baudelaire. For Continental literature had been thoroughly Byronized, and it is not surprising that Baudelaire's distant contemporary, the Empress Eugénie,[14] should cite as her three favorite poets: Calderón,[15] Shakespeare, and Byron.

The feminine attachment to the Byronic in life and art may be significant, but the lure is not limited to women or to fictional beings; it points to a common emotion, that of nineteenth-century man who, as soon as freed by enlightenment and revolution, found himself locked in a life-and-death struggle with the democratic nation-state and industrial society. The more than individual importance of this struggle is borne out by the fact that with the progress of the

[10] Julien Sorel is the hero of *The Red and the Black,* by Stendhal.
[11] Jean Jacques Rousseau (1712–1778), French philosopher, author, political theorist, and composer; he is sometimes thought of as the father of romanticism, sometimes as the inspiring genius of the French Revolution.
[12] James Boswell (1740–1795), English author, best known for his biography of Samuel Johnson.
[13] Rochester is the leading male character in *Jane Eyre* (1847) by Charlotte Brontë (1816–1855). The demonic hero of *Wuthering Heights* (1847), by Emily Brontë (1818–1848), is Heathcliff.
[14] Born Eugenia Maria de Montigo de Guzman (1826–1920), Empress of France (1853–1870), consort of Napoleon III.
[15] Pedro Calderón de la Barca (1600–1681), Spanish dramatist.

century the figure of the mysterious evil-doer who is also the vindicator of justice
draws to itself every important acquisition of psychology and social thought.
Post-Byronic despair-plus-rebellion takes us so far that—as the later Dickens bears
witness—it threatens altogether the ordinary notions of identity and morality.
One thinks of the ambiguous Harmon-Handford-Rokesmith[16] in *Our Mutual
Friend* or the unresolved who's who of *Edwin Drood*.[17] Dostoevsky's Raskolnikov[18] owes his very name (the rebel) to the spirit of revolt that underlies the
Byronic, though his compulsive ethical need for crime would doubtless have
revolted Byron. In Nietzsche, the hero gains a foothold *beyond* good and evil,
but he has not wholly lost the Byronic traits of lofty brooding and lonewolf
pugnacity. And meantime "the herd" has multiplied, so that to be alone
Zarathustra[19] requires a mountaintop, like Byron's Manfred.

To trace this circuit is but to say that the nineteenth century's passion for
liberty called into being many models of the free spirit. The Byronic model,
early and crude as it was, owed its long career to a persistent need in the hearts
of men and the structure of society. It ceased to have meaning only when the
triumph of political democracy made group action possible and necessary, thereby dwarfing the value of individual acts and rendering "the hero" ridiculous. One
might say, harking back to Shaw, that the Byronic hero comes to an end when
he joins the Fabian Society.[20] The dedicated man of today, though no longer
endowed with heroic qualities, has nonetheless retained some of the signs of
apartness and superiority. He is not an outlaw but he is an artist. His guilty
brooding (now called neurosis) and his outlaw feeling (called alienation)
are, according to a widely accepted belief, the source of his creative power and
of his claim on our regard. His psychic "wound"[21] makes Byron's look like a
scratch, but (as in Auden's "Letter to My Wound") the modern poet seems just
as much in love with it. In this he is doubtless making the most conspicuous
use of his circumstances, as did the Byronic hero.

In retrospect, then, we can grant that Byronism was a pose, but we must
immediately add that a pose is simply the way men meet the dilemmas of
conscious life. Each epoch has its characteristic or prevalent pose by which we
name it: the Puritan, the Man of Reason, the Spartan revolutionary, the
Democrat, the Decadent—all are named after poses which were affectations
until they became the human nature of the moment or the place.

To observe in passing that the Byronic was a *crude* model of the free spirit
is to point out that the plot, motives, and especially the verse of Byron's oriental
tales lack finish and solidity. *The Giaour, Lara, The Corsair* were hastily
composed. But in saying this one means also that, like *Childe Harold*, these

---

[16] The name and pseudonyms of the hero of *Our Mutual Friend* (1865), by Charles
Dickens (1812–1870).

[17] Dickens never completed *Edwin Drood,* which, as it exists, is a mystery novel
without detection.

[18] Raskolnikov is the protagonist of *Crime and Punishment* (1866) by Dostoevski.

[19] See *Thus Spake Zarathustra* (1883–1891), by Frederich Wilhelm Nietzsche
(1844–1900).

[20] Society of English socialist reformers.

[21] See "Letter to a Wound," in *The Collected Poetry of W. H. Auden* (New York,
1945), p. 191.

narratives do not disclose Byron's full mind—merely his sharp eye and quick sensibility. The author was telling the truth about his regard for fact when he wrote to his publisher: "I don't care one lump of sugar for my *poetry*: but for my *costume* and my *correctness* I will combat lustily." He was improvising instead of working, storing up experience, possibly with no particular purpose in view, but at any rate reserving his powers for a later day and a more exacting genre. We know that he had powers to reserve because, once again, we have the letters. When they deal, as many of them do, with high matters, they show even in that early period none of the weaknesses we find in the tales. The firm, rather stiff prose forecasts the master observer of life and of himself who will later write *Don Juan*. The purely Byronic is thus—in spite of its hold upon contemporaries—a mere outline sketch for the fully Byronian.

This early maturing was no doubt due to the circumstance of Byron's deplorable parentage and childhood. Born in the year before the French Revolution, George Gordon Byron was the offspring of a rakehell father and a harassed, tempestuous, and selfish mother. The Byrons were proud of their Norman descent, and the poet on occasion would also lay claim to the tough fiber of his Scottish ancestors on his mother's side. He grew up at any rate in Aberdeen, and was there equipped with a Calvinist sense of sin, no doubt against the day when he would be old enough to do something requiring its exercise. Being both an ill-loved, fatherless child and a poor lordling of uncertain prospects, Byron came early in touch with the most scarifying ills of life: lack of steady affection and shabby gentility. As if this were not enough, he suffered a deformity of the lower leg.* This put him at a disadvantage except perhaps as a rider and swimmer, and made him especially self-conscious in society. Eighteenth-century manners, we must remember, were not gentle to such "disgrace," and crude derisive comments might be openly passed. Entering a room where he was not known was a torture to the crippled youth. Fortunately, he was handsome of face and of good figure, though inclined to stoutness; and in 1798 (the date of his first letter) he inherited from his great-uncle the title and estates of the Byrons. A peerage was protection for tender pride; Newstead Abbey, though a partial ruin, was a home to cling to; and the magnetism of a title would help people his life.

At Harrow and Cambridge, which were his next stopping places, Byron's intellectual education followed the pattern of his time, but he read a good deal more than was required and scribbled much English and Latin verse, without being thought academically brilliant. He made friends, fell in love,

---

* Basing myself on an elaborate review of the evidence by Prothero, Byron's admirable editor, I stated earlier that this deformity was not a clubfoot but a sequela of infantile paralysis. A friendly reader, who is a physician at Stanford University Medical School, wrote to me to say that he had gone back to the medical literature published on the subject and was persuaded that the trouble was a perfectly "classical" clubfoot. Since Prothero had also followed the best medical judgment, since despite drawings in *The Lancet* there seems to be strong doubt as to which leg was affected, since—in short—all conclusions emerge from mixed inferences at second hand from the words of bootmakers, surgeons, and other witnesses now inaccessible, I find in the state of affairs an excellent opportunity to desist from conjecture and to enjoy the luxury of having no opinion whatever. [Barzun's note.]

quarreled with his mother, his solicitor, and his guardian, and wasted time and money in the usual college dissipations. Although his good fortune had not overcome his genuine modesty, he persuaded himself that some of his verses should see the light of day, at least in a private edition. This soon became a public one under the title *Hours of Idleness*—and with a note of apology to say that the author was only nineteen.

The reviewers were for the most part kind, but Lord Brougham in the *Edinburgh Review* seized the chance for elaborate mockery. The sensitive author at once set about revenging himself by satire. He worked for a year at *English Bards and Scotch Reviewers,* a witty excoriation in the style of Pope's *Dunciad,* taking in nearly all the eminent poets and critics then living. This sequence of actions is characteristic. The title *Hours of Idleness* had hinted at the tradition of a noble lord who merely plays at the arts: Byron never for a moment conceded that he might be a professional writer; his concern was rather to infuse genuine nobility into aristocratic pride. Now this same pride impelled him to challenge the entire forces of the British Parnassus.[22] He soon earned his reward—enmity, fear, and a certain degree of admiration. He had moreover found his satirical vein and learned to work it in patience like a good craftsman. As Goethe later said, every stroke told, and Byron was now master of at least one conventional genre. The satirist, to be sure, was to regret many of his harsh judgments, but the main thing was that he had survived the first of his duels with the public. His zest for high deeds had been satisfied and he had lived up to the idea of himself which as a boy he had confided to his mother—that of a man who could not rest under an affront and never calculated the chances of success in following the dictates of honor. Will power must supply the lack of strength, experience, or friends.

This Quixotic strain often goes with genius and sometimes with great physical or sexual power, all of which Byron possessed; but he also had what rarely goes with the Quixotic, a passion for facts, itself accompanied by a singularly cool judgment. If one considers that Byron was barely twenty-one and fresh to any world, English or Mohammedan, when he wrote home the remarkable account of his meeting with Ali Pasha, one can only echo his own surprise: "I have learnt to philosophise in my travels." He had, one must suppose, learned his part of *grand seigneur*[23] quickly and easily because he had somehow known how to make circumstance serve ambition, instead of more prudently adapting his desires to his opportunities.

He wanted above all to be what his title implied, a lord among men. This required the gift of action and made poetry secondary, a by-product of action— hence disposed to be political and autobiographic, though not invariably or literally so. What Byron increasingly asked of life was not subjects for poems but opportunities for doing. This is what makes it a cruel misrepresentation to find in him the source of a mere literary attitude. Nothing was farther from him at any time than pretense to virtues (or sins) that he was not ready to act out. Nor did he ever let the discharge of obligations go by default. When some lines in *English Bards* offended the Irish poet and musician Thomas Moore,

---

[22] Parnassus was the ancient Greek name for the mountain now known as Liakura, then sacred to Apollo and the Muses.
[23] "Great lord."

Byron showed himself eager to give him "satisfaction," though the journey to the Near East intervened. Home again two years later, Byron sought out his opponent and renewed his offers of "service," which happily turned the projected duel into a lifelong friendship. Proud of his blood, he was always willing to spill it—not perhaps the surest test of a proposition's truth, but a fair index of the propounder's commitment. Byron was from the start *engagé*.

Reading, as one does in the letters, of many similar challenges and leaps into action, one might veer to the other extreme from the charge of attitudinizing and conclude that Byron was a real swashbuckler, from vanity or bad temper. All the evidence goes to show that on the contrary his disposition was cheerful, even gay, and that in the daily business of life he was neither touchy nor vain. He was, according to Shelley who knew him well, gentle and unassuming. Byron's promptness in attack was quite simply courage, but courage cultivated by habit. A high-spirited nature that had undergone such trials as Byron's in childhood would be likely to fall into the habit of constantly testing itself and would do so in a series of apparent aggressions against the world. The small boy who wants to make friends does not approach a strange schoolmate affectionately: he kicks him in the shins and sees what happens. It is in fact an accepted knightly tradition that great friendships begin in great fights, and so it happened in Byron's life. But this argues a large fund of affection, not resentment, behind the attack. Having left boyishness behind, he achieved a manliness unusual among authors and even among fighters. Chivalry sits on him naturally—as witness the controversy with Bowles,[24] or the instant suppression of polemical pages about Keats on hearing of his death.

The unity of Byron's life thus comes out of his character. Convinced that deeds were nobler than words, he had in his own black moods a further incentive to brush aside verbal anodynes and *re-act*. With increasing wisdom and age, the objects of his challenges and sorties become more and more significant and disinterested. By 1815, when to Byron's regret Napoleon lost Waterloo, and when the poet was himself on the verge of exile—cast off by his wife, by English society, and by a part of his reading public—he had run through the cycle of his formative experiences. He had seen both sides of life, the smooth and the seamy, twice over; and he had become—as nearly as anyone can be who still lives and feels—proof against surprises. He knew what he might expect and what he must do, which was: counterattack with all his wits about him but with diminishing animus—a lord among men because dispassionate in the face of facts.

Byron's politics similarly embody the results of generalized experience. He hates injustice and tyranny regardless of party. At twenty-four he rises in the House of Lords to make his maiden speech, the first of three in defense of the Nottingham weavers who were rioting against the new machinery:

> I have traversed the seat of war in the Peninsula, I have been in some of the most oppressed provinces of Turkey; but never under the most despotic of infidel governments did I behold such squalid wretchedness

---

[24] In *English Bards and Scotch Reviewers* Byron had called William Lisle Bowles "the maudlin prince of mournful sonneteers." He later got into a controversy with Bowles over the latter's edition of Alexander Pope, but, according to Bowles, Byron "acknowledged how wrong he had been very ingenuously." Letter of April 4, 1813.

as I have seen since my return in the very heart of a Christian country. And what are your remedies? After months of inaction, and months of action worse than inactivity, at length comes forth the grand specific, the never-failing nostrum of all state physicians . . . these convulsions must terminate in death. . . . Setting aside the palpable injustice and the certain inefficiency of the Bill, are there not capital punishments sufficient in your statutes? . . . Will the famished wretch who has braved your bayonets be appalled by your gibbets? When death is a relief, and the only relief it appears that you will afford him, will he be dragooned into tranquillity?

His counterproposal is financial aid to those displaced by machinery and amnesty for the rioters. Again, Byron speaks in favor of removing disabilities against Catholics and Jews. In Italy later, he carries on single-handed a war of invective against British and foreign reactionaries—Wellington, Castlereagh, the two Georges, and the Holy Alliance. The Austrian police who open his letters and trace his connections with liberal groups can scarcely understand why he joins secret societies "whose objects seem foreign to his own purposes." For all the while Byron continues to behave like a ruler of men, not like an agitator. He hates demagogy and has no illusions about underdogs, whether in Nottingham or in Italy. He is an egalitarian in liberty but no farther, at one with Milton in despising overprotection and a cloistered virtue. The hero of Byron's *Cain* is for that very reason dissatisfied with the politics of Paradise. In righting wrongs Byron unites the dedicated spirit of the knight-errant with the practical ability of the Tory Democrat. In his last fight in Greece we find him writing clear-eyed reports of the Greeks' corrupt mismanagement and making the shrewdest use of his own "barrels of dollars," but also treating the Turkish enemy as if the times had been those of Saladin and Richard the Lion-Hearted. In short, Byron must be classed with those few influential men of rank who have taken the aristocratic ideal seriously. In obedience to it they have defied their own class and all other majorities, and braved scandal and obloquy for a cause that they also knew how to blazon forth. Such men give the words "independence" and "example" the fullest meaning they are capable of, and this is so rare that the world can neither quite believe nor ever forget it.

In Byron's life, of course, scandal applied to him on other grounds than politics, and it is usual to say that the final Greek adventure redeems by its noble selflessness the ignoble self-indulgence of earlier years. Byron's reputation is so familiar to those who ignore his poetry and have never read his letters that he can be made to appear as a tragicomic Don Giovanni who reforms in the last act. Chronology itself disallows this interpretation. For what we find between his burst into fame as the creator of *Childe Harold* and his departure for Greece is not a downhill course arrested at the last minute, but four distinct periods, twice alternating between dissipation and concentration. From 1812 until his engagement to Anne Milbanke late in 1814, Byron yielded himself to friendship and fashionable life, easy love affairs and easy riming. This is the time of his Byronizing in verse tales and of his capture of the Continental imagination. The two years of courtship and marriage that followed mark the first return to self-discipline. It produced only lyrics, but they include his finest, chiefly in the collection of *Hebrew Melodies.* Byron becomes a father and seems altogether settled.

Then comes the disastrous break with Lady Byron, grounded on a rumor which alienated all but a handful of his friends. Byron goes into exile, fleeing popular wrath. Fifteen years later, the poet being dead, Macaulay[25] could pour scorn on the British public's fit of moral indignation, but at the time it was a hurricane not to be withstood. On the Continent, and chiefly at Venice, Byron gave himself once again to the pursuit of sensual pleasure. Solace or pastime, a succession of mistresses and casual companions occupied his days and nights; but clearly not his heart and mind, since even at this time his words and deeds show no relaxation of his grip on personal, political, or artistic reality. He took up *Childe Harold* and added two more cantos greatly superior to the first, began writing verse plays, studied Italian (Dante in particular), read copiously in science and history, and wrote incessantly both verse and prose.

Within less than two years, he has emerged still stronger and wiser, the ultimate Byron of history. His new liaison, with the Countess Teresa Guiccioli, coincides with a new period of domestic regularity, abundant and marvelous poetic output, increasing political commitments, and serious, indeed philosophical, friendships—notably with Leigh Hunt, Shelley, Trelawny, Medwin, and his future companion in the Greek war, Teresa's brother Pietro.

Any mention of the final adventure ending in death usually has the effect of checking somewhat the public's enjoyable disapproval of Byron's relations with women, but this is not enough. The going off to war throws no light on the one interesting aspect of Byron's amorousness, which is its place not in his biography but in his soul. The sheer extent of his lustful devastation has of course been exaggerated, so that the French, who like sobriety in these matters, have been put to the trouble of producing a work of scholarship entitled: *Les Maîtresses* AUTHENTIQUES *de Lord Byron.*[26] The fact is plain that other great figures have led far more disordered lives and received far less censure. One reason for this is that Byron's career came at a time of stiffening moral standards and increasing hypocrisy. What we call Victorian morality antedates Victoria's accession by at least two decades, and although Byron's social circle did not in fact obey the rigid middle-class code of sexual behavior, they paid it the respect of concealment. His impatience with every kind of fraud made him on the contrary ostentatious, communicative, defiant; thereby implying what other men before and since Dante have seriously believed, that incontinence is not among the gravest sins. When he looked upon the new moralism from afar, Byron told the British quite justly:

> The truth is, that in these days the grand *primummobile* of England is *cant;* cant political, cant poetical, cant religious, cant moral; but always cant multiplied through all the varieties of life. . . . I say cant because it is a thing of words, without the smallest influence upon human actions; the English being no wiser, no better, and much poorer, and more divided

[25] Thomas Babington, first Baron Macaulay (1800–1859), English historian, essayist, statesman. His essay on Byron appeared in the *Edinburgh Review,* June 1831.

[26] "The AUTHENTIC Mistresses of Lord Byron."

among themselves, as well as far less moral, than they were before the prevalence of this verbal decorum.

For thus preaching what he practiced Byron again suffered the penalty meted out to minds complex and courageous. The paradox is that during his marriage he remained a faithful husband and meant to be a good father, and that he has been pilloried as a sinner without regard to time and circumstance. To this day he is "the bad Lord Byron" because people prefer him so; or else he is condemned, like Admiral Byng, *pour encourager les autres—*[27] and principally on the ground of his presumed affair with his half-sister Augusta. It is unnecessary to enter the maze of motives, declarations, and events surrounding this alleged cause of Byron's separation from his wife. It is enough to remember that he himself always invited the fullest investigation of the facts and was never given satisfaction by his accusers.

What matters more, because it takes us back into Byron's inner self, is that late in his life, without shuffling for a moment about his past errors, he made it a claim to consideration that he had never been a seducer, and no evidence has ever turned up to contradict him. His statement must be taken together with what he feared might happen during the Greek campaign, namely, that a woman would be thrown at his head to influence his decisions. He says in so many words that he is "easy to govern" ("by a woman" is here understood), and he had every reason in past experience to be apprehensive once again. This fear and this governance unmistakably suggest that his career of love means something more complicated than promiscuous appetite— just the opposite in fact, as Byron doubtless meant to show in the story of his own Don Juan.

He knew that a disorder of the feelings was at the root of most of his troubles. As early as his twenty-third year, he writes to a friend: "The latter part of my life has been a perpetual struggle against affections which embittered the earliest portion." Whether this refers to his mother or to his unhappy first love for Mary Chaworth, an older girl who made fun of him, Byron felt the need to overcome attachment. He "flatters himself that he has conquered," but now and again he has a relapse, characterized by depression of spirits and savage temper. This certainly describes the sort of relation in which he stood to his mother: he could not help loving and hating her and resenting the ambiguity of his feelings. He tried to conquer his affection and fell into gloom, despair, and savagery at the inevitable promptings of guilt. That this unfortunate cycle of ideas repeated itself throughout his life seems established by his frequent disclaimer of the capacity to love.* Though he had many friends he spoke of only one, Lord Clare, as being close to his heart, and Lord Clare was a childhood friend.

And yet Byron was wise enough to feel no shame when the full tide

---

[27] "To serve as an example for others." John Byng (1704–1757), a British admiral, was executed for neglect of duty.

* It is interesting to speculate whether Shaw's Cashel Byron, whose grand cry of liberation, "Two things I hate: my duty and my mother," is here so apposite, owes anything to his historic namesake. Lord Byron, too, was a boxer, though not a professional like Cashel. [Barzun's note. See Shaw's novel, *Cashel Byron's Profession* (1886).]

of a genuine emotion mastered him. He wept on taking leave of England, and Lady Blessington, thinking it tactful, suggested that she, too, often broke down from nervousness. Byron angrily scouted the excuse: "nerves!" But in acknowledging true feeling on another occasion, he cautions the witness: "Don't imagine that because I feel I am to faint." To these crosscurrents of passion and repression another force must be added. As the cripple George Byron became a handsome young nobleman, he was subjected not alone to the temptations of his age and station, but more regrettably to the almost automatic aggression of women. Lady Caroline Lamb was only the wildest of those who captured (rather than captivated) the poet. His letters include a good many replies to the unknown authors of provocative messages, and in the accounts of other love-exchanges the reader notes how an English icicle, such as Lady Frances Webster, proved as active a menace as the Italian volcanoes of his Venetian period. It could make little difference to Byron that his eyes were open and his judgment unclouded, for it is the characterisic of damaged emotions that they are liable to the same hope and hurt endlessly. Every new proffer of love meant to him the possibility of recouping the loss felt in childhood, and when he himself sought love (or brought it), what we call his immoral act was undoubtedly part of an attempt to shut out the memory of rejection and stave off despair.

Perhaps the most striking feature of this not unusual involvement is the attraction Byron felt for Miss Milbanke, about the same time as he found a kind of substitute mother in Lady Melbourne. Annabella Milbanke was to become Lady Byron and Lady Melbourne was her aunt, besides being the mother-in-law of Byron's former love, Caroline Lamb. But the older woman's judgment and affection were not deflected by these relationships, and she gave Byron a taste of the solid and *intelligent* love that he wanted. He addresses her, one notes, in a different voice from any he uses to other correspondents. The woman Byron married should have been like her aunt. Annabella was unfortunately "mathematical" rather than passionate, and he seems to have chosen her chiefly because she stood out from the giddy, flirtatious crowd and did not pursue him. In marriage her tranquillity proved to be more conventional and sanctimonious than consoling and affectionate, and somehow—perhaps because Byron was still in search of elusive love—he goaded her into thinking of him as a godless reprobate. This belief justified to her, first her separation from him, and then his total exclusion from her life. Byron was denied all access to their daughter Ada, as well as direct communication with herself by letter. His self-exile is thus in part the repetition of her act by his will, in part the symbol of his original situation in relation to his mother: baffled love, hate, and resentful guilt. No wonder he fell into the habit of grinding his teeth in his sleep!

It follows from all this that the "cynical" Byron who wrote *Don Juan,* who affected coldness now and again, and judged La Guiccioli as if she had been somebody else's mistress, is not a new man, disillusioned at long last. He is the same man showing his armored side. Nor is he a cynic in the sense of being meanly hardened. He is, if anything, too full of affection to be able to consume or convert it for his own use; he finds his warmth of feeling difficult to share because he thinks it unwanted or sees it undervalued. True, he lavished much of it on Lady Melbourne until her death, and again on Allegra, his little daughter by another Amazon, Jane Clairmont. To his great grief the child died in her sixth year.

His friends, of course, could count on his good will to an uncommon degree, as the elaborate financial rescue of Thomas Moore proves.[28] But the misfortune of such an education of the feelings as Byron had is that it develops the observer at the expense of the enjoyer. Byron mentions with a kind of shudder the "microscopic eye" one is endowed with at the end of a liaison. He might have added that with each accrual of insight the affections become more demanding. In childhood, he would have been content with any reasonable mother, and he could repose trust and affection in his "dearest sister Augusta." But as Augusta turned into a thoughtless and incoherent matron, he found it harder to feel anything for her but lost love's loyalty. Similarly, his friends could command his devotion but they requited it according to their lights and not his, which he could not help regretting, given the pain and trouble this entailed. It is exasperating, in reading Byron's replies, to see Hobhouse, Kinnaird, Murray, and the rest badgering and patronizing the poet, almost purposely disturbing his work and his mind—all this ostensibly in friendship's name, actually out of indulgence toward their own limitations.

Yet it is in those same documents—about a poem, a remittance, or a tin of toothpowder—that Byron's intrinsic greatness, matching his outward heroism, appears most true and winning. Harassed on all sides by worry, grief, lawsuits, ill-fame, literary squabbles, stupid or malicious friends, he keeps his head and his good temper. In the biography of an artist, Judgment is as notable as Genius. With Byron at the last, the two are in equilibrium. Every successive crisis finds him as understanding of others as he is lucid about himself, and his impulse is truly magnanimous. This is what Carlyle—almost alone in England, and despite his dislike of Byronism—understood when he praised the poet for making light of "happiness" and preferring to be, in the honorific sense, "a man."

Seen in this light, the spectacle of Byron's life is the reverse of a tragedy. Tragedy shows original flaws bringing an acknowledged hero to his downfall. In Byron the original flaws belong to a character whom we cannot help acknowledging as great in the last act. The flaws are not in the end obliterated, they are transcended, transcended exactly as the purely Byronic, which was brooding self-pity, is not obliterated but transcended in the satiric poetry and the moral poise of Byron's later life. The serenity of the comic spirit informs the closing scenes. He had written to his friend in that early piece of self-analysis already quoted: "I am not one of your dolorous gentlemen: so now let us laugh again." Twelve years later, within sight of death, he writes to Thomas Moore: "On the 15th (or 16th) of February I had an attack of apoplexy, or epilepsy,— the physicians have not exactly decided which, but the alternative is agreeable. My constitution, therefore, remains between the two opinions, like Mahomet's sarcophagus between the magnets."

The spectacle of such a life can only be called edifying—unless, as often happens, one confuses "edifying" with "blameless" and a great man with a

---

[28] Byron gave Thomas Moore (1779–1852), English poet and biographer, his memoirs, which, according to Shelley (in a letter of August 10, 1821), Moore sold for £2000.

saint. The distinction is in place here, because it is needed for judging Byron's work in prose and verse and extracting from it all the pleasure it holds for us. It is all too likely, for instance, that the reader who comes to the letters with the preconceptions of today concerning art and artists will be as shocked and scornful as the Victorians were, though for different reasons. The modern reader will have learned leniency toward the sinful artist, but he will unconsciously require him to be disabled, crushed by "his society." The critic will also require that the work which came out of the conflict be what he calls "fine," that is, delicate and suggestive rather than strong and explicit. From fellow-feeling our hearts go out to Keats, Baudelaire, and others whose triumph was almost wholly spiritual, whose strength spent itself in communicating to us the worth of their latent powers, and who did this largely by impressing upon us the reality of the obstacles that stood in their way. As a result, we are tempted to resent Byron's boisterous health and positive capability, his sixteen servants, eight horses, barrels of gold, and yachts in the offing. Whatever he did looks too easy, just because he did it. And we take out our resentment on the work: it seems too easy, too, in form and contents. The wisdom of the letters is, after all, but worldly wisdom. When the writer comes close to one of the great problems, such as religion or esthetics, he either declares himself baffled or cuts Gordian knots with blunt strokes instead of setting us thinking by rich allusive ambiguities. And it completes the indictment to add that in whatever he wrote Byron needs virtually no exegesis. His meaning lies on the surface, and we are not disposed to thank him for having worked hard to put it there within easy reach.

The rejoinder at large must be that we have to take poets as history makes them, rather than as we wish them for our comfort. But there is a more particular reason why, even with our strictly contemporary interest, we should assimilate the rough dose that Byron compounded. For what we honor, say in Baudelaire, is the genuine passion in his desire to be a dandy, a world-scorner, a man superior to the unhappy "Belgians" that he so viciously slandered. We cannot suppose that he preferred degradation and obscurity any more than Keats preferred tuberculosis. And however valuable the by-product of these calamities when they take effect on the imagination of genius, no amount of poetry can make them anything but deplorable and disgusting. Since every genius must carry, besides the burdens of life, the burdens of *his* life, he who triumphs over adversity otherwise than by embellishing defeat deserves equal regard for *his* circumstances; he may be equally instructive and possibly even more inspiriting.

These reflections are implied when we describe Byron's last phase as belonging to the comic spirit, and as expressed in the genre that he forged to his own use, the comic epic. *Don Juan* owes its eight-line stanza to the Italian parodists of the heroic romances, but apart from this and a hint from Hookham Frere,[29] it is an original creation. Byron could feel confident of its lasting qualities because it brought into synthesis all that he had ever tried or learned to do: narrative, satire, description, and disquisition. He could pour his worldly experience into characters, dissect the varieties of love, lyricize about nature,

---

[29] John Hookham Frere (1769–1846), English journalist and poet, whose mock-romantic Arthurian poem, written under the pseudonym "Whistlecraft" provided the "hint" for Byron.

preach social and political doctrine, retell sieges and shipwrecks with factual fidelity, attack his enemies, and versify with the gusto of a virtuoso who knows when to be careless. The work is to nineteenth-century Europe what *Tom Jones*[30] is to eighteenth-century England—a mirror like a comedy, a voyage like an epic, and a store of facts like a history—in short, a novel; only, *Don Juan* is a novel in verse. This should have insured its popularity with the readers of Byron's earlier tales. But by comparison with these, "Donny Johnny" (as Byron affectionately called it) was a failure. Whereas *The Corsair* sold thirteen thousand copies in one day, the best of *Don Juan* went at the rate of twelve hundred a month. The public's resistance is hardly accounted for by Byron's "disgrace"; it was due to the intrinsic qualities of the comic poem.

Easy as it looks, *Don Juan* has never been successfully imitated, and not even the shorter flights that preceded it—*Beppo* and *The Vision of Judgment* —have communicated the secret of their making to later comers. This should suffice to establish Byron as a "great" poet, the great being defined in any art as those who have produced intelligible works of a certain magnitude which no one else could make even if they would. Yet in spite of our century's leaning toward the colloquial, there persists a doubt whether Byron is a great poet after all. He is held wanting, once again, in fineness, also in depth and in technique— which is what Matthew Arnold[31] complained of a long while ago. Arnold was going about with his "touchstones" and hunting for verbal magic. Sir Herbert Read,[32] a modern critic not to be lightly disregarded, compares Byron's lines:

> She walks in beauty, like the night
> Of cloudless climes and starry skies

with Donne's:

> No Spring, nor Summer Beauty hath such grace
> As I have seen in one Autumnal face

and concludes that Byron's mind was not fundamentally poetic because he was incapable of using a reverberating epithet like "autumnal."

The danger of such a conclusion is that it reduces the species "poetry" to one of its subvarieties, the magical or evocative; and again that it perverts criticism into an illicit kind of sampling for plums. Arnold has done incalculable harm by encouraging with his authority the connoisseur's pose of valuing a work for its scattered "moments"; one is reminded of those "lovers of opera" who come for one aria. The result is to force every poet or musician into the role of lyricist and to judge him by the frequency with which he satisfies a desire that is not his. Byron unquestionably cannot be read through the slots of such a stencil. Had "autumnal face" come to his pen he would doubtless have struck it out and found a "straight" adjective. For it was his intention to be simple and *rapid* without banality. The perfection of "cloudless climes" and "starry skies" is precisely that they are obvious and clear and yet rejuvenated

---

[30] The novel of 1749 by Henry Fielding (1707–1754).

[31] Arnold's essay first appeared as an introduction to a selection of Byron's poems in 1881; it was re-published in *Essays in Criticism, Second Series* (1888).

[32] Herbert Read makes this comparison in *Byron,* a pamphlet in the *Writers and Their Work* series, published in London in 1951.

by the context. The "poetry" lies in the conception, which from "walks in beauty" to "starry skies" is a picturable image. To a lover of natural fact like Byron, it would matter that cloudless climes and starry skies exist, whereas autumnal faces must forever remain a subjective possibility.

Again, in our sensuous abandon to "lines" in poetry we are all too likely to be swayed by quite superficial association, as Arnold was, for example, in bidding the reader glow with him over such a fragment as:

> Presenting Thebes or Pelops' line
> Or the tale of Troy divine.

One can surely dream as happily over Byron's:

> The rock, the vulture, and the chain
> All that the proud can feel of pain. . . .

Right or wrong, Byron was aiming at the effect of bare projection, which needs no fringe of associations to seem valuable. Watching a Venetian sunset with Moore, he exclaimed "Damn it, Tom, don't be poetical!" We recognize here the principle of one device of Byron's that we may approve because our poets use it a great deal. Before Eliot, and even before Heine, Byron expanded the comic syllepsis[33] of the Augustans* into the contrast of eloquence and matter-of-fact:

> Sooner shall this blue Ocean melt to air,
>   Sooner shall Earth resolve itself to sea,
> Than I resign thine image, oh my fair!
>   Or think of anything, excepting thee;
> A mind diseased no remedy can physic—
> (Here the ship gave a lurch, and he grew sea-sick.)

The frequent collapse of the lofty into the common-place for critical—as against merely comic—effect marks a kinship between Byron and the moderns that can scarcely be denied. He and they insist on seeing everything from at least two points of view. This amounts to saying that Byron reintroduced wit into poetry at a time when the art seemed to have succumbed to the desire for profundity. The importance of the step lay in showing that serious thought may use the light tones. And that demonstration, taken together with his defense of Pope against Keats and the Lake Poets, has lent color to the belief that Byron was at heart a classicist, in full reaction against the Romanticism of his own time. It is true that he repudiated his early work (like many other artists) and took upon himself a large share of blame for corrupting the public taste. But this seems no more than a polemical—and polite—exaggeration: Romanticism is something bigger than those early tales and than Byron himself.

If, moreover, we really wish to know his mind in its fullness—which is the sole reason for examining in this detail his poetical theory and practice—we must avoid quoting sallies on one side only. How unlike the neo-classic, for example,

---

[33] A figure of speech in which the same word (a verb or preposition) is applied to two others in different sense; e.g., the word "take" in the example from Pope.

* E.g., Pope in *The Rape of the Lock:* "Here, thou, great Anna! whom three realms obey, Dost sometimes counsel take—and sometimes tea." [Barzun's note.]

is this outburst, which occurs precisely in Byron's first pamphlet on Pope: "I do hate that word *invariable*. What is there of *human,* be it poetry, philosophy, wit, wisdom, science, power, glory, mind, matter, life or death, which is *invariable?*" And to the last Byron kept his admiration for unmistakably romantic work such as Scott's tales in verse and prose and Coleridge's "Christabel": "I won't have anyone sneer at 'Christabel,' it is a fine wild poem."

No doubt Byron defended Pope, but he did not think or write like Pope—except of course in the youthful *English Bards*. Byron's intense (and romantic) love of nature, his double or dialectical view of life, art, and religion, his intellectual Satanism parallel to Blake's—all are at odds with the corresponding notions in Pope and the Augustans generally. Thomas Moore grasped the truth—though giving it a moralizing twist—when he said: "Byron was the first very great poet who did not range himself on the *right* side of human things." By first, Moore meant first to his knowledge, Blake being unknown to him, and Shelley being forgotten by reason of his relative obscurity.

To put the facts in truer perspective than Moore could: Rousseau and the French Revolution come between Pope and Byron, and the mark of those new forces remains indelible on the later poet. What then is the meaning of the Pope controversy? Why did Byron write two pamphlets and a good many letters of aggressive vindication? One reason is Byron's unusual sense of solidarity with the defenseless, (even, at times, with his enemies), a feeling here sustained by his genuine humility toward the great dead. He was shocked that the Reverend William Bowles should, on the strength of some agreeable sonnets, assume the right to displace Pope from Parnassus altogether. The apparently unanimous rallying to Bowles's view on the part of other poets and critics made Byron all the more eager to take up the challenge.

Two other motives were at work. Pope's poetry was being dismissed as prosaic, because it was declarative and this-worldly instead of sensuous and transcendental. If the condemnation went unchallenged, Byron's own work would be deemed no poetry. Byron was therefore fighting to keep a place open for the kind of verse which, being written for the eye as well as the ear, withholds no secret from the mind. Byron could have championed Swift[34] just as appropriately: the genre of verse Byron was trying to reinstate is that which embodies the visible movement of life—narrative verse, and discursive as well, the verse which works upon the trivial and through intellect fits it for poetic uses: was not Byron the first poet to make literature out of contemplating the subject of money? His verse must allow the poet to pass from wit to invective, from meditation to parody, and from eloquence to doggerel, in short, his is dramatic verse, as against lyrical or elegiac.

The mention of drama introduces Byron's second motive, and with it a paradox characteristic of Romanticism. In the same period as the Pope controversy and the production of *Don Juan,* Byron composed no less than eight plays in verse, which he published and explicitly proffered as closet dramas. Their plan, as the letters make clear, was to be "classical" according to the French rules: observing the unities, beginning the conflict *after* the embroilment has occurred, and working toward the tragic denouement by means of introspective tirades.

---

[34] That is, Jonathan Swift (1667–1745).

Byron felt that the loose construction of the Elizabethans would not do for a reading play. He was nonetheless compelled to borrow their blank verse for his proposed hybrid, and like nearly all the Romanticists he produced only still-born dialogues of very uneven quality. In relation to these works, Byron's battle for Pope is a battle against the universal Shakespeare worship. Byron too knew his Shakespeare by heart and could not get rid of him completely enough to succeed in the French genre,* but he correctly judged that the great idol was an incubus on contemporary playwrights.

The genuine drama that Byron felt in the life of his times and in his own soul found no theatrical form. He put it into his loose "Shakespearian" tales, from *Childe Harold* to *Don Juan.* Almost any passage at random, even one taken from an ode (which we should not require to be in any sense dramatic) shows how the dramatic vision can enliven alien forms:

> Oh Venice! Venice! when thy marble walls
>   Are level with the waters, there shall be
> A cry of nations o'er thy sunken halls,
>   A loud lament along the sweeping sea!
> If I, a northern wanderer, weep for thee,
> What should thy sons do?—anything but weep:
> And yet they only murmur in their sleep.
> In contrast with their fathers—as the slime,
> The dull green ooze of the receding deep,
> Is with the dashing of the spring-tide foam
> That drives the sailor shipless to his home,
> Are they to those that were; and thus they creep,
> Crouching and crab-like, through their sapping streets.
> Oh! agony—that centuries should reap
> No mellower harvest! Thirteen hundred years
> Of wealth and glory turned to dust and tears;
> And every monument the stranger meets,
> Church, palace, pillar, as a mourner greets;
> And even the lion all subdued appears,
> And the harsh sound of the barbarian drum,
> With dull and daily dissonance repeats
> The echo of thy Tyrant's voice along
> The soft waves, once all musical to song,
> That heaved beneath the moonlight with the throng
> Of gondolas—and to the busy hum
> Of cheerful creatures, whose most sinful deeds
> Were but the overbeating of the heart,
> And flow of too much happiness, which needs
> The aid of age to turn its course apart
> From the luxuriant and voluptuous flood
> Of sweet sensations, battling with the blood. . . .

---

* With his usual self-criticism at work, he said that his own tragedies were "fit only for the ——— closet." [Barzun's note.]

The principle, here and elsewhere, is motion, the pressing forward of scenes and traits as if we were moving among a crowd whose own bustling now obscures, now reveals the inanimate décor. The rhythm, rugged on the surface, is irresistible and right beneath—as one will find on reading pages instead of lines or stanzas. For like any story teller, whether on the stage or in print, Byron should be taken in as far as possible at one sitting. He is not to be parsed or queried but read and reread—provided pleasure accompanies the repetition. Not the analytic, but the synoptic view gives us the measure of his mind. And if we are asked to define still more closely his special power, it is that he gives us not so much the illusion or the total harmony of life but rather its *animation*. On his own ground he has few equals and no superiors. In English verse other than the strictly dramatic, one can only think of Burns's sublime comedy of "Tam O' Shanter." In foreign literatures, despite the models which Byron furnished through translation, he still reigns alone in the realm he created, and he is still read as a unique master. That his peculiar power should survive translation is not surprising, given the transparency and factuality of his verse. But that the translations should leave him his character of poet shows that this resides, once again, in his conceptions—and hence that his mind was fundamentally poetic.

It remains to say a word of his letters as examples of the genre. They belong, of course, to the spontaneous and not the prepared kind that are meant to be published. Byron's extended travels and long exile, coupled with the happy preservation of the hundreds of letters that he was thus occasioned to write, make it possible to follow his life in his correspondence with a minimum of annotation. Almost any sizable extract from it is an open diary. One regrets all the same that his publisher and friends highmindedly destroyed the Memoirs that he composed and did want published: the first-person narratives in the letters whet our appetite for the continuous story. Indeed, Byron was born for autobiography, and in what may be called "egotistical prose," displays consummate tact; he neither boasts nor deprecates, but simply fulfills the purpose of a letter, which is to tell what the writer has thought and done since he last wrote.

Bryon's letters are also correspondence in the literal sense of being subtly different for each person addressed. They vary with mood and occasion—curt, rambling, expostulatory, formal; and in the most difficult sort, which is the long letter on a single subject, he is peerless. The only type missing from the series is the love letter. The fact is not so odd as it seems. If there is truth in what was said earlier about the probable causes of Byron's self-distrust in matters of affection, then we should expect him to write rather conventional billets such as the few that have survived—or else what may be termed sensual scenarios not likely to be preserved.

In any case, the bulk of his extant correspondence is with his friends, his family connections, and his business acquaintances, including John Murray his publisher. The letters to Murray form a little saga in themselves and a social document. With the possible exceptions of William James[35] and Shaw, Byron

---

[35] The American philosopher and psychologist (1842–1910).

was the last man who wrote to his publisher as an author should, giving due regard to the inescapably duplex character of publishing, and addressing the man therefore with a friendliness ready to topple into contempt; this being the fit counterpart of the publisher's devotion always ready to cut its losses. Byron's variations on the theme of "Do as I tell you" are notable for the conscious handling of his irritation and the amusement he manages to draw from it.

It is obvious that letter writing often gave Byron the opportunity to be outrageous and gay in a degree that no civilized society allows. A letter is in fact the only device for combining solitude and good company. And for some obscure reason, letters are also the proper medium for extravaganza. Byron, whom we know to have been remarkably adaptable to his surroundings, ready to take the tone of those about him, would be most himself in tête-à-tête with his notepaper. We detect this in the free association of ideas that leads us from one paragraph to the next and beyond the signature to the frequent P.S. In this last he explains himself further, or redoubles an injunction at the risk of weakening it; just as in the bad habit of his period, excessive underlining, he strains titanically to put his inflections on paper. This vagary is no harder to accept than Keats's anarchical punctuation, and perhaps those who judge Byron harshly for his irregular life will in their charity remember that he always *dated* his letters like a truly good man.

He need not have been afraid that his voice would not carry. His style and diction, becoming freer and suppler as time goes on, do all the work of recording his half of a perfect conversation. Unlike almost all his contemporaries—and this again makes him kin with our times—Byron writes in a speaking tone, yet with that coherence and equilibrium that speech never attains. The occasional bad grammar of which so much has been made by his detractors is usually nothing more than eighteenth-century aristocratic colloquialism: "lay" for "lie," "you was," "the business *don't* go on." What matters more than right grammar is that nothing is forced or cramped. Epigrams, puns, humorous spellings, quotations from Shakespeare or the classics, facts from his omnivorous reading of science and history, argument about business or politics, details of dueling or proofreading—Byron's prose accommodates them all, high and low as well as the transitions from one to the other. It is a medium of feeling and also of thought, transparent from any point of view and, by its frequent descent into the colloquial, entirely modern—past 1920. We notice the new direction as early as 1804, when he was only sixteen. He begins in the limbered up Johnsonese that his elders (like Southey) and his juniors (like Shelley) would continue to write all their lives; then shifts to his own rhythm for eight lines, and pulls out of it again into decorum:

> I left my mother at Southwell, some time since, in a monstrous pet with you for not writing. I am sorry to say the old lady and myself don't agree like lambs in a meadow, but I believe it is all my own fault, I am rather too fidgety, which my precise mamma objects to, we differ, then argue, and to my shame be it spoken fall out a *little,* however after a storm comes a calm; what's become of our aunt the amiable, antiquated Sophia? is she yet in the land of the living, or does she sing psalms with the *Blessed* in the other world. Adieu. I am happy enough and Comfortable

here. My friends are not numerous, but select; among them I rank as the principal Lord Delawarr, who is very amiable and my particular friend. . . .

In epigram the Byronian speed generates a style not elsewhere to be met with; it is equidistant from Swift (or Pope) and Shaw (or Wilde). Here is Byron to his estranged wife: "Deep resentments have but half recollections"; and again: "Men died calmly before the Christian aera. . . . A deathbed is a matter of nerves and constitution, and not of religion. Voltaire was frightened, Frederick of Prussia not." The same bullet-like meaning is discharged at his friends with the intent to rouse, not kill, as in this opening sentence to Moore: "You owe me two letters—pay them. I want to know what you are about." But the weapon also serves self-criticism: "The printer has done wonders; he has read what I cannot—my own handwriting." Byron may make us think of Johnson or Shaw when his sarcasm is more elaborate and conscious, for example in defining negus, a mild hot drink, as "a wishy-washy compromise between the passion for wine and the propriety of water." But in the prose as in the poems, it is the movement, the pace—and the change of pace—that are inimitable. In the letters of the final period freedom goes with the power both to sustain and to skip; the thought winds itself about the many relevant objects and fixes them for our inspection. Once the writer has shown where the argument is going, intermediaries are leaped over:

> In answer to your note of page 90 I must remark from *Aristotle* and *Rymer,* that the *hero* of tragedy and (I add *meo periculo*)[36] a tragic poem must be *guilty,* to excite *"terror and pity,"* the end of tragic poetry . . . [yet] in the Greek tragedy, innocence is unhappy often, and the offender escapes. I must also ask you is *Achilles* a *good* character? or is even Aeneas anything but a successful runaway? It is for Turnus[37] men feel and not for the Trojan. Who is the hero of *Paradise Lost?* Why Satan,—and Macbeth, and Richard, and Othello, Pierre,[38] and Lothario,[39] and Zanga?[40] If you talk so, I shall "cut you up like a gourd," as the Mamelukes say. But never mind, go on with it.

The dots in the passage just quoted represent an omission for brevity's sake. Unfortunately, a good many omissions in his letters have not so good an excuse. Apart from obliterated proper names, the blanks stand for words and passages that Byron's early editors could not stomach, and that (one surmises) we could. They are now irrecoverable, and their absence of course lends to certain pages a suggestiveness far worse than the full text could possibly be. Expurgation invariably boomerangs in this way, but in its recoil misrepresents a writer who was outspoken only because he was addressing a friend and not a public meeting. It would seem the merest justice not to censor what we have pried into.

[36] "At my risk."
[37] Opponent of Aeneas in the *Aeneid.*
[38] A character in *Venice Preserv'd* (1682), a blank verse play by Thomas Otway (1652–1685).
[39] A character in *The Fair Penitent* (1703), a blank verse tragedy by Nicholas Rowe (1674–1718).
[40] A character in *The Revenge* (1721) by Edward Young (1683–1765).

Byron would certainly be the last to resent our full scrutiny. He invites it in many forms; he was almost as self-critical as we, who are perfectionists in that line, could require. And if he entrusted his Memoirs to his survivors instead of braving the public with his disclosures, it was only because he believed that an autobiography published in midcareer persuades everybody the author must be dead. Neither as author nor as hero is Byron dead yet. Nor can the valet-like intimacy afforded by reading his daily thoughts do anything but increase his stature in our eyes. When we think of him away from the text of his tribulations (so to speak), we cannot help being aware of more, much more than the accepted attributes of fame—genius, wit, resourcefulness; more even than the characteristics of heroism—courage, superior mind, forgetfulness of self. We see rather a being in whom virtues and powers fused with vices and weaknesses in so imposing a fashion that we are tempted to ascribe to the presence of grosser earths the great strength of the alloy, and to feel that it was he whom the Prince of Denmark apostrophized as the archetype of Man, wonder and paradox of Nature.[41]

---

[41] *Hamlet*, II. ii. 300 ff.

Northrop Frye

MYTH, FICTION, AND DISPLACEMENT

Northrop Frye was born in 1912 in Sherbrooke, Quebec, and was educated at Emmanuel College of the University of Toronto and at Merton
College, Oxford. In 1947 the publication of his study of William Blake,
Fearful Symmetry, established him as one of the preeminent scholar-critics
of his generation. A decade later he published *The Anatomy of Criticism*
which has been compared, in point of its influence upon critical theory,
with I. A. Richards' *Principles of Literary Criticism* (1924). The two
books are alike in their strong evangelical purpose—both undertake to
bring criticism and critics to a consciousness of their being deficient in
grace and derelict in duty and to point out the path to salvation. The
influence of Richards was in all likelihood the wider to begin with and
will probably continue the longer, for the principles with which he was
concerned are those that govern not only criticism but also an activity
much more commonly practiced: in the first instance they are the principles of reading. Frye does of course have the common reader in mind,
at least ultimately, and he does indeed envisage criticism's advancing the
cause of "culture . . . and liberal education" and bringing about "the
systematic progress of taste and understanding," but this good purpose,
we gather, must wait upon the creation of a systematically progressing
discipline of criticism, an enterprise which of its nature is restricted to
professional practitioners, to whom, in effect, *The Anatomy of Criticism*
is addressed.

In his vivacious "Polemical Introduction" to the *Anatomy* Professor
Frye sets forth the premises upon which his conception of the critical
discipline is to be based. "If criticism exists," he says, "it must be an
examination of literature in terms of a conceptual framework derivable
from an inductive survey of the literary field." And he goes on: "The
word 'inductive' suggests some sort of scientific procedure. What if criticism is a science as well as an art? Not a 'pure' or 'exact' science, of
course, but these phrases belong to a nineteenth century cosmology
which is no longer with us." Of the two kinds of workers in the field
of criticism, the research scholar and what Professor Frye calls the "public critic," neither satisfies the demands made by criticism conceived as
a science. The scholar, although he proceeds on assumptions that are
derived from science, does not contribute to a coherent, systematic, and
developing study, which is what a science must be. The "public critic"
(such as Lamb, Hazlitt, Matthew Arnold, Sainte-Beuve) makes only

"random and haphazard use of what the scholar offers," and, what is more, is too much concerned with formulating value-judgments and taking "positions" about authors and literary tendencies which, upon examination, are found to have more reference to social and moral concerns than to literature itself. The only hope for criticism as "a field of genuine learning" is to become a coherent theory which has reference to literature regarded as a whole and as being susceptible to systematic and objective study. Although Professor Frye does not remark it, the intellectual ethos he proposes for literary criticism is in some considerable degree established in the study of the fine arts: possibly the nature of the subject-matter makes its objectification relatively easy as compared with literature, which has a way of asserting its subjectivity and exciting ours.

Professor Frye has taught English at Victoria College of the University of Toronto since 1939 and served as Principal of the College from 1959 until 1967, when he was appointed University Professor. Among his works are *The Well-Tempered Critic* (1963), *Fables of Identity: Studies in Poetic Mythology* (1963), *A Natural Perspective: The Development of Shakespearean Comedy and Romance* (1963), *The Return to Eden* (1965), *Fools of Time* (1967), and *The Modern Century* (1967). The essay reprinted here was first published in the Summer 1961 issue of *Daedalus,* the journal of the American Academy of Arts and Sciences, and reprinted in *Fables of Identity.*

"Myth" is a conception which runs through many areas of contemporary thought: anthropology, psychology, comparative religion, sociology, and several others. What follows is an attempt to explain what the term means in literary criticism today. Such an explanation must begin with the question: Why did the term ever get into literary criticism? There can be only one legitimate answer to such a question: because myth is and has always been an integral element of literature, the interest of poets in myth and mythology having been remarkable and constant since Homer's time.

There are two broad divisions of literary works, which may be called the fictional and the thematic. The former comprises works of literature with internal characters, and includes novels, plays, narrative poetry, folk tales, and everything that tells a story. In thematic literature the author and the reader are the only characters involved: this division includes most lyrics, essays, didactic poetry and oratory. Each division has its own type of myth, but we shall be concerned here only with the fictional part of literature, and with myth in its more common and easily recognized form as a certain kind of narrative.

When a critic deals with a work of literature, the most natural thing for him to do is to freeze it, to ignore its movement in time and look at it as a completed pattern of words, with all its parts existing simultaneously. This approach is common to nearly all types of critical techniques: here new and old-fashioned critics are at one. But in the direct experience of literature, which is something distinct from criticism, we are aware of what we may call the persuasion of continuity, the power that keeps us turning the pages of a novel and that holds us in our seats at the theatre. The continuity may be logical, or pseudo-logical, or psychological, or rhetorical: it may reside in the surge and thunder of epic verse or in some donkey's carrot like the identity of the murderer in a detective story or the first sexual act of the heroine in a romance. Or we may feel afterwards that the sense of continuity was pure illusion, as though we had been laid under a spell.

The continuity of a work of literature exists on different rhythmical levels. In the foreground, every word, every image, even every sound made audibly or inaudibly by the words, is making its tiny contribution to the total movement. But it would take a portentous concentration to attend to such details in direct experience: they belong to the kind of critical study that is dealing with a simultaneous unity. What we are conscious of in direct experience is rather a series of larger groupings, events and scenes that make up what we call the story. In ordinary English the word "plot" means this latter sequence of gross events. For a term that would include the total movement of sounds and images, the word "narrative" seems more natural than "plot," though the choice is a matter of usage and not of inherent correctness. Both words translate Aristotle's *mythos*, but Aristotle meant mainly by *mythos* what we are calling plot: narrative, in the above sense, is closer to his *lexis*.[1] The plot, then, is like the trees and houses that we focus our eyes on through a train window: the narrative is more like the weeds and stones that rush by in the foreground.

We now run into a curious difficulty. Plot, Aristotle says, is the life and soul of tragedy (and by implication of fiction generally): the essence of fiction, then, is plot or imitation of action, and characters exist primarily as functions of the plot. In our direct experience of fiction we feel how central is the importance of the steady progression of events that holds and guides our attention. Yet afterwards, when we try to remember or think about what we have seen, this sense of continuity is one of the most difficult things to recapture. What stands out in our minds is a vivid characterization, a great speech or striking image, a detached scene, bits and pieces of unusually convincing realization. A summary of a plot, say of a Scott novel, has much the same numbing effect on a hearer as a summary of last night's dream. That is not how we remember the book; or at least not why we remember it. And even with a work of fiction that we know thoroughly, such as *Hamlet,* while we keep in mind a sequence of scenes, and know that the ghost comes at the beginning and the duel with Laertes at the end, still there is something oddly discontinuous about our possession of it. With the histories[2] this disappearance of continuity is even more striking. *The Oxford Companion to English Literature*[3] is an invaluable reference work largely because it is so good at summarizing all the fictional plots that one has forgotten, but here is its summary of *King John:*

> The play, with some departures from historical accuracy, deals with various events in King John's reign, and principally with the tragedy of young Arthur. It ends with the death of John at Swinstead Abbey. It is significant that no mention of Magna Carta appears in it. The tragic quality of the play, the poignant grief of Constance, Arthur's mother, and

[1] The word as it appears in Aristotle is usually translated by the word "diction"; Frye uses the word to mean something like the "texture or rhetorical aspect of a work of literature"—Frye's definition from *Anatomy of Criticism* (1957).
[2] Shakespeare's history plays, that is.
[3] Edited by Sir Paul Harvey; first published in 1932; 4th ed. 1967.

the political complications depicted, are relieved by the wit, humour and gallantry of the Bastard of Faulconbridge.

This is, more or less, how we remember the play. We remember Faulconbridge and his great speech at the end; we remember the death scene of Prince Arthur; we remember Constance; we remember nothing about Magna Carta; we remember in the background the vacillating, obstinate, defiant king. But what *happened* in the play? What were the incidents that made it an imitation of an action? Does it matter? If it doesn't matter, what becomes of the principle that the characters exist for the sake of the action, the truth of which we felt so vividly while watching the play? If it does matter, are we going to invent some silly pedantic theory of unity that would rule out *King John* as legitimate drama?

Whatever the final answer, we may tentatively accept the principle that, in the direct experience of fiction, continuity is the center of our attention; our later memory, or what I call the possession of it, tends to become discontinuous. Our attention shifts from the sequence of incidents to another focus: a sense of what the work of fiction was all *about*, or what criticism usually calls its theme. And we notice that as we go on to study and reread the work of fiction, we tend, not to reconstruct the plot, but to become more conscious of the theme, and to see all incidents as manifestations of it. Thus the incidents themselves tend to remain, in our critical study of the work, discontinuous, detached from one another and regrouped in a new way. Even if we know it by heart this is still true, and if we are writing or lecturing on it, we usually start with something other than its linear action.

Now in the conception "theme," as in the conception "narrative," there are a number of distinguishable elements. One of them is "subject," which criticism can usually express by some kind of summarized statement. If we are asked what Arthur Miller's *The Crucible*[4] is about, we say that it is about—that is, its subject is—the Salem witch trials. Similarly, the subject of *Hamlet* is Hamlet's attempt at revenge on an uncle who has murdered his father and married his mother. But the Olivier movie of *Hamlet*[5] began with the statement (quoted from an unreliable memory): "This is the story of a man who could not make up his mind." Here is a quite different conception of theme: it expresses the theme in terms of what we may call its allegorical value. To the extent that it is an adequate statement of the theme of *Hamlet*, it makes the play into an allegory and the chief character into a personification of Indecision. In his illuminating study of *The Ancient Mariner*, Robert Penn Warren[6] says that the poem is written out of, and about, the general belief that the truth is implicit "in the poetic act as such, that the moral concern and the aesthetic concern are aspects of the same activity, the creative activity, and that this activity is expressive of the whole mind" (italicized in the original). Here again is allegorization, of a kind that takes the theme to be what Aristotle appears to have

---

[4] *The Crucible*, by Arthur Miller (b. 1915), American playwright, was first produced in 1953.

[5] Sir Laurence Olivier played the lead role and directed his film version of *Hamlet*.

[6] Robert Penn Warren, "A Poem of Pure Imagination," in *The Rime of the Ancient Mariner* (New York, 1946).

meant primarily by *dianoia,* the "thought" or sententious reflexion that the poem suggests to a meditative reader.

It seems to me that a third conception of "theme" is possible, less abstract than the subject and more direct than an allegorical translation. It is also, however, a conception for which the primitive vocabulary of contemporary criticism is ill adapted. Theme in this third sense is the *mythos* or plot examined as a simultaneous unity, when the entire shape of it is clear in our minds. In *Anatomy of Criticism* I use *dianoia* in this sense: an extension of Aristotle's meaning, no doubt, but in my opinion a justifiable one. The theme, so considered, differs appreciably from the moving plot: it is the same in substance, but we are now concerned with the details in relation to a unity, not in relation to suspense and linear progression. The unifying factors assume a new and increased importance, and the smaller details of imagery, which may escape conscious notice in direct experience, take on their proper significance. It is because of this difference that we find our memory of the progression of events dissolving as the events regroup themselves around another center of attention. Each event or incident, we now see, is a manifestation of some underlying unity, a unity that it both conceals and reveals, as clothes do the body in *Sartor Resartus.*[7]

Further, the plot or progress of events as a whole is also a manifestation of the theme, for the same story (i.e., theme in our sense) could be told in many different ways. It is, of course, impossible to say how extensive the changes of detail would have to be before we had a different theme, but they can be surprisingly extensive. Chaucer's *Pardoner's Tale* is a folk tale that started in India and must have reached Chaucer from some West-European source. It also stayed in India, where Kipling picked it up and put it into the *Second Jungle Book.*[8] Everything is different—setting, details, method of treatment—yet I think any reader, on whatever level of sophistication, would say that it was recognizably the same "story"—story as theme, that is, for the linear progression is what is different. More often we have only smaller units in common, of a kind that students of folklore call motifs. Thus in Hawthorne's *The Marble Faun*[9] we have the motif of the two heroines, one dark and one light, that we have in *Ivanhoe* and elsewhere; in *Lycidas* we have the motif of the "sanguine flower inscrib'd with woe," the red or purple flower that turns up everywhere in pastoral elegy, and so on. These smaller units I have elsewhere called archetypes, a word which has been connected since Plato's time with the sense of a pattern or model used in creation.

In most works of fiction we are at once aware that the *mythos* or sequence of events which holds our attention is being shaped into a unity. We are continually, if often unconsciously, attempting to construct a larger pattern of simultaneous significance out of what we have so far read or seen. We feel confident that the beginning implies an end, and that the story is not like the soul in natural theology, starting off at an arbitrary moment in time and going on

[7] *Sartor Resartus: The Life and Opinions of Herr Teufelsdröckh* (1833–1834), by Thomas Carlyle.

[8] *The Second Jungle Book,* by Rudyard Kipling (1865–1936) was published in 1895. The earliest known analogue of the *Pardoner's Tale* is one of the Jatakas, or birth-tales of Buddha. Kipling's tale is called "The King's Ankus."

[9] *The Marble Faun,* by Nathaniel Hawthorne (1804–1864), was published in 1860.

forever. Hence we often keep on reading even a tiresome novel "to see how it turns out." That is, we expect a certain point near the end at which linear suspense is resolved and the unifying shape of the whole design becomes conceptually visible. This point was called *anagnorisis* by Aristotle, a term for which "recognition" is a better rendering than "discovery." A tragic or comic plot is not a straight line: it is a parabola following the shapes of the mouths on the conventional masks. Comedy has a U-shaped plot, with the action sinking into deep and often potentially tragic complications, and then suddenly turning upward into a happy ending. Tragedy has an inverted U, with the action rising in crisis to a peripety and then plunging downward to catastrophe through a series of recognitions, usually of the inevitable consequences of previous acts. But in both cases what is recognized is seldom anything new; it is something which has been there all along, and which, by its reappearance or manifestation, brings the end into line with the beginning.

Recognition, and the unity of theme which it manifests, is often symbolized by some kind of emblematic object. A simple example is in the sixteenth-century play, *Gammer Gurton's Needle*,[10] the action of which is largely a great to-do over the loss of the needle, and which ends when a clown named Hodge gets it stuck in his posterior, bringing about what *Finnegans Wake*[11] would call a culious epiphany. Fans, rings, chains and other standard props of comedy are emblematic talismans of the same kind. Nearly always, however, such an emblem has to do with the identification of a chief character. Birthmarks and their symbolic relatives have run through fiction from Odysseus' scar to the scarlet letter, and from the brand of Cain to the rose tattoo.[12] In Greek romance and its descendants we have infants of noble birth exposed on a hillside with birth-tokens beside them; they are found by a shepherd or farmer and brought up in a lower station of life, and the birth-tokens are produced when the story has gone on long enough. In more complex fiction the emblem may be an oblique comment on a character, as with Henry James's golden bowl;[13] or, if it is only a motif, it may serve as what T. S. Eliot calls an objective correlative.

In any case, the point of recognition seems to be also a point of identification, where a hidden truth about something or somebody emerges into view. Besides the emblem, the hero may discover who his parents or children are, or he may go through some kind of ordeal (*basanos*) that manifests his true character, or the villain may be unmasked as a hypocrite, or, as in a detective story, identified as a murderer. In the Chinese play *The Chalk Circle* we have almost every possible form of recognition in the crucial scene. A concubine bears her master a son and is then accused of having murdered him by the wife, who has murdered him herself, and who also claims the son as her own. The concubine is tried before a foolish judge and condemned to death, then tried again before a wise one, who performs an experiment in a chalk circle resembling that of the judgment of Solomon in the Bible, and which proves that the concubine is the mother. Here we have: (a) the specific emblematic device which gives

[10] The play, by William Stevenson, dates from about 1580.
[11] *Finnegans Wake* (1939), by James Joyce (1882–1941), is a steady stream of puns and portmanteau words. For a sample, see the footnote to p. 384 of this volume.
[12] *The Rose Tattoo* (1951) is the title of a play by Tennessee Williams (b. 1914).
[13] *The Golden Bowl* (1904) is the title of a novel by Henry James (1843–1916).

the play its name; (b) an ordeal or test which reveals character; (c) the re-union of the mother with her rightful child; and (d) the recognition of the true moral natures of concubine and wife. There are several other elements of structural importance, but these will do to go on with.

So far, however, we have been speaking of strictly controlled forms, like comedy, where the end of the linear action also manifests the unity of the theme. What shall we find if we turn to other works where the author has just let his imagination go? I put the question in the form of this very common phrase because of the way that it illustrates a curious critical muddle. Usually, when we think of "imagination" psychologically, we think of it in its Renaissance sense as a faculty that works mainly by association and outside the province of judgment. But the associative faculty is not the creative one, though the two are frequently confused by neurotics. When we think of imagination as the power that produces art, we often think of it as the designing or structural principle in creation, Coleridge's "esemplastic" power. But imagination in this sense, left to itself, can only design. Random fantasy is exceedingly rare in the arts, and most of what we do have is a clever simulation of it. From primitive cultures to the *tachiste*[14] and action paintings of today, it has been a regular rule that the uninhibited imagination, in the structural sense, produces highly conventionalized art.

This rule implies, of course, that the main source of inhibitions is the need to produce a credible or plausible story, to come to terms with things as they are and not as the story-teller would like them to be for his convenience. Removing the necessity for telling a credible story enables the teller to concentrate on its structure, and when this happens, characters turn into imaginative projections, heroes becoming purely heroic and villains purely villainous. That is, they become assimilated to their functions in the plot. We see this conventionalizing of structure very clearly in the folk tale. Folk tales tell us nothing credible about the life or manners of any society; so far from giving us dialogue, imagery or complex behavior, they do not even care whether their characters are men or ghosts or animals. Folk tales are simply abstract story-patterns, uncomplicated and easy to remember, no more hampered by barriers of language and culture than migrating birds are by customs officers, and made up of interchangeable motifs that can be counted and indexed.

Nevertheless, folk tales form a continuum with other literary fictions. We know, vaguely, that the story of Cinderella has been retold hundreds of thousands of times in middle-class fiction, and that nearly every thriller we see is a variant of Bluebeard.[15] But it is seldom explained why even the greatest writers are interested in such tales: why Shakespeare put a folk-tale motif into nearly every comedy he wrote; why some of the most intellectualized fiction of our day, such as the later works of Thomas Mann,[16] are based on them. Writers are interested in folk tales for the same reason that painters are interested in still-life arrangements: because they illustrate essential principles of storytelling.

---

[14] Action painting.

[15] The tale was first collected from some popular source and re-told by Charles Perrault (1628–1703), French critic and poet.

[16] Later works by Thomas Mann (1875–1955) with a folktale base are *Joseph and his Brothers* (1933–1943), *Doctor Faustus* (1947), *The Holy Sinner* (1951).

The writer who uses them then has the technical problem of making them sufficiently plausible or credible to a sophisticated audience. When he succeeds, he produces, not realism, but a distortion of realism in the interests of structure. Such distortion is the literary equivalent of the tendency in painting to assimilate subject-matter to geometrical form, which we see both in primitive painting and in the sophisticated primitivism of, say, Léger or Modigliani.[17]

What we see clearly in the folk tale we see less clearly in popular fiction. If we want incident for its own sake, we turn from the standard novelists to adventure stories, like those of Rider Haggard or John Buchan,[18] where the action is close to if not actually across the boundary of the credible. Such stories are not looser or more flexible than the classical novels, but far tighter. Gone is all sense of the leisurely acquiring of incidental experience, of exploring all facets of a character, of learning something about a specific society. A hazardous enterprise is announced at the beginning and everything is rigorously subordinated to that. In such works, while characters exist for the sake of the action, the two aspects of the action which we have defined as plot and theme are very close together. The story could hardly have been told in any other narrative shape, and our attention has so little expanding to do when it reaches the recognition that we often feel that there would be no point in reading it a second time. The subordination of character to linear action is also a feature of the detective story, for the fact that one of the characters is capable of murder is the concealed clue on which every detective story turns. Even more striking is the subordinating of moral attitude to the conventions of the story. Thus in Robert Louis Stevenson's tale, *The Body-Snatcher*,[19] which is about the smuggling of corpses from cemeteries into medical classrooms, we read of bodies being "exposed to uttermost indignities before a class of gaping boys," and much more to the same effect. It is irrelevant to inquire whether this is really Stevenson's attitude to the use of cadavers in medical study or whether he expects it to be ours. The more sinister the crime can be felt to be, the more thrilling the thriller, and the moral attitude is being deliberately talked up to thicken the atmosphere.

The opposite extreme from such conventionalized fiction is represented by Trollope's *Last Chronicle of Barset*.[20] Here the main story line is a kind of parody of a detective novel—such parodies of suspense are frequent in Trollope. Some money has been stolen, and suspicion falls on the Reverend Josiah Crawley, curate of Hogglestock. The point of the parody is that Crawley's character is clearly and fully set forth, and if you imagine him capable of stealing money you are simply not attending to the story. The action, therefore, appears to exist for the sake of the characters, reversing Aristotle's axiom. But this is not really true. Characters still exist only as functions of the action, but

[17] Fernand Léger (1881–1955), French cubist painter, and Amedeo Modigliani, (1884–1920), Italian painter, who moved from an early style influenced by cubism and African art to one not associated with any school or movement.

[18] Sir Henry Rider Haggard (1856–1925), best known for *King Solomon's Mines* (1886) and *She* (1887); John Buchan (1875–1940), best known for *The Thirty-Nine Steps* (1915).

[19] The tale was first printed in the *Pall Mall Gazette* in 1884.

[20] The *Last Chronicle of Barset* by Anthony Trollope (1815–1882), was published in 1867.

in Trollope the "action" resides in the huge social panorama that the linear events build up. Recognition is continuous: it is in the texture of characterization, the dialogue and the comment itself, and needs no twist in the plot to dramatize a contrast between appearance and reality. And what is true of Trollope is roughly true of most mimetic[21] fiction between Defoe and Arnold Bennett. When we read Smollett or Jane Austen or Dickens, we read them for the sake of the texture of characterization, and tend to think of the plot, when we think of it at all, as a conventional, mechanical, or even (as occasionally in Dickens) absurd contrivance included only to satisfy the demands of the literary market.

The requirement of plausibility, then, has the apparently paradoxical effect of limiting the imagination by making its design more flexible. Thus in a Dutch realistic interior the painter's ability to render the sheen of satin or the varnish of a lute both limits his power of design (for a realistic painter cannot, like Braque or Juan Gris,[22] distort his object in the interest of pictorial composition) and yet makes that design less easy to take in at a glance. In fact we often "read" Dutch pictures instead of looking at them, absorbed by their technical virtuosity but unaffected by much conscious sense of their total structure.

By this time the ambiguity in our word "imagination" is catching up with us. So far we have been using it in the sense of a structural power which, left to itself, produces rigorously predictable fictions. In this sense Bernard Shaw spoke of the romances of Marie Corelli[23] as illustrating the triumph of imagination over mind. What is implied by "mind" here is less a structural than a reproductive power, which expresses itself in the texture of characterization and imagery. There seems no reason why this should not be called imagination too: in any case, in reading fiction there are two kinds of recognition. One is the continuous recognition of credibility, fidelity to experience, and of what is not so much lifelikeness as life-liveliness. The other is the recognition of the identity of the total design, into which we are initiated by the technical recognition in the plot.

The influence of mimetic fiction has thrown the main emphasis in criticism on the former kind of recognition. Coleridge, as is well known, intended the climax of the *Biographia Literaria* to be a demonstration of the "esemplastic" or structural nature of the imagination, only to discover when the great chapter arrived that he was unable to write it. There were doubtless many reasons for this, but one was that he does not really think of imagination as a constructive power at all. He means by imagination what we have called the reproductive power, the ability to bring to life the texture of characterization and imagery. It is to this power that he applies his favorite metaphor of an organism, where the unity is some mysterious and elusive "vitality." His practical criticism of work he admires is concerned with texture: he never discusses the total design, or what we call the theme, of a Shakespeare play. It is really fancy which is his

---

[21] The word as Frye uses it here means roughly "realistic."

[22] Georges Braque (b. 1882), French painter, who also moved from cubism to an unclassifiable style of his own; Juan Gris (pseudonym of José Victoriano González; 1887–1927), Spanish cubist painter.

[23] "Marie Corelli" was the pen-name of Mary Mackay (1855–1924), English writer of popular novels.

"esemplastic" power, and which he tends to think of as mechanical. His conception of fancy as a mode of memory, emancipated from time and space and playing with fixities and definites, admirably characterizes the folk tale, with its remoteness from society and its stock of interchangeable motifs. Thus Coleridge is in the tradition of critical naturalism, which bases its values on the immediacy of contact between art and nature that we continuously feel in the texture of mimetic fiction.

There is nothing wrong with critical naturalism, as far as it goes, but it does not do full justice to our feelings about the total design of a work of fiction. We shall not improve on Coleridge, however, by merely reversing his perspective, as T. E. Hulme[24] did, and giving our favorable value-judgments to fancy, wit, and highly conventionalized forms. This can start a new critical trend, but not develop the study of criticism. In the direct experience of a new work of fiction we have a sense of its unity which we derive from its persuasive continuity. As the work becomes more familiar, this sense of continuity fades out, and we tend to think of it as a discontinuous series of episodes, held together by something which eludes critical analysis. But that this unity is available for critical study as well seems clear when it emerges as a unity of "theme," as we call it, which we can study all at once, and to which we are normally initiated by some crucial recognition in the plot. Hence we need a supplementary form of criticism which can examine the total design of fiction as something which is neither mechanical nor of secondary importance.

By a myth, as I said at the beginning, I mean primarily a certain type of story. It is a story in which some of the chief characters are gods or other beings larger in power than humanity. Very seldom is it located in history: its action takes place in a world above or prior to ordinary time, *in illo tempore*, in Mircea Eliade's[25] phrase. Hence, like the folk tale, it is an abstract story-pattern. The characters can do what they like, which means what the story-teller likes: there is no need to be plausible or logical in motivation. The things that happen in myth are things that happen only in stories; they are in a self-contained literary world. Hence myth would naturally have the same kind of appeal for the fiction writer that folk tales have. It presents him with a ready-made framework, hoary with antiquity, and allows him to devote all his energies to elaborating its design. Thus the use of myth in Joyce or Cocteau,[26] like the use of folk tale in Mann, is parallel to the use of abstraction and other means of emphasizing design in contemporary painting; and a modern writer's interest in primitive fertility rites is parallel to a modern sculptor's interest in primitive woodcarving.

The differences between myth and folk tale, however, also have their im-

[24] Thomas Ernest Hulme (1883–1917), theorist of the imagist movement, friend of T. S. Eliot and Ezra Pound, is chiefly known for the posthumous collection of essays, *Speculations* (1924), which describes romantic theories of literature and the mind as "spilt religion."

[25] Mircea Eliade (b. 1907) uses the phrase in *Cosmos and History, the Myth of the Eternal Return*, first published in French in 1949–1950.

[26] Jean Cocteau (1889–1963), French poet, novelist, painter, playwright, and film-maker. Best known to speakers of English for his film, *The Blood of a Poet* (1932).

portance. Myths, as compared with folk tales, are usually in a special category of seriousness: they are believed to have "really happened," or to have some exceptional significance in explaining certain features of life, such as ritual. Again, whereas folk tales simply interchange motifs and develop variants, myths show an odd tendency to stick together and build up bigger structures. We have creation myths, fall and flood myths, metamorphosis and dying-god myths, divine-marriage and hero-ancestry myths, etiological[27] myths, apocalyptic myths; and writers of sacred scriptures or collectors of myth like Ovid[28] tend to arrange these in a series. And while myths themselves are seldom historical, they seem to provide a kind of containing form of tradition, one result of which is the obliterating of boundaries separating legend, historical reminiscence, and actual history that we find in Homer and the Old Testament.

As a type of story, myth is a form of verbal art, and belongs to the world of art. Like art, and unlike science, it deals, not with the world that man contemplates, but with the world that man creates. The total form of art, so to speak, is a world whose content is nature but whose form is human; hence when it "imitates" nature it assimilates nature to human forms. The world of art is human in perspective, a world in which the sun continues to rise and set long after science has explained that its rising and setting are illusions. And myth, too, makes a systematic attempt to see nature in human shape: it does not simply roam at large in nature like the folk tale.

The obvious conception which brings together the human form and the natural content in myth is the god. It is not the connexion of the stories of Phaethon[29] and Endymion[30] with the sun and moon that makes them myths, for we could have folk tales of the same kind: it is rather their attachment to the body of stories told about Apollo and Artemis[31] which gives them a canonical place in the growing system of tales that we call a mythology. And every developed mythology tends to complete itself, to outline an entire universe in which the "gods" represent the whole of nature in humanized form, and at the same time show in perspective man's origin, his destiny, the limits of his power, and the extension of his hopes and desires. A mythology may develop by accretion, as in Greece, or by rigorous codifying and the excluding of unwanted material, as in Israel; but the drive toward a verbal circumference of human experience is clear in both cultures.

The two great conceptual principles which myth uses in assimilating nature to human form are analogy and identity. Analogy establishes the parallels between human life and natural phenomena, and identity conceives of a "sungod" or a "tree-god." Myth seizes on the fundamental element of design offered by nature—the cycle, as we have it daily in the sun and yearly in the seasons—and assimilates it to the human cycle of life, death, and (analogy again) re-

[27] Myths explaining the origin of a custom, artifact, or social institution.
[28] Publius Ovidius Naso (43 B.C.–A.D. 18), Roman poet. Frye is thinking of such works by Ovid as the *Metamorphoses* and the *Fasti,* both of which are collections of myths loosely held together by a unifying theme.
[29] Son of Helios, God of the sun, Phaethon drove his father's chariot of the sun, but could not control the horses. Zeus had to blast Phaethon with a thunderbolt to prevent the careening chariot from burning up heaven and earth.
[30] Endymion was loved by Selene, the Goddess of the moon.
[31] Apollo was connected with the sun and Artemis with the moon.

birth. At the same time the discrepancy between the world man lives in and the world he would like to live in develops a dialectic in myth which, as in the New Testament and Plato's *Phaedo*, separates reality into two contrasting states, a heaven and a hell.

Again, myths are often used as allegories of science or religion or morality: they may arise in the first place to account for a ritual or a law, or they may be *exempla*[32] or parables which illustrate a particular situation or argument, like the myths in Plato or Achilles' myth of the two jars of Zeus at the end of the Iliad.[33] Once established in their own right, they may then be interpreted dogmatically or allegorically, as all the standard myths have been for centuries, in innumerable ways. But because myths are stories, what they "mean" is inside them, in the implications of their incidents. No rendering of any myth into conceptual language can serve as a full equivalent of its meaning. A myth may be told and retold: it may be modified or elaborated, or different patterns may be discovered in it; and its life is always the poetic life of a story, not the homiletic life of some illustrated truism. When a system of myths loses all connexion with belief, it becomes purely literary, as Classical myth did in Christian Europe. Such a development would be impossible unless myths were inherently literary in structure. As it makes no difference to that structure whether an interpretation of the myth is believed in or not, there is no difficulty in speaking of a Christian mythology.

Myth thus provides the main outlines and the circumference of a verbal universe which is later occupied by literature as well. Literature is more flexible than myth, and fills up this universe more completely: a poet or novelist may work in areas of human life apparently remote from the shadowy gods and gigantic story-outlines of mythology. But in all cultures mythology merges insensibly into, and with, literature. The Odyssey is to us a work of literature, but its early place in the literary tradition, the importance of gods in its action, and its influence on the later religious thought of Greece, are all features common to literature proper and to mythology, and indicate that the difference between them is more chronological than structural. Educators are now aware that any effective teaching of literature has to recapitulate its history and begin, in early childhood, with myths, folk tales and legends.

We should expect, therefore, that there would be a great many literary works derived directly from specific myths, like the poems by Drayton and Keats about Endymion[34] which are derived from the myth of Endymion. But the study of the relations between mythology and literature is not confined to such one-to-one relationships. In the first place, mythology as a total structure, defining as it does a society's religious beliefs, historical traditions, cosmological speculations—in short, the whole range of its verbal expressiveness—is the matrix of literature, and major poetry keeps returning to it. In every age poets who are

[32] Plural of *exemplum*, a moralized tale.

[33] "Two jars stand upon Zeus' threshold, full of the gifts he gives—one of evil, one of good. He to whom Zeus, that rejoices in the thunder, gives a mixture, meets sometimes evil, sometimes good; him to whom he gives hateful gifts he makes contemptible and an evil, raucous hunger pursues him upon the glorious earth, and he wanders about, honored by neither gods nor mortals."

[34] *Endimion and Phoebe*, a pastoral, was written by Michael Drayton (1563–1631) in 1595. Keats's *Endymion* was written in 1818.

thinkers (remembering that poets think in metaphors and images, not in propositions) and are deeply concerned with the origin or destiny or desires of mankind—with anything that belongs to the larger outlines of what literature can express—can hardly find a literary theme that does not coincide with a myth. Hence the imposing body of explicitly mythopoeic poetry in the epic and encyclopaedic forms which so many of the greatest poets use. A poet who accepts a mythology as valid for belief, as Dante and Milton accepted Christianity, will naturally use it; poets outside such a tradition turn to other mythologies as suggestive or symbolic of what might be believed, as in the adaptations of Classical or occult mythological systems made by Goethe, Victor Hugo, Shelley, or Yeats.

Similarly the structural principles of a mythology, built up from analogy and identity, become in due course the structural principles of literature. The absorption of the natural cycle into mythology provides myth with two of these structures; the rising movement that we find in myths of spring or the dawn, of birth, marriage and resurrection, and the falling movement in myths of death, metamorphosis, or sacrifice. These movements reappear as the structural principles of comedy and tragedy in literature. Again, the dialectic in myth that projects a paradise or heaven above our world and a hell or place of shades below it reappears in literature as the idealized world of pastoral and romance and the absurd, suffering, or frustrated world of irony and satire.

The relation between myth and literature, therefore, is established by studying the genres and conventions of literature. Thus the convention of the pastoral elegy in *Lycidas* links it to Virgil and Theocritus,[35] and thence with the myth of Adonis. Thus the convention of the foundling plot, which is the basis of *Tom Jones* and *Oliver Twist*,[36] goes back to Menandrine comedy formulas[37] thence to Euripides and so back to such myths as the finding of Moses and Perseus.[38] In myth criticism, when we examine the theme or total design of a fiction, we must isolate that aspect of the fiction which is conventional, and held in common with all other works of the same category. When we begin, say, *Pride and Prejudice*,[39] we can see at once that a story which sustains that particular mood or tone is most unlikely to end in tragedy or melodrama or mordant irony or romance. It clearly belongs to the category represented by the word "comedy," and we are not surprised to find in it the conventional features of comedy, including a foolish lover, with some economic advantages, encouraged by one of the parents, a hypocrite unmasked, misunderstandings between the chief characters eventually cleared up and happy marriages for those who deserve them. This conventional comic form is in *Pride and Prejudice* somewhat as the sonata form is in a Mozart symphony. Its presence there does not account for any of the merits of the novel, but it does account for its conventional, as distinct from its individual, structure. A serious interest in structure, then, ought naturally to lead us from *Pride and Prejudice* to a study

[35] Third-cent. B.C. writer of pastoral poetry.

[36] *Tom Jones* (1749) by Henry Fielding (1707–1754); *Oliver Twist* (1837–1838), by Charles Dickens (1812–1870).

[37] Formulas derived from Menander (c. 342–291 B.C.), Greek comic playwright.

[38] Perseus and his mother were committed to the sea in a wooden box by his grandfather Acrisius.

[39] A novel, published in 1813, by Jane Austen (1775–1817).

of the comic form which it exemplifies, the conventions of which have presented much the same features from Plautus[40] to our own day. These conventions in turn take us back into myth. When we compare the conventional plot of a play of Plautus with the Christian myth of a son appeasing the wrath of a father and redeeming his bride, we can see that the latter is quite accurately described, from a literary point of view, as a divine comedy.

Whenever we find explicit mythologizing in literature, or a writer trying to indicate what myths he is particularly interested in, we should treat this as confirmatory or supporting evidence for our study of the genres and conventions he is using. Meredith's *The Egoist*[41] is a story about a girl who narrowly escapes marrying a selfish man, which makes many references, both explicitly and indirectly in its imagery, to the two best-known myths of female sacrifice, the stories of Andromeda and Iphigeneia.[42] Such allusions would be pointless or unintelligible except as indications by Meredith of an awareness of the conventional shape of the story he is telling. Again, it is as true of poetry as it is of myth that its main conceptual elements are analogy and identity, which reappear in the two commonest figures of speech, the simile and the metaphor. Literature, like mythology, is largely an art of misleading analogies and mistaken identities. Hence we often find poets, especially young poets, turning to myth because of the scope it affords them for uninhibited poetic imagery. If Shakespeare's *Venus and Adonis* had been simply a story about a willing girl and an unwilling boy, all the resources of analogy and identity would have been left unexplored: the fanciful imagery appropriate to the mythical subject would have been merely tasteless exaggeration. Especially is this true with what may be called sympathetic imagery, the association of human and natural life:

> No flower was nigh, no grass, herb, leaf, or weed,
> But stole his blood and seem'd with him to bleed.[43]

The opposite extreme from such deliberate exploiting of myth is to be found in the general tendency of realism or naturalism to give imaginative life and coherence to something closely resembling our own ordinary experience. Such realism often begins by simplifying its language, and dropping the explicit connexions with myth which are a sign of an awareness of literary tradition. Wordsworth, for example, felt that in his day Phoebus and Philomela[44] were getting to be mere trade slang for the sun and the nightingale, and that poetry would do better to discard this kind of inorganic allusion. But, as Wordsworth

---

[40] Titus Maccius Plautus (c. 254–184 B.C.), Roman comic poet, whose plays are largely adoptions from Greek New Comedy, as written, say, by Menander.

[41] *The Egoist*, by George Meredith (1828–1909), a novel that came out in 1879.

[42] Andromeda was chained by her father to a rock where a sea-monster could get at her because an oracle had said that Andromeda was the only thing that would get the monster to cease his depredations. Perseus saved her. Iphigeneia was sacrificed by her father Agamemnon when the Greek fleet was stalled at Aulis by a calm caused by Artemis. In some versions of the myth Iphigeneia was indeed sacrificed; in other versions she was spirited away to Taurus by Artemis.

[43] *Venus and Adonis,* lines 1055–6.

[44] "Phoebus" is an epithet of Apollo's, meaning bright, life-giving, holy; Philomela was changed into a swallow by the gods when her brother-in-law Tereus was on the verge of killing her.

himself clearly recognized, the result of turning one's back on explicit myth can only be the reconstructing of the same mythical patterns in more ordinary words:

> Paradise, and groves
> Elysian, Fortunate Fields—like those of old
> Sought in the Atlantic Main—why should they be
> A history only of departed things,
> Or a mere fiction of what never was?
> For the discerning intellect of Man,
> When wedded to this goodly universe
> In love and holy passion, shall find these
> A simple produce of the common day.[45]

To this indirect mythologizing I have elsewhere given the name of displacement. By displacement I mean the techniques a writer uses to make his story credible, logically motivated or morally acceptable—lifelike, in short. I call it displacement for many reasons, but one is that fidelity to the credible is a feature of literature that can affect only content. Life presents a continuum, and a selection from it can only be what is called a *tranche de vie*:[46] plausibility is easy to sustain, but except for death life has little to suggest in the way of plausible conclusions. And even a plausible conclusion does not necessarily round out a shape. The realistic writer soon finds that the requirements of literary form and plausible content always fight against each other. Just as the poetic metaphor is always a logical absurdity, so every inherited convention of plot in literature is more or less mad. The king's rash promise, the cuckold's jealousy, the "lived happily ever after" tag to a concluding marriage, the manipulated happy endings of comedy in general, the equally manipulated ironic endings of modern realism—none of these was suggested by any observation of human life or behavior: all exist solely as story-telling devices. Literary shape cannot come from life; it comes only from literary tradition, and so ultimately from myth. In sober realism, like the novels of Trollope, the plot, as we have noted, is often a parody plot. It is instructive to notice, too, how strong the popular demand is for such forms as detective stories, science fiction, comic strips, comic formulas like the P. G. Wodehouse stories,[47] all of which are as rigorously conventional and stylized as the folk tale itself, works of pure "esemplastic" imagination, with the recognition turning up as predictably as the caesura in minor Augustan poetry.[48]

One difficulty in proceeding from this point comes from the lack of any literary term which corresponds to the word "mythology." We find it hard to conceive of literature as an order of words, as a unified imaginative system that can be studied as a whole by criticism. If we had such a conception, we could

---

[45] From the conclusion of the first book of *The Recluse*, an unfinished poem, which Wordsworth quotes in the Preface to the 1814 edition of *The Excursion*.

[46] "Slice of life."

[47] Pelham Grenville Wodehouse (b. 1881) author of stories in which the principal character is Jeeves, the "man" or valet.

[48] That is, poetry in the main written during the reign of Queen Anne (1702–1714) or, in a broader sense, during the life of Alexander Pope (1688–1744), or, loosely, in the first half of the eighteenth century.

readily see that literature as a whole provides a framework or context for every work of literature, just as a fully developed mythology provides a framework or context for each of its myths. Further, because mythology and literature occupy the same verbal space, so to speak, the framework or context of every work of literature can be found in mythology as well, when its literary tradition is understood. It is relatively easy to see the place of a myth in a mythology, and one of the main uses of myth criticism is to enable us to understand the corresponding place that a work of literature has in the context of literature as a whole.

Putting works of literature in such a context gives them an immense reverberating dimension of significance. (If anyone is worrying about value-judgments, I should add that establishing such a context tends to make the genuine work of literature sublime and the pinchbeck one ridiculous.) This reverberating significance, in which every literary work catches the echoes of all other works of its type in literature, and so ripples out into the rest of literature and thence into life, is often, and wrongly, called allegory. We have allegory when one literary work is joined to another, or to a myth, by a certain interpretation of meaning rather than by structure. Thus *The Pilgrim's Progress* is related allegorically to the Christian myth of redemption, and Hawthorne's story, *The Bosom Serpent*,[49] is related allegorically to various moral serpents going back to the Book of Genesis. Arthur Miller's *The Crucible*, already mentioned, deals with the Salem witch trials in a way that suggested McCarthyism to most of its original audience. This relation in itself is allegorical. But if *The Crucible* is good enough to hold the stage after McCarthyism has become as dead an issue as the Salem trials, it would be clear that the theme of *The Crucible* is one which can always be used in literature, and that any social hysteria can form its subject matter. Social hysteria, however, is the content and not the form of the theme itself, which belongs in the category of the purgatorial or triumphant tragedy. As so often happens in literature, the only explicit clue to its mythical shape is provided by the title.

To sum up. In the direct experience of a new work of literature, we are aware of its continuity or moving power in time. As we become both more familiar with and more detached from it, the work tends to break up into a discontinuous series of felicities, bits of vivid imagery, convincing characterization, witty dialogue, and the like. The study of this belongs to what we have called critical naturalism or continuous recognition, the sense of the sharply focused reproduction of life in the fiction. But there was a feeling of unity in the original experience which such criticism does not recapture. We need to move from a criticism of "effects" to what we may call a criticism of causes, specifically the formal cause which holds the work together. The fact that such unity is available for critical study as well as for direct experience is normally symbolized by a crucial recognition, a point marking a real and not merely apparent unity in the design. Fictions like those of Trollope which appeal particularly to critical naturalism often play down or even parody such a device, and such works show the highest degree of displacement and the least conscious or explicit relationship to myth.

---

[49] In *Mosses from an Old Manse* (1854).

If, however, we go on to study the theme or total shape of the fiction, we find that it also belongs to a convention or category, like those of comedy and tragedy. With the literary category we reach a dead end, until we realize that literature is a reconstructed mythology, with its structural principles derived from those of myth. Then we can see that literature is in a complex setting what a mythology is in a simpler one: a total body of verbal creation. In literature, whatever has a shape has a mythical shape, and leads us toward the center of the order of words. For just as critical naturalism studies the counterpoint of literature and life, words and things, so myth criticism pulls us away from "life" toward a self-contained and autonomous literary universe. But myth, as we said at the beginning, means many things besides literary structure, and the world of words is not so self-contained and autonomous after all.

Jorge Luis Borges

PARTIAL ENCHANTMENTS OF THE *QUIXOTE*

Jorge Luis Borges was born in Buenos Aires in 1899. His father, a writer, poet, and translator, came from an old Argentinian family of mixed Spanish, Portuguese, and English descent. Borges spent his childhood in the Palermo district of Buenos Aires, but moved with his family to Geneva in 1914. There and while traveling to France and Spain after the war he became acquainted with writers committed to *avant garde* movements such as Futurism, Expressionism, Cubism, and Dada. In Madrid he became associated with a new *avant garde* group, the Ultraists, and in Seville with the older Modernist group. In the periodicals edited by members of these two movements Borges published his first poems and essays.

When he returned to Argentina in 1921 he introduced Ultraism to Buenos Aires literary life and founded with a number of sympathetic young writers the literary reviews *Prisma* (1921–1922) and *Proa* (first series: 1922–1923; resumed 1924). His first volume of poems, *Fervor de Buenos Aires: poemas,* was published in 1923. But in 1928 Borges published his first story; and three collections, *The Universal History of Infamy* (1935), *The Garden of Forking Paths* (1941), and *Fictions* (1945), established him as one of the greatest, if also one of the most idiosyncratic, of short-story writers.

Because of his growing fame as poet, essayist, and writer of stories, the dictatorial Argentinian government did not dare to punish him more severely when during World War II Borges was outspoken in his criticism of fascism than by demoting him from municipal librarian to chicken inspector. After the revolution against Peronism in 1955, the new government made amends by awarding to Borges the directorship of the National Library. In the same year he joined the Faculty of Philosophy and Letters at the University of Buenos Aires, where he has since become Professor of English and American literatures.

The year 1961 brought to Borges the International Publishers' Prize and world-wide recognition. His blindness, which became complete in 1955, has not prevented him from lecturing on literary subjects in a number of European countries and in the United States; in 1968–1969

From *Other Inquisitions,* by Jorge Luis Borges, translated by Ruth L. C. Simms. Austin, Texas: University of Texas Press, 1964. Reprinted by permission of the University of Texas Press.

he served as the Charles Eliot Norton Visiting Professor of Poetry at Harvard University.

His most important collections of prose, aside from those listed above, are *El Aleph* (expanded edition, 1952; stories) and *Other Inquisitions, 1937–1952* (1952; translated 1964; essays), from which "Partial Enchantments of the *Quixote*" is reprinted.

It is probable that these observations have been made before at least once and, perhaps, many times; the novelty of them interests me less than their possible truth.

In comparison with other classics (the *Iliad*, the *Aeneid*, the *Pharsalia*,[1] the Dantesque *Comedy*, the tragedies and comedies of Shakespeare), the *Quixote* is realistic; but this realism differs essentially from the nineteenth-century variety. Joseph Conrad[2] was able to write that he excluded the supernatural from his works, because to include it would seem to be a denial that the quotidian was marvelous. I do not know whether Miguel de Cervantes shared that idea, but I do know that the form of the *Quixote* caused him to counterpose a real, prosaic world with an imaginary, poetic one. Conrad and Henry James incorporated reality into their novels because they deemed it poetic; to Cervantes the real and the poetic are antonyms. To the vast and vague geography of the *Amadís*,[3] he opposes the dusty roads and sordid inns of Castile; it is as if a novelist of our day were to sketch a satirical caricature of, say, service stations, treating them in a ludicrous way. Cervantes has created for us the poetry of seventeenth-century Spain, but neither that century nor that Spain were poetic for him; men like Unamuno or Azorín or Antonio Machado,[4] whose emotions were stirred by the evocation of La Mancha,[5] he would have found incomprehensible. The plan of his work precluded the marvelous, but still the marvelous had to be there, if only indirectly, as crime and mystery are present in a parody of the detective story. Cervantes could not have had recourse to amulets or sorcery, but he insinuated the supernatural in a subtle and therefore more effective way. In his heart of hearts, Cervantes loved the supernatural. In 1924 Paul Groussac observed: "With his cursory smattering of Latin and Italian, Cervantes derived his literary production primarily from pastoral novels and novels of chivalry, fables that had given solace to him in his captivity."[6] The *Quixote* is less an antidote for those tales than a secret nostalgic farewell.

---

[1] The *Pharsalia* is an epic poem written by Lucan (Marcus Annacus Lucanus; A.D. 39–65) on the civil war between the forces of Pompey and Caesar.

[2] Joseph Conrad (1857–1924), the famous English novelist of Polish birth.

[3] The *Amadís de Gaula*, chivalric romance of uncertain date and unknown authorship. *Don Quixote* parodies, otherwise makes fun of, and in a subtle way affirms the ideals of, the *Amadís*.

[4] Miguel de Unamuno (1864–1936), Azorín (pseudonym for Jose Martinez Ruiz; 1875–1967), Antonio Machado (1875–1939), Spanish authors, all of whom wrote works on or inspired by *Don Quixote*.

[5] Region of central Spain, where most of the adventures in *Don Quixote* occur.

[6] Cervantes was captured at sea by Turks and taken off to Algiers as a slave in 1575. He was ransomed in 1590. He was later imprisoned a number of times, when, as a tax collector, his accounts did not balance. Paul Groussac is an Argentinian writer who preceded Borges as director of the National Library.

Every novel is an ideal depiction of reality. Cervantes delights in fusing the objective and the subjective, the world of the reader and the world of the book. In the chapters that consider whether the barber's basin is a helmet and the packsaddle a harness, the problem is treated explicitly; other parts, as I mentioned before, merely hint at it. In the sixth chapter of Part One the priest and the barber inspect Don Quixote's library; astonishingly enough, one of the books they examine is the *Galatea*[7] by Cervantes. It develops that the barber is a friend of his who does not admire him very much, and says that Cervantes is more versed in misfortunes than in verses. He adds that the book has a rather well-constructed plot; it proposes something and concludes nothing. The barber, a dream of Cervantes or a form of one of Cervantes' dreams, passes judgment on Cervantes. It is also surprising to learn, at the beginning of Chapter IX, that the whole novel has been translated from the Arabic and that Cervantes acquired the manuscript in the marketplace of Toledo. It was translated by a Morisco, who lived in Cervantes' house for more than a month and a half while he completed the task. We are reminded of Carlyle, who feigned that the *Sartor Resartus* was a partial version of a work published in Germany by Dr. Diogenes Teufelsdröckh;[8] we are reminded of the Spanish Rabbi Moisés de León, who wrote the *Zohar* or *Book of the Splendor*[9] and divulged it as the work of a Palestinian rabbi of the third century.

The set of strange ambiguities culminates in Part Two. The protagonists of the *Quixote* who are, also, readers of the *Quixote*, have read Part One. Here we inevitably remember the case of Shakespeare, who includes on the stage of *Hamlet* another stage, where a tragedy almost like that of *Hamlet* is being presented. The imperfect correspondence of the principal work and the secondary one lessens the effectiveness of that inclusion. A device analogous to Cervantes' and even more startling, appears in the *Ramayana*, epic poem by Valmiki,[10] which relates the deeds of Rama and his war with the evil spirits. In the last book Rama's children, not knowing who their father is, seek refuge in a forest, where a hermit teaches them to read. That teacher, strangely enough, is Valmiki; the book they study is the *Ramayana*. Rama orders a sacrifice of horses; Valmiki comes to the ceremony with his pupils. They sing the *Ramayana* to the accompaniment of the lute. Rama hears his own story, recognizes his children, and then rewards the poet.

Chance has caused something similar to occur in *A Thousand and One Nights*. That compilation of fantastic stories duplicates and reduplicates to the point of vertigo the ramification of a central tale into subordinate ones, without attempting to evaluate their realities; the effect (which should have been profound) is superficial, like that of a Persian rug. The first story is well known: the desolate oath of the Sultan, who marries a maiden each night and then orders her to be beheaded at dawn, and the courage of Scheherazade, who delights him with fables until a thousand and one nights have gyrated about them

[7] Cervantes' first novel, of 1585.

[8] *Sartor Resartus: The Life and Opinions of Herr Teufelsdröckh,* by Thomas Carlyle (1795–1881), was published in 1833–1834.

[9] The *Zohar,* one of the two main sources of the Cabala, is a mystical commentary on the Pentateuch, written by Moisés de León in the thirteenth century.

[10] The Ramayana is a Sanskrit epic of India, perhaps written in the third century B.C. and traditionally ascribed to Valmiki, one of the characters in the poem.

and she shows him their son. The need to complete a thousand and one sections obliged the copyists of the work to make all sorts of interpolations. None is so disturbing as that of night DCII, magic among the nights. That is when the Sultan hears his own story from the Sultana's mouth. He hears the beginning of the story, which embraces all the other stories as well as—monstrously—itself. Does the reader perceive the unlimited possibilities of that interpolation, the curious danger—that the Sultana may persist and the Sultan, transfixed, will hear forever the truncated story of *A Thousand and One Nights,* now infinite and circular?

The inventions of philosophy are no less fantastic than those of art. In the first volume of *The World and the Individual* (1899) Josiah Royce[11] has formulated the following one:

> . . . let us suppose, if you please, that a portion of the surface of England is very perfectly levelled and smoothed, and is then devoted to the production of our precise map of England. . . . But now suppose that this our resemblance is to be made absolutely exact, in the sense previously defined. A map of England, contained within England, is to represent, down to the minutest detail, every contour and marking, natural or artificial, that occurs upon the surface of England . . . For the map, in order to be complete, according to the rule given, will have to contain, as a part of itself, a representation of its own contour and contents. In order that this representation should be constructed, the representation itself will have to contain once more, as a part of itself, a representation of its own contour and contents; and this representation, in order to be exact, will have once more to contain an image of itself; and so on without limit.

Why does it make us uneasy to know that the map is within the map and the thousand and one nights are within the book of *A Thousand and One Nights?* Why does it disquiet us to know that Don Quixote is a reader of the *Quixote,* and Hamlet is a spectator of *Hamlet?* I believe I have found the answer: those inversions suggest that if the characters in a story can be readers or spectators, then we, their readers or spectators, can be fictitious. In 1833 Carlyle observed[12] that universal history is an infinite sacred book that all men write and read and try to understand, and in which they too are written.

---

[11] Josiah Royce (1885–1916) was an American philosopher, teacher, and essayist.
[12] In *Sartor Resartus.*

Alain Robbe-Grillet

NATURE, HUMANISM, TRAGEDY

Alain Robbe-Grillet was born in Brest, France, in 1922, the son of an
engineer. He received his education at the Lycée St. Louis and the
Institut National Agronomique. He worked first for the National Institute of Statistics (1945–1950) and then for the Institut de Fruits et
Agrumes Coloniaux (1950–1951), for whom he studied tropical fruits
in Africa and the Antilles. Since 1954 he has been literary advisor to
Les Éditions de Minuit, a Paris firm and Robbe-Grillet's own publishers.

His first novel, *Les Gommes* (1953; trans. 1964 as *The Erasers*),
brought Robbe-Grillet instant attention, much of it abuse from old guard
critics. Roland Barthes, one of the most influential of the French "new
critics," praised *The Erasers* for a method as revolutionary in its consequences as "the surrealist attack on rationality." His second novel, *Le
Voyeur* (1955; trans. 1958 as *The Voyeur*) won Robbe-Grillet a wider
public and the important Prix de Critiques; but the controversy over his
work thickened with passion and ideology.

Robbe-Grillet's next three novels, *La Jalousie* (1957; trans. 1959 as
Jealousy), *Dans le labyrinthe* (1959; trans. 1960 as *In the Labyrinth*),
and *La Maison de rendez-vous* (1965; trans. 1966); and his two films,
L'année dernière à Marienbad (1961; it appeared in the United States
as *Last Year in Marienbad*) and *L'immortelle* (1963) did nothing to
change the minds of his detractors or champions, but they considerably
increased the number of the latter, and at the moment he ranks as one
of the most highly regarded of Europe's living writers of fiction.

It is against the background of heat, abuse, misunderstanding, and
partisanship inspired by his novels that Robbe-Grillet's collection of
essays, *Pour un nouveau roman* (1963; trans. 1965 as *For a New Novel*,
from which "Nature, Humanism, Tragedy" has been reprinted) is most
intelligibly read. In his introductory essay, Robbe-Grillet argues that the
novel's forms must evolve to remain alive, that "literature too is alive,
and that the novel, ever since it has existed, has always been new," that
"each novelist, each novel must invent its own form." And in the body
of the book he employs the term *New Novel* to designate the work of
"all those seeking new forms for the novel, forms capable of expressing
(or of creating) new relations between man and the world, to all those
who have determined to invent the novel, in other words, to invent man.

Such writers know that the systematic repetition of the forms of the past is not only absurd and futile, but that it can even become harmful: by blinding us to our real situation in the world today, it keeps us, ultimately, from constructing the world and man of tomorrow."

Tragedy is merely a means of "recovering" human misery, of subsuming and thereby justifying it in the form of a necessity, a wisdom, or a purification: to refuse this recuperation and to investigate the techniques of not treacherously succumbing to it (nothing is more insidious than tragedy) is today a necessary enterprise.

—Roland Barthes

As recently as two years ago, trying to define the direction of a still tentative development in the art of the novel, I described as a constant factor "the destitution of the old myths of depth." The violent and almost unanimous reactions of the critics, the objections of many readers of apparent good faith, the reservations formulated by several sincere friends have persuaded me that I went too far too fast. Apart from several men themselves engaged in comparable investigations—artistic, literary, or philosophical—no one would grant that such an assertion did not necessarily involve the negation of Man himself. Loyalty to the old myths showed itself to be, as matter of fact, quite tenacious.

That writers as different as François Mauriac and André Rousseaux,[1] for example, should concur in denouncing the exclusive description of "surfaces" as a gratuitous mutilation, the blind folly of a young rebel, a kind of sterile despair leading to the destruction of art nonetheless seemed quite in order. More unexpected, more disturbing, was the position—identical, from many points of view—of certain materialists who, in order to judge my enterprise, referred to "values" remarkably similar to the traditional values of Christianity. Yet for them there was no question of a confessional *parti pris.*[2] But on either side, what was offered as a principle was the indefectible solidarity between our mind and the world, while art was reduced to its "natural," reassuring role as mediator; and I was condemned in the name of the "human."

Finally I was quite naive, it was said, to attempt to deny this depth: my own books were interesting, were readable, only to the degree—and the degree was disputed—to which they were, unknown to me, its expression.

That there is no more than a rather loose parallelism between the three novels I have published up to now[3] and my theoretical views on a possible novel of the future is certainly obvious enough. Moreover, it will be regarded as only natural that a book of two or three hundred pages should be more complex than an article of ten; and also, that it is easier to indicate a new direction

---

[1] François Mauriac (b. 1885), French novelist, dramatist, critic. Rousseaux is a literary journalist. A typical collection of his studies is *Ames et visages du XX siècle* (1944).

[2] "Taking of sides."

[3] *The Erasers* (1953); *The Voyeur* (1955); *Jealousy* (1957).

than to follow it, without failure—partial or even complete—being a decisive, definitive proof of the error committed at the outset.

Finally, it must be added that the characteristic of humanism, whether Christian or not, is precisely to recover *everything*, including whatever attempts to trace its limits, even to impugn it as a whole. This is, in fact, one of the surest resources of its functioning.

There is no question of seeking to justify myself at any price; I am merely trying to see the matter more clearly. The critical positions cited above help me do so in a notable way. What I am undertaking today is less to refute their arguments than to define their scope, and to define at the same time what separates me from such points of view. It is always futile to engage in polemics; but if a true dialogue is possible, one must on the contrary seize the opportunity to engage in it. And if dialogue is not possible, it is important to know why. In any case, we are doubtless all, on one side as on the other, interested enough in these problems to make it worth while discussing them again, however bluntly.

Is there not, first of all, a certain fraudulence in this word *human* which is always being thrown in our faces? If it is not a word quite devoid of meaning, what meaning does it really have?

It seems that those who use it all the time, those who make it the sole criterion of all praise as of all reproach, identify—deliberately, perhaps—a precise (and limited) reflection on man, his situation in the world, the phenomena of his existence, with a certain anthropocentric atmosphere, vague but imbuing all things, giving the world its so-called *signification,* that is, investing it from within by a more or less disingenuous network of sentiments and thoughts. Simplifying, we can summarize the position of our new inquisitors in two sentences; if I say, "The world is man," I shall always gain absolution; while if I say, "Things are things, and man is only man," I am immediately charged with a crime against humanity.

The crime is the assertion that there exists something in the world which is not man, which makes no sign to him, which has nothing in common with him. The crime, above all, according to this view, is to remark this separation, this distance, without attempting to effect the slightest sublimation of it.

What could be, in other words, an "inhuman" work? How, in particular, could a novel which deals with a man, and follows his steps from page to page, describing only what he does, what he sees, or what he imagines, how could such a novel be accused of turning away from man? And it is not the character himself, let us make that clear at once, who is involved in this judgment. As a "character," as an individual animated by torments and passions, no one will ever reproach him with being inhuman, even if he is a sadistic madman and a criminal—the contrary, it would seem.

But now suppose the eyes of this man rest on things without indulgence, insistently: he sees them, but he refuses to appropriate them, he refuses to maintain any suspect understanding with them, any complicity; he asks nothing of them; toward them he feels neither agreement nor dissent of any kind. He can, perhaps, make them the prop of his passions, as of his sense of sight. But his sense of sight is content to take their measurements; and his passion, similarly, rests on their surface, without attempting to penetrate them since there is nothing inside, without feigning the least appeal since they would not answer.

To condemn, in the name of the human, the novel which deals with such a man is therefore to adopt the *humanist* point of view, according to which it is not enough to show man where he is: it must further be proclaimed that man is everywhere. On the pretext that man can achieve only a subjective knowledge of the world, humanism decides to elect man the justification of everything. A true bridge of souls thrown between man and things, the humanist outlook is preeminently a pledge of solidarity.

In the literary realm, the expression of this solidarity appears chiefly as the investigation, worked up into a system, of analogical relations.

Metaphor, as a matter of fact, is never an innocent figure of speech. To say that the weather is "capricious" or the mountain "majestic," to speak of the "heart" of the forest, of a "pitiless" sun, of a village "huddled" in the valley, is, to a certain degree, to furnish clues as to the things themselves: shape, size, situation, etc. But the choice of an analogical vocabulary, however simple, already does something more than account for purely physical data, and what this *more* is can scarcely be ascribed only to the credit of belles-lettres. The height of the mountain assumes, willy-nilly, a moral value; the heat of the sun becomes the result of an intention. . . . In almost the whole of our contemporary literature, these anthropomorphic analogies are repeated too insistently, too coherently not to reveal an entire metaphysical system.

More or less consciously, the goal for the writers who employ such a terminology can only be to establish a constant relation between the universe and the being who inhabits it. Thus man's sentiments will seem alternately to derive from his contacts with the world and to find in that world their natural correspondence if not their fulfillment.

Metaphor, which is supposed to express only a comparison, without any particular motive, actually introduces a subterranean communication, a movement of sympathy (or of antipathy) which is its true *raison d'être*.[4] For, as comparison, metaphor is almost always a useless comparison which contributes nothing new to the description. What would the village lose by being merely "situated" in the valley? The word "huddled" gives us no complementary information. On the other hand it transports the reader (in the author's wake) into the imagined soul of the village; if I accept the word "huddled," I am no no longer entirely a spectator; I myself become the village, for the duration of a sentence, and the valley functions as a cavity into which I aspire to disappear.

Taking this possible adherence as their basis, the defenders of metaphor reply that it thereby possesses an advantage: that of making apparent an element which was not so. Having himself become the village, they say, the reader participates in the latter's situation, hence understands it better. Similarly in the case of the mountain: I shall make it easier to see the mountain by saying it is majestic than by measuring the apparent angle from which my gaze registers

4 "Reason for being."

its height. . . . And this is true sometimes, but it always involves a more serious reversal: it is precisely this participation which is problematical, since it leads to the notion of a hidden unity.

It must even be added that the gain in descriptive value is here no more than an alibi: the true lovers of metaphor seek only to impose the idea of a communication. If they did not possess the verb "huddle," they would not even mention the position of the village. The height of the mountain would be nothing to them, if it did not offer the moral spectacle of "majesty."

Such a spectacle, for them, never remains entirely *external*. It always implies, more or less, a gift received by man: the things around him are like the fairies in the tale, each of whom brought as a gift to the newborn child one of the traits of his future character. The mountain might thus have first communicated to me the feeling of the majestic—that is what is insinuated. This feeling would then be developed in me and, by a natural growth, engender others: magnificence, prestige, heroism, nobility, pride. In my turn I would refer these to other objects, even those of a lesser size (I would speak of a proud oak, of a vase of noble lines), and the world would become the depository of all my aspirations to greatness, would be both their image and their justification, for all eternity.

The same would be true of every feeling, and in these incessant exchanges, multiplied to infinity, I could no longer discern the origin of anything. Was majesty to be located first within, or around me? The question itself would lose its meaning. Only a sublime communion would remain between the world and me.

Then, with habit, I would easily go much farther. Once the principle of this communion was admitted, I would speak of the melancholy of a landscape, of the indifference of a stone, of the fatuousness of a coal scuttle. These new metaphors no longer furnish appreciable information about the objects subject to my scrutiny, but the world of things has been so thoroughly contaminated by my mind that it is henceforth susceptible of any emotion, of any character trait. I will forget that it is I, I alone, who feels melancholy or suffers solitude; these affective elements will soon be considered as the *profound reality* of the material universe, the sole reality—to all intents and purposes—worthy of engaging my interest in it.

Hence there is much more involved than describing our consciousness by using things as raw material, as one might build a cabin out of logs. To identify in this way my own melancholy with that which I attribute to a landscape, to admit this link as more than superficial, is thereby to acknowledge a certain predestination for my present life: this landscape existed *before* me; if it is really the landscape which is sad, it was *already* sad before me, and this correspondence I experience today between its form and my mood were here waiting for me long before I was born; this melancholy has been fated for me forever. . . .

We see to what point the idea of a human *nature* can be linked to the analogical vocabulary. This nature, common to all men, eternal and inalienable, no longer requires a God to establish it. It is enough to know that Mont Blanc has been waiting for me in the heart of the Alps since the tertiary era, and with it all my notions of greatness and purity!

This nature, moreover, does not merely belong to man, since it constitutes the link between his mind and things: it is, in fact, an essence common to all "creation" that we are asked to believe in. The universe and I now have only one soul, only one secret.

Belief in a *nature* thus reveals itself as the source of all humanism, in the habitual sense of the word. And it is no accident if Nature precisely—mineral, animal, vegetable Nature—is first of all clogged with an anthropomorphic vocabulary. This Nature—mountain, sea, forest, desert, valley—is simultaneously our model and our heart. It is, at the same time, within us and around us. It is neither provisional nor contingent. It encrusts us, judges us, and ensures our salvation.

To reject our so-called "nature" and the vocabulary which perpetuates its myth, to propose objects as purely external and superficial, is not—as has been claimed—to deny man; but it is to reject the "pananthropic" notion contained in traditional humanism, and probably in all humanism. It is no more in the last analysis than to lay claim, quite logically, to my freedom.

Therefore nothing must be neglected in this mopping-up operation. Taking a closer look, we realize that the anthropocentric analogies (mental or visceral) are not the only ones to be arraigned. *All* analogies are just as dangerous. And perhaps the most dangerous ones of all are the most secret, those in which man is not named.

Let us give some examples, at random. To discover the shape of a horse in the heavens may, of course, derive from a simple process of description and not be of any consequence. But to speak of the "gallop" of the clouds, or of their "flying mane," is no longer entirely innocent. For if a cloud (or a wave or a hill) possesses a mane, if later on the mane of a stallion "flings arrows," if the arrow . . . etc., the reader of such images will emerge from the universe of forms to find himself plunged into a universe of significations. Between the wave and the horse, he will be tempted to conceive an undifferentiated profundity: passion, pride, power, wildness. . . . The idea of a nature leads infallibly to that of a nature common to all things, that is, a *superior* or *higher* nature. The idea of an interiority always leads to the idea of a transcendence.

And the task extends step by step: from the bow to the horse, from the horse to the wave—and from the sea to love. A common nature, once again, must be the eternal answer to the *single question* of our Greco-Christian civilization; the Sphinx is before me, questions me, I need not even try to understand the terms of the riddle being asked, there is only one answer possible, only one answer to everything: man.[5]

This will not do.

There are *questions,* and *answers.* Man is merely, from his own point of view, the only witness.

[5] The Sphinx's riddle was, "What walks on four feet in the morning, on two at noon, and on three in the evening?" The answer: man.

Man looks at the world, and the world does not look back at him. Man sees things and discovers, now, that he can escape the metaphysical pact others had once concluded for him, and thereby escape servitude and terror. That he can . . . that he *may*, at least, some day.

He does not thereby refuse all contact with the world; he consents on the contrary to utilize it for material ends: a utensil, *as* a utensil, never possesses "depth"; a utensil is entirely form and matter—and purpose.

Man grasps his hammer (or a stone he has selected) and pounds on a stake he wants to drive into the ground. While he uses it in this way, the hammer (or the stone) is merely form and substance: its weight, the striking surface, the other extremity which allows him to hold it. Afterward, man sets the tool down in front of him; if he no longer needs it, the hammer is no more than a thing among things: outside of his use, it has no signification.

And man today (or tomorrow) no longer experiences this absence of signification as a lack, or as a laceration. Confronting such a void, he henceforth feels no dizziness. His heart no longer needs an abyss in which to lodge.

For if he rejects communion, he also rejects tragedy.

Tragedy may be defined, here, as an attempt to "recover" the distance which exists between man and things as a new value; it would be then a test, an ordeal in which victory would consist in being vanquished. Tragedy therefore appears as the last invention of humanism to permit nothing to escape: since the correspondence between man and things has finally been denounced, the humanist saves his empire by immediately instituting a new form of solidarity, the divorce itself becoming a major path to redemption.

There is still almost a communion, but a *painful* one, perpetually in doubt and always deferred, its effectiveness in proportion to its inaccessible character. Divorce-as-a-form-of-marriage is a trap—and it is a falsification.

We see in effect to what degree such a union is perverted: instead of being the quest for a good, it is now the benediction of an evil. Unhappiness, failure, solitude, guilt, madness—such are the accidents of our existence which we are asked to entertain as the best pledges of our salvation. To entertain, not to accept: it is a matter of feeding them at our expense while continuing to struggle against them. For tragedy involves neither a true acceptance nor a true rejection. It is the sublimation of a difference.

Let us retrace, as an example, the functioning of "solitude." I call out. No one answers me. Instead of concluding that there is no one there—which could be a pure and simple observation, dated and localized in space and time—I decide to act as if there *were* someone there, but someone who, for one reason or another, will not answer. The silence which follows my outcry is henceforth no longer a *true* silence; it is charged with a content, a meaning, a depth, a soul—which immediately sends me back to my own. The distance between my cry, to my own ears, and the mute (perhaps deaf) interlocutor to whom it is addressed becomes an anguish, my hope and my despair, a meaning in my life. Henceforth nothing will matter except this false void and the problems it raises for me. Should I call any longer? Should I shout louder? Should I utter different words? I try once again. . . . Very quickly I realize that no one will answer; but the invisible presence I continue to create by my call obliges me to hurl my wretched cries into the silence forever. Soon the sound they make begins to stupefy me. As though bewitched, I call again . . . and again. My solitude, aggravated, is ultimately transmuted into a superior necessity for my alienated consciousness, a promise of my redemption. And I am obliged, if this redemption is to be fulfilled, to persist until my death, crying out for nothing.

According to the habitual process, my solitude is then no longer an accidental, momentary datum of my existence. It becomes part of me, of the entire world, of all men: it is our nature, once again. It is a solitude forever.

Wherever there is distance, separation, doubling, cleavage, there is the possibility of experiencing them as suffering, then of raising this suffering to the height of a sublime necessity. A path toward a metaphysical Beyond, this pseudo-necessity is at the same time the closed door to a realistic future. Tragedy, if it consoles us today, forbids any solider conquest tomorrow. Under the appearance of a perpetual motion, it actually petrifies the universe in a sonorous malediction. There can no longer be any question of seeking some remedy for our misfortune, once tragedy convinces us to love it.

We are in the presence of an oblique maneuver of contemporary humanism, which may deceive us. Since the effort of recuperation no longer bears on things themselves, we might suppose, at first sight, that the divorce between them and man is in any case consummated. But we soon realize that nothing of the kind is the case: whether the pact is concluded with things or with their distance from us comes down to the same thing; the "bridge of souls" subsists between them and us; in fact it is actually reinforced from the operation.

That is why the tragic sense of life never seeks to suppress the distances: it multiplies them, on the contrary, at will. Distance between man and other men, distance between man and himself, between man and the world, between the world and itself—nothing remains intact: everything is lacerated, fissured, divided, displaced. Within the most homogeneous objects as in the least ambiguous situations appears a kind of secret distance. But this is precisely an *interior distance,* a false distance, which is in reality a well-marked path, that is, already a reconciliation.

Everything is contaminated. It seems, though, that the favorite domain of tragedy is the narrative complication, the romanesque. From all mistresses-turned-nuns to all detective-gangsters, by way of all tormented criminals, all pure-souled prostitutes, all the just men constrained by conscience to injustice, all the sadists driven by love, all the madmen pursued by logic, a good "character" in a novel must above all be *double.* The plot will be "human" in proportion to its *ambiguity.* Finally the whole book will be true in proportion to its contradictions.

It is easy to ridicule. It is less so to free oneself from the tragic conditioning our mental civilization imposes upon us. One might even say that the rejection of the ideas of "nature" and of predestination lead *first* to tragedy. There is no important work in contemporary literature that does not contain at the same time the assertion of our freedom and the "tragic" germ of its abandonment.

Two great works at least, in recent decades, have offered us two new forms of the fatal complicity: absurdity and nausea.

Albert Camus,[6] as we know, has named *absurdity* the impassable gulf which exists between man and the world, between the aspirations of the human mind and the world's incapacity to satisfy them. Absurdity is in neither man nor things, but in the impossibility of establishing between them any relation other than *strangeness*.

Every reader has noticed, nonetheless, that the hero of *The Stranger* maintains an obscure complicity with the world, composed of rancor and fascination. The relations of this man with the objects surrounding him are not at all innocent: absurdity constantly involves disappointment, withdrawal, rebellion. It is no exaggeration to claim that it is things, quite specifically, which ultimately lead this man to crime: the sun, the sea, the brilliant sand, the gleaming knife, the spring among the rocks, the revolver. . . . As, of course, among these things, the leading role is taken by Nature.

Thus the book is not written in a language as *filtered* as the first pages may lead one to believe. Only, in fact, the objects already charged with a flagrant human content are carefully neutralized, and *for moral reasons* (such as the old mother's coffin, whose screws are described in terms of their shape and the depth they penetrate into the wood). Alongside this we discover, increasingly numerous as the moment of the murder approaches, the most revealing classical metaphors, naming man or infected by his omnipresence: the countryside is "swollen with sunlight," the evening is "like a melancholy truce," the rutted road reveals the "shiny flesh" of the tar, the soil is "the color of blood," the sun is a "blinding rain," its reflection on a shell is "a sword of light," the day has "cast anchor in an ocean of molten metal"—not to mention the "breathing" of the "lazy" waves, the "somnolent" headland, the sea that "pants" and the "cymbals" of the sun. . . .

The crucial scene of the novel affords the perfect image of a painful solidarity: the implacable sun is always "the same," its reflection on the blade of the knife the Arab is holding "strikes" the hero full in the face and "searches" his eyes, his hand tightens on the revolver, he tries to "shake off" the sun, he fires again, four times. "And it was—he says—as though I had knocked four times on the door of unhappiness."

Absurdity, then, is really a form of tragic humanism. It is not an observation of the separation between man and things. It is a lover's quarrel, which leads to a crime of passion. The world is accused of complicity in a murder.

When Sartre[7] writes (in *Situations I*) that *The Stranger* "rejects anthropomorphism," he is giving us, as the quotations above show, an incomplete

---

[6] Albert Camus (1913–1960), French novelist, dramatist, essayist. Best known for *The Stranger* (1942), *The Plague* (1947), *The Myth of Sisyphus* (1942), *The Rebel* (1952).

[7] Jean-Paul Sartre. See p. 495 of this volume. *Situations I* is a collection of his essays published in 1947 and followed by *Situations II* and *III* in 1948 and 1949.

view of the work. Sartre has doubtless noticed these passages, but he supposes that Camus, "unfaithful to his principle, is being poetic." Can we not say, rather, that these metaphors are precisely the explanation of the book? Camus does not reject anthropomorphism, he utilizes it with economy and subtlety in order to give it more weight.

Everything is in order, since the point is ultimately, as Sartre points out, to show us, according to Pascal's[8] phrase "the natural unhappiness of our condition."

And what does *Nausea* offer us? It is evidently concerned with strictly visceral relations with the world, dismissing any effort of description (called futile) in favor of a suspect intimacy, presented moreover as illusory, but which the narrator does not imagine he can avoid yielding to. The important thing, in his eyes, is in fact to yield to it as much as possible, in order to arrive at self-awareness.

It is significant that the three first perceptions recorded at the beginning of the book are all gained by the sense of touch, not that of sight. The three objects which provoke revelation are, in effect, respectively, the pebble on the beach, the bolt of a door, the hand of the Self-Taught Man. Each time, it is the physical contact with the narrator's hand which provokes the shock. We know that the sense of touch constitutes, in everyday life, a much more *intimate* sensation than that of sight; no one is afraid of contracting a contagious disease merely by looking at a sick man. The sense of smell is even more suspect: it implies a penetration of the body by the alien thing. The domain of sight itself, moreover, involves different qualities of apprehension: a shape, for example, will generally be more certain than a color, which changes with the light, with the background accompanying it, with the subject considering it.

Hence we are not surprised to note that the eyes of Roquentin, the hero of *Nausea*, are more attracted by colors—particularly by the less determined shades —than by outlines; when it is not his sense of touch, it is almost always the sight of an ill-defined color which provokes the nausea. We recall the importance assumed, at the beginning of the book, by Cousin Adolphe's suspenders, which are scarcely visible against the blue of his shirt: they are "mauve . . . buried in the blue, but with false humility . . . as if, having started out to become violet, they had stopped on the way without abandoning their pretensions. One feels like telling them: 'Go on, *become* violet and get it over with.' But no, they remain in suspension, checked by their incompleted effort. Sometimes the blue that surrounds them slides over them and covers them completely: I remain without seeing them for a moment. But this is only a transition, soon the blue pales in places, and I see patches of the hesitant mauve reappearing, which spread, connect, and reconstitute the suspenders." And the reader will continue to be ignorant of the suspenders' shape. Later, in the park, the famous root of the chestnut tree finally concentrates all its absurdity and its hypocrisy in its black color: "Black? I felt the word draining, emptying out its meaning with an extraordinary rapidity. Black? The root

---

[8] Blaise Pascal (1623–1662), French philosopher and physicist, best known for his *Pensées* ("Thoughts"), published in 1670.

was not black, *that* wasn't black there on that piece of wood . . . but rather the vague effort to *imagine black* on the part of someone who had never seen it and who could not have decided on it, who would have imagined an ambiguous being, beyond colors." And Roquentin comments on himself: "Colors, tastes, smells were never real, never truly themselves and nothing but themselves."

As a matter of fact, colors afford him sensations analogous to those of the sense of touch: they are for him an appeal, immediately followed by a withdrawal, then another appeal, etc.; this is a "suspect" contact accompanied by unnamable impressions, demanding an adherence and rejecting it at the same time. Color has the same effect on his eyes as a physical presence on the palm of his hand: it manifests above all an indiscreet (and, of course, double) "personality" of the object, a kind of shameful insistence which is simultaneously complaint, challenge, and denial. "Objects . . . they touch me, it's unbearable. I'm afraid of entering into contact with them, just as if they were living creatures." Color changes, hence it is *alive;* that is what Roquentin has discovered: things are alive, *like himself.*

Sounds seem to him similarly corrupted (aside from musical tunes, which do not *exist*). There remains the visual perception of outlines; we feel that Roquentin avoids attacking these. Yet he rejects in turn this last refuge of coincidence with himself: the only lines which coincide exactly are geometric lines, the circles for example, "but the circle too does not exist."

We are, once again, in an entirely *tragedified* universe: fascination with doubling, solidarity with things *because* they bear their own negation within themselves, redemption (here: accession to consciousness) by the very impossibility of achieving a true correpondence; in other words, the final recuperation of all distances, of all failures, of all solitudes, of all contradictions.

Hence analogy is the only mode of description seriously envisaged by Roquentin. Facing the cardboard box containing his bottle of ink, he discovers the futility of geometry in this realm: to say that it is a parallelepiped is to say nothing at all "about it." On the contrary, he tells us about the *real* sea which "crawls" under a thin green film made to "fool" people, he compares the "cold" brightness of the sun to a "judgment without indulgence," he notices the "happy gurgle" of a fountain, a streetcar seat is for him "a dead donkey" drifting, its red plush "thousands of tiny feet," the Self-Taught Man's hand is a "big white worm," etc. Each object would have to be cited, for all are deliberately presented in this fashion. The one most charged with transformations is, of course, the chestnut root, which becomes, successively, "black nail," "boiled leather," "mildew," "dead snake," "vulture's talon," "sealskin," etc., until nausea.

Without trying to limit the book to this particular point of view (though it is an important one), one can say that *existence* in it is characterized by the presence of interior distances, and that nausea is man's unhappy visceral penchant for these distances. The "smile in complicity with things" ends in a grimace: "All the objects that surrounded me were made of the same substance as myself, of a kind of shoddy suffering."

But are we not incited, under these conditions, to accord Roquentin's melancholy celibacy, his lost love, his "wasted life," the lugubrious and laughable fate of the Self-Taught Man—all the malediction weighing on the terrestrial world—the status of a superior necessity? Where, then, is freedom? Those who are unwilling to accept this malediction are all the same threatened with the supreme moral condemnation: they will be "filthy swine," *salauds*. Everything happens, then, as if Sartre—who can nonetheless hardly be accused of "essentialism"—had, in this book at least, brought the ideas of *nature* and of *tragedy* to their highest point. Once again, to struggle against these ideas is initially to do no more than to confer new powers upon them.

Drowned in the *depth* of things, man ultimately no longer even perceives them: his role is soon limited to experiencing, in their name, totally *humanized* impressions and desires. "In short, it is less a matter of observing the pebble than of installing oneself in its heart and of seeing the world with its eyes . . ."; it is apropos of Francis Ponge[9] that Sartre writes these words. He makes the Roquentin of *Nausea* say: "I *was* the chestnut root." The two positions are not unrelated: it is a matter, in both cases, of thinking "with things" and not *about* them.

Ponge too, as a matter of fact, is not at all concerned to describe. He knows perfectly well, no doubt, that his texts would be of no help to a future archaeologist seeking to discover what a cigarette or a candle might have been in our lost civilization. Without our daily frequentation of these objects, Ponge's phrases concerning them are no more than lovely hermetic poems.

On the other hand, we read that the hamper[10] is "annoyed to be in a clumsy position," that the trees in spring "enjoy being fooled" and "release a green vomit," that the butterfly "takes revenge for its long amorphous humiliation as a caterpillar."

Is this really to take the "side" of things, to represent them from "their own point of view"? Ponge obviously cannot be deceiving himself to this degree. The openly psychological and moral anthropomorphism which he continues to practice can have as its goal, on the contrary, only the establishment of a human, general, and absolute order. To assert that he speaks *for* things, *with* them, in their *heart*, comes down, under these conditions, to denying their reality, their opaque presence: in this universe populated by things, they are no longer anything but mirrors for a man that endlessly reflect his own image back to him. Calm, tamed, they stare at man with his own gaze.

Such a *reflection*, in Ponge, is not of course gratuitous. This oscillating movement between man and his natural doubles is that of an active consciousness, concerned to understand itself, to reform itself. Throughout his subtle pages, the smallest pebble, the least stick of wood gives him endless lessons, expresses and judges him at the same time, instructs him in a progress to be made. Thus man's contemplation of the world is a permanent apprenticeship to life, to happiness, to wisdom and to death.

So that ultimately it is a definitive and smiling reconciliation that we are

[9] Sartre makes this remark about Francis Ponge (b. 1899), French poet and essayist, in "Man and Things," an essay in *Situations I.*
[10] "Le Cageot" ("The Hamper") is the title of one of the prose poems in Ponge's *Le parti pris des choses* ("Taking the Side of Things"; Paris, 1942), p. 38.

being offered here. Again we have come back to the humanist affirmation: the world is man. But at what cost! For if we abandon the moral perspective of self-improvement, Ponge's *Le parti pris des choses* is no longer of any help to us. And if, in particular, we prefer freedom to wisdom, we are obliged to break all these mirrors so artfully arranged by Francis Ponge in order to get back to the hard, dry objects which are behind them, unbroached, as alien as ever.

François Mauriac, who—he said—had once read Ponge's *Hamper* on Jean Paulhan's[11] recommendation, must have remembered very little of this text when he baptized *Hamper Technique* the description of objects advocated in my own writings. Or else I had expressed myself very badly.

To describe things, as a matter of fact, is deliberately to place oneself outside them, confronting them. It is no longer a matter of appropriating them to oneself, of projecting anything onto them. Posited, from the start, as *not being man,* they remain constantly out of reach and are, ultimately, neither comprehended in a natural alliance nor recovered by suffering. To limit oneself to description is obviously to reject all the other modes of approaching the object: sympathy as unrealistic, tragedy as alienating, comprehension as answerable to the realm of science exclusively.

Of course, this last point of view is not negligible. Science is the only honest means man possesses for turning the world around him to account, but it is a material means; however disinterested science may be, it is justified only by the establishment, sooner or later, of utilitarian techniques. Literature has other goals. Only science, on the other hand, can claim to know the *inside* of *things.* The interiority of the pebble, of the tree, or of the snail which Francis Ponge gives us ridicules science, of course (and even more than Sartre seems to think); hence it in no way represents what is *in* these things, but what man can put into them of his own mind. Having observed certain behavior, with more or less rigor, Ponge is inspired by these appearances to human analogies, and he begins talking about man, always about man, supporting himself on things with a careless hand. It matters little to Ponge that the snail does not "eat" earth or that the chlorophyllic function is an absorption and not an "exhalation" of carbon gas; his eye is as casual as his recollections of natural history. The only criterion is the truth of the sentiment expressed in terms of these images—of the human sentiment, obviously, and of the human nature which is the nature of all things!

Mineralogy, botany, or zoology, on the contrary, pursue the *knowledge* of textures (internal and external alike), of their organization, of their functioning, and of their genesis. But, outside their domain, these disciplines too are no longer of any use, except for the abstract enrichment of our intelligence. The world around us turns back into a smooth surface, without signification, without soul, without values, on which we no longer have any purchase. Like the workman who has set down the tool he no longer needs, we find ourselves once again *facing* things.

To describe this surface then is merely to constitute this externality and

[11] Jean Paulhan (b. 1884), French fiction writer and critic.

this independence. Probably I have no more to say "about" the box my ink bottle came in than "with" it; if I write that it is a parallelipiped, I make no claim to defining any special essence of it; I have still less intention of handing it over to the reader so that his imagination can seize upon and embellish it with polychrome designs: I should prefer to keep him from doing so, in fact.

The most common criticisms made of such geometric information—"it says nothing to the mind," "a photograph or a diagram would show the shape better," etc.—are strange indeed: wouldn't I have thought of them first of all? As a matter of fact, there is something else involved. The photograph or the diagram aims only at reproducing the object; they are successful to the degree that they suggest as many interpretations (and the same errors) as the model. Formal description, on the other hand, is above all a limitation: when it says "parallelipiped," it knows it achieves no Beyond, but at the same time it cuts short any possibility of seeking one.

To record the distance between the object and myself, and the distances of the object itself (its *exterior* distances, i.e., its measurements), and the distances of objects among themselves, and to insist further on the fact that these are *only distances* (and not divisions), this comes down to establishing that things are here and that they are nothing but things, each limited to itself. The problem is no longer to choose between a happy correspondence and a painful solidarity. There is henceforth a rejection of all complicity.

There is, then, first a rejection of the analogical vocabulary and of traditional humanism, a rejection at the same time of the idea of tragedy, and of any other notion leading to the belief in a profound, and higher, nature of man or of things (and of the two together), a rejection, finally, of every pre-established order.

The sense of sight immediately appears, in this perspective, as the privileged sense, particularly when applied to outlines and contours (rather than to colors, intensities, or transparencies). Optical description is, in effect, the kind which most readily establishes distances: the sense of sight, if it seeks to remain simply that, leaves things in their respective place.

But it also involves risks. Coming to rest, without preparation, on a detail, the sense of sight isolates it, extracts it, seeks to develop it, fails, insists, no longer manages either to develop the detail or return it to its place . . .; "absurdity" is not far away. Or else contemplation is intensified to the point where everything begins to vacillate, to move, to dissolve . . .; then "fascination" begins, and "nausea."

Yet these risks remain among the least, and Sartre himself has acknowledged the cleansing power of the sense of sight. Troubled by a contact, by a suspect tactile impression, Roquentin lowers his eyes to his hand: "The pebble was flat, dry on one side, wet and muddy on the other. I was holding it by the edges, my fingers far apart to keep from getting dirty." He no longer understands what has moved him; similarly, a little later on, at the moment of entering his room: "I stopped short, because I felt in my hand a cold object which attracted my attention by a kind of personality. I opened my hand, I looked: I was simply holding the doorknob." Then Roquentin attacks colors, and his eye no longer manages to exercise its displacing action: "The black root did not *get through*, it remained there in my eyes, as a piece that is too big remains stuck in the throat. I could neither accept nor reject it." There has already been the "mauve" of the suspenders and the "suspect transparency" of the glass of beer.

We must work with the means at hand. The sense of sight remains, in spite of everything, our best weapon, especially if it keeps exclusively to outlines. As for its "subjectivity"—principal argument of the opposition—how is its value diminished thereby? Obviously I am concerned, in any case, only with the world as *my point of view* orients it; I shall never know any other. The relative subjectivity of my sense of sight serves me precisely to define *my situation in the world*. I simply keep myself from helping to make this situation a servitude.

Thus, though Roquentin thinks "the sense of sight is an abstract invention, a scoured, simplified idea, a human idea," it nonetheless remains, between the world and myself, the most effective operation.

For effectiveness is the point. To measure the distances—without futile regret, without hatred, without despair—between what is separated will permit us to identify what is *not* separated, what *is one*, since it is false that everything is double—false, or at least provisional. Provisional with regard to man, that is our hope. False already with regard to things: once scoured clean, they no longer refer to anything except to themselves, without a flaw for us to slip into, without a tremor.

One question persists: Is it possible to escape tragedy?

Today its rule extends to all my feelings and all my thoughts, it conditions me utterly. My body can be satisfied, my heart content, my consciousness remains unhappy. I assert that this unhappiness is *situated* in space and time, like every unhappiness, like everything in this world. I assert that man, some day, will free himself from it. But of this future I possess no proof. For me, too, it is a wager. "Man is a sick animal," Unamuno wrote in *The Tragic Sense of Life*;[12] the wager consists in believing he can be cured, and that it would therefore be a mistake to imprison him in his disease. I have nothing to lose. This wager, in any event, is the only reasonable one.

I have said that I possessed no proof. It is easy to perceive, nonetheless, that the systematic *tragedification* of the universe I live in is often the result of a deliberate intention. This suffices to cast a doubt on any proposition tending to posit tragedy as natural and definitive. Now, from the moment doubt has appeared, I cannot do otherwise than seek still farther.

This struggle, I shall be told, is precisely the tragic illusion par excellence: if I seek to combat the idea of tragedy, I have already succumbed to it; and it is so natural to take objects as a refuge . . . perhaps. But perhaps not. And, in that case. . . .

---

[12] Miguel de Unamuno (1864–1936), Spanish philosopher, fiction writer, poet, Professor of Greek Language and Literature, then Rector, at Salamanca University. *The Tragic Sense of Life* was published in 1913.

Susan Sontag

AGAINST INTERPRETATION

Over the last century the history of literature—of the arts in general—has been one of extreme mutations in theory and practice which have made considerable difficulty for the public. It was natural to suppose that, in relation to works which disappoint habitual expectations and are recalcitrant to "comprehension," criticism ought to assume a pedagogic role, instructing a disadvantaged public in how to be easy with works that at first baffle and distress it. And this is indeed what criticism has supposed its duty to be. But Susan Sontag's essay exemplifies a view which in recent years has gained some ground: that in carrying out its function of serving as intermediary between the work and the public, criticism reduces the autonomy and power of the work itself as well as of those who experience it. Miss Sontag was born in New York in 1933 and grew up in Tucson, Arizona, and in Los Angeles. Graduated from high school at the age of fifteen, she attended the University of California at Berkeley and the University of Chicago, receiving her B.A. from the latter institution in 1952. She has studied philosophy at Harvard, where she was a teaching fellow, and at Oxford and has held teaching posts (in English, philosophy, and religion) at the University of Connecticut, The City College of New York, and Columbia University. Her first book, *Against Interpretation,* a collection of the influential essays she had published in the preceding two years, appeared in 1965. Another collection of essays, *Styles of Radical Will,* was published in 1969. She has also written three novels, *The Benefactor* (1963), *Death Kit* (1967), and *Duet for Cannibals* (1969).

Content is a glimpse of something, an encounter like a flash. It's very tiny—very tiny, content.

WILLEM DE KOONING,[1] *in an interview*

It is only shallow people who do not judge by appearances. The mystery of the world is the visible, not the invisible.

OSCAR WILDE, *in a letter*

[1] An American painter, born in the Netherlands in 1904.
Reprinted with the permission of Farrar, Straus & Giroux, Inc., from *Against Interpretation* by Susan Sontag. Copyright © 1964, 1965 by Susan Sontag.

The earliest *experience* of art must have been that it was incantatory, magical; art was an instrument of ritual. (Cf. the paintings in the caves at Lascaux, Altamira, Niaux, La Pasiega, etc.) The earliest *theory* of art, that of the Greek philosophers, proposed that art was mimesis, imitation of reality.

It is at this point that the peculiar question of the *value* of art arose. For the mimetic theory, by its very terms, challenges art to justify itself.

Plato, who proposed the theory, seems to have done so in order to rule that the value of art is dubious. Since he considered ordinary material things as themselves mimetic objects, imitations of transcendent forms or structures, even the best painting of a bed would be only an "imitation of an imitation." For Plato, art is neither particularly useful (the painting of a bed is no good to sleep on), nor, in the strict sense, true. And Aristotle's arguments in defense of art do not really challenge Plato's view that all art is an elaborate *trompe l'oeil*,[2] and therefore a lie. But he does dispute Plato's idea that art is useless. Lie or no, art has a certain value according to Aristotle because it is a form of therapy. Art is useful, after all, Aristotle counters, medicinally useful in that it arouses and purges dangerous emotions.

In Plato and Aristotle, the mimetic theory of art goes hand in hand with the assumption that art is always figurative. But advocates of the mimetic theory need not close their eyes to decorative and abstract art. The fallacy that art is necessarily a "realism" can be modified or scrapped without ever moving outside the problems delimited by the mimetic theory.

The fact is, all Western consciousness of and reflection upon art have remained within the confines staked out by the Greek theory of art as mimesis or representation. It is through this theory that art as such—above and beyond given works of art—becomes problematic, in need of defense. And it is the defense of art which gives birth to the odd vision by which something we have learned to call "form" is separated off from something we have learned to call "content," and to the well-intentioned move which makes content essential and form accessory.

Even in modern times, when most artists and critics have discarded the theory of art as representation of an outer reality in favor of the theory of art as subjective expression, the main feature of the mimetic theory persists. Whether we conceive of the work of art on the model of a picture (art as a picture of reality) or on the model of a statement (art as the statement of the artist), content still comes first. The content may have changed. It may now be less figurative, less lucidly realistic. But it is still assumed that a work of art *is* its content. Or, as it's usually put today, that a work of art by definition *says* something. ("What X is saying is . . . ," "What X is trying to say is . . . ," "What X said is . . ." etc., etc.)

II

None of us can ever retrieve that innocence before all theory when art knew no need to justify itself, when one did not ask of a work of art what it said

[2]A deception; the phrase is used of exceptionally realistic and detailed still-life paintings.

because one knew (or thought one knew) what it *did*. From now to the end of consciousness, we are stuck with the task of defending art. We can only quarrel with one or another means of defense. Indeed, we have an obligation to overthrow any means of defending and justifying art which becomes particularly obtuse or onerous or insensitive to contemporary needs and practice.

This is the case, today, with the very idea of content itself. Whatever it may have been in the past, the idea of content is today mainly a hindrance, a nuisance, a subtle or not so subtle philistinism.

Though the actual developments in many arts may seem to be leading us away from the idea that a work of art is primarily its content, the idea still exerts an extraordinary hegemony. I want to suggest that this is because the idea is now perpetuated in the guise of a certain way of encountering works of art thoroughly ingrained among most people who take any of the arts seriously. What the overemphasis on the idea of content entails is the perennial, never consummated project of *interpretation*. And, conversely, it is the habit of approaching works of art in order to *interpret* them that sustains the fancy that there really is such a thing as the content of a work of art.

III

Of course, I don't mean interpretation in the broadest sense, the sense in which Nietzsche (rightly) says, "There are no facts, only interpretations."[3] By interpretation, I mean here a conscious act of the mind which illustrates a certain code, certain "rules" of interpretation.

Directed to art, interpretation means plucking a set of elements (the X, the Y, the Z, and so forth) from the whole work. The task of interpretation is virtually one of translation. The interpreter says, Look, don't you see that X is really—or, really means—A? That Y is really B? That Z is really C?

What situation could prompt this curious project for transforming a text? History gives us the materials for an answer. Interpretation first appears in the culture of late classical antiquity, when the power and credibility of myth had been broken by the "realistic" view of the world introduced by scientific enlightenment. Once the question that haunts post-mythic consciousness—that of the *seemliness* of religious symbols—had been asked, the ancient texts were, in their pristine form, no longer acceptable. Then interpretation was summoned, to reconcile the ancient texts to "modern" demands. Thus, the Stoics,[4] to accord with their view that the gods had to be moral, allegorized away the rude features of Zeus and his boisterous clan in Homer's epics. What Homer really designated by the adultery of Zeus with Leto, they explained, was the union between power and wisdom. In the same vein, Philo of Alexandria[5] interpreted the literal historical narratives of the Hebrew Bible as spiritual paradigms. The story of the exodus from Egypt, the wandering in the desert for forty years, and the entry into the promised land, said Philo, was really an allegory of the

[3] Friedrich Wilhelm Nietzsche (1844–1900) makes the remark in a number of places, but see the collection of notes published posthumously as *The Will to Power*.
[4] Stoicism was a school of philosophy founded by Zeno of Citium in the third century B.C.
[5] Sometimes called Philo Judaeus (c. 20 B.C.–A.D. c. 40); only fragments of his work survive.

individual soul's emancipation, tribulations, and final deliverance. Interpretation thus presupposes a discrepancy between the clear meaning of the text and the demands of (later) readers. It seeks to resolve that discrepancy. The situation is that for some reason a text has become unacceptable; yet it cannot be discarded. Interpretation is a radical strategy for conserving an old text, which is thought too precious to repudiate, by revamping it. The interpreter, without actually erasing or rewriting the text, *is* altering it. But he can't admit to doing this. He claims to be only making it intelligible, by disclosing its true meaning. However far the interpreters alter the text (another notorious example is the Rabbinic and Christian "spiritual" interpretations of the clearly erotic Song of Songs), they must claim to be reading off a sense that is already there.

Interpretation in our own time, however, is even more complex. For the contemporary zeal for the project of interpretation is often prompted not by piety toward the troublesome text (which may conceal an aggression), but by an open aggressiveness, an overt contempt for appearances. The old style of interpretation was insistent, but respectful; it erected another meaning on top of the literal one. The modern style of interpretation excavates, and as it excavates, destroys; it digs "behind" the text, to find a sub-text which is the true one. The most celebrated and influential modern doctrines, those of Marx and Freud, actually amount to elaborate systems of hermeneutics, aggressive and impious theories of interpretation. All observable phenomena are bracketed, in Freud's phrase, as *manifest content*. This manifest content must be probed and pushed aside to find the true meaning—the *latent content*—beneath. For Marx, social events like revolutions and wars; for Freud, the events of individual lives (like neurotic symptoms and slips of the tongue) as well as texts (like a dream or a work of art)—all are treated as occasions for interpretation. According to Marx and Freud, these events only *seem* to be intelligible. Actually, they have no meaning without interpretation. To understand *is* to interpret. And to interpret is to restate the phenomenon, in effect to find an equivalent for it.

Thus, interpretation is not (as most people assume) an absolute value, a gesture of mind situated in some timeless realm of capabilities. Interpretation must itself be evaluated, within a historical view of human consciousness. In some cultural contexts, interpretation is a liberating act. It is a means of revising, of transvaluing, of escaping the dead past. In other cultural contexts, it is reactionary, impertinent, cowardly, stifling.

IV

Today is such a time, when the project of interpretation is largely reactionary, stifling. Like the fumes of the automobile and of heavy industry which befoul the urban atmosphere, the effusion of interpretations of art today poisons our sensibilities. In a culture whose already classical dilemma is the hypertrophy of the intellect at the expense of energy and sensual capability, interpretation is the revenge upon art.

Even more. It is the revenge of the intellect upon the world. To interpret is to impoverish, to deplete the world—in order to set up a shadow world of "meanings." It is to turn *the* world into *this* world. ("This world"! As if there were any other.)

The world, our world, is depleted, impoverished enough. Away with all duplicates of it, until we again experience more immediately what we have.

V

In most modern instances, interpretation amounts to the philistine refusal to leave the work of art alone. Real art has the capacity to make us nervous. By reducing the work of art to its content and then interpreting *that,* one tames the work of art. Interpretation makes art manageable, comfortable.

This philistinism of interpretation is more rife in literature than in any other art. For decades now, literary critics have understood it to be their task to translate the elements of the poem or play or novel or story into something else. Sometimes a writer will be so uneasy before the naked power of his art that he will install within the work itself—albeit with a little shyness, a touch of the good taste of irony—the clear and explicit interpretation of it. Thomas Mann[6] is an example of such an overcooperative author. In the case of more stubborn authors, the critic is only too happy to perform the job.

The work of Kafka,[7] for example, has been subjected to a mass ravishment by no less than three armies of interpreters. Those who read Kafka as a social allegory see case studies of the frustrations and insanity of modern bureaucracy and its ultimate issuance in the totalitarian state. Those who read Kafka as a psychoanalytic allegory see desperate revelations of Kafka's fear of his father, his castration anxieties, his sense of his own impotence, his thralldom to his dreams. Those who read Kafka as a religious allegory explain that K. in *The Castle* is trying to gain access to heaven, that Joseph K. in *The Trial* is being judged by the inexorable and mysterious justice of God. . . . Another *oeuvre* that has attracted interpreters like leeches is that of Samuel Beckett.[8] Beckett's delicate dramas of the withdrawn consciousness—pared down to essentials, cut off, often represented as physically immobilized—are read as a statement about modern man's alienation from meaning or from God, or as an allegory of psychopathology.

Proust, Joyce, Faulkner, Rilke, Lawrence, Gide . . . one could go on citing author after author; the list is endless of those around whom thick encrustations of interpretation have taken hold. But it should be noted that interpretation is not simply the compliment that mediocrity pays to genius. It is, indeed, the modern way of understanding something, and is applied to works of every quality. Thus, in the notes that Elia Kazan published on his production of *A Streetcar Named Desire,*[9] it becomes clear that, in order to direct the play, Kazan had to discover that Stanley Kowalski represented the sensual and vengeful barbarism that was engulfing our culture, while Blanche Du Bois was Western civilization, poetry, delicate apparel, dim lighting, refined feelings

---

[6] Thomas Mann (1875–1955), German novelist and essayist, best known for *Death in Venice* (1912) and *The Magic Mountain* (1927).

[7] Franz Kafka (1883–1924), Austrian fiction writer, author of *The Castle* (1926) and *The Trial* (1925).

[8] Samuel Beckett (b. 1906), Anglo-French playwright and novelist, best known for *Waiting for Godot* (1952).

[9] A play of 1947, by Tennessee Williams, pseudonym of Thomas Lanier (b. 1914), the cinema version of which was directed by Elia Kazan.

and all, though a little the worse for wear to be sure. Tennessee Williams' forceful psychological melodrama now became intelligible: it was *about* something, about the decline of Western civilization. Apparently, were it to go on being a play about a handsome brute named Stanley Kowalski and a faded mangy belle named Blanche Du Bois, it would not be manageable.

VI

It doesn't matter whether artists intend, or don't intend, for their works to be interpreted. Perhaps Tennessee Williams thinks *Streetcar* is about what Kazan thinks it to be about. It may be that Cocteau in *The Blood of a Poet* and in *Orpheus*[10] wanted the elaborate readings which have been given these films, in terms of Freudian symbolism and social critique. But the merit of these works certainly lies elsewhere than in their "meanings." Indeed, it is precisely to the extent that Williams' plays and Cocteau's films do suggest these portentous meanings that they are defective, false, contrived, lacking in conviction.

From interviews, it appears that Resnais and Robbe-Grillet consciously designed *Last Year at Marienbad*[11] to accommodate a multiplicity of equally plausible interpretations. But the temptation to interpret *Marienbad* should be resisted. What matters in *Marienbad* is the pure, untranslatable, sensuous immediacy of some of its images, and its rigorous if narrow solutions to certain problems of cinematic form.

Again, Ingmar Bergman may have meant the tank rumbling down the empty night street in *The Silence*[12] as a phallic symbol. But if he did, it was a foolish thought. ("Never trust the teller, trust the tale," said Lawrence.)[13] Taken as a brute object, as an immediate sensory equivalent for the mysterious abrupt armored happenings going on inside the hotel, that sequence with the tank is the most striking moment in the film. Those who reach for a Freudian interpretation of the tank are only expressing their lack of response to what is there on the screen.

It is always the case that interpretation of this type indicates a dissatisfaction (conscious or unconscious) with the work, a wish to replace it by something else.

Interpretation, based on the highly dubious theory that a work of art is composed of items of content, violates art. It makes art into an article for use, for arrangement into a mental scheme of categories.

VII

Interpretation does not, of course, always prevail. In fact, a great deal of today's art may be understood as motivated by a flight from interpretation. To

---

[10] Jean Cocteau (1889–1963), French writer, artist, musician, and film-maker. *The Blood of a Poet* and *Orpheus* are films of 1932 and 1949 respectively.
[11] Alain Robbe-Grillet (b. 1922), French novelist and Alain Resnais (b. 1922), French film director, collaborated on *Last Year at Marienbad* (1961).
[12] A film of 1963, by Ingmar Bergman (b. 1918), Swedish director.
[13] D. H. Lawrence (1885–1930) made this remark in *Studies in Classic American Literature* (1922).

avoid interpretation, art may become parody. Or it may become abstract. Or it may become ("merely") decorative. Or it may become non-art.

The flight from interpretation seems particularly a feature of modern painting. Abstract painting is the attempt to have, in the ordinary sense, no content; since there is no content, there can be no interpretation. Pop Art[14] works by the opposite means to the same result; using a content so blatant, so "what it is," it, too, ends by being uninterpretable.

A great deal of modern poetry as well, starting from the great experiments of French poetry (including the movement that is misleadingly called Symbolism) to put silence into poems and to reinstate the *magic* of the word, has escaped from the rough grip of interpretation. The most recent revolution in contemporary taste in poetry—the revolution that has deposed Eliot and elevated Pound —represents a turning away from content in poetry in the old sense, an impatience with what made modern poetry prey to the zeal of interpreters.

I am speaking mainly of the situation in America, of course. Interpretation runs rampant here in those arts with a feeble and negligible avant-garde: fiction and the drama. Most American novelists and playwrights are really either journalists or gentlemen sociologists and psychologists. They are writing the literary equivalent of program music. And so rudimentary, uninspired, and stagnant has been the sense of what might be done with *form* in fiction and drama that even when the content isn't simply information, news, it is still peculiarly visible, handier, more exposed. To the extent that novels and plays (in America), unlike poetry and painting and music, don't reflect any interesting concern with changes in their form, these arts remain prone to assault by interpretation.

But programmatic avant-gardism—which has meant, mostly, experiments with form at the expense of content—is not the only defense against the infestation of art by interpretations. At least, I hope not. For this would be to commit art to being perpetually on the run. (It also perpetuates the very distinction between form and content which is, ultimately, an illusion.) Ideally, it is possible to elude the interpreters in another way, by making works of art whose surface is so unified and clean, whose momentum is so rapid, whose address is so direct that the work can be . . . just what is it. Is this possible now? It does happen in films, I believe. This is why cinema is the most alive, the most exciting, the most important of all art forms right now. Perhaps the way one tells how alive a particular art form is, is by the latitude it gives for making mistakes in it, and still being good. For example, a few of the films of Bergman—though crammed with lame messages about the modern spirit, thereby inviting interpretations—still triumph over the pretentious intentions of their director. In *Winter Light*[15] and *The Silence,* the beauty and visual sophistication of the images subvert before our eyes the callow pseudo-intellectuality of the story and some of the dialogue. (The most remarkable instance of this sort of discrepancy is the work of D. W. Griffith.)[16] In good films, there is always a directness that entirely frees us from the itch to interpret. Many old

[14] As instanced, say, by Andy Warhol's Campbell Soup cans.
[15] Another film by Bergman (1962).
[16] Classic American director (1875–1948), best remembered for his *Birth of a Nation* (1915).

Hollywood films, like those of Cukor, Walsh, Hawks,[17] and countless other directors, have this liberating anti-symbolic quality, no less than the best work of the new European directors, like Truffaut's *Shoot the Piano Player*[18] and *Jules and Jim*, Godard's *Breathless* and *Vivre Sa Vie*,[19] Antonioni's *L'Avventura*,[20] and Olmi's *The Fiancés*.[21]

The fact that films have not been overrun by interpreters is in part due simply to the newness of cinema as an art. It also owes to the happy accident that films for such a long time were just movies; in other words, that they were understood to be part of mass, as opposed to high, culture, and were left alone by most people with minds. Then, too, there is always something other than content in the cinema to grab hold of, for those who want to analyze. For the cinema, unlike the novel, possesses a vocabulary of forms—the explicit, complex, and discussable technology of camera movements, cutting, and composition of the frame that goes into the making of a film.

VIII

What kind of criticism, of commentary on the arts, is desirable today? For I am not saying that works of art are ineffable, that they cannot be described or paraphrased. They can be. The question is how. What would criticism look like that would serve the work of art, not usurp its place?

What is needed, first, is more attention to form in art. If excessive stress on *content* provokes the arrogance of interpretation, more extended and more thorough descriptions of *form* would silence. What is needed is a vocabulary— a descriptive, rather than prescriptive, vocabulary—for forms.* The best criticism, and it is uncommon, is of this sort that dissolves considerations of content into those of form. On film, drama, and painting respectively, I can think of Erwin Panofsky's essay, "Style and Medium in the Motion Pictures," Northrop Frye's essay "A Conspectus of Dramatic Genres," Pierre Francastel's essay "The Destruction of a Plastic Space." Roland Barthes' book *On Racine* and his two essays on Robbe-Grillet are examples of formal analysis applied to the work

---

[17] George Cukor (b. 1899), director of, for example, *My Fair Lady* (1965); Raoul Walsh (b. 1892), *High Sierra* (1941) and *White Heat* (1950); Howard Hawks, (b. 1896), *The Big Sleep* (1946) and *To Have and Have Not* (1944).

[18] François Truffaut (b. 1932), French director; *Shoot the Piano Player* (1960), *Jules and Jim* (1961).

[19] Jean-Luc Godard (b. 1930), French director; *Breathless* (1960), *Vivre Sa Vie* ("My Life to Live," 1962).

[20] Michelangelo Antonioni (b. 1912), Italian director; *L'Avventura* (1959).

[21] Hernnano Olmi (b. 1931), Italian director; *The Fiancés* (1962).

* One of the difficulties is that our idea of form is spatial (the Greek metaphors for form are all derived from notions of space). This is why we have a more ready vocabulary of forms for the spatial than for the temporal arts. The exception among the temporal arts, of course, is the drama; perhaps this is because the drama is a narrative (i.e., temporal) form that extends itself visually and pictorially, upon a stage. . . . What we don't have yet is a poetics of the novel, any clear notion of the forms of narration. Perhaps film criticism will be the occasion of a breakthrough here, since films are primarily a visual form, yet they are also a subdivision of literature. [Sontag's note.]

of a single author.[22] (The best essays in Erich Auerbach's *Mimesis,* like "The Scar of Odysseus," are also of this type.) An example of formal analysis applied simultaneously to genre and author is Walter Benjamin's essay, "The Story Teller: Reflections on the Works of Nicolai Leskov."[23]

Equally valuable would be acts of criticism which would supply a really accurate, sharp, loving description of the appearance of a work of art. This seems even harder to do than formal analysis. Some of Manny Farber's film criticism,[24] Dorothy Van Ghent's essay "The Dickens World: A View from Todgers',"[25] Randall Jarrell's essay on Walt Whitman[26] are among the rare examples of what I mean. These are essays which reveal the sensuous surface of art without mucking about in it.

IX

Transparence is the highest, most liberating value in art—and in criticism—today. Transparence means experiencing the luminousness of the thing in itself, of things being what they are. This is the greatness of, for example, the films of Bresson and Ozu[27] and Renoir's *The Rules of the Game.*[28]

Once upon a time (say, for Dante), it must have been a revolutionary and creative move to design works of art so that they might be experienced on several levels. Now it is not. It reinforces the principle of redundancy that is the principal affliction of modern life.

Once upon a time (a time when high art was scarce), it must have been a revolutionary and creative move to interpret works of art. Now it is not. What we decidedly do not need now is further to assimilate Art into Thought, or (worse yet) Art into Culture.

Interpretation takes the sensory experience of the work of art for granted, and proceeds from there. This cannot be taken for granted, now. Think of the sheer multiplication of works of art available to every one of us, superadded to the conflicting tastes and odors and sights of the urban environment that bombard our senses. Ours is a culture based on excess, on overproduction; the result is a steady loss of sharpness in our sensory experience. All the conditions of

[22] Erwin Panofsky, "Style and Medium in the Motion Pictures," *Explorations: Reading, Thinking, Discussing, Writing,* eds. T. C. Pollock and others (Englewood Cliffs, N.J.: Prentice-Hall, 1965). Northrop Frye, "A Conspectus of Dramatic Genres," *Kenyon Review,* XIII (Autumn, 1951), 143–162. Pierre Francastel, *Peinture et société: Naissance et destruction d'un espace plastique, de la renaissance au cubisme* (Lyon: Audin, 1951). Roland Barthes, *Sur Racine* (Paris: Éditions du Seuil, 1965); "Littérature Littérale," in *Essais Critiques* (Paris: Éditions du Seuil, 1964), pp. 63–70; "Objective Literature: Alain Robbe-Grillet," in *Two Novels,* tr. Richard Howard (New York: Grove Press, 1965).
[23] In *Illuminations,* ed. Hannah Arendt (New York, 1968), pp. 83–109.
[24] American free-lance film critic.
[25] In *Sewanee Review,* LVIII (Summer, 1950), 419–438.
[26] Originally entitled "Walt Whitman: He Had His Nerve," most easily available as "Some Lines from Whitman" in *Poetry and the Age* (New York, 1953), pp. 101–120.
[27] Robert Bresson (b. 1907), French director; Yasujiro Ozu (1903–1963), Japanese director.
[28] Jean Renoir (b. 1898), French director; *Rules of the Game* (1939).

modern life—its material plenitude, its sheer crowdedness—conjoin to dull our sensory faculties. And it is in the light of the condition of our senses, our capacities (rather than those of another age), that the task of the critic must be assessed.

What is important now is to recover our senses. We must learn to *see* more, to *hear* more, to *feel* more.

Our task is not to find the maximum amount of content in a work of art, much less to squeeze more content out of the work than is already there. Our task is to cut back content so that we can see the thing at all.

The aim of all commentary on art now should be to make works of art—and, by analogy, our own experience—more, rather than less, real to us. The function of criticism should be to show *how it is what it is*, even *that it is what it is*, rather than to show *what it means*.

X

In place of a hermeneutics we need an erotics of art.

Annotated Index of Names